Idolatry and Its Enemies

Idolatry and Its Enemies

COLONIAL ANDEAN RELIGION

AND EXTIRPATION, 1640–1750

• *KENNETH MILLS* •

PRINCETON UNIVERSITY PRESS

PRINCETON, NEW JERSEY

Library of Congress Cataloging-in-Publication Data

Mills, Kenneth (Kenneth R.)
Idolatry and its enemies : colonial Andean religion and
extirpation, 1640–1750 / Kenneth Mills.
p.   cm.
Includes bibliographical references and index.
ISBN 0-691-02979-2 (cl : alk. paper)
1. Quechua Indians—Religion.   2. Quechua Indians—Missions—Peru—
Lima Region.   3. Catholic Church—Missions—Peru—Lima Region—
History.   4. Catholic Church. Archdiocese of Lima (Peru)—History.
5. Christianity and other religions—Peru—Lima Region.
6. Christianity and culture—Peru—Lima Region.   7. Spain—Colonies—
America—Administration.   I. Title.
F2230.2.K4M56 1997
200'.985'09032—dc20   96-28847

This book has been composed in New Caledonia

Printed in the United States of America by Princeton Academic Press

1   3   5   7   9   10   8   6   4   2

FOR LIBBIE, FELIX, AND ALDOUS

• CONTENTS •

• A C K N O W L E D G M E N T S •

I AM PERHAPS the first historian of Peru to write any part of a book in Bangladesh, at two tables in Dhaka: one in the sweltering library of the National Museum, and the other, in the comparative cool of the air-conditioned library of the British Council. My first thanks go to the many people there, whose curiosity—I like to think—provided the perfect atmosphere for my beginning.

I am grateful to the Rhodes Trust for the scholarship which took me to the University of Oxford, where this book began as a doctoral dissertation (submitted at the end of Michaelmas term, 1991, and defended on 28 February 1992). The Trust's support also made possible my research program. I am mindful, too, of the generous assistance of Doctoral and Postdoctoral Fellowships from the Social Sciences and Humanities Research Council of Canada. These awards provided essential time for reflection and writing. The research support at Balliol College, Oxford, from the Adam and the Browning funds were much appreciated and, I hope, profited from. I am grateful, too, for the Junior Research Fellowship in Latin American History at Wadham College, Oxford, which provided a welcome and interesting home. And I thank the University Committee on Research in the Humanities and Social Sciences, the Program in Latin American Studies, and the Department of History, all at Princeton University, for support that has allowed me to revise and reconstruct this book in the midst of other pursuits.

Many people have helped me in one way or another. More names spring to mind than I can possibly acknowledge here. But I should like to single out Roger Highfield, whose knowledge, counsel, and thoughtful teas provided much comfort. I thank Terence Ranger, whose lectures on religious change in Africa were nothing short of inspiring, and for the warm reception afforded this Andeanist interloper by the Africanist circle at Oxford. John Fisher listened to early versions of a few of this book's chapters with great patience. Felipe Fernández-Armesto read an earlier draft of this book, and I thank him for his perceptive comments and useful nudges. I am grateful also to Malcolm Deas, Maurice Keen, and Penry Williams for their encouragement and support. And I thank Olivia Harris, Tristan Platt, Anthony McFarlane, Stuart Clark, Penny Dransart, Denise Arnold, and Rosaleen Howard-Malverde for their extraordinary generosity. I would also like to thank the gracious folks in the Bodleian Library, and in the British Library, for their consistent smiles, and their efficient—and often patient—assistance.

In Lima, Peru, I reserve special gratitude for Luis Millones, whose interest, encouragement, and comments on my writing since my first, wide-eyed visit to Peru in 1986 have been crucial; he and his wife, Renate, and their family are true friends who have helped me a great deal. I am also grateful for the kind reception and advice I received from María Rostworowski de Diez Canseco at the Instituto de Estudios Peruanos, and for timely spurs from David Cahill and

Erwin Salazar in Cusco. I thank the former director of the Archivo Arzobispal de Lima, Mario Ormeño, for his understanding. Also at the AAL, I would like to thank Hernán Remy Barúa, who was rarely without a smile and a joke, Melecio Tineo Morón, and a gruff but agreeable man I knew only as Carlos. The staff in the Investigations Room in the Biblioteca Nacional del Perú are also appreciated.

In Rome, my work was made easier by P. Wictor Gramatowski S. J. and P. Joseph de Cock S. J. at the Archivum Romanum Societatis Iesu, Fathers Josef Metzler and Charles Burns at the Archivio Segreto Vaticano, and by the helpful staff in the Vatican Library. The Archivo General de Indias in Seville is an excellent place to conduct research, and I wish warmly to thank its director and staff for their courtesy and help. I am indebted to Pedro Rubio Merino and his assistant for allowing me access to the fascinating material in the archive of the Cathedral of Seville. The library and facilities at the Escuela de Estudios Hispano-Americanos are also superb, and I thank all those responsible for maintaining such excellent living and working conditions for visiting scholars. Finally, I thank the staffs in the Biblioteca Nacional de España and the Archivo Histórico Nacional in Madrid, for their help.

There is an eccentric cast of historians and investigators whose words and examples have influenced my research and writing, and whom I would like to acknowledge: Pierre Duviols, Emmanuel Le Roy Ladurie, John V. Murra, John H. Rowe, and George Kubler deserve initial mention, as do Inga Clendinnen, Nancy Farriss, Karen Spalding, William B. Taylor, Frank Salomon, and Sabine MacCormack. And I thank an excellent teacher, David C. Johnson of the University of Alberta, for helping to set me on this path, and for his constant encouragement. I am grateful also to John Langdon, Philip Lawson, and Kenneth Munro for their teaching, encouragement and friendship, and to Inge Bolin and Ruth Gruhn for their kindness and subtle introductions to how anthropology and history might work together.

Libbie Mills deserves more gratitude than I can bestow. I will say that a few years ago, with all my good fortune, I did not know I was marrying a reader and critic of such care and skill. And, quite apart from editorial abilities, I thank her for her love. It is to Libbie and to the welcome young Felix and Aldous that the book is dedicated.

I am grateful to Anthony Pagden for his careful attention to an early version of this book and for his continued support. Terry Ranger, too, made welcome suggestions early on. Peter Lake helped me to see a title that should have been staring me in the face. Discussions with and encouragement from Peter Brown, Natalie Davis, Bill Jordan, and Tony Grafton have been much appreciated, and I thank Ben Weiss for his suggestions in the late stages of revision. Ignacio Gallup-Diaz has helped with timely reactions and in preparation of the index. My students, in courses ranging from a freshman to a graduate seminar, also deserve a word of thanks even if they must go unnamed; this is my opportunity to acknowledge how much they teach me. Bill Taylor's reading of the manuscript, the wealth of his prompts and the generosity of his suggestions have been inspirational; the warmth of his friendship and our communications are the stuff of life. I owe my deepest debt of gratitude to Sir John Elliott, for sharing his knowledge and experience of the Spanish world, and for the privilege of his friendship. His unfailing diligence and infectious enthusiasm for history have made this book much finer than it ever could have been without him.

I thank Margaret Case for her creative and editorial vigilance. And, finally, I thank the editors of *Past and Present* for the permission to use material in Chapters Eight and Nine which first appeared in my article, "The Limits of Religious Coercion in Mid-Colonial Peru," no. 145 (November 1994), pp. 84–121. Part of Chapter Six appears in a different form in my essay "Seeing God in Mid-Colonial Peru," in *Andean Art: Visual Expression and its Relation to Andean Beliefs and Values*, edited by Penny Z. Dransart (Aldershot, Avebury: World Archaeology Series, 1995). And I thank both William B. Taylor and Stuart Clark for permission to discuss their important works in progress; in both cases, I cite chapters and parts of these manuscripts and not page numbers. Taylor's *Magistrates of the Sacred: Priests and Parishioners in Eighteenth-Century Mexico* is forthcoming from Stanford University Press, while Clark's *Thinking with Demons: The Idea of Witchcraft in Early Modern Europe* is being published by Oxford University Press.

AAL   Archivo Arzobispal de Lima. Lima, Peru.
ACS   Archivo de la Santa Metropolitana y Patriarchal Iglesia Catedral de
        Sevilla. Seville, Spain.
AGI   Archivo General de Indias. Seville, Spain.
AHN   Archivo Histórico Nacional. Madrid, Spain.
ARSI   Archivum Romanum Societatis Iesu. Rome, Italy.
ASV   Archivio Segreto Vaticano. Rome, Italy.
BL   British Library. London, Great Britain.
BNM   Biblioteca Nacional de España. Madrid, Spain.
BNP   Biblioteca Nacional del Perú. Lima, Peru.
BOD   Bodleian Library. Oxford, Great Britain.

Idolatry and Its Enemies

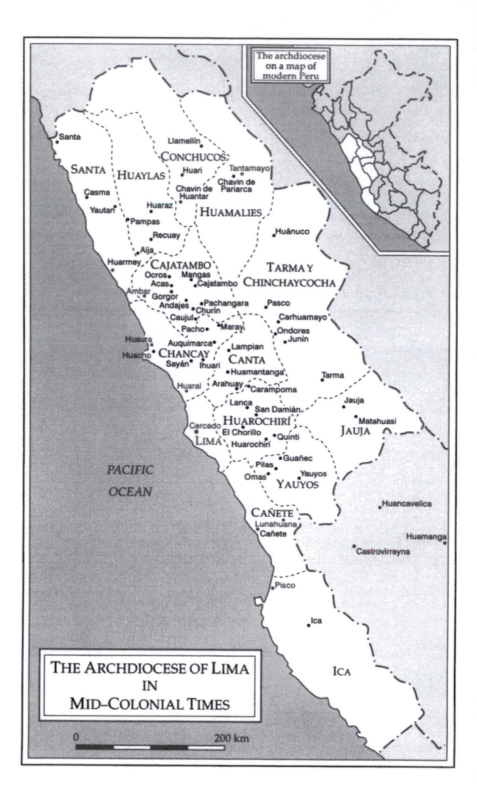

The archdiocese on a map of modern Peru

Santa

Llamellín

CONCHUCOS

SANTA   HUAYLAS   Huari   Tantamayo

Casma   Chavin de Pariarca

Yautan   Chavin de Huantar

Huaraz   HUAMALIES

Pampas   Huánuco

Recuay

Aija

Huarmey   CAJATAMBO   TARMA Y CHINCHAYCOCHA

Ocros   Mangas

Acas   Cajatambo

Ambar   Pasco

Gorgor   Pachangara

Andajes   Churín   Carhuamayo

Caujul   Maray   Ondores

Pacho   Junín

Huaura   Auquimarca   Lampian

Huacho   CHANCAY   CANTA

Sayán   Ihuari   Tarma

Huamantanga

Huaral   Arahuay   Carampoma   Jauja

Lanca   Matahuasi

San Damián   JAUJA

Cercado   HUAROCHIRÍ

El Chorillo   Quinti

LIMA   Huarochirí

Pilas   Guañec

Omas   Yauyos

YAUYOS   Huancavelica

CAÑETE

Lunahuana   Huamanga

Cañete   Castrovirreyna

PACIFIC OCEAN

Pisco

Ica

THE ARCHDIOCESE OF LIMA
IN
MID–COLONIAL TIMES

ICA

0   200 km

Introduction

THIS BOOK is primarily about Andean religion in the mid-colonial Archdiocese of Lima, Peru. I use "mid-colonial" as a shorthand to refer to people, events, and the religious atmosphere between 1640 and 1750. Although recognizable over a pan-Andean zone, colonial Andean "religion" (which Spanish Christians often called the Indians' idolatry) was neither unitary nor fixed in time. It was predominantly regional and local in character, however much the religious system of one region or community might resemble that of its neighbor in structure and emphasis. Most importantly, colonial Andean religion, like its prehispanic forebears, was changing while it was enduring. Colonial Andeans resisted Christianity at the same time as they reacted to its presence and included aspects of what began as the invader's religion into their emerging and reinterpreted ways of seeing and managing the world.

The book is also about the Christian faith as it was carried, and as it appeared, to the indigenous inhabitants of the central Andes in these times. I write about "faces" of Christianity in an attempt to displace the monolithic images that studies of evangelization too often spawn, and to capture instead the different undercurrents and approaches that coexisted and jostled each other in the central Andes. Through the controversial reinvigoration of an investigatory and penal process, the Extirpation of idolatry, in the middle of the seventeenth century, the Church in the Archdiocese of Lima sought to bring about a belated and highly ambitious religious reform of the indigenous peoples of the vast realm. The documentation that resulted from this enterprise is a rich and still largely untapped source of information about Andean religion and life in mid-colonial times.

Andeans did much to determine what constituted colonial religion, but their religion, like their history, interlocks with that of Spaniards and Christianity. The evidence allows the examination of what Quechua-speaking Andeans said about what they believed and practiced and what Spanish Christian judges and interpreters heard them say. My fundamental approach joins those of others, first, in identifying the ill effects of polarized conceptions of colonial religious history (in this context, the idea of a Spanish Christianity locked in mortal combat with Indian religion), and second, in trying to move beyond them.[1] I do

---

[1] I have in mind Nancy Farriss, Inga Clendinnen, and William Taylor, even though the list might easily be longer. See their works in the bibliography.

not portray a neat sort of struggle in which there are clear victors and vanquished or in which the would-be "opponents" keep to their own sides of the ring. Andean beliefs and practices survived because they changed and were adapted to colonial realities (such as being declared forbidden and demonic) by the people themselves, and because people assimilated Christian terms, ideas, rituals, and explanations into an expanding religious framework. Thus, my exploration of fundamental dimensions of colonial Andean religion is combined with my consideration of the extirpators' Christianity and what systematic extirpation might actually have achieved in its mission to eradicate suspect Indian religiosity and to advance the Indian parishioners' acceptance of an approved Christianity. This is a study in which native Andeans and Spaniards inhabit the same analytical space.[2] Although I do not pretend to have created a complete picture of colonial Andeans' and Spaniards' shared (if not harmonious) history, I have selected what I believe are some fundamental elements in their cultural and religious interrelations, and I have attempted to examine their significance.

There is no denying that aspects of Christianity were being embraced voluntarily by some Andean people and even incorporated into the sacred repertoires of religious ministers and specialists. But significantly, it was neither the kind of embrace nor the kind of Christianity desired by the Church at the time. Andean traditions of religious assimilation—favored famously by the Inkas and pre-Inkaic regional powers but also characteristic of more local patterns—had not disappeared in just over a century of Spanish Christian presence. Andeans in colonial times resisted the compartmentalization of their religious ideas and options. Most people could not live comfortably within the frequently dichotomous categories of the extirpators (the *visitadores generales de idolatría*, or idolatry judges and inspectors). So-called idolatry and Christianity could meet as well as compete, especially when the increasingly faint line that separated the two "religions" was less rigorously monitored than during an idolatry investigation, and especially when colonial religion is viewed as a developing manner of living and thinking instead of a stark arena for the cosmic battle of antithetical worlds. Thus the stark oppositions in the book's title and subtitle are meant to draw you, the reader, toward the discovery of a more complicated story—a story in which the poles of idolatry (colonial Andean religion) and its enemies (Christianity and Christian extirpators) frequently look artificial and out of place.

Andean people were selective in their religious assimilations. There were often good, sound reasons for colonial Andeans to worship a patron saint, to invoke Jesus Christ, or to ally with the parish priest. Yet, just as often, religious mixtures were as unintended by native Andeans as by Spaniards. Incidents of mixture could be the gradual, inadvertent results of many years' experience,

---

[2] The phrase is indebted to Ashis Nandy's formulation of "colonialism as a shared culture," and follows William Taylor's work toward a "colonial situation . . . in which European colonists and native peoples are united in one analytical field." W. B. Taylor, "Colonial Religion," p. 33. A. Nandy, *The Intimate Enemy*, p. 5.

practice, and contestation in an Indian parish. As will become more clear, I believe that Andean religious change in the colonial period and beyond was an uneven, fitful, and unpredictable experience. The formulation of stages, like typological classifications, works brilliantly to concentrate the mind and to stimulate discussion,[3] but encourages a unidirectional and unvarying way of thinking about not only religious change but colonial history in general. Historians of religion and society in colonial Spanish America may be too conditioned to expect a certain kind and scope of change to occur, an essentially teleological process set off by the moment of Columbus's landfall.[4]

One cannot explain satisfactorily Andean religious endurance simply by invoking such things as the Andean people's remarkable determination or the strength of their reciprocal relationship with their ancestors, as important and real as such things were. Recognizably Andean religious patterns retained their significance because they changed. In many parts of the mid-colonial Archdiocese of Lima, Andean religious survival was as much about a dynamic and gradual emergence as about a more basic persistence.[5] There were conscious religious adaptations to the conditions of colonial life, and there were many other, often slower, transformations that were imperceptible to the people themselves. Andean religion was adapted and reconstructed in colonial times, and change occurred as much from within as from exposure to the gradual and sometimes inadvertent effects of Christianity's varied presence.

I offer a new reading of some familiar sources for the mid-colonial period and on the theme of colonial religion in particular. Yet my researches into sources such as ecclesiastical correspondence, missionary and other chronicles, catechisms and other pastoral tools, books of sermons, and the Jesuits' reports primarily complement, test and enrich the religious information I derive from a diverse body of idolatry trial documentation. I undertake a close description and analysis of what is often only said to be complex and syncretic, a description and analysis drawn from the so-called idolatry testimonies, the sources derived from the Lima Church's efforts to eradicate suspect Andean religion and reform its Indian parishioners in the seventeenth and eighteenth centuries. Many of the declarants' testimonies surmount the legalistic formulae of the trial proceedings and the linguistic, cultural, and ideological filters through which they passed. In addition to their invaluable religious content, they are often compelling and passionate narratives. The vitality of colonial Andean religious life is

---

[3] The phrase is Peter Hulme's, from his memorable discussion of the influence of typology and other classifications on Caribbean ethnology in *Colonial Encounters*, p. 51. See James Lockhart's cogent argument for three stages in "the general postconquest evolution of the Nahuas" of central Mexico in *The Nahuas after the Conquest*, ch. 7, and pp. 428–36, and also his discussion of stages 1 and 2 in "Sightings," which revises a portion of his Introduction to *We People Here*, pp. 1–21. On degrees of change see also S. Gruzinski, *The Conquest of Mexico*.

[4] O. Harris, "The Coming of the White People."

[5] A collection of essays which employs these concepts to good effect is R. V. H. Dover, K. E. Seibold, and J. H. McDowell, eds., *Andean Cosmologies*.

best captured at the level of the individual in his or her community and region, thus my study frequently focuses on people with names who tell engaging and meaningful stories. My larger hypotheses about religious change and persistence rely, first, on native Andeans' descriptions of their own ritual actions and beliefs and those of others and, second, on my careful consideration of these statements as rendered in the documentation. Their imagery and often surprising voices can replace some of the misrepresentative and simple depictions that have so often been used in the portrayal of colonial Andean history.

I have tried, as much as possible, to allow the richness of the source material to shine through the two main intervening filters, the inquisitorial genesis and formulaic recording of this evidence, and my own retelling and analysis. The witnesses before the extirpators were predominantly Quechua-speaking, so their testimonies often passed through an interpreter before a bilingual notary recorded them in Spanish (occasionally using a few Quechua words). As scholars from diverse fields consistently warn, any reconstruction that depends on records of inquisition and recrimination for its evidence must be conducted with the utmost caution, mindful of the realities of the historical context that brought the information into being.[6]

The documentation produced by such policing bodies as the Inquisition and the Extirpation can poison the well in other ways. An historian can be led to unwarranted generalizations out of enthusiasm for a rich case study. Attention to only certain kinds of information in these documents might persuade an incautious observer to conclude, for instance, that native Andeans were resisting and countering Christianity whenever possible. Poignant cries of resistance to forms of domination have issued from Amerindian peoples from the earliest colonial times to the present, but these cries have not existed alone, nor do they tell what may be the more significant parts of the story about indigenous cultural survival and dynamism in the face of any number of pressures and influences.[7] The idolatry judges' questions and preoccupations, for their part, often forced the Indian witnesses' answers in certain directions. And one has to be just as aware of the fact that witnesses themselves did not always speak accurately for others; indeed, for good reasons, Andeans were often enterprising in the misrepresentation of themselves. I have tried to use the Indians' testimonies and other assembled information to show not only what the people's alleged offenses were but also many other things that emerge about the encounters between extirpators and native Andeans in mid-colonial times, employing what I have come to know about these documents and the situations

---

[6] See, for instance, the memorable piece by R. Rosaldo, "From the Door of His Tent."

[7] I am thinking, for example, of Ruth Behar's excellent discussion of the case of an old Guachichil visionary in San Luis Potosí, northern Mexico, in the late sixteenth century. The woman's resistance and agression toward Spaniards and Christianity is undeniable, yet her visions and urgings reveal her creative mixing of Christian symbolism into Guachichil patterns and the genesis of new cultural meanings. "Visions of a Guachichil Witch," esp. p. 123.

they describe, and following what Eric Van Young called "the humane scholar's traditional map of reasonableness"—what another might call his nose.[8]

Connected with the historian's challenge of what intermediaries and scenario might do to the evidence is the dilemma of terminology. The notaries' occasional use of Quechua words and expressions when their constant search for approximating Spanish synonyms proved hopeless points to a problem that persists today. I record a large number of expressions and names of Andean religious beings and locations in the indigenous language because their translation so often proves inadequate or impossible (a full glossary follows the text). In the case of other words I have chosen to concede. My use of the terms "god," "divinity," and "force" to describe Andean numina is uncomfortable and tentative, reflecting a decision made in the interest of the text's general accessibility and to express—however crudely—entities of great importance to people. I am the first to admit, and to want to demonstrate, just how different even a Christian Andean's idea of divinity might be from a Judeo-Christian's orthodox understanding of a supernatural God. With the same hesitation, I use "Andean" adjectivally not only to refer to place, but also to the experience of a range of different peoples, and I write of "Indians" and "Andeans" in order to tell of things in more than one locality and affecting more than one group of people. So the words are imperfect, and usages in English are in a state of flux. The Spanish use of the connotative rubrics of "idolatry" or "superstition," not to mention "religion," to refer to Andean systems of belief and practice spawns other significant problems that are recognized and discussed, even if they will not be dwelt upon in great detail here. The thread, for example, which links the original context of the charge of idolatry against others in the monotheism of Israel, through its use in the expansion of Latin Christianity in Europe, to the points of its renewed currency in the Iberian endeavors in the Atlantic islands, on the west coast of Africa and, eventually, in the Americas and Pacific islands, is the important subject of another book. It bears remembering that the distortion of realities through language is part of my book's subject, an integral piece of a screen which can obscure the interactive colonial terrain.

On its western border, the mid-colonial Archdiocese of Lima stretched more than 140 leagues (approximately 420 miles or 675 kilometers) along the Pacific coast of South America (see the map facing page 3). It extended from the Santa River Valley (latitude 9 degrees south) in the *corregimiento* (tribute district) of Santa, its northern border shared with the Diocese of Trujillo, to the Nazca River Valley (latitude 15 degrees south) in the province of Ica, the boundary with the Diocese of Arequipa. The City of the Kings, or Lima as it came to be known, rested at the coastal center (latitude 12 degrees south). Further inland, the northernmost boundaries of the jurisdiction were at the extent of the mountainous *corregimientos* of Conchucos and Huamalíes. The eastern fringe

---

[8] "The Cuautla Lazarus," p. 21.

was the least clearly defined border from the perspective of Spanish Catholic administration. According to contemporary sources the outer limits of the colonial provinces of Tarama and Chinchacocha (modern Tarma and Junín) and Jauja, some 150 to 200 miles (or 250 to 300 kilometers) from the coast, gave way to lands inhabited by "infidels" and "warlike" peoples. The southeastern boundary with the Diocese of Huamanga (modern Ayacucho) was defined by the southern limits of the *corregimientos* of Jauja and Yauyos.

Pedro de Villagómez's estimate of the Indian population in the archdiocese in November of 1664 counted over 131,000 native Andean parishioners.[9] This reckoning would seem to correspond roughly with the figures for differently defined regions covering this area given by Noble David Cook for 1630.[10] Even after the great resettlements of the 1560s and 1570s and over a century of integration of Andean peoples into parish networks, the population of the central Andes, still stuttering in its recovery from the onslaughts of disease and displacement, represented a substantial challenge for the Spanish state and the Catholic Church.

As in the sixteenth century, the prime vehicle of Spanish contact with native Andeans in the towns, villages, and countryside that together provide the principal settings for this book continued to be the parish priest. From the point of view of the order-seeking European administrator, the principal towns, the smaller villages (parish annexes), and the settlements around small silver mines, *obrajes* (workhouses, usually for textiles) and fertile plots of land (*chacras*) were scattered over a wide and difficult terrain. Moreover, as will become evident, the prehispanic landscape, replete with sacred and historical meanings, had not been completely superseded by the grid-patterned *pueblos* of the first colonial century, as in Cajatambo, where the villages of Nanis and Chamaz were described, even by Villagómez and his seventeenth-century informants, in terms of ancient, out-settled *ayllus* (kin groups) of Mangas.[11] In addition to the challenge to Catholic supremacy that this intertwined geographical and religious continuity represented in the Andes, there was the sheer magnitude of the clergy's task. One cannot but remark at the impossible obligations of lone clerics administering to populous parishes with up to eleven

---

[9] Significantly, this number neither takes into account the fluctuating population in Lima's principal Indian quarter, the *Cercado*, and its environs, nor does it provide anything but approximate ideas of "reduced" and "Christianized" numbers in the eastern frontier regions of the realm. The tentative figure of 131,491 represents my calculations based on the details within AGI Lima 304, Letter from Villagómez to the king, Lima, 20 November 1664.

[10] Cook estimated a population of 106,125 in the northern Sierra and 109,801 in the central Sierra, numbers which had fallen from 1570 totals, which had been almost double those. The Archdiocese of Lima straddled both of Cook's territorial regions and included a northern and central coastal area where, apart from a few areas around Lima and the upper valleys, the purely Indian population would have been negligible in the mid-seventeenth century. See *Demographic Collapse*, pp. 94, 198, and 209.

[11] On the traditional "archipelago" pattern of Andean settlement and kin relations, see the seminal work of J. V. Murra, *Formaciones económicas y políticas*, pp. 59–116.

or twelve annexes, spread over a number of rugged mountain ranges and deep river valleys.

In 1583, the Third Provincial Council of Lima decreed, amid its many ideals reflecting the pastoral concerns expressed at the Council of Trent (1545–1563), that one priest should serve no more than two to three hundred families in Peru. It appears, however, that in spite of the increasing numbers of qualified clergy in the early seventeenth century, this ideal ratio was not achieved.[12] According to Villagómez, in 1664 the Church's presence over the vast space and population in the sixteen *corregimientos* that made up the Archdiocese of Lima asserted itself in the form of 162 parishes (or *doctrinas*). These were administered by 108 secular priests and 67 friars from four religious orders— 35 Dominicans, 16 Mercedarians, 15 Franciscans, and 1 Jesuit.[13] In addition to these *doctrineros* (priests who instructed and administered to Indians), the majority of whom were based in the most sizeable Andean communities, there were various itinerant missions conducted intermittently by small groups of religious. In the mountain communities, the official Christian presence in the seventeenth and eighteenth centuries was frequently bolstered during the Lenten season—commonly by Jesuits—when native parishioners were required to confess their sins, often in large congregations, ayllu by ayllu. At a glance, and certainly from the point of view of a Catholic Church that was generally over-stretched in the Andes, as in many other parts of Spanish America, this amounted to a brave dispersal of resources in one of the better covered regions of Peru. But even the archbishop's most hopeful calculations could not conceal a basic predicament. Such numbers meant that the average priest of Indians in the 1660s, working in some of the most difficult conditions in Spanish America, was entrusted with far more parishioners than he could care for or monitor. A characteristic request in many of the letters sent by contemporary Jesuit provincials, echoed by other kinds of churchmen, had not altered since the arrival of the Society in 1568: the plea for more able bodies to assist in a task only begun.

A few more words are needed to explain my approach, and how my emphases contribute to what is known and surmised about this place and time. The agents of the Extirpation were meant to operate throughout the Archdiocese of Lima; yet, in practice, their extirpating efforts did not cover anything close to every parish or annex. Even with the remarkable dispersal of visitadores that did occur, my investigations can follow only where the *visitas* (idolatry trials and inspections) passed, and can profit only from the documentation that has survived. Worry over these limitations is diminished when one

---

[12] R. Levillier, *Organización de la Iglesia*, 1: 273–415 and A. Vázquez de Espinosa, *Compendio y descripción de las Indias occidentales*, cited in G. Kubler, "The Quechua," p. 403.

[13] In a few cases, two friars or priests might occupy a particularly large parish. For details see AGI Lima 304, Letter from Villagómez to the king, Lima, 20 November 1664. Almost sixty years earlier P. Antonio Vázquez de Espinosa wrote of 15 corregimientos with 179 doctrinas, 113 of which were ministered by secular priests and 67 by friars. See *Compendio*, p. 319.

considers the detail and abundance of the religious information for parts of the Lima region in comparison with what has thus far been uncovered for most of colonial Peru. Not surprisingly, numerous reports and references in correspondence, along with the occasional set of proceedings from a religious inquiry, confirm that "idolatry," as the Spanish broadly defined it, existed throughout the viceroyalty.[14] However, persistent Indian ways and alleged perversions of Catholicism in other regions never met with an organized fury comparable to the Extirpation in the Lima region. As appears to have been the case in much of contemporary New Spain, an evident concern over Indian religious error from various individuals and places did not translate into a sustained and centrally directed Extirpation akin to the process in the Archdiocese of Lima.[15]

It could be argued that a concentration upon the religious documentation from a particular province—or perhaps even one parish that had been visited three or four times in the course of a century—would be more useful than an examination of people and actions within the larger swath of the archdiocese as a whole. There is no doubt that much is learned from focusing upon regions, valleys, and communities where, among other things, precise moments of religious change can be investigated. But, with the possible exception of the region of Huarochirí, or possibly Cajatambo—where other texts and kinds of documents complement a notable abundance of trial information[16]—the evidence would not seem adequate to support the endeavor.

The quality of the information in these sources is uneven, and dependent on such things as the care and patience of a given visitador and the cunning and moods of certain key informants. Rich details emerge in one parish that are contradicted only two leagues away. In one locality there will be a band of persons eager to tell of anything that might contribute to the downfall of a set of village enemies, while in another there will arise a wall of silent solidarity so thick that the inspectors find that even denials of religious crimes are difficult to wrench from witnesses' lips. In one place a visitador's questions—or what the Indians are inclined to reveal—might deal especially with the survival of reverence for *malquis* (the mummified remains of important ancestors), while in another place the investigation will focus upon rites of divination or the visitations of so-called demons. The religious information is thus fragmented;

---

[14] Examples could be cited from all corners. Most important are perhaps the many oblique references made to a short but busy anti-idolatry campaign led in the Cusco diocese by a contemporary and an admirer of Villagómez's initiatives, Bishop Juan Alonso Ocón (1644–1651). See AGI Lima 332, Letter from the College of the Society of Jesus to the king, Cusco, 14 July 1648. Correspondents from both the Franciscan and Dominican orders sent letters of approval to Madrid concerning Ocón's zeal. See also a Franciscan's claims from what is modern Bolivia in AGI Lima 302, Letter from Fr. Juan Valero to the king, La Paz, 20 September 1632. For a later period in Arequipa, see P. Duviols, "Un procès d'idolâtrie," and F. Salomon, "Ancestor Cults." José Dammert Bellido has studied investigations into "superstition" in the late seventeenth- and late eighteenth-century Diocese of Cajamarca: "Procesos . . . siglo XVII," and "Procesos . . . siglo XVIII."

[15] The comparison has not yet been systematically treated, though see J. F. Schwaller "The Extirpation of Idolatry." I thank him for letting me read this essay in progress.

[16] See K. Spalding's *Huarochirí*, and, in much more limited way, my *An Evil Lost to View?*

what can be surmised from one parish or one region, even over the space of many years, rarely provides enough kinds of detail to build a coherent understanding of either the character of religious life in that place or the resulting religious existence for colonial Andean peoples.

Nonetheless, the problems of fragmentation and the unevenness of the evidence are outweighed by its richness as a whole and the fascinating opportunities for comparison. Thus the difficulties I have noted, and doubtless many others, can be at least partially surmounted by considering that whole, by establishing some larger themes for discussion and then carefully comparing and contrasting the beliefs and experiences of different regions, valleys, parishes, and even individuals. The comparative and classificatory process is made easier by the fact that centuries of prehispanic contact between regions, not to mention the incorporative nature of Andean religion, contributed to a fundamental base of beliefs and rituals that was similar, irrespective of a given people's diverse traditions and local idiosyncracies. Still, generalizations must be cautious and informed. The investigative competence or preoccupations of one visitador differed from those of another, and colonial Andean religion in the Lima region was neither fixed in time nor uniform over some geographical entity stretching from Conchucos in the north to Ica in the south. I show common patterns where I believe they exist, but I also capture the apparently contradictory, the ambiguous, and ponder the less easily connected and peculiar cases.

The decision to cast my net wider than, say, the province of Cajatambo or the Chillón River Valley is an accurate reflection of what the idolatry sources offer and how—at least in this early stage of their investigation—they can best be presented. To put the matter in the more familiar terms of European religious historiography, the evidence has more in common with what William Christian has pieced together about local religion from the answers to a questionnaire of Philip II in sixteenth-century Castile than with what was available to Emmanuel Le Roy Ladurie in Fournier's Inquisition Register for fourteenth-century Montaillou.[17]

My decision to focus on a period from 1640 to 1750 is easier to explain. Changing religious demands forced Spanish Christians to confront and investigate the realities of colonial Andean religious life, and this confrontation and investigation produced rich documentation that bears directly on the interlocking histories of Spaniards and Andeans in the center of the Peruvian viceroyalty. 1640 was the year that Pedro de Villagómez set out from Arequipa (where he was bishop) to take up the metropolitan see of Lima (1641–1671). His revitalization of the Extirpation of idolatry, and the recognizable (if more sporadic and changed) continuation of this mechanism of repression after his death, appears to have run most of its course by about 1750.[18] The period

---

[17] W. A. Christian, *Local Religion*; E. Le Roy Ladurie, *Montaillou*.

[18] Idolatry investigations were pursued in the region after this time, and at least into the middle of the nineteenth century; see Chapter Five. Almost any choice of beginning and end dates is

inaugurated by Villagómez in Lima set off the most systematic and sustained attempt to eradicate colonial Indian religion that Peru, or any other part of colonial Spanish America, had ever seen.

The mid-colonial period has been neglected by scholars, and not only in the study of colonial religion. Only relatively recently have writers identified open fields of inquiry in between the much-investigated era of the military conquest and its aftermath, on the one hand, and the period of the late colonial rebellions and the eventual Spanish defeat, on the other. This book is meant as a contribution to the stream of literature that is telling the stories of the colonial middle.

The weight of assumptions and neglect has, not surprisingly, also touched the narrower history of the Extirpation of idolatry in the Lima region. Although the Extirpation has been a subject of serious inquiry for a number of years, study has consistently focused upon the reasons and motivations behind the initiation of organized persecution and upon the phenomenon and mechanisms of the campaigns, particularly those in the time of Archbishop Bartolomé Lobo Guerrero (1609–1622), and only more recently on the time of Archbishop Pedro de Villagómez and beyond.[19] Interest has tended to fall off quite abruptly around the decade of the 1660s. There has been an impression that, as in the history of witchcraft repression in Europe (at its height between about 1560 and 1650), the extirpation of idolatry in Peru ceased to be a religious phenomenon of any importance by the late seventeenth century. Why? Partly because the Indians were said to have accepted Roman Catholicism at last, and partly because the hold of Andean religion on the hearts of the people was said to have been successfully wrenched away, that is to say, extirpated. And even more central to this argument has been the assumption that the Church had lost its appetite for campaigns of religious repression.

By the second half of the seventeenth century, Hispanic churchmen, like other members of the intellectual élite in Europe and Spanish America, are said to have begun to absorb ideas like those of Benedict de Spinoza (1632–

---

problematic, as Duviols observed in the forward to *La Lutte*, p. 15. Neither my starting point of 1640 nor my end point of 1750 are meant to suggest either that colonial Andean religious practices were nonexistent, dormant, or crystallized, or that idolatry investigations of some description (often local initiatives) were not pursued, before and after.

[19] The most essential readings for orientation and interpretation include P. Duviols, *La Lutte*; P. Duviols, "Prefacio," in *Cultura andina*; A. Acosta Rodríguez, "Los doctrineros" and "La extirpación"; L. Huertas Vallejos, *La religión en una sociedad*; and L. Millones, "Introducción al estudio de las idolatrías." See also the survey essays introducing a number of valuable collections of relevant documentation, by A. Sánchez in *Amancebados, hechiceros y rebeldes*; J. C. García Cabrera in *Ofensas a Dios*; and for the interpretations of H. Urbano, especially in "Introducción: Idolos, figuras, imágenes," and "Estudio preliminar." Two dissertations, focusing on ancestor worship and the "Andean priesthood," respectively, are also of note: M. E. Doyle, "The Ancestor Cult," and G. Cock Carrasco, "El sacerdote andino." Other recent essays include N. Griffiths's pondering of Duviols's lines in "Inquisition of the Indians?" and "Los *hechiceros idólatras*." In the bibliography of the latter essay, Griffiths cites his Ph.D. dissertation, "Religious Repression and Adaptation in the Archbishopric of Lima ca. 1640–ca. 1788" (University of Cambridge, 1993).

1677), rather as Catholic Christendom is said to have absorbed the doctrines of the Council of Trent a century earlier. An increasing desire for strategies of explanation that involved reason and for the application of the scientific method frustrated belief in such phenomena as the dark powers of witches.[20] In the same way, enlightened and skeptical attitudes were supposed to have calmed the Church's anxiety over Indian idolatry in mid-colonial Peru. The fact that extant information about Andean religion and its extirpators becomes more sparse after the 1660s has also greatly influenced the treatment of this subject. Influential, too, has been the date of the death of the Extirpation's greatest proponent, the Archbishop of Lima Pedro de Villagómez, in 1671. Without a pleasing and easily accessible cache of evidence, and deprived of the attraction provided by the prelate who revived systematic extirpation in the middle of the seventeenth century, the subject is more elusive. The pertinent conclusions within a bold and influential article still much cited as an English-language survey of the Andean colonial experience, George Kubler's "The Quechua in the Colonial World" (1946), offer further instruction about the guiding historiographic assumptions.[21]

The historiography of colonial Latin America is rooted in Kubler's landmark essay. Although usually without explicit reference to Kubler, and perhaps even without recalling his precise propositions on the subject, many historians have been inclined to turn 1660, or at least the decade of the 1660s, into a watershed in the religious and cultural history of Peru.[22] Kubler argued for two related

[20] Sabine MacCormack argues that in the last third of the seventeenth century the vocabulary and concepts of Spinoza—which would have even more impact after his death—were "part of the philosophical culture of the time." For her thoughts on his views and their influence on contemporaries' thinking about "demonic manipulation of sense perception and imagination," see the Epilogue to *Religion in the Andes*, p. 435. Fernando Cervantes brilliantly charts similar intellectual developments as they affected diabolism in New Spain in particular; see *The Devil in the New World*. See the explanations of changing views in the European context in J. Delumeau, *Catholicism between Luther and Voltaire*, esp. p. 174, and K. V. Thomas, *Religion and the Decline of Magic*, pp. 681–98. And within a massive literature, see also R. Muchembled, *Culture populaire et culture des élites*; C. Larner, *Enemies of God*, pp. 15–28; and E. Le Roy Ladurie, *Jasmin's Witch*, part one.

By making the analogy with the spread of reformist zeal after the Council of Trent, I mean only to ponder in passing the comparability of two massive processes of change that affected the Church and its faithful through this period. The influence of the Tridentine program of reform, as received in Spain especially through the decrees of the Provincial Council of Toledo (1565–1566), is explored in detail for the diocese of Cuenca by Sara Nalle in *God in La Mancha*, ch. 2. For a comparative examination of the spread of Tridentine influence to other regions, and an argument that emphasizes, among other aspects, the unevenness of reformist measures in Spain, see A. D. Wright, *Catholicism and Spanish Society*.

[21] In *The Handbook of South American Indians*, edited by J. Steward, 2: 331–410.

[22] Kubler gained much from the treatise by the contemporary bishop of Quito, Alonso de la Peña Montenegro, the *Itinerario*. For more on the bishop's background, see M. Bandín Hermo, *El Obispo de Quito*. For those more or less accepting this periodization and its suggestions, see, for instance, P. Duviols, *La Lutte*; M. Marzal, *La transformación religiosa peruana*, pp. 61–63; and most recently, S. MacCormack, *Religion in the Andes*, p. 5 and ch. 9.2. Duviols, as I have already noted, recognized "a certain arbitrariness" in his choice of 1660 as a cut-off date; *La Lutte*, p. 15.

transformations taking place in Peru in the second half of the seventeenth century.

First, he held that after about 1667, when an aged Villagómez's campaigns against Andean religion slowed, Peruvian churchmen began to look more tolerantly upon idolatry, viewing it as "nonheretical" and essentially harmless. Although Andean beliefs and practices were still to be discouraged as pollutions of the Christian atmosphere, he held that the Indian concepts and rituals were increasingly seen only as misguided ideas and mere superstition. For Kubler, a terrible chapter in the religious history of the Andes had ended; the hungry zeal of the extirpator to seek and destroy all obstacles to Christian orthodoxy among the Andean new Christians had been sated. His second point grew from his first. Kubler proposed that roughly concurrent with the Peruvian Church's change of attitude came a genuine acceptance of Christianity by native Andeans. In the course of the seventeenth century, he asserted, improved religious education and the repeated efforts at extirpation had finally borne their intended fruit: in the eyes of the Quechua-speaking faithful, the chief Andean gods had lost what Kubler memorably called their "divine essence."[23]

Pierre Duviols's periodization of the Extirpation's history into certain epochs or "campaigns" in the seventeenth century (1609–1621; 1625–1626; 1646–1667), has been just as influential.[24] The Spanish attitude to idolatry was to have softened on the eve of Villagómez's death, just as the battle against a serious idolatry was won. As a result, the idolatry investigations conducted in the Lima region after the Kublerian watershed have been cordoned off, treated as somehow different from and by implication as less substantial in a religious sense than those which preceded them.[25] This view is understandable, given the sources that have hitherto been emphasized, but if tested more rigorously it emerges as only a small part of the answer. It runs the risk of mistaking shifts in the terminology employed by mid-colonial proponents of the Extirpation for

---

M. Burga argues for a slightly later turning point in the late seventeenth century; see *Nacimiento*, pp. 162–65. As hinted above, compare with the periods set down in Keith Thomas's influential *Religion and the Decline of Magic*.

[23] "The Quechua," p. 403. Kubler works out similar views of religious change in the native context in his pioneering studies of early colonial architecture, especially *Mexican Architecture*. Another work that pursues an argument about the imposition of religion from the point of view of architecture in early colonial Peru is V. Fraser, *The Architecture of Conquest*.

[24] *La Lutte*, pp. 147–69.

[25] The relegation of the later trials is often related to the separation of certain supposedly "magical" practices from "religion." One of the most accomplished modern Andeanists, Frank Salomon, writes, for instance: "After the waning of the 'extirpation' campaigns, the record becomes thinner but still workable through, for example, trials of shamans implicated in political assassination via magic." "Introductory Essay," *The Huarochirí Manuscript*, translated and edited by F. Salomon and G. L. Urioste, p. 28. On the problems with "magic" as a basic category for discussion of colonial Andean religion see Chapter Four below. The more "political" nature (again, interestingly, separated from "religion") is another feature often identified and emphasized in investigations of these themes in the later colonial period as well. F. Salomon, "Shamanism and Politics," and "Ancestor Cults"; L. Millones, "Shamanismo y política"; and J. Dammert Bellido's two articles cited above, "Procesos . . . siglo XVIII" and "Procesos . . . siglo XVIII."

evidence of changes in attitude. More seriously, it can cause research to slide into a search for signs that Christianity was "replacing" Andean religion in the Indians' minds or that a syncretic synthesis had been reached. The sources from the Villagómez era and beyond, however, provide new and surprisingly detailed information on Andean religious dimensions, that allows for many different views and demonstrates a more uneven pace of change than has often been supposed.

A number of the best recent monographs on colonial Andean history have analyzed a smattering of idolatry trial evidence,[26] while still others have dealt with selected information from the documents in their discussion of wider themes.[27] But considerations of the Extirpation have been dominated, first by treatment of the machinery of repression—dutifully connected to that well-known forebear, the Inquisition, and also to bodies of theoretical work which prove that religious investigations, like religion itself, can be a form of social control, especially in colonial settings. And second, the field has also seen its share of reflections on the fascinating circumstances surrounding the initiation of the idolatry campaigns in the early seventeenth century. There is a need to go beyond these contributions, to establish what else the idolatry trials themselves reveal.

In the process of searching beyond the depictions of contemporary treatises and the idolatry testimonies from the better-understood regions and periods, and also beyond the prevalent narratives of opposition between official Christianity and the colonial religion of Andean peoples, I hope to challenge and complicate previous renderings. But, as the reader will appreciate, I advance not a step without making plain the many and obvious debts to the seminal work of the historians who have gone before.

[26] The shining example is K. Spalding, *Huarochirí*, pp. 252–69.

[27] Examples are L. Millones, *Historia y poder*; M. Burga, *Nacimiento*, pp. 123–96; A. Flores Galindo, *Buscando un Inca*, pp. 79–100; and S. MacCormack, *Religion in the Andes*, pp. 406–33.

Valverde to Villagómez

THE INKA state cults, their lavish objects and monumental sites of worship, had offered the quickest riches to the Spanish conquerors of Peru and proved the easiest to locate and tear down in the name of God. And what the Spaniards learned about the overarching divinities of Inkaic religion could, with a little imagination, be seen as nearly analogous to the invaders' monotheistic categories.[1] The concentration upon Inka religion, coupled with the Spaniards' internecine struggles, their quest for riches and mineral wealth, and the ruggedness of the Peruvian terrain would keep the Spanish Catholic Church from reaching the heart of Andean religion in early colonial times. Despite their grandeur and impressive ubiquity, the Inkaic cults were the least rooted in the hearts and traditions of the subject peoples outside the Cusqueño élite.

That said, the state cults of Tawantinsuyu and the regional expressions of Andean religion were related. Thus the assumption that a degree of religious convergence between the two would have occurred after the Spanish conquest is sensible; indeed, it would be surprising if this convergence had not begun before the upheaval that followed the confrontation between Francisco Pizarro and his accompanying Dominican Vicente Valverde and the Inka Atahuallpa on 16 November 1532.[2] The Inkas and their subject peoples sprang from, and developed belief systems amidst, similar environments and historical contexts. Moreover, the Inkas' style of religious expansion involved the superimposition of state cults and the careful incorporation of the important divinities of subject areas, where regional religious networks were left mostly intact.[3] Still, the case for the perceptible convergence of Inkaic and Andean religions, self-evident to a degree, can be taken too far. As Frank Salomon writes, "the equation between Inca religion and Andean religion is an ideological slight," a misrepresentation of an intensely local and regional point of view in Andean religion.[4]

---

[1] See the vivid portrayal of Hernando Pizarro's destruction of the coastal shrine of Pacha Camac in S. MacCormack's *Religion in the Andes*, pp. 55–58. On the attraction of Andean "creators," and parallels offered by classical antiquity, see S. MacCormack, "Limits of Understanding," pp. 98–102.

[2] Interpretations of this event are weighed by S. MacCormack, "Atahuallpa and the Book," and P. Seed, "Failing to Marvel."

[3] See M. Rostworowski de Diez Canseco, *La historia de Tawantinsuyu*.

[4] F. Salomon, "Introductory Essay," in *The Huarochirí Manuscript*, edited and translated by F. Salomon and G. L. Urioste, pp. 4–5. Concentrating largely on the persistence of rites devoted to the sun, Sabine MacCormack argues that Andean and Inka religion were "fused" or "converging" after 1533. But she goes on to complicate this image of an Inka-Andean fusion by also noting that Inka religion was gradually stripped away in early colonial times and, moreover, that other changes were occurring. See *Religion in the Andes*, pp. 3–6, 13–14, 179–81 and 404–5. For further thoughts

How much did the comparatively small numbers of sixteenth-century churchmen in Peru know of these local and regional religious worlds?[5] The chronicles of the mendicant orders claim miraculous conversions and great Christian triumphs but, generally speaking, the contacts of the friars with Andean peoples (let alone their religious systems) in the early post-conquest period were minimal and their moments of missionary success hard won. In Peru, the search for the fruits of a missionary era—much less a "spiritual conquest"—comparable to the early evangelization of New Spain is made in vain.[6]

Although the evangelization of Indians in Peru can be traced back to a point soon after the military conquest, historians know surprisingly little about how the gospel was preached in the different Andean regions concurrently with the era of the struggles between Spaniards and their respective Indian allies.[7] For the earliest years after 1532, there is little to go on beyond the fleeting mentions of various friars' movements between the first monasteries, mission stations, and the parishes set up for the Indians' indoctrination (*doctrinas de indios*). The early Dominican provincial, Fray Tomás de San Martín, was said to have dispatched his friars "two by two" into the mountainous areas northeast of Lima where a few schools were begun.[8] Another Dominican, the great Quechua lexicographer and informer of Bartolomé de Las Casas, Fray Domingo de Santo Tomás, was said to have won "admirable fruits through his preaching and in the conversion of towns and entire provinces."[9] Although some of the reli-

---

on the theme, see S. MacCormack, "From the Sun of the Incas." On the cult of the sun, see also an earlier article by G. Cock Carrasco and M. Doyle, "Del culto solar."

[5] The maintenance of the Christian faith among Andeans after baptism and some intitial instruction was an acknowledged problem, particularly in remote mountain regions. In September of 1583, the third session of the Third Provincial Council of Lima decreed that no *cura* should administer to more than 400 Indian parishioners, and stated its objective of one pastor for every 200 or 300 people. See Francesco Leonardo Lisi, tr. and ed., *El Tercer Concilio Limense*, Actio tertia, caput 11m.: Quoto numero Indorum præficiendus sit parochus, 172–73. In the early seventeenth century, however, the church appears still to have been falling short of its goals. See G. Kubler, "The Quechua," p. 403.

[6] R. Ricard, *The Spiritual Conquest of Mexico*, and J. L. Phelan, *The Millennial Kingdom*. A wide-ranging study of sixteenth-century evangelization in the Andes remains to be written, though a seminal piece is S. MacCormack's "The Heart Has Its Reasons." There have been suggestions that Andeans of certain regions did receive pastoral attention comparable to that seen in early New Spain. Valerie Fraser's architecturally driven allusions to the Dominicans' missionary achievements before and during the 1560s in the south Andean province of Chucuito offer one example: see *The Architecture of Conquest*, pp. 11–15, 160–62. For a different interpretation of the results of evangelization in the environs of Lake Titicaca—based primarily on ecclesiastical sources—see N. Meiklejohn, *La iglesia y los Lupaqas*.

[7] For general histories of the Catholic evangelization in this troubled era we are still largely reliant on F. de Armas Medina, *Cristianización del Perú* and "El clero en las guerras civiles"; and P. Borges, *Métodos misionales* and *El envío de misioneros*.

[8] San Martín arrived in Peru in 1538, two years before Francisco Toscano and twelve other Dominicans, among whom would be Fr. Domingo de Santo Tomás, mentioned below. See A. de Egaña, *Historia de la Iglesia*, p. 48.

[9] J. Melendez, *Tesoros verdaderos de las Indias*, 1: 328.

gious chroniclers such as the Augustinian, Antonio de la Calancha, noted difficulties that the early missionaries encountered, far more common were their
repetitive and even formulaic references to amazing feats of baptism and conversion.[10] The Mercedarian, Diego de Porres, for example, wrote that he had
worked for two years among the peoples of the province of "Caxatambos," and
that "with the help of Our Father and my instruction [I] baptized more than
two thousand souls and married more than five hundred."[11] Of course, Andean
peoples had not been as passive and unproblematic in their reception of the
basic Christian tenets as was often pretended. Many of the religious chroniclers
of the sixteenth and seventeenth centuries, not unlike other contemporary
churchmen to be discussed below, were less interested in producing an accurate portrayal of the vicissitudes of their Peruvian endeavors than they were in
fitting their supposed achievements into an existing framework of Christianization that stretched deep into the history and identity of the Roman Church.[12]

Regardless (for the moment) of the "predicaments" for the Church that
arose from the realm of the potential converts themselves, the missionaries
were simply not present in sufficient quantity—and often, quality—to achieve
their goals.[13] Beyond administering baptisms, the occasional marriage or con-
firmation, and what could be achieved through the patchy proselytization of
these early Andean encounters, the bulk of the efforts to incorporate the In-

[10] By Calancha's account, Fr. Francisco Martínez de Viedma, for example, found that in the
mountains to the north and west of Lima there were "swarms (*enjambres*) of witches, magi, and
sorcerers who made the conversion of these people very difficult." A. de la Calancha and B. de
Torres, *Crónicas agustinianas del Perú*, 1: 47. On early Franciscan efforts see D. de Córdova y
Salinas, *Corónica*, and the survey of Antonine Tibesar, *Franciscan Beginnings in Colonial Peru*.

[11] Porres, like many of his day, was one for conveying impressive statistics. See the letter dated
1586 from him to the king claiming, among other things, the baptism of between seventy to eighty
thousand Indians in his thirty-three years of service. AGI Charcas 142. See also "Memorial de Fr.
Diego de Porres de la Orden de Nuestra Señora de la Merced a S.M., en el que expone los meritos
y servicios de su ministerio en los reinos del Perú," without date, in *Los Mercedarios en el Perú*,
edited by V. M. Barriga, 3: 195; or R. Levillier, *Organización de la Iglesia*, 1: 394–98. For more on
the Mercedarians see P. Nolasco Pérez, *Historia de las misiones mercedarias*.

[12] An exceptional early account is that prepared about 1560 by Fray Juan de San Pedro, the
Augustinian prior of a small monastery his order had established at Huamachuco in the region
north of the central Andes in 1552. See *Relación de la religión y ritos del Perú* in Colección de
documentos inéditos, 3: 5–58 and, in a new edition, *La persecución del demonio*. Three interpretative essays by José Luis González, John R. Topic and Luis Millones precede the latter transcription.

Sabine MacCormack has recently pondered this source, and especially the adaptations that the
peoples of Huamachuco appear to have made to their own mythic histories of origin as early as the
1550s. Just as Europeans interpreted the native inhabitants of the Americas in accordance with
their own knowledge and past experiences, these Andeans made sense of the Spaniards by observing them, judging their worth, and integrating them into their own historic vision—in MacCormack's view—by "applying a familiar mythic motif to a new situation"; *Religion in the Andes*,
p. 145. This formulation gains another dimension in what Frank Salomon, working from Waud
Kracke's thoughts on dreams and myths among the Kagwahib people of the Amazon region, has
characterized as the ways in which Andeans in colonial times might succeed in "making the found
world their own." See F. Salomon, "Nightmare Victory," p. 5; and W. Kracke, "Myths in Dreams."

[13] The word is borrowed from the subtitle of MacCormack's "The Heart Has Its Reasons."

dians into Christendom and into the political creation the Spanish had named the Viceroyalty of Peru would come decades later, in the late 1560s, the 1570s, and thereafter.

In the 1560s, an ecclesiatical *visitador general*, Cristóbal de Albornoz, was commissioned to conduct an investigation in south-central Peru in response to the spread of an Andean religious movement known as the Taki Onqoy. Its adherents were itinerant dancers and teachers whose cosmology showed a creative blending of indigenous traditions of cataclysm and rebirth with the Christian symbolism of destruction and resurrection, and who foretold the imminent triumph of Andean gods and the end of Spanish rule. The local investigations, sentences, and the public punishment of the principal agents of this movement, in connection with the execution in Cusco of the last of the so-called neo-Inka rebels, Túpac Amaru, in 1572 must have sent a strong message to Andeans about the Spanish Catholic presence. An ambitious viceroy, Francisco de Toledo, accelerated the resettlement of Andeans into towns and villages (*reducciones*) that were conceived as crucial not only to the exploitation of Indian labor but also to the twin processes that could make "conquest" complete: the Christianization and Hispanicization of the Indian peoples. In 1568, the first padres of the Society of Jesus arrived in Peru, beginning a period during which they would greatly affect the character of evangelization.[14] And, finally, the archbishop of Lima, Toribio Alfonso de Mogrovejo, convened the enormously influential Third Provincial Council of that city in 1582–1583. These events, among others of a similar ilk, signaled the belated arrival of Spanish Catholicism in the Andes in more than just name.[15]

As far as the relationship between Christianity and Andean religion was concerned, the last event was perhaps the most crucial. The constitutions of this provincial council responded to the observation of some of the best-informed Spanish contemporaries—people such as the lawyer Juan Polo de Ondegardo—that the conversion of the indigenous peoples to Christianity remained an objective rather than an accomplishment.[16]

It was agreed that Christian proselytizers had much to learn about what they were up against. As recommended by St. Augustine's timeless injunction to the Church Militant, research would have to be conducted into the false beliefs

---

[14] See Manuel Marzal's *La utopía posible*, vol. 1, ch. 3.

[15] On the Taki Onqoy see L. Millones, comp. *El retorno de las huacas*; on Toledo's life and achievements, see R. Levillier, *Don Francisco de Toledo*; on the most influential of the first Jesuits, J. de Acosta, see his *De Procuranda Indorum Salute*, upon which he would base his advice for the Third Provincial Council of Lima; the decrees of that council are published in R. Vargas Ugarte, *Concilios limenses* 1: 259–377. A recent bilingual edition (Latin and Spanish) is F. L. Lisi, tr. and ed., *El Tercer Concilio Limense*. See also E. T. Bartra, *Tercer Concilio Limense*; J. G. Durán, *El catecismo*; and P. Tineo, *Los concilios limenses*.

[16] See J. Polo de Ondegardo, "Instrucción contra las ceremonias" and "Los errores y supersticiones" in *El catecismo*, edited by J. G. Durán, pp. 447–78. In the facsimile edition, *Doctrina Christiana*, see pp. 253–83. See also Pedro de Quiroga, *Libro intitulado*, p. 115ff.

and practices of the peoples who were to be gathered into the fold.[17] This process of finding out about Andean religion in order to eradicate it guided and inspired the labors in particular of those in the Peruvian Church who advocated that a measure of force was necessary to wrest the Indians from their error-filled ways.

The image of a persuasive, experimental style of evangelization draining away with the sixteenth century, and being replaced by the flood of a more forceful approach in the seventeenth century, is as misrepresentative as it is prevalent in the colonial historiography of the Andes and elsewhere in Spanish America. Coercive actions that were meant to advance the conversion of Andeans to Christianity had been present from the beginning of the evangelization in Peru. The Indians' sin of idolatry in particular was seen by many in the conquering parties as justification enough for acts of wanton destruction, acts that could always be portrayed by Spanish Christians as instructive demonstrations of the powerlessness of the wicked gods to defend themselves against the agents of the true religion. Yet systematic exertions of force ran against the grain of a more patient and gradualist tradition that was simultaneously present. This evangelical stance stressed its emulation of the apostles, its benevolence. Sanctioned by Pope Alexander VI in 1493 and thereafter, peaceful evangelization was recognized by contemporary Spanish thinkers as the foundation upon which rested the entire edifice of legitimate Spanish control.[18] Thus the aggressive undercurrent favored by some churchmen in their relations with non-Christians could be at least partly held back by a determined regional leader of the Church and his supporters. This appears to have been the case during the long prelacy in Lima of Archbishop Toribio Alfonso de Mogrovejo (1581–1605), who called the Third Provincial Council of Lima (Figure 1).

Many of the constitutions of this council were directed inward, faithfully reflecting Tridentine concerns about doctrinal ignorance, absenteeism, and poor conduct on the part of prelates and parish clergy. If the priests were able, devout, and numerous enough, the constitutions affirmed, the goals of Christianization might be reached. When its reforming gaze turned outward, although it is true that the churchmen did recommend separating Andean "ministers of the devil" from other new Christians whom they might "infect," the Council more characteristically stressed the "timid nature" of the Indians and advocated moderation in the punishment of them for religious and other er-

---

[17] *City of God*, Book 6. Similar motivations—mixed with ethnographic curiosity—inspired impressive compilations of information on indigenous culture, religion, and history in Mexico, most notably those of Andrés de Olmos and Bernardino de Sahagún. See Olmos, *Tratado de hechicerías y sortilegios*, and Sahagún's *Florentine Codex*, esp. vol. 1. See also D. Durán, *Historia de las indias*, 1: 7–8.

[18] James Muldoon convincingly stretches discussion of this point from its usual sixteenth-century setting in discussion of the Salamancan theologian Francisco de Vitoria and the Dominican protector of the Indians, Bartolomé de Las Casas, among others, to consideration of Juan de Solórzano Pereira's seventeenth-century *De Indiarum Jure*, in *The Americas in the Spanish World Order*.

Figure 1. Toribio Alfonso de Mogrovejo, the Archbishop of Lima (1581–1606). Drawing by Don Carlos Fabbri from the oil portrait in the cathedral chapter of Lima.

rors.[19] Over and above its deliberations, this council elaborated a precise catechism for Indians new to the faith, as well as one for those who were more
advanced in their knowledge. It published a standard *doctrina* (doctrinal manual) for regular instruction, a guide for the confession of Indians, the first official book of thirty bilingual sermons for Indian congregations (with two texts
devoted largely to the error of idolatry), and a whole host of other contemporary works meant to serve as pastoral complements for parish priests and pious
persons.[20] As I will show in Chapter Six, the guidelines and pastoral tools provided by the Third Provincial Council formed a trusted archive from which
colonial churchmen and jurists would long draw inspiration and practical directions in their labors.[21]

For a quarter of a century, at a time when the Spanish had finally stopped
fighting each other and turned their attention to the consolidation and organization of their rule in the Andes,[22] Mogrovejo was the chief representative and
visionary of the contemporary Church in Peru. He embodied a number of the
most crucial features of the model prelate as defined by the Council of Trent—
charity, personal piety and conviction, the promotion of seminaries, and fervent
protection of ecclesiastical jurisdiction in the face of viceroys, the audiencia,
and even the monarch himself (Mogrovejo often chose to inform the pope
before, or in place of, the Spanish sovereign), all of which would later speed his
canonization.[23] More to the point, on the basis of his experiences on repeated

[19] On the separation of Andean ministers, see the Actio secunda, caput 42m.: "Ministros diaboli
a consortio cæterorum Indorum separandos esse"; on the themes of moderation and protection of
Indian parishioners, see Actio quarta, caput 8m.: "De moderatione servanda in punitione Indorum," and Actio tertia, caput 3m.: "De protectione et cura Indorum," in *El Tercer Concilio*, edited
and translated by F. L. Lisi, pp. 154–55, 206–7 and 164–65, respectively.

[20] See J. G. Durán, *El catecismo*, pp. 368–513 in the facsimile, *Doctrina Christiana*, pp. 189–
777. The guidance and advice of the Jesuit P. José de Acosta was instrumental at this council and in
the publication of its pastoral texts. See the collection of essays published in *Doctrina cristiana*,
edited by A. García y García and F. Maseda.

[21] If the seventeenth-century record is correct, then the publication and distribution of these
pastoral complements to the conciliar decisions—the guides and manuals for priests and
confessors—went considerably more smoothly in Mogrovejo's Peru than in the contemporary New
Spain of the archbishop of Mexico, Pedro Moya de Contreras (1571–1591). On the comparison,
and on the atmosphere of Moya's New Spain, see the excellent study by Stafford Poole, *Pedro
Moya de Contreras*, pp. 160–62.

[22] The secular side of this moment is epitomized by the activities of the fifth viceroy of Peru
already mentioned, Francisco de Toledo (1569–1581). The classic study of his career is R. Levillier,
Don Francisco de Toledo. The best recent assessments have not found reason to question Toledo's
centrality to the establishment of Spanish aims. See esp. S. J. Stern, *Peru's Indian Peoples*, pp. 76–
79 and ch. 4; and K. Spalding, *Huarochirí*, pp. 156–68 and 209–27.

[23] The formal collection of reports on his life and virtues began in 1631. Helped along by the
steady encouragement of Mogrovejo's nephew, the sixth archbishop of Lima Pedro de Villagómez
(1641–1671), and the lobbying of his agents in Rome, Mogrovejo was beatified in 1679 and finally
declared Santo Toribio by Pope Benedict XIII in 1726; Egaña, *Historia de la Iglesia*, p. 280.

The figure of Mogrovejo recalls the career of, and similar challenges faced by, a contemporary
in New Spain, the archbishop of Mexico Pedro Moya de Contreras. No study of which I am aware
has examined and compared exhaustively these two Tridentine prelates, although the potential

and ambitious pastoral tours, Mogrovejo took an optimistic view of Andeans as Christians and potential Christians. He found the Indians, for the most part, not only content in what they already understood of the new religion, but desirous of both the sacraments of the Church and greater knowledge of Christianity.[24] Mogrovejo believed that Andeans needed reform that would be advanced only through better instruction and more careful pastoral surveillance by adequately trained clergy.[25]

Still, even with the considerable influence of the long-serving Mogrovejo's opinions, and the Third Provincial Council's laying of the theoretical and pastoral groundwork and directives for Andean Christianization, the real task, and the discussion over how it would best be approached, had only begun. Moreover, the omnipresent tension between peaceful and forceful evangelization only became more acute with the passage of time. The two traditions, never separate in Christian Europe, blurred just as completely in Spanish America. Churchmen in Peru were agreed that, ideally, conversion was to be a voluntary and blessed experience: the gospel was to call its own through careful teaching and the beginning of a personal transformation at baptism. Yet there was a recognition among a growing number of churchmen that Peru was not proving ideal—that is to say predictable—soil for the growth of Christianity. There was a breaking point, for some, after which patience with persistent Indian religious error and seemingly fruitless missionary effort would run out.

Supporters of a more forceful approach to Indian religious error, who had either known part of Archbishop Mogrovejo's archiepiscopate or who had followed immediately in his wake—people such as the parish priest Francisco de Avila and the Jesuit padres Diego Álvarez de Paz and Pablo José de Arriaga—grew critical of aspects of Mogrovejo's tenure not long after he was gone. They saw Mogrovejo as a pious and ambitious churchman who, for all his good intentions and aspirations, had been deceived.

Padre Arriaga was perhaps the most explicit. He wrote in the preface to his manual for extirpators of idolatry in 1621 of the need to demonstrate the

---

importance of the connection is hinted at by Stafford Poole in *Pedro Moya de Contreras*, pp. 5–6, and the task is begun by Victoria H. Cummins in her "Blessed Connections." The most detailed studies of Mogrovejo are quite old and sometimes lacking in critical perspective. See V. Rodríguez Valencia, *Santo Toribio de Mogrovejo*, and R. Levillier, "Santo Toribio Mogrovejo: Arzobispo de Los Reyes (1581–1606)," in his *Organización de la Iglesia*, 1: lxiii–xcii.

[24] ASV, Ad Limina 450, Relación y memorial, Thuribius to the pope, Lima, 28 April 1599, fol. 338v. In this letter, one of a number that discuss different dimensions of the "state of his archdiocese," Mogrovejo emphasized that since his arrival in Lima in 1581, he had confirmed over 600,000 Andean souls and had traveled over 6,000 leagues (sometimes on foot, and often to remote regions in difficult terrain); see fol. 338.

[25] A good sense is provided by the constitutions of the Third Provincial Council of Lima that he convened. See F. L. Lisi, ed. and tr., *El Tercer Concilio Limense*, esp. Actio secunda. I have also found useful the parish-by-parish relation of Mogrovejo's 1601 tour in "Carta del Arzobispo, enviando la razon de los diezmos del Arzobispado y clerigos doctrineros, 30 abril de 1602," edited by R. Vargas Ugarte in his *Biblioteca peruana*, 2: 10–21. Antonio de Egaña summarizes Mogrovejo's ambitious itineraries over twenty-four years in his *Historia de la Iglesia*, pp. 273–74.

simple truth about Andean religion. He glorified the "discoveries" of idolatry made by Francisco de Avila in Huarochirí, and added accounts of his own, along with those of early seventeenth-century extirpators such as Fernando de Avendaño, Diego Ramírez, and others in different regions of the archdiocese. Arriaga sought to challenge the contradictions and doubts planted by those "serious and learned persons" who argued that the diverse peoples of the Andes "are all good Christians," and to prove instead that "there is idolatry among the Indians."[26] In the eighth chapter of his treatise, although Arriaga remained respectful of the former archbishop, he was also frank about what, in his opinion, Mogrovejo had failed to do and about the damaging influence of this failure. "Señor Don Toribio, who is in Heaven," may have personally visited even the smallest Andean communities in his archdiocese repeatedly, showing "the great zeal of a holy prelate," Arriaga stated, but he had not perceived the secret idolatry; indeed, "he knew nothing about that which is now known."[27] The verdict on Mogrovejo's misplaced optimism, his blindness, and his legacy was clear: the great man had moved too quickly, with too much hope, too little information from his parish priests, and at too great a distance from the evil realities of colonial Andean religiosity.[28]

By the early seventeenth century, it had become difficult for many churchmen fully to understand, let alone to look tolerantly on, widespread Indian religious error in the archdiocese that surrounded the viceregal capital. Certainly, it was known that there were still "barbarous infidels" in remote places of this realm as in others: it was agreed that these neglected peoples, who enjoyed a constant place in colonial ecclesiastical correspondence, needed to be reached by the agents of their salvation. But they were increasingly viewed as a different problem. In the Archdiocese of Lima, the Indian who was viewed as a pagan or an idolater, and whose errors derived from complete ignorance of the Christian truth, had for the most part become a distant figure of an early colonial past. This Indian's replacement, both in reality and especially in the minds of many Spanish Christians, was a "new Christian"—an American *converso*—a baptized and at least superficially instructed convert of whom certain things could now be expected. This Indian's persistent participation in the vast array of crimes and evils called idolatry, superstition, and error was seen as considerably more serious. Andeans were losing the defense of ignorance.

Pierre Duviols's thoughtful work on the early development of the Extirpation of idolatry has established the importance of the argumentative line that would grant the status of apostate or heretic to Indian religious offenders. A few characters emerge as the chief proponents of this shift. For instance, the parish priest from Huarochirí, Francisco de Avila, a crucial figure in the early history of seventeenth-century extirpation, found his parishioners to be apostates in

[26] P. J. de Arriaga, "*La extirpación*," pp. xxx-xxxi.

[27] Ibid., pp. 80–81.

[28] A. de Egaña, in his *Historia de la Iglesia*, makes the same point, referring to the critical attitudes of Avila and Álvarez de Paz; see p. 274.

the early seventeenth century. And a host of seventeenth-century voices—ranging in importance from the first two archbishops to support systematic extirpation, Bartolomé Lobo Guerrero (1609–1622) and Gonzalo de Campo (1625–1626), to individual priest-extirpators—began referring to the Indians' crimes of apostasy, heresy, and idolatry in the same breath.[29] Wording in the constitutions of the synod convened by Lobo Guerrero in Lima in 1613 are a good representation of this inclination. Lobo set down that "the majority (*casi los más*) of the Indians who have been investigated since I began my tenure in this archdiocese are idolaters and apostates from Our Holy Catholic faith who maintain the rites and ceremonies of their paganism."[30]

Yet, in spite of these collapsing distinctions, many churchmen continued to recognize a complex set of reasons—some of them plainly to do with Spanish pastoral negligence—for the existence of Andean religious error (by whatever name) and for the delays in these new Christians' collection into the fold. The point after which an originally non-Christian society—militarily defeated and, for the most part, politically subjugated, baptized, and at least to some degree introduced to the Christian faith—would be considered fully subject to Christian rule was not reached unanimously or without ambiguity. The views of Spanish Christian commentators and participants were not clear and they would continue to oscillate through the mid-colonial period.

Both this ambiguity and the prejudicial nature of the Indians' apparent inclusion into Christendom can be clearly demonstrated. First, although some Indian parishioners might work as catechists in their communities, Indians were not being ordained as Christian priests. No amount of Christian education or evidence of understanding entitled an Indian to that confidence or kind of inclusion. Second, and even more pertinent to this discussion, there was judged to be no point after which Indians would be treated as the heretics and apostates they were being called. That is, Indians did not fall within the jurisdiction of the Holy Office of the Inquisition—the institution that policed belief, practice, and manners of living among all full-fledged Catholics. Judging inclusion by such a measure may seem curious at a glance, as if being subject to the Inquisition was some kind of privilege. But it is a symbol. It is as significant that Andean Christians in the seventeenth and eighteenth centuries who strayed off the path of orthodoxy would be treated differently from other Christians—by episcopal processes like the Extirpation of idolatry—as it is that certain people from the same communities were not being ordained. Andean

---

[29] P. Duviols, *La Lutte*, pp. 221 and 148, and his discussion of the charges of Luis de Mora y Aguilar in "La visite des idolâtries." Gonzalo de Campo wrote to his sovereign telling about the existence of "idolatry and heresy among the Indians," and about the urgent need for the "extirpation of idolatry and heresy, and the reform and correction of customs." See two letters written on the same day—the first of three folios, and the second of six: AGI Lima 302, Campo to the king, Llamellin, 8 October 1626.

[30] "Constituciones synodales del arçobispado de los Reyes . . . ," Libro 1, titulo 1, capitulo 6, published in facsimile as "Sínodo de Lima de 1613," in B. Lobo Guerrero and F. Arias de Ugarte, *Sínodos de Lima*, edited by H. Santiago-Otero and A. García y García, p. 38.

"new Christians" were regarded as still, and perhaps perpetually, beneath the grade. They were being allowed a place on the edge of the edge of the Christian laity; in the post-Tridentine era, their failures and errors were increasingly taken as willful noncompliance with Christian strictures.

Spanish Christians in Peru were faced with the task of judging precisely which aspects of colonial Andean culture were offensive to God and detrimental to the people's religious and cultural improvement. At the point that these were determined, due force might be employed in the interest of reformation. Such developments were ultimately dependent on the emergence of a religious atmosphere that favored extirpation, a climate of enthusiasm among religious and secular authorities that had transformed Indian religious error from a collection of survivals, adaptations, and deviations from a prescribed Christian norm among a newly converted people into a perceived enemy that the Church was obliged to attack decisively and whose reform it was emphatically to encourage.

Local phenomena—the most important of which were perceived changes in Indian religious practices and the collapse of established understandings between the parochial representatives of Spanish Christianity and Andean converts—were important variables that could affect the nature of relations between Indians and official Christianity. But systematic extirpating initiatives grew from an atmosphere that relied ultimately upon the authorities in Lima. The development of a widespread extirpating atmosphere hinged most crucially upon how a prelate, perhaps a viceroy—as well as a supporting cast of inspectors, colonial officials, important secular priests, and friars—viewed and defined idolatry and, moreover, upon what portions of Andean life and thought the people at the center of the political and religious power structure chose to gather under that flexible concept.[31]

The use of a centrally organized investigative and penal body to achieve evangelical ends in the Andean parishes of the Archdiocese of Lima took root especially during the tenure of Mogrovejo's successor, Bartolomé Lobo Guerrero

---

[31] I acknowledge a debt to Robert Moore's arguments about the importance of religious authorities in the organization of the "machinery of repression" in Latin Christendom. Moore, along with other medievalists, has helped me to rethink this moment in which the extirpating initiatives began in Lima. Without denying the ways in which individuals and society at large might shape the attitudes of churchmen and secular officials, Moore emphasizes that at points in the eleventh and twelfth centuries "deliberate and socially sanctioned violence began to be directed, through established governmental, judicial and social institutions, against groups of people defined by general characteristics such as race, religion or way of life." R. I. Moore, *The Formation of a Persecuting Society*, p. 5, and also pp. 4 and 10. Moore puts his view in reaction to the nearly opposite opinions and suggestions of Bernard Hamilton and Sir Richard Southern. Both found that the origins of organized violence against perceived enemies of Christianity grew from "the people," more than from the holders of ecclesiastical power who, Southern argued, "were not free agents." B. Hamilton, *The Medieval Inquisition*, esp. pp. 33 and 57; R. W. Southern, *Western Society and the Church*, p. 19. In a later, Spanish context, see the treatment of similar subject surrounding the Inquisition by H. Kamen, *Inquisition and Society in Spain*.

(1609–1621; Figure 2).[32] After moving from Spain to Mexico as an official of the Inquisition, Lobo was passed over once as the preferred candidate for archbishop of Santa Fe de Bogotá in New Granada, before eventually being promoted to that see in 1599. During his time in New Granada (1599–1607), Lobo demonstrated a particular desire to work with the Society of Jesus in the investigation and destruction of Indian religious error. Lobo was much affected by the evidence that he and his assistants uncovered that the indigenous people's conversion to Christianity had not proceeded according to the Church's design. Moreover, Lobo's own words written from Lima confirm that, at least by 1611 and probably much earlier, he was connecting what he had heard and seen in his new archdiocese with his experiences in northern South America. The Indians of the Lima region venerated a whole range of natural objects, he wrote, "and they proceed in the same manner as the Indians of the kingdom of New Granada, having priests (*saçerdotes*) among themselves who preach and teach the followers of their evil sect (*su mala çeta*) in opposition to the indoctrination and teaching of the ministers of the Church."[33] When Lobo Guerrero arrived in Lima in October of 1609, his convictions and inclinations toward the forceful reform of Indian religiosity would be significantly encouraged by a seemingly small series of events already in progress in the vicinity of the principal city of the archdiocese.

In October 1609, an ambitious priest to whom I have already referred, Francisco de Avila, who had administered to the Checa people at San Damián de Huarochirí in the mountains southeast of Lima since 1597, became involved in a protracted investigation of his conduct. The outline of Avila's story is well known; Antonio Acosta's meticulous work on this figure, in particular, has emphasized the discrepancy between the moment when evidence suggests that Avila's extraordinary interest in the eradication of persistent Andean religion began and when, after the fact, he claimed it began. Avila, eager both to deflect attention away from the serious charges that his own parishioners had brought

---

[32] Lobo had grown up in Andalusia in southern Spain, part of the Guerrero family that had moved into the region of Ronda after its Islamic rulers had surrendered to the Christian armies of King Ferdinand in May of 1485. AHN, Sección de Inquisición, Leg. 1207, caja 3, exp. 37, "Genealogia de la limpieza del Doctor Lobo Guerrero, 1578." On Ferdinand's deployment of troops under Rodrigo Ponce de León and the siege and surrender of Ronda in 1484 and 1485, see esp. L. P. Harvey, *Islamic Spain*, pp. 285–86. Lobo studied at the universities of Osuna and Salamanca, and at the Colegio de Santa María de Jesús in Seville, where he ultimately obtained a doctorate in canon law and became rector. By 1578, he appears to have been headed for a promising career in the Holy Office of the Inquisition. There is no record of his service on a tribunal in Spain, but he traveled to Mexico in 1580 to take up an appointment as a *fiscal* of the Inquisition. Three years later, he was made an inquisitor. AHN, Inquisión, Leg. 1207, caja 3, exp. 37, and *Consejo de la Suprema Inquisición*, p. 201. See also M. de Mendiburu, *Diccionario histórico-biográfico del Perú*, 11: 71, and J. M. Soto Rábanos, "Contexto histórico" in *Sínodos de Lima*, p. xxiii. See also J. M. Pacheco, "Don Bartolomé Lobo Guerrero," and P. Castañeda Delgado, "Don Bartolomé Lobo Guerrero."

[33] AGI Lima 301, Lobo to the king, Lima, 20 April 1611. An excerpt from this letter has been transcribed and published by Pierre Duviols in the appendix to *Dioses y hombres*, pp. 253–54.

Figure 2. Bartolomé Lobo Guerrero, Archbishop of Lima (1609–1622). Drawing by Don Carlos Fabbri from the oil portrait in the cathedral chapter of Lima.

against him and to capitalize on the prestige and vindication which might be granted the "discoverer" of Andean idolatry and the "initiator" of systematic Christian efforts to uproot this evil, engaged in the fabrication of the origins of his own "special zeal."[34] Avila's misrepresentation of history to cast his own actions in a more favorable light began surprisingly early, even if his most systematic effort in this regard awaited the reemergence of a favorable, extirpating climate at the end of his career.[35]

Avila's grasp of the roles that the discovery and existence of idolatry might be made to play in his own defense and retaliation against his accusers, however useful, did not exhaust their potential for him. Perhaps as few as ten days after the entrance of Bartolomé Lobo Guerrero into Lima, Avila paid the new prelate a visit. The priest brought with him from the mountains a sizeable collection of Andean gods—including a number of malquis (mummified bodies of ancestors), the care of one of whom was said to have passed from one generation to the next for over eight hundred years—some other "idols" and religious objects from the region, and Hernando Pauccar, the chief minister of Chaupi Ñamca (an important regional divinity) from San Pedro de Mama, Huarochirí. Avila also delivered at least the implicit offer of an agenda to a prelate whom he seems to have known would be sympathetic to his concerns.[36]

Avila's material evidence of persistent Andean religion seems to have made an immediate impression on Archbishop Lobo Guerrero, the viceroy the marquis of Montesclaros, Juan de Mendoza y Luna (1607–1614), and other authorities. On Sunday, 13 December 1609, before the notables of the Church, the secular government, and the university in Lima who had assembled in the cathedral, Avila delivered a sermon in Latin, dedicated to the new archbishop. Draped in the worshipful style of its day, this sermon was noteworthy for its particular tone and contents. The parish priest denounced the Indians' idolatry and the dissimulation he said he had suddenly discovered in Huarochirí; he heaped praises on Lobo Guerrero and presented his prelate with a glorious opportunity. In what was not the first, and what would not be the last, rhetorical connection between colonial Peru and the deep past of the Christian religion, Avila suggested that the venture which Lobo had the power to initiate

---

[34] "Francisco de Avila;" p. 563. Earlier studies of Avila by Pierre Duviols, who provided some different emphases, are *La Lutte*, pp. 146–61 and "Estudio bio-bibliográfico," in *Dioses y hombres*, pp. 218–29. See also K. Spalding, *Huarochirí*, pp. 252–55.

[35] A preface ("Prefación") to a collection of of his sermons, the *Tratado de los evangelios*, was written in 1645 and published posthumously (for Avila died in 1647) with the *Tratado* in Lima in 1648. This preface became the perfect vehicle for a last attempt at self-aggrandizement, for those were the very years when the new archbishop of Lima, Pedro de Villagómez (1641–1671), was asserting the need for a revitalized campaign of visitas de idolatría as the best remedy for the persistence of Andean religious error.

[36] It is conceivable, as Acosta suggests, that through his close contact with the Jesuits (who had assisted Lobo, and who had been Avila's teachers) Avila had gained a notion of the new prelate's predilections. Avila's later recollection of Lobo Guerrero as an official "very experienced" in matters of idolatry suggests some knowledge of his record or opinions while in New Granada. F. de Avila, "Prefación," p. lxviii–lxix, as cited in A. Acosta Rodríguez, "Francisco de Avila," p. 589.

among the erring Indians of Peru would be nothing less than an emulation of the apostolic zeal of the earliest Christians. Avila presented a vision of the future in Andean Peru that was triumphantly Christian, but a future that would require great efforts at "uprooting, and tearing out from the Indians' hearts that hollow and false religion of demons."[37]

In the space of a few months, Avila's fortunes had improved considerably. Although his sentence was still pending in the investigation of his alleged misconduct as the pastor of San Damián, the charges of his parishioners were fast receding into a problematic past that could be all too easily reinterpreted by a man enjoying political and religious favor. Avila's exhibitions of zeal were being noticed and appreciated. He was suddenly cleared of all charges against him by the *Juez Provisor* Feliciano de Vega on Christmas eve, 1609, just four days after Avila's most successful cultivation yet of his attentive audience.

On Sunday, 20 December, a public act of faith had been held in the central square of Lima. This *auto de fe*—modeled on well-oiled Inquisition procedures but tempered to correspond to the perceived needs of Andean new converts—marked the theatrical genesis of a systematic extirpating initiative in the archdiocese. Held just before Lobo Guerrero had completed his third month in Lima, the event sent a clear public signal to churchmen and their assistants throughout the archdiocese about the arrival of a new official mood with respect to Indian religious error.[38]

Most of the secular officials, the members of the *cabildo* (municipal council) and the senior *alcalde* (chief magistrate) met at the home of the *corregidor* (regional Crown inspector) of the Indians, before entering the main plaza together on horseback at four in the afternoon. The viceroy and the archbishop enjoyed the vantage points of the balconies on their respective palaces overlooking the square. A pulpit and two platforms had been constructed, surrounding a raised portion of earth on which a generous supply of firewood had been placed. The idols, ancestors' bodies, and other objects that had been collected in Huarochirí were set amidst the wood. The focus of the event, the Andean religious offender Hernando Pauccar, was tied to a pole, above and just out of reach of the things that were to be burned.

From the pulpit, Avila delivered a sermon first in the Quechua language and then in Spanish.[39] Following the sermon, and adhering to a formal procedure

---

[37] "ac Demonum inauem ac falsam religionem è cordibus Indorum extirpaueris atque euelleris." F. de Avila, "Orati habita in ecclesia cathedrali Limensi ad Dominum Bartholomæum Lupum Gerrerum Archiepiscopum . . . ," in *Tratado de los evangelios.*

[38] My description of the scene is informed mostly by Rubén Vargas Ugarte's brief but vivid passage in his *Historia de la Iglesia*, 2: 306–7. Other descriptions are those of Pierre Duviols in *La Lutte*, pp. 153–54, and Antonio de Egaña in his *Historia de la Iglesia*, p. 283.

[39] The text of this sermon is not known, though one suspects that the *auto* provided the opportunity for a public and less formal airing of an oration similar to the one Avila had delivered in the cathedral a week before. There are also other hints of his style. As mentioned above, Avila made a selection of his anti-idolatry sermons available just before he died in 1647. The sermons were published posthumously in 1648 as his *Tratado de los evangelios.*

that would be repeated intermittently for over a century in the humbler settings of the central squares of Andean villages and towns, a notary read out the sentence against Hernando Pauccar. This "much feared and respected" chief minister from San Pedro de Mama, Huarochirí, who had admitted his obstinate attachment to forbidden cults of the gods Chaupi Ñamca and Paria Caca in particular, and whose teachings and very presence encouraged other Andean Christians to backslide into error, would suffer public shame and castigation. In addition to the endurance of his time on the pole, his hair was shorn and he was given two hundred lashes before the assembled crowd. Finally, he was sent into exile to the Jesuit college in Santiago de Chile, where he might learn to reform his ways in a place far from the region where his influence was such that he could further corrupt other new Christians.[40]

Avila preached in Quechua before the hundreds of Indians who had been assembled in the square to hear the words and witness the spectacle. But what were the messages conveyed to them by this unknown priest in his methodical *runa simi* ("human speech")?[41] How edifying and meaningful would the destruction of the regional gods and religious objects that had been carried from Huarochirí have been to the people who formed the bulk of the audience that Sunday afternoon in 1609? They would have understood, of course, that Andean religion was being vilified and that a Christian interpretation of things Andean—an interpretation that, while recognizable, was shriller in tone and

---

[40] R. Vargas Ugarte, *Historia de la Iglesia*, 2: 307.

[41] In his pioneering study of Quechua since 1532, Bruce Mannheim explains that the idea of languages having names was, like many other things, brought to the Andes by the Spanish, and then "borrowed back" into common Andean usage. He suggests that the term "Quechua" (from the sixteenth-century rendering "qhechwa") may have come from the Europeans' mistaken early assumption that the coastal linguistic varieties with which they were first coming into contact, "qheswa simi" or "valley speech," was the name of the overarching Peruvian language. Largely because of the astounding lexicographic work of missionaries such as the Dominican Domingo de Santo Tomás (1560) and later the Jesuit Diego González Holguín (1607 and 1608), the word came into common usage.

Growing up and being educated in Cusco, having taken formal classes in Quechua at the university in Lima, and having been rigorously examined for his competence as a *doctrinero de indios* (a priest in an Indian parish, charged especially with instruction), Francisco de Avila would have had a considerable command of southern Peruvian Quechua, a language that, in 1609, Andeans of the Lima region would have understood. This south Peruvian linguistic variety had been the lingua franca of the Inka dominion, Tawantinsuyu, before the Spaniards' arrival, and it had been called, since the conquest, the "lengua general del ynga." Although the Inka state had used southern Peruvian Quechua for administrative purposes and had taught the language, along with other things, to the sons of local lords in their far-flung lands, Mannheim finds "no evidence that it ever became hegemonic or was ever standardized" in pre-Pizarran times. Ironically, Spanish colonial policies championed the language of the Inkas to a far greater extent than the Inkas had done and, thus, changed the linguistic map of the Andes during the period under discussion. For the purposes of evangelization and economic convenience, the Spanish encouraged the replacement of a "linguistic mosaic" with a "relative homogeneity." Mannheim notes how "covert" linguistic variation was achieved in colonial and later times, but otherwise presents a forceful case for what he dubs "linguistic oppression," the Spanish promotion of one native Andean language, "the language of a subjugated people." B. Mannheim, *The Language of the Inka*, pp. 6, 8, and 108–9.

different in emphases from others with which they would have been familiar—
was being shared with them. They would have been told that what they were
about to witness was the destruction of some worthless idols and fetishes—
powerless natural things that, before the advent of Christ's gospel to Peru, the
Devil had deceived Andeans into believing were entities capable of great feats
and deserving of veneration, rituals, and offerings. And they would have witnessed the punishment of an Indian from a place in the mountains, a man
being described as an idolater and sorcerer who had resisted genuine conversion to the Christian religion.

Yet it is unclear whether the Indians present had any attachment to Andean
religious practices. If they did, it was certainly not an attachment to the ancestral beings and family divinities from the region of Huarochirí. These gods
were not their gods, and the people knew nothing, apart from what they had
been told, about Hernando Pauccar. The people in the square were Indians
who had been summoned from the Cercado district of Lima and from settlements within four leagues of the city.[42] They were necessary extras in a dramatic production that needed a crowd but was meant primarily for other eyes,
the eyes that watched from balconies and horseback.

Like the *autos* organized by the contemporary Inquisition across the Spanish
world, this ceremony had its most vital role to play in reinforcing and informing
the faith of the Spanish Christians who observed it and later heard about its
occurrence. The *auto* established both the gravity of the problem of Indian
idolatry and a commitment to overcome it, a commitment that would now
emanate not simply from a mountain parish in Huarochirí but from the very
center of the viceregal and archiepiscopal power structure. The august assembly, the solemn and rousing words of the sermon, public prayers, display and
destruction of the vile evidence, the public sentencing, flogging, and banishment of the Andean minister Hernando Pauccar, were all parts of a performance announcing a new agenda that was meant to supplant old approaches.
The sermon dedicated to Lobo Guerrero the week before had cleared the path,
as had a number of earlier actions, such as Avila's rallying of support and assistance from the most influential missionaries in Peru at the time, the Society of
Jesus. Moreover, the auto of 20 December, despite its departures from standard inquisitorial procedure, was similar enough in form to contribute to a
mounting sense of legitimacy for a new priority. Lobo and Avila placed the
issue of idolatry before the religious and secular officialdom and intelligentsia
of Lima, employing existing structures and expressions of religious authority
and orthodoxy. Their aim was to display a convincing need for a struggle against
Andean religion and inject it smoothly into the heart of the religious climate
and Spanish Christian identity in seventeenth-century Lima.

The formal theatrics were also calculated to convince, or at least disarm,
existing opponents of the use of systematic force as a buttress in the ongoing
evangelization of Indians in Peru. Thus the cascade of solemn events in De-

[42] R. Vargas Ugarte, *Historia de la Iglesia*, 2: 306.

cember 1609 also demonstrates that Avila, his main Jesuit supporters, and the newly arrived Lobo were anticipating the criticism they might receive.

Opposition to the fledgling Extirpation of idolatry was expressed in the context of a tension between religious approaches that had deep roots not only in Peruvian but also in Christian history—the tension between persuasion and force in evangelization, that is, between peaceful and forcible conversion.

A first source of discord between purveyors and maintainers of Christianity in an originally non-Christian setting such as the central Andes concerned drawing a distinction between what constituted the survival of Andean religion and what were the regrettable but natural and less threatening survivals of Andean culture or custom. Certain experienced and well-informed sixteenth-century missionaries and chroniclers in Peru, as elsewhere in Spanish America, demonstrated their unease with this distinction. Some attempted to differentiate between the endurance of prehispanic religion—which would have to be eliminated—and the persistence of practices which, even if they had once been part of a religious framework, were believed to have lost their religious meaning and thus might be tolerated, even if not encouraged.[43] For some evangelists, there were even patterns of indigenous religious and festive behavior that might be salvaged, turned into effective vehicles for Christianization.

Ideally, the missionary had to make distinctions between what was and was not, from a Christian point of view, permissible in the Indian ways of living and conceiving of the world. Combining as sure a knowledge of prehispanic traditions and structures as he could muster with an instinctive sympathy for the stutters of religious and cultural change, he needed to apply a vigilant but discerning eye. In sixteenth-century Cusco, Cristóbal de Molina, the long-serving priest of Nuestra Señora de los Remedios, was an observer who used his first-hand experience and familiarity with knowledgeable Andean informants to face the possibility of distinctions between religion and culture. Although Molina was as concerned as any other contemporary churchman about what he defined as manifestations of Andean idolatry, chiefly the "guacas [huacas, Andean sacred places, often gods themselves] and temples where the Devil gives his responses," he was prepared to think differently of other practices. Andean rites connected to the human life cycle (for example, rituals of giving names, first hair cuts, and rites of puberty) or communal life (for example, rites for the building of a new couple's home) he deemed the essentially unthreatening "customs that these peoples have."[44] The Cusqueño's purpose, like that of others who shared or partly shared his views, was not to approve of such cus-

---

[43] Carmen Bernand and Serge Gruzinski have discussed Cristóbal de Molina the Cusqueño (c.1530–c.1595) and Diego Durán (c. 1537–1588) as suggestive examples of this distinguishing tendency. *De l'idolâtrie*, esp. pp. 111–15. On Durán in the context of other missionary chroniclers of Mexican "religion" see Inga Clendinnen, "Ways to the Sacred."

[44] C. de Molina, "Relación de las fábulas y ritos," 1: 19, 22–23, and 87. A more recent edition of Molina appears in H. Urbano and P. Duviols, eds., *Fábulas y mitos de los Incas*.

toms so much as to separate them from the beliefs and practices he found truly sinister and antagonistic to the Indians' Christianization.[45]

In contrast to Molina, the supporters of systematic extirpation as a solution to Andean religious error used idolatry as a considerably wider category. There was much they could detect in Andean life that hindered and threatened the spread of Christianity. Many churchmen felt the reconciliation of much of Andean culture with what they regarded as acceptable Christian behavior a virtual impossibility. Such observers for the most part disregarded the hope of other commentators—especially earlier ones such as Molina but also others at the time—that the meanings and forms of Andean culture might be changing for Andean peoples in colonial times. The extirpators' inclusion of the Indians into Christendom became characterized, quite simply, by their exclusion of things deemed Indian.

Although opponents of systematic extirpation believed that idolatry or Indian religious error existed, they were prepared to judge many originally non-Christian practices less harshly. And they examined the new Christians' rate of apparent religious and cultural transformation more patiently. They saw features in Andean society that—however much they may have once constituted parts of a prehispanic religious complex, and however reprehensible or "superstitious" they remained on an absolute Christian scale—had altered through a general process of cultural change that involved, among other things, integral places for kinds of Christianity.

This supposed line between religion and culture, however, was a distinction meaningful to Christian (and Christianized) minds; it did not descend from the rarefied air of theory to the realm of people's lives and practices where religion and culture were intertwined. Most mid-colonial Andeans—whose lives, structures of authority, and world views had come to operate within a framework influenced by Spanish Christianity—still saw the world differently from their priests and extirpators. One should be cautious, then, in finding distinctions such as the one between religion and culture, and the equally important supposed separations between supernatural and natural, good and evil, even resistance and acculturation. The actual identification of which aspects of culture fell on which side of a line that would separate those aspects from religion is the game of analysts—now as much as then.[46] Such identifications often would

---

[45] See discussion in S. Grunzinski and C. Bernand, *De l'idolâtrie*, p. 114, and referring to C. de Molina, "Relación de las fábulas y ritos," p. 88. Although such matters receive ample discussion below, it is worth stating briefly here that evidence of these and other rites associated with the rhythm of life for pastoralists and agriculturalists turns up in the idolatry trials conducted in Andean parishes as much as a century after Molina's observations. These rites appear to have remained intimately connected with regional Andean gods and their ministers, and they turn up conspicuously as aspects of regular communal practice in parishes where undeniably religious networks (Andean officialdoms, organized cults, regular ceremonies, and high degrees of community participation) were strongest. For numerous examples, in San Pedro de Acas in Cajatambo, see the transcription in P. Duviols, ed. *Cultura andina*, pp. 135–261. See also K. R. Mills, *An Evil Lost to View?*

[46] A similar point is emphasized by Inga Clendinnen in her essay "Ways to the Sacred."

have been unclear to colonial Andeans, some of whom considered themselves better Christians than the Spaniards they knew.

Yet defining the characteristics of the enemy was only part of a continuous challenge that very much concerned both extirpators and their opponents. A second fundamental matter upon which the veneer of ecclesiastical agreement frequently cracked was the problem of finding idolatry's most effective remedy. Churchmen who favored a gradual approach to evangelization, and who emphasized the ultimate importance of establishing and maintaining excellent indoctrination at the parish and individual level, viewed the claims of the extirpators and the methods of the nascent Extirpation with skepticism and even fear. They believed that "idolatry" was not the problem into which it was being turned by certain archbishops and official circles in Lima. Moreover, these opponents of systematic extirpation drew attention to the questionable motivations of some extirpators in their midst. Many of the opponents wondered what purpose the Extirpation was serving, what effects it was having on the larger process of evangelization of Indians. A few general points about their opposition shed some preliminary light on the question of why these opposing voices were sometimes drowned out by the proponents of systematic extirpation, and why similar extirpating initiatives did not spring up elsewhere in Peru and in Spanish America.

First, the critique of the Extirpation was rarely expressed in a coherent form by one or another commentator, even if a relatively consistent message can be pieced together from a number of remarks. Second, many of the strident critics of the Extirpation spoke up only when high-powered support for systematic *visitas de idolatría* in Lima had waned. Moreover, a number of the critics weighed in from regions outside the archdiocese, where it must have seemed more possible to oppose the approaches, and point out the deficiencies, of others, for a forceful prelate and his closest supporters might command considerable power over the prevailing ecclesiastical opinion within a given realm.[47]

---

[47] In 1619, the viceroy of Peru, the prince of Esquilache, stated his desire that the visitas generales de idolatría be raised by prelates in Cusco, Arequipa, Huamanga, La Paz, La Plata, and Santa Cruz de la Sierra. Yet nothing like the organized series of idolatry inspections seen in Lima seem to have developed. See AGI Lima 38, Esquilache to the king, Lima, 23 March 1619, and P. J. de Arriaga, *La extirpación*, ch. 19, pp. 186–87, and discussion by P. Duviols, *La Lutte*, p. 210. Pedro de Villagómez (1641–1671) harbored similar hopes, but raised little response beyond the efforts of an admiring contemporary prelate in Cusco. See Chapter Five.

Furthermore, the correspondence from the bishops of the surrounding dioceses of Arequipa, Huamanga, Trujillo, and Cusco—often sent after the cessation of Lobo's Extirpation in the Lima region—offer clear instances of a fairly uniform criticism of extirpating methods, if not an outright denial of serious religious error (idolatry) in the Indian parishes in their realms. Significantly, these churchmen did not deny the existence of difficult pastoral challenges in the ongoing evangelization of Andeans; they held the Church (effectively themselves) to be partly to blame for the inadequacies they perceived in the indigenous people's reception of Christianity. The prelates' quarrel (more often implicit than explicit) was with the wisdom and efficacy of the approach of the extirpation of idolatry as it had been practiced in the Archdiocese of Lima and as it had been recommended to them by the viceroy, the prince of Esquilache. Some of the principal commentators

This is clear in the records of the seventeenth-century Archdiocese of Lima. Only the backing of Archbishop Lobo Guerrero, the Viceroy Esquilache, and the Jesuits turned Francisco de Avila's personally motivated and regional initiative into an intermittent archiepiscopal enterprise. Correspondingly, opponents of systematic extirpation became conspicuously vociferous only after the departure of Esquilache in 1621 and the deaths of first, Arriaga in a shipwreck in 1622, and then Lobo Guerrero on 11 November of the same year, and before the arrival of the new archbishop Gonzalo de Campo in 1625.[48] The cathedral chapter of Lima waited only one day after the death of Archbishop Lobo to call a halt to all idolatry investigations. Moreover, there was begun, at the same time, a secret investigation into the alleged excesses and corruption in the conduct of a number of the idolatry inspectors.[49] The timing of the chapter's actions bespeaks an opposition to the Extirpation that had been suppressed while Lobo and his supporters had held sway. The new atmosphere seems to have emboldened those in the mendicant orders—particularly the Dominicans—who now raised their voices against the approach that had been championed by the diocesan establishment and, notably, by a prominent faction within the rival Society of Jesus.[50]

---

were the bishop of Arequipa, the Augustinian Pedro de Perea (1619–1630), who preceded Pedro de Villagómez in this post; the bishop of Huamanga, Francisco de Verdugo (1623–1637); the Dominican bishop of Trujillo, Francisco de Cabrera (1615–1619); and the bishop of Cusco, Lorenzo Pérez de Grado (1620–1627). See esp. AGI Lima 309, Perea to the king, Arequipa, 1620; AGI Lima 308, Verdugo to the king, Huamanga, 20 April 1621 and AGI Lima 308, Verdugo to the king, Huamanga, 2 February 1626; AGI Lima 38, Cabrera to the Assembly and Father General of the Society of Jesus, Trujillo, 9 July 1618; and AGI Lima 305, Pérez de Grado to the king, Cusco, 18 March 1623.

[48] P. Duviols, *La Lutte*, p. 160.

[49] AGI Lima 310, The ecclesiastical chapter to the king, Lima, 8 May 1623. The secret investigation implicated Francisco de Avila, who was by this time a canon in the cathedral of La Plata, Diego Ramírez (who had died), Fernando de Avendaño, and six other visitadores. See particularly AAL Leg. 2, exp. 6, "Preguntas por las quales sean de examinar los testigos que fueren llamados en la visita secreta que se hace contra los visitadores que an sido de la ydolatria en este arçobispado del tiempo que fue arçobispo del el señor D. Bartolome Loboguerrero de buena memoria, La villa de Carrion de Velasco, Chancay," 1622, and AAL Leg. 4, exp. 7, "Información y pesquisa secreta contra los visitadores del pueblo de Santiago de la Nazca," 1623. P. Duviols discusses the Chancay questionnaire that formed part of this investigation in *La Lutte*, pp. 329–30. As Duviols notes, the actual proceedings have not been found. P. Duviols, ed., *Cultura andina*, p. xlvi.

[50] This aspect of the story has been skillfully told by Pierre Duviols. Briefly, provincials of the Dominicans, Augustinians, and Mercedarians reasserted the need for Christian authorities to distinguish between religion and culture, between what had been uprooted from the Andean parishes (idolatry and formal allegiances to false gods) and what remained (superstitions and remnants of culture). Especially significant sources are the letters written to the king by the Augustinian provincial Francisco de la Serna (AGI Lima 325, de la Serna to the king, Lima, 9 May 1622) and his equal in the Peruvian province of the Order of Mercy, Gaspar de la Torre, (see AGI Lima 302, de la Torre to the king, Lima, 30 October 1626). De la Serna presented evidence, writing that an ambitious investigation of the order's parishes conducted by the Dominican provincial Luis Cornejo had found Andean parishioners innocent of idolatrous rites. And de la Serna agreed with Cornejo that the Indian peoples of Peru were guilty only of rather meaningless "rites and abuses" to which they clung more out of respect for their elders and the example of their ancestors than out of any

Yet the oscillation would continue. It was not long after Gonzalo de Campo arrived in Lima as the next archbishop that he formed his plan to organize the assistance of "learned" and "experienced" Jesuits and secular priests, and to incorporate a sweeping investigation of Andean religiosity into his personal visit of the archdiocese—"going out," as he put it, "and leaving no corner neglected." His extirpation, however short-lived, would have this modified, personal touch, for at least two reasons. First, Campo was listening to the Extirpation's critics. A number of Lobo's visitadores were being investigated for excesses and abuses, so to commission a body of similar officials would have been ill-advised. Second, concerned people were calling into question the gravity and very nature of colonial Andean religious error, and these people clearly had Campo's ear from an early moment in his tenure. The prelate commented on the ecclesiastical discord he perceived over the issue of idolatry and its remedy in the Lima region, writing to the king of his determination

> to know it [the idolatry and heresy of the Indians] and see it in order to be able to inform Your Majesty with the certainty of a truth witnessed and examined by me, because I found a variety of opinions about this when I arrived in Lima; and among the serious and most important men there were those who told me there was much idolatry, and most of these were theologians, preachers, and persons with great zeal for the salvation of souls; others told me that it [idolatry] was the invention and [a product of the] greed of the visitadores who used their titles to enrich themselves, and that this did serious injustice to the Indians when they were thus accused [of being idolaters]; others said that they believed well enough (decían que bien creían) that there was some idolatry, but not as much as was claimed.[51]

As even his few letters from the mountains attest, there was a canny and cautious side to Campo. Yet he followed Lobo's tradition in conceiving of an extirpation of idolatry as a vital part both of his pastoral function and of the more general ecclesiastical reform he began immediately after his arrival in Lima in April 1625. His own investigations confirmed for him the existence of errors that would require force to uproot them. Campo enlisted experienced help from Fernando de Avendaño, now rector of the metropolitan cathedral, and from the Jesuits. He even proposed that the padres of the Society consider upgrading their roles in the enterprise of extirpation from being essentially pedagogical assistants to the visitadores to becoming the visitadores generales de idolatría themselves, but to no avail. The actions of his retinue before his sudden death in the village of Recuay in the north-central Andes on 19 December 1626—perhaps as a result of poisoning—demonstrate that while the Extirpation of Lobo, Avila, and Arriaga was seeing modifications under Campo, its basic approach enjoyed a short but ambitious revival.[52]

---

coherent religious conviction. On de la Serna and Cornejo see P. Duviols, La Lutte, pp. 170–72 and P. Duviols, ed., Cultura andina, pp. xlv–xlvi.

[51] AGI Lima 302, Campo to the king, Llamellin, 8 October 1626.

[52] See P. Duviols, La Lutte, pp. 161–62.

The tenure of Campo's successor in the metropolitan see, Hernando Arias de Ugarte (1630–1638)—who was skeptical about both the danger represented by idolatry and the motives of the men its extirpation attracted—is the exception that may prove the rule.[53] Arias was seventy years old when he arrived in Lima, a Creole and an experienced colonial official in Spanish South America.[54] During Arias's tenure, no campaigns against idolatry were sponsored directly from Lima, and there is an accompanying dearth of negative comment on the matter either from eclipsed, former extirpators or from others.[55] It is tempting to explain Arias's skeptical attitude toward idolatry and the Extirpation as an effective remedy for Indian religious error by stressing his Creole background and experience, assigning him a place in the Creole culture that criticized peninsular incompetence which was emerging during his lifetime.[56] Yet what one learns about Arias's attitudes links him as much with earlier and current opponents of the Extirpation who were *peninsulares* as with the words on wider themes written by contemporary Creole religious in the Andes. The new archbishop's views on idolatry, extirpation, and aspiring extirpators appear in relief not because they were very different from existing and previous opponents' ideas but because they represent an official departure from the argumentative lines taken, and temporarily institutionalized, by Lobo Guerrero and, with some innovation, Campo.

Arias's skepticism in the 1630s did not spell the end for the extirpation of idolatry. In fact, the period of its most frenetic activity lay just ahead, when there would be a radical swing back in favor of a centrally organized Extirpation—as well as yet another corresponding and conspicuous drying of oppositional ink—with the establishment in Lima of another extirpating prelate, Pedro de Villagómez, in 1641.

[53] See especially AGI Lima 302, Letter from Arias to the king, Lima, 27 May 1632 and AGI Lima 302, Letter from Arias to the king, Lima, 13 May 1633. Pierre Duviols discusses the possible shaping of Arias's attitudes through his experiences among Indian peoples during his other postings, and notes the conspicuous lack of concern with idolatry in the constitutions of the synod convened by Arias in 1636 (in comparison with those of Lobo Guerrero's 1613 synod) in *La Lutte*, p. 163.

[54] A. de Egaña, *Historia de la Iglesia*, p. 289. He had previously served as a judge on the Audiencia of Panama (1595–1597), on the Audiencia of La Plata de Los Charcas (1597–1608), and on the Audiencia of Lima (1603–1613). He had been bishop of Quito (1613–1616), archbishop of Santa Fe de Bogotá (1616–1624), and he was named archbishop of La Plata de Los Charcas in 1623, though he was only present there briefly from 1627 to 1629. He was not the first and would not be the last churchman to reach his archiepiscopate in Lima as a culmination and last stop in his career. E. Schäfer, *El Consejo Real*, vol. 2, Appendices, pp. 468, 481, 506, 572, 593, and 594. On Arias's time in La Plata, see A. de Egaña, *Historia de la Iglesia*, p. 372.

[55] On Arias, see P. Duviols, *La Lutte*, pp. 162–64. Noting that Arias promoted no campaigns from Lima is, of course, different from claiming there were no visitas de idolatría during the Arias period or, for that matter, when an extirpating prelate was not in office. The documentation of idolatry investigations that were initiated locally by clergymen and "concerned citizens," sometimes in contravention of the opinions of an archbishop like Arias de Ugarte, was the least likely to survive. Yet there are hints of the existence of such investigations. I discuss and feature one such trial in "Persistencia religiosa en Santiago de Carhuamayo (Junín), 1631."

[56] See, for instance, B. Lavallé, *Las promesas ambiguas*, pp. 79–153.

Huacas

ONCE A YEAR, "on the night of the moon," a little after the Catholic feast day of Corpus Christi, the men and women of the village of San Pedro de Quipan in the province of Canta came out in their best new clothes. Their chief minister (*huacapvíllac*, or *ministro mayor*) wore a black shirt of *cumbe* and a many-colored head-piece made of wool and the plumage of the pariona bird of the high plateaus (*punas*). Men and women walked separately, and the minister assumed his place in the center as a procession wove its way out of the village and into the surrounding hills. Young women who were virgins carried the sacred *chicha* (corn beer) they had prepared, and others followed, laden with the other offerings that constituted the food of the gods: on this occasion, *cuyes* (Andean guinea pigs), potatoes, maize cakes, colored powders made from shells and earths, and llama fat.[1]

When the assembly reached the special place on the mountain, the chief minister would enter the presence of a male god (a huaca) and address him on behalf of all. Although his words show signs of Christian influence, the minister's objectives were those of his own land and people:

> Father and Our Creator,
> Here we come,
> All your children,
> To celebrate your festival.
> We bring you food and drink.

The minister poured a bit of chicha out of a cup used only for this purpose, a libation to the god, and then he drank before passing the chicha on, so that everyone present could perform the same ritual until the drink was gone. Each person would then offer whatever he or she had brought, gathering it before the god and burning it in sacrifice with the help of dry íchu grass.[2]

Participation in the festival devoted to the principal god of Quipan was mandatory in the mid-seventeenth century and it was viewed with the greatest seriousness. Ceremonies were, of course, less elaborate and public than they had been in prehispanic times. But necessary simplification and attention to degrees of secrecy must be carefully interpreted. Postconquest indigenous contexts in Spanish America could be different; similar evidence might suggest

---

[1] P. J. de Arriaga, *La extirpación*, ch. 3, p. 32. Cumbe is a finely woven and often colorful textile. The pariona or parihuana, the Chilean flamingo (*Phoenicpterus chilensis*), is an intensely pink wading bird of the puna; see M. Koepcke, *The Birds of the Department of Lima*. According to Arriaga, the virgins were called *açuac* or *accac*. The chicha in the indigenous tongue was *asua* or *aka (acca)*; *La extirpación*, ch. 3, p. 34. See also D. González Holguin, *Vocabulario*, p. 470.

[2] AAL Leg. 2, exp. 11, fol. 8v.

that the deterioration of religious and cultural meaning, apparently straight-forward in one place, was more complicated somewhere else. In this Andean instance, observances were not so impoverished as to be accurately charac-terized as "sad little do-it-yourself ritual(s)."[3] The people of mid-colonial Quipan, along with many other predominantly Indian communities, main-tained Andean religious organizations of remarkable complexity. Subordinate to a chief minister, each *ayllu* (the social and economic unit of extended kin-dred) had one or two ministers who, in turn, had ritual assistants (*yanápac*, whom the Spanish notary rendered as *sacristanes* [sacristans] or *ayudantes* [helpers]).[4] The keepers of the cults and traditions rigorously punished the negligent in the community. The ministro mayor told of a general rebuke he delivered to the people; it effectively encapsulates the attitude toward those who broke with community religious practice in a place such as Quipan: "You wicked ones, you will not have children, and you will have neither *chacras* [plots of land] nor livestock because you have not fulfilled the obligation and given the worship that you must. You have an obligation to your God [cap-italized and rendered *Dios*] for the fortunes of everyone."[5] Even though Don Cristóbal Java, the mayor (*alcalde ordinario*, and often a Hispanicized indige-nous official in a locality) expressed his concern as a Christian and did not wish to attend with those of his ayllu, he was said to have agreed that the people's well-being was connected to the Andean festivals and worship.[6]

Because the festival was also the time of community purification, the minis-ters were also "confessors" (according to an Indian code), exhorting the people to reveal all their wrongs that they might receive pardon and not run the risk of greatly angering the huacas against them.[7] Only after the confession of wrongs and a ritual bathing at the confluence of two rivers was pardon achieved and a regenerative purification complete. The god himself provided the check, infor-ming the minister of those who had concealed their wrongs. The reticent were flogged with a twisted cord called *coilla cusma*, which had a sheepskin tip (*aco*) with small rocks in it. The ordeal continued until the wrongs were deemed confessed or the guilty party fainted "as if dead."[8]

---

[3] I. Clendinnen, "Ways to the Sacred," p. 127.

[4] P. J. de Arriaga, *La extirpación*, ch. 3, p. 33.

[5] AAL Leg. 2, exp. 11, fol. ff.8v–9.

[6] Ibid., fol. 9.

[7] The Quechua word *aucachic* (most often *ichuri* in the Cusco area) was taken by Spaniards who had experience in these regions, and in the Andean languages, to mean "confessor." P. J. de Arriaga, *La extirpación*, ch. 3, p. 33; J. de Acosta, *Historia natural y moral*, book 5, ch. 25, p. 260; B. Cobo, *Historia del Nuevo Mundo*, vol. 2, book 13, ch. 33, p. 225. See AAL Leg. 2, exp. 11, fol. 8 and fols. 15–15v.

[8] AAL Leg. 2, exp. 11, fol. 8. Rites for determining the members who concealed wrongs varied from region to region in the mid-colonial archdiocese. It is not possible to determine the "Andean-ness" of one practice over another. Indeed, it is probable that most rituals (those of purification and scores of others) had developed and changed gradually over many years, and that the arrival of the Spanish and Christianity, although a particularly demanding and enduring impetus for change, was not the only such impetus experienced by these peoples.

A common form of purification ritual (more widespread than the one described by the chief

This short relation summarizes part of the testimony given by Hernando Caruachin before the idolatry inspector Pedro Quijano Zevallos in Quipan in 1656. In addition to his mediation with the village's main god, Hernando Caruachin fulfilled an organizational role as the chief minister in his community.[9] This role put him at the head of a spiritual hierarchy that included not only the ministers and confessors from other ayllus in the village and immediate region but also a diverse assemblage of guardians and teachers of religious knowledge (*dogmatizadores*, or dogmatizers), and specialists who might deal in divination, the interpretation of dreams, the hurling of curses and spells, the healing of sicknesses and injuries, or a number of combinations of these things and many more. This spiritual power structure had eluded the uneven Christian attempts to make it disappear. By the seventeenth century, the structure was often intertwined with the so-called secular administration of the village by Andean officials. The village offices were either transformed "traditional" ones (according to family lineage, kin group, and regional settlement), those imposed by the Spanish (especially the municipal council [*cabildo*] and various church offices), or both. Thus the extent of Caruachin's knowledge is not surprising.

Although not all mid-colonial parishes of the Archdiocese of Lima had a religious system with recognizably prehispanic traits to rival Quipan's, a surprising number did. In the Archdiocese of Lima fundamental aspects of the traditionally Andean local and regional religious structures maintained vital places in the people's lives well into the colonial era and beyond. This is not to say that observances did not change. But rituals, practices, and explanations—however affected by the necessity of clandestinity and the penetrations of Catholicism— were neither a disjointed nor a residual assortment of beliefs. Most importantly, their survival was not accidental.

What manner of gods held sway in this mountain community over a century after Francisco Pizarro and his accompanying Dominican, Fray Vicente de Valverde, had ostensibly initiated the region's Christianization?[10] Physically,

---

minister of Quipan, Canta) was performed regularly by the people of San Pedro de Acas in Cajatambo, to the northwest of Canta. The peoples of each ayllu would confess to particular minister-confessors in open clearings near their local gods. Each person carried a handful of straws (íchu grass) and, after confessing his or her wrongs, the confessor would choose a bunch of these at random. Inés Julca Colque elaborated thus: "Those who are confessed bring in their hands pieces of straw in order that the confessors might see if they have revealed their sin. They draw out a little of the straw with their hands, and if the number is even it has been a good confession, while if it is odd it is not good and the confessant must tell more sins." The drawing of straws and demands on the people's consciences would be repeated until an even number was drawn. Cristóbal Pampa Condor spoke of a frequently lengthy procedure. He related that he had seen two of the region's most well-known minister-confessors, Hernando Hacas Poma and Cristóbal Hacas Malqui, "confess men and women until the emergence of the bright star of the morning that they called Atumguarac." See P. Duviols, ed. *Cultura andina*, Julca Colque at p. 179, and Pampa Condor at p. 219. On the rites of purification in and around Acas see also the testimonies of Hernando Chaupis Condor at p. 157, Cristóbal Hacas Malqui at p. 166, and Hernando Poma Quillai at pp. 206–7.

[9] See AAL Leg. 2, exp. 11, fols. 7v–8.

[10] An illuminating discussion of the events at Cajamarca in 1532 is S. MacCormack, "Atahuallpa

the huacas being worshiped were most often natural stone forms, although these were occasionally sculpted or painted upon by human hands. The word *huaca* seems to have had a wider meaning as well; to say that an object or place was huaca implied that it was sacred and deserved reverence. Yet like so many Quechua religious terms, huaca defies succinct description. The first Spanish lexicographers in Peru obviously struggled with this conception of divinity, among them noting that huacas could be both small figures or idols, as well as peaks of mountains, important places, shrines, ancestor's bodies (*malquis*), or burial sites.[11] In addition, by at least the second half of the sixteenth century, many Spanish commentators writing of huacas meant almost exclusively treasures that had been buried or concealed with dead Andean nobles.[12] But, Diego de Torres Rubio's eventual assertion that a huaca was, above all, "an extraordinary thing, [something] outside of the common," captured the wider, essential aspect of its physical nature which was elaborated upon by his nineteenth-century successors.[13]

In the early seventeenth century, El Inca Garcilaso de la Vega had offered some nine possible meanings, going to pains to establish solid reasons that would differentiate *huaca* from the Spanish gloss of *ídolo* (idol). Garcilaso stressed that all things which, either in their "beauty or excellence" or their capacity to "inspire horror and alarm," set themselves apart from others of their kind were thought of as huaca.[14] Yet even the Spanish churchmen and administrators who perceived far more than buried treasure in this concept could not but interpret the huacas from their own cultural and religious perspective. They continued to dredge up notions of the idols that had sat in the temples of classical Greek and Roman pagans, and of the false gods of infidels recounted in Judeo-Christian tradition.[15]

Calling huacas "ídolos" (idols), and interpreting them largely in terms of Greco-Roman and biblical traditions, did them more than just a passing injustice. For it was not as if huacas—or a host of other indigenous concepts—would become better appreciated by judgmental European intruders with time. The observers' interpretations and terms of reference might shift in significant ways,

---

y el libro." Particularly helpful on another meeting of Europeans with an alien culture is D. F. McKenzie, "The Sociology of a Text."

[11] D. de Santo Tomás, *Léxico o vocabulario*, fol. 109; D. González Holguín, *Vocabulario*, p. 165; and L. Bertonio, *Vocabulario*, p. 149.

[12] Thus in 1589, in his curious report on the native Peruvians' lack of writing, Doctor Murillo de la Cerda defined *guacas* as the "great funerary edifices of the Indian governors and notables," filled with "cups of gold and silver," rich decorative clothing, and many other things; BNM Ms. 5938, "Sobre la escritura de los indios del Perú," fol. 433v. In his entry for 1561, Fernando Montesinos's "Memorias antiguas i nuebas del Pirú" of 1642 noted the discovery of many guacas in the Cusco region; by these he meant burials and treasures (entierros) in which gold and other precious things could be found. BNM Ms. 3124, fol. 187v.

[13] D. de Torres Rubio, *Arte y vocabulario*, fol. 6. J. J. Von Tschudi, *Die Kechua-Sprache*, p. 91 and E. W. Middendorf, *Die einheimischen Sprachen Perus*, p. 413.

[14] *Royal Commentaries*, translated by H. V. Livermore, book 2, ch. 4, pp. 76–77.

[15] See, for example, P. de Villagómez, "Carta pastoral," chs. 6 and 7, pp. 21–27. On this theme see esp. S. MacCormack, "Limits of Understanding."

but rarely in the direction of an objective, let alone an Andean, perception. As Sir John Elliott has written on the wider reception of America in European consciousness, there was no such thing as a "linear advance in understanding as observers disencumbered themselves by degrees of their traditional constraints and belatedly got to grips with an American 'reality.'"[16] What to seventeenth-century Europeans seemed a vain cult of stone was in fact a present embodiment—albeit often in natural, petrified forms—and reinterpretation of a long cultural past.[17] What the huacas and their histories meant and represented to mid-colonial Andeans, the paths these gods followed to their clandestine religious positions in the seventeenth and eighteenth centuries, and how they were venerated and consulted, can best be approached through a return to Quipan, Canta, and their environs in 1656, and an introduction to a regional set of huacas' subtle blend of physical reality and divine omnipresence.

A half a league above the village of Quipan was the peoples' principal huaca, Guara Cani (alternatively referred to as Chonta Bilca who lives at Guara Cani). He was an ancient stone form evoking the shape of a man, but only about half the height of an official's staff. It was to Guara Cani that the rituals described in the opening of this chapter were directed. Scarcely two paces away from him was a white stone in the shape of a woman. Her name was recorded in Spanish as Mama Criadora (Mother Nurturer or Mother Creator)—reflecting either her current name or the interpreter's and notary's agreement on a suitable Spanish translation. She was the wife or consort of Guara Cani. In the mid-seventeenth century both huacas were kept within enclosures, buried beneath stones and grass with caches of their offerings. Two widows joined Hernando Caruachin as the principal ministers who would officiate at ceremonies and take the peoples' requests to the gods at this place. A virgin named Catalina Llama Suyo prepared the huacas' chicha. The cult of Guara Cani and Mama Criadora could boast a sizeable material wealth: twenty llamas, fifty Castilian sheep, two painted silver *tembladeras* (wide, round dishes with handles on the sides); two cumbe shirts, colored and with black wool; two cumbe blankets; two llicllas (shawls) of colored cumbe; and the possession of a choice plot of land called Llaquabamba, where the special black maize, *araguai*, was grown for the huaca's sacred chicha.[18]

Guara Cani and Mama Criadora were far from unique in the local and regional landscape. The principal huaca, and his wife and family members, were

[16] "Final Reflections," p. 397.

[17] Studies that examine oral traditions, non-European conceptions of history, and the constant reinterpretation of the past (written and otherwise) now abound. Two that I have found particularly helpful are G. Dening's *Islands and Beaches*, and G. Prakash's *Bonded Histories*, esp. ch. 2, "True Stories," on Bhuinya oral traditions. Influencing Prakash's approach, see particularly J. Miller, "Listening for the African Past." These works, and many others, suggest the value of careful comparative study for Americanists working to understand colonial situations.

[18] AAL Leg. 2, exp. 11, fols. 6v–7v. The dedication of Castilian livestock to a huaca represents a change wrought by the depletion of llama herds and the growing viability of sheep herding in the area. In some places, San Pedro de Acas in Cajatambo for instance, the incorporation of European livestock into sacred ritual was resisted. Hernando Caruachin of Quipan explains his village's and their huacas' decision to diversify ibid., fol. 7v.

only the top level of the huaca numina, the regional divine population. Descent or birth groups—which did not always conform to, and often subdivided, the ayllus—usually traced their lineage back to a divine forefather, a progenitor from a dim past who, upon making some contribution to the world, would be transformed into part of the landscape, living on as an eternal force, a protector and a threat. The huacas' superhuman exploits, when they had lived and breathed both before and after the advent of normal men and women, were often recalled in their names or, even more commonly, in the epithets that spoke of their associations. Guachu Cara, a rough, black, half-flattened huaca of the Chuclla ayllu, for example, was known as "God of the chacras," and lived at a place called Pariasca Culpi.[19]

About a league from Quipan, on a hill called Pomabamba, the Julcachuri ayllu worshiped Yaropalpa and, only a short distance away, a stone roughly the shape of a person, the huaca Chinchaypalpa. Like the other gods in this region, these huacas had substantial possessions in livestock, carefully seeded chacras, coins and special clothing.[20] The widow Catalina Chumbi served as their minister, and a virgin of fifty years of age made their chicha and even instructed a young apprentice in the art. Both the Chaupin and Yanac ayllus of Quipan looked to yet another huaca, an outcropping of rock named Marca Aura, and beneath him they had long kept their malquis, the mummified bodies of their more recent, illustrious dead.[21]

Maria Ticlla Guacho of the Sigual ayllu in the neighboring pueblo of Huamantanga reported that in the middle of the high lake bed of Curcuy Cocha, in the old town of Purumarca was the huaca Poma Guato whom, it was said, the Indians worshiped "like a God" (capital in original).[22] Although this huaca's

---

[19] AAL Leg. 2, exp. 11, fols. 11–12.

[20] Minted money is another obvious addition during colonial times. An erudite and wonderfully wide-ranging discussion of the ritual use of coins and their possible meanings for Andean peoples from colonial to modern times is Olivia Harris's "The Earth and the State," see pp. 254–57.

[21] AAL Leg. 2, exp. 11, fols. 7–7v. The malquis deserve a proper discussion of their own, and I recognize that I do them no great service by treating them alongside the huacas. That said, the cults of the malquis and huacas are intimately related, as is suggested by the proximity of the more recent dead to the principal huaca of the two ayllus from Quipan, and by the fact that observances were often shared. It was common for colonial Andean peoples of the Archdiocese of Lima to keep their malquis in cave tombs called *machayes*. Although the mummified bodies had once been carried into open spaces for ritual performances and consultation, this practice was constrained by increasing Christian surveillance in the colonial years. Offerings and nourishment were taken to the malquis in their resting places, and here, too, they would be consulted by a minister (*malquipvíllac*) on behalf of their people.

The attitudes of Christian priests toward the persistence of Andean peoples' attention to their non-Christian dead were precarious. In many cases, these attitudes were definitely hardening in the seventeenth century as the extent of this attention and its connectedness to what was being called "idolatry" was considered.

[22] "Old town" is my rather literal rendering of the Spanish notaries' *pueblo viejo*, which referred to the "settlements of the ancients," those who had lived before Andeans were resettled into the grid-patterned towns and parishes. The resettlement process was begun soon after the Spaniards consolidated their political control of Peru, but was pursued unevenly until Viceroy Francisco de

wife had been destroyed and burned by a previous visitador, Poma Guato's son, Malmay, still stood at his base. María was Malmay's faithful minister.[23] Yet another huaca, a black and white god named Yunga, stood in a cave above Curcuy Cocha and, like his fellows, could boast numerous possessions.

In mid-seventeenth-century Quipan and Huamantanga, the religious system that centered upon the huacas in natural surroundings was very much alive. This system both antedated and persisted through the Spanish military conquest and feats of colonial reorganization of peoples and boundaries. Different degrees of secrecy and modification had been forced upon the system's keepers by the uneven hand of priestly vigilance and the intermittent efforts of official persecution, but Spanish pressure had not eradicated it by mid-colonial times. Huacas such as Guara Cani and Mama Criadora might have been buried or even moved from their original sites, and the large gatherings of public ritual and performance may have become a thing of the past; but the network of indigenous ministers (often referred to as priesthoods by their interpreters) was maintained, and the witnesses' detailed knowledge shows that the people's vital attachment to the huacas had not died out and was, in fact, flourishing in many places.

Examples from other regions add depth to the picture sketched by the Cantan information. Indeed, the evidence suggests similar degrees of persistence throughout much of the Archdiocese of Lima. The testimonies of Andeans collected by churchmen in the successive visitas de idolatría in the Indian parishes reveal the survival of this fundamental dimension of Andean religion well into the first half of the eighteenth century. Some people who were interrogated by the idolatry inspectors knew little—or revealed little—about the huacas beyond their names and the maintenance of their cults, yet other people were veritable founts of religious information. In the tense inquisitorial atmosphere, motivated by such things as fear, suspicion, hope for escape, greed, and revenge on others, some witnesses and accused offenders reveal themselves and others in great detail to have been the guardians of local religious knowledge and the performers of the oral histories of the huacas and malquis. Their testimonies must be read with great care, for there is much contained between the lines; and what they suggest must be tested against the information given by others and against the particular backdrop of context in each idolatry investigation. But answers to important questions do surface. Where did these divine beings come from, and how does one explain their enduring authority into mid-colonial times? Fortunately, the huacas' ancient histories do not remain a complete mystery.

Toledo's initiatives in the 1570s. Andean communities, villages or hamlet organizations within the ayllu exchange networks of extended kin relations, were called *llacta*. The clearest account of these of which I am aware appears in Frank Salomon's "Introductory Essay" to *The Huarochirí Manuscript*, edited and translated by F. Salomon and G. Urioste, (hereafter *Huarochirí*), pp. 23–24. On the reducción process see A. Málaga Medina, "Las reducciones en el Perú."

[23] AAL Leg. 2, exp. 11, fols. 11–11v.

In ancient times, long before the years of Inka hegemony or the arrival of the Spanish invaders, the Andean world was said to have been inhabited by a succession of powerful beings or god-men who were called huacas by their descendants. After a certain point ordinary men and women existed as well, though their lives were much affected by the roaming huacas and the *villcas*, the demigodlike humans whom the huacas held in particular favor. Divine intervention in earthly affairs was a fact of life in these times, in a fashion that would rival any Olympian machinations: entire landforms were raised from dust; irrigation and agricultural systems were cut out of the sides of mountains; unjust men were ruined and put to shame; beautiful virgins were seduced; and whole worlds were washed into the sea only to be reconstituted afresh.

From the mid-colonial Andean point of view, there was no doubting that the huacas had once lived upon the earth, where they had carried out their various feats. They had been the organizers of the known world. And thus the world could be both explained and managed. The physical surroundings, local agricultural traits and preferences, the order of society and its institutions—all attested to the huacas' initiatory actions and guiding influence. What was more, the landscape displayed what amounted to living proof. When the huacas' exploits on earth were completed, when their particular deeds had been accomplished or when they had been superseded by huacas more crafty or powerful than themselves, it was common for them to turn to stone, either in their own shapes or in those of animals or appropriate symbols. This divine lithomorphosis hardly spelled the end of their power over the lives of their "children," the generations of men and women who would inhabit the land in their wake and gaze upon them every day; on the contrary, lithomorphosis made their power everlasting. The huaca ancestors represented an otherworldly stability and permanence, but—as Millones has expressed it—they were simultaneously "active" and "living" forces that remained "integrated" in the world of their people. The extent of their fixity was possible because of their fluidity.[24] The Cantan huacas discussed above were just such active, permanent beings.

The transformation into stone usually occurred at some conspicuous site in a god's mythical wanderings, at the point where the huaca had made a most lasting contribution or where he or she had been overcome by a better. Capac Huanca in the region of Huarochirí, for instance, was frozen in stone and promised coca offerings in perpetuity from his peoples in reward for his kind treatment of the principal regional god Paria Caca. Similarly, two of Paria Caca's sons took up eternal positions of honor and responsibility that they might ward off forever the gods whom they had defeated and banished to the jungle and sea.[25] In their places, charged with meaning, the huacas would live on as an eternal forces, and often as arbiters.[26] Such sites became sacred,

[24] L. Millones, *Historia y poder*, pp. 117–18. On their "fluidity" see also C. K. Columbus, "Immortal Eggs," pp. 183–84.

[25] See *Huarochirí*, chs. 25 and 8, secs. 102–5 and 107–9, respectively.

[26] Sabine MacCormack discusses the equation with classical oracles in *Religion in the Andes*, pp. 58–59.

inseparable from the memory of the huacas themselves. Frank Salomon writes that a prehispanic llacta settlement "is not the simple equivalent of our 'town' or 'village,' which denote a portion of territory or the legal corporation that governs it. A *llacta* in its old sense might be defined as a triple entity: the union of a localized *huaca* (often an ancestor-diety), with its territory and with the group of people whom the *huaca* engendered."[27] Huacas became places of religious pilgrimage and congregation, shrines where the peoples who believed themselves descended from these divine progenitors would bring offerings, give regular worship, and look for continuing support and guidance. The landscape—its mountain peaks, outcroppings of rock, peculiar boulders, and life-giving springs—was thus full of religious meaning. Sacralized natural forms made sense of the world and the peoples' origins, recalling the lives and deeds of the divine ancestors which were regularly commemorated at festivals. In Acas, Cajatambo, for instance, the festivals of Pocoimita and Caruamita were two of a number of ceremonial occasions that punctuated the year in the middle of the seventeenth century; the central objects of these observances included the regional huacas.[28]

We do not know of the ancient lives and adventures of most of the huacas who survived into the colonial period. However, rich information about a few of them does survive; it would be wrong to assume that the lack of such information in the case of others indicates that sacred histories were forgotten. Andeans were, at times, understandably reluctant to share these histories, what are usually referred to as their *tradiciones*, with missionaries and priests. Indeed, we may safely assume that often considerably more than the histories was withheld. Numerous huacas escaped the sporadic Spanish efforts at extirpation, and their names and whereabouts—and thus their histories and meanings—were concealed by faithful Indian witnesses. Other huacas, although betrayed in name by the large number of declarants who recognized exactly how much they needed to say to satisfy a given visitador's need for material results from his inquest, otherwise remained enigmas both to Spanish investigators and posterity. They were simply the names of "idols" recorded in the idolatry documentation, idols never found, or smashed and burned in one of the innumerable *autos de fe* before a visita left a village. The possibility of the huacas' complete or partial concealment from the inquisitorial view varied from region to region, village to village, ayllu to ayllu, and even depended on which individual became the visitador's targeted source of information. Huacas such as the ones I have noted from Canta are among the mysterious kind; one searches almost in vain for clues to their ancient pasts. As is frequently the case in the study of the idolatry documentation, it is necessary to supplement the evidence for particular cases with that about neighboring huacas and their histories.

In the Andes, because historians for the most part lack sources equivalent to the splendid historical and geographical information contained within the few

---

[27] *Huarochirí*, p. 23.
[28] See K. R. Mills, *An Evil Lost to View?*, esp. ch. 5.

Mesoamerican codices that date from just before and after the arrival of the Europeans in the Mexica realm, it is necessary to employ the "regressive method" so well known to historians of European popular culture, among other fields.[29] One must learn what one can of earlier, prehispanic histories by cautiously reading backward from later, colonial sources. Much of the possible insight into the world of the huacas derives from Indian oral traditions (often called myths) recounted in the late sixteenth and seventeenth centuries. When these sacred histories were committed to writing they could not escape a number of interpretive filters, the most obvious of which were provided by a Spanish notary or a Hispanicized indigenous editor or redactor. Moreover, the written word also represented something of a sentence of imprisonment. Traditions recorded in alphabetic Quechua or "Quechuaized" Castilian in early colonial times—like native-language sources in Nahuatl or Mixtec—offer important perspectives for the colonial investigator, but as translations from an originally oral medium by Indian scholars and informants in the colonial years, they are as problematic and challenging (even if in different ways) as Spanish-language sources. Confinement to text denied the huaca histories' spirit and nature, both of which were suited to the more fluid medium of oral, performative expression.[30] Despite these drawbacks, the indigenous voice and convictions concerning the ancestor beings and their histories are not completely lost. When they are not loud and clear in testimonies before visitadores or in the historical relations that exist, they are often perceptible just beneath the surface of the written text, obscured only by a thin veneer of Christian prudence and prejudice.

The age of the huacas, as retold, appears to have been an unstable time when anything from cataclysm to creation might occur. Good battled evil and did not always win; huacas pitted themselves against one another to establish dominance in region after region in the Andes. The survival of both gods and men was precarious in a world that could suddenly be overturned only to be created again.[31] Like great ancestral figures, heroes, tricksters, and chapbook characters the world over, these Andean ancients depended upon their wits and the cultivation of cleverness, ingenuity, irreverence, self-confidence, strength, physical beauty, and a host of other particular abilities. Numerous are the morals that emerge from the traditions that extolled such virtues in their cultural founders.

Of all the huacas who might be highlighted, Paria Caca (or Pariaqaqa) is perhaps the most illuminating prototype. A being of celebrated wisdom, his predominant characteristic was without a doubt his terrific power. His exploits are a main feature in the foremost collection of myths and sacred histories in

---

[29] See especially P. Burke, *Popular Culture*, pp. 81–87.

[30] See G. Henningsen and J. Tedeschi, eds., *The Inquisition*, pp. 3–12. On what writing can do to modern versions of huaca histories, see R. Howard-Malverde, "The Speaking of History."

[31] Some thoughtful work has been done with the Quechua concept of *pachakuti*, meaning the world turned upside down. See especially O. Harris, "De la fin du monde"; S. MacCormack, "*Pachacuti*"; T. Bouysse-Cassagne and P. Bouysse, "Volcan indien, volcan chrétien"; and T. Bouysse and O. Harris, "Pacha."

the Andes from late sixteenth-century Huarochirí.[32] His dramatic birth, or emergence, which saw him "fly forth" from five eggs in the form of five falcons or hawks who become five men "who are at once sons and brothers," foretold a certain greatness.[33] This fivefold nature would do him no end of good as a divine presence upon the earth. Paria Caca's rise involved a number of mighty actions, among both humans and rival huacas who had held sway in the times before his emergence. Among men and women, his force took the form of a wide civilizing power and an ordering force. His cult grew to include a great number of different peoples who inhabited regions from the coastal shrine of Pacha Camac south of Lima, inland and into the mountains through Huarochirí to Yauyos.

In keeping with a salient motif in this body of myths, Paria Caca was in the habit of traveling about the ancient world incognito as a friendless beggar, testing peoples' goodness and charity toward a poor stranger. Because of their selfishness, the village people of a place such as Huagui Usa, for instance, could be lashed by his torrential rains and washed out to sea.[34] The communities of Cupara and Quinti were more fortunate, chiefly because the ever-amorous Paria Caca had espied a beautiful virgin in their midst. It also happened that there was an acute water shortage in the region. In exchange for the opportunity to sleep with the young woman, Chuqui Suso, Paria Caca extended and widened the existing irrigation network to assist her fields. When even these heroics proved insufficient to win her charms, he promised to channel the water directly from the river, a task superintended for him by a ready crew of animal allies. In the end, Paria Caca enjoyed his prize, and the communities had an explanation for a greatly improved—if somewhat quirky—irrigation canal. The animals, it seems, were not the smoothest of operators. The fox, who was in charge, was scared by a bird and fell down the mountain. The narrator/redactor continues:

> If the fox hadn't fallen, that canal of theirs
> would run at a higher level.
> But now it runs somewhat lower.
> The spot from which the fox fell is clearly visible to this day.
> In fact the water flows down the course the fox's fall opened.[35]

[32] G. Taylor's edition, *Ritos y tradiciones*, has been widely regarded as the best scholarly edition since its appearance in 1987. Its main Castilian predecessor, J. M. Arguedas's translation, the *Dioses y hombres*, is a more poetic rendering that is still widely cited and, by some, preferred. I shall, however, make reference to the newest edition by F. Salomon and G. E. Urioste, *Huarochirí*. The accessible style and careful notation of the latter (often building upon Taylor's previous analyses) commend it for future use. I make chapter and section references to assist readers locating passages in Taylor, Arguedas, or other editions.

[33] The last, apt phrase belongs to Claudette Kemper Columbus. See her "Immortal Eggs," p. 176.

[34] *Huarochirí*, ch. 6, secs. 76–80.

[35] This aetiological story is at *Huarochirí*, ch. 6, secs. 82–87. For Chuqui Suso's histories see *Huarochirí*, ch. 6, secs. 88–89 and ch. 7, secs. 91–95.

By recalling the story as part of their regular worship of the huaca in later times, the people of the region expressed their gratitude and reinvigorated their relationship with their founder and benefactor.

In what was perhaps the most glorious victory over other huacas in his steady rise to regional supremacy, Paria Caca's five selves attacked the highland domain of the fearsome god Huallallo Caruincho. This huaca took the form of a giant fire reaching almost to the heavens. Even the great rains that Paria Caca was able to unleash from five directions could not quite extinguish Huallallo. The waters uselessly rushed away to the sea until Llacsa Churapa, one of the Paria Cacas, dismantled a mountain and dammed up the water to form the lake of Mullo Cocha. Lightning bolts were hurled at the besieged huaca, until he finally fled in defeat to the lowlands, the Antis, where he lived out his sentence—to be worshiped forevermore by the "dog-eating" Huanca peoples. Another of the selves of Paria Caca, Paria Carco, guarded the pass to the highlands in case Huallallo should attempt a return.[36]

Other huacas in the Huarochirí collection feature as incidental beings, the heroes of interpolated myths that form chapters within the larger history of Paria Caca's ascendancy. The histories of their important deeds, though less earth-shattering than Paria Caca's, became just as embedded in regional Andean tradition. The incidental huacas of Huarochirí were much like their brethren in other regions (such as the huacas from Quipan and environs). There was, for example, a humble figure named Huatya Curi who was fortunate enough to witness Paria Caca's fantastic birth, and whom Paria Caca assisted in a series of contests with an arrogant prospective brother-in-law who had been harassing him. With help from the principal god, the poor man's revenge would be complete. The brother-in-law was put to shame by Paria Caca's favorite, and eventually turned into a brocket deer in his fright, condemned to be forever hunted by men in the forest. His wife, in even more standard Andean mythical fashion, was turned to stone standing on her head, with her legs and private parts, her shame, immortalized for all to see.[37]

The Huarochirí myths are beautiful and sometimes stunningly coherent. But the cultural archives and memories of other regions preserved similar, if less completely known, histories to explain the features of their natural world. The numinal population and apparent hierarchy among the huacas still clearly visible in Canta in the seventeenth century are a set of examples. One by one, the huacas took their places in many regional landscapes, their histories entering the oral traditions and festival calendars. Both the idolatry evidence and the letters of missionary observers complement our growing appreciation of colonial Andeans' conceptions of ancient times and of themselves.

Only a year later than the idolatry trial in Canta noted above, in San Pedro

---

[36] *Huarochirí*, ch. 8, secs. 102–5 and the beginning of ch. 9.

[37] *Huarochirí*, ch. 5, secs. 57–72, especially 69–70. The vivid history of the huaca Cuni Raya (who was often associated with Vira Cocha and even referred to as Cuni Raya Vira Cocha) at ch. 2, sec. 26, demonstrates how even thwarted adventures were full of significance.

de Acas, Cajatambo, Visitador Bernardo de Novoa's notary recorded many such histories. One of these was the Quirca and Canta ayllus' tradición of the mythical battle between two great huacas in their region's past. Cristóbal Hacas Malqui testified that two ancient founders named Corcui Callan and Capa Bilca had entered the region from the lowlands (los llanos)[38]. A chivalric contest to establish supremacy was said to have begun when Capa Bilca began assuming for himself the chacras that Corcui Callan had under cultivation. Both showed remarkable abilities to transform the living environment around them. Recognizing themselves equally brave and capable in this respect, they were said to have announced: "We will see which of us has the greater power to create springs." The places where each proceeded to urinate became the famous life-giving springs that dotted the high Andean landscape and provided water for the chacras. In the end, determining a winner was seen as futile, and the tradición ends with a fascinating comment on the philosophy of confidence and power. The notary recorded:

> The ídolos, realizing and knowing fully
> the power and wisdom that they possessed,
> became friends and they shared the chacras between them.
> When they died they both changed to stone,
> and the people of the ayllu have worshiped (mochado) them always."[39]

Writing from Ocros in the same province of Cajatambo in 1619, a group of Jesuit padres had told of a prevalent explanatory history they had encountered in the visita conducted in twenty-two villages through two entire parishes and part of a third. There had once been a giant huaca named Huari Viracocha who, after emerging from Lake Titicaca in southern Peru, had set his course for the north-central Andes, turning the people in his path into stone. The peoples in the regions of Cajatambo and los Conchucos, hoping to avoid their fate, built a house as if to welcome him. Inside, they fashioned a trap door, through which they planned his fall into a deep hole where he would die. The great Huari was, of course, soon wise to their trick, and hid himself behind a thicket near the meeting place appointed for his welcome. When his Andean hosts finally appeared to check their trap, he turned them into stones in the shapes of various animals. The Jesuits reported that the "house of the huacas" was still much revered, a place to which the ministers of different localities would return to converse with their ancestors (the zoomorphic huacas) according to their needs. The Cajatambinos, it seems, also employed the story as a means of explaining the shift from what had been a public cult in prehispanic times to the necessarily more secret one of the colonial era.[40]

---

[38] Coming from the lowlands and being primarily agriculturalists, these ancients were the important Huari founders. The thunder and lightning-worshiping Llacuaz, who formed the other major moiety in this region, were pastoralists who later invaded and conquered the area from the high mountains. On this dualism, see particularly P. Duviols's seminal "Huari y Llacuaz."

[39] The testimony of Cristóbal Hacas Malqui appears in P. Duviols, ed., Cultura andina, p. 172.

[40] This particular letter is published in P. Duviols, ed., Cultura andina, pp. 452–53.

Huacas such as Paria Caca, Cuni Raya, Capa Bilca, and their less illustrious colleagues were found throughout the Andean landscape of the archdiocese; they might have been hidden and the importance of many of them might have been concealed in the colonial era. But, from the information that has survived, it is clear that in the eyes of their people they had been neither defeated nor replaced. Moreover, as entertaining as they are, the collected histories of the huacas were more than a mere assemblage of fond memories and tales of a few fanciful beings who had once been thought of as ancestors. The evidence from the seventeenth and early eighteenth centuries affirms that the huacas' religious dominion had lasted, and suggests that understanding the nature of their persistence is an important step in comprehending colonial Andean religion.

The bulk of the idolatry documentation from the mid-colonial Lima region suggests that—at least for a time—the worship, if not the memory, of the great Inkaic cults had all but faded away. This was not to be the fate of the regional huacas, who were more deeply rooted in both the people's hearts and their landscape; they would prove more difficult to destroy.[41] At the very time that historians of the mendicant orders recorded the miraculous triumphs of their missionaries in the conversion of the heathen, there occurred a dramatic sign of life from the indigenous gods: the spread of a religious movement in the center and south of Andean Peru.

The Taki Onqoy, the so-called "dancing sickness" of the 1560s, was so named because of the gyrations enacted by the itinerant preachers—the *taquiongos*—who were said to be taken over by the huacas when they delivered their prophecies.[42] The message of the taquiongos could hardly have been more distressing from the Spanish point of view, given the continued threat of a massive Andean rebellion, perhaps led by the rebel neo-Inka state that was still at large in the jungles of Vilcabamba. The huacas possessed the taquiongos in order to spread the word of their imminent and glorious return. Perhaps, just as the dancing prophets claimed, the time was nigh when the Christian God would be defeated and the Spanish would be driven into the sea.

However, the new viceroy, Francisco de Toledo, responded with the firm hand that would characterize his tenure in Peru. A visitador general, Cristóbal

[41] The Extirpation's findings in the Archdiocese of Lima are, for the most part, a stumbling block for the wide-ranging studies of Inka messianism and rebirth, which tend understandably to gravitate toward the eighteenth century for documentation more propitious to their theses. It is probable, as these studies assert, that the days of Inka hegemony and the prospect of an Inka's return became more fondly viewed and more widely received with the passage of time. See especially the late A. Flores Galindo's *Buscando un Inca*; M. Burga, *Nacimiento*; and A. Zarzar, "Apo capac huayna."

[42] The Taki Onqoy has drawn considerable academic attention, especially since Luis Millones's 1964 article "Un movimiento nativista." Among the recent scholarship, see particularly Rafael Varón Gabai's "El Taki Onqoy," in *El retorno de las huacas*, compiled by L. Millones, and the published documents in this same collection; and also L. Millones, ed., *Las informaciones de Cristóbal de Albornoz*. Also, S. J. Stern, *Peru's Indian Peoples*, pp. 51–79, and, on a related phenomenon, M. Curatola, "El culto de crisis del Moro Oncoy."

de Albornoz, was commissioned to search out the movement's leaders and de-
fuse any threat to Spanish authority. Shortly after his investigations and punishments ceased, the last of the sixteenth-century neo-Inkas, Túpac Amaru, was
captured and executed before a large crowd in the central plaza of the old Inka
capital of Cusco. His death marked the symbolic if not the practical end of
renascent Inka hopes in the sixteenth century, and ushered in an era of great
upheaval in the Andean provinces. Toledo began a massive resettlement of the
Indian population into towns (*reducciones*) and a coherent parish network,
rejuvenating a process that had periodically flagged before his time. In addition
to its obvious advantages for the Spanish exaction of tribute and manual labor,
the policy was designed to allow for a closer religious control of the Indians. As
the agents of the crown attempted to tighten their grip, the Andean gods and
their people were punished for their rising.[43]

The increasing rigor of Spanish control in the later sixteenth century had its
effects on Andean religion. The regional huacas and their people were forced
to adopt more pragmatic, less frontal and injurious, methods of survival than
those taken in the Taki Onqoy episode in the south. But to suggest that the
allegiances to huacas waned or temporarily withdrew, only to experience a revival or resurgence in the early seventeenth century, thus prompting the
Church's campaigns of extirpation and further huaca revival, imparts far more
significance to surviving documentation than should ever be claimed for it.[44]

Because of what the Extirpation would later find, historians puzzle over the
huacas' comparative silence after the suppression of the Taki Onqoy. There is
little mention of them and related "idolatry" in the Indian parishes in the late
sixteenth and the beginning of the seventeenth centuries. As I noted in the
previous chapter, the archbishop of Lima, and later saint, Toribio Alfonso de
Mogrovejo, made some four pastoral visits over the vast expanses of his archdiocese during his long tenure, yet he expressed conspicuously little suspicion
about the nature of Andean faith. Where were the people who had provided
the taquiongos with an audience? And where were their successors and some
of the very same huacas and ministers who would make such a dramatic re-
entry into the Spanish religious imagination only a few years later, when some
of these churchmen's successors would "unmask" idolatry and whip up fervor
in support of the Extirpation?[45]

---

[43] As will be discussed in more detail in Chapter Eight, the people who had been rounded up
by administrators and resettled in the pueblos do not seem to have lost their connections with the
old settlements and sacred places in the regional geography. Many reducciones appear to have
been gradually abandoned as Indians drifted back to their old places. For examples and wider
discussion, see A. M. Wightman, *Indigenous Migration*, pp. 4–73; W. G. Lovell, "Surviving Conquest," pp. 33–35; and I. Clendinnen, *Ambivalent Conquests*, pp. 139–53.

[44] See Manuel Burga's provocative arguments that distinct waves of anti-idolatry campaigns
rose to meet "idolatry" as it "revitalized" and threatened, and that huaca cults tended to rejuvenate
in the places where they were most set upon by the Extirpation; *Nacimiento*, esp. pp. 122, 151, and
155.

[45] F. de Armas Medina's "desenmascara" (to unmask or expose something already there) seems

The answer is suggested by mention of the Spanish religious imagination, and by recalling that the late sixteenth and early seventeenth centuries, the alleged period of dormancy, was precisely the time when Francisco de Avila organized the collection of religious information that would form the Huarochirí manuscript. The huacas were where they had always been, and not only in the province of Huarochirí. They were a little battered and worn from intermittent persecution by priests and missionaries, but many of them still stood above and around the resettled Andean villages throughout the arch-diocese. The people passed them on the way to their chacras, celebrated their festivals in secret if this was necessary, and consulted them through their minis-ters both regularly and in times of great need. Any impression of a change in the huacas' importance to Andeans, just like the signs of continued reverence afforded them by the people, come to us not because of any sudden decline or resurgence in huaca worship, but largely thanks to shifts in official Church attention in Lima.

One can momentarily direct one's gaze away from the Andean villages and towns to recall the tenures of five archbishops of Lima spanning nearly a cen-tury: the approaches to Andean religiosity in Mogrovejo's time were markedly different from those under Bartolomé Lobo Guerrero (1609–1622) or Gonzalo de Campo (1625–1626), just as the relative inactivity against "idolatry" by Her-nando Arias de Ugarte (1630–1638) would contrast sharply with the vigor of the Extirpation encouraged by Pedro de Villagómez (1641–1671). The person-alities of three of these archbishops, and their shifting concerns, were not the sole reasons for the campaigns undertaken against the huacas and Andean reli-gious practices, but there can be little doubt that the centralized initiatives and influential sponsorship of Lobo, Campo, and Villagómez, in particular, were crucial to the organization of systematic persecution efforts. These efforts, in turn, provoked mounting zeal and hysteria in the region, which determined not only the ebb and flow of the idolatry trials but the character of much of the surviving evidence. Even clergy who abused their local positions and made false idolatry accusations against Indian enemies might benefit from the official climate of opinion, the extirpating atmosphere, during the Lobo Guerrero or Villagómez years. Thus it is from the documentary survivals of increased per-secution that one gains points of entry, once more, into the history of the An-dean gods.

The huacas responded to increased ecclesiastical pressures in much the same way as their traditions suggest they had always done in difficult times—with a notable adaptability. It had been no easy matter for Paria Caca to banish Huallallo to the jungle, and even then the rival had not completely disap-peared. The genesis of a religious coexistence—sometimes tense and combat-ive, but at other times covertly cooperative—similar, perhaps, to the kind of

---

a far more accurate expression to describe Francisco de Avila's theatrics in the central plaza in Lima than "discover," which is most commonly used. See "La pervivencia de la idolatría," p. 20. On Avila's role, see A. Acosta, "Francisco de Avila."

coexistence of peoples that resulted after the mythical clash of Corcui Callan and Capa Bilca in Cajatambo, was a more common result in the Andean parishes. It was in the huacas' nature to transform their existence and modes of worship, to endure and negotiate contemporary circumstances, rather than to be beaten down and stripped away by alien newcomers. Thus the huacas encountered by the Spanish investigations in the seventeenth and first half of the eighteenth centuries were not gods who had been brought to their knees by over a century of living with a domineering Christian presence. Yet neither were they the huacas of the Taki Onqoy, the vengeful possessing spirits of the crisis of the 1560s who were thought to represent a direct menace to Spanish Catholic hegemony. The continued existence of the huacas had come to depend on subtler forms of response to pressures. New responsibilities fell upon their devotees. The cults, and the huacas themselves, had to be more pragmatic and less conspicuous; ritual had to be concentrated and concealed instead of protracted and public.[46]

The indigenous editor(s) of the Huarochirí manuscript captured the climate of necessary diminution perfectly in describing the festival celebrated in the community of San Pedro de Mama in the lower Rímac valley in honor of the huaca Chaupi Ñamca: "If somebody says 'How did you worship before the Spanish Viracochas appeared?' we know how they reply: 'People used to drink for five days in the month of June, wearing their most splendid clothes. Later, for fear of the Spaniards, they worshiped on Corpus eve.'"[47] The changing lifestyle and demands of colonial rule meant that the huacas' hold upon, and very relevance to, their adherents depended upon their ability to conceal much of themselves, absorb innovation, and prove an integral part of the emerging colonial religious reality.

Many mid-colonial Andean people believed that their gods had the power to affect their prosperity and happiness. In most of the Lima region, the local economies operated from an agricultural and pastoral base in the seventeenth and eighteenth centuries. Reflecting this, the huacas and the more personal and familial gods to be met with below were primarily agricultural divinities, concerned with crops and their seeding, irrigation, soil fertility, and harvest, and access to pasture, streams, and springs. The huacas in their oldest but

---

[46] For elaboration on some of the forms that this kind of "resistance" has taken in the historical Andean framework, see S. J. Stern's introductory essay in his edition, *Resistance, Rebellion, and Consciousness*, pp. 3–25, and F. Salomon's "Ancestor Cults" in the same volume. An insightful examination of the manipulation of symbols as a means of survival and a motor of change in New Spain is W. B. Taylor's "Santiago's Horse." In a lecture delivered at St. Antony's College, Oxford on 18 January 1989, Terence Ranger captured what for me has always been the most vivid example of the tragic reality of the alternatives to these subtler forms of resistance for many subjugated peoples in a colonial framework. He described the prophet Kinjikitele and the Maji Maji uprising of 1905 against German colonialism in Africa. Religious prophecy, millenarian promises, and myths of invincibility saw the people rush straight into the German line of fire. For more see G. Gwassa, "Kinjikitile and the Ideology of the Maji Maji."

[47] *Huarochirí*, ch. 13, sec. 175.

persistently relevant roles as protectors and providers of herders and farmers expressed the sacred character of all subsistence activity in the Andean world, and often the apparent absence of the distinction that contemporary Spanish Christians would have drawn between the natural and the supernatural.

Yet, as Karen Spalding and others have demonstrated, Andeans' prosperity and happiness were under considerable threat through most of the period studied here. Vertical relationships of exhange between ayllu members living in different conditions and altitudes had been altered, and many networks that had partially survived were under constant strain. The effects of massive de-population could still be noted in the mid-colonial period, and intermittent plagues and onslaughts of disease continued to devastate. Resettlement schemes, the forced contribution of manual laborers to mines and different work *mitas* (a rotational labor system) also contributed to the disruption of the Indians' lives. Segments of the population could not resist the lead of many of the local nobles who had embraced new standards of wealth and prestige, who had been lured by the cities and markets, and who had entered into Hispanic Christian culture and pursuits as far as they might in the years after the military conquest.[48] Yet, however much they might appear to be colonial pragmatists— the willing agents of cultural and religious transformation or even rupture— certain individuals' apparent breaks with indigenous ways are not matters about which to generalize idly. Accommodation to the dominant society's wishes could be both prudent and calculated. Change did not necessitate a complete break with Andean tradition.

Contact with Europeans and the burgeoning mestizo population had ines-capable effects on Andean society. Hispanicization is found in many spheres of the mid-colonial people's existence, and not least in the ways that the people made their livings. Many Indian people, for instance, embraced the new oppor-tunities offered by more extensive trade outside the exchange within the ayllu and regional frameworks. For them, meeting the increasing demands of the larger towns in the valleys, or even the capital, meant entering a wider world. Lima is mentioned many times in the mid-colonial testimonies, suggesting that it was not so foreign or distant a place as might be imagined. If a person had not been there himself on business, then some relative, a neighbor, or the region's *kuraka* (native lord and governor) surely had. The increasing connections with the lowland towns and the capital city were symbolic of the fact that Andean people's social and economic lives were expanding beyond their valleys and mountains, and that they were acquiring priorities beyond what might be called their traditional concerns.

What was to become of the gods whose histories and functions were so rooted in caring for the chacras, strengthening irrigation canals, and maintain-

---

[48] See S. R. Ramírez, "The '*dueño de indios*'"; K. Spalding's "Defendiendo el suyo," and also her earlier essays, especially "Social Climbers" and "*Kurakas* and Commerce." See also S. Rivera C., "El Mallku y la sociedad," and works by F. Pease G.Y., especially *Curacas*, and by S. J. Stern, *Peru's Indian Peoples*, pp. 27–50.

ing the health of the herds of camelids, in the midst of this change? Out of necessity, the gods' mirroring of their society continued; their peoples' needs included, but also transcended, agricultural and pastoral endeavors, and so too did the huacas' abilities to respond. Like their people, without fully departing from their traditional base the huacas appear to have diversified and absorbed change. However, there is a foundation of belief and practice that needs to be understood before these transformations can be adequately appreciated.

Even in mid-colonial times, an examination of the expanding realm of competence of the Andean gods begins with the earth. The central preoccupations of many people in the communities of the Archdiocese of Lima were their chacras, the plots of land in the surrounding countryside that fed them and others. It was of the utmost importance for the soil's fertility that it be properly prepared, ritually as well as in the sense of practical cultivation. In a well-known and widespread Andean rite, a libation of chicha was poured out to the earth (*pacha mama*) and coca leaves were scattered in hope of abundant crops. Thus in Caujul in Cajatambo in 1652, Martín Curi Poma was sentenced to participate in a procession of public shame and to suffer a year's exile from the town for believing in his ancestors' teaching that the casting of the two ritual substances assisted fertility.[49] Ritual offerings with similar goals could also be more elaborate; people like Juan Rinri Chagua in Utcas, Cajatambo, in the same year invoked the gods of the surrounding mountain peaks and hills, as well as the more localized huacas on the spot.[50] The latter were common, and the following example is illustrative of many more.

María Llano of the Qiuma Marca ayllu in the village of Santo Domingo de Oteque, an annex of Ihuari in the province of Chancay, came before the visitador, Don Juan Sarmiento de Vivero, in 1665 and twice denied making offerings to a huaca at her own chacra. She admitted worshiping for the abundance of the chacras in the early mornings before she began her work, but was eager to distract attention from any god who might be close to her own fields. María claimed that she performed her rites at a huaca called Ana Guilca, who stood by a field called Corotayoc above the neighboring settlement of Ñaupay. María conducted her observances all alone "at the time of the chacras," that is, at the time of cultivation, when the seedbed was being prepared. María offered Ana Guilca chicha, sango, and the parpa made from white maize.[51]

Her husband, she said, had taught her that this was a huaca of the ancients,

---

[49] AAL Leg. 6, exp. 4, fol. 2v.

[50] AAL Leg. 6, exp. 9, fol. 2. Juan was a chief minister. The mountains were nearby Copa and Ychacos.

[51] AAL Leg. 5, exp. 12, fols. 14 and 15. Sarmiento would eventually burn Ana Guilca in a village *auto de fe*. She also states that the huaca at Corotayoc was offered only chicha. The contradiction might be her own blending of descriptions of other huacas' rites. Sanco and parpa are small cakes of maize, the former soft and the latter cooked with salt and *ají* (a chili pepper). Both are often noted among the foods of the gods and were prohibited in the Edict against Idolatry. See Villagómez, "Carta pastoral," ch. 60, p. 207.

and she claimed that it was his family who had encouraged her in the cult. María Llano's incantation to Ana Guilca, a simultaneous request for fertility and sustenance and a deflection of guilt, was recorded as follows:

> My in-laws tell me to commend myself to you
> that you will give me good maize crops so I may eat.
> Thus I offer you this that you
> will give me good chacras and [food] to eat.[52]

When Visitador Sarmiento asked if she actually believed that the stone huaca possessed the power to grant bountiful chacras, María replied that yes, she believed it did.

Sowing inspired just as much ritual care in indigenous practice, often involving not only the huacas but other gods.[53] Some fields had their own specialized protectors nearby in the large immovable stones called huancas.[54] In many places, Andean ministers also consulted the important malquis, taking them food and drink, and seeking encouragement to begin sowing. In 1725, the people of San Pedro de Palpas in Cajatambo spoke of a giant and ancient malqui named Apu Casa Paico, who sat in a house amidst the ruins of the ancients' old town of Cotomarca. Each year the community notables and religious officials (recorded as the "maestros and principales") would ascend to the place to ask Casa Paico's permission to sow their fields.[55]

As mentioned above, sacred objects, very different from the stone figures or mountain peaks, could also achieve a religious status akin to that of the lesser huacas. In the late seventeenth century, Martín Phelipe of Pachangara, Cajatambo, guarded a large earthen jar (*tinaja*) named Tinlla Cocha, which was worshiped by all the people in the pueblo. It was endowed with certain anthropomorphic features and no one viewed it without the special consent of its guardian and minister. At the time of the preparation of the chacras, Martín and the principal elders would fill Tinlla Cocha with chicha and cover (or, perhaps more appropriately, dress) it with an assortment of objects—the hide of a black llama, decorated blankets, belts, large pins—while putting llama fat and colored wool in what were referred to as the "ears" (presumably the handles) of the jar. It was said that the chicha inside would soon turn various colors,

[52] Ibid., fol. 14v. Of course the accusatory beginning, perhaps recited for the visitador and his notary, was probably not included in her actual incantation.

[53] María Guassa of San Pedro de Guandaro in Canta, to cite only one example, told of a small white stone (a *conopa*), inherited from her *maestra* (female teacher) as a "great relic," which she put amidst the seeds she would plant in the hope that her harvest would be bountiful. The same woman carried along another larger stone—either a movable huaca or, more likely, a *chanca* or lineage divinity—to the sowing of her chacra. AAL Leg. 5, exp. 25, 1696, fol. 12. See Chapter Three below.

[54] P. J. de Arriaga noted the huanca's designation as *chacrayoc*, "lord of the chacra," and its veneration at seeding time. *La extirpación*, p. 28. Commonly, huancas were obscured by the generic use of the term huaca both by recording notaries and by other Spanish commentators. The best focused study of which I am aware is P. Duviols, "Un symbolisme de l'occupation."

[55] AAL Leg. 3, exp. 11, fols. 8v–9.

forming an arc like a rainbow on its surface. At that point all would drink from the jar and this act would give them strength. Then they would go "in common" to the sowing of their chacras which, in turn, would produce much fruit.[56]

There were also sacred musical instruments that were huacas—shell trumpets or horns were the most common, it seems—and there were associated dances that characterized the season of the preparation of the earth and sowing of the crops in different regions. Some of the most detailed information comes from the province of Cajatambo. In Santo Domingo de Nava in the parish of Churín, the people cherished an eight-pound sea shell called Cara Guarca that was played when the common lands were seeded and the irrigation canals were cleared of debris. Antonio Ripas said that the mighty shell could be heard for three leagues. One might wonder what the Mercedarian friars who ministered to the parish thought was meant by the sounding of this great shell. We know from testimonies taken in 1725 by Visitador Pedro de Celis y la Vega that the sounding of a similar horn inaugurated a ceremony that had survived from prehispanic times, culminating in a dance called the Airigua.[57] In Nava, Ripas described the performance in colonial times, saying that the dancers would dress up as devils.[58] This description and others, too, suggest that the dances were survivals of ritual performances similar to those described in vivid detail in Huarochirí, in which *huacsas* (dancing ministers) would effectively embody the huacas whose deeds and personalities they portrayed. In the region around Caujul and Andajes in Cajatambo, another dance called the Mallco was also celebrated in connection with the seeding of the chacras to maize. These dances frequently involved the reenactment and singing of the huacas' traditions.[59]

Water was, of course, a central concern at the time of seed germination as well as during the growing season. Although most of the mountainous region in the archdiocese enjoyed, as it still enjoys, a defined rainy period each year, droughts were not unknown. An equally serious problem was caused in times of excessive rainfall, when mountainside plots were often washed away by water and mudslides. As with the quest for fertility of soil and seed, people—then as now—sought means by which rainfall could be influenced by their own ritual actions.

The ancestors of the community of Pachangara had passed down a sacred horn, much like the shell from Nava, which was played especially to bring rain.[60] In Santiago de Carampoma in Huarochirí one accused man, Don Francisco Gulca Rilpo, seeking to deflect attention from the charges against himself, told of rites allegedly carried on in nearby La Ascención de Guanza. An annually elected official called a *marcayoc* was said to have led a ceremony that

[56] Ibid., fols. 4v–5.
[57] See Juana María, ibid., fol. 5.
[58] Ibid., fol. 6v.
[59] AAL Leg. 6, exp. 4, fols. 2 and 2v. And see *Huarochirí*, esp. ch. 9, secs. 117–40.
[60] AAL Leg. 4. exp. 37, fols. 9–9v.

involved dancing and drums. The young men cried out as they danced, either for or against rain, as the situation demanded. Gulca Rilpo said that spies ensured that the parish priest was asleep or otherwise unaware, in order that the day-long festival could be performed in secret.[61] Although this witness, near the end of his statement, claimed "he did not know that which he declared for certain," his description bears a striking resemblance to the traditional rites of the Chanco season in another part of Huarochirí.

For the Checa people of the region near colonial San Damián—the parish that had been administered by Francisco de Avila—the time when "the heavens will rain" began with a ritual hunt which retraced the mythical path of the divine ancestor, Tutay Quiri. The huaca himself had once moved over the route as red and yellow rain. Their journey complete, the hunters were ceremoniously received in the community by the rest of the villagers. "When they danced the Chanco," the narrator related, "the sky would say 'Now!' and the rain would pour down." The success of the ritual was thought to augur the harvest and well-being of the people for the year to come.[62]

But prudent farmers knew that the sky might not always be as compliant as it was said to have been in the mythical past. Water from highland springs and lakes, conducted to the chacras through a system of irrigation canals, was a crucial necessity. Thus the annual cleaning and maintenance of the canals, too, took on a festive and religious significance. As I have noted, some communities conceived of their irrigation networks as divinely inspired, that is to say, the ancient work of the cultural heroes, the huacas. One Andean man explained as much to an incredulous Spaniard who worked beside him during the annual canal cleaning in the parish of Santiago de Lunahuana in Cañete. The man said that the water's course, the very placement of the boulders and crags that formed the workers' obstacles, had been arranged by divine ancestors who had "driven" everything into place.[63] A number of the people sentenced by Visitador Felipe de Medina in Caujul, Cajatambo, in 1652 were accused of having offered "chicha, coca, and other things" to the main canal of that town, Cocha Pareco. The rites were meant to secure the channel from breaks and leakage. In Andajes, the same visitador had his notary record that they were struggling against a teaching which had corrupted so many innocents—the transmission

[61] AAL Leg. 3, exp. 15, 1730–1732, fols. 11–11v.

[62] *Huarochirí*, ch. 11, secs. 159 and 164. See also P. Duviols, "Huari y Llacuaz." A similar ritual hunt was carried out by the Llacuaz men, who were then received by Huari villagers in the community of San Pedro de Acas, Cajatambo, in 1657. See the testimonies of Cristóbal Hacas Malqui at p. 173, and Hernando Chaupis Condor at p. 161, in P. Duviols, ed., *Cultura andina*. The intimate concern with rainfall, of course, continues in modern Peru. For modified rites incorporated into drama in Carhuamayo, Junín, see L. Millones, *El Inca por la Coya*. For practices in Canta, see J. M. Arguedas's posthumous "Folklore del pueblo de Araguay."

[63] AAL Leg. 7, exp. 1, fols. 6–7. Rosaleen Howard-Malverde has collected some fascinating modern oral history from San Pedro de Pariarca in Huamalíes, in which an ancient figure called "the Inka's old man" is described as having brandished his whip and sling, and thus driven the boulders into their places in the natural landscape. See "The Speaking of History," pp. 63–65.

of a belief that by offering chicha, coca, and sanco, and by "pagan superstitions and actions," the water could be guided and directed.[64]

The huacas were never far removed from these regular proceedings, as is evident from one typical instance from Navan, Cajatambo. A minister named Ysabel Rosa in 1725 said she had inherited a dark stone figure named Rayguan (alternatively Raiguasa) from her deceased aunt. Rayguan was brought down from a dwelling place in the old town of Guatec and taken to the chacras at Lipli each year when the principal canal was being cleaned. Ysabel said she spoke to the god, offering it animals' blood and "other things."[65] The priest of the benefice, Fray Gregorio Marin, had finally managed to take Raygaun from Ysabel, "at great risk to his life" according to him. However, he had not sent the stone god to the provisor in Lima as eighteenth-century parish priests were instructed to do by the centralizing authorities of the time; Marin had simply left Rayguan in the possession of the town's indigenous governors.[66]

Regular rituals to secure water were also performed at the sources where the water came out of the earth, the mouths of the canals and springs. Divine protectors often resided at these spots. One can recall the ancient huaca in Huarochirí, Chuqui Suso, who gained irrigation canals for her region and turned to stone at the mouth of the canal called Choco Calla. She was worshiped at every canal cleaning with "a major festival, [at which there was] dancing and drinking all night long."[67] Perhaps the most fascinating example of a huaca protector at a spring bids us return to the province of Canta.

In 1650 in Pomacocha, the indigenous maestra Catalina Suyo allegedly told her charges of a divine encounter at a water source that she had experienced as a girl. One day while tending her llamas, the spring had "opened up and taken her for five or six days." Within, Catalina said she had met "a man with colored [or red] hair" whom she had soon asked for something to eat. The man proved generous, not only feeding her once, but giving her *mazamorra* (maize porridge) on each of the days she was there. The man told her that after she left she must be certain to provide for him. Thus, with the passing of each five-month span (an interesting extension of the "five days" of her possession expe-

---

[64] AAL Leg. 6, exp. 4, fols. 1v–2v. Similar rites performed near a channel named Conoc are noted in an investigation in Utcas in the same year. See AAL Leg. 6, exp. 9, fol. 2.

[65] AAL Leg. 3, exp. 13, fol. 6. Strictly speaking, this may not have been a "huaca proper," but a lineage god (see Chapter Three) given the more common designation. Ysabel also stated that it was customary to lay the body of a child over the huaca. It is unclear whether any action was taken with the body, if this refers to a human sacrifice, or if this was a ritual enactment of an ancient practice.

[66] AAL Leg. 3, exp. 13, fols. 7v–8. See also Ysabel Sallan at fol. 6v. Although there is not space to treat them properly here, María Rostworowski de Diez Canseco's conclusions about Mama Raiguana's relationship with food and sustenance open up important comparisons. See her "Mitos andinos relacionados con el origen de las subsistencias." I thank Luis Millones for this reference.

[67] *Huarochirí*, ch. 7, secs. 93–94 and ch. 6, secs. 88–89. Another spring in the Anchi Cocha ravine had a mythical two-headed toad as its protector. See *Huarochirí*, ch. 5, sec. 54. As Salomon observes in his note 161 (ch. 7, sec. 91), canal cleaning ceremonies, *y'arq'a hasp'iy*, have long been important in many parts of the Andes.

rience), Catalina was said to have taken an ample offering of sanco, coca, crushed maize, fat, cooked potatoes, and chicha to the spring.[68] In the Andes, these regular rites ensured the water supply that sustained the crops on the hillsides, and they honored the interdependence of the people and their natural source of water. The reciprocal relationship is neatly captured in the maestra's story of her abduction and the development of a vital link with the guardian of the spring.

Such sacralized springs and sources were, not surprisingly, often referred to as huaca. They might be regularly propitiated, but like other huacas they could also be visited in times of special need. For example, every dry season, the men of Nava, Cajatambo, would proceed to the mouth of their main canal with offerings of chicha, asking that the water be abundant.[69] The parish of San Juan de los Sondores in colonial Tarama (modern Junín) provides a superb illustration of rites on the banks of a life-giving spring (*puquio*). In 1668 the parish priest, Francisco de Alevardo, was led by a contingent of local Spaniards and Indian officials to a spring at the beginning of a long underground channel that provided water for the fields of the parish's annex of San Blas. While the party scrutinized the darkest corners of the place by torchlight, a young boy who accompanied them made a discovery. Beneath some large rocks was the body of a white *cuy* (an Andean guinea pig) with a grain of colored maize in its mouth. Beside the cuy were some cooked goods on three small clay plates, and some spun colored wool. The cuy and food appeared to be only a few days old. The assumed offerings and implements were taken and solemnly destroyed in a fire before the people in the plaza of San Blas, thus setting in motion an investigation into the practices of the chief perpetrators.

Forty-year-old Pedro Quispi Rima (alias Pedro Ynga) admitted that it was he who ministered to the spring, periodically refreshing the offerings to ensure that the water from the source would always increase. Pedro was described by another witness as one who was much respected as the "owner and dispenser" of the water. Pedro's wife, Ana Sija, added that making the offerings was "a custom of their ancients from time immemorial."[70] This is the language of Spanish law, a language that carried particular weight in the assertion of property rights; thus, the customs of "time immemorial" were invoked repeatedly by Amerindian litigants against each other and Spaniards in the seventeenth and eighteenth centuries.[71] Thus, the notary's record of Ana Sija's invocation of

[68] AAL Leg. 4, exp. 14, fol. 16. The being in the spring is described as "un hombre con unos cavellos colorados" and "este hombre del cavello colorado." Irene Silverblatt, in her treatment of this case, calls him "a devil, of golden-red hair." Because of his alleged blondeness, his sex (he was a man when, in Andean tradition, water is usually the province of the feminine) and "his truly extraordinary powers," Silverblatt interprets this being as a masculine symbol of a Spaniard. See *Moon, Sun, and Witches*, pp. 189–90.

[69] AAL Leg. 3, exp. 11, fol. 5.

[70] Juan Masco at AAL Leg. 4, exp. 37, fol. 6; Ana Sija at fol. 5.

[71] On land and property rights in general, see the selection of case abstracts offered by Woodrow Borah in *Justice by Insurance*, pp. 128–48.

"time immemorial" as a justification for Andean religious practices in colonial times is perhaps significant. Of course, her own—or possibly the notary's— application of the concept to explain and defend the veneration of a huaca would have stretched it beyond breaking for a colonial judge. Yet the widening usage of "time immemorial"—as seen in Ana Sija's testimony—to approximate the importance of maintaining Andean traditions suggests a mixing of European and Andean strategies of legitimation. It hints at how at least Ana Sija may have been conceiving of, and justifying, her religious practices.

Still, neither Ana nor her husband was pretending that an ignorance of what was proscribed by the Church had resulted in the persistence of their activities. Pedro admitted to being afraid of performing rites that were forbidden by the Catholic Church, but he told his inquisitor he was even more "fearful to stop it." The people's dependence on the spring was profound and, it seems, for more than just water. Ninety-year-old Bernabé Guaranga noted that the puquio was also a crucial provider of salt.[72]

The witnesses from San Blas spoke of a respected elder named Don Pasqual, now deceased, who had taught that "the Inka had ordered the rites to be performed at that spring." Pedro's alias, Pedro Ynga (a common notarial rendering of "Inka"), suggests his office's association with an Inkaic, and perhaps even a pre-Inkaic, injunction.[73] There had also been other teachers and opportunities for religious mixture in colonial times. As a child, Pedro Quispi Rima recalled learning that the blessing of the spring was to be a regular celebration following the festival of the Catholic patron, San Blas. If a llama was not readily available for sacrifice, one was to be purchased with a collection taken from the Christian festival's celebrants. The animal was ritually killed, and its meat was shared among the people, who were said to have responded "with a great clamor and celebrative cries and shouts."[74]

The spring of San Blas was a divine personality that reflected colonial religious realities. Once again, explicit reference to the Christian God and the slightly "Christian" description of the spring's importance add to its Andean meanings. Juan Masco explained that the sacrifice of a llama to the puquio was done "in veneration of him to whom they gave worship as to God (Dios), holding him as such in their estimation, [and] attempting in this way to give him thanks that he would not fail them in [granting] his abundance."[75] The visitador may have called the ritual the "superstitious anniversary of the devil," but only one Andean witness to come before Pedro de Cardenas y Arbieto expressed clear skepticism or disgust at the proceedings. Alonso Callan said he had defied his kuraka's order to cooperate with the community's custom, claim-

---

[72] AAL Leg. 4, exp. 37, fol. 8v.

[73] Ibid., fols. 4–4v. As noted above, when the Inka spread their influence they frequently subsumed existing Andean gods and rituals into an expanding religious amalgam.

[74] Rodrigo Guamallanqui at AAL Leg. 4, exp. 37, fols. 9v, 4v, and 5.

[75] Ibid., fol. 6. Other witnesses also said that "they venerated the puquio as God" [the notary wrote Dios]. See Juan Nina Guara at fol. 7; Bernabé Guaranga at fol. 8v; and Alonso Callan at fols. 7v–8.

ing that the rites at the spring represented nothing but "following the illusion of his ancestors."[76] In this Los Sondores trial there is no mention of a huaca standing over or near the spring, nor is one referred to in connection with the regular rites at the irrigation canal. In this case the god was the puquio itself. According to an ancient practice sanctioned by the Inka, but perhaps dating from a time before their control, the huaca-spring was worshiped with fresh offerings on its banks. In mid-colonial times, it seems to be have been nourished with annual sacrifices and ceremonies of a festive nature in conjunction with the feast day of San Blas—one of many convergences and gradual mixtures that we will encounter.

Implicit in the ritual attention to sowing, land fertility, and access to water was the concern for the fruit of the people's labors, the harvest. Similarly, the water level of springs and streams, and the amount of rainfall, affected pasture and the health of the peoples' herds. No matter how much the onset of the colonial system had altered the business of life, in most of the Andean villages in the seventeenth and eighteenth centuries crop failure and herd sickness were serious matters. Hard times would mean the difference between life and death for some families, whereas for many others the fate of foodstuffs and livestock contributed directly to their standard of living, their personal prosperity, and ultimately their happiness.

Andean villagers in much of the Lima region practiced huaca worship, which was directly concerned with assuring a bountiful harvest. Antonio Tapaojo was over seventy years old when he appeared before Visitador Celis y la Vega in San Antonio de la Lancha in the parish of Andajes in Cajatambo, in 1725. He recalled a trip he had made to Lancha with his grandmother some forty years earlier. All of the people of Lancha, he remembered, were busy in their fields of sweet potatoes (*camotes*). Their concern for the harvest meant strict veneration of the village's two principal gods, Auqui Libiac (or Auquillay Libiac) and Mama Raiguay. As at Quipan, Canta, in the middle of the seventeenth century, the observances in eighteenth-century Lancha, Cajatambo, were treated with the utmost seriousness. At the time when the crops were sown, people abstained from sleeping with their spouses, and one woman—a huaca minister— did not speak or eat. Antonio Tapaojo explained that these abstinences and those which he observed personally had been taught by their forefathers; "by not doing these things," he said, "they do not lose the harvest."[77]

María Poma Ticlla of the Quiripa ayllu in the town of Huarochirí, in the province of the same name, came before Juan Sarmiento de Vivero in 1660 and told of a sacred place (*mochadero*) on a hill called Chanqui. The place had a minister who tended his llamas nearby, one Juan Payco Guaman. María said that on the summit she had seen fresh coca leaves, a cob of maize, the straw

[76] Ibid., fols. 5v, 8.

[77] AAL Leg. 3, exp. 13, fol. 4v. María Catalina claimed that no person spoke or ate during the special time for fear of losing the harvest. See fol. 5.

called Guaylla Ocsa which "spoke like a person" in the wind, and two small jugs of Tuclli, the "chicha which the huacas drink." People gathered at the place "at the time of harvests," offering these things to the "huaca and mochadero" so that "the maize might ripen" and the crops would be augmented. Furthermore, when the town's much-remembered kuraka Don Sebastian Quispe Nina Bilca had been alive, he had allegedly told María of an annual vigil, a kind of harvest festival, that had been carried out at this huaca on the mountain. People moved (probably in a dance or winding procession) round and round the harvested piles of husked maize, without ceasing, for an entire night.[78]

As important as agriculture was to mid-colonial Andeans of the Lima region, many people in these communities were still dedicated primarily to related pastoral pursuits. Thus the huacas were also approached to increase the size of the herds and to ensure good pasture and sources of water for their maintenance. Although camelid numbers were on the decline in the Lima region by the middle of the seventeenth century, and they were certainly not the people's exclusive livestock, the testimonies suggest that llamas were still tended by many Andeans. They continued to constitute an important asset toward a person's wealth and prestige. In the Huarochirí region, the owners of llama herds were said to have danced wearing puma skins to flaunt their wealth at festivals.[79]

In eighteenth-century San Sebastián de Tinta, at a cliff a short distance from the village, was a large stone form resembling a llama. María Juana stated that a recent outbreak of disease and the subsequent deaths had greatly reduced a cult that had once thrived. There had been elders who had often spoken with the llama-huaca. Even so, she said that a persistent group kept up these observances.[80] One learns no more of the worship or its function, perhaps because María chose the path of prudence and self-preservation, distancing herself from any personal attachment to the cult. Yet based on what can be discovered about similar gods in nearby places, this was probably a huaca whose mythical path had ended with its transformation into stone. Perhaps its animal form was a commemoration of some founding deed pertaining to the llama herds in the area, and was meant to eternalize its protection of their well-being. But huacas did not need such obvious forms to direct the pastoralists of the archdiocese to their cults.

According to Juan Chapa, he and his consort, María Ticlla, had long made specific offerings to the peak of a mountain called Pata Caca (or alternatively Cataa Caca) in the province of Yauyos. The place had once been a shrine of the

---

[78] AAL Leg. 4, exp. 32, fols. 6–6v. In addition to this late kuraka's knowledge and apparent sponsorship of these harvest rites, it was said that two old women served as his religious consultants. We learn little about them, but even their names, Paria Caca and Chuya Guaya, confirm deep connections with the Andean religious world.

[79] *Huarochirí*, ch. 10, sec. 150. Fascinating continuities are explored in P. Z. Dransart, "Fibre to Fabric."

[80] AAL Leg. 3, exp. 11, fol. 6v.

ancients. There was a small clearing or plaza, Juan explained, where the old ayllus of Guanpara and Tamara had always gathered to give worship.[81] The rites that were continued in veneration of this ancient place related especially to the benefit of the llama herds.

Juan Chapa would clip the tips of the young llamas' ears and cook these in a fire. Then he would mix them with coca leaves and white and colored maize, before offering the mixture in honor of Pata Caca. This rite was performed twice a year, notably at the feast of San Juan and at Christmas.[82] Both of the accused said that they carried out the offerings in their corral, Uchupa Cancha, in the ravine where their llamas were, and from which the peak of Pata Caca was clearly visible. María said that she and Juan spoke in unison, addressing the mountain by another of its names:

> Antanama Hurco,
> receive this which we offer to increase the llamas.
> I wish for it so much.[83]

There seems to have been no question in the minds of Juan or María about the mountain-huaca's power and there is a disarming forthrightness in the ways they explained their belief to a judge whom they knew would disapprove. The pair were devout believers who had returned to their practices after no fewer than three castigations by successive parish priests. Visitador Juan Sarmiento confronted Juan Chapa frankly: "Did he believe that the mountain had the power to increase the said herds?" The notary recorded his answer: "Yes, [he believed] that through the sacrifices made to the mountain the herds increased." For her part, María Ticlla concurred that the reason she had kept up the offerings each year, even after her punishment, was because she believed in the power of Pata Caca to augment the herds.[84]

My attention to the diversity of the the huacas' forms and to the breadth of their connection to the agricultural and pastoral base of their people is meant to build a case for their extraordinary degree of persistence into mid-colonial times. The case, however, is not complete without some reflection on the capacity of these gods, and the religious system of which they are a part, to absorb

[81] AAL Leg. 1, exp. 2. San Pedro de Pilas in Omas, 1660, fols. 7v, 8v, and 6–6v.

[82] AAL Leg. 1, exp. 2, fols. 6–6v. This might well have been an established ancient custom. When Paria Caca set down the provisions with which one of his five "selves," Chuqui Huampo, would be worshiped forevermore, he included the "slitted ears" of a young llama. See *Huarochirí*, ch. 8, sec. 108.

[83] AAL Leg. 1, exp. 2, fol. 11.

[84] Juan Chapa had been punished by Fray Alvaro de Lugares some eighteen years before Sarmiento de Vivero's visita. María had been punished and absolved independently by the same friar in Santiago de Guandaro. Chapa's persistent reverence for Pata Caca had later led to a public whipping by another priest, Francisco López. Juan Chapa's wife had reportedly fled in fear to the puna with her llamas, and he claimed to have never seen her again. Since the point when Juan and María began living together, the offerings had been resolutely started again. See Ibid., fols. 6v–7v, 10–10v, 11, and 12.

new things and to change. I have already noted the huacas' participation in the Christian calendar and their responsiveness to their people's priorities and preoccupations.

The theme of pastoralism offers itself, once again, as a ready point of entry. The huacas in most of the Archdiocese of Lima seem to have been willing and able to expand their area of competence to include European strains of livestock, in accordance with the changing character of their peoples' husbandry. In the middle of the seventeenth century at Pomacocha in the province of Canta, the mountain god at Chinchay Cocha named Apo Quircay Capac Quircay was invoked with offers of white and black lambs. In one of his aspects, the huaca lord, Quircay, was called the "Maestro of the sheep," a significant adaptation of an epithet such as "Lord of the chacras" noted above. Worship was given to Quircay that the flocks might keep well and not die off.[85] A nearby mountain named Yachuqui Quilca received similar invocations and offerings. In a place called Colpa in Cajatambo, Francisco Quipo admitted to sacrificing lambs on or near a stone in the countryside that one may suspect was a huaca, on the express orders of the majordomo of his Christian confraternity, asking that other "lambs would not die." Quipo also stated that blood was sprinkled on the rock as a means of intercession to the souls in purgatory.[86]

The Andean gods' expanded repertoire did not end with people requesting the huacas' protection of flocks of sheep. In the parish of Santiago de Carampoma, Huarochirí, in 1723, three stone divinities—although less famous numina than the regional huacas—were given offerings in order that the cattle in Juan de Rojas's care should not perish. Like the sheep of Colpa, Cajatambo, mentioned above, these cattle were also confraternity property, this time of Our Lady of the Nativity.[87] Eight years later, an old woman named Juana Agustina of San Francisco de Rapas, Huarochirí, told of a stone huaca in the form of a large toad (sapo) near the village. "For many years" she had been devoted to it; among other things, she asked it for "all kinds of livestock."[88]

Such examples abound, and the religious accretions that they seem to represent among a fundamentally agricultural and pastoral people might seem so natural as to appear unremarkable. Yet the huacas' spiritual province in the middle of the colonial period did not stop with agrarian concerns. Some excellent illustrations of the expanding realities of colonial huaca religion survive in the little-known documentation of Pedro de Celis y la Vega's visita of the eighteenth-century parishes of Santiago de Maray in Checras and neighboring San Juan de Churín in Cajatambo.[89] In this region in 1724 and 1725, an elaborate regional religious structure centered on two huacas named Apu Libiac and Apu Libiac Cancharco. The more important of the two, Libiac Cancharco,

[85] Ynes Carua Chumbi, ibid., fol. 4v.

[86] AAL Leg. 3, exp. 11, fol. 6.

[87] AAL Leg. 3, exp. 9, fols. 4 and 5. See Chapter Three on these divinities.

[88] AAL Leg. 3, exp. 11, fol. 11v. Another witness, María Josepha, also of Rapas, told of the multi-purpose "little huaca" (guaquilla) as well. See fols. 11v–12.

[89] AAL Leg. 3, exp. 10, 1724–1725 and Leg. 3, exp. 11, 1725, respectively.

stood in a concealed hollow or niche on a *pampa* (open grassy area) called Cayaioc (or Cayanyayoc) near the village of Pachangara. Libiac resided in another ravine.[90]

In 1724, Libiac Cancharco and his cult were in the hands of an extraordinary minister named Pedro Quiñones (alias Pedro de la Cruz) whose religious authority extended over a territory that included at least two surrounding parishes. He claimed to be 115 years old, and to be the guardian and keeper (*quipucamayoc*) of a *quipu* in his town that accounted for some four hundred souls.[91] Quiñones' grandson, an adolescent named Francisco Bartolomé, was clearly the preferred successor and the youth was gradually learning the rites and practices from the old man. The cult following of this principal huaca seems to have been a healthy one—this evidence, along with much else, flying in the face of suggestions that little more than religious remnants and superstitions were to be found in Andean parishes after the late seventeenth century. Martín Phelipe of Pachangara said that the people of that place all went in common to worship the huacas and that "they made feasts and observed penitence to keep the said idols [*huacas*] content."[92]

There is graphic detail of the rites of propitiation in Quiñones' own testimony. The sustaining drinks of the god were blood from a llama, cuy, and perhaps even a human being, and chicha mixed with the powder of a crushed sea shell.[93] The favored food of the god was uncooked wheat, meat jerky, and dense cooked cakes of crushed maize. Once the offering was made, Quiñones and the other ministers would ensure the huaca had partaken of the food. The custom was "to wait until some small part had disappeared which was the sign that the offering had been accepted." Whatever was left would be burned to finish the offering, and the rest of the sacrificial meat would be shared out among the celebrants.

---

[90] AAL Leg. 3, exp. 10. See the second testimony of Pedro Quiñones at fol. 21v, and that of Francisco Bartolomé, at fol. 27.

[91] Ibid., fol. 8. The *quipu* were intricately knotted cords that the Inkas and other prehispanic Andean cultures seem to have used for accounting and more complex mnemonic purposes.

[92] AAL Leg. 3, exp. 11, fols. 9–9v. See also Juan Ramos at fol. 10. The increasing Christianization of the language and descriptions is entirely characteristic, and seems attributable to more than simply the notary's insensitive gloss.

[93] AAL Leg. 3, exp. 10, fol. 7. One of the visitador's preoccupations in this trial becomes the issue of human sacrifice. Though no physical evidence was turned up, it is possible that an old man named Martín de la Cruz from the village of Acain was ritually killed on 8 September 1724, in Antonio Alexo's home in Puñun. According to Pedro Quiñones in his first confession, the man's blood was offered in sacred cups to the huaca Cancharco (fol. 7v). Later in the same testimony, Quiñones claimed that he could remember having sacrificed some fourteen persons to different huacas over the years (fol. 8). However, when the trial passed to the ecclesiastical tribunal in Lima (as the post-Villagómez era idolatry investigations tended to do), Pedro denied most of what he had said before Visitador Celis in Maray, stating that he had spoken out of fear of the whip (fol. 23v). The act of the 8 September sacrifice, however, was not denied. Pedro blamed it on Antonia (alternatively Josepha) Rosa, Antonio Alexo's wife (fol. 23). Francisco Bartolomé added to the confusion by speaking of "a woman from Arinpay" as the one who had performed the sacrifice in Puñun (fol. 29).

These rites were the culmination of what, for the regional religious officials, was a time of strict observance in honor of the huaca. There were five days in which salt, *ají*, and any food considered sweet or savory were not taken, and in which people refrained from having sexual relations.[94]

Libiac Cancharco would speak only with his minister, Pedro Quiñones. To approach the huaca, Pedro dressed in "the way of the ancients," and with a sling on the back of his head and neck. He would then uncover his head and sink down to his knees before the god.[95] Once again, the language is interesting and potentially important. It is impossible to say for certain if the description is faithful to Pedro's testimony. The notary may have written an account of this profound worship using the only language of description he knew. Alternatively, the Christian echoes might have been Pedro's way of trying to get across to the visitador the solemnity and seriousness of the adoration and consultation process. Perhaps most plausibly of all, by the eighteenth century (and even earlier) the ways of giving worship and seeking contact with the sacred— Andean and Christian—were blending. As if to provide further food for thought, Francisco Bartolomé, the young apprentice minister who had been to Libiac Cancharco with his grandfather, presented an alternative description of the proceedings that was considerably less influenced by Christianity. The boy said that "many other men and women" assembled before the huaca with their requests, but that the god responded only to his grandfather, who sat separated from all the others in a niche or corner called guanaca. The huaca's responses were almost oracular in the Greco-Roman sense, adding force to Sabine Mac-Cormack's pioneering work on perception and analogy noted above. The responses were described as "sometimes clear and at other times confused"; their success rate—things coming out as the huaca had said—appears to have been moderate.[96]

Libiac Cancharco and Libiac received a variety of entreaties, confirming the portrayal of the huacas' growing network of responsibilities. The people's requests tell us much about the issues of importance in their lives. In addition to the usual petitions for abundant harvests of the different foodstuffs, there were requests for a range of personal things such as the preservation of health or

---

[94] Ibid., fol. 7.

[95] Ibid., fol. 7.

[96] Ibid., fols. 27v, 7v. In his study of Andean "priests," G. Cock examines the applicability of Mircea Eliade's conclusions concerning the role of ecstasy in shamanic experience to the Andean huaca ministers' consultations. Cock suggests that, apart from one case that he includes in an endnote (that of Hernando Hacas Poma), the ecstatic trance does not form a regular part of Andean communications with the gods. Cock's larger thesis in this instance (that huaca ministers were more than simply shamans or medicine men) is commendable, but abundant evidence such as this example involving Pedro Quiñones brings Cock's claim about the communicative sessions into question. Like Quiñones and Hacas Poma, other ministers seem to have customarily separated themselves from the other faithful to speak to the huacas and receive their responses. It is the documentation which often fails us at the crucial moments. The specific accounts of mediation with the gods were rarely told to the visitadores, or were not appreciated by the notaries. See G. Cock Carasco, "El sacerdote andino," pp. 48–49 and 76–77; and M. Eliade, *Shamanism.*

protection from adulterers, "that women do not steal good husbands." Most importantly, the huacas were pleaded with to assist people in difficulties that arose between them and the current parish priest, Joseph de Veramendi. One person asked "that the priest not demand lambs from the confraternities," while another requested "that the priest, who had gone to Lima, would not return."[97] The information is all too brief, but these examples and many others are suggestive of at least two things. First, that the better-studied tensions between Francisco de Avila and his Andean parishioners over a century earlier in Huarochirí were far from unique. And second, that when the Extirpation was in favor, religious tensions between the alleged idolaters and their enemies revolved less around persistent prehispanic beliefs and practices than around religious mixture (with the blanket term "idolatry" often obscuring the distinction). The huacas' malleability was an integral part of Andeans' more general capacity for religious adaptations that made the proponents of the Extirpation, along with many other Spanish Christians, distinctly uncomfortable.

One learns that some Indians had raised official complaints against the priest Veramendi, but that the provisor in Lima had sided with the doctrinero. Don Andrés de Munibe ruled that in this instance a group of idolatrous Indians had denounced a zealous soldier of God who was steadily uncovering their forbidden practices. Munibe wrote that the Indians' allegations were unfounded and "amount to no more than particular claims concerning some cows and mules that they say the priest has taken from their lands." As frequently happened in such cases, the Indians who had sacrificed much to pursue the litigation and avail themselves of the official channnels of justice went away frustrated. Even in the 1720s, the alleged idolatry became the issue of first importance, completely overriding the chance of a reprimand for the priest, or any compensation to Andean parishioners who might have been wronged.[98] One does not learn of Libiac Cancharco's response on the Veramendi question. But the fact that the principal huaca was approached with such colonial, or at least nontraditional, matters was part of a larger general trend.

Antonio Ripas of Nava appeared before the same visitador in Churín, Cajatambo, in 1725 and spoke of two other huacas of dark stone, Apullanu Guara and Mama Guanca, who were worshiped in a cave on a high mountain called Llanu Guaina. The gods regularly consumed an assortment of offerings, and were consulted for a multitude of things that transcended agricultural and pastoral preoccupations. Some people asked for luck in love, others for material goods, mules, and money, and still others that "things might go well" with the priests and corregidores.[99]

The descriptions of the variety of the huacas and their modes of worship from other witnesses in the same trial in Cajatambo are striking. Juan Bautista

---

[97] AAL Leg. 3, exp. 10, fols. 7v, 27v, and the Promotor Fiscal's charges at fol. 32v.

[98] AAL Leg. 3, exp. 10, fols. 1–2v. The similarities with the situations described by Antonio Acosta Rodríguez for over a century earlier are striking; see "Los doctrineros."

[99] AAL Leg. 3, exp. 11, fol. 6.

told of a darkish stone in the old town that one would pass on the way from Mallay to Tinta, upon which there were "various pictures of men and women." The people who made the journey to this place searched its surface for the figures they thought most resembled themselves, before making their many different requests of the huaca. This god was said to have spoken many times to the old man, Diego Quisguar, who was now deceased.[100]

Long journeys, especially those to the lowlands or the coast, were thought extremely perilous. Many highlanders grew sick or died during their stays in warmer climes, often from exposure to infectious diseases to which their bodies were not accustomed. Thus, one had to be religiously prepared. A special appeal for protection from the huacas seems to have been an integral rite of departure in many regions of the archdiocese. Eighty-year-old María Quillay (alias Puyron), who lived in Guandaro, Canta, in 1696, said that people in her region were in the custom of bringing the powders called *poco* (from a sea shell) to her that she might ensure that they and their loads of potatoes would travel safely to Lima.[101] She does not mention an object of worship, but because of similar and more direct evidence from other places one may assume that the powders—a common offering—sought the blessings of an Andean god.

To the northeast of Canta, for instance, in the parish of Santiago de Andajes in the province of Cajatambo, was a mountain which, in the eighteenth century at least, the people called "The Inquisitor." At its summit was a great boulder or outcropping named Juchapa Maman (alternatively Mama Pajuchan or Juchapa Man), which the notary rendered rather ominously as "Mother of Sin." María Catalina, who was over sixty years of age, recalled that when she was a small girl, her parents—laden with "cuyes, blood, and other preparations"—had taken her to this place, where "each one asked for what they needed."[102] Most other witnesses, however, noted the huaca Juchapa Maman in light of more specific roles. Antonio Tapaojo defined these precisely as travelers seeking safe journeys down the valley and immunity from diseases. Ysabel Rosa confessed that many times she had seen her father take offerings to the huaca before his trips to the valleys, and she told of another great stone called Marca Aparac near the town of Caujul that served the same purpose. Ysabel Sallan confirmed what was said and added that everyone in this region knew that when Juchapa Maman was passed, something had to be offered.[103]

In spite of the urgent assertions of Christian preaching—to which I will return in a later chapter—and between one and two hundred years of Spanish Christian presence, the Andean landscape, its spaces and heights, its surrounding

[100] Ibid., fol. 7.

[101] AAL Leg. 5, exp. 26, fol. 43.

[102] AAL Leg. 3, exp. 13, 1725. For the best descriptions of the place, see the testimonies of Antonio Tapaojo at fol. 4v, María Catalina at fol. 5 and Ysabel Rosa at fol. 6. María Quillay also remembered being taken to the place as a child; see fol. 7.

[103] Ibid., fols. 4v, 6, and 6v.

natural forms and even its ancient settlements, were believed by Andeans to be endowed with meaning.[104] A dividing line between sacred and profane did not separate the natural from the supernatural. This is not to say that a stone or a spring was thought to be divine or sacred simply because of what it was, or because of an extraordinary form or conspicuous location. The regional *tradiciones* prove that natural objects and places became objects of adoration also because of what they represented and were thought to embody. Often, they were an ancestor or an evocative reminder of a divine action in the past. These huacas remained sacred into colonial times because of the permanence of their meaning and religious power in the lives of generation after generation of their people, many of whom still conceived of themselves as the huacas' descendants, a people whose lives continued to be animated and influenced by autochthonous gods.

The religious belief in huacas was a means of comprehending and coping with human defenselessness in the face of drought, pestilence, crop failure, disease, death, and even the existence of pain in life. Conceiving of themselves as living among their gods and their land, Andean peoples could seek both to control what happened to them and to explain their dangers and misfortunes through appealing to their huacas.[105] Like major gods from many religious traditions, the huacas could be both benevolent and vengeful. The divine mood depended on the literal feeding of a profoundly mutual relationship. The community of persons who looked to a given huaca believed they would meet with her protection or his wrath depending on their measure of attention and care for the huaca's needs. These founts of sacred energy could either be nourished or neglected, and colonial Indians were very much beset with the choice. And choosing became that much harder when exclusivist Christian pressures and demands on their allegiances increased.

The evidence from the mid-colonial idolatry documentation suggests that the huacas made the choice easier for a large number of people by proving themselves even more adaptable than some of their faithful ministers were prepared to admit before their persecutors.[106] Many Andeans persisted in their huaca worship, not to mention in their observance of other dimensions of Andean religion, because a relationship of religious interdependence was perceived as vital to their existence. As a result of forced resettlement that had complicated a sacred landscape in which communities now also functioned as parts of a Catholic parish this reality changed but was not diminished. The new faith had not managed to supplant its principal rivals, the huacas—not, at least, in many parts of the vast Lima region.

One can take the case of the rediscovered huaca of San Damián de los Checa

---

[104] The statement is not a romantic conception of some nearly lost indigenous world. Indeed, William Christian portrays a remarkably similar—albeit popular Christian—"nature invested with . . . sensitivity" in roughly contemporary rural Castile. See *Local Religion*, p. 208.

[105] The idea of "liminality," especially in Victor Turner's work, is convincingly explored by T. Platt in "The Andean Soldiers of Christ." See also V. W. Turner, "Liminality and the Performative Genres."

[106] I explore this idea further in *An Evil Lost to View?*, especially ch. 6.

in Huarochirí, Llocllay Huancupa, as an instructive example of why. His name and ancestry suggest an association with rain and water, probably signaling a mythical past and purpose that can now be only dimly perceived. But after he was "rediscovered" in a field, and after his cult rose in the area in colonial times, his faithful beseeched him according to the widest of their current needs. He was asked not only for abundant water but also for safety from enemies and natural calamities like disease and earthquakes, freedom from grief and sorrow and, finally, "well-being." His purpose was simultaneously simple and all-encompassing: he was "to watch over the village."[107]

The notaries, Quechua interpreters and visitadores of idolatry seem to have struggled with what the Indians confessed about the breadth of their huacas' spiritual jurisdictions. The Andean gods were supposed by their extirpators to be almost laughably limited in their value and effectiveness, yet Andeans consistently testified that their worship was pursued to procure what the Extirpation officials most often recorded only fleetingly as variations of "a good life."[108] Juan Ramos was the minister of Apu Macac in Pachangara, Cajatambo, and in 1725 he described a flourishing cult in which "nearly everyone" participated in Macac's adoration. The town's *alcaldes* (local magistrates) and *camachicos* (heads of lineage groups) ordered the worship "so there would be good fortune." María Ticlla Guacho in Huamantanga, Canta, in 1656 was adamant about the function of the huacas in her area. She said that she and her *compañeros*, the farmers and herders "from her ayllu and other ayllus," did not go to the huacas with offerings so much to affect rainfall nor when they had specific needs. They went to the huacas for "assistance" or "relief" (*el socorro*). Similarly, María Josepha from the village of Rapas spoke of worshiping a nearby huaca in order "to procure good fortune and advantage (*conveniencias*)." The offerings, she said, were made just as her ancestors had done. She recognized great value in the rites and carried them out so that "she would not lose the custom."[109]

[107] *Huarochirí*, ch. 20, secs. 236–43 and note 472. Another example of a general protector was Guara Cani, a huaca of San Pedro de Quipan in the doctrina of Huamantanga in Canta. See AAL Leg. 2, exp. 11, 1656, esp. fol. 8.

[108] "Buena vida" and "buen suceso" were the most common expressions. It is possible that the statements about "a good life" and "well-being" were partly the result of the interpreters and notaries who sought to summarize quickly that upon which a Quechua-speaking witness was elaborating. Yet this possibility does not cancel the point that the witnesses' testimonies spurred the summaries in the first place. Moreover, there is enough alteration in the ways that "well-being" and "a good life" were rendered to indicate strongly that the sentiments, and perhaps even roughly equivalent phrases, were coming from the witnesses themselves. Andeans' repetitive variations on the same concepts in their testimonies and related tradiciones strike me as related to what Gyan Prakash, following Joseph Miller, identifies as "cliché" or "stereotype" in oral histories, "a highly compressed and deceptively simple statement of meaning that refers to a much more complex reality." My point is not to claim that the fragmented testimonies of Andeans before idolatry inspectors represent a perfect analogy to people in India or Africa performing oral histories on ritual occasions, but only to suggest that mid-colonial Peruvians may have had similarly high charged, simplified expressions of what their religion was about. G. Prakash, *Bonded Histories*, pp. 42–43 and n. 26.

[109] AAL Leg. 3, exp. 11, fols. 10, 12–12v, 11v–12.

In the mid-colonial era, the huacas survived the arrival and consolidation of Spanish Christianity among their people. The huacas' spiritual realm—like that of Llocllay Huancupa from the Huarochirí manuscript—fit into an emerging religious system that was considerably wider, more dynamic, and able to reinterpret itself than has usually been supposed.

Chancas and Conopas

To LEARN of the huacas in the mid-colonial period, I have asked the reader to make a mental journey to the ancient settlements, peaks, cliffs, and springs that dotted the Andean countryside surrounding the villages and towns of the Arch-diocese of Lima. Many of these gods stood in the open, whereas others were buried on sacred lands or hidden in caves. But just as they represented a re-gional dimension of Andean religion beneath, as it were, more pan-Andean forms such as Pacha Camac or even Paria Caca, there were other gods who operated in smaller circles within the spiritual orbits of the huacas. Though for considerably less intrusive ends than those of the visitadores' henchmen, like them the reader must enter the houses, rooms, alcoves, and gardens of the historical subjects to gain a vision of a more personal or familial dimension of Andean religion.

Two kinds of gods deserve special attention in this context: chancas (or lin-eage gods) and conopas (personal gods of fecundity). The first, usually figures of stone, occasionally adorned with wax, coins, and other things, were common in the Andean parishes of the Lima region in the seventeenth and eighteenth centuries. Very little has been written about chancas—particularly in a histori-cal sense—for a number of reasons.[1] I have already alluded to the principal reason in my discussion of the huacas. These chanca gods are at times difficult to distinguish from the many lesser huacas described in the Indians' testi-monies because most Spanish investigators and (as I shall discuss below) not a few Andeans failed to make the distinctions. Arriaga's reference in *La extirpa-ción* of 1621 to the visitador Juan Delgado's discovery in a town in Conchucos of "a Huaca named Chanca, a stone in the form of a person," to whom a "girl of rare beauty and less than fourteen years" was devoted, is entirely typical.[2] In colonial times, both types of god might at times be called "idol," and both might be hidden and protected close to the domestic hearth. Because the inter-preters and notaries of the Extirpation were inclined to call almost any divinity or burial site a huaca, or an idol, Andean meanings become difficult to deter-mine. The term conopa, too, took on a general usage and was frequently em-

---

[1] Although see Jorge Flores Ochoa's essay, "Enqa," primarily a study of contemporary practices in the Cusco region. See also Max Uhle's brief "Las llamitas de piedra de Cuzco." Flores Ochoa describes the *enqaychu*, a modern version of what we discuss, as composed of "natural stones of no more than eight centimetres in length, elongated or rounded in form, of a very brilliant granite or quartzite." These are ideally passed down from father to eldest son as part of a large "bundle" of religious inheritance. Similar sacred or "medicine" bundles have been handed down in the families of other Amerindian peoples; see Å. Hultkrantz, "The Religious Life of Native North Americans," p. 7, and H. L. Harrod, "Blackfeet," pp. 36–37.

[2] P. J. de Arriaga, *La extirpación*, p. 36.

ployed to describe what were clearly chanca gods. The matter is most compli-cated by the Andeans' own natural tendency, particularly by mid-colonial times, to apply broadly such terms as huaca and even idol. Thus, there are perhaps even more than the usual layers of distortion with which the historian must contend. What began some four hundred years ago as a problem of termi-nological comprehension becomes one of accurate identification. My inter-pretation rests largely on searching the people's testimonies for these gods' distinguishing features and for the meanings Andeans attributed to them; the gods' forms, manner of inheritance, location, and spiritual spheres are the prin-cipal features I have sought.

The chancas were generally small and moveable, most often found within the dwelling of the individual who had inherited their care. From here they would be revered by an extended family or lineage group, usually but not always that of the minister. These collections of faithful seem to have been patrilineal groups that existed within the larger ayllu network that continued to make up most Andean communities. The depopulation and exigencies of colo-nial Indian life (agricultural labor and mita service in mines and other projects) seem to have threatened the maintenance of many of these groups and begun to force less rigid criteria for membership during the mid-colonial period.[3]

Francisco de Avila encountered these lineage gods in the late sixteenth and early seventeenth centuries, both as a priest in the parish of San Damián in Huarochirí and as an extirpator over a wider area of the archdiocese. In the preface to his bilingual sermons published in Lima at the dawn of Archbishop Villagómez's rekindling of the Extirpation one encounters their possible names and most basic description. Avila wrote of "con churis and chancas," describing them only as "lesser idols," and adding that "there is not an Indian family . . . which lacks its particular god in its house."[4]

It is possible to gain insight into their position in the prehispanic religious network through a section in the Huarochirí manuscript that seems to bear out the depiction of them as immediate and familial gods. In this episode the huaca-sisters of Chaupi Ñamca admonish the people who come straight to them with their consultations, asking: "Have you come on the advice of your Con Churi, your father, or your elders?" Evidently, like parents and wise rela-tives, the gods of the home were to be respected and consulted first. Only then was it considered appropriate to approach the huacas in order that they might respond to the people's concerns.[5] Although one receives no direct indication that the household gods were the huacas' intermediaries, no sign that—as with the popular worship of saints in much of contemporary Europe—getting their

---

[3] I know of no better or more engaging description of what the ayllu was or might have become in colonial times than Karen Spalding's in *Huarochirí*, esp. pp. 28–34 and 43–59.

[4] F. de Avila, *Tratado*, "Prefación." See also J. M. Arguedas, tr. and ed., *Dioses y hombres*, p. 255. The statement is a fascinating echo of what the Augustinian friars claimed about the ubiq-uity of these "idols" in Huamachuco to the north as early as 1560. See "Relación de la religión," p. 27.

[5] *Huarochirí*, ch. 13, secs. 185–86.

ear might somehow advance a person's requests to a god on high, one must be alive to the interrelationship between these more public (*huacas*) and private (*chancas*) dimensions of Andean religion.[6] Less grand and sweeping in their authority than the huacas, the gods we shall call chancas were part of the sacred family group and were considerable powers in their own right.[7]

One is on slightly firmer ground in considering a second type of household divinity called, in most of our colonial documentation, *conopa* and, in much of the current ethnography from more southerly regions of the Andes, *illa*.[8] Once again, it was the shrewd Jesuit, Pablo José de Arriaga, who contributed most to what became the accepted seventeenth-century description. His account was for the most part either copied or closely echoed in Pedro de Villagómez's anti-idolatry treatise almost thirty years later. Arriaga told of small stone forms, usually representational in shape and kept in the home or on one's person.[9]

Because of their size and sculpted features, these gods were associated by Spanish observers with compulsive fetishism and the Indians' allegedly boundless credulity. In the Huarochirí manuscript, colonial Indians who possessed these "pretty illa amulets" were also said to finger piously their rosaries, exhibiting their supposed need to be inspired to devotion by things they could hold in their hands.[10]

---

[6] See W. A. Christian, *Local Religion*; K. V. Thomas, *Religion and the Decline of Magic*, pp. 28–31, 53 and 81; and J. Bossy, *Christianity and the West*, pp. 11–19. Again the friars of the Huamachuco region in the middle of the sixteenth century provide early indications of what later evidence suggests. On the relationship between the "small stone" Tantaguayanai and the supreme huaca of the region, Catequil, see the "Relación de la religión," pp. 26–27.

[7] Avila suggested two names for these powers. I choose chanca rather than con churi for the following reasons. P. Arriaga, in *La extirpación*, pp. 26–28, mentions chancas as the term for "household gods" in the Cusco area even when, for the sake of simplification, he views them as analogous to the conopas of the Lima region (p. 26). In Extirpation evidence to be discussed below, "chanca" is used by an important Andean witness to describe an actual god in her possession. Although it is impossible to determine whether chanca was her god's type or its actual name, or both, it seems a less problematic choice than con churi. In the Huarochirí manuscript, con churi appears to refer not only to a "lesser god" (ch. 13, sec. 185, and Frank Salomon's note 366) but also to the title of an indigenous minister in the context of twin rituals; see *The Huarochirí Manuscript*, edited and translated by F. Salomon and G. L. Urioste (hereafter *Huarochirí*), suppl. I, sec. 462. Finally, choosing chanca seems further justified in light of the difficulties the Spanish had in consistently recognizing the different Andean gods. As if to underscore this point, as late as 1649 Archbishop Villagómez was clearly in some confusion concerning the conopa, chanca, and caullama distinctions. He escaped by the common route: he followed his most knowledgeable predecessors' assumptions, notably those of Arriaga. Villagómez labeled most small, portable gods simply "conopas;" see the *Carta pastoral*, ch. 42, pp. 147–48.

[8] See J. Flores Ochoa, "Enqa"; also, C. Delgado de Thays, *Religión y magía*, pp. 252–53.

[9] P. Arriaga, *La extirpación*, pp. 28–29, and Villagómez, *Carta pastoral*, ch. 42, p. 148. One of P. Arriaga's Jesuit colleagues, P. Felipe de Tapia, described the pervasiveness in similar terms, writing that "there is not an Indian who does not have his secret idol"; see ARSI, Carta anua de 1610, *Peru* 13, vol. 2, fol. 78v.

[10] *Huarochirí*, ch. 9, sec. 134. A good concise discussion of the origins and connotations of "fetishism" is Mesquitela Lima's "Fetishism." For more on the extirpators' critique of the Andeans' alleged fetishism, see Chapter Six below.

Conopas are easier to identify in the testimonies from the Lima region than are the chancas. The former were usually small stones, sometimes natural but often sculpted to represent certain animals (commonly llamas and alpacas) or produce (usually maize or potatoes). Conopas, like huacas, could have specific and general realms of competence. Those that were representational often depicted their purpose, and often had a direct connection with fertility. The most elaborate had an indentation or space on their surfaces (or backs) where an offering (often llama fat) could be placed. Like the chancas, conopas were passed down from one generation to the next, which added, of course, to their value. Andeans in the mid-colonial era frequently told of both these types of gods; they seem, as Avila claimed, to have been maintained in the homes of many extended family groups. Extirpators often compiled detailed inventories to prove the ubiquity of the Indians' gods and to show material results to their superiors. Even given the probability of self-serving exaggerations on the part of extirpators, from these tallies one gains some idea of how common these particular gods were. In 1617, for example, three Jesuit padres reported that they had collected 2,500 conopas in the Chancay region alone.[11]

The Indians' testimonies introduce us to the first type, the chancas, their ministers, and to both the setting for and mode of the rituals associated with their worship. In 1660, a set of idolatry investigations conducted by perhaps the most tireless extirpator of the Villagómez era, Juan Sarmiento de Vivero, in and around San Lorenzo de Quinti in Huarochirí—close to the area from which Avila's intelligence had sprung—affords a beginning.[12]

One woman named María Guanico testified to Sarmiento in secret, perhaps in hope of leniency from her judge. She told him of a stone which she called Chanca and kept near the head of her bed. Chanca, she said, was "white, about the size of a hen's egg with eyes and a mouth."[13] The visitador sent his notary and the defensor to confirm this account and seize the god. In an attempt to hide their confessant's collaboration from the other townspeople, the officials went in disguise and under cover of night. Burning straw to make their way inside her dark home, they found a white object in an alcove by the head of her bed. Their written report states that it was "a little bigger than a coconut from Chile, and formed in the stone was a face with eyes and a mouth."[14]

---

[11] ARSI, Carta anua de 1617, *Peru* 14, vol. 3, fol. 52.

[12] AAL Leg. 2, exp. 21, and Leg. 2, exp. 23.

[13] AAL Leg. 2, exp. 21, fols. 2v–3. It was a common inquisitorial method to encourage secret denunciations, even through bribery, from knowledgeable persons whose own religious doubts or fear for their personal safety often triumphed over their reticence when an idolatry inspector was in the region. Padre Arriaga (1621) and Archbishop Villagómez (1649) both recommended the procedure for visitadores generales de idolatría in Peru. "The first thing is to win over some intelligent Indian (*algón Indio de razón*)," P. J. de Arriaga advised, "and keeping all this a great secret offer him sizeable rewards, saying that no living person will ever know, and persuade him to divulge the principal huaca of his pueblo."; *La extirpación*, ch. 14, p. 133.

[14] AAL Leg. 2, exp. 21, fol. 4.

The domestic place where María Guanico kept her chanca corresponds with the practices of others in Huarochirí and beyond. Seventy years after the extirpating sweep of the 1660s, an Andean governor in the parish of Carampoma in the same province was accused of keeping stone gods in a hollow beneath his bed and in a storehouse.[15] In 1648, Juan Alonso Ocón, the bishop of Cusco— and one of the most vociferous contemporary supporters of Villagómez's initiatives outside the Archdiocese of Lima—reported a similar example of such intimacy and proximity in a relationship between a minister and the "stone idol" with which she had lived "for many years."[16]

In 1646, in the parish of San Jerónimo de Pampas in the province of Huaylas, Visitador Juan Gutiérrez de Aguilar made a tour of the homes of a number of suspected persons. In the home of Ynes Yaco Caxo, he and his retinue of town officials found a large assemblage of "suspicious things." These "things" were either the instruments used for making offerings or the offerings themselves, and they make for an illuminating and detailed inventory. There were *mates* (gourds), hairs wrapped up with plants, and a number of tied bundles: one of feathers from different birds; another of llama and "lion" (puma) fat; one of white maize and pieces of yellow herb; and another of maize leaves and tiny black sea shells. There was yet another *mate* filled with yellow powders, and there were many separate hairs, parts of blankets, pieces of bread mixed with meat, fat, and coca, all of which was dried, "and many other things of this kind."[17] Again, the materials were near the head of the bed, along with the objects of veneration. Most striking of all were the six stones, three which were round and blue, and three which were longer, yellow and white. The town officials managed to look "greatly frightened" at the revelation, and they were said to have asked the judge to punish the woman.

Most of the Andean witnesses were not forthcoming when it came to describing the variety of rites that were observed in worship of the chancas. A few remarkable exceptions have to suffice. In a remote village in the parish of Bombon in Cajatambo in the mid-1660s, Jesuit padres from the College of San Pablo in Lima encountered a number of celebrated chancas. One stood out from the rest, and was described as a "small, well-fashioned pitcher . . . dressed like a queen" with a shawl of precious cumbe and intricate pins. This god, along with others, was regularly taken to the shores of a lake where offerings were performed and the gods were consulted and gave responses.[18]

An investigation in Santiago de Carampoma, Huarochirí, in 1723 reveals more elaborate details. Within the home of a chanca minister named Juan de Rojas was said to be a niche hidden by a large stone. In the document the notary persistently describes it as a "chapel" (*capilla*). There dwelt a principal

---

[15] AAL Leg. 3, exp. 15, fols. 8–9, and his self-defense at fols. 10v–11.

[16] ARSI, Carta anua de 1649, *Peru* 15, vol. 4, fol. 236. And see two of the bishop's letters to Villagómez on the "leprosy of idolatry" (Cusco, 14 October 1648, and Cusco, 14 December 1648), published as appendices to Villagómez's *Carta pastoral*, pp. 272–76.

[17] AAL Leg. 6, exp. 8, fol. 6v.

[18] ARSI, Cartas anuas de 1664, 1665 y 1666, *Peru* 16, vol. 5, fol. 109.

god of stone and three smaller gods, as well as a large shell and small tied bags of other things.[19]

Sizeable and regular gatherings were convened by Juan de Rojas in his chapel. Juan's two sisters could both remember hearing the sea shell trumpet that was played when the meetings came together.[20] His wife, María Melchora, said that her mother-in-law came to the house with a great jug of chicha for those in attendance, and that "they all drank and sang and performed their acts of idolatry (*idolatrías*)."[21] Not surprisingly, Juan de Rojas and his activities became the primary target of the extirpator, but it seems that his chapel was not the only such gathering place in town.

Juan's mother, María Josepha, who was integral to the ritual practices and seems once to have possessed the principal chanca found in Juan's home, convened similar meetings in her house. There was no love lost between María Melchora, the declared enemy of these practices, and her mother-in-law. Melchora said she had once pursued her husband to his mother's home only to find him drunk with all the others. She claimed that when she asked "why he got drunk and did not come [home] or work," María Josepha had told her that "he was working," and threatened to "break her to pieces" if she did not leave him to it.[22]

Another group of people from the Julca ayllu in the same town possessed a god that was kept in a clay jar. It had been ministered to in the home of Francisco Julca Libiac until his recent death. Francisco Libiac Condor told of ceremonies in the deceased minister's dwelling, noting that he and others of the ayllu took chicha and coca to sacrifice. Similar practices seem to have been carried out by this witness, Libiac Condor, who seems to have decided that denouncing others was the best way to save himself. He, too, had a little clay jar, in which two stone forms were kept. Different witnesses referred to gatherings in his home, and Ynes Llango, who was Francisco Julca Libiac's widow, went so far as to say that Libiac Condor now possessed the group's chanca. Alonso Poma Michuy, who lived near Libiac Condor's house and was a member of the same ayllu, confirmed that meetings were conducted there. Alonso declared that on some nights he could hear the noise of voices issue from within, and he said that he had heard that "the idols of the ancestors" were there. The people of his ayllu, he asserted, were led by Francisco Libiac Condor and would "come together and drink and worship idols."[23]

All of these chancas, and many others, were cared for by one individual who

[19] AAL Leg. 3, exp. 9. It is possible that the declarants used the term themselves. In any event, most of the witnesses in this trial discuss the "chapel." The most informative descriptions are at fols. 1 and 34.

[20] AAL Leg. 3, exp. 9, Ynes Poma Sacsa at fol. 8 and Petrona Francisca at fol. 8v. The ceremonial playing of these shells seems to have been common in many places of the Lima region.

[21] Ibid., fols. 3–3v. María noted the names of ten people in attendance, including her husband and his mother.

[22] Ibid., fols. 29v–30.

[23] Ibid., fols. 13, 14–14v (see Juan de Rojas at fol. 24 and Pedro Osorio at fols. 14v–15), and 16v.

was the mediator of the needs and concerns of a defined group of people to the god in question. Avila had stressed this aspect when he stated that "the most important person of each family guards this [chanca] and he is the person who has the right of succession." He wrote that when there was no blood relation to whom it could be bequeathed, the minister could give it to an appropriate person or close friend. Failing this, the minister was to deposit the god in an ancestor's tomb.[24]

In the case of the white chanca from Huarochirí, a man from San Cristóbal de Guañec in the neighboring province of Yauyos, Juan Acso, whom María Guanico referred to as the "great doctor," had passed the god on to her. Juan taught her how to care for it, as he had taught others with other chancas.[25] Although this information provides a general image of how most indigenous ministers assumed their roles and learned their special rituals, one learns a good deal more about the history and inheritance of the unnamed chanca and other gods found in Juan de Rojas's domestic *capilla* (chapel or shrine) in Carampoma in 1723.

In his idolatry investigation there, Toribio de Mendizábal followed a rigid eight-question interrogation that has survived in the documentation. His seventh query asked "if the idols were invented by the said Juan de Rojas or his wife." The question is fascinating because it is so loaded; it begs brief comment upon the preconceptions that a visitador might bring to his labors, which would be challenged by the religious information in the people's testimonies. The question reflects, among other things, the common Spanish assumption that a good number of the Andean ministers (*hechiceros* or sorcerers) were crafty charlatans, deceivers who invented divinities out of crude and vile things and who thus took advantage of Indian credulity. However, as Mendizábal interrogated one of Juan de Rojas's sisters, the visitador found little evidence of devious invention. Instead, he stumbled upon the chanca's antiquity and familial importance. Ynes Poma Sacsa declared that the "idols" found in her brother's chapel had been with the family at least all of her life, which was more than forty years. And she later revealed that these gods had been maintained by her relatives "since their gentility."[26] One can add this family member's testimony to what is learned of the chanca's more recent history, in the years before the arrival of Mendizábal's visita de idolatría in 1723.

There existed a certain amount of discrepancy among the declarants as to the immediate path of the chanca god (or "great stone" as it is most often referred to by the notary) to Juan de Rojas's home. María Melchora claimed that the chanca, as well as the other stones and things, had all been given to her husband by his mother, María Josepha. But because of María Melchora's appar-

---

[24] *Tratado de los evangelios*, "Prefación." Salomon quotes an even lengthier passage in his discussion of con churi in *Huarochirí*, sec. 185, note 366. Villagómez recorded similar succession rules in his *Carta pastoral*, ch. 42, pp. 147–48.

[25] Juan Acso's fame is noted at AAL Leg. 2, exp. 21, fols. 2v–3. Isabel Pulpu Saxsa is mentioned as another who was knowledgeable in chanca rites.

[26] AAL Leg. 3, exp. 9, fols. 2, 8.

ently negative attitude to her husband's religious role and her transparent hatred for María Josepha, her words need careful interpretation. For reasons—
perhaps domestic as much as religious—that remain mostly unknown to us,
María Melchora became one of Mendizábal's principal witnesses against her
husband, mother-in-law, and the other local "idolaters." The most convincing
alternative to María Melchora's on the matter of the god's provenance was
offered by Ynes Poma Sacsa, Juan's sister, who said that the "idol" found in her
brother's little chapel had originally been in their father's home. When he died,
the "great stone" had begun its journey, reportedly passing to Antonio Rique,
then to the home of Francisco Tanta Cunia, and finally to the chapel from
which it was removed by the extirpator.[27] Other testimonies support the crucial
parts of this story.

Most notably, Francisco Gulca Rilpo laid to rest any doubt about the late
father's sacred position in the community when he said that "it was public
knowledge to all the Indians in the parish that Juan de Rojas's father had been a
witch (brujo)."[28] Thus, it seems probable that the chanca followed a
common—if curiously complicated—route of succession from father (the late
Francisco Poma Cacha) to son (Juan de Rojas).

What about the other stones and sacred items found in the little alcove?
They had diverse origins. But, like the "great stone," they seem to have been
solemnly passed to Juan de Rojas's care. Juan said that he and Antonio Rique
had found the large sea shell trumpet on Malambo Street, and that it had only
come to reside with him after a temporary stay in the house of a widow named
Juana de la Cruz. According to María Josepha, the same Juana de la Cruz had
also given Juan the other, smaller stones when her husband had died because
the widow thought "that men should have these idols."[29] The widow's husband
must have been their former minister, and it seems likely that it was he who
arranged that they be bequeathed to Juan de Rojas.

The little chapel or home shrine had become something of a center for the
kin divinities, a place where religious observances could be conducted and
meetings could occur in private, away from the gaze of the parish priest and
other potential enemies of these practices. As the eldest son of a famous regional minister, Juan's succession and effective appointment as chanca minister
were in accordance with established local practice. The fact that others from
his extended lineage group also naturally entrusted gods to his care is additional proof of the legitimacy of this as an example of chanca inheritance.

[27] Ibid., fols. 3, 7v–8.

[28] Ibid., fol. 7. Brujo (witch), like hechicero (sorcerer), was a common term in extirpating language. The labels I choose in English, perhaps more accurate and suggestive of possibilities than
those chosen by the extirpators, are "minister," "specialist," "adept," and "practitioner."

[29] AAL Leg. 3, exp. 9, fols. 4 and 4v; Malambo was probably the street of this name in contemporary Lima, which the men must have visited. Ibid., María Josepha at fol. 9v, a curious statement
in the wider context in which women were often ministers. Perhaps María Josepha referred only to
her late husband's wishes for his successor.

There is less information in the case of the Julca people's chanca in the same town of Carampoma, but it would appear that a similar succession occurred there. As recounted above, although Francisco Libiac Condor was too prudent to admit it directly to the visitador, the late minister Francisco Julca Libiac's widow claimed that Libiac Condor had indeed inherited the care of this group's god in its small clay pot. Another witness, Francisco Quispi Condor, confirmed this claim, stating that the "idol" of the Julca people was the very one so closely guarded by Libiac Condor. It was he "who was the priest (saçerdote) who sacrificed to this idol." Quispi Condor even claimed that once he had been scolded by the minister for violating his secrecy and for having seen this god in the sanctum of his home. Francisco Libiac Condor was also said to be of great fame and to have been renowned in the region for his orations or "prayers."[30] Like Rojas, Libiac Condor seems to have been revered within his social unit as the natural, or at least the most suitable, candidate for the inheritance of the principal chanca. And other gods, too, had found their way into his custody. In an inheritance story strikingly reminiscent of the one told by Rojas and his mother above, Libiac Condor told the visitador that, about a year and a half before, a widow named Juana Sacsa had, on her death bed, entrusted him with two stone gods and a sacred small pot (ollita). Her last wish was that they "would never lack what they needed to maintain them." An Andean maestro named Juan Guaman from the annex of La Ascención de Guanza was said to have taught Libiac Condor the words he had to say to the little stones and pot that had come under his care.[31]

As noted above, one of the principal difficulties in presenting a satisfying picture of so personal a dimension of Andean religion in the colonial era stems from the relative ease with which Indians could conceal these small home gods and the rituals and beliefs associated with them from the idolatry investigations. It was not always so with the huacas, as I have shown. Once one or two witnesses had confessed a name or even alluded to a cult's existence, the most alert visitadores could ferret out the locations of the huacas, who were often conspicuous stone forms in the Andean countryside. Chancas, however, were much less vulnerable to both priestly surveillance and the average visita. From the point of view of their indigenous faithful, such ease of concealment was a fortunate circumstance; the depth of the peoples' attachment to these gods appears to have been considerable.

The chancas' most distinguishing feature was their human connection, their vital interrelationship with human "relatives." In this sense, the bond was perhaps even stronger than that fostered by the people with the huaca and malqui ancestors. The case in which María Guanico of Quinti, Huarochirí, stepped forward to make a secret and detailed confession and betray her Chanca to the

---

[30] Ibid., fol. 16.

[31] Ibid., fols. 13v–14. Like the smaller stones in Juan de Rojas's capilla, it is possible that these were not chancas proper. They may have been conopas, like those to be discussed below.

Extirpation stands as an anomaly. This, along with other instances when María provided the extirpator with vital information, suggest that the god's former minister, Juan Acso, had not chosen his heiress wisely.

A related set of proceedings conducted by Juan Sarmiento de Vivero in the same pueblo of Quinti in 1660 illustrates what the evidence suggests was a more common degree of allegiance to these gods of the home. In pursuing a line of investigation against a man named Lorenzo Llaxsa Yauri and his wife, Juana Tanta Mallau, the judge unleashed an inquisitorial zeal that extended far beyond that required of the visitador in the case of the compliant townswoman, María Guanico.

The summary of the preliminary investigations recorded that one day Juana Tanta Mallau had walked into her home to find her husband seated on the ground before two stones laid on top of some straw. He was reportedly doing something with his hands. Juana was said to have asked what he was doing, at which he hushed her, saying: "Be quiet silly, one looks for food in this manner." During her first interrogation, Juana claimed that her husband had immediately concealed his things with his hands, and that all she had in fact been able to see were a few small beads (*chaquiras*). Later, when Lorenzo Llaxsa Yauri was threatened with the torture session that had already been suffered by his wife, he did confess to having had some "beads." However, when he was asked to produce them for inspection, he replied that "if he had possessed them he would have handed them over [already], and that the visitador should not tire himself as he [Lorenzo] had no idols."[32] Sarmiento, however, clearly did not believe he had heard all from either Lorenzo Llaxsa Yauri or Juana Tanta Mallau.

Cords were tightened on to the fleshy parts of Juana's arms, which prompted her to confess that she had actually seen coca leaves, llama fat, and some hairs that her husband was holding and combing in his hands. The cords were further tightened and she declared that Lorenzo had asked her for "a stone that is called Panti Pequeña," with which she swore that she knew no more.[33] Lorenzo's reticence met with even more severe measures. He was threatened with torture upon the rack and was smugly warned according to standard inquisitorial formula that if limbs were broken, as so often happened, it would be no one's fault but his own. In the face of this threat, he staunchly maintained that he had done no more than he had already said, with which he was stripped, put astride a burro and twice given the same exhortation and warning. The ordeal, and perhaps a procession of shame, awaited if he persisted.

An obligatory third exhortation dictated by the precepts of a well-oiled procedure met with the same answer. The notary's grim record states that on the second turn of the cords attached to his arms, Lorenzo confessed that he had spoken of his beads to his Jesuit confessor who had told him "to throw them

---

[32] AAL Leg. 2, exp. 23, fols. 7, 8, 11v.
[33] Ibid., fols. 8–8v.

away, and that he had duly tossed them in the river." A turn on the cords attached to his legs achieved nothing further, and this torture session ceased.[34]

As the investigation delved deeper, the extent of Lorenzo Llaxsa Yauri's determination to keep a special god, or perhaps two, concealed from the Extirpation comes to the fore. An Indian named Juan Mateo declared that before his arrest Lorenzo had managed to visit his wife in the town jail where the visita had imprisoned her. He was said to have warned her not to tell of their "idols," lest they both end up in the Cercado.[35] Juana Tanta Mallau had already admitted to receiving her husband's counsel, making the meeting in jail something that Lorenzo could deny no longer. He held, however, that he had not mentioned anything about the concealment of "stones and huacas." He said that he had done no more than bring his wife a cup of water and utter a phrase to her in their mother tongue: "Ancha huchanchi," which the notary, presumably hearing more information than he recorded, translated as: "we are very guilty and they will take us to the Cercado."[36]

It was the additional testimony provided by the already proven informant from Sarmiento's related investigation, María Guanico, that caused the resistance of Lorenzo Llaxsa Yauri to be put to further tests. Unfortunately for the couple, María had been one of the prisoners in the jail with Lorenzo's wife. She claimed to have witnessed his visit and to have heard him warn "not to say more than what had to be said." She also supplied the visitador with some damning new evidence. María claimed that Lorenzo had "a small, elongated stone idol" and that once, when she was sick, he had come to her offering a remedy to return her to health. She alleged that he had said that for two reales he would "commend her to their relatives, their huacas." Three times, she said, he had

---

[34] Ibid., fols. 12–13.

[35] Ibid., fol. 15v. The Cercado was a district of Lima where Andean workers, servants, and people of mixed race lived. Lorenzo, however, would have been referring specifically to the infamous Casa de Santa Cruz within this quarter; it is interesting to learn of an Andean minister's knowledge and dread of the sorcerers' prison. Santa Cruz was established in the second decade of the seventeenth century by the viceroy of Peru, the prince of Esquilache, to incarcerate Indian hechiceros (so-called "sorcerers") who were believed to be beyond the hope of reform and thus had been banished from their realms of spiritual influence. Sentences were in theory up to eight years, and included manual labor and intensive instruction in the Christian faith. Because many of the prisoners were already aged when they were taken there, because the Lima climate rarely agreed with highland peoples, and because release often depended on complete repentance and acceptance of Christianity, most terms were, in effect, life sentences.

[36] Ibid., fol. 14v. Lorenzo's denial is at fol. 15. As Regina Harrison has discussed, the general verb that contemporary Spanish translators took from Quechua to capture sinning (pecar in Castilian) was huchallicuni, the noun hucha being taken to mean pecado (sin), but also pleito (a law suit or petition, or a business contract). Hucha and its derivations appears from time to time in the idolatry documents from different regions, an expression—I think—of the notaries' or interpreters' uneasiness with the straight translation as "sin" or "to sin." See the seventeenth-century definition in D. González Holguín, Vocabulario, pp. 199–200 and 619–20, and Harrison's pondering of possible ramifications in "The Theology of Concupiscence," pp. 141–43, that connect usefully to Louise Burkhart's emphases in the Nahua evangelization setting in The Slippery Earth.

returned to her with the same basic message and solicitation of offerings, asking "that she should give him coca, a cuy, and chicha." She claimed that, on at least one occasion, he had "shown her two bundles, saying that these were their relatives." Lorenzo, for his part, admitted only to visiting her and taking her pulse in his capacity as healer in the community. He said he had merely recommended that she seek "some remedy." María claimed that she had dispatched him, telling him "to return to God."[37]

Brought face to face with María Guanico as she told this to the visitador and his retinue, Lorenzo was left with few options when Sarmiento once again made him the center of attention. Again the man took intelligent refuge behind the sacrament of penitence he performed with the Jesuit padres.[38] Lorenzo said that the bundles which María had mentioned had been handed over to the passing missionaries after confession. Yet once again the visitador did not believe him, and Lorenzo was tortured for his alleged lack of sincerity. The notary records that after about a half an hour the ordeal finally ceased. The confessant had finally agreed to surrender an "idol," perhaps a chanca, that he had hidden just outside his house, or else a stone substitute that might get him some relief. Lorenzo described it briefly to his tormentors as round, one part of it white and the other colored. Its name was rendered only in Spanish as "Ventura": luck, fortune, happiness and well-being.[39] The surviving trial documentation ends at this point, so it is not possible to learn whether Ventura or any other god was discovered, or if Lorenzo ended up in the Casa de Santa Cruz as he feared.

The effect of torture on truth is, of course, a subject often discussed by students of the Inquisition and related ecclesiastical procedure. The capacity of torture to provoke fabrications from witnesses eager to secure any escape from their predicament is one famous possibility to consider. But, when a witness's resolve is strong, torture—however brutal—might still prove itself ineffectual and it might even strengthen an individual's resistance. In his history of the Moriscos of Spain (new converts to Christianity from Islam), Henry Charles Lea wrote that in the 190 heresy cases he examined in a set of representative Inquisition documents, torture was employed to extract a confession 55 times (in four of which it was applied twice). In "a considerable portion of those [cases] which were suspended or discontinued," Lea states, "the accused had been tortured without extracting a confession."[40] One wishes the historian

---

[37] AAL Leg. 2, exp. 23, fols. 13–14v. Huaca, of course, as used by María Guanico, could be used generically and thus might refer to a chanca or other god.

[38] The Andeans' preference and even affection for Jesuit confessors was frequently expressed in different ways in these documents. Felipe Guaman Poma de Ayala's early seventeenth-century chronicle, which otherwise contained a fairly vigorous condemnation of priests and friars, was also strikingly kind to the Jesuits. See *El primer corónica y buen gobierno*, 2: 532–636.

[39] AAL Leg. 2, exp. 23, fol. 16.

[40] *The Moriscos of Spain*, p. 108. In the Spanish-American context, see I. Clendinnen's excellent discussion of the effects of Franciscan excesses, and torture in particular, in sixteenth-century Yucatan, in which 4,500 Indians were tortured during a three-month religious investigation; *Ambivalent Conquests*, pp. 74–77.

were more communicative about his final statistics and case sample, but his suggestive point is pertinent to our case in seventeenth-century Quinti, Huarochirí. For here torture secured two sure aims: the hope of material evidence, the supposed chanca Ventura, and the confession of idolatry. That seems to have been sufficient for this extirpator; his zeal had produced results. But what of the possibility that the accused, who had already shown determination and no small awareness of confessional strategy, was attempting a final ruse? Was Ventura, or the stone which was said to be Ventura, the legitimate chanca? One will probably never have certain answers, but the questions lead us away from the contemplation of torture and back to the principal subject at hand. For the main revelation from this case is surely the length to which the defiance of Lorenzo Llaxsa Yauri extended.

A few deductions provide us with a clearer view of the kind of religious relationship people had with their chancas. The two "bundles" said to be Lorenzo's "relatives" were surely the two stones, wrapped up, which he was said to have worshiped on the straw in his home. As noted above, the Indians frequently wrapped their small gods, religious instruments, and offerings in tied and sacred bundles.[41] The chancas' designation as relatives fits well with the peoples' larger beliefs in kin interrelationships and in their descent from a common huaca ancestor. It also concurs with the status I have already associated with the chancas from the Huarochirí example in which the huacas admonished their faithful for not first consulting their fathers, elders, and con churis (chancas). As relatives, these gods were protected and cared for and, in turn, depended upon by their people; the cases are as good an expression of the religious principles behind Andean reciprocity as can be found.

It seems probable that one of the "relatives" was the chanca Ventura (or the god protected by Ventura's invention), while the other was perhaps the mysterious stone, Panti Pequeña, whose name was revealed by Juana Tanta Mallau under torture. Lorenzo claimed that his visit to the jail and his risky counseling of his wife was done out of fear that they would be sent to the sorcerers' prison in Lima. María Guanico, on the other hand, said that the prime content of his message had concerned the necessity of their concealment of the gods. Both messages were undoubtedly related; if the latter was not actually uttered it was certainly implied. Lorenzo's visit to the jail was but the first of a number of demonstrations of the distress he felt at the possibility that the chancas would be revealed and destroyed.

Both Lorenzo and Juana had attempted to play dumb about the charges raised against them in the ensuing interrogation. But imprisonment, the constant pressure of singular and group cross examination, repeated torture, and the information provided against them by the loose-tongued María Guanico eventually wrenched at family ties and brought fragments of confession from

---

[41] The possibility that these "relative bundles" were ancestor mummies (*malquis*) seems remote in this context. See J. A. Flores Ochoa's fascinating discussion of the significance of the bundles in the modern Cusco region. "Enqa," pp. 213–16.

their lips. The Panti Pequeña lead, extracted from Juana by torture, does not appear to have been followed up by the busy visitador, and it is clear that Lorenzo was severely tortured before he betrayed the alleged hiding place of Ventura outside his home.

The reader might feel inclined to think that the strong loyalties to the chancas exhibited in the above case are exceptional. It is true that these chancas' protectors were pushed by the methods applied in investigation to extreme lengths. But the genuineness of their attachment to the gods is underscored by even a cursory glance at other similar cases.

Jesuit correspondence to Rome in the mid-1660s told of an Indian in Cajatambo who concealed a small "idol" in a bag strung around his neck until his death. The persistent padres claimed to have instilled a "fear of Hell" in him that proved sufficient to make him confess of the god and other things. In Copa in the same province, another man suffered threats and subsequent torture at the hands of the missionaries in his attempt to conceal a god described as a "round smooth stone . . . with two eyes." Only when she believed her husband would be killed did this man's wife relinquish the chanca god to the Jesuits. The provincial's letter records that "when the Indian saw the idol brought in the hands of his wife he started to cry."[42]

In the eighteenth century, too, the chancas retained their importance, as evidence from two investigations in Huarochirí attests. In 1723 in Carampoma, the prospect of his imminent imprisonment spurred Juan de Rojas, to whom I have referred above, to take desperate measures to ensure the safety of the family gods under his care. A crisis had arisen when, one night, the Andean governor's deputy (*segunda persona*), Don Lorenzo Baptista, discovered a group of Indians "worshiping idols" near a lake. His rebuke, or perhaps only the detection of his presence, had prompted the group to reply with a flurry of stones that was said to have seriously injured him. A leader of those Indians was known to have been Juan de Rojas. That very night, Juan set about preparing for the reckoning that was bound to follow the unfortunate confrontation.

Petrona Francisca confessed that her brother Juan had appeared at their mother's door with the "idols" wrapped in a blanket, asking that she protect them "because he was going to die." Juan was said to have explained his actions by saying that "he had wrapped them [the gods] in a *manta* (blanket or cloak) that they might [continue to] be worshiped in his town." María Josepha confirmed this statement, adding that on the night that Don Lorenzo was stoned, her son "had entered her home and told her not to untie what he had put in the blanket, that they were idols, and if they were removed she would die."[43]

The chanca minister was arrested just as he had feared; witnesses concurred that he was publicly whipped in the village of Matucuna for his role in the forbidden adoration and in the stoning of the official. His quick attention to

---

[42] ARSI, Cartas anuas de 1664, 1665 y 1666, *Peru* 16, vol. 5, fols. 103–103v, 108v.
[43] AAL Leg. 3, exp. 9, fols. 8v, 10.

the safety of the gods when he was in danger may have saved them, but only for the moment. After the pressure had lifted, Juan's sister said he had returned them to the alcove in his home, the place where, as I have shown, they were later found by the visitador and his retinue.[44]

Seven years later another idolatry investigation was begun in the same parish. There is much evidence to indicate that, beneath the tense atmosphere and charged enmities in this case, there existed a similarly deep concern for the fate of some important familial gods. Although the evidence is somewhat less certain, this additional instance tests what one has learned in the clearer chanca cases in an interesting way.

The "bitter enemies" of the accused kuraka Don Francisco Gulca Rilpo included a rival named Juan Mango, a corregidor's teniente (deputy or assistant)-turned-visitador named Don Manuel Márquez, and the Indian alcaldes of both La Ascención de Guanza and Carampoma. These officials formed a united opposition which insisted that Don Francisco and his wife, Doña Petrona, held idolatrous gatherings in their home. The house concerned, as well as other family homes, were said to contain many "idols." A house by the church, in particular, was said to hold the principal divinity in a room that contained many such gods. Another denunciator described Petrona's attendance at elaborate rites in devotion to a special idol in the shape of a man.[45] But in the face of these and many other accusations, the husband and wife consistently protested their innocence, claiming that their enemies were motivated by envy and ill will. Moreover, the couple paraded their considerable knowledge of Christianity as evidence of their integrity.

Indeed, the local enmities appear so strong that we might well dismiss the idolatry charges as nothing but the evil brain-child of Juan Mango, the apparent leader of a conspiracy against the kuraka's reputation, wealth, and power.[46] But certain hard facts call into question Don Francisco's all-too-convenient self-portrayal as the classic Christian Andean scapegoat framed by an idolatry accusation.

In his maize granary smooth, blood-stained stones and small niches were found. A vault concealed beneath his bed, too, seems a rather suspicious, not to say elaborate, place for a regional lord to hide "tribute money" as he claimed. Moreover, when the visita arrived to investigate the charges against him, Don Francisco fled, and even tried to bribe his eventual captor for his freedom. His sister-in-law's house—one of those under suspicion as a local hub of idolatry—had been carefully locked up before his flight. And in the testimony he made after his arrest, he sought to deflect attention from the charges against him by revealing a striking amount of detail concerning the traditional rites performed by others in the neighboring village of La Asención de Guanza.

Ultimately, because of the difficulty in separating truth from slander in this

---

[44] Ibid., María Josepha at fol. 10 and Petrona Francisca at fol. 9; 8v.

[45] AAL Leg. 3, exp. 15, 1730–1732, Ana María at fols. 33v–34.

[46] See Mango ibid., fols. 2–2v and 31–31v.

case, one can do no more than cautiously speculate. Don Francisco might well have been framed, either by covetous enemies or fearful observers of Andean religion—people such as those who had worshiped with Juan de Rojas in the same region seven years earlier. It is conceivable that the kuraka fled simply because he was afraid of being accused and of not being able to prove his innocence once the machinery of persecution was rolling.[47] On the other hand, one might well wonder why so powerful a man as Don Francisco, if innocent, should have behaved so erratically and have known so much about the forbidden religious observances of his neighbors. Moreover, any worry on the kuraka's part about not being able to disprove an idolatry accusation against him once it had been planted is less convincing in the early 1730s than it would have been seventy years earlier, in the days of widespread support for centralized extirpation campaigns. Perhaps an influential chanca minister and a lineage god (or gods) were being desperately protected behind the screen of legitimate authority and a convincing knowledge of Christianity. If Don Francisco himself was not that minister and keeper of the gods, then his wife, her sister, or some other person they were protecting, might well have been.

What, in the end, was it about these chancas that saw their inheritance so carefully looked after, and made their preservation a matter of such dire importance? Their place in the home, as the god of a relatively close-knit lineage group, more intimate with their faithful than the huacas in the mountains, springs, and sky, is an initial and obvious clue. An examination of the chancas' worship allows a closer understanding of their significance to colonial Andeans.

Not too surprisingly, María Guanico of Quinti emerges as the most revealing of the individual chanca ministers I have treated. She related that, following an instructive apprenticeship with the minister who had been her predecessor, she had gone into the countryside to find another stone out of which she fashioned a sort of base for the purposes of her observances. On this base she scratched four furrows: one for coca leaves, the second for offerings of money, the third for llama fat, and in the final furrow sat Chanca. María said that she then brought out a cup of chicha she had prepared in a new pot. The god Chanca was sprinkled with the chicha and also received some coca, before the minister herself partook of the ritual sustenance. The appeal she would then make to the god underscores the familial nature of the chancas, and once again harks back to the first step in the consultation of the gods demanded by the huacas in the Huarochirí manuscript.[48] María said to her Chanca:

---

[47] See Don Francisco's sophisticated and detailed second and third petitions outlining his enemies' enmities and his accusation of his first judge's greed, ibid., fols. 43v–44 and 51–51v. For consideration of the complex of errors associated with notables accused of idolatry, see K. R. Mills, "Bad Christians."

[48] AAL Leg. 2, exp. 21, fol. 2v. Compare also the case of a Guamachucos woman described by Augustinian friars in the middle of the sixteenth century: she came to possess a small stone named Tantaguayanai who communicated with its discoverers and turned out to be the child of none other than the supreme deity of the region, Catequil. "Relación de la religión, pp. 26–27.

Father, Son, Nephew,
As I am poor
give me maize and potatoes to eat.

In response to a specific query from Visitador Sarmiento concerning the god's communications, María said that the chanca did not speak to her, "but [that] what she asks turns out for certain."[49] She believed her poverty to have been made less acute through the satisfaction of Chanca's needs.

References to the rites performed in honor of other chancas are not as descriptive as in the above case. However, they offer verification and one can make a number of observations from what was recorded. The careful rites and drinking that might have been conducted in the open air in prehispanic times were moved indoors, into domestic space. The depiction of regular offerings presided over by the chanca minister in the privacy of the home seems an accurate mid-colonial portrayal. In addition to María Guanico's above description, we can recall the image of Lorenzo Llaxsa Yauri of Quinti seated alone on the floor with the chancas on some straw before him; in Carampoma there was Francisco Libiac Condor's stern rebuke to the man who had set eyes on the Julca ayllu's god without the minister's permission; and, above all, there was the household niche of Juan de Rojas's "great stone" and the set of accompanying gods or "relatives." Direct reverence seems to have been the privilege of only a select few besides the chanca minister, the group whom the extirpators would often call the principal "accomplices to idolatry." The intimacy and secrecy of the Andean gatherings greatly bothered the investigating churchmen, recalling perhaps the ways that many non-Christian peoples in Spain had not long before been suspected of withstanding and resisting the increasing Old Christians' demands for absolute cultural change through, among other things, the strength of their hearths. In typical fashion, the prosecutor in Lima who reviewed the information from Carampoma, Huarochirí, in 1723 found the privacy of the worship—centered on stone gods hidden in an alcove behind a stone and attended by a select few—particularly abhorrent.[50] Moreover, there was the Indians' organization of ritual practices to consider; the cults were not

---

[49] AAL Leg. 2, exp. 21, fol. 2v. It was common for ministers of huacas and chancas, when faced with this question, to deny that their god spoke to them, while admitting that it had spoken with certain elders or perhaps a deceased predecessor. Partly, this was prudent testimony before a persecutor, but the prevalence of such portrayals seems worthy of further investigation. It is possible that colonial Andeans were also finding it increasingly difficult to decipher their gods' messages. Alternatively, perhaps the gods' messages had always been hard to follow, and people in mid-colonial times supposed that venerated ancestors had understood what they could not. The food for thought is plentiful: Juana Ycha of Pomacocha in Canta was screamed at and beaten by her maestro for not understanding the crackling of the fire (AAL Leg. 4, exp. 14, 1650, fol. 6v; see Chapter Seven below); and the rumblings of Llocllay Huancupa, the returned huaca from Huarochirí noted near the end of Chapter Two, are described as inarticulate by the seventeenth-century editor/redactor.

[50] See AAL Leg. 3, exp. 9, fol. 34.

haphazard. Ritual observances were held at regular intervals. The rites observed in the little chapel in Juan de Rojas's home, for instance, fell on distinct days assigned for sacrifices of cuyes and the offering of their blood to the gods.[51] Similar rites to other chancas—many of whom are recorded as being blood-spattered when they were found by the extirpators—were normal, expected features of the local religious life of the lineage groups and their ministers who were unfortunate enough to come to the Extirpation's attention.

Much of what I noted in the last chapter about the general function of the huacas in indigenous society applies to the chancas and, for that matter, to the conopas. The religious spectrum, no matter how varied its different dimensions, served a range of common human aims. The gods of the home were simply more immediate, more accessible, and personable repositories of the power that might assist in daily life. The familiar goal of well-being, and all of its possible physical and spiritual ingredients: fertility, fecundity, abundance, prosperity, good fortune, strength, confidence, happiness, and so on, was sought from the chancas, too—and, because of the intimacy people shared with them, perhaps even more vigorously than from the huacas. For, the chancas were the more immediate "relatives," the more cherished sources of sacred energy for the average family network in the mid-colonial Andean parishes. A comparable European parallel in contemporary, popular Catholic practices is, of course, the devotion surrounding saints and other images of the Holy Family.[52]

To return to the chancas, one might drop in, one last time, on Carampoma, Huarochirí, in 1723. The prosecutor of Juan de Rojas accused him of officiating at gatherings at which his "special purpose" was to see that "these two stones be truly worshiped, [and] that through them one could ensure a tranquil life, the increase and permanence of one's livestock, and the copious abundance of fruits of the earth in one's farms in the countryside." The offerings, in the fiscal's (prosecutor's) view, sprang from an enduring Andean conviction that by "sacrificing animals of distinct species and offering the blood to the stones, and giving them the smoke, rosemary, and other resins," all these benefits would be obtained. The opinions in these passages—though admittedly part of a longer document in which the fiscal recommends torture to obtain more information and severe penalties to all the Church's perceived religious transgressors—are most valuable, for the moment, in isolation.[53]

---

[51] Ibid., fol. 5.

[52] See particularly J. Bossy, *Christianity and the West*, chs. 1 and 2, and also W. A. Christian, *Local Religion*. For a brief consideration of the place of saints and holy images in the emerging religious universe of a particularly well-documented region of the north-central Andes, Cajatambo, see K. R. Mills, *An Evil Lost to View?*

[53] AAL Leg. 3, exp. 9, fol. 34. As I shall argue more directly in Chapter Eight, the often elaborate arguments of fiscales, defensores (advocates or defense attorneys), and protectores generales de los naturales (Protector of the Indians) have consistently been underestimated as a historical source for the shades of Spanish Christian opinion they express concerning "idolatry" during the Extirpation's active years. These officials' views often transcended the formulaic and legalistic

Superficially, the prosector's words are an example of a contemporary Spanish Catholic gloss of Andean belief bent on demonstrating the extent of the indigenous error and better facilitating its eradication. But on another level, the passage is a valid attempt by a committed official and follower of another—and a particularly exclusivist—religion to offer a concise, synthetic description of Andean chanca worship. The seeking of tranquillity through true worship of the stone gods or, to use his words from yet another passage in the document, the Indians' desire "to preserve their lives from disquiet," are not such bad beginnings to a synopsis of mid-colonial Andean religious purpose.[54]

The conopas are another vital dimension of mid-colonial Andean religion in the Archdiocese of Lima. Their rituals were on an even more personal and portable level than those of the chancas, in the sense that although ministers might be employed, they do not appear to have been necessary intermediaries between these gods and ordinary people.[55] The conopa was the god that a person might carry, with the god in turn carrying the person's preoccupations and priorities. Despite the terminological confusion, the identification of the conopa had more successfully entered the extirpating churchman's imagination than that of the chanca, which, as I have noted, was often called simply an *ídolo* or a *huaca* in the documentation.[56] Consequently, the extirpators' interrogations about conopas could usually be more specific and penetrating. Andeans who came before visitadores generales de idolatría could expect questions about both their huacas and conopas. This, along with the fact that conopas were clearly much more numerous than the chancas, meant that declarants were bound to yield a considerable quantity of information about these ubiquitous small divinities.

Conopas are immediately more tangible for the historian, as well. Their shapes and crafted forms often denoted a special significance or competence, and invited the visitador's questions about their functions and meanings. In the 1660s, for example, in a village in Cajatambo called Chamas, Jesuit missionaries encountered gods of many forms: "some were the shape of cobs of maize, others of potatoes and *ocas* [edible tubers] . . . and others . . . of different types of things that they [the people] grew." These gods would be carried to the appropriate fields at the time of sowing. There, the gods would be offered the blood of cuyes, chicha, maize, and other foods in the hope that the harvests

---

bounds that admittedly constrain them at many points. Prosecutors of alleged Andean religious offenders did not always debate within the confines of some latter-day version of the *Malleus Malificarum*, and defenders of parties did not always resort to pleas that alleged the ill will of certain witnesses, or the Indians' simplicity and ignorance of what was proper.

[54] AAL Leg. 3, exp. 9, fol. 34v.

[55] Historical treatment is scarce, usually in the form of short prefaces to ethnographic work. Anthropological references, however, are more numerous and many are noted in J. A. Flores Ochoa's indispensable chapter, "Enqas," in *Pastores de puna*, esp. p. 212.

[56] See, for instance, the "Edict against Idolatry" in Villagómez, *Carta pastoral*, ch. 55, pp. 208–9. Arriaga's earlier version is published in P. Duviols, *Cultura andina*, pp. 514–17.

would be copious. Other conopas, resembling camelid families (often a llama mother with her little ones) were similarly revered in the interests of herd fertility. The same Jesuit missive to the Father General in Rome records that in the Arequipa region in the south of Peru, the padres had even found gods in the form of a "goose or duck."[57]

As adaptable to new demands and pressures as the huacas and chancas had proven to be, the mid-colonial conopas' powers were conspicuously not limited to traditional Andean livestock. Nor, apparently, did they avoid association with Christian institutions. Another line of investigation in the trial affecting Santiago de Carampoma, Huarochirí, in 1723 involved cattle owned by a local religious association of men and women (a *cofradia*), that of Our Lady of the Nativity.[58] Both Juan de Rojas and Francisco Libiac Condor, figures already familiar to us as chanca ministers, were accused of observing rites in honor of three small stones at the place where the cattle of the cofradía were pastured. When Juan de Rojas appeared before the *provisor* in the ecclesiastical court in Lima, he explained that the stones had been inherited by him, coming from "the time of his father."

Juan said that he had always kept them in a bag (*talega*), along with a ball of fat and some cattle hairs of different colors, which his mother had given to him.[59] The man clearly traveled and went about his daily tasks, accompanied by his specialized kit of conopas and basic materials for their ritual nourishment. Other necessary offerings could be obtained along the way. The blood on the stones, Juan had explained some two weeks earlier to the visitador in Carampoma, had come from a cuy he and Libiac Condor had sacrificed.

Throughout his ordeal, Juan maintained that the true expert with these cattle-conopas was Francisco Libiac Condor. Juan implied that Francisco's assistance had been specifically solicited by the owners of the cattle in the town. There were said to be some "special words," known only by Libiac Condor, which were incanted to the conopas when offerings were made. Libiac Condor, however, steadfastly denied taking part in any such sacrifices or knowing any secret "prayers." Like Don Francisco Gulca Rilpo seven years later in the same place, in 1723 Libiac Condor endeavored to hide behind a life that might seem legitimate to his interrogators. He was currently serving as the town's chief magistrate (*alcalde*). And, in spite of some rather glaring errors during his demonstration of his understanding of Christianity, he emphasized his honest living as a tailor.[60]

A mestizo witness named Juan de Medina, however, strengthened Juan de

---

[57] ARSI, Cartas anuas de 1664, 1665 y 1666, *Peru* 16, vol. 5, fols. 107v, 157v.

[58] AAL Leg. 3, exp. 9, fol. 4.

[59] We do not learn that the stones were formed like cows, but the existence of cattle hair in their midst suggests the association. Alternatively, these conopas might have been general fertility gods, venerated according to current needs.

[60] AAL Leg. 3, exp. 9, fols. 24, 27–28v. It was common for certain people in Andean communities to be entrusted with the supervision of songs and "prayers," the order and precision of which were essential in observances.

Rojas's claim about Libiac Condor's position, noting a separate occasion on which the members of the cofradía had put some cattle in the care of another Indian man named Francisco Tanta Cunya. Medina said that he had heard from the townspeople that Libiac Condor was "a priest who makes consultations." Medina claimed that the cofradía's new cowherd had asked Libiac Condor to "increase the herd of cattle," and that the minister had agreed. Just what observances, if any, had gone on at the pasture, the mestizo declarant was not sure of. He estimated only that there had been some "witchcraft (brujería) to ensure that the cattle would not die out."[61]

The judges of this case, however, seem ultimately to have considered the information about Libiac Condor as something of a complication, perhaps even a maneuver of distraction by Juan de Rojas and his allies. Pedro de la Peña, the provisor and vicar general of the archdiocese in Lima, like Toribio de Mendizábal, the priest-turned-visitador before him in Carampoma, focused on Rojas as the prime perpetrator. The narrowing scope of this special ecclesiastical investigation in Huarochirí in 1723 mirrored the procedures followed by the idolatry inspectors of the Villagómez era a half-century before, and—for that matter—by their predecessors during the Extirpation's operations during the archiepiscopates of Bartolomé Lobo Guerrero and Gonzalo de Campo.

Extirpators among seventeenth- and eighteenth-century Andeans were conditioned to seek out corrupters of the flock, heresiarch equivalents who were partly to blame for the imperfect Christianization they perceived all around them. The tendency of an idolatry inspector or provisor to avoid a number of possible lines of enquiry, in order to focus an investigation on the activities of one person or a small group of people, is extremely common in the trials of the Extirpation. The assertion will not surprise students of the Peruvian cases or either investigators of extirpation initiatives in New Spain or scholars familiar with Inquisition records in America and Europe. In Peru, as presumably elsewhere at other times, the telescoping attention was expedient for officials desperate for evidence and concrete results.

In a larger sense, however, the inclination to concentrate on a prime perpetrator reflects something far more important than the simple hunger for material proof. It reflects a basic assumption about how the evangelization of non-Christians should proceed. The Limeño Church—like the slightly older establishment in Mexico, the same institution installed in the Iberian kingdom of Granada after the Muslim capitulation of 1492, and a seemingly endless host of earlier manifestations of the Church Militant in European history, the ready examples of which easily extend back to the projections of the gospel by the earliest missionaries among the Irish, Norse, or Germanic tribes—believed that by converting the élite in a target population and subverting the hold of that people's spiritual leadership, success in the task of evangelization would be only a matter of time. In the Andes, the sixteenth-century conciliar constitutions were as theoretically adamant on this point as were the more practical

<hr>

[61] Ibid., fol. 15v.

machinations of the seventeenth- and eighteenth-century idolatry inspectors. The destruction of the local ministers of Andean gods and other native religious specialists, along with the conversion of the Andean governors and principales, seemed to offer the shortest route to a successful and widespread Christianization of the Indian population.

Thus the churchmen's natural concentration on the latest principal rival in Carampoma, Huarochirí, in 1723. Juan de Rojas, as I noted, was a *relapso*. He was a person judged to have accepted Christianity at least once, but then to have backslid into religious error. He had been found guilty of many idolatrous crimes and was even known to have acted violently against a magistrate who threatened his illicit activities. The ecclesiastical judge asked Juan de Rojas how, as a Catholic Christian, he could so obviously break the first commandment to worship only God? Although he had attempted to share the blame for the observances with Francisco Libiac Condor among others, Juan de Rojas was remarkably straightforward in his answer. It seemed to come down to his beliefs concerning the cattle-conopas. Simply put, in a time of extreme need he had looked to indigenous religious solutions. Juan explained that "many of the confraternity's cattle were dying, and that he had consulted different Indians to help him [so] they might not die. The sacrifice was made to this effect."[62]

As in other dimensions of colonial Andean religion, the specific purposes of certain conopas did not preclude more general, and adapted, colonial functions in others. Examples are plentiful, but the point is perhaps best illustrated by concentrating, first, on a number of testimonies heard in San Pedro de Quipan in the parish of Huamantanga, Canta, in 1656 and, to the northeast of this place, in San Jerónimo de Pampas in the province of Huaylas, almost a decade earlier.

Hernando Caruachin—who will be recalled as the chief huaca minister in mid-seventeenth-century Quipan, Canta—declared that about thirteen years before the visita's arrival in his village a woman who was now his fellow-prisoner, Ynes Guacai Suyo, had called him to her home. There, she had shown him three small figures that she said she had inherited from her deceased grandmother, Doña Ana Casa. The first was black, about the size of an almond, with the face of a man and an indentation in its back.[63] His name was Sulca Vilca. The second was called Choque Ticlla, and she was a green figure, somewhat larger than the first and with the face of a woman. The third was different from the pair, and in the shape of a *choclo* (a large maize cob). This conopa also appears to have been female, though obviously not anthropomorphic; she was Sara Mama.

On the occasion of his meeting with Ynes Guacai Suyo, Hernando said that

---

[62] Ibid., fols. 24–24v.

[63] Flores Ochoa explains that in modern Cusco these spaces are called, in Quechua, *qochas* (literally, "lakes"), and that they are frequently seen in the backs of llama-conopas, symbolizing the pastoralists' dependence on water for the herds. See "Enqa," p. 215.

he and the woman had burnt llama fat in offering to the gods. Then Ynes had presented him with "the man-idol Sulca Vilca" as his own conopa, who, he explained, "is the same as a god of the home." Taking him to his own home, Hernando said he filled Sulca Vilca's indentation with llama fat as he had been taught to do, and in this space he stuck a half-*real* coin. It was to the conopas, Hernando Caruachin said, that people turned for "their needs." He himself now cared and provided for Sulca Vilca and asked him for many things, but most of all, for "good fortune."[64] This case can be compared with those from the earlier investigation conducted in Huaylas, to the north of Canta, in 1646.

I have already told of the six stone gods discovered at the head of Ynes Yaco Caxo's bed by Visitador Juan Gutiérrez de Aguilar in Pampas, Huaylas, during this investigation. On this same occasion only the parish priest's intervention had saved her from a severe flogging at the hands of the Extirpation officials. The parish priest, Gonzalo Cano Gutiérrez, in gaining her cooperation, had also persuaded the old woman to betray some of her other personal gods. To date, I have been able to discover precious little about this Cano Gutiérrez, but—on the basis of his actions with Ynes Yaco Caxo and with another accused offender to be discussed just below—it is tempting to wonder both how much he knew about his parishioners' colonial religious lives in the years before the Extirpation arrived in town and what he thought of the methods being employed by the temporary intruders in his parish. Cano seems to have counseled Ynes and others that the best way forward was to give in.[65]

Hand in hand with the priest, Ynes guided the visitador and town officials to a storehouse (*colca*) in which there was "a small window walled in with clay." Within this niche was a medium-sized pot containing four stone figures. Two were described as very dark in color and distinctly shaped—the one like a heart and the other, a tobacco pouch. The other two were white and appeared, in either the visitador's or the notary's estimation, to have been "brought from the ocean." The judge learned from Ynes that the "largest and most important" stone was named Micuy Conopa, the next two were Damiay Conopa and Pachay Carae, and the smallest was Guaga Conopa. Around them in the space, the notary recorded the evidence of many types of offerings. There was llama and cuy fat, coca, the hairs of many persons, colored wool and cotton, maize flour, what were referred to mysteriously as "little rocks broken from the huaca," and three cobs of maize—two white and the other colored.[66]

That same day the visitador wisely enlisted the persuasive powers of Gonzalo Cano Gutiérrez yet again, this time with a reticent suspect named Diego Guaman Poma. The two were permitted some time together. An hour and a half later, the visitador found them, in the notary's words, "very happy," the priest

[64] AAL Leg. 2, exp. 11, fol. 6; "el buen suceso."

[65] Ibid., fols. 6v–7. Another priest named Diego Cano Gutiérrez was later commissioned as one of Pedro de Villagómez's visitadores generales de idolatría.

[66] AAL Leg. 6, exp. 8, fols. 7–7v.

with the Indian, and the latter carrying a small crystalline stone carefully wrapped in black and white wool and tied with a white string. Guaman Poma said he had brought it from a corner in his home.

The judge asked him for its name and an explanation of why he kept it. The man responded that this was his conopa, Mayguanco, "with whom he had lived all his life, hiding it from the visitadores." Diego Guaman Poma explained that he regularly provided Mayguanco with food and drink, and had even provided him with a female companion (*palla*) named Aclla. The counterpart evidently had propitious powers all her own; Diego told of these in response to questions. One time he had carried Aclla with him to the city of Lima and, that night, found no fewer than four *patacones* (small coins) in the plaza. He claimed he had also come upon a knife that later had enabled him to kill a tiger.[67]

Among other things, the examples demonstrate the way the conopas were integrated into the Andean home, to the extent that, like many of the huacas, they often appear to have had mirroring "family" relationships of their own. Sulca Vilca had a mate in Choque Ticlla, and we know that Aclla was especially provided for Mayguanco by his minister. The arrangements have strong resonances not only with the huaca families—the multiple personages (like Paria Caca or Chaupi Ñamca) and tendency toward divine pairing in several of the cases I have described—but also with the status of relatives that people granted to the chancas, who were part of the extended home, the religious dimension of the Andean domus.

Most contemporary Spanish Christians, of course, recoiled at the thought of devotions being directed at such an apparently pantheistic medley, especially by supposedly Christian Andeans. But the Indian families and kin groups do not appear to have felt particularly crowded or confused by the complex of divine beings and their interrelationships with them. On the contrary, people seem to have felt the different dimensions of the system quite necessary. A given minister (take Hernando Caruachin of Quipan, Juan de Rojas or Francisco Libiac Condor of Carampoma, or Ynes Yaco Caxo of Pampas as examples to hand) served a chanca or principal huaca, and took part in conopa worship. Indeed, in the next chapter I show how the obligations of many ministers could stretch even further, demonstrating a capacity to take on more in colonial times without losing what was deemed irreplaceable. At a certain point, too, one must differentiate between the ministers of Andean gods and other people in these communities, for the ministers—however much they themselves absorbed change and adapted to new pressures—were charged with the maintenance of a measure of religious coherence that was still defined more strictly

---

[67] AAL Leg. 6, exp. 8, fol. 8. *Aclla* could be translated as "the chosen one"; see D. González Holguín, *Vocabulario*, pp. 15 and 513. Patacones appear sometimes to have been included in offerings to Andean gods; see P. J. de Arriaga's description of Diego Ramírez's findings in Recuay in *La extirpación*, p. 44, and Olivia Harris's discussion in "The Earth and the State," pp. 256–59.

than that of most people. The religious allegiances and responsibilities of the people who might tentatively be called the "ordinary faithful" appear to have been even more comfortably multifarious.

The extirpators, who so often latched on to a piece of information about one huaca or a set of conopas and proceeded to focus long investigations on the pursuit of this one aspect or even a single god, rarely produced documentation that adequately reflects the indigenous commitment to a number of religious dimensions at once. The practical, Spanish interpretation that radically diminished the scope, variety, and interconnections of the Andean religious system was especially prevalent when a god such as a conopa was confronted. Isolated from their contexts, conopas became easier to demean. It appears to have been easy to trivialize, to think of a conopa as a "fetish" or "idol," or as an object of merely superstitious attachment. It was true that a god such as Ynes Guacai Suyo's Sara Mama, sculpted to the form of a large maize cob, was a personal god of maize abundance, analogous to the apparent unidimensionality and temporality of a llama-, cattle- or potato-conopa described elsewhere. But Sulca Vilca, and perhaps his green counterpart Choque Ticlla, were, by contrast, virtually omnipotent. According to what might be advanced as a central principal of Andean religious philosophy, the good that came from their worship assisted in the fulfilment of the more general, unpredictable needs and wants of everyday life. As in the cases of huaca and chanca worship, the testimony of Hernando Caruachin asserted that Sulca Vilca, "the god of the home," was cared for and provided for that he might bring "good fortune" and help people meet "their needs."

One does not learn enough about the principal Micuy Conopa or the three others found in Ynes Yaco Caxo's storehouse in Pampas, Huaylas, to state their purposes with much certainty. Yet their location and names might indicate a relationship with maize or other foodstuffs, even if the grouping together of such a number suggests that perhaps they were only being hidden there. Their peculiar appearances point toward a variety of functions, probably according to the noted pattern of specificity and generality seen in others like them.[68]

Diego Guaman Poma's conopas provide a most interesting case in this respect. One can tell that the second part of one of the visitador's questions to the man, "and why did he keep it [his conopa]?" was seriously pondered by this Andean who had been coaxed into confession by his parish priest. The importance of his gods seems to have been difficult for Diego to capture in words. Perhaps he knew only too well the estimation with which his words would likely be received.

Diego had recourse to reciting personal anecdotes to explain that he attributed fortuitous occurrences in his life to his conopas' satisfaction and pres-

---

[68] *Micuy* means "food," whereas *pachay* might well be a rendering of *pacha*, implying a relationship with the earth and its fertility. See González Holguín, *Vocabulario*, pp. 239 and 454 for the gloss of the former. Guaga Conopa confounds me, unless it means huaca, which was often written "guaca."

ence. He saw his fortune and condition as being directly related to his ritual attention to them. One can imagine the highlander, perhaps in Lima very rarely, carrying Mayguanco's companion, Aclla, in his bag, shuffling about the empty central plaza in the late evening, finding coins and even a knife that had been dropped on the ground, and that would allow him to do great things. Lest these memorable good-luck stories be taken too literally by the visitador, Diego seems to have further tried to evoke accurately the conopas' nature and significance. The conopas were so much more than simple lucky charms or amulets. Diego related that the crystalline Mayguanco was kept to enable him "to live a long life, and to be very rich, and for women to be well-loved by men and many other things."[69] The reader of his testimony feels that his list might have gone on for some time, and that it was perhaps only an overworked notary who chose to cut it short.

Conopas and chancas were not gods with generative powers on a massive scale. The creation and "animation" of the natural landscape, men and women, llamas and other animals, foodstuffs, even of social institutions and structures—all this had been the ancient business of the huaca heroes like Paria Caca, or a "worldmaker" and "worldshaker" like Pacha Camac. Huacas were regularly worshiped by people who conceived of themselves as their children. Huacas enjoyed regular festivals, and they could be appealed to through their ministers in times of great need or personal crisis. But they were far from the exclusive forces affecting people's lives. The responsibilities of the chancas and conopas fit into a religious world and a human society that already existed, but one that required vigilant maintenance to ensure its survival.

　　Procreation, augmentation, revitalization—the stuff of fertility, prosperity, well-being, and happiness—these were and are the rewards of everyday human life. In the mid-colonial Archdiocese of Lima these rewards could be sought especially from the gods who were cherished as personal relatives in the home. Jorge Flores Ochoa's explanation of Andean pastoralists' belief in the interconnectedness of camelid health and human happiness applies equally well to the other things over which the indigenous gods watched.[70] The determined protection and worship of these gods in the Andean parishes in the seventeenth and early eighteenth century, and their survival in some Andean regions until today, is a testament to their durability as part of a vital religious base.

[69] AAL Leg. 6, exp. 8, fol. 8.
[70] Noted in "Enqa," p. 235. See also *Los pastores de Paratía*, pp. 103–5.

Specialists

ONE COMMON ASSUMPTION in much of what has been written on the subject of Andean—not to mention wider Amerindian—religious change is surprisingly similar to that expressed by the archbishop of Lima, Pedro de Villagómez, in a letter to King Philip IV in 1652. In describing the efforts of four of his visitadores de idolatría in the regions of Cajatambo, Checras, Conchucos, and Huaraz, he claimed that only the first region had yielded significant evidence of "idolatrías formales." By formal idolatry he meant organized religious networks involving "many idols, huacas, shrines . . . and backsliders (*relapsos*)." In the three other areas, his agents were said to have encountered "few instances of formal idolatry," but "much superstition and error."[1]

This was not the only way to view and to subdivide Andean religion. The knowledgeable sixteenth-century commentator, the Jesuit P. José de Acosta, had not seen the need to make such a distinction.[2] In referring to the "sorcerers" in Andean society, in a treatise appended to the 1585 "Confesionario para curas de indios," Juan Polo de Ondegardo was careful to point out that "there are a great number, and there are also many differences [between them]."[3] And P. Bernabé Cobo, in the mid-seventeenth century, warned his readers against creating careless and ill-informed categories. "The priests [of the huacas] were," he said, "at the same time, confessors, doctors, and sorcerers. Because of this, even though we divide these officials, treating each one in its own chapter, one should not assume them to have always been distinct."[4] Yet at this very time, when Andean religiosity was made most manifest before the tribunals of Villagómez's Extirpation, genuine exploration was being abandoned by those who were turning their minds to persecution in Peru. Extirpators in line with the attitude of their prelate in Lima, tended to detach what were to be regarded as superstitious beliefs from false religion. The simplification and denigration of elements within Andean religion served political and personal ends. Whereas idolatry among supposed Christians implied a rejection of God, superstition was a less tangible enemy that might have many causes. In the Andes, as in both Catholic and Protestant Europe at the time,

[1] AGI Lima 303, Villagómez to the king, Lima, 16 August 1652. Felipe de Medina was visiting Cajatambo; Br. Bartolomé Jurado, Checras; Br. Esteban de Aguilar worked in Conchucos; and Br. Diego Tello spent some three and a half months with two Jesuit padres in Huaraz.

[2] Acosta wrote of two types of idolatry: one that involved the worship of "natural" things and another of "imagined" things. Although he glossed some indigenous tenets as superstitious, he did not completely separate them from the rest of the Amerindian belief systems, however deluded he believed them to be. See *Historia natural y moral*, book 5, ch. 2, pp. 218–19.

[3] "Los errores y superstiticiones de los indios," ch. 10: "De las hechicerías," p. 469.

[4] *Historia del Nuevo Mundo*, vol. 2, book 13, ch. 34, p. 225.

"superstition" had become a common term of abuse when applied to a belief or practice; it signified excessive, vain, defective, and irrational behavior.[5]

The ramifications of this inclination to divide were felt even outside Villagómez's realm of Lima. The bishop of Quito, Alonso de la Peña Montenegro, was a man well aware of the extirpating ventures in the Lima region. Writing in 1668, his treatment of "idolatry" distinguished between cults that were consciously "false," and therefore of the gravest offence to God, and those that were "superfluous," the simply perverse or mistaken.[6] The idolatry/superstition distinction recalls some other observers' separation between activities that were considered religious and those that were custom. But the difference is that superstition, while a lesser enemy in the minds of many extirpators, was still to be stripped away.

The path that a person such as Villagómez must have taken in arriving at his distinction between idolatry and superstition is an interesting one. Early modern churchmen rarely presented Indian religion in anything but their own terms. At the most obvious level, analogies brought interpretative comfort. Even vague similarities to Catholicism tended to make an aspect of the indigenous system less loathsome. Thus, huaca worship, replete with its established traditions, its ministers, guardians, attendants, offerings, regular festivals, and purification rituals, was at least an entity that a Spanish Christian observer could conceive of and distort as religion—however misguided and false—through recourse to his own religious categories. It followed, then, that a variety of popular beliefs and practices might be otherwise classified.

That which was least understood, that which was supposedly primitive and unseemly, became degraded even below the status of false religion. There were numerous dimensions of the Andean religious system that Spaniards of the extirpating era discarded in this way, intellectually severing them from the body of Indian belief and practice. Colonial Andeans' conceptions of health, illness, and human nature, interpretations of causality, and its connections to collective social and religious behavior were not comprehended by many of their Hispanic and Hispanicized observers. Indeed, the Indians' reliance on apparently mystical agency to explain human events as well as natural and biological processes was taken to be one of the surest signs of their inferior, credulous minds. The Indians had been confused and deceived; much of their ritual structure was thus in vain and could never be thought to form coherent parts of a religion. In making these critical judgments, of course, Spanish Christians declined to recall the functions that so-called "magic" had played and continued to play in their own religious tradition, not to mention the traditions of many other peoples. There was a "magic that persisted," "a magic that was needed" in

[5] M. R. O'Neil surveys these European attitudes in "Magical Healing," pp. 88–89, and in "Superstition."

[6] A. de la Peña Montenegro, *Itinerario*, book 2, treatise 4, fols. 175–76. Discussing similar distinctions and themes, see W. B. Taylor, *Magistrates of the Sacred*, ch. 3, and R. Behar, "Sexual Witchcraft."

the medieval European conceptions of religion that had suffered a denial and rejection (tempered only partly by rehabilitation) similar to that which lay in store for the perceived magical and superstitious aspects of mid-colonial Andean religion.[7] Terms of opprobrium made poor descriptions of religious dimensions.

An archbishop of Lima, like many other officials, was governed and affected by the relatively rigid dictates of the contemporary Catholic Church as well as by the idealistic decrees of the Spanish crown. Yet there was a sense in which official Christian views did not move in unison with real knowledge and opinion. This gulf forced contradictions in the interest of expediency. There are strong clues, for instance, that Archbishop Villagómez knew that his portrayal of the state of mid-colonial Andean religion in his letter to the king in 1652 amounted to a gross simplification.

Much of the compendium of Andean beliefs and practices within the second part of his own *Carta pastoral* of 1649 was borrowed directly from the 1621 treatise by Arriaga, evidence that the archbishop knew the contents of the Jesuit's treatise well enough to copy them and add to them. In the *Carta,* Villagómez was markedly less insistent on the separation between idolatry and superstition for which he argued in his letter. Following Arriaga, who—as MacCormack has noted—had drawn analogies from the predictable supply of European titles (priests, confessors, diviners, and so on), he describes the offices of the Andean specialists.[8] His chapter 43 on "the ministers of idolatry" includes numerous religious officials besides the huaca ministers and Indian confessors. In chapter 46, which ostensibly treats the Andeans' "abuses and superstitions," Villagómez writes that these things permeated all of Indian life. The wide range of rituals and beliefs he describes are, to employ his familiar motif, the "branches and leaves that issue from the trunk of their gentility and idolatry."[9]

Historians of the Inquisition in Spain and other parts of Europe have made much of the institution's careful exaggeration of the threats posed to society by different groups of heretics, witches, and other perceived enemies of orthodoxy.[10] Exaggeration and embellishment aroused interest and fear that, in turn, strengthened the position of the Inquisition to supply the remedies. Because the revived extirpating initiatives of Villagómez were controversial, similar rhetorical tactics were being practiced in the middle of the seventeenth century in Lima. The archbishop's approach was calculated to justify himself and his policies. Making, and reiterating to Madrid, the distinction between idolatry and superstition proved useful for the Peruvian prelate in a number of ways. If it

[7] V. I. J. Flint, *The Rise of Magic*, chs. 5, 6, and 7.

[8] *Religion in the Andes*, p. 392. But, as will be demonstrated below, Arriaga made an extraordinary effort to record the Quechua names—frequently with a number of orthographic possibilities—of the ministers and specialists he described.

[9] *Carta pastoral*, pp. 151–56 and 174, respectively.

[10] For a concise example see, for instance, J. Contreras's essay, "The Impact of Protestantism in Spain."

could be made to appear that organized Andean religion—Christianity's true rival, idolatry—was being eradicated in most of his archdiocese, the ongoing policy of extirpation would seem an effective remedy. Making the alleged distinction, and even noting how widespread "superstition" was, amounted to declaring the main stage of the battle all but won. Those aspects of the Andean religious tradition that fell into the loose and lower category of "superstition and error" became generic and almost insignificant items of secondary concern. Their widespread existence was only enlisted to demonstrate the sorry state to which the idolaters' religion was said to have been reduced. The "branches and leaves" were waiting to be lopped from a "trunk" that was already dead. For certain seventeenth-century churchmen, it was most comfortable and convenient if Andean religion proper was being steadily converted into a memory. Villagómez, who needed not to be alone in his mental endeavor, degraded his enemy both to win royal support for his practical measures and to embolden his supporters in Peru.

In particular, Villagómez appended to his *Carta pastoral* letters from the contemporary bishop of Cusco and a respected Jesuit missionary of the same region, letters that underscored his point. They were written to him in late 1648, on the eve of the publication of the *Carta*, and just as Villagómez was transforming a few visitas de idolatría into more ambitious tours of duty.[11] Here were experienced churchmen, in a south-central Andean region that had not yet seen systematic extirpation campaigns, telling of the ubiquity of idols and organized Andean priesthoods, the very "formal idolatry" that had allegedly been brought to its knees by extirpating efforts in the Lima region.[12] The lessons that Villagómez meant to be learned are obvious.

By the mid-colonial period, the so-called "magical" elements in Andean practice (principally healing, divination, the interpretation of dreams, omens and signs, and the assortment of rituals and procedures called sorcery and witchcraft) had acquired a dubious reputation as a jumbled assemblage of cultural remnants and twisted traditions of mixed Andean and European provenance. According to most shades of this interpretation—both contemporary and modern—the superstitious perversions arose in the Andean parishes that were subjected to the visitas de idolatría as a result of two broad factors: the vacuum left by uprooted indigenous cults and the infusion of European ideas about witches, Satanism, black magic, and the like.

Any of the Andean customs thought to resemble the practices associated

---

[11] The archbishop himself, in one of his few ascents to the mountains during the early years of his tenure, had begun the idolatry investigation discussed in the last chapter in the village of Yautan in the parish of San Jerónimo de Pampas, Huaylas, on 27 December 1646. See AAL Leg. 6, exp. 8, 1646–1648. Another related investigation in the same Yautan, Huaylas, is AAL Leg. 4, exp. 11, 1646–1647. There had also been a trial of an accused sorcerer, Isabel Huanay, in Huarochirí in 1642, AAL Leg. 2, exp. 8.

[12] Two letters from Juan Alonso Ocón to Villagómez, Cusco, 14 October and 14 December 1648, respectively; two letters from P. Francisco Patiño to Villagómez, Cusco, both dated 14 October 1648, in *Carta pastoral*, pp. 272–86.

with European religious deviants were consistently viewed as either fundamentally non-Andean or so perverted from what was deemed pure as to have become virtually so. One European observer in early seventeenth-century Peru went so far as to heap the entire weight of the blame for sorcery and superstition on corrupting European influences, saying that the Indians (as well as the African slaves) had become "more barbarous now than before they came into contact with the Spaniards, because then they had no one to show them the way, and now they are sorcerers and laden with superstitions."[13] Guillermo Cock has suggested something similar, namely, that the infiltration of these kinds of "exogenous" European conceptions through the sixteenth, seventeenth, and first half of the eighteenth centuries brought about the end of a recognizably Andean religion, or what he calls the Andean "sacerdotal system." The pastoral rhetoric of the evangelizers and extirpators which had sought to marginalize Andean ministers and specialists from functioning religion and society finally succeeded, Cock believes, in convincing Andeans of the legitimacy of these judgments, and in bringing about a "self-marginalization."[14]

Any traditionally Andean components within ritual practices that were transforming in colonial times were thought to have been transmuted beyond useful recognition. A standard image of the time, which has prevailed in many scholarly studies, runs roughly thus: superstitions and witchcraft were seized by confused Andean elders and sorcerers who groped about their "destructured" religious universe, searching for anything that might help them to maintain a semblance of their traditional legitimacy and religious power.[15] Unlike the huaca and chanca worship networks, which because of their resemblance to what Europeans called religion had to be confronted vigorously and refuted by the pastoral of the Extirpation, Andean ritual specializations were devalued, cast onto a lower plane. Colonial Andeans are meant to have internalized uniformly the extirpators' separation.

But how do these images fit the mid-colonial Andeans who are some of the historical subjects of this book? It is possible to read through the extirpators' judgments, and around the sides of many later interpretations, to find out. All the different elements that constituted the specialists' dimension within colonial Andean religious life deserve a book of their own. Here, however, we can identify a few of the most important specializations to contemporary Andeans, and disentangle these as much as possible from the stereotypical labels and connotations that have long encumbered them. Mid-colonial Andeans were careful people rather than superstitious ones, and I want to demonstrate that these specializations and their practitioners were integral—as opposed to marginal—parts of the colonial Andean religious system.[16]

---

[13] *Descripción del virreinato del Perú*, p. 73.

[14] G. Cock Carrasco, "El sacerdote andino," pp. 62–64.

[15] The depiction of the contemporary Andean minister or specialist as a charlatan who played upon the Indians' credulity for his own financial and vain ends is a common one in extirpation literature; see Chapter Six below. The idea of "destructuration" in the Andean cultural context is borrowed from its wider application by N. Wachtel in *The Vision of the Vanquished*, pp. 159–60.

[16] I do not mean to imply that I am alone here, or that closer scholarly examination of the

The picture one gets of the prehispanic Andean religious specialists within local and regional societies is of a highly differentiated association of persons performing functions that were as important in local and regional life as were those of the ministers of the gods. As Bernabé Cobo expressed in the quotation given above, huaca, malqui, and chanca ministers often carried out these and other exercises in addition to administering to the gods. The breadth of these people's ritual activities does not appear to have been only a colonial adaptation, although the evidence does frequently suggest that depopulation and concomitant pressures did result in many ministers and specialists extending their general coverage. The early seventeenth-century Andean chronicler Felipe Guaman Poma de Ayala told of pre-Inkaic "wise men" who recommended propitious times for planting and harvest, and who foretold the future through the observation of heavenly bodies, the flights of birds, and other things.[17] Guaman Poma, the editor(s) or redactor(s) of the Huarochirí manuscript, and other early colonial commentators included descriptions of Indian diviners who met to take auguries before the Spanish conquest.[18]

Pedro Cieza de León and El Inca Garcilaso de la Vega wrote admiringly of the Andeans' accumulated medical knowledge. They described herbalists and healers who maintained ancient curing practices and whom they had watched perform operations.[19] Garcilaso also noted that certain members within society were known for their abilities to concoct philtres and poisons, and to cast bewitching spells. Similarly, Guaman Poma's catalogue of traditional Andean "sorcerers" included persons who could cast a number of ingenious curses, influence love, and command spirits to do their bidding. Sources from the first years of the viceroyalty (1540s) tell of Andean "sorcerers" being commissioned to bring about deaths.[20] And P. Arriaga noted the survival of these and many other

---

"sorcerer" in wider contexts has not already begun. Yet there are few published works that treat the Andean specialists in detail. M. Rostworowski de Diez Canseco's *Estructuras andinas del poder*, is an original contribution. See also a number of suggestive works by Luis Millones: Millones and G. Solari, "Males del cuerpo"; Millones with M. Pratt, *Amor brujo*; and the contributions in the volume edited by Millones and M. Lemlij, *En el nombre del Señor*. Two theses, G. Cock Carrasco's B.A. thesis, "El sacedote andino," and I. Gareis's Ph.D. dissertation, "Religiöse Spezialisten," provide some analysis. For Mesoamerica see particularly N. M. Farriss, *Maya Society*, pp. 287–89, 296, and 317–18; the interpretations of R. Behar in "Sexual Witchcraft" and "Visions of a Guachichil Witch"; and S. Gruzinski, *The Conquest of Mexico*, esp. pp. 177–87, 198–200, and 259–62.

Ritual divination, healing, and magic in the contemporary European setting, which the Inquisition branded "superstitious error," have recently been scrutinized by numerous scholars and have been placed generally within the sphere of popular religion. See the pointers offered, for instance, by M. R. O'Neil in her "Magical Healing," p. 90, and by the eccentric and fascinating observations by C. Ginzburg in "The European (Re)discovery of Shamans."

[17] *El primer nueva corónica*, 1: 54–55.

[18] Ibid., 2: 353–54 and *The Huarochirí Manuscript*, edited and translated by F. Salomon and G. L. Urioste (hereafter *Huarochirí*), ch. 18, secs. 221–25, and Salomon's note 428. On diviners who inspected spiders see also J. Polo de Ondegardo, "Los errores y supersticiones", ch. 11: "De los sortilegos y adivinos," p. 472; and *Huarochirí*, ch. 28, sec. 370.

[19] P. Cieza de León, *La crónica del Perú*, ch. 112; and Garcilaso de la Vega, *Royal Commentaries*, book two, chs. 24 and 25, pp. 120–23.

[20] See Garcilaso de la Vega, *Royal Commentaries*, book I, ch. 14, pp. 39–40, and F. Guaman

practitioners, whose Quechua titles he recorded whenever he could, in one of the portions of his 1621 treatise that was copied assiduously by Villagómez in the *Carta pastoral* of 1649. There was the *macsa* or *viha* who cured people with the help of offerings to "huacas and conopas," the *sócyac, rípiac,* and *pacharícuc* (or, alternatively, *pacchacátic* or *pachacuc*), who were specialized diviners, the *hacarícuc* or *cuyrícuc,* who performed similar functions through examining the entrails of cuyes, the *móscoc,* who interpreted dreams, and the *cuachos* or *runapmícuc,* who were the "sorcerers" or "type of witches" that people were said to fear greatly (see Figure 3).[21]

The most important among the cadre of prehispanic specialists appear to have operated within much wider geographical boundaries than those suggested by the colonial confinements of resettlement (the people from a number of llacta rounded up into a reducción) and the parish network (the central town or *cabecera* of the doctrina linked to its annexes). Their prehispanic operational zones would seem to have approximated to those of a hereditary group of indigenous ministers and guardians of culture about whom little is known, and who were called *yancas* in the Huarochirí region.[22] The yancas appear often to have been associated with the control of important shrines at lakes and sources of water, places such as the puquio of San Blas discussed in Chapter Two. As Frank Salomon's researches have indicated, these ministers seem, through their knowledge of ceremonial observance, history telling, and their fulfillment of other religious offices, to have embodied their regional religious systems on the western side of the Andes. This formulation is what Salomon dubs the "unifying proposition" or "yanca synthesis," a principle that assists greatly any comprehension of the conspicuous regionalism that is so predominant in the activities of the mid-colonial adepts to be discussed below.[23] For even when there is no colonial evidence identifying a specialist as yanca, or some analogous term in regions outside of Huarochirí, there is often plenty of information to suggest a similar kind of expert.

The different specializations engaged in by certain persons, and even entire regions, had their origins in the same mythical past as the huacas and other gods. In fact, the gods themselves frequently imparted the powers, knowledge, and techniques of the practitioners and their descendants. One particular sa-

---

Poma de Ayala, *El primer nueva corónica,* 1: 247–53. A section on "bad omens" and "superstitions" follows this at pp. 253–57. For two cases of sorcerers causing deaths from AGI Justicia 451, see F. P. Bowser in *The African Slave,* p. 252 and notes on pp. 402–3.

[21] P. J. de Arriaga, *La extirpación,* ch. 3, esp. pp. 34–41, and P. de Villagómez, *Carta pastoral,* ch. 43, pp. 151–56.

[22] The authority of yanca ministers over vital resources and people's actions is most clearly exemplified in *Huarochirí,* ch. 31, secs. 434–35. In his "Introductory Essay," Salomon quotes another vital source on this official, Francisco de Avila's own paraphrasing of Hernando Pauccar's confession concerning his yanca position and its responsibilities; see p. 18, and the quotation from Avila's "Prefación" to the *Tratado de los evangelios.* On Pauccar, the prominent minister of early seventeenth-century San Pedro de Mama and environs, see also A. Acosta Rodríguez, "Francisco de Avila," pp. 575–76.

[23] F. Salomon, "Oral and Redactorial Makeup of a 'Native Chronicle,'" pp. 2–9. I thank Frank Salomon for sharing this essay in progress.

Figure 3. Sorcerers. From Felipe Guaman Poma de Ayala, *El primer nueva corónica*, edited by John V. Murra and Rolena Adorno. Original manuscript in the Royal Library, Copenhagen.

cred history recounted to the Jesuits in Cajatambo in 1619 captures beautifully the genesis of such a regional religious network. Its emphasis on an important huaca's sharing and bestowal of healing powers also demonstrates how such functions might have been consolidated into the larger religious system of huaca worship.

The padres were told of the bold huaca Vrau, who was worshiped in Lampas. In addition to his other powers, Vrau was much revered for his ability to restore the health of those who were ill. However, on one of his triumphant journeys abroad, he was said to have been detained in Canta, "where the Indians received him with great applause and began to worship him as God (Dios)." (On this occasion he cleverly deceived the sun and his wife, the moon, out of the coca seeds that they jealously guarded, and thus carried the sacred coca plant to his people.) Of course, it was not long before his curative skills and powerful presence were missed in the region nearer to Lampas. A kuraka from one of the villages came to him and asked that Vrau might return to heal a sister who was seriously ill. The great huaca agreed to heal the woman, but not before conceiving of a plan that would benefit the people of all the regions which desired his powers. He left a son in Canta and another in the kuraka's village, before he was requested to pass to yet another community six leagues further on. The Jesuit report concluded that "this is the reason that the padres find huacas named Hurau (Vrau) in many of the towns in the region."[24]

Subsequent ministers and specialists within the realms of Vrau and his children would thus inherit their specific chores and responsibilities. Although there is no further evidence on this case, one can presume that such persons would have been sought out by those in need, and that the divinely empowered individuals would have made offerings to, and invoked the assistance of, these gods in the interests of their people's health.

The idolatry documentation, like the Jesuit correspondence, does not always explicitly establish the religious specialists' direct links with a given region's huacas or their origins in the mythical past. The divine connection is poorly recorded principally because most mid-colonial extirpators and commentators did not believe in it. Those intruders who penetrated most deeply into regional Andean religion, the most tireless collectors of information, were also among the most prejudiced observers. In their minds, as in their commentaries, the specialists and specializations were completely detached from the trunk of idolatry. Yet in spite of the presence of such interpreters as judges, and the Andeans' understandable reticence in such matters, these officials' persistent importance and their resemblances to predecessors who had fulfilled similar functions in prehispanic times are not completely obscured. The evidence of linkage is in their actions, about which a careful reader can still learn a great deal.[25]

---

[24] "Misión a las provincias de Ocros y Lampas," pp. 453–54.

[25] The visitadores' notaries did not always use the term curandero(a) to describe the healers. They frequently wrote only of hechiceros or hechiceras, or of persons who claimed to heal (usually

The aged Francisco Malqui of San Pedro de Guaroquin in Canta was re-nowned as the "wiseman" and "doctor" in at least two parishes in the late 1650s. What is more, although many men and women sought him out as the one "who knows the most," he claimed that in providing his services (primarily healing), he was hardly unique. Each of the principal ayllus in his town had one or two such "doctors" and "wisepersons," and a similar pattern extended to the ayllus in the neighboring communities of Santiago de Chisque, Santa Cruz de Cormo, and San Cristóbal de Guascoy. In Guaroquin, Francisco explained, there were Isabel Magaai and Elvira Suio of the Allauca ayllu, and, in addition to himself, Andrés Llana of the Quisal ayllu; in Chisque, Pablo Capcha minis-tered to the Sancar ayllu, while a certain Pedro looked to those of ayllu Chaupis, and there was a woman named María of the Tunas ayllu; in Cormo he noted two women, one of whom was named Magdalena, from the Allauca ayllu; and in Guascoy he knew of a man named Vilca Poma of the Cuchi ayllu, along with Martín Condor, who was apparently among the most famous of all.[26]

Archbishop Villagómez's population estimates for the archidiocese five years later (1664) make possible a general indication of the range and numerical responsibilities of these specialists. The eleven Cantan "doctors" and "wiseper-sons" noted by Francisco Malqui, including himself (and one cannot be certain he mentioned anyone beyond the most important specialists), would have cared for just over 500 persons between them: Guaroquin had 182 parishio-ners, Chisque 150, Cormo 70, and Guascoy 110, for a total of 510.[27] This was a ratio that would have been much envied by almost any set of eleven parish priests or catechists of the Catholic Church in the mid-colonial Andes. In addi-tion to the decentralized network of specialists who were committed to serve their social groups, the last one mentioned, Martín Condor of Guascoy, who "traveled to all the towns and doctrinas that were close to his pueblo," came closest to replicating Francisco Malqui's own regional reputation.[28]

Similar patterns existed throughout the Archdiocese of Lima, as even a small sampling of evidence shows. In the visita conducted in the parish of San Jer-ónimo de Sayan, Chancay, in 1662, an accused man named Pedro Guamboy, perhaps in hope of deflecting attention from himself, compromised seven other regional specialists.[29] In the same trial, a herbalist and healer, María Ynes, told

---

curar, but sometimes *sanar* or *remediar*) with superstition and *hechizos* (spells, curses). In this instance, the extirpators were partly correct in their wider designation. The Andean healers, like their gods, often did far more than heal, and they frequently also had the power to harm.

[26] San Juan de Lampian and Atavillos. AAL Leg. 4, exp. 23, 1659, fols. 7–7v..

[27] AGI Lima 304, Letter from Villagómez to the king, Lima, 20 November 1664.

[28] AAL Leg. 4, exp. 23, fol. 7v.

[29] AAL Leg. 5, exp. 8, fols. 13v–14v. He did so after his own practices had been uncovered and in response to Visitador Juan Sarmiento de Vivero's request for information on others like him. These specialists were almost universally called "sorcerers." Most of those whom Pedro denounced appear to have been, among other things, important regional healers. He compromised Juan Caxa and María Manco of Quintay; two crippled men, one named Santiago from Guamboy and another, Lloclla, who was said to be a *yanacona* (an Indian servant without local ayllu affiliations) of a Spanish overlord named Captain Castillo; Domingo Guaman and Alonso Martín, also of Guamboy;

of how a magistrate (alcalde) of Chambara and a slave owned by the *encomendero* (Spaniard to whom Indian laborers have been entrusted), Don Juan de la Adaga, had not only heard of her skills and knowledge but had climbed from the valley to be cured by her. As was the case with many of her colleagues in the Archdiocese of Lima, María had found it impossible to respect the repeated demands of Christian authorities that she reform her ways and neglect her calling. María Ynes said she had been punished some twenty years before in the town of Supe by the idolatry visitador Felipe de Medina. She said that he had sentenced her to a procession of shame and "four blows on her knees with a staff," but she had returned to her practices.[30] In 1690, it emerged that thirty-nine-year-old Pedro Guaman, a longtime resident of Mataguasi in the province of Jauja, was clearly a healer of similar regional renown. Guaman's dedication was such that on one occasion he had traveled all night to reach his ailing kuraka.[31]

These regional networks of specialists did more than heal, and they involved more than simply famous healers. Moreover, the practitioners were not always on the road; people also traveled to them. A remarkable woman to be discussed further below, María Poma Ticlla of the Quiripa ayllu in Huarochirí, in the district of Huarochirí, was said to have attracted people from throughout the entire province because of her competence in divination and matters of love. Receiving parcels of maize, potatoes, and other goods in kind for her services, she was said to hold secret consultations with all those who came to her.[32] Juana Maca Culqui of San Lorenzo de Quinti, Huarochirí, explained the commonness of such transactions, stating that these goods and a few others were what "they were accustomed to bring to the doctors when they saw to their affairs."[33] A voluminous trial conducted in San Jerónimo de Sayan, Chancay, in 1662 revealed a similarly acclaimed figure of María de Arriero. When Arriero was not traveling between the towns and villages of her clients, her home was reportedly inundated with visitors seeking consultations.[34] In the same region there was much talk of a great man called only Cojo, who worked in the priest's pottery workshop. Sebastian de Palacios claimed that all the people went to Cojo and "at night they carried him on a litter in the town of Oteque, where

---

and Bartolomé Pérez, a native of Huamanga who lived in Cañas. According to Villagómez's tally, the settlements with which these specialists were associated were all tiny at this time: Quintay had 40 parishioners, Guamboy 30, and scattered Spanish haciendas (Captain Castillo's undoubtedly among them) and chacras had 20, 50, and 20 persons, respectively. AGI Lima 304, Letter from Villagómez to the king, Lima, 20 November 1664.

30 AAL Leg. 5, exp. 8, fols. 5–7.

31 AAL Leg. 1, exp. 9, fols. 19v–21.

32 AAL Leg. 4, exp. 32. See particularly María Conolla's petition at fol. 9 and the confessions of Juana Maca Culqui and Sustacha (alias María Justa) at fols. 8–8v and 10–10v. See also AAL Leg. 2, exp. 21, 1660, Juana Maca Culqui's testimony at fols. 6–7, and AAL Leg. 2, exp. 15, 1660, María Choqui Suyo and María Poma Ticlla at fols. 1v–4.

33 AAL Leg. 4, exp. 23, fol. 8.

34 AAL Leg. 5, exp. 7; see Cristóbal Guaman at fol. 17; Juan Brigida at fols. 9v–10; Doña Ursula de los Ríos (a native of Seville) at fol. 8; and Juan Chamorro at fol. 11.

they call him the doctor, because there is no one more famous in the province of Checras."[35]

Apart from the specialists' participation within regional religious networks, it is striking how pervasive the influence of these adepts continued to be in the seventeenth and eighteenth centuries. Although some of these persons were hounded by zealous priests and shunned by "Christian" factions within certain communities, the number of colonial specialists who either assumed or who were cast into roles as peripheral nonconformists in and by their communities— in the classic fashion of stereotypical witches, scapegoats, and maleficents of society—was a distinct minority.[36]

The bulk of the idolatry evidence complicates the uni-directional tack that has tempted some scholars in presenting selected parts of this material. This tack seeks, more than anything else, a kind of resistance that is pure and simple, and that excludes other kinds of Andean actions. For example, one of the lasting impressions left by Irene Silverblatt's pioneering comparative study of gender ideologies in Inka- and Spanish-controlled Peru is that, during colonial times, anti-Christian feelings contributed to the separation of supposed witches from their society, and that many women, in particular, fled to the high plateaux (*puna*) in protest against "colonial ideology" and "Catholic dogma." They fled that they might return "to their native religion and, as best they could, to the quality of social relations which their religion expressed."[37]

Although some indigenous ministers and specialists in the Lima region certainly did foster anti-Christian and, by extension, anti-colonial sentiments— and although many of these persons were feared, at the same time as they were respected, by others—these feelings were often not the only dimensions of their religious lives. It is not accurate to suggest that the tendency of a few

[35] Ibid., fols. 3v–4; see also Raphaela de los Ríos at fol. 2v.

[36] G. Cock Carrasco, in his "El sacerdote andino" at p. 40, also argues that the Andean figures were not marginal figures in society. I. Silverblatt suggests similarly, if more tentatively, that "the sorcery and witchcraft that the Spanish chroniclers claimed to have witnessed in the Andes . . . were very likely a Spanish invention," and that "perhaps spells, spirits, and magic, which many anthropologists impute to all cultures, were also part of Andean belief systems." She goes on to argue that through a "forced acculturation of ideas" (an expression borrowed from the work of Michael Taussig), colonial Andean women in particular, came to take on and use the "Western norms" (especially those associated with diabolism, she suggests) that had been imposed on them; see *Moon, Sun, and Witches*, pp. 174 and 177–81, and M. Taussig, *The Devil and Commodity Fetishism*, pp. 40–43. Treating some related themes in the context of colonial Mexico, see also the work of F. Cervantes, especially *The Devil in the New World*. Sir Keith Thomas, in *Religion and the Decline of Magic*, gives a good synthesis of the problems and process of marginalization in the English and European context, with some references to the findings of anthropologists studying similar figures in African societies; see pp. 599–637. For more on the supposed "witches" and "diabolists" in the Andes, see Chapter 7 below.

[37] *Moon, Sun, and Witches*, pp. 197 and 207–9. Similar lines are pursued within the same author's "El surgimiento de la indianidad," 475–76. See Chapter 8 below.

persons to flee was a manifestation of a generalized "culture of resistance" or rejection. These accentuations run the risk of misrepresenting the religious information in the idolatry documentation. Most mid-colonial people's lives— apparent complexities and contradictions included—took place both within their communities and within expanding religious frameworks.[38]

As in most societies, there were some perceived evildoers in the mid-colonial communities. They were often conspicuous and extraordinary people, about whom stories circulated. But too narrow a fixation upon certain aspects of their lives and practices can be detrimental to an accurate interpretation. Even with the outpouring of an increasingly sophisticated literature on the contemporary European witch trials and the phenomenon of witch beliefs in both learned and popular culture, it remains all too easy to succumb to the inquisitors'—or in the Peruvian cases, the extirpators'—ways of seeing and categorizing such things. Witchcraft, along with demonology, had become something of a science in its own right, and thus offered Hispanic churchmen plenty of convenient points of reference and authority.[39] One still has to chip vigorously to break through the Spanish, not to mention modern academic culture's assumptions about witches and witch beliefs. When one does break through, in the mid-colonial Andes it is possible to find specialists and practitioners, both women and men, whose roles as mediators between members and groups within communities, and between people and the perceived divine causal forces, were viewed as vital to the functioning of society.

The Extirpation documents provide numerous examples of the kinds of specialization that were widely practiced in the communities of the mid-colonial Archdiocese of Lima. These included the rituals and practices of healing (to which I have already alluded briefly and to which I will return in Chapter Eight) and the different customs of divination; here I want to focus on two themes that were, not surprisingly, fundamental: love and hate.

Treatment of the practitioners in matters concerning love demonstrates the persistent vitality of one particular ritual specialization.[40] Like their colleagues noted above, these specialists were inheritors of a long tradition in the Andes. Sexual enticement, trickery, and the acquisition of love were predominant motifs in the ancient histories of the huacas that were enacted and collected in written form in the Huarochirí region. When Tutay Quiri led Paria Caca's chil-

---

[38] See my An Evil Lost to View?

[39] See particularly S. Clark, "The Rational Witchfinder," and the collection of essays within B. Ankarloo and G. Henningsen, eds., Early Modern European Witchcraft Centres and Peripheries.

[40] Little has been written about this in the Andes. L. Millones and M. L. Pratt, Amor brujo, explores the transformation of love magic in what is today the Ayacucho region, largely through the utilization of fieldwork and close examination of a popular art form, the tablas de Sarhua; on the older roots see especially pp. 51–54. Some useful comparisons with similar arts in the European context arise with the examination of "love magic" in late sixteenth-century Italy by M. O'Neil in her "Magical Healing," especially pp. 98–105.

dren out of the highlands in conquest of Yunca lands, one of Chuqui Suso's sisters waylaid him in a style that was nothing if not forward. She

> waited for him in her field thinking to seduce him by showing off her private parts and her breasts.
>
> "Rest a while, sir; have a little sip of this maize beer and a taste of this *ticti* [chicha residue]," she said.
>
> At that moment, in that way, he fell behind.[41]

The playful eroticism in the ancient histories could work both ways. When Cuni Raya found Collquiri, the huaca of Yansa lake, bemoaning his loneliness, he provided a prospective partner in the person of the beautiful, dancing llamaherd, Capyama. The successful seduction which ensued involved enticing her up the mountainside with a story that one of her llamas had given birth. Collquiri, possessing a huaca's prodigious powers of metamorphosis, turned himself into a *callcallo* (either a small bird or grasshopper), which the woman placed inside her dress for safekeeping. From there the callcallo entered her womb, which began to grow and "ache terribly."

> "What could this be?" she said when it hurt her; she looked, and there on the ground where he'd fallen, appeared a man, a fine handsome youth.
>
> He immediately greeted her in his sweetest way, saying, "Sister, I'm the one you stuck in your dress. What can we do about it now? It was me who sent for you."
>
> The woman for her part immediately fell in love with him.[42]

For the ancestral founders and heroes, at least, love was subject to manipulation, conquerable through effort. But ordinary people could hardly expect to be as clever and successful as the huacas were said to have been. Thus, the attempts to control the intricacies and mysteries of love became the exclusive province of certain specialists. Although some of these practitioners appear to have made regular rounds between the villages and homes of their clientele, private consultations held in their own homes were most common. They might use any number of traditional means to achieve an astonishing variety of ends.

Perhaps the most famous method involved the subtle employment of a *huacanqui*, a powerful object believed to command the passions of a person if properly administered.[43] Descriptions of their constitution and usage through-

---

[41] *Huarochirí*, ch. 12, secs. 170–71 and Millones and Pratt, *Amor brujo*, at p. 52.

[42] *Huarochirí*, ch. 31, secs. 408–16 and Salomon's suggestion of a grasshopper in note 780. See also J. M. Arguedas, tr. and ed., *Dioses y hombres*, p. 175, and Millones and Pratt, *Amor brujo*, p. 52.

[43] Both J. Santa Cruz Pachacuti Yamqui and F. Guaman Poma de Ayala specifically mention huacanquis in reference to prehispanic times and practices. See "Relación de anitigüedades deste reyno del Perú," p. 289, and *El primer nueva corónica*, 1: 247 and 249, respectively. As Regina Harrison notes, churchmen, ever worried about "lustful encounters," included references to huacanqui in catechisms and guides for priests. See the "Confessionario" included in the *Tercero catecismo* (1585) and an informative list of ingredients in Juan Pérez Bocanegra's *Ritual formulario* (1631), discussed in R. Harrison, "The Theology of Concupiscence," p. 147.

out the vast Lima region in the mid-colonial era prove remarkably similar. In 1656 in Huamantanga, Canta, Hernando Caruachin—the chief minister of this region, discussed in Chapter Two—told the visitador Pedro de Quijano Zevallos of one of his successes involving the use of a typical huacanqui. He explained that a married man from Quipan named Marcelo Guaman had once come to him to confess his unrequited love for a young widow named Catalina Chumbi and ask for some assistance (*rremedio*) whereby she might love him. Hernando instructed Marcelo to collect some of his own hairs along with some of Catalina's. The specialist then plaited these through a brilliant feather from a pariona bird. The incantation he made, which he recalled to Quijano, reveals at least some of the metaphoric possibilities of the object: "Beautiful and gorgeous feather, in you I have threaded the hair of the beloved. Allow that this woman will love him and not look at any other man but him, and that once together they will remain so and not part, one from the other, just like their hairs in you."[44] The incantation has the distinct ring of a Christian marriage vow, which also emphasizes ties, joining and not parting, and the union of "two in one flesh."[45] Yet the symbolic weaving of the prospective lovers' hairs through a feather seems more distinctly Andean. Again, it is virtually impossible to comment with certainty about the provenance of the rhetoric and expressions—just how much came from the speaker and how much from the notary's attempt to capture what he heard in a language that he knew. But one can establish that Hernando did not doubt that the huacanqui had taken effect when the two, Marcelo and the widow Catalina, came together soon after. Moreover, when Marcelo's unfortunate wife died, Hernando said that Catalina and Marcelo had married, adding that they lived happily in Quipan to that day.[46]

In San Lorenzo de Quinti, Huarochirí, in 1660, Catalina Chuqui Ticlla (alias Calaguaya) admitted to having attempted to bring about the return of María Poma Ticlla's errant husband some three years before. She described the art she employed, having learned it from a woman named Juana from the Jauja valley. "Two small sticks (*palitos*) from the tiny trees that grow in the irrigated ravines" were carefully tied together with the hairs of both Poma Ticlla and her unfaithful husband. Catalina added that the small construction was then "spoken with . . . in the mother tongue"; she implored the huacanqui that the husband and wife might "live well."[47]

Some specialists employed herbs, flowers, water, and colored earth. The information collected by Juan Sarmiento de Vivero in two trials, the visitas to

---

[44] AAL Leg. 2, exp. 11, fols. 6–6v.

[45] Genesis 2:21–24 and Matthew 19:5–6. The suggestions of religious mixture in incantation and prayers is taken up again in Chapter Eight.

[46] AAL Leg. 2, exp. 11, fol. 6v.

[47] AAL Leg. 4, exp. 32, fols. 12–12v, 13. Antonio Guaman was believed to be living with a concubine. See also an investigation in Ambar, Cajatambo, two years later, AAL Leg. 6, exp. 18, 1662, fols. 2–2v, Ana María at fols. 37–37v, and Juana Mayguay at fols. 22v–23; and from Sayan in Chancay see AAL Leg. 5, exp. 7, 1662, fol. 30.

Ambar in Cajatambo and Sayan in Chancay, both in 1662, provide particularly vivid accounts of regional love ritual in action. The Ambar trial came to focus on the activities of no fewer than seven women: Juana Mayguay, Juana de los Reyes, María Canchan, Ana María, María Juliana, María Julía, and Catalina Yauca Choque. Although some seem to have been involved only as assistants or clients, all were knowledgeable and to some degree active in a flourishing trade in special commodities. The second investigation in Chancay revolved around the renowned figure of María Arriero (alias María Susa Ayala).[48]

In Ambar, the widow Juana Mayguay's speciality was the collection of certain herbs, flowers, and yellow earth, which she distributed to persons throughout the Ambar and Gorgor regions. The herbs and flowers came from a place on the puna called Yopanqui, about three leagues from the town of Ambar. The knowledge appears to have been passed down to her from an elder or maestra. Juana said that she had learned of the virtues of the flowers and herbs of Yopanqui from a local woman, long deceased, named María Capia. The earth called Anaipuyu (otherwise rendered as Anaypujo) was found in a cave near the ancients' settlement of Ayllon.[49] Juana Mayguay had been punished by the Extirpation ten years before for lying about her practices; she had been found guilty of "raising false testimony." Juana said she had been just a girl (*muchacha*) when Lic. Felipe de Medina had visited (1652) and punished her along with "many women." In particular, she recalled how Catalina Yauca Choqui (another whom Sarmiento had once again imprisoned) had been whipped in the church. Despite the ordeals of a decade ago, she confessed that soon after Medina's visita had departed she had returned to her activities. Her collection of the yellow earth, however, was a new addition to her repertoire, she claimed, something she had begun some five years before.[50]

María Juliana had accompanied Juana Mayguay on a number of the collection trips, and it was this accomplice who provided Sarmiento with the most descriptive information about these excursions. Two bunches (handfuls) of plants "with blue flowers" were carefully chosen from the spot at Yopanqui. These, it was said, "would be good for getting men." Then the two women would pass on to the cave at Ayllon "which turned the earth to orange," where two handfuls—"a little more or less"—of soil would also be taken. At first, María Juliana attempted to maintain that the earth was only collected "because it was pretty (*vonita*)," but after successive interrogations she confessed that it had famous alluring properties just like the flowers and herbs: "the earth was good," she said, and was sought "that men would love her." The chief specialist,

[48] AAL Leg. 6, exp. 18, 1662, and AAL Leg. 5, exp. 7, 1662, respectively.

[49] AAL Leg. 6, exp. 18; see especially Juana Mayguay's first testimony at fols. 22–22v. See also the confused letter of denunciation from the interim parish priest and Augustinian friar, Bernabé López de Burgos, to Archbishop Villagómez and the visitador, Sarmiento de Vivero, at fol. 2v. Clearer are the following: the first testimony of María Julía at fols. 19v–20; and the second testimony of Juana Mayguay, the fourth of Ana María, and the second of María Julía, all on folios without numbers, but at fols. 39v–40, 40v, and 41v–42, respectively.

[50] Ibid., folios without numbers but fols. 40–40v in succession.

Juana Mayguay, later testified similarly, saying that the primary reason for their collection of the elements was "to make men greatly desire them."[51]

A common way of securing their advantages involved washing with these ingredients.[52] For example, in reference to the Anaipujo earth, Juana Mayguay said "[in order] to ensure that the men they wanted would be attracted, they would bathe in it." The addition of special water carried from a place near the town of Gorgor was thought to make the bath a particularly potent mixture. According to one witness, María Canchan had generated no fewer than two relationships with married men (one of whom was said to be Don Gaspar Rodríguez Pilco, her own sister's husband) "because she washed with the waters of Gorgor." Catalina Yauca Choque explained that Juana de los Reyes made similar claims for the amorous benefits to be derived from covering oneself with the special flowers. And, in case her investigator was too scandalized, Catalina added that she knew "it was not good to cover oneself with flowers because those are what should adorn the Virgin."[53]

Some similarities present themselves when one shifts focus from Cajatambo to a contemporary's operations in the province of Chancay. It was said to be common knowledge in the parishes of Sayan, Auquimarca, and Ihuari that a woman named María Arriero traveled through the neighboring pueblos carrying three small gourds (*porongillos*). These contained the following commodities: a "white water" from Gorgor known as Iuraciacu; another kind of water that was either not named or not recorded by the notary; and the famous yellow earth, Anaypujo. Although the famed water of Gorgor, Cajatambo, is noted yet again, María Arreiro mentioned a different source for her Anaypujo earth than the cave in the pueblo viejo near Ambar. She made regular visits to an old shepherd's wife in a small settlement near Caujul (in the parish of Andajes) in Cajatambo. The herbs called Tupa Sayre, which in her testimony she often associated with the yellow earth, had yet another Cajatambino provenance near San Antonio de la Lancha in the same parish of Andajes. The waters in her gourds were said to have been produced mostly for female clients who, as Doña Ursula de los Ríos put it, would "wash their private parts (*partes venereas*) so that men might love them."[54] De los Ríos was a Spaniard, a native

[51] AAL Leg. 6, exp. 18; see María Juliana's first, second, and third testimonies at fols. 14v–15 and folios without numbers, but fols. 43 and 44–44v in succession, respectively. María Juliana claimed that these were things which Juana Mayguay had taught her. Mayguay, in her second testimony, also attempted to pass over the virtues of Anaipuyu, saying that the earth from Ayllon was brought "to look at, no more." See a folio without number, but fol. 39v in succession, and f. 22v.

[52] The bathing practices seem to have been widespread. See, for instance, AAL Leg. 6, exp. 9, Cajatambo, 1652, fol. 2; or AAL Leg. 7, exp. 6, Lima, 1668, at fols. 1–1v. On the latter see L. Millones and G. Solari, "Males del cuerpo."

[53] AAL Leg. 6, exp. 18, folio without number, but fol. 45 in succession; Juana de los Reyes at a folio without number, but fol. 55v in succession; and folio without number, but fol. 51 in succession.

[54] AAL Leg. 5, exp. 7; see Doña Ursula de los Ríos at fol. 8; Isabel Nuna Quillay at fol. 15v; and María herself at fol. 21v; see also Juan Chamorro at fol. 11; Isabel Nuna Quillay at fol. 15v, and María Arriero at fol. 21v. In this trial, the earth is often "Anaypuia."

of Seville, who provided information similar to that gained from the primary Andean witnesses, suggesting that María Arriero's arts were appreciated by a more diverse public than most scholars have grown to expect in a rural setting.[55]

Men might also seek a specialist like María Arriero for her expertise, or alternatively, as seen in the case of Hernando Caruachin from Canta, they might practice their own arts. A notorious character named Sebastián Quito was rumored to have treated some four of his previous wives poorly, to the point of even killing one or two. He traveled with María Arriero to obtain the Anaypujo earth in the hopes of winning the heart of a woman who had refused his proposition of marriage because of his ghastly reputation.[56] Yet the dividing line between Sebastián's role as client (which the notary rendered here, and elsewhere, *mingador*) and assistant practitioner becomes blurred. The evidence suggests his own active participation in the ritual practices, and that he was not alone. An even clearer case of a male specialist, as famous in these practices as Caruachin from Canta, is that of Pedro Guamboy from the parish of Sayan in Chancay. According to his kuraka, Guamboy (whom I will discuss further below) operated just like his colleagues: mostly, he "moved among women, giving them herbs so that men might love them."[57] Other male specialists, as I will show, performed rituals with purposes that ranged more widely.

In order to understand better the function and services of the love specialists within the regional communities of the mid-colonial era, it is useful to divide discussion of their most common objectives into a few broad categories: influencing love's genesis in attraction, securing and rekindling love, causing the return of truant love, the maintenance of familial reputation, and love manipulation for the purposes of deception. Inevitably, my categories are imperfect, but they do the specialists' range of ritual functions considerably more justice than most of the contemporary categorizations imported from Europe. The Roman Inquisition at this time, for example, made the simple division of "love magic" into rites that either incited and or discouraged attraction, the *incanti ad amorem* and *superstitiones ad amore impendendo*.[58]

Arousing passionate love and obtaining desirable marriage partners were, of course, subjects of concern among many young people in Andean society. As a

---

[55] The study of intercultural influence in these spheres has been investigated mostly in the urban zones in colonial Peru. See L. Millones and G. Solari, "Males del cuerpo," and also I. Gareis, "Religión popular y etnicidad."

[56] AAL Leg. 5, exp. 7; see María Arriero at fols. 22v–23. The rumors were that this man poisoned his unfortunate wives. In addition, the rancorous testimony of Quito's own father, Sebastián Quito el viejo (who expressed forcefully his overriding preoccupation that his son wished him dead so that he could inherit his chacra), contained an account of his son's alleged beatings of previous wives; See fols. 34v–35.

[57] AAL Leg. 5, exp. 8, 1662, Don Francisco Carlos at fol. 17.

[58] See M. R. O'Neil, "Magical Healing," pp. 98–105.

consequence, a correspondingly high proportion of love ritual seems to have pertained to what one might call the consolidation of initial attractions. Apparently, this could be done for oneself and for others. It was commonly believed in Sayan, Chancay, for example, that María Arriero had "bewitched" a well known local Mulatto named Nicolás de Acosta to make him love her. Similarly, in 1662 the specialist Agustín Carvajal (or Ricapa) of León de Huánuco was said to have performed an unspecified form of love ritual to lure a man away from his mistress, and into the arms of the woman (Agustín's client) who wanted to marry him.[59]

A case from Quinti, Huarochirí, in 1660 involving María Guanico (the same chanca minister and informer discussed in Chapter Three), and another from the province of Canta in 1696 provide valuable information on the exchange between practitioner and client. María Guanico was found to have sought the expert assistance of two regional specialists, the famed María Poma Ticlla of Huarochirí and María Cancho Ticlla of San Pedro de Guancayri, to win the favors of her brother-in-law, a man who was described as "very spirited (*muy bravo*)." First, Poma Ticlla provided María Guanico with a drink containing some unnamed herbs that she had crushed, and some *quinua* (a high-altitude grain) to put in the bed where her brother-in-law slept. In exchange for these things, María Guanico gave the specialist four balls of spun black wool.[60] In a related investigation by the same visitador, María Poma Ticlla denied this interaction. María Guanico said that on a second occasion, the "gran hechicera," María Cancho Ticlla, had told her she would "bewitch (*enhechisaria*)" her brother-in-law into having "a good heart (*buen coraçon*)" and "good desire (*buena gana*)."[61] In 1696, in Canta, Don Juan de Guzmán admitted to having approached a local specialist saying he wished to marry a woman named Lucia. Knowing just what the maestra would require, he had arrived with powder ground from a poco shell which she was said to have used "to commend him" to the sun.[62] When the visitador, Juan de Saavedra y Osorio, asked this specialist, eighty-year-old María Puyron (alias María Quillay), if she knew why she had been denounced, the octogenarian declared astutely to her Spanish Christian interrogator that it did not seem so evil a thing to have sought to bring about a marriage. As mentioned above, the specialists were frequently accused by the visitadores of employing "diabolic arts." This might be why María's pragmatic answers sought to assuage her judge even further; she added that she had

---

[59] AAL Leg. 5, exp. 7, 1662, fol. 4; and AAL Leg. 3, exp. 3, folios without numbers, but fols. 8v–9 in succession. Agustín steadfastly denied the charge and would only admit to having performed healing practices.

[60] AAL Leg. 2, exp. 21; see the combined testimonies of Juana Maca Culqui and María Guanico before Juan Sarmiento de Vivero at fols. 6v and 7v–8.

[61] See AAL Leg. 4, exp. 32, 1660, fol. 11v.

[62] The Jesuit Bernabé Cobo noted the prevalence of this rite when venerating and asking for something of the Andean gods in his *Historia del Nuevo Mundo*, vol. 2, book 13, ch. 35, pp. 228–29.

offered the poco dust "with no more art than believing in her heart that there would be a marriage."[63] It is also possible that María Puyron was at least partly confounded by the accusations against her, genuinely believing that what she was doing, the ends she had in sight, were what an Andean Christian might do.

Some young Indian women in the parishes of the Lima region sought liaisons with Spaniards and Mestizos, an inclination that aroused considerable concern among many Andean elders and parents. When a woman named Quillay came in search of Hernando Caruachin of Quipan, Canta, it had been in the hope that he would "do something [to ensure] that her eldest daughter, Catalina, would not trouble herself with Spaniards." To quiet the restless daughter and "get her to marry," Hernando requested her mother to bring him "a little of her hair, together with the hairs of a fox and a lion [jaguar]." The specialist then advised Quillay to keep the collection of hairs in the house, thus ensuring that "her daughter would be loathed (*aborrecida*) and nobody would want to enter."[64] Similarly, Juana Ycha of Pomacocha in the same province, was prompted to use the powerful means at her disposal to protect her notoriously wayward daughter, Violante. The girl apparently showed little interest in anything except the "*viracochas* (Spaniards, or, more generically, non-Indians)." She was said to have had tumultuous affairs with at least two Mestizos in the region. Juana Ycha actually came to approve of one of these Mestizos as a suitor, until the fickle Violante tired of him and employed her mother's expertise to ease her escape. Violante's less popular second Mestizo, one Francisco Ramírez of Huánuco, had been foolish enough to ask Juana's help in forgetting a past love. Juana claimed that the rogue had said to her: "I am reminded a lot of a woman I once had. You, who know so much, must do something to make me forget her so that I may always be with your daughter."[65]

Women more distant from the eyes of disapproving parents, however, would endeavor to employ love rites to bolster their own intentions with certain men. Leonorilla of Quinti, Huarochirí, for example, seems to have felt insecure in her status as the town notary's "concubine (*amiga*)." María Guanico claimed that Leonorilla frequently enlisted the assistance (*hechizos*) of María Poma Ticlla to keep Don Juan de Avila with her. "And that is why they are so dear to each other," María concluded.[66] Back in the parish of Sayan in Chancay, when Visitador Sarmiento accused María Arriero of the grave sin of sorcery (*hechicería*) in her first appearance before his tribunal, she replied smoothly that she continued her trade in herbs, waters, and earth "because all the young women involved [in relationships] with Spaniards told her that they enjoyed good fortune (*bentura*), and it is no sin to enjoy good fortune."[67] María Arriero appears to have lived what would have seemed a scandalous life from the per-

---

[63] AAL Leg. 5, exp. 26; see María Puyron at fols. 42v–43.

[64] AAL Leg. 2, exp. 11, 1656; Hernando Caruachin at fols. 4–4v.

[65] AAL Leg. 4, exp. 14, 1650, fols. 15 and 13v. Juana Ycha's practices involved much more than love rituals; see Chapter Seven below.

[66] AAL Leg. 2, exp. 21, 1660, fol. 7.

[67] AAL Leg. 5, exp. 7, fol. 22v.

spective of her confessors and the visitador de idolatría. Indeed, her case seemed almost to beg the extirpators to make their already frequent connection between the Indians' religious practices and the inclination toward immorality. This specialist publically cohabited with the Mulatto Nicolás de Acosta, and was said to have had an ongoing affair with a married man. Further, Juana Brígida claimed that María carried on intricate love rituals involving four small decorated pitchers with human faces, which were meant to ensure that "Spaniards would love her and give her money."[68] But, in her own terms and perhaps in those of others around her, María Arriero was also a notorious success. She appears to have made many of her own rules, and to have enjoyed what she herself called "good fortune." And some of her adherents were judged similarly. An Andean woman, Isabel, who was married to a Spaniard named Don Diego in San Juan de Churín in Cajatambo, and who advocated the virtues of bathing in the special waters, was a prominent example of success, a living advertisement, to whom María Arriero seems to have referred with some pride.[69]

However important the rituals were believed to be in the genesis of love, the specialists' variety of substances and rites were thought to produce equally precise effects upon the passions at many stages in a relationship. Love rituals were thought as effective in securing, rekindling, or ending attraction as they were in helping to initiate it. So it was revealed to Juana Brígida when the same renowned María Arriero of Sayan demonstrated her range of plants, saying (and presumably pointing),

> this is to love,
> this is to hate;
> this is to make men go,
> and this is to make them stay.[70]

A typical example from this same region involved a married woman named Catalina who sought to improve an unstable, and perhaps brutal, marital life.[71] In Ambar, Cajatambo, in 1662, Juana Roque was suspected of employing her arts and implements to win quarrels with her husband, a church sacristan named Jerónimo. The husband's covert search of their home for her materials proved successful. He uncovered "a cloth [bundle] in which there were ten stones of diverse colors, the earth that shone brilliantly and another [kind of earth] called Anaypuio, hairs from a man's beard as well as head [which he assumed to be his own], pieces of clothing, llama fat, herbs, and [the bodies of]

---

[68] Ibid., see Ursula de los Ríos at fols. 8–8v; Isabel Nuna Quillay at fol. 16; Cristóbal Guaman at fols. 17v–18, and the said Juana Brígida at fol. 10. It is worth remembering the possibility that, in the interest of shifting attention from their own participation in forbidden activities, some of these witnesses may have exaggerated María's promiscuity.

[69] Ibid., fol. 21v.

[70] Ibid., fol. 10.

[71] Ibid., Sebastián Quito at fol. 30v.

two colorful birds."[72] Another common practice was recommended by Catalina Chuqui Ticlla (alias Calaguaya) from Olleros in Huarochirí to guard against being abandoned. Among other things, she advised the sewing of a huacanqui into the clothing of any husband who was in the habit of going away.[73]

Similarly truant husbands and their often aggressive mistresses provided problems of their own. In Huamantanga, Canta, in 1656, for example, María Ticlla Guacho of the Sigual ayllu told of how she and another widow, Jauja María, had successfully pooled their expertise and caused the kuraka, Don Rodrigo, to abandon the Mestiza with whom he was living and return to his proper life with this declarant's daughter, María Magdalena. The example offers a clear demonstration of the interconnection between the love rituals and huaca worship. For the women made an offering and gave two *reales* to "the God and huaca," and then proceeded to the corral, where a common practice ensued. They blew powders into the air "to the day (*al día*)" (in other places: the sun, or *punchao*), and asked for what they wanted.[74]

Ritual endeavors in which especially active passions might be curbed or extinguished to preserve reputations were also well within the spheres of these specialists. I have already noted a few representative examples of daughters whose amorous exploits with non-Indians worried parents and prompted entreaties to the regional practitioners. But no portrayal of mid-colonial Andean love rituals in the Archdiocese of Lima would be complete without reference to a particular mother and specialist named María Guassa. She was apprehended in her home in 1696 in San Pedro de Guandaro, Canta.

Foreshadowing the more dangerous forms of ritual to be discussed below, her case shows that specialists might also use their spells and collections to ruin relationships. The visitador asked María Guassa to explain the significance of a number of careful groupings of hairs that had been found among her belongings. It turned out that three of the four collections described were from men who had been involved with her daughter, Juana. María had disapproved of these men and sought to dispatch them. Some blonde hairs were those of a man named Don Gonzalo Mazuelos, who was said to have "deceived" Juana and invoked her mother's wrath about two years ago. Another group were those of an Indian named Don Juan de Ugalde Cargua Capcha, who had allegedly lived with Juana and maltreated her about a year before. The third collection of hairs was said to belong to none other than a promiscuous former priest, Pedro Guissado de Contreras, who, María said, had been removed from the parish because of his importunity. The last grouping eluded her memory. Like a shoe repairer whose shop's clutter has long surpassed any hope of control, the specialist María Guassa tried in vain to recall the provenance of the fourth bunch

[72] See AAL Leg. 6, exp. 17, fols. 1–1v.

[73] AAL Leg. 4, exp. 32, San Lorenzo de Quinti, 1660. See María Poma Ticlla at fol. 11v, and Catalina Choqui Ticlla at fol. 13. This particular huacanqui will be recalled from the above discussion.

[74] AAL Leg. 2, exp. 11, fols. 12v–13. See also AAL Leg. 4, exp. 32, Quinti, Huarochirí, 1660, fols. 8–8v and 10v for another similar case.

of hairs, which, she ventured, might have been brought by Gonzalo Bisca's wife. The woman had long been dead, and María could not remember for certain whose hairs they were or for what purpose they had been collected.[75]

The wide and powerful reputations of some of these regional love specialists seems to be confirmed in the final category of common objectives: love ritual for the purpose of deception. On this subject, Visitador Sarmiento de Vivero's 1662 investigation of Pedro Guamboy of San Pedro de Guamboy, in the parish of San Jerónimo de Sayan, Chancay, affords a lively illustration.

It was revealed that two fugitives from justice, a Creole (a Spaniard born in America) known as "the Dancer (el dansarin)" and his Mestizo associate, Marcos, had traveled to highland Chancay in search of Pedro Guamboy's services. Domingo Guaman gave voice to the vague local rumor that the two were outlaws who sought a magical invincibility to evade capture.[76] But Pedro Guamboy described a purpose more compelling and immediate than that. He said that the man called the Dancer had come to him in search of some means to protect himself from detection in a dangerous love affair he was having with a married woman named Doña Catalina Saldana in the coastal town of Huaura. Huaura had a sizeable Spanish population, which was listed as "fifty homes of Spaniards" two years later in 1664. The climb up the Huaura valley to Guamboy—an annex of Sayan consisting of only thirty parishioners at this time—would have been over eighty miles (fifty kilometers).[77] Pedro Guamboy said he had concocted a drink in which he inserted the root of a special plant called "tusi" which would render the Dancer "invisible," and thus immune from detection and any eruption of the cuckold's rage.[78]

The word "invisible" was introduced by the visitador in his own query. However, according to the notary's account, Pedro agreed with its usage when questioned, and also employed it himself in his answers. Tusi was said to have grown wild in the irrigation channels. Pedro confessed that he had learned of its powers ("that the said yerba [plant] was good for turning invisible") long ago from a now-deceased Indian man named Santiago from his ayllu. Although the Dancer had promised to pay the specialist for the potion, Pedro at first claimed that the man had returned to Huaura and that he had never seen him again.[79] The story, however, saw a few changes as the interrogation wore on.

Francisco Morejon Pérez de Idiaguez, a native of Quito (the capital city of what is modern Ecuador) who had acquired his nickname in Lima where he had been taught to dance, also proved to be something of an actor. He pleaded for mercy from Juan Sarmiento "as a fragile and miserable sinner," claiming that it was his lover in Huaura who had told him to seek the Andean hechicero's magic. The Dancer explained that Doña Catalina had encouraged him so that

---

[75] AAL Leg. 5, exp. 25, 1696–1697, Huamantanga and environs. See the testimony and ratification of María Guassa at fols. 11v–12 and 18–18v, respectively.

[76] AAL Leg. 5, exp. 8, fol. 22.

[77] AGI Lima 304, Letter from Villagómez to the king, Lima, 20 November 1664.

[78] AAL Leg. 5, exp. 8, fols. 25v–26.

[79] Ibid., fol. 26.

"her husband would not deprive her of him, nor get cross with her, and that she might have freedom to 'communicate' with him [the Dancer]." Francisco claimed he had paid Pedro Guamboy twelve pesos in advance and had received nothing in return, a story which contradicted the specialist's own version of events, but with which Pedro was quick to agree when Sarmiento interrogated them face to face. Although it is impossible to know for certain, this second version of events seems a transparent ploy by both a cunning creole rake and a quick-witted Andean specialist to extricate themselves from a collusion that would have brought at least the visitador's punishment for the Andean, and perhaps that of the Inquisition for the Creole.[80]

In the case in Chancay, the ploy helped only the errant Creole lover. The dubiously repentant Dancer was ordered to give a peso in alms and do the light penance of a prayer on his knees before the Host. Pedro Guamboy was condemned, for his involvement in love rituals along with a host of other charges, to one of the more rigorous sentences the Extirpation handed down. Pedro was to wear a wooden cross around his neck for the rest of his life, to endure one hundred lashes in public, and to participate in a procession of shame, wearing a *coroza* (pointed headgear worn by a religious offender) and naked to the waist astride a beast, while a crier broadcast his crimes for all to hear; finally he was to be banished for four years to the Casa de Santa Cruz, the sorcerers' prison, in the Cercado of Lima. He was informed that any lapse in his reform would lead to more lashes and assignment to the galleys of Callao in the service of the king.[81]

Unfortunately, it is not so large a step from discussion of rites that govern love, jealousy, and deception to those pertaining to the human propensities toward envy, rivalry, and hate. The latter were also attended to by a type of Andean specialist who had practiced the trade since prehispanic times.[82] Like the practitioners of love rituals, in the mid-colonial era these persons continued to operate within regional networks and usually performed other religious functions. Hernando Caruachin of Quipan in Canta or Hernando Hacas Poma of Acas, Cajatambo, are good examples. Both were noted specialists of rituals related to love, healing, and throwing curses, in addition to their fulfillment of established positions as ministros mayores of the huacas, and *aucaches* or confessors of the people in their ayllus. Their skills and offices were common features in Andean communities throughout the archdiocese, even if certain

[80] Interethnic religious collusions of this kind in the Andes—usually with the Amerindian cast by the documentation as the peripheral and "magical" influence on the European, Creole, and Mestizo elements of society—deserve a discussion all their own, linked to what is now a provocative literature that treats New Spain. See, for example, F. Cervantes, *The Devil in the New World*, and R. Behar, "Sexual Witchcraft," pp. 192–94.

[81] AAL Leg. 5, exp. 8, fols. 29–29v and 58–58v.

[82] See Iris Gareis's discussion, "Brujos y brujas."

regions do appear gradually to have established reputations for particular specializations.[83]

People were said to travel "from diverse parts" for the assistance of the experts who lived in the environs of late seventeenth-century Huamantanga in Canta.[84] The most notorious among those whom they sought there were two men, Francisco Guaman and Domingo Cacha, who were widely known by their popular names Ismay Matanga and Coillon, respectively. They practiced the two related arts to be discussed below, namely, the casting of spells or curses (*maleficios*) as well as their removal or cure. But the two specialists were hardly alone. Numerous confessions revealed a substantial list of such officials throughout this region, and an even greater number of people who sought their services. The principal names derive from three testimonies.

According to the accused Francisco Guaman, others apart from Domingo Capcha who were adepts in the same faculties as himself included: Magdalena Suyo of Rauma, María Du . . . yno (record unclear) of the *ingenio* (sugar plantation and mill) at Chicheguasi, Ysabel Yacine of San Luis de Chaupis, Atoc Guaman of Pallac, a woman from Raran whose name he forgot, the wife of a man named Toribio in Sumbirca, María Candelaria's mother in Guandaro, and the wife of the elder, Mendoza, from Pariac. After he was tortured to persuade him to reveal the names of others like him, eighty-year-old Domingo Capcha of the Asiento de Cocha Cocha confirmed a number of these same officials. María Pascuala added María Pilco Suyo of San Miguel, María Quillay (alias Puyroa) and Maray (or María) Guassa from Guandaro,[85] María Verona and two other women of the Sigual ayllu in Huamantanga, Juan Baptista Rata of Marco, a woman called Peca María in Raran, and Andrés Guaman of Sumbirca. María Pascuala's memory was keener, or her fear and desire for leniency greater, than either Francisco Guaman's or Domingo Capcha's, and she noted that the "mother" from Guandaro was named Magdalena, that the "woman from Raran" was Doña María, and that the said "Mendoza's wife" was named María. Some of these denounced persons, seeking to deflect attention from themselves, in turn revealed even more *mingadores*, those who came in search of their ritual knowledge and services.[86]

[83] See AAL Leg. 2, exp. 11, and K. R. Mills, *An Evil Lost to View?*, esp. ch. 3. The anthropologist Joseph Bastien has described a situation of regional expertise in divination among the Aymara-speaking Kaatans of modern, mid-western Bolivia, to the northeast of Lake Titicaca; *Mountain of the Condor*.

[84] AAL Leg. 5, exp. 25, 1696–1697. See, for example, Cristóbal Francisco's testimony at fols. 3–3v, and that of Magdalena Suyo at fol. 4v. Ysabel Aco of Rauma testified at fol. 4 that people came "not only from this province, but from the neighboring provinces" as well. María Llano at fol. 18 specified that people came in groups of "sometimes two and three together" from places "like Checras and Chancay."

[85] The same María Guassa discussed above.

[86] AAL Leg. 5, exp. 25, Francisco Guaman at fols. 6–6v; Domingo Capcha at fols. 7–7v; and María Pascuala at fols. 9–10; María Petrona at fols. 10v–11; María Guassa at fols. 12–12v; María Pilco Suyo at fol. 13v; and Juan Baptista at fols. 14v–15.

The presentation and corroboration of so elaborate a regional network of specialists in curses affected the language and perhaps even the views of the idolatry inspector Juan de Saavedra y Osorio and his notary. As if in deference to their sheer numbers and established positions within regional society, Saavedra y Osorio began to refer to these offenders not by the standard term, "hechiceros," but as "curse doctors (*doctores de maleficios*)."[87] The concession to their significance may not have been much, but it hints at a grudging awareness of these officials' importance and their undeniable place in regional religious life.

In spite of such evidence, one's view of these individuals and their networks becomes consistently obscured. The chief difficulty in representing the specialists as integral parts of the regional religious systems stems largely from the now familiar Spanish Christian inclination toward placing these people on some loathed and fearsome periphery. Spanish jurists, Hispanicized Indian chroniclers, and extirpators of idolatry found in the Andes, as they had found in Mexico and in many other places, evidence that could be made to fit their own preoccupations.[88] Because of their association with disabling deeds and even deaths, these particular specialists and the many others who were often lumped in with them were seen much as witches and wizards were seen in contemporary Europe, as unidimensional traffickers in evil. Just as many ritual practices, which to many mid-colonial European observers and Hispanicized Andeans smacked of superstitious magic, were seen as separate from (or degraded remnants of) the Indians' false religion, the curse specialists of the Andean past and present were intellectually reconstituted as dreaded brujos and hechiceros. Similar fates, of course, befell contemporary European "cunning folk" who were often accused of sorcery and witchcraft in light of their perceived capacity to harm as well as heal.[89]

Spanish commentators were quick to pick up on suggestions that the Inkas had not only recognized but occasionally punished evil sorcerers and witches who were thought to kill people with their arts and powers. Before the time of the Third Provincial Council of Lima (1582–1583), Polo de Ondegardo had in fact written that many kinds of sorcerers who were like witches (*como brujos*) had been permitted by the Inkas. But far more than the "sorceries permitted by their laws," what certain seventeenth-century readers of Polo's detailed information noticed was his claim about the Inkas' attitude toward the Andean practitioners who killed with poison and other arts. According to Polo, the Inkas arrested and killed these specialists, visiting capital punishment even on their descendants.[90] The Hispanicized Mestizo El Inca Garcilaso de la Vega,

[87] See, for example, the notary's rendering of his first question to Juan Baptista of Marco at AAL Leg. 5, exp. 25, fol. 14.

[88] See J. de Solórzano Pereira, *Libro primero*, vol. 1, tit. 4, law 7, pp. 130–37; and F. Guaman Poma, *El primer nueva corónica*, 1: 247.

[89] P. Burke, *Popular Culture*, pp. 107–8.

[90] "Los errores y supersticiones de los indios," ch. 10, p. 470. Polo was explicit about why he thought the Andean specialists to be like witches. They could fly through the air over great dis-

for his part, made no secret of his disgust at what he presented as the pre-Inkaic Andeans' use of poisons, curses, and spells. For Garcilaso, these practitioners and their techniques compared poorly with the enlightened "medicinal" techniques that were supposedly instituted throughout the Andes by the conquering Inka.[91] In this, of course, the Inkaic lords of Cusco might resemble many other states and societies who expressed their divinely sanctioned authority by persecuting their witches within, the supposed enemies of God and man.[92] Thus when, in the early seventeenth century, Pablo José de Arriaga examined the various practitioners in the regions of the Archdiocese of Lima, he drew on a tradition of interpretation that had already been honed in Peru as well as in other contexts, and he saw the curse specialists, in particular, through eyes that sought parallels that would help to explain. Arriaga interpreted the Quechua *queta runamicu* as a "killing witch" or "man eater," and in his reports from 1617 to his Jesuit provincial in Lima, he elaborated on Andean practices that to him recalled malevolent witchcraft and even the witches' sabbat.[93]

In the seventeenth and early eighteenth centuries, both Andeans and Spaniards partook of cultural systems that sought to explain the existence of evil and, more importantly, to understand the human capacity to do evil. People drawing from either the Spanish Christian or Andean tradition—and increasingly from a mixture of both traditions—believed that certain individuals managed, through an ability to harness unseen powers, to achieve various aims. As is well known from an abundant literature on the western European sixteenth and seventeenth centuries, and a fast-increasing one on Mexico, such beliefs and practices—whether they were attributed to superstitious imaginings or diabolic intervention—were thought worthy of energetic persecution in the interests of religious purity and public safety.[94] At certain times in the late prehis-

---

tances, they could divine what happened in "remote places," and they could speak with the Devil, "who would respond to them in stones and other things" (ibid). In her "Brujos y brujas," pp. 586–91, Iris Gareis discusses some of Polo's influences drawn from the European tradition of witch-beliefs and stereotypes from the *Malleus maleficarum* (c. 1486, with twenty-eight editions between 1486 and 1600) of Johann Sprenger and Heinrich Kraemer through to the most famous Spanish treatises on these and wider subjects by Pedro Ciruelo, *Reprovacion de las supersticiones y hechicerías* [1530], and Martin de Castañega, *Tratado de las supersticiones y hechicerías* [1529].

[91] *Royal Commentaries*, book 1, ch. 14, pp. 39–40, and book 2, chs. 24 and 25.

[92] I am indebted to Stuart Clark's formulations in *Thinking with Demons*, Part 5, "Politics." Further afield, the widespread "witchcraft eradication" movements in nineteenth-century Africa offer a fascinating parallel that points to the universality of cultural attempts to deal with evil as it is perceived; see T. O. Ranger, "The Problem of Evil in Eastern Africa," and C. Brantley, "An Historical Perspective."

[93] See *La extirpación*, pp. 38–40, and ARSI, Carta anua de 1617, *Peru* 14, vol. 3, fols. 55–55v. For discussion of the famous, roughly contemporaneous, trials of witches from the Spanish villages of Zugarramurdi and Urdax (on the north side of the Pyrenees) by the Inquisition at Logroño in 1610 see esp. G. Henningsen, *The Witches' Advocate*, ch. 2.

[94] For Spain, see especially S. Cirac Estopañán, *Los procesos de hechicerías*. One need not doubt that peninsular beliefs in such things were frequently applied in the New World, and not just within the Indians' realms. A letter from Cusco, dated 4 July 1571, tells of the imprisonment and subsequent proceedings against one P. Juan de Luna, allegedly a relative of the current viceroy of

panic period, the Inkas may well have grown similarly concerned with individuals they perceived as malevolent among their constituent peoples.

But far beneath the homogenizing and purifying apparatus of state systems and their orthodoxies, the perpetual uncertainties of agricultural and pastoral life remained inseparable from the natural tensions that brewed between persons. Exceptional illnesses, misfortune, deaths, and calamities demanded both explanations and protection. In the regional Andean zones, certain individuals' reputations for perpetrating or remedying evil were believed in. Such specialized knowledge was respected, trusted, and even revered as much as it was feared.

This Andean respect for the curse specialist is richly documented in the mid-colonial period. Some people could turn their herbal knowledge to potent use and became experts in the concoction of poisons and venoms.[95] More generally, people throughout the Archdiocese of Lima regularly looked to curses as causes of everything from agricultural failure to personal misfortune to political difficulties. At least two characteristics emerge clearly. The first is the essential role that the curses played in people's explanations for the problems and challenges they faced. Similar to, and often related to, breaches in the relationships with Andean gods, curses were recognized as meaningful causes of misfortune and obstacles. Thus in Yautan in the province of Huaylas in 1646–1647, for example, the kuraka Francisco Mallqui Guaman and his wife Elvira Yauca were accused of contaminating and cursing the irrigation canals and chacras of Andrés Díaz Calderon. Similarly, the visita to Sayan, Chancay, in 1662 learned of a man named Santiago of Guanangi who was believed to have caused an infestation of worms in Pedro Capcha's plot of land in envy of the bountiful chacra.[96] Curses in revenge and those that were meant to incapacitate political rivals (particularly in disputes over *kurakazgos*, the offices of kurakas) were common. There are as many aspirant officials who end up in the specialists' homes seeking means to assist their rise as there are authority holders trying to explain or prevent their own demise. In Huamantanga, Canta, in 1696—to suggest only one typical example—Don Juan de Campos believed that the curses solicited by the kuraka Don Miguel Menacho were affecting his entire family's health,

---

Peru, who was said to have undertaken to curse the king's representative; AGI Lima 314, "Informe contra el P. Luna." On the applications to Andeans see S. MacCormack, *Religion in the Andes*, ch. 2, 1 and ch. 5, 2. On Indian specialists in New Spain receiving similar treatment to that of our Peruvian examples, see R. Behar, "Visions of a Guachichil Witch," pp. 123–25; S. Gruzinski, *Man-Gods in the Mexican Highlands*; and F. Cervantes, *The Devil in the New World*, chs. 1 and 2.

[95] For cases involving alleged poisonings, see information pertaining to Sebastian Quito in AAL Leg. 5, exp. 7, Sayan, Chancay, 1662; the accused camachico in Leg. 6, exp. 23, San Pedro de Acas, Cajatambo, 1665; and the kuraka in Leg. 6, exp. 24, Ocros, Cajatambo, 1665–1669. Jesuit missionaries from the colleges of San Pablo in Lima and that of Huamanga reported attempted poisonings, as well. See ARSI, Carta anua de 1638, *Peru* 15, vol. 4, fol. 155 and Carta anua de 1646, *Peru* 15, vol. 4, fol. 194.

[96] See AAL Leg. 4, exp. 11, folios without numbers, but fols. 2v–3 in succession; and AAL Leg. 5, exp. 7, fols. 31v–32v.

and thwarting his legitimate bid for the governorship of the *repartimiento* (regional administrative district).[97]

The second characteristic is the level of regard for the specialists' powers. When seemingly wanton threats emanated from certain persons—even if they were made in fits of rage—these threats were taken seriously. And if some wrong had been done to a neighbor or kinsman or woman, it surprised no one if some malady or misfortune befell the guilty party. I hesitate to refer to local or regional systems of divine and human justice because of the formality that seems to imply. Yet there can be little doubt that men and women called on gods and their powers to use against other men and women. The wording in the documentation consistently relegates this system of communal inspection, and divine arbitration and enforcement, to imported categories of the irrational or purely evil. It was a system with flaws and contradictions but also knowledge and tradition, and the ability to change.

María Poma Ticlla of Huarochirí was one of the respected persons about whom tales were told in the communities of her region. A few of these were recounted to the idolatry inspectors and judges. Juana Maca Culqui, for instance, told of how her own father had suddenly fallen dead on the road outside of town immediately after a bitter dispute with Poma Ticlla over the inheritance of a cloak.[98] Some thirty years later, Teresa Aguado of Santa Fe de Jauja was said to have threatened Juan de Rojas, whose statements and seizure of her "bundle" of religious objects had brought about her imprisonment by the Extirpation. Less than three weeks after her release, Juan was said to have fallen gravely ill and died. Just as mysteriously, his mother, Jacinta Curi Chumbi, who had visited Teresa to accuse her of causing his death, became crippled.[99]

Similarly, in 1662 in Sayan, Chancay, Pedro Guamboy (mentioned above in connection with love specialism) described an elaborate ritual that he used to kill Lorenzo Ruiz (or Clavito) and his father, Lorenzo Muños, in response to the evil the former was said to have done him. Lorenzo Ruiz had apparently humiliated Pedro one day in a violent pushing match. It was the healer, María Ynes, who was said to have diagnosed the illness that presently incapacitated Lorenzo (severely swollen legs which she lanced and to which she applied herbs) as Guamboy's curse. Under threat of torture, Pedro Guamboy admitted

---

[97] AAL Leg. 2, exp. 33, esp. fols. 36–37v. See also AAL Leg. 3, exp. 15, Santiago de Carampoma, Huarochirí, 1730–1732, fols. 2–2v and 4–4v.

[98] They were both of the Quiripa ayllu. The two had laid claim to Juana's grandfather's cloak, and Juana's father had taken it because "he was a man." According to Juana, "everyone said" that María had killed him "with hechizos" because of his greed. AAL Leg. 4, exp. 32, San Lorenzo de Quinti, 1660, fol. 8v.

[99] See AAL Leg. 7, exp. 6, 1689–1691; the testimonies of Joseph Ambrosio at fols. 3v–4 and Juana María at fols. 4v–5v. In Quinti, Huarochirí, María Chumbi Ticlla was accused of "crying to the ancients" (in songs) and indulging in similar deadly rites against her enemies; see AAL Leg. 2, exp. 22, Juan Bautista at fols. 2–2v. In yet another case investigated in Ambar, Cajatambo, in 1662, among her other religious crimes, Francisca Leonor was said to have killed "many people" (one witness said four) with poison and sorcery; see AAL Leg. 6, exp. 19; the testimonies of Pedro Santiago at fol. 4, Juan Villar at fols. 2–3, and Sarmiento de Vivero's judgment at fols. 8–8v.

to reneging on an agreement to lift the curse from Lorenzo Muñoz's son. Pedro said that just as his father had taught, he collected a piece from a new pot, in which he made a candle of llama fat. Then he scattered the earth from a footprint left by Ruiz over the fat, and lit the candle. Finally, with another piece of new pot, he extinguished the flame. The specialist said that a month after the son's death he had begun another ritual session to kill Lorenzo Muñoz, the father, employing the words: "that one will die."[100]

One form that Andean curse ritual could take, the insertion of pins or bristles into wax or clay renderings of targetted persons, was sufficiently reminiscent of the image magic commonly associated with contemporary European witches that extirpators and other churchmen could place it within their existing mental categories with even fewer scruples than usual.[101] Yet the Andean cursing through *bultos* (figures or forms) or small collections of *hechizos* (often tied bundles of hairs and other objects with sacred and powerful properties) that appears in our evidence from the Archdiocese of Lima was, in reality, pursued differently. The basic difference was that the maker or specialist did not retain possession of the bulto, but instead planted it in or near the dwelling place of the person to be affected. In Lunahuana, Cañete, in 1661, for example, one learns from Alonso de Casas's testimony of how Magdalena Callao (alias Condoriana) was severely punished for, among other things, having placing two small figures of a man and woman smeared in excrement beneath her kuraka's bed. Through a procedure that was related to the love rituals I have described above, Don Diego Jacobo was meant to come to detest the concubine with whom all the pueblo knew him to be living. There is no evidence in this case to suggest that Condoriana carried a particular grudge against Don Diego for any other reason. His moral misconduct, perhaps a reflection of wider abuse of his kurakazgo, seems to have met with local condemnation and action from an eminent specialist. For her offence, the interim priest Melchor de Leyba, together with Don Diego, had taken Magdalena to the home of another, Don Alonso Guaytara, and "hung her from a board in the ceiling and whipped her," before shaving off all her hair.[102] The ordeal was obviously meant to cause Magdalena, and other specialists who would see her and hear of her example, to think again before they took the reform of the local political élite upon themselves. Yet I cannot help but wonder whether the churchmen and their supporters had not interrupted a regional Andean means of monitoring conduct. Other examples reveal the ubiquity of such specialists, and attest to the widespread belief in their abilities to affect outcomes. The information is fre-

---

[100] AAL Leg. 5, exp. 8, 1662, Luisa Díaz at fol. 8v and Pedro Guamboy at fols. 11v–12v.

[101] See, for instance, K. V. Thomas, *Religion and the Decline of Magic*, p. 612. The bishop of Quito, Peña Montenegro, made the direct connection in describing a case from his region in which espinas (thorns or bristles) were said to have been removed from "a wax statue" before the victim would return to health. See *Itinerario*, trat. 5, sess. 4, fol. 195. R. Behar notes beliefs in image magic in a fascinating case from early eighteenth-century Mexico in "Sexual Witchcraft," pp. 194–99.

[102] AAL Leg. 7, exp. 1, Alonso de Casas at fols. 12v–13. Condoriana was also accused of many other curses, discussed throughout these proceedings.

quent, brief, and focused. In 1660, for example, in San Pedro de Pilas in Yauyos, a healer removed a tied bundle of "ashes and crushed maize" from a corner in the home where a man named Juan Ramos was said to have been suffering.[103]

What we learn of Pedro Vilca Guaman's activities in Huarochirí in 1700 provides the best illustration of all. Here, it was said that within four days of having revealed some suspicious objects to the local priest, Juan Ylario had fallen seriously ill with two peculiar maladies. After much bartering over his price to cure the illnesses, the specialist Vilca Guaman proceeded to remove two objects, a dried toad (*sapo*) with bits of glass around its neck and wrapped in baize, and a stone adorned with silver and gold from where they were concealed in the ceiling (presumably thatched) of the victim's home. He ascended a ladder twice to get the objects down from two distinct places, one for each illness. Juan Ylario explained that the sapo's glass was crucial and was what "caused this declarant [him] to begin to die." When he asked Pedro Vilca Guaman why the pieces of glass were needed, the specialist was said to have made the apparently metaphoric connection to the evils of drink. To consume a lot of *aguardiente* (a particularly strong liquor, perhaps from a glass bottle) did one evil as well.[104] Pedro Vilca Guaman's reputation for afflicting certain people in this way was well established. At the time when the visita passed through, an alcalde said he knew for certain that the pains in his body, from which he suffered "much more at night than during the day," were the result of the vengeful Pedro Vilca Guaman. He recalled with horror the threat Pedro was said to have spoken: "Look Don Marcelo, you are against me and have advised the Señor Vicar [of my practices]. You watch, because the day will come, before I close my eyes to die, when I will have my revenge."[105] One learns little else about the alcalde Don Marcelo and his possible relationship to Vilca Guaman and perhaps other practitioners of Andean religion in the town. Was Marcelo protecting himself by pretending a previous zeal in informing the priest about Pedro's activities, which had angered the specialist? Does the brief mention in Marcelo's testimony of a tension between the two local men over the alleged denunciation uncover a factionalism that was common in mid-colonial Andean parishes?

If the evidence from the above case does not answer such questions with any certainty, the descriptions of persons believed to have been afflicted by curses provide insight into the Andean view of the infirmities the curses were thought to cause. The examples from diverse parts of the mid-colonial Archdiocese of Lima bear a marked similarity to an Andean rendering of illness that can be gleaned from the account of a prehispanic incident in the Huarochirí manuscript. When Huatya Curi, the son of the huaca Paria Caca, addressed the

---

[103] AAL Leg. 4, exp. 29, San Jerónimo de Omas, Yauyos, 1660. See Ynes Tarpo at a folio without a number but fol. 2v in succession.

[104] AAL Leg. 1, exp. 13, Santa María de Jesús de Huarochirí, 1700. This case, in particular, deserves much closer attention. See fols. 1–2v and 5–5v; 3v–4; and 6.

[105] Ibid., fol. 6.

illness of the rich man, Tamta Ñamca, he began thus: "*camta micucri*, 'as for what's eating you'. . . ."[106] The eventual remedy, the removal of two snakes and a toad from the sick man's dwelling, confirms the appropriateness of my comparison with a host of mid-colonial instances.

In 1661, Alonso de Casas of Lunahuana in Cañete described his son's ailment as a "strange illness (*enfermedad singular*)" characterized by the nearly complete inability to pass food and water down his throat. It had been "consuming him" for over a year and a half, to the point at which his suffering was such that "he wished to die." What is more, Juan Aylli, Diego Allaucan Poma Canchi, Francisco Allaucan, and Juan Sánchez were all said to have suffered from an affliction that killed "little by little." Juan Tinton declared, for example, that he had seen "Juan Aylli sick for a long time with a dry throat (*tener seca la garganta*), and that he got thinner and thinner until he died." All of the afflicted persons in Lunahuana had maltreated or otherwise wronged a local specialist's daughters.[107] In 1700, the former alcalde of Huarochirí, Don Marcelo Macuy Chauca (the man who claimed to have been cursed by Pedro Vilca Guaman above), expressed his dread of a similar insidiousness in the malady commonly associated with curses, saying, "we can just waste away and not know the evil from which we are suffering."[108] Infectious growths also seem automatically to have been blamed on curses.[109] A Spaniard named Joseph de Ayala, who kept an inn (*tambo*) at the town of La Rinconada near Lima, told an investigation in 1695 of how frustrated Indian healers in the pueblo and the capital had convinced him that his wife's strange illness was the result of "diabolic curses." According to his horrifying description, "three worms, with the hair of a pig and wool" had grown from her nostrils. Ayala had tried Spanish doctors and medicines in the beginning, but to no avail. According to Juana López de la Cueba, the woman's "nostrils had descended and pig's hairs, the scales of fish, and other filthy things had grown from them." The same witness believed that a Mestiza named Agustina, who envied the couple their prosperous tambo, worked with a well known specialist named María Antonia, to effect the curse.[110]

Such sensational stories of curse hurlers inevitably stuck in people's memories, and some even entered regional oral traditions. These episodes had a shock value for their audiences, and were also packed full of the sort of damning

---

[106] *Huarochirí*, ch. 5, secs. 50–51. I am indebted to Frank Salomon's careful pondering on the Quechua phrase in note 115.

[107] AAL Leg. 7, exp. 1, 1661, fols. 11v–12. See Alonso de Casas at fols. 12–12v, Isabel de Atabalos at fol. 20, and Juan Tinton at fols. 21v–22.

[108] AAL Leg. 1, exp. 13, fol. 6.

[109] In note 115 on p. 57 of *Huarochirí*, Salomon suggests the connection of the "what's eating you" incident with leishmaniasis, "an infectious disease often pictured in Mochica [coastal culture, precursors to the Chimu, in the Trujillo area] ceramics, which eats away at the soft tissues of the nose and lip."

[110] AAL Leg. 7, exp. 21, 1695, folios without number, but fols. 2–2v in succession, and Juana López de la Cueba at fols. 6–6v.

evidence that most interested many visitadores de idolatría. Time and again these specialists, thinly disguised in the documentation by the labels of sorcerer, charlatan, or witch, became the center of attention. Amidst all of the evidence is the Andean view of these persons. For the curse hurlers in the Andes were clearly more than what they seemed to the extirpating mind, more than a simple scourge on society, and more than the convenient vehicles of personal vengeance. These specialists were part of the religious network to which people turned, both regularly and in times of particular trouble. This turning only rarely involved a move away from the people whom many Andeans still recognized as religious officials in their communities, for many mid-colonial curse specialists were also ministers and healers who involved huacas and malquis in their ritual actions. The specialists' perceived capacity for unleashing wraths and maladies was balanced by their often proven ability to rein in the very evil that they, and others like them, might set in motion. They controlled forces in the world that ordinary people could not hope to harness without them.

However much they might channel evil for their purposes or the purposes of their clients, the existence of evil was not believed to be the curse specialists' fault. Evil was a floating, omnipresent force in the Andean world, more ambiguous than constant.[111] Most of the manifestations of evil in the Andean world, especially disease and drought, were intimately associated with a community's religious neglect and the subsequent displeasure of the ancestors and huacas. Evil, in the form of misfortune and threats to well-being, was believed not to descend on people, villages, and entire regions without reason.

Three witnesses in Acas, Cajatambo, in 1657, for instance, spoke of offerings they made that winds would stop carrying sicknesses to the village. The depopulation of their relatives' lands, which had seen entire ayllus wiped out and others on the verge of disappearance, caused distress and demanded explanation and remedy. According to many of the accounts collected in Acas by Bernardo de Novoa in 1656–1657, the Yunga people of nearby Cochillos were wasting away. According to Pedro Poma Guras, the highlanders had raised what amounted to a religious relief effort that had continued for some "ten or twelve years that he could remember." Hernando Chaupis Condor of the Yanaqui and Alonso Chaupis the Blind of the Quirca ayllu had organized the people of Acas to descend annually to Cochillos with a llama and many cuyes. There, the two ministers and specialists would assist the depleted population of the village. Closer to Acas itself, similar situations threatened as villagers noted how chacras lay uncultivated and irrigation channels had become obstructed by debris.[112] In a mental frame in which spells, maledictions, and divine displeasure represented the coherent explanations for adver-

---

[111] See the discussion of the Andean concept of Supay in Chapter Seven below.

[112] In P. Duviols, ed. *Cultura andina*. On the winds, see Juan Raura at p. 193, Ynes Julca Colque at p. 182, and Pedro Guaman Vilca at p. 228. On Cochillos, see Hernando Chaupis Condor at p. 162, Pedro Guaman Vilca at p. 228, Francisco Poma y Altas at p. 188, Alonso Quispi Guaman at p. 199, Hernando Poma Quillai at p. 207, Pedro Sarmiento at p. 211, and Juan Chaupis at p. 240. The quotation from Pedro Poma Guras is at p. 237.

sity and affliction, specialists in their capacity as "curse doctors" were absolutely essential.

The evidence suggests that they were widely understood and employed as such by Andeans, and that any blame they were apportioned in sensational cases was offset by the larger solutions—both explanatory and practical—they provided. The Spanish Christian pigeonhole for evil proved too narrow to contain the adepts' range of expertise and functions. The examples are legion but the point is sufficiently clear if one confines investigation, for the moment, to the frequent coexistence of curse and remedy.

María Pilco Suyo from Punacoto in Canta was said to use the same substances for her curse rituals and her healing, and the specialist known as Ismay Matanga (Francisco Guaman) of Rauma in the same province acquired renown for removing curses as well as making them. "In both faculties," Ysabel Aco said of the latter, "he is skilful (*diestro*)." The trial of Ismay Matanga demonstrates the power of a few of these specialists to push their idolatry inspectors to put the practitioners' skills to the test: the visitador's demand that the Andean specialist remove his disabling curse from a dying man in the presence of the ecclesiastical retinue made for a fascinating scene. The victim, Cristóbal Francisco, had, however, already been pronounced incurable by Ismay Matanga. An entire night's efforts to revive him failed.[113]

Even Pedro Vilca Guaman of Huarochirí who, if one believes half of what the townspeople claimed, was responsible for a string of specialist killings was also reputed to "travel about healing those he has cursed."[114] Pedro's exaction of sums of money for his cures offers a profit-oriented twist that reminds one of the specialists' changed context. When payments to practitioners are mentioned in other cases they tend to be in kind (and often in materials needed for offerings or countercurses), or in the form of a spoken promise that the victim would utter as proof that he or she has appreciated the power of the specialist. In Huarmey in 1650, it was widely believed that the famous Santiago Tañedor (alias Michan) was responsible for the serious illness that had befallen the region's kuraka "two or three years ago," after he had whipped Santiago in the plaza for previous ritual endeavors. Only this Hispanicized kuraka's double threat to the specialist's security—that he would denounce Santiago to Visitador Felipe de Medina who was nearby, and that he would send "his two Mulattos" to visit him with knives—persuaded Santiago to bring about the governor's miraculous recovery.[115]

The many stories of successful curses and cures were, of course, useful to the specialists. As the testimonies prove so vividly, the tales entered the popular

---

[113] On María Pilco Suyo, see AAL Leg. 5, exp. 26, 1696, fol. 35v; on Ismay Matanga, see AAL Leg. 5, exp. 25, 1696–1697, fols. 4 and 8–8v.

[114] AAL Leg. 1, exp. 13, 1700;. see Don Marcelo Macuy Chauca at fols. 6v–7, Ana María at fol. 10v, María Teresa Puma Chumbi at fol. 11v, and María Macuy Sacsa at fols. 18v–19.

[115] AAL Leg. 5, exp. 1. See Don Francisco Guaman at fols. 2v–3v, and Rodrigo Guañez at fol. 4v. I have written about an even more graphic case involving similar pressures in mid-seventeenth-century Acas, Cajatambo, in *An Evil Lost to View?*, pp. 93–95.

imagination, enhancing the reputations of the greatest practitioners and strengthening the people's belief in them. But one must not get carried away with the portrayal of the success rate in these endeavors. The curse healings, in particular, seem to have occasioned some famous failures that only fueled the arguments of colonial Andeans who, encouraged by the pastoral drummings of their priests and the extirpators, were looking more skeptically at aspects of the Andean religious system. In events that transpired in late seventeenth-century Rauma in Canta, for example, three elaborate attempts to cure Juan Cristóbal of a "deadly curse," two of which were conducted by María Pilco Suyo—the specialist who had been employed to curse him in the first place—failed.[116] As in the case of Ismay Matanga noted above, such an apparent failure was easily seized upon by the extirpating preacher as evidence of the impotence of the specialists and the futility of Andean beliefs and practices. But how were such deaths and failures explained by Andeans? Specialists like María Pilco Suyo had an equally easy time in explanation. They almost invariably blamed the failure of a cure or curse on divine displeasure caused by the religious negligence of their clients—though a few claimed they had not been consulted in time. In the mid-colonial years, with so much pressure on Andean religion and its practitioners, their principal reason for failure would have rung true.

Bernabé Cobo explained in his *Historia del Nuevo Mundo* how Andean hechiceros had learned of the particular virtues of plants, and how they could employ diverse materials in their "sorceries" to achieve different and precise effects. Even the specialization that did evil and killed, he observed, had its complement that restored health and life. For this reason, in this society, Cobo earnestly stated, specialization, like the religion of which it was a part, "was held to be necessary."[117] Yet the careful Padre Cobo could not hide his skepticism and distaste for some of the practices he described. Like his seventeenth-century European contemporaries, he had his own crowded explanatory framework that he employed to make sense of an alien religion and tradition. His experience in America bashed at this frame and, as I have tried to show in Cobo's case, it sometimes managed to establish a foothold in his writing. But, when pushed too far by what he saw of, and heard about, Andean religion, Cobo took a common intellectual escape route, attributing most of the evil in the Indians' arts to the Devil. Even so, it is something of a tribute to a Spanish Jesuit writing in the middle of the seventeenth century that, however much he doubted and disapproved, he rarely seems to have stopped granting at least a measure of legitimacy to colonial Andean ways of seeing or to have stopped thinking about the practices as the Indians' established customs—however false.

But Cobo was no extirpator. Moreover, as a member of an order which, at

---

[116] See AAL Leg. 5, exp. 25, María Pilco Suyo at fols. 13–13v and 15; and in related proceedings, AAL Leg. 5, exp. 26, 1696, Juan Cristóbal at fols. 35–35v.

[117] Vol. 2, book 13, ch. 35, p. 228.

the time of his publication, was involved in a quiet feud with Pedro de Villagómez over official Jesuit participation in the Extirpation among other things, he could hardly be said to have had the ear of the archbishop who vowed for nearly three decades to destroy the allegedly sorry vestiges of Andean religion.

The skills, the lore, knowledge, and rituals which, for Andean societies, were vital parts of the revered specializations increasingly became superstition and error under the scrutiny of churchmen in the extirpating era. The specialists' survival and continued roles in regional religious networks, the protocol of their consultations, their enormous, comparable repertoires of rituals and observances, the sheer number of people who sought their wisdom and services, were consistently overlooked and explained away. Like the practitioners of "popular technique" in contemporary Europe, the Andean adepts were categorized as the debased and sometimes laughable rivals of the parish priests.[118] These specialists were fitted into already bursting categories of depraved and deviant traffickers, those who were thought to have overstepped the ordained limits of human conduct and set the protective powers of civilized society against them.

As a well-educated Hispanic of the early modern era, the mid-colonial extirpator could envisage a witch, or the equivalent of his own society's wise-yet-wicked Celestina figure, eking out a living on the fringe of local life. He could envisage that old hag, that instrument of evil, in the Andes or anywhere else. Yet Amerindian specialists who behaved like doctors, who often communicated with the gods, and who remained so vitally involved in the forbidden and clandestine religious affairs of their communities and regions, presented a problem. Too many specialists were serving too many Indians for their practices to be peripheral or insignificant, superstitious remnants. Moreover, in most of the cases I have read, their traditional inheritance, their organization, their careful rites, were by no stretch of the imagination the stuff of confused or desperate charlatans. The existence of a few deceptive fakes does not invalidate the rest, who assuaged anxiety and helped people to make sense of a complex world. The real and undeniable proximity of what were called "formal idolatry" and "superstition," the two things which the extirpating rhetoric had so expediently separated, became distinctly uncomfortable, even for active extirpators.

The note of dismay in the penned words of a Catholic priest's assistant (*teniente de cura*), Don Antonio Cáceres, as he summarized two lengthy investigations in the Mercedarian parish of Caujo in 1650 was not atypical. A number of Andeans had been imprisoned, interrogated, whipped, and banished to Lima, while only a few had been successfully "saved" from their errors. Cáceres ended by damning the religious offenders, but doing so within a recognition of the specialists' indispensable roles in mid-colonial Andean society. Referring to the specialists and the people they served, he judged that "they are maestros, all of them, and all are *mingadores* [clients], wicked *mingadores*."[119]

---

[118] S. Clark, "The Rational Witchfinder," pp. 229–30. See also P. Burke, *Popular Culture.*
[119] AAL Leg. 2, exp. 10, fol. 9.

Villagómez and After

THE IDOLATRY evidence from between 1640 and 1750 demonstrates the changing foundations of mid-colonial Andean religious life. This chapter and, to a certain extent, the one that follows it concentrate on a few of the tasks begun in Chapter One: the contemplation of different kinds of churchmen, the Extirpation, and the mid-colonial face of Christianity. For the evidence offers an understanding not only of Andean religion but also of the extirpators of idolatry, those priests and ecclesiastical judges who have all too often emerged as cardboard historical figures who destroyed but did not think. To understand the character of the mid-colonial attempts to eradicate idolatry—revived in the 1640s, flourishing until the late 1660s, and continuing more sporadically through the 1690s and 1720s to the 1740s—it is necessary to learn something more about the sixth Archbishop of Lima, his idolatry inspectors, and their successors.

Pedro de Villagómez y Vivanco was born in 1589 in Castroverde de Campos, Zamora, in the Diocese of León, northern Spain.[1] The family blood was judged, in the language of the day, "noble and clean," having been subjected to countless investigations (*pruebas de sangre*) for Jewish or Muslim ancestors as family members steadily accumulated offices and honors in both the secular and religious realms. Pedro's father, Don Francisco de Villagómez, was a knight of the military order of San Juan and had served Philip II both as an infantry captain in Portugal and at the head of a company of horsemen against the French at Perpiñán. Inspection of the rest of the paternal blood line, in descent from the great grandfather, yet another Francisco de Villagómez, and this man's brother, Diego de Ordas y Villagómez, reveals a veritable parade of secular and religious servants of the early modern Spanish state.[2] The lineage of

---

[1] No adequate study of this crucial figure in Peruvian history exists, and there are numerous inaccuracies in what has been written of his Spanish background. See Q. Aldea Vaquero and T. Marin Martínez, eds., *Diccionario*, 4: 2,760. The best synthesis of his Peruvian career is still in R. Vargas Ugarte's *Historia de la Iglesia*, 3: 1–34.

[2] To note only the principal figures in the Villagoméz line, Pedro's grandfather's brother, Pedro de Villagómez Castañón, was a knight of San Juan and later a canon in the cathedral of León. Pedro's great uncles, Dr. D. Diego de Villagómez and Lic. D. Sebastián de Villagómez, served in various capacities on the tribunals and councils of Charles V and Philip II. One uncle, Lic. Hernando de Villagómez, served on the Council of the Indies from 1604 as well as the Council of Castille. In the former capacity he carried on the compilation of laws and edicts until his death in 1612. Another uncle, Lic. D. Pedro de Villagómez, alumnus and then rector of the *colegio mayor* of Oviedo, a house of education or college within the University of Salamanca, became an inquisitor in Seville. Pedro's cousins, D. Pedro and D. Francisco de Vivanco y Villagómez, were knights of Santiago, and the former served as *consultor* to the Holy Office in Granada. Pedro's own brother,

Pedro's mother, Doña Inés Correal de Quevedo, though less illustrious in the military and bureaucratic sense, furnished the family's strong ecclesiastical and inquisitorial tradition. The most luminous figure, and one whom Pedro de Villagómez would come to invoke tirelessly in pursuit of his ends, was his maternal grandmother's brother, the later saint, Toribio Alfonso Mogrovejo. As I have already noted, after his time with the Inquisition in Granada, Don Toribio had preceded Pedro as the long-serving second archbishop of Lima (1581–1606).[3]

It must have been clear to all those who participated in his upbringing that Pedro's future was to be in the Church or, failing that, among the armies of bureaucrats who now fanned out across the Spanish empire (Figure 4). Having attended grammar school in Montilla near the end of the sixteenth century, he followed in his famous uncle Toribio's steps in pursuing his studies at the College of San Salvador de Oviedo at the University of Salamanca. There he was recognized for his aptitude in jurisprudence and theology, apparently catching the eye of those in the faculties of Law and Canon Law. His doctorate in the latter would come from the University of Seville in 1624.[4] Pedro's move to Andalucía in 1611 or 1612 came when, "at the age of twenty years and eleven months," he received a canonry in the Cathedral of Seville by order of Philip III and a brief from Pope Paul V.[5] During his time as canon in Seville (1612–1632), Villagómez served in a number of capacities, including visitador to the College of Santa María de Jesús, secretary of the ecclesiastical chapter and deputy of the festival of Corpus Christi. He was also appointed *consultor*, and later judge, of the Holy Office of the Inquisition in the Arch-

---

D. Diego de Villagómez, had led an infantry company in Naples before entering the armada. Pedro later claimed that two from his paternal clan, Diego de Ordas Villagómez and D. Alvaro de Ordas Villagómez, had participated in the discovery and conquest of Peru and Chile, "being among the first of the military orders to come to these parts." See, in particular, AGI Lima 302, Letter from Villagómez to the king, Lima, 17 July 1647. I have checked the facts, where possible, against E. Schäfer's invaluable *El Consejo Real*, 1: 76, 105, 236, 242, 258, 309, 354, 358, 367, 378, and 408. On the difficulty of identifying and separating names and individuals among slightly earlier Spanish families, see Helen Nader's preface to *The Mendoza Family*.

[3] Inés's father, D. Bernardo Correal de Quevedo, was a founder of the Inquisition's tribunal at Valladolid, while his brothers, Lic. Fabian de Quevedo and Antonio de Quevedo, were an inquisitor in Valladolid and a commisary of the Holy Office in the ancestral home of Castroverde, respectively. On Don Toribio, see AGI Lima 302, Letter from Villagómez to the king, Lima, 17 July 1647. Basic, short depictions of Santo Toribio's career include A. de Egaña's *Historia de la Iglesia*, pp. 268–80 and R. Levillier, ed. *Organización de la Iglesia*, 1: lxiii–xcii.

[4] He received his baccalaureate from Salamanca in 1610. AGI Lima 57, Letter from Villagómez to the king, Lima, 14 August 1653. J. Rezabel y Ugarte, *Biblioteca*, p. 432; M. M. Mendiburu, *Diccionario histórico-biográfico del Perú*, vol. 11 (1934), p. 315; and R. Vargas Ugarte, *Historia de la Iglesia*, 3: 1.

[5] AGI Lima 303, Letter from Villagómez to the king, Lima, 29 August 1658; ACS Secc. I, Secretaría: Autos Capitulares, book 46, 1611–1612, Presentación de bullas de D. Pedro de Villagómez, 20 January 1612, fol. 60; and Pruebas de Sangre, book 18, 1612, Información de Don Pedro de Villagómez. See also R. L. Kagan's discussion of the influence of colegio mayor education in obtaining ecclesiastical and other positions in contemporary Spain; *Students and Society*, pp. 102–4.

Figure 4. A portrait of Pedro de Villagómez, the Archibishop of Lima (1641–1671).
Drawing by Don Carlos Fabbri from the oil portrait in the cathedral chapter of Lima.

diocese of Seville and the Diocese of Cádiz, though little is yet known of his work there.[6]

Assiduous in the tasks he was given, in Spain and later in Peru Villagómez acquired a reputation as a zealous and independent man of scholarly bent. He was also adept at making and fostering enemies. During his Lima prelacy he was accused of everything from pastoral negligence to unseemly pretension and unbridled nepotism.[7] He nursed a fervent distaste for religious error and, even in the second half of the seventeenth century when ecclesiatical repression was becoming increasingly unfashionable in the larger Catholic world, he displayed few scruples about using compulsion to achieve a recognizably Tridentine religious reform. Those inclined to attribute the mid-seventeenth-century revival of the campaigns against Andean religion in the Archdiocese of Lima largely to internal quarrels and priestly corruption at the parish level have only part of the answer. They run the risk of seriously underestimating Villagómez's role, his ideals, and his charismatic ability to influence and even manipulate his contemporaries. This is particularly the case with respect to the approaches of churchmen to idolatry and what many viewed as suspect Andean religiosity (to them, worrisome perversions of Catholicism). If the proposed agenda of this ambitious archbishop had been followed to the letter, the Extirpation of idolatry would have been far stronger and even more systematic in the archdiocese between 1646 and 1671, and it would have spread beyond the Lima region, not only to Cusco where a fawning bishop was ready and waiting, but through all of Peru.[8]

In spite of his numerous ecclesiastical commissions in Seville and the votes of support from his chapter, Villagómez proved unable to win promotion to any of the dioceses for which he was recommended in Castile.[9] Oddly enough, his passage to America came as a result not of a Church appointment but of a secular one. In any event, he would not wait long for the honor of the former.

In May of 1632, Villagómez became the royal visitador of the Audiencia of Lima and the other tribunals, as well as San Marcos University in the Peruvian capital. He was the king's replacement for the recently deceased Don Fray

---

[6] ACS Autos Capitulares, book 47, 17 August 1614, fol. 141; book 52, 25 August 1625, fol. 105; book 54, 9 December 1630, fol. 431. Book 55, 1631–1634, fols. 1–160 are in the hand of secretary Villagómez. Other sources give unreferenced mention of his visita of convents, but I found no record of it in the Cathedral books. See R. Vargas Ugarte, *Historia de la Iglesia*, 3: 1–2; M. M. Mendiburu, *Diccionario histórico-biográfico del Perú*, p. 315; and C. Romero, "Nota bio-bibliográfica" in *Colección*, edited by H. H. Urteaga, 11: vi.

[7] A list of his publications appears in J. Rezabel y Ugarte, *Biblioteca*, p. 432. Nepotism was common in his day, and in his archiepiscopate it began early and finished only with his death. See the allegations in AGI Lima 332, Letter from Sancho Pardo de Cárdenas to the king, Lima, 1643, and the last of a series of attempts to further the career of his nephew and namesake in AGI Lima 304, Letter from Villagómez to La Señora, Lima, 4 February 1671.

[8] See AGI Lima 303, Letter from Villagómez to the king, Lima, 9 March 1650. For idolatry trials that did occur outside the archdiocese see P. Duviols, *La destrucción*, pp. 263–67.

[9] AGI Lima 5, Consulta from the Council of the Indies to the king, Madrid, 29 January 1631.

Juan Gutiérrez Flores, the former inquisitor in Mexico and Lima. By August of 1632, however, Philip IV's petitions to Rome also bore fruit for the forty-three-year-old canon of Seville, when Pope Urban VIII approved him as bishop of Arequipa in southern Peru.[10] Villagómez thus became one of the thirty-two bishops, and six archbishops, administering to the religious needs of Spanish America. As a peninsular of privileged education and Iberian experience in mid-career, he was a typical high official of his time, in both the secular and ecclesiastical sphere. The creole Hernando Arias de Ugarte—the archbishop of Lima at the time of Villagómez's visitations in the capital and of his episco-pacy in Arequipa—had been an exception, one of a handful of American-born prelates in the first half of the colonial period.[11]

Despite his election to the Arequipan diocese, Villagómez did not rush to finish his secular responsibilities. In fact, once busy with his visitation of the secular tribunals in Lima, Villagómez wrote prudently appreciative letters to his superiors asking for permission to be absent from his southern see and actually to extend his tenure in Lima. In the end, he spent a good deal more than the stipulated year completing his investigations. One learns from his letter to the king in April of 1636 that it had taken the royal cédula of 17 July 1635 to send him to Arequipa. With characteristic precision, Villagómez fur-nished insight into both his manner and the inspecting procedures of the day. He wrote that he had pursued his brief with the maximum care, and that "the papers concerning my secret investigation" are in the possession of the viceroy, protected by a "strongbox requiring three keys" held by three different per-sons. If one believes his own words, Villagómez's industry, incorruptibility, and the stiffness of his "condemnations and penalties" had earned him the "hatred" of the officials on the tribunals in the capital, and not least of the *letrados* (judges and bureaucrats) of the Audiencia.[12] Villagómez already demonstrated what would become a much-practiced penchant for portraying himself as the righteous servant of king and pope, the man who did not play the game and whose pure agenda was constantly assailed by a corrupt world, led—not too surprisingly—by self-serving bureaucrats. Clashes between peninsular prelates and the ranks of colonial officialdom were routine, but even so Villagómez was able to attract more than his share of critics. His enmity with the Audiencia, for instance, would prove to be longstanding. It would be renewed during Vil-

---

[10] Ibid., 17 April 1632. R. Vargas Ugarte, *Historia de la Iglesia*, 3: 2 and M. M. Mendiburu, *Diccionario histórico-biográfico del Perú*, p. 315. The Councillors of the Indies had ranked Vil-lagómez second among the proposed candidates for the diocese. Notably, the great jurist of Peru-vian experience and now royal councillor Dr. Juan Solórzano Pereira recommended three others before him. See AGI Lima 5, Consulta, Madrid, 29 January 1631.

[11] See J. L. Mecham, "The Church," pp. 216–17 and J. M. Barnadas, "The Catholic Church," 1: 517–18, 527.

[12] AGI Lima 309, Letter from Villagómez to the king, Arequipa, 11 April 1636. The summary of his visita in Lima was given to the king in AGI Lima 309, Letter from Villagómez to the king, Lima, 30 April 1635.

lagómez's tenure in the metropolitan see, and not before still more feathers would be ruffled in the white city to the south.[13]

Villagómez's excitement on finally taking up his first diocese was palpable in a letter written from Arequipa to King Philip IV in 1636. Having been visited by the viceroy at six in the evening to confirm his intentions, Villagómez wrote, "I set out at four the next morning on the road to this city."[14] Viewed in the light of his later initiatives in Lima, his first see seems to have provided of a brief provincial testing ground for his ambitions and dreams. Villagómez did not rest. He supervised the completion of a new cathedral and episcopal residences in the Sevillian architectural style, and he sponsored improvements to the famous convent of Santa Catalina in the city. In the spirit of his great-uncle, Bishop Villagómez became known for his charity, reportedly giving two-thirds of his income in alms to the poor. Moreover, as befitted a post-Tridentine churchman, there was always a tone of seriousness and urgency in his pastoral pursuits.[15]

Villagómez set out almost immediately on an eight and a half month pastoral tour (*visita general*) to survey his southern Andean realm. Little seems to have escaped his gaze. He condemned the regional corregidores' failure to maintain the provisions of the hospitals for the Indians, and he railed against Franciscan, Mercedarian, and Dominican friars whom he found to be administering sacraments, begging alms, and operating as doctrineros when appointed only by the independently minded provincials of their orders, and without his own formal permission or that of the king through the Royal *patronato* (the papal granting of Crown control over the Church). The inflexibility and perfectionism of the peninsular Villagómez seem to have come as a shock to the churchmen of the Arequipa region, some of whom wrote to the Council of the Indies in protest.

Villagómez also expressed his nascent views on Andean idolatry. It was presumably on this early tour that he gained his first close experience of Andean religion, although his descriptions of the types of gods and practices suggest that he already had more than a nodding acquaintance with writings on the subject by earlier chroniclers and extirpators. Villagómez was already a reader; it was at this point that he became also an observer. In an early exhibition of the zealous sense of purpose for which he would later be known, Villagómez encountered the Andean belief system not as its student or patient enquirer, but as its intrusive destroyer. "In some Indian towns," he informed his king, "I found many tombs or ancient *guacas* (*huacas*) that preserve the pagan and idolatrous superstitions among these barbarous people. To eliminate these memories and the *guacas*, which numbered more than 3,000, I had them all destroyed at my own cost. I have also erased the other traces of idolatry which

---

[13] On his differences with his chapter and prebendaries in Arequipa see ASV, Ad Limina, Lima 450, Letter from Villagómez to Urban VIII, Lima, 2 June 1642, fols. 678–678v. Villagómez's episcopate in Arequipa extended from 1633 to 1640, though he did not arrive until 1635.

[14] Ibid.

[15] G. González de Avila, *Teatro eclesiástico*, p. 48, and M. M. Mendiburu, *Diccionario histórico-biográfico del Perú*, p. 316.

we have discovered—all for the glory of God and the good of these new plants of the faith."[16] The end of the "pagan and idolatrous superstitions" of these "barbarous people" required force, according to the bishop, and it was necessary even if the cost of raising that force had to be personally borne. But, as would be shown to even greater effect during his later endeavors in Lima, in Arequipa Villagómez was convinced of the need to balance the firm hand of repression with intensified teaching. If the Catholic faith did not enter the field as an intellectual combatant, he seemed to assert through his words and actions at this early stage, the Andean would never truly be changed. Again, Villagómez showed himself eager to contribute personally to the religious reform he perceived as vital to the spiritual health of Andeans: he composed a simple catechism, printing two thousand copies to be used in the parishes of the diocese and, in time-honored, Tridentine fashion, he opened a school in his own residence where kurakas' sons might learn the Spanish language and Christian doctrine.[17] Finally, in 1638, on the eve of his promotion to the metropolitan see, Villagómez convened a synod.

His own priorities, among which was a growing concern with the problem of suspect Indian religiosity, are readily apparent in the voluminous set of constitutions from the Arequipan deliberations. In its Tridentine preoccupations with priestly conduct, the content of sermons, doctrinal instruction, sacramental obedience, morality, and the interrelated "pestilent vice of drunkenness" and "crime of idolatry," the Arequipa document recalled the character of Lobo Guerrero's Lima synod of 1613.[18] More importantly, the 1638 constitutions foreshadowed Villagómez's more famous tract published in Lima a decade later.

The *Carta pastoral* of 1649 (see Figure 5), even if better known than the Arequipa constitutions, has suffered from its own kind of neglect: a consistent underestimation by investigators who have grown accustomed to discussing it similarly and in passing. The common and contagious reason given for diminishing the work's importance centers on Villagómez's verbatim use of entire sections of Pablo José de Arriaga's 1621 treatise on idolatry extirpation. This claim is perfectly correct, but only for part of the treatise. Moreover, the suggestion that Villagómez lacked originality misses the point of the churchman's work.

Even the fruits of his synod in Arequipa had proven Villagómez a keen student of the Jesuit's earlier work.[19] The second part of Villagómez's *Carta*

---

[16] AGI Lima 309, Letter from Villagómez to the king, Arequipa, 18 April 1638.

[17] AGI Lima 309, Letter from Villagómez to the king, Lima, 27 April 1635.

[18] BNP B1742, "Sinodales de Pedro de Villagómez," Cuaderno 22, Arequipa, 5 May 1639. See book 1, tit. 1 and 2, and especially the chapters within book 4, tit. 4–9. In the addition of their attention to Andean religious error, Villagómez' constitutions from Arequipa are markedly different from those issued by Hernando Arias de Ugarte at the synod he convened only two years before in Lima (1636). See B. Lobo Guerrero and F. Arias de Ugarte, *Sínodos de Lima*.

[19] "Sinodales," book 4, tit. 4, ch. 3, fols. 262v–265, for example, restated the "Edict against Idolatry."

CARTA PASTORAL

DE EXORTACION

E INSTRVCCION CON-
TRA LAS IDOLATRIAS DE
LOS INDIOS DEL ARÇOBISPADO
DE LIMA.

POR EL ILLVSTRISSIMO SEÑOR
DOCTOR DON PEDRO DE VILLAGOMEZ,
ARZOBISPO DE LIMA.

A SVS VISITADORES DE LAS
IDOLATRIAS, Y A SVS VICARIOS, Y CV-
ras de las Doctrinas de Indios.

Año de ⟨⟨⟩⟩ 1649.

Iuan Cortes
1649

CON LICENCIA.

En Lima, Por Iorge López de Herrera, Impreſſor de Libros, en la calle de la carcel de Corte.

Figure 5. Title page of Pedro de Villagómez, *Carta pastoral* (Lima, 1649). Courtesy of the John Carter Brown Library at Brown University.

pastoral, the *instrucción (manual on procedure)*, borrowed heavily from the recommendations of his experienced predecessor and from P. Arriaga's compendium of Indian beliefs and practices, *La extirpación de idolatría en el Perú*. Given the detailed quality of Arriaga's treatise, its contemporary influence in Peru, and the fact that the new archbishop of Lima was bent on reinvigorating the very institution for which the Jesuit had been a prime theoretician and proponent, the quotation and paraphrasing is hardly surprising.[20] Villagómez's authority depended on being well informed, and his text also exhibits a familiarity with the relevant writings of José de Acosta and Antonio de la Calancha.[21] In explanation of his tract, Villagómez informed Philip IV that his personal experiences among Andean peoples in Arequipa, combined with the reports he had received from "all types of persons" about rampant idolatry in the metropolitan see, had obliged him to assemble an instrucción against this evil. His own treatise would be, as he put it, "of great service to God and to Your Majesty."[22] P. Arriaga's work was simply a prime resource for this urgent purpose, this task left unfinished by his clerical predecessors. And the work was not bereft of Villagómez's own touches, though always as a contribution to a recognizable Christian pastoral tradition.

In particular, the polemical *exhortación*, the first part of the *Carta pastoral*, which included thirty-six of the total of fifty-six chapters, is worth closer consideration. The exhortación is at once both a defensive declaration of purpose and a strident manifesto. Villagómez was shrewdly aware of the criticism he and his pastoral letter would meet, and his work was calculated, reasoned, exegetical, and authoritative. Amidst the caution there was a pronounced triumphalism as he chiseled himself a glorious place in the grand sweep of Christian history. After passages from the Old Testament, his most quoted sources were the works of Gregory the Great, the late sixth-century pope whose scholarly achievements and attitude toward persistent paganism and heresies were a powerful inspiration to the Peruvian prelate over a thousand years later.[23]

But Villagómez had a king, a council, and hundreds of churchmen to bring over to his side. Availing himself of the mantle of Gregory was only the first step in a deeper employment of the "authoritative canon" and a skilful appeal to the contemporary ecclesiastical imagination.[24] In what was perhaps his most potent analogy and metaphor, Villagómez portrayed the monster that chal-

---

[20] Many instances from part two of the pastoral letter might be cited. For one clear example, compare the discussions of Andean ministers in P. de Villagómez, *Carta pastoral*, ch. 43 and P. J. de Arriaga, *La extirpación*, ch. 3.

[21] See, for instance, P. de Villagómez, *Carta pastoral*, ch. 23, pp. 72–73 and ch. 20, p. 61.

[22] AGI Lima 303, Letter from Villagómez to the king, Lima, 9 March 1650. Over the years, the archbishop would make frequent proud references to the use of his *Carta pastoral* by his agents. See especially AGI Lima 303, Letter from Villagómez to the king, Lima, 12 August 1652.

[23] On Gregory see particularly C. Straw, *Gregory the Great*; R. A. Markus, "Gregory the Great"; P. Brown's suggestive synthesis in *The Rise of Western Christendom*, ch. 8; J. Barmby, tr. and ed., "The Book of Pastoral Rule"; and the now venerable classic, F. H. Dudden, *Gregory the Great*.

[24] See A. R. Pagden, "*Ius et Factum*."

lenged the Church's supremacy in the Andes as a latter-day, collective equivalent of the Philistine god Dagon, the father of the Biblical Baal. The image he created in his text took what was most useful from the well-known organic conception of the tree of idolatry—with its less important branches and leaves—and moved a memorable step beyond.

The image of Dagon, whose head and trunk were in human form but whose lower parts were those of a fish, offered a suitably horrible symbol of religious error. In an adaptation that recalled, among other things, the millenarian prophecies of Joachim de Fiore, the archbishop wrote of three ages of the faith in Peru, the third and most triumphant of which was—not surprisingly—going on around him. The account in the fifth chapter of the first book of Samuel, in which the presence of the Ark of God in Dagon's temple brings about the gradual humiliation and dismemberment of the idol before the wondering eyes of its priests, was deployed to great effect by the archbishop. Matters were put in the most apocalyptic of terms; read in the context of the Catholic Reformation, and with the imagination of a seventeenth-century Spanish churchman in the New World, the exhortación was an official incitement to zeal. Under Archbishop Villagómez's care and supervision, the program of religious reform by means of repeated visitas through the infected parishes offered the only opportunity to reduce Andean idolatry to the pitiful impotence of Dagon's fishy stump.[25]

The people meant to respond to the call for visitadores de idolatría were the more fervent of the parish priests and vicars in the Indian areas. Villagómez had written that, although all ordained priests and their assistants should be paragons of virtue in service to God, "His watchmen (*atalayas*)" on earth, the visitadores would have to be a cut above even this.[26] The departure of the first seven commissioned extirpators in September of 1649, clutching their copies of the *Carta pastoral* and a special book of anti-idolatry sermons to guide them, was to be a departure of the holy.[27] The triumphal seven included the veteran extirpators of Lobo Guerrero's time, Fernando de Avendaño and Alonso Osorio, along with Francisco Gamarra, Pablo Recio de Castilla, Felipe de Medina, Alonso Corbacho, and Bartolomé Jurado.

The day of departure was exquisitely timed to coincide with the installation of a holy relic, a piece of wood from the Holy Cross, which had been sent to

[25] P. de Villagómez, *Carta pastoral*, especially chs. 1, 2, 6, and 7. In addition to 1 Samuel 5, see Judges 16:23, and 1 Chronicles 10:10.

[26] On the watchmen, see *Carta pastoral*, chs. 23 and 35, pp. 73–76 and 120–22, respectively. The probable source of the "watchmen" image is Isaiah 62:6. For more on the Spanish use of "atalaya" see M. Cavillac, *Gueux et marchands*, pp. 296ff. I thank Sir John Elliott for the latter reference. On the visitadores, see *Carta pastoral*, ch. 26, pp. 86–88, and chs. 38, 39, and 41, pp. 130–42.

[27] Visitas de idolatría, in fact, had begun soon after Villagómez's arrival. I have already discussed evidence from investigations as early as 1642. The *sermonario* was written by the experienced extirpator and preacher Fernando de Avendaño; see Chapter Six below.

Villagómez as a present from Pope Urban VIII—very much recalling the confluence of saintliness and repression in the days of Avila's theatrics at the inception of Lobo Guerrero's Extirpation.[28] The public spectacle and great, capitoline event were being used again to stir an extirpating atmosphere. Present were the aging Fernando de Avendaño, who had authored the book of anti-idolatry sermons appended to the *Carta pastoral*, though not the recently deceased Francisco de Avila, who had finally received his place on the cathedral chapter in Lima in 1632.[29] Supported by a new archbishop, the Extirpation was retaking its place on the official agenda and in the minds of certain churchmen in Lima. A timely sermon made all the right connections between the glorious arrival of the holy relic and the exodus of the idolatry inspectors.[30] As the visitadores processed from the metropolitan cathedral on 19 September 1649, Archbishop Villagómez blessed their white banners, emblazoned with a green cross in the center and red characters at the border that read: *Ecce crucem Domini jugite partes adversae* (Behold the cross of the Lord uniting adverse factions).[31]

Yet all the dramatic coincidence could not erase the fact that ecclesiastical opinion in Peru was not unified on the matter of extirpation. Moreover, the "campaigns" against Andean idolatry were not yet ready to be launched, at least not in the manner Villagómez intended. Unbeknownst to many who watched the solemn send-off in Lima, the event marked a false start. Only one of the seven original visitadores, Felipe de Medina, was able to proceed at once. The delay seems to have occurred for a number of reasons. If one believes Villagómez, this early difficulty—as well as others the Extirpation would face through the 1650s—arose partly because there was a lack of funds provided for the visitadores' allowances.[32]

But Villagómez's claim that the launching of his campaigns and their later maintenance were hindered by lack of financial resources should be considered cautiously for at least two reasons. First, in the 1650s and 1660s he does not appear to have had great difficulty persuading competent priests to accept the promotion and prestige carried by the office of visitador de idolatría. And second, priest-visitadores enjoyed enormous powers in regions remote from supervisory eyes. Many of them seem not to have taken seriously the crown's prohibitions on exactions from the resources of the Andean communities. In

---

[28] The holy Lignum Crucis was set to be installed on 14 September, the day of the Exaltation of the Holy Cross on the Catholic calendar, but the installation was postponed until the following Sunday, 19 September, the day when the seven visitadores were to leave. R. Vargas Ugarte, *Historia de la Iglesia*, 3: 6–7.

[29] A. Acosta, "Francisco de Avila,," pp. 609–11.

[30] Fr. Blas d'Acosta, *Sermon*, fols. 11v–12, 13v, and 14–15. For insight into the contemporary thirst for religious spectacle that Spanish Lima inherited from its metropolis, see J. H. Elliott, "The Court of the Spanish Habsburgs," pp. 147–48.

[31] R. Vargas Ugarte, *Historia de la Iglesia*, 3: 7.

[32] See Villagómez's apologetic missive, AGI Lima 303, Letter from Villagómez to the king, Lima, 9 March 1650.

spite of the difficulties and delays, Villagómez's ambition was great, and eventually a number of small investigation teams did set out. One of the principal reasons for the slow start in 1649 emerges quite naturally from the evidence. Villagómez had chosen a number of visitadores who—as much as they brought prestige, experience, and perhaps legitimacy, to his enterprise—brought little in the way of health and energy. The majority of the original seven were not able to meet Villagómez's expectations of them.

The frequent, informative letters of this archbishop who was so practiced in the arts of imperial bureaucracy and eager for royal recognition provide us with a reasonable picture of the main visitadores' paths through the archdiocese. Between 1649 and 1652, Felipe de Medina climbed from Huacho in Chancay into the province of Cajatambo, discovering much "formal idolatry" as he went.[33] Avendaño, the declared "superintendent of idolatry," who left accompanied by the Jesuit P. Francisco Conde, conducted a few investigations in the Cercado quarter of Lima and in the vicinity of the capitol before succumbing to old age and a hardening of the mental arteries. In 1653, the aging extirpator recommended in a letter to the king and Council of the Indies that the worst Andean idolaters should be transferred to the jurisdiction of the Holy Office of the Inquisition.[34] Documentary evidence on Alonso Osorio's activities is slight, though he was commissioned ambitiously to visit the mountain district of Huarochirí and to proceed into Huamanga. Corbacho, who was to have visited communities in the tribute district of Santa, appears not even to have departed. Bartolomé Jurado passed from the Conchucos region to the parishes in Checras, where Pablo Recio de Castilla also worked, though Jurado too was soon stricken by illness and forced to retire.

Apart from Medina (who was originally commissioned to visit the districts of Yauyos, Jauja, Chancay, and Huaylas, and who turns up mostly in documents that survive from Chancay and Cajatambo), the busiest visitadores between late 1649 and 1655 appear to have been Diego Tello—who, along with the Jesuit PP. José de Torres and Juan del Portillo, visited parishes in the Huaylas region for three and a half months—and two additional commissions, Esteban de Aguilar—who, along with two priests as his assistants, picked up where Jurado had left off in Conchucos—and a Dominican about whom little is known, Francisco de Lugares, who accepted the task of visiting the parishes in Yauyos that were administered by friars of his order. There was also a Dr Andrés García de Zurita, formerly a priest in the Diocese of Huamanga, who took up a short commission in an undefined region.[35]

---

[33] Medina was accompanied to Chancay by two Jesuits, PP. Lorenzo de Tapia and Jerónimo de Herrera, and he described his investigations in a valuable report, AGI Lima 303, "Relación que hizo Felipe de Medina de las idolatrías descubiertos en Huacho, 25 March 1650." For a transcription in print see J. T. Medina, *La imprenta en Lima*, 2: 215–21.

[34] See the upbeat epistle in AGI Lima 332, Letter from Avendaño to the king, Lima, without date but on a 1651 armada. And on the recommended transfer, AGI Lima 332, Letter from Avendaño to the king, Lima, 5 August 1653. See also R. Vargas Ugarte, *Historia de la Iglesia*, 3: 13–14.

[35] R. Vargas Ugarte, *Historia de la Iglesia*, 3: 7–8; see also P. Duviols, *La Lutte*, pp. 164–66.

It is worth noting parenthetically that visitadores Tello and Medina each enjoyed the assistance of two Jesuit padres, as was customary for extirpators and set down as recommended procedure by Arriaga and Villagómez. Avendaño was accompanied by one Jesuit during his brief stints of work. Aguilar, though he had no Jesuits with him, appears to have made alternative arrangements to share the duties and to shore up the pedagogical and reformative side of his visitas. He traveled with two other secular priests as his assistants.

A number of temporary or one-time visitadores filled in for officials whose commissions had not been started or whose labors were not completed. These judges included Villagómez's own nephew, another Pedro de Villagómez, who took time away from his prestigious urban parish of Our Holy Lady Santa Ana in Lima to begin an idolatry investigation in 1650 in Huarmey, Santa.[36] There were also the occasional priests' assistants or deputies in the provinces of the archdiocese who—seized by varying degrees of zeal and/or opportunism—decided to initiate idolatry investigations that in basic procedure, at least, conformed to the prescriptions set down by the *Carta pastoral* and Arriaga's *La extirpación*, and the proceedings of which were carefully recorded and passed to Lima.[37] A good example of one of these zealous parish deputies is Don Antonio de Cáceres, the teniente of the Mercedarian priest Fray Pedro de Zárate in the parish of Caujo, Canta.[38] The existence of unofficial enemies of idolatry who might mount investigations that, however limited in geographical range, could be thorough in their probing of colonial Andean religion, serves a reminder that the climate of zeal encouraged by the Extirpation could result in trials that were not sponsored from or by Lima.[39] The less systematic, noncentralized efforts at extirpation remind one of the kinds of extirpation occurring in seventeenth-century Mexico, supported by individual priests and officials and most often at the local or regional level.

By 1654 Diego Barreto had replaced the now deceased Medina, and he conducted visitas in the vast Jauja region and in Huarochirí until his own health began to fail. The visitadores de idolatría who became especially active in the middle of 1650s are, with one exception, the group most representative of

---

AGI Lima 303, Letter from Villagómez to the king, Lima, 16 August 1652; AGI Lima 332, Title of Visitador given to Lic. Pablo Recio de Castilla, Lima, 18 September 1649; and AGI Lima 53, Letter from Villagómez to the king, Lima, 20 October 1648.

[36] On 6 December 1650, Lic. Villagómez handed his commission to the priest and vicar of Huarmey at the time, Bernardo de Novoa, who would go on to be one of the busiest and most careful of Archbishop Villagómez's idolatry inspectors. AAL Leg. 5, exp. 1, fols. 5–5v.

[37] W. B. Taylor gives a thorough discussion of ecclesiastical officialdom in the Diocese of Guadalajara and Archdiocese of Mexico, which is also suggestive for the rest of colonial Spanish America, in *Magistrates of the Sacred*, ch. 4. In this context, see particularly his treatment of the *coadjutor*, the often temporary assistant to a priest and, as Taylor notes, frequently synonymous with *teniente de cura*, lieutenant.

[38] See AAL Leg. 4, exp. 14, 1650 and AAL Leg. 2, exp. 10, 1650. Cáceres's investigation will be discussed in Chapter Seven.

[39] For the evidence of a trial from the era of Hernando Arias de Ugarte, who did not support the Extirpation, see K. R. Mills, "Persistencia religiosa."

Villagómez's Extirpation. The prelate, it seems, had learned the cost of appointing agents who were frequently ailing and unable to undertake protracted tours of investigation in difficult conditions. Villagómez's new agents were generally drawn from among the middle-aged parish priests of the Lima region and included, in addition to Barreto, such figures as Bernardo de Novoa. Novoa—the former priest of Huarmey, Santa, who had already been involved in one idolatry trial there in 1650–1651—received the first of his idolatry commissions in Cajatambo. Novoa's extirpating career would continue intermittently into the mid-1660s.[40] There were also Diego Tello (the priest of Huaraz), who expanded his inspections to cover the entire province of Huaylas; Estanislao de Vega Bazán (who went to Conchucos and Huamalies); and Pedro de Quijano Zevallos (the priest Canta, who visited the region of the same name).[41]

The notable exception, and perhaps the most significant of the later commissions, was Juan Sarmiento de Vivero, the former chaplain of the Convent of the Incarnation in Lima and general visitor of the Diocese of Huamanga and the Archdiocese of Lima. Sarmiento was named visitador general de idolatría in 1660, and much documentation from his idolatry investigations in the 1660s survives.[42] He visited Huarochirí, Yauyos, Checras, and the Cercado in Lima. Juan Ignacio de Torres y Solis was active in Huánuco, while Sebastián de Vitoria and Joseph Laureano de Mena conducted visitas in Jauja and Huamalies, respectively. Vega Bazán seems to have been reinstated in Cajatambo in the late 1660s, taking over from Bernardo de Novoa, who had been operating there since the end of the previous decade. Pedro Cárdenas y Arbieto worked in Tarama, and Ignacio de Castelvi conducted at least one investigation in Cajatambo in 1671, the year of Villagómez's death.

Certain churchmen who had no commissions enthusiastically took up Villagómez's call for "watchmen" and proceeded with independent idolatry investigations before seeking their prelate's support. Although the work of the uncommissioned agents might be less restricted in method and sometimes more surprising in results than that of the visitadores proper, their efforts were still recognizable emulations of official procedure.[43] The actions of these priests

---

[40] AGI Lima 303, Letter from Villagómez to the king, Lima, 28 August 1654; AGI Lima 59, Letters from Villagómez to the king, Lima, 28 March 1655 and 24 June 1656; and AGI Lima 59, Letter from Villagómez to the king, Lima, 26 June 1657. Ten of Novoa's investigations are published, although with parts omitted and some folio errors, in P. Duviols, ed., *Cultura andina*.

[41] One can learn much about what Vega Bazán found from his *Testimonio auténtico de una idolatría muy sutil que el demonio avia introducido entre los indios de las provincias de Conchucos y Guamalies* . . . , Rockefeller Library, Brown University, Providence, Rhode Island, Medina Collection of microfilm FHA.210.5. P. Duviols has printed a transcription from the microfilm copy in the National Library of Peru in Lima as the eighth document in his appendix to *La Lutte*, pp. 386–89. See also the same visitador's later letter to Villagómez, written from Lima and dated 16 December 1662, at pp. 390–92.

[42] See K. R. Mills, "The Limits," esp. notes 45 and 46 on p. 103; also seven of Sarmiento's Chancay trials transcribed in Ana Sánchez ed., *Amancebados, hechiceros y rebeldes*.

[43] In discussing the "idolatry trials" at the center of her study of Maya-Spanish relations in sixteenth-century Yucatán, Inga Clendinnen ponders usefully the differences between the Inquisi-

remind one of how much unofficial extirpation may not have been carefully recorded, and encourages caution in snap judgments about what was going on in contemporary dioceses outside of the Lima region, not to mention in New Spain and elsewhere.

Villagómez's personality and appetite for paperwork made him the undisputed commander of the activities of the agents who were central to the renewed Extirpation. Yet recurrent illness kept Villagómez from first-hand involvement in the Andean parishes during all but the beginning of his thirty-year tenure. The health problems that clearly had begun to restrain him even during his time in Arequipa were worsening. In 1646, he had made at least one foray as far as Huaylas but, because of a hernia and other vaguely defined ailments, he was soon confined to Lima and those places on the coast to which he could travel in a litter. Villagómez's enemies over the next decades seized upon his afflictions as evidence that he was not fulfilling his pastoral function, and there is a corresponding mountain of documentation debating the proper course of action in the light of his inability to conduct the personal visitas generales that were expected of post-Tridentine prelates.[44]

Villagómez's dependence upon his fluctuating group of visitadores (ordinarios as well as those who specifically investigated idolatry) to be his eyes and ears in the mountain areas was acute, and for this dependence too he was roundly criticized. But the archbishop's tireless letters and his devotion to executive detail went beyond self-justification, and are proof of his close involvement in each action that was undertaken in his realm, especially in the struggle against idolatry. Indeed, I believe that his inability to make personal visitations caused him to spur the activity of others, which at least partly explains the significant rise in idolatry trials during his tenure.[45] Like many people who

---

tion's well-oiled investigative and coercive procedure and those that might be employed in a remote region by an episcopal process. *Ambivalent Conquests*, pp. 76–77.

[44] He admitted to being struck down by ill health after his excursions in the southern diocese in 1637–1638 and again in 1640. Moreover, after he was officially informed of his promotion to the see in Lima on 22 November 1640 he was, for a time, too ill to receive the pallium. ASV, Ad Limina, Lima 450, Letter from Villagómez to Urban VIII, Lima, 2 June 1642, fols. 678–80. A sense of the much wider controversy is gained from AGI Lima 59, Letter from the viceroy, Conde de Alva, to the king, Lima, 14 December 1657.

[45] The number of idolatry investigations we know of is, of course, mostly dependent on documentary survival. Yet, even with this qualification, the anti-idolatry activity in this period c. 1649–1671 is striking. Manuel Burga's attempt to capture the idolatry trials conducted between 1600 and 1749 in a table, and Ana Sánchez's conversion of Burga's data between 1600 and 1699 into a bar graph, offer striking visualizations of this fact. Of the 135 idolatry trials noted by Burga (1600–1749), 88 occurred between 1640 and 1669, with 7 in the 1640s, 15 in the 1650s, and some 66 in the 1660s. Villagómez died in 1671, and for the following decade (the 1670s), Burga records 6 trials. M. Burga, *Nacimiento*, p. 153, and A. Sánchez, "Mentalidad popular," p. 4.

Burga wisely cautions that numbers can be deceiving. The trials are very unequal in length, and in depth and range of investigation. Thus, a single idolatry trial can occasionally "do more"—that is, investigate the religiosity of more people and turn up more information on the dimensions of colonial Andean religion and culture—than a series of, say, a half-dozen precise investigations.

suffer from lengthy or recurring illnesses, Villagómez more than made up for his infirmity through written and organizational effort. In an imperial culture renowned for its addiction to documentation, no seventeenth-century Peruvian prelate examined and authorized as many *autos* and initiatives as Villagómez.[46] Moreover, at times he was clearly the experienced constant around which the other, more fleeting powers in the viceroyalty were forced to revolve. In the course of his long tenure the throng of secular and religious officials changed and no fewer than five viceroys represented the crown in Peru. With many of these men, Villagómez would clash bitterly, principally over issues of protocol and responsibility, but also over the direction of policy. Their correspondence— not only to each other, but also to the king and Council of the Indies—reveals much in this regard. The professional relationship between the count of Salvatierra (viceroy, 1647–1653) and Villagómez was, for example, especially cordial and mutually supportive, whereas the enmity between the prelate and Mancera, and later Alva, was thinly veiled in the case of the former and naked in the case of the latter.[47]

When it came to his own immobility and the corresponding furore over pastoral tours, Villagómez argued much as his Creole predecessor, Hernando Arias de Ugarte (1630–1638), had done. Although the former prelate had spent much of his time on visitas generales, Arias, on this issue and many others, showed himself to be a shrewd man with few illusions about what might be achieved on an official tour. Arias believed that clerical scoundrels and religious criminals could easily conceal themselves from peripatetic prelates and thus that the obligatory visitations produced little benefit beyond the granting of dispensations and the good that might come from the dutiful, public performance of innumerable confirmations. Villagómez was forced to take his predecessor's disarming reasoning one step further. He held that those to whom he delegated responsibility—his carefully chosen and well-monitored visitadores—could more than adequately perform the mobile aspects of a prelate's work. Indeed, in the case of the priest-inspectors of idolatry, he had a point. Their linguistic training in Quechua, their familiarity with the Andean parishes and the fact that they might be commissioned to perform precise functions such as the

---

Also, largely because of the patchiness of documentary survival and the understandably imperfect attention to the holdings of regional and local archives since the recent atmosphere of violence began in the Andes in the 1980s, it has not proved possible for any scholar to claim a complete survey of the idolatry material in the Lima region or beyond.

[46] See J. H. Elliott, "Spain and America," 1: 303.

[47] The five viceroys were the marquis de Mancera (1638–1648) and the counts of Salvatierra (1647–1653), Alva de Aliste y Villaflor (1653–1660), Santisteban (1660–1666), and Lemos (1666–1672); E. Schäfer, *El Consejo Real*, p. 442. See AGI Lima 303, Letter from Villagómez to the king, Lima, 10 August 1652 (on Salvatierra); AGI Lima 302, Villagómez to the king, Lima, 20 October 1648 (on Mancera); AGI Lima 303, Villagómez to the king, Lima, 28 June 1657 (on Alva); AGI Lima 303, Letter from Alva to the king, Lima, 5 July 1657 and AGI Lima 59, Alva to the king, Lima, 30 June 1655 (on Villagómez). P. T. Bradley has concentrated on a range of matters between 1655 and 1661 from the point of view of Viceroy Alva in *Society, Economy and Defence*, chs. 1, 4, and 6.

extirpation of idolatry in defined regions, made them a good deal better suited to investigate and to judge Indian religious error than almost any peninsular prelate who had much to do in many places in a limited time.[48]

The people who would keep the engine of Villagómez's extirpating enterprise running for the next two decades, and in some cases well beyond his death, were predominantly experienced, creole secular clergy. They were the aspirants to the upper reaches of at least the regional, and often the viceregal, religious hierarchy, although the Andean chronicler Guaman Poma used spiteful, ringing words to describe their striving sort in quite another way.[49] Becoming a visitador de idolatría was a smart career move, particularly in the Villagómez era, and these churchmen knew it. Not much else beyond an extra dose of ambition and a decision to channel anti-idolatrous zeal, both genuine and affected, into the advancement of their careers separated the eventual visitadores de idolatría from the other parish priests in the competitive religious climate of the mid-seventeenth-century archdiocese. There were not many to whom the office was offered who did not already desire it.

One can easily chart how the commission and the inclusion of a difficult or particularly fruitful tour of duty as an idolatry inspector on a priest's professional résumé (*relación de méritos y servicios*) might help an ecclesiastical career. A priest might not always rise as high as he desired, but Villagómez's recommendations of clergy who could fill benefices or cathedral canonries in this period did not fail to emphasize services rendered in the extirpation of idolatry. In fact, Villagómez usually mentioned this position last, as a crowning achievement, when putting forward his visitadores for ecclesiastical vacancies. Pablo Recio de Castilla, though noted for his abilities in the pulpit, had failed in six attempts over twelve years (1634–1646) to gain a parish in the archdiocese. Yet soon after his promotion to visitador general de idolatría in 1649 came a remarkable change of fortune; he was offered the enviable position of provisor and vicar general of the Diocese of Cusco. Estanislao de Vega Bazán, whose extirpating career was most distinguished by its interruptions and one fascinating report, shamelessly used the office in his attempts to secure a place in the Cathedral of Lima.[50]

Where did these ambitious priests come from? A survey of fifteen of Villagómez's busiest visitadores de idolatría finds fourteen Creoles and one peninsular Spaniard: twelve natives of Lima, one of Cusco, one of Chachapoyas in the Diocese of Trujillo, and one of Toledo in Spain (Diego Tello). These were Fernando de Avendaño, Diego Barreto de Castro, Diego Cano Gutiérrez, Pedro Cardenas y Arbieto, Francisco de Gamarra, Bartolomé Jurado Palomino,

---

[48] AGI Lima 302, Letter from Arias de Ugarte to the king, Lima, 13 May 1633.

[49] See the *El primer nueva corónica*, 2: 638–53, especially 640, 642–43, and 648. On colonial churchmen, I have found valuable P. B. Ganster's work on mid-eighteenth-century priests in the archdiocese, "A Social History"; and particularly inspiring, W. Taylor's *Magistrates of the Sacred*.

[50] On Regio de Castilla, see AGI Lima 303, Letter from Villagómez to the king, Lima, 26 August 1651, and AGI Lima 332, Testimonio, Cusco, 24 May 1652. On Vega Bazán, see AGI Lima 332, Letter from Vega Bazán, Huamalies, 2 May 1656.

Joseph Laureano de Mena, Felipe de Medina, Bernardo de Novoa, Alonso Osorio, Pablo Recio de Castilla, Juan Sarmiento de Vivero, Diego Tello de Gúzman, Diego de Torres y Zúñiga, and Estanislao de Vega Bazán. These men were of an average age of almost fifty-two years when they were active agents of the Extirpation.[51] Ten had parents who were said to have definitely been born in Spain (*peninsulares*) and to have been of proven "noble and pure" blood, while the five others were of undefined but always "honored" parentage. Five claimed descent from the conquerors of Peru and Chile but according to Villagómez only two had either the papers or conciliar recognition to prove it.[52]

Most of these men were trained in the humanities by the Jesuit teachers from the College of San Pablo in Lima. Ten were alumni of the College of San Martín, and the full fifteen obtained bachelors degrees (usually in arts, Theology, Canon Law, or a combination of these) from San Marcos University. Six were licentiates, and three of the men graduated with doctorates, two in theology and one in canon law. All would have been more or less fluent in Latin, and would have translated from a classical canon of authors. And any who sought a benefice in the Andes would have taken instruction in Quechua at the university from professors who were often themselves frustrated in their climb up the same ecclesiastical ladder.

The visitadores were not only well-educated men for their place and time; they were the fortunate products of seventeenth-century schools whose teachers included the humanist and founding theoretician of the Extirpation, Pablo José de Arriaga; the linguist and preacher, Fernando de Avendaño; one of the greatest compilers of Indian jurisprudence, Diego de Avendaño; and the moral theologian, Pedro de Oñate, disciple of Francisco Suárez and superior of the great Jesuit experiments in Paraguay, among many others.[53] Thus any impression that would-be extirpators were poorly trained or that their intellectual

---

[51] Avendaño's age of seventy years in 1651 and Cardenas y Arbieto's of twenty-nine in 1663 balance each other out, but should be seen as uncharacteristic to either extreme. This is not a complete list, but a list of the principal actors. Other figures, such as Esteban de Aguilar or the friar-visitador Francisco de Lugares, served sporadically and often as replacements for resting or retired prefects. This information and that which immediately follows derives, unless otherwise indicated, from a series of recommendations for ecclesiastical vacancies. All were written from Lima and addressed to the king: AGI Lima 302, 31 May 1643; AGI Lima 302, 23 October 1648; AGI Lima 303, 26 August 1651; AGI Lima 59, viceroy, Conde de Alva to the king, 15 September 1655; AGI Lima 303, 22 July 1657; AGI Lima 303, 29 August 1658; AGI Lima 303, 8 June 1663; and AGI Lima 304, 5 December 1664.

[52] The five were Barreto, Novoa, Sarmiento, Torres y Zúñiga, and Vega Bazán. See J. Lockhart's second appendix, "Mistakes, Lies, and Legends: Men Who Were Not at Cajamarca" in *The Men of Cajamarca*, pp. 464–70 on unproven claims of *conquistador* descent.

[53] See especially, L. Martín and J. A. Pettus, eds., *Scholars and Schools*. Apart from the Extirpation treatise of 1621, Arriaga wrote a textbook on effective oration for the Jesuit college of San Pablo, the *Rhetoris Christiani Partes Septem*. The sermons of F. de Avendaño are discussed in Chapter Six below. D. de Avendaño's *Thesaurus Indicus* sits alongside the collections of legal and moral precedent in Spain's American experience by Juan de Matienzo and Juan de Solórzano Pereira. Oñate wrote about international ethics in his *De Contractibus*, and was the author of a much-cited letter to the viceroy, the count of Chinchón, in 1629, condemning the use of Indian labor in the mines at Huancavelica. See R. Vargas Ugarte, ed. *Pareceres jurídicos*, pp. 140–53.

background was misrepresentative of that of a contemporary, educated Spaniard or Creole should be abandoned. Certain lieutenants and assistants in the parishes, men of more uncertain instruction and training, would occasionally involve themselves in idolatry investigations, of course, but the average visitador was a lettered man.[54] This, however, is different from saying they were satisfied.

Extirpators of idolatry, even more than other priests, have often been tarred with the same brush, presented as rather flat figures carved out of some cultural and religious monolith. Subtleties of difference within their ranks, so often passed over, should provoke more interest than they have. That said, the effects of the future visitadores' education—or of that of Archbishop Villagómez for that matter—are as difficult to measure systematically as the impact of their first-hand experiences as priests among the Indians. Colonial prelates and other commentators made no secret of the degradation and loss of learning and competence they believed would set in once a priest had been set in his parish for a number of years. And the transmission of these beliefs would not have been the only thing making life difficult. Ordination, like taking the vows of a religious order, represented a common way forward for educated Andean creoles whose other possibilities were frequently blocked by peninsular privilege and prejudice. Yet their sights were often set on ends other than, say, a small parish of Indians in Yauyos.[55]

Being a learned person, and perhaps a frustrated Creole, could have had its disadvantages for an individual whose life might be spent in remote Andean parishes. It would have hindered enjoyment, increased impatience, and conceivably hardened attitudes about the "rustic" parishioners one ostensibly served. For aspiring priests such as Francisco de Avila (irrespective of whether he was Creole or Mestizo), and doubtless the others who followed him, the extirpation of idolatry represented a way out—and one taken often at the expense of Andean parishioners. One's participation in the Extirpation could reasonably be seen as a step in the direction of Lima or an urban parish of Spaniards that men like Recio de Castilla, Vega Bazán, and many others sought.

In the ecclesiastical climate of the mid-colonial Archdiocese of Lima, a commitment to a more coercive means of conversion and civilization of the Andean became common among many churchmen. Perhaps more surprisingly, however, the inclination away from standard missionary methods and toward more coercive forms was not simply an automatic recipe for benightedness or belief in diabolic agency.[56] One should not dismiss lightly, for example, Villagómez's own emphasis on the education that Andeans would need to lead them back to

---

[54] Although the preacher Fernando de Avendaño was not entirely typical, the inventory of his library surveyed by Pedro Guibovich is revealing; see "La carrera."

[55] See W. B. Taylor, *Magistrates of the Sacred*, ch. 4; B. Lavallé, *Las promesas ambiguas*.

[56] Work on the imposition and influence of a penitential regime among the Nahua in colonial New Spain reminds us that missionary strategies could, in the end, be coercive in their own insidious and effective ways. See especially L. Burkhart, *The Slippery Earth*, and J. J. Klor de Alva "Colonizing Souls" and "Sin and Confession." Also, by S. Gruzinski, "Individualization and Acculturation."

proper observance of the Christian faith. It was his contention that his extirpating program, properly implemented and followed up, would rapidly transform Andean society for the better largely because of the instructional dimension. Furthermore, a man like the visitador Cano Gutiérrez was commended by his prelate not only for his extirpating zeal but also for a discourse he once presented (in the tradition of Oñate's more famous letter) on the necessity of alleviating the appalling working conditions at the mine of Huancavelica.[57] But most striking of all are the impressions gleaned from the interrogations, sentences, and arguments in the trial documentation, which confirm that all extirpators were not of a piece on the matter of Andean religious reform. Fascinating differences in their characters and arrays of priorities come to light.

Two principal routes appear to have been open to these young priests after ordination and the almost obligatory baccalaureate. First, there were parish appointments for the best and brightest who managed to impress a stern tribunal of examiners in the oposiciones. These were the examination interviews in which the candidates would be asked to expound upon selected passages and concepts, often from the corpus of Aristotle, in competition with as many as twenty others of similar qualifications and connections.[58] The second route was academic. Many of these fifteen visitadores had been professors, or at least interim teachers of Quechua, or else lecturers in one of the faculties at San Marcos University. A few had served as rector. But this second option was usually temporary or a side interest while the men waited to win an oposición and begin their ecclesiastical careers. Archbishop Arias de Ugarte had tried to eliminate the tendency for studious churchmen to divide their time between sacerdotal duties and professorships at the university. In contrast, in the era of Villagómez, a man with scholarly interests and pretensions, this practice was esteemed.[59]

Before long, these men secured their first benefice, or some other appointment.[60] As trusted parish priests with good records of service and perhaps some contact with, or friends close to, Villagómez, they became vicars with regional supervisory responsibilites. Many were also regional agents for the Inquisition and the Santa Cruzada. Some would examine for the oposiciones in Quechua, and many clearly set their sights on a coveted office in the Cathedral of Lima. Selection as visitadores generales de idolatría in their late forties or

[57] AGI Lima 302, Letter from Villagómez to the king, Lima, 31 May 1643.

[58] Late in his term, Villagómez complained of the high numbers of clerical contestants. This is a good indication of the intense competition for ecclesiastical preferment and also explains why the friars' doctrinas, portrayed by many as the leftovers of the earlier missionary age, were so coveted. AGI Lima 304, Letter from Villagómez to the king, Lima, 26 February 1668. See also L. Martín, and J. A. Pettus, eds., *Scholars and Schools*, pp. 179–80; W. B. Taylor, *Magistrates of the Sacred*, ch. 5, and D. A. Brading, *The First America*, pp. 321–22.

[59] See AGI Lima 302, Letter from Arias to the king, Lima, 28 May 1630.

[60] As I noted briefly above, Juan Sarmiento de Vivero, whose extirpating career is well known, followed a slightly more unorthodox path to his idolatry commission in 1660. He spent twelve years as chaplain in the Convento de la Encarnación in Lima (1637–1649) before serving as a visitador general in the Diocese of Huamanga (1649) and the Archdiocese of Lima (1655).

early fifties, as I have mentioned, did much to enhance their career prospects. As visitadores they were often dispatched to the Andean regions with which they were familiar as doctrineros, although this practice was often criticized because of justifiable fears about conflict of interest.

By the late 1650s and early 1660s, despite the fact that Pedro de Villagómez had extirpating teams operating in a number of regions and much evidence to show for his efforts, all was still not well on the tactical and political front in his war against Andean idolatry. Villagómez's correspondence betrays the mounting strains on a man whose plans and ideals were beleaguered by complications. Problems that can be described as internal to the renewed Extirpation gave way to problems caused by criticism from those on the outside.

Internally, the sporadic trials through the 1640s, and especially the false start after the theatric "departure" in 1649, were not the end to the difficulties.[61] Visitador Tello was detained by ordinary visita obligations in Huaylas; Vega Bazán, the archbishop wrote bitterly in the mid-1650s, "has deserted me totally"; both Barreto and Quijano were doing little on account of poor health; Barreto himself had been charged with corruption in Yauyos, and Novoa had ceased operations to face even more serious charges of cruel excesses committed in the course of duty. Although at this point Villagómez could only fear it, other idolatry inspectors would soon draw similar complaints and lawsuits. The archbishop's principal response was to raise once again the delicate issue of his visitadores' allowance, the *procuración*. How could he be expected to attract and maintain trustworthy and incorruptible subordinates if they were not properly provided for?[62]

Not only was it proving difficult for him to attract the best and most suitable clergy to act as idolatry inspectors, he claimed, but those priests he did secure were virtually obliged to take "contributions" in kind and in money from the Andean communities they investigated. Villagómez was adept at pleading his case and at drawing enough royal support to allow him room to maneuver in Lima. But how detrimental to the visitas de idolatría was the lack of financial support? As Antonio Acosta has pointed out, the Crown, through the viceregal government, had helped with the visitadores' expenses during the first campaigns of the Extirpation under Lobo Guerrero, thus the suspension of this assistance was a departure and could be represented a handicap. Still, the solution that Villagómez suggested at least twice in his correspondence—that the

---

[61] For example, as early as 26 September 1642, Villagómez supported the visita conducted by Rodrigo Gómez Bravo, the priest and vicar of Pampacolca in Huarochirí. AAL Leg. 2, exp. 8. The trial records are incomplete. And I have already discussed above the idolatry investigation initiated by Villagómez himself and continued by Juan Gutiérrez de Aguilar in the environs of Yaután, Huaylas, between 29 December 1646 and 27 January 1647. AAL Leg. 4, exp. 11.

[62] AGI Lima 59, Letters from Villagómez to the king, Lima, 24 June 1656 and 26 June 1657. The case against Novoa is in P. Duviols, *Cultura andina*, pp. 303–21, and the visitador's defense of himself a decade later in AGI Lima 304, Letter from Br. Bernardo de Novoa to the king, La Barranca, 20 February 1669.

visitadores be permitted to receive goods and contributions for their upkeep drawn from the Andean communities—was rejected as too open to abuse.[63] There is evidence to suggest at least two things about the effect of this decision by the crown. First, a number of visitadores clearly could not have cared less. And, second, betraying Villagómez's defensive complaint, the lack of official funding was not keeping able clergy from the visitadores' ranks. Many idolatry inspectors funded their operations with money from their own pockets, but many seem also to have considered it their right to make up as much of this expense as they might in the course of their duties. And visitadores were clearly not always careful to restrain the greed and cruelty of their petty officials. As priests in Andean parishes, a number of the visitadores were accustomed to living beyond the edge of the law, augmenting their small stipend with goods and produce from the labor of the Indian community and with charges for their religious services. As visitadores, at least some abused their new powers and turned the force they could justify in their own terms into violence, committing unwarranted acts against the Andeans they were charged to reform.

The examples here are legion. There is no doubt that many mid-colonial Andeans perceived the usefulness of raising an allegation (whether false or genuine) of corruption against Christian authorities who threatened their lives, or negotiated arrangements and their very livelihoods. But this ever-present possibility does not obscure the cases in which a lawsuit or filed grievance appears to have been one of the few means of public defense Andean parishioners had against a rapacious priest or set of visiting officials. As is indicated by the work of Duviols, Acosta, and others on Andeans' legal grievances against their priests and visitadores in the seventeenth century, Andean claims and fears of the visitadores' corruption often had basis in fact.[64]

One learns frequently of the Andean parishioners' fear of the extirpators. María Poma Ticlla of the Quiripa ayllu in the town of Huarochirí, for instance, informed Juan Sarmiento de Vivero in 1660 that she, Doña Francisca Melchora, and Isabel Llaxa (of the Huarochirí ayllu) had traveled to Lima to inform the "Señor Protector" (the Protector of the Indians, *protector general de los naturales*) that they had heard that the idolatry visitador (Sarmiento) was not only torturing people but that he was imprisoning "sorcerers" and charging them "twenty and thirty pesos." The Protector persuaded the three women not to speak these "wounding remarks." He dispatched them back to Huarochirí

---

[63] AGI Lima 303, Villagómez to the king, 28 August 1654 and AGI Lima 59, Villagómez to the king, Lima, 10 July 1658. See A. Acosta, "La extirpación de las idolatrías," pp. 185–86.

[64] A. Acosta's essays treat this theme exhaustively in one form or another, most systematically with respect to the visitadores of the Lobo Guerrero period. He offers information and interpretation on the Villagómez period in his 1987 response to Duviols's *Cultura andina* in "La extirpación de las idolatrías," esp. pp. 184–92. For Duviols's evidence on corruption in the Extirpation during the Villagómez period see for example his discussion of the charges that Andeans brought against three prominent visitadores, Diego Barreto (accused in Yauyos in 1655), Bernardo de Novoa (accused in Cajatambo in 1658), and Juan Sarmiento de Vivero (accused in Canta in 1665), to be discussed just below, in *La Lutte*, pp. 324–29, and more broadly ch. 4, pp. 299–333.

with assurances that the "Señor visitador was a saint who would not harm them."[65]

It was not long, however, before the saint himself, Juan Sarmiento de Vivero, faced two lengthy petitions against his alleged abuses and excesses in the region of Canta in 1665. His accusers were embarassingly specific about his officials' demands for money, among other things, making the truth of Poma Ticlla's fears of five years earlier in a relatively distant place seem all the more plausible. Don Cristóbal Pariasca, the kuraka of San Juan de Lampian, said that Sarmiento's entourage (the visitador, his notary, two fiscales, two interpreters, one magistrate, one defensor, two female and two male servants) had been in Canta for more than a year "causing much expense and discomfort to the Indians." None of the retinue received any payment, so all, he said, had to be provided for by the people of the area. They had stayed in Lampian itself for more than a month and a half, using mules, forcing the Indians to do manual labor and "other things." Pariasca continued, detailing the excessive charges that Sarmiento demanded for performing marriage ceremonies (twelve or more pesos), and noting how Indians who were accused of cohabitation were imprisoned and charged sometimes as much as twenty-five pesos. Additionally, an excessive payment, a procuración of over 120 pesos, was demanded of the pueblo, the confraternities, and Cristóbal Condorato, the *mayordomo* (chief attendant) of the church. Pariasca also accused the visitors of violence and flagrant moral crimes. Five houses and other property belonging to Juan Jiménes were said to have been burnt or otherwise destroyed by the visitadores' officials, and single Andean women were allegedly lured for "obscene purposes (*usos torpes*)" to the houses where the ministers and justices of the visitador were staying.[66]

Such avowals and evidence of the visitadores' abuses and exploitation of the Indians and their resources, of course, did no good to the revived Extirpation's reputation.[67] Moreover, it was compounded by the wider criticism Villagómez was receiving from both outside and within his extirpating circle. The archbishop referred to ruthless adversaries who, he said, were "undoubtedly motivated by the Devil," and who had redoubled their attacks on his spiritual administration. A principal problem, from Villagómez's point of view, was Don Juan de Padilla, the chief criminal attorney (*alcalde del crimen*) on the Audiencia of Lima who began his ongoing, general denunciation of the spiritual and temporal state of affairs in the central Andes with a letter to Philip IV on 15 October 1654. Among other things, Padilla complained of the great number of Indians in Peru who not only were ignorant of Christian doctrine but who

---

[65] AAL Leg. 4, exp. 32, fol. 4. Before making the trip they had gone first with their account to the local priest, Juan Bernabé de la Madriz.

[66] AAL Leg. 5, exp. 10, San Juan de Lampian, Canta, 1665, fols. 1–1v. Also P. Duviols, *La Lutte*, p. 327. This case is placed in a wider context in my "Bad Christians."

[67] Actual payments might be taken from the *cajas de comunidad* (the holding boxes where many Andean repartimientos kept money and important documents); See S. J. Stern, *Peru's Indian Peoples*, pp. 81 and 97–100.

seemed unlikely ever to learn of it, given the incompetence and idleness of most of the clergy. What the indigenous peoples of Peru required—according to this missive from the *alcalde del crimen* and his later correspondence—were teachers, able doctrineros who knew the Andean languages and who could be trusted.

Padilla's letter received attention in Spain. Philip IV responded with three royal decrees (to Padilla; to the viceroy, the count of Alva; and to Archbishop Villagómez), which requested explanations and—already sensing the political divisions among his subordinates on the ground in Lima—directed his officials to cooperate in finding means to solve these problems. The *real cédula* (royal decree) of 20 May 1656 sent to Villagómez told of the stir Padilla's words had caused among the Councillors of the Indies, and of their concern that the Indians of Peru, who had been regarded as "so rooted in the Catholic faith," were not being administered properly.[68] Villagómez could not but have felt challenged by Padilla's general insinuations and by the crown's acceptance of the official's claims in response. And Padilla was not yet finished. A *memorial* (report) included with his letter of 20 July 1657 condemned again the lack of pastoral achievement among Andean peoples, many of whom, he said, died without ever having received the Holy Sacrament of Communion. Furthermore, he suggested that the Jesuits be encouraged to take over a key parish in each region in order that they might act as examples to the clergy who were failing miserably in their tasks. What was most damaging to Villagómez, however, was Padilla's attention to the prelate's immobility and failure to undertake personal visitations in his realm. Padilla, of course, had larger evils in mind than Villagómez's administration, or the Extirpation of idolatry in particular. He was diplomatic enough to note that these pastoral "deficiencies" were "not a private evil of the Archdiocese of Lima." Yet here he protested too much and made his principal target clear.[69] The criticism had Villagómez foremost in mind, and it indirectly pertained to the Extirpation, in that the use of visitadores generales de idolatría formed a central part of Villagómez's approach to evangelization, his preferred solution to his own immobility and the religious error in the Indian parishes.

[68] AGI Lima 59. See M. M. Marzal, *La transformación religiosa peruana*, pp. 119–20, and R. Vargas Ugarte, *Historia de la Iglesia*, 3: 15–16.

[69] R. Vargas Ugarte, *Historia de la Iglesia*, 3: 15–16. Padilla's memorial, the "Trabajos, agravios e injusticias que padecen los indios del Perú en lo espiritual y temporal," which accompanied his letter to the king of 20 July 1657, is at AGI, Audiencia de Charcas 266. Rubén Vargas Ugarte has published a transcription in the appendix to vol. 3 of his *Historia general del Perú*, pp. 391–420. The memorial, the rush of correspondence it provoked, and its ramifications have been much discussed. A *junta* was eventually convened in Lima on the express orders of a royal *cédula* dated 21 September, 1660. The conference of many sessions included the viceroy, Archbishop Villagómez, the judges (*oidores*) of the Audiencia, and Padilla; the meetings resulted in a report prepared by the current general protector of the Indians, Diego de León Pinelo (1608–1671). The best and most entertaining discussion of the flurry of correspondence, and the point-by-point analysis of the memorial by the junta, is Manuel Marzal's in *La transformación religiosa peruana*, pp. 119–71.

There were other contemporary critics whose words and actions are even more easily seen as differing from Villagómez's Extirpation. Indeed, in appending to his *Carta pastoral* the adulatory and supportive letters of the contemporary bishop of Cusco, Juan Alonso Ocón, and of the Jesuit P. Francisco Patiño, both of whom wrote in 1648, Villagómez sought to paper over serious disagreement and create the impression of a unity of purpose in important parts of Peru. Anyone who surmised that movements of systematic extirpation, copied from the Limeño process, were about to be inititiated in neighboring dioceses would have been mistaken. In fact—as Villagómez knew well enough and could not conceal—neither the Peruvian prelates (ostensibly represented by Ocón) nor the Jesuits (ostensibly spoken for by Patiño) were accurately depicted as uniformly supportive of systematic extirpation as the best solution to idolatry. Villagómez himself framed three chapters of the *Carta pastoral* around the "objections" raised by unnamed opponents and doubters of the Extirpation's renewal. He portrayed their disapproval as unsurprising and nothing new in the history of Peru or elsewhere, but the attention he gave them and the strenuous efforts of denial betray a certain preoccupation with their case.[70]

The archbishop's religious critics in the 1650s and 1660s should be differentiated from the kind of opposition to the Extirpation that was perhaps best characterized by Archbishop Arias de Ugarte in the 1630s. Arias had questioned the motivations of prospective visitadores and enemies of idolatry, but he had also questioned the very existence of idolatry as a problem. He seemed to take a more patient and tolerant view of what others were calling serious religious errors, believing—like Mogrovejo and others both before and after him—that most Andeans who lived in parishes and missions were genuine converts to Christianity. What they required, from a Catholic point of view, was more teaching and more time to make the faith a steadfast (and orthodox) part of their religious lives. The critics of the renewed Extirpation in the 1650s and 1660s were more like the churchmen who had raised their voices against the Extirpation in the earlier seventeenth century. Neither group disputed the existence and evil of Andean religious error. What they challenged were the appropriateness and efficacy of the campaigns of the Extirpation as a means of reform. The principal remedy for the errors of baptized Andeans, some of whom had received substantial Christian instruction, they seemed to say, needed to be chosen carefully at this mid-colonial stage. Very much as was the case in the era of Lobo Guerrero, the most focused religious criticism in the time of Villagómez was somewhat veiled and came from outside the metropolitan see.

The letters of Francisco de Godoy, a Chilean Creole, and the sixth bishop of Huamanga (1652–1659) who was consecrated by Villagómez himself in Lima in 1652, reveal significant disagreement, and are perhaps the richest example. His belief in the existence of serious errors in Indian parishes and in the need for their remedy was clearly expressed. Bishop Godoy's pastoral visitations had uncovered much idolatry, particularly in July of 1656 in the town of Vilca in the

---

[70] *Carta pastoral*, chs. 8–10. The letters of Ocón and Patiño are at pp. 272–86.

region of Huancavelica, and he declared himself not averse to employing threats of extreme punishments in order to persuade Indians to reveal the details of their false religions that they might be speedily eradicated.[71] Yet, as seen in Padilla's denunciation and in the earlier criticisms of the Extirpation after Lobo Guerrero's death, Godoy placed most of the blame for Andean idolatry on the church's failure to uproot it through a strong presence, efforts in instruction, and the demonstration of a better way. Idolatry, in Godoy's opinion, was rampant in Huamanga mostly due to the scarcity of clergy in many parts of the diocese and to the related lack of intensity and good example in teaching the doctrine.

Less than a league from the city of Huamanga, Godoy had found few Indians who had ever taken communion; in the twenty-four leagues that separated the towns of Huanta and Sintihuailas, there were peoples who never saw the one priest charged with their pastoral care. Godoy began a school where Indians might learn the faith, but he strongly implied that he was overburdened and that more effort and personnel were needed. Thus, like others before him—and at the very time that the Extirpation was in operation in the neighboring Archdiocese of Lima—the bishop of Huamanga stressed definite priorities in his words, in the constitutions of the synods he convened, and in his actions. He saw the need for teachers and effective sermons rather than judges and corporal punishment. As Rubén Vargas Ugarte put it in 1960, Godoy believed the Eucharist the best remedy for idolatry.[72]

Contemporary Jesuit reservations over their continued participation in the visitas de idolatría were related to Godoy's subtle departures from the path recommended by the archbishop of Lima, but they were also a good deal more significant from Villagómez's point of view. It would have been troubling that the prelate of a nearby diocese, a man one had consecrated, was not responding favorably to the exhortation in the *Carta pastoral* he would surely have received and studied. Yet the bishop of Huamanga was not an immediately serious threat. Villagómez could view him simply as a neighboring prelate who favored a different approach to the same end. The Society of Jesus was another matter. The Jesuits had supplied the Extirpation's prime theoretician and first superintendent, Pablo José de Arriaga, and Jesuit padres had become essential features in an extirpator's entourage. Even the threat of their withdrawal of participation in his idolatry investigations was a blow from within.

A visitador, of course, might take it upon himself to preach during his stay in an Andean community, but alone he could not hope to deliver enough sermons to those in need. Moreover, while he was heading idolatry investigations he hardly had time to direct enough classes in elementary doctrine or absolve

---

[71] A. de Egaña, *Historia de la Iglesia*, pp. 344–45; and AGI Lima 308, Godoy to the king, Huamanga, 10 July 1656.

[72] AGI Lima 308, Godoy's letters from Huamanga of 15 June 1652, 30 August 1653, 18 June 1656, 10 July 1656, and 18 June 1657. R. Vargas Ugarte, *Historia de la Iglesia*, 3: 171–73; largely derivative of Vargas's points but also with a few other emphases, see A. de Egaña's *Historia de la Iglesia*, pp. 344–45.

enough parishioners of their sins to complement his stern hand with the reforming hand of a teacher. A Jesuit presence among the retinues of each visitador gave instruction a prominent place in the investigations. For the sake of
more than just appearances—but for appearances' sake as well—a pair of Jesuits provided considerable justification for action. The padres ensured that the
juridical and penal side of the visita de idolatría would have its necessary pedagogical complement.

Villagómez began complaining in writing about the Jesuits in the archdiocese—and he mentioned in particular their reservations about participating
in the Extirpation—in August of 1654.[73] Were the Jesuits seeking to frustrate
Villagómez's Extirpation just as it was beginning to pick up a momentum of its
own? If they were, their timing could hardly have been worse from the point of
view of Villagómez's rejuvenated initiative. The reasons behind the apparent
cooling of relations between the Society and the prelate are complicated, as are
the ways in which these particular relations sit within the context of Jesuit
attitudes and approaches to idolatry over a longer span of time.

It is useful to return briefly to Villagómez's own explanations for the difficulties in his relationship with the Jesuits. Villagómez estimated in 1658 that
the Jesuits were feeling increasingly anxious that their positions as the Indians'
trusted confessors and missionaries were being jeopardized through association
with the visitas de idolatría. The Indians, it is implied, were growing distrustful
of searching their consciences before the very same missionaries who walked
on the right side of the Extirpation; true confession required trust and, quite
conceivably, the involvement of the confessors with the Extirpation tainted that
trust. The Jesuit padres in the Lima region, Vargas Ugarte contends from the
explanation offered by Villagómez, chose to return to the pedagogical and missionary methods for which they were already famous.[74]

Although it is true that a conscious shift away from the relatively random
investigations and punishments of inquisitorial regimes toward missionary regimes of instruction and "penitential discipline" had, from the point of view of
many churchmen, a far greater chance of reaching evangelical objectives
among the Indians, it is misrepresentative of both Jesuit opinions and actions to
pretend that the Society was making a clean break in these years, rejecting
systematic extirpation and returning to missionary persuasion. The subject of
Jesuits' reservations about their own participation in the extirpation process in
the middle of the seventeenth century must be approached more carefully. As
Duviols in particular has hinted, there was much more to mid-colonial Jesuit
policy toward idolatry in Peru—both within and outside of the Villagómez
era—than has generally been suggested. It is worth noting that some members
of the Society were never completely comfortable with its close association
with the Extirpation. Furthermore, the Jesuits' alleged withdrawal of official

---

[73] AGI Lima 303, Villagómez to the king, Lima, 28 August 1654.
[74] R. Vargas Ugarte, *Historia de la Iglesia*, 3: 9–11. See also P. Duviols, *La Lutte*, ch. 2, esp.
pp. 181–86, and *La destrucción*, pp. 225–28.

collaboration with the Extirpation campaigns in the 1650s was neither definite nor straightforward.[75]

There is both implicit and solid evidence that some Jesuit missionaries continued to team up with Villagómez's commissioned idolatry inspectors well after relations were said to have fallen off. The provincial in Lima in the early 1660s, for instance, seems to have felt no painful rift and no reason to distance the Jesuits' current activities from the Extirpation. He told of how "our missionaries (*nuestro missioneros*)" preached among the peoples of the Cajatambo region and how pleased they were to find that the Andeans had become good Christians, "no longer living as they [and their predecessors] had done." He wrote proudly and specifically to Rome of what "our padres" had achieved "in past times" in Cajatambo; during the time of Archbishop Lobo Guerrero and Viceroy Esquilache the Jesuits had not only raised their regular missions, but they had, in the company of idolatry inspectors, "found many idolaters." After the punishment of the Andean "maestros," the offenders had been reconciled, and "two beautiful crosses had been erected on the site of the ancient Andean sacred place (*el adoratorio antiguo*)."[76] Jesuits may not have been proceeding out from Lima as part of the official retinues of the Extirpation after the middle of the 1650s, but while pursuing their independent missions in the standard pairs, some visitadores working in the same regions appear to have been able to gain their assistance.[77]

In spite of the early delays, the charges of corruption, implicit criticisms, and the imperfect assistance of Jesuit assistants, Villagómez's Extirpation continued—albeit more quietly. In a remarkable shift in his ways, Villagómez became distinctly less forthcoming with information about his extirpators' exploits in the 1660s, at precisely the time of their busiest operations.[78] The comparative silence that surrounds the movements of the Extirpation's agents in Villagómez's last decade has, no doubt, contributed to the impression that attitudes were beginning to change and that, by 1671 at least, the repressive campaign against idolatry was on its last legs. Reflecting these assumptions, Villagómez's death has customarily marked the end of the study of the Extirpation of idolatry, not to mention of mid-colonial Andean religion.[79] Although there can be no doubting the loss of a major promoter of a centrally organized assault against idolatry, and that less information can be derived from élite sources and ecclesiastical correspondence, extirpation continued.

[75] On "penitential discipline," see J. J. Klor de Alva, "Colonizing Souls." On Jesuit policy toward idolatry, P. Duviols, *La destrucción*, pp. 228 and 225.

[76] ARSI, Carta anua de los años de 1660, 1661 y parte de 1662, *Peru* 16, vol. 5, fols. 69v–70.

[77] See, for example, evidence from Huaylas in ARSI, Cartas anuas de los años de 1664, 1665 y 1666, *Peru* 16, vol. 5, fol. 107v.

[78] See R. Vargas Ugarte, *Historia de la Iglesia*, 3: 15–34, and A. Egaña, *Historia de la Iglesia*, pp. 294–97, for the most detailed presentations of these eras from an ecclesiastical viewpoint.

[79] Spalding's brief attention to early eighteenth-century trials in the Huarochirí region is a notable exception; *Huarochirí*, pp. 263–65.

The idolatry investigations pursued in the period after 1671—their changes in methodology, their different and similar preoccupations, their divergent and familiar findings—are not yet well known. The religious information from a number of the post-Villagómez trials, however, can provide a suggestive frame.

Archbishop Villagómez's immediate successor, an elderly native of Córdoba, Andalucía, the Trinitarian friar Juan de Almoguera (1674–1676), had, like his predecessor, served as bishop of Arequipa (1659–1674) before his accession to the metropolitan see. Almoguera made a reforming and moralizing mark on both lay and clerical society in Arequipa and during his short tenure in Lima.[80] He seems to have done little to hinder or otherwise affect the Extirpation of idolatry in the archdiocese while it was in his care. There is evidence of at least two idolatry investigations in Cajatambo in 1671, one in 1672 in Huaylas, three in 1675 (in Chancay, Canta, and Cajatambo), another one in Chancay in 1676 (which expressly notes his archiepiscopate), and two in 1677, the year after Almoguera's death and before the arrival of his successor.[81] The trials seem to have occurred more because the institutional machinery and concerned personnel were in place than because of any particular encouragement from either the ecclesiastical cabildo or, after 1675, Almoguera.

The evidence is ambivalent. Yet there is a hint that Almoguera might have been less than perfectly sympathetic to organized extirpation. A letter written to the king from Arequipa by then Bishop Almoguera on 16 May 1663 suggests that although the future archbishop of Lima was pessimistic about the spiritual state in which many mid-colonial Andeans existed, he was not personally prone to view Andean idolatry as an evil requiring radical investigative action. "The Indian caste, my lord, has perverse tendencies," he wrote, "they are excessively inclined to lie, to get drunk, and not to work." Yet unlike Villagómez, who, during his time in the southern diocese three decades earlier, claimed to have found thousands of idolaters and many huacas being venerated, Almoguera stated categorically that "there are no idolatrous Indians in this diocese, not even in its outermost parts." When Almoguera had heard about a "few" peoples who were living in the "remote mountain passes," he had dispatched Jesuits to

---

[80] In a letter to the king in 1668, Fr. Almoguera spoke of the continuing animosity toward friars who retained parishes, and he demonstrated a sophisticated understanding of the temptations and conditions that many religious faced outside the cloister. AGI Lima 309, Almoguera to the king, Arequipa, 28 November 1668. On his character and priorities see also P. Guibovich Pérez, "Evangelización y sociedad." More generally, see A. de Egaña, *Historia de la Iglesia*, pp. 298–300 and R. Vargas Ugarte, *Historia de la Iglesia*, 3: 175–82.

[81] AAL, Legajo and expediente unnumbered (but Leg. 7, exp. 9 by the new classification), Cajatambo, Cajatambo, 1671; AAL Leg. 4, exp. 41 and Leg. 5, exps. 10 and 17, Mangas, Cajatambo, 1671; BNP, B 612, Santiago de Aija, Huaylas, 1672; AAL Leg. 1, exp. 6 and Leg. 4, exp. 11, San Francisco de Ihuarí, Chancay (repartimiento of Checras), 1675; AAL, Legajos and expedientes unnumbered, but Leg. 5, exp. 24, Canta, 1675, and Leg. 7, exp. 16, Churín, Cajatambo, 1675, according to the new classification; AAL Leg. 5, exp. 14, Villa de Chancay, Chancay, 1676; AAL Leg. 5, exp. 15, Santiago de Maray, Chancay (repartimiento of Checras), 1677; and AAL Leg. 7, exps. 13, 14, and 24, Pararín, Recuay, 1677. For the new numbers of trials that were without clear designation when I conducted my research, I have relied on L. Gutiérrez Arbulú, "Indice."

ensure their knowledge of the true faith. He seems to have viewed persistent Andean religion—in the Arequipa region at least—as something that required a steady mopping up and not a campaign of repression. His presentation was not aggressive, and in his implications Almoguera was not much distant from other contemporary prelates such as Godoy in Huamanga—not to mention others who were implicitly or explicitly critical of Villagómez's Extirpation— who saw the need for teachers rather than judges.

Almoguera's accent fell consistently on the good that would come from the reform of the clergy; he considered better-trained and morally sound doc-trineros as the key to the evangelization of Indians. Baptized Andeans, he wrote, tend to slide back to "their natural condition" largely because of a lack of guidance from Spanish Christians; the Indians' misguided customs had been "poorly repressed" and the people had "never been properly indoctrinated."[82] Yet, in spite of Almoguera's apparent views, the movements of Extirpation did not end, and of this fact he was undoubtedly aware. From extant documenta-tion, at least five individuals—Ignacio de Castelvi, Domingo Francisco del Castillo, Joseph Morán Collantes, Juan de Esquivel y Aguila, and Francisco Alvarado y Tovar—conducted visitas de idolatría in the archdiocese between 1671 and 1677. As was the case with the deaths of Lobo Guerrero and Arriaga in an earlier time, the passing of Pedro de Villagómez may have provided the Extirpation's critics room to maneuver, but a number of Andean parishes did not gain much of a reprieve. Evidently, a new group of parish priests-turned-visitadores were replacing the cadre that had been led especially by Juan Sar-miento de Vivero in the 1660s.[83] If the immediate post-Villagómez years were a time to consider the approach to evangelization that had been officially fa-vored, even if not universally supported, over the last three decades, there is precious little evidence that much had changed in practice.

The archiepiscopate of Melchor de Liñán y Cisneros (1678–1708), an expe-rienced peninsular from near Madrid offers another thirty-year span to con-sider. Liñán does not contrast sharply with Almoguera, and cannot emerge as a strong candidate for the line of extirpating Peruvian prelates that already in-cluded Lobo Guerrero, Campo, and Villagómez. Indeed, Liñán's official priori-ties appear to have been moral and reformative of the secular and ecclesiastical establishment in ways that Almoguera's also had been, and his admiration for the Jesuits was considerable.[84] The archbishop lamented the fact that his own

---

[82] AGI Lima 309, Almoguera to the king, Arequipa, 16 May 1663. The bishop wrote in reponse to three royal cédulas, one of which (27 June 1662) exhorted him to renew his efforts "to convert Indians who were infidels and to conserve in the faith those who were already 'reduced.'"

[83] Sarmiento's last recorded idolatry trials were in 1668–1669 in the city of Lima. Also partic-ularly active in Lima in 1669–1670 was Luis Fernández de Herrera. In 1669, Cristóbal de Vargas Garrido led a visita in Ocros, Cajatambo (AAL Leg. 2, exp. 31), and Rodrigo de Molina conducted an investigation in Atavillos Alto, Canta (AAL Leg. 7, exp. 10).

[84] See esp. ASV, Ad Limina 450, Liñán to the pope, Lima, 30 November 1692, and his request for the power to appoint a commission to investigate the abuses of Indians by corregidores, local magistrates, and governors. AGI Lima 304, Liñán to the king, Lima, 28 June 1678. See also ASV,

"watchmen" in the provinces informed him that the "Indian *miserables* and other parishioners" were often subjected to much misery because of the misdeeds of "their own priests," as well as by the "regular clergy" who took advantage of their measure of independence from ordinary jurisdiction to do as they wished in the Indian parishes they administered.[85]

Yet on the subject of Andean religious error Archbishop Liñán y Cisneros, too, kept his options open. He clearly believed that the indigenous peoples of the archdiocese needed, more than anything, better Christian instruction, but this view did not translate into aversion for extirpation. Liñán himself wrote approvingly of at least one former extirpator, Bernardo de Novoa, by this time the oldest canon in the metropolitan cathedral. And he does not appear to have awakened negative emotion in Lima toward either the memory of Villagómez or the Extirpation that he had revived and that continued to be active. A letter with eight signatories from the municipality of Lima, in reference to the merits of another of Villagómez's former visitadores generales, Ignacio de Castelvi, by now the treasurer of Cusco's cathedral, noted his "good example" to the Indians with whom he worked incessantly, "teaching them in the Catholic faith and separating them from the errors of paganism."[86] Liñán's tenure saw a definite resumption of extirpating operations, albeit slightly more sporadically and with some procedures clearly altered from the Villagómez years.

At least twenty-three idolatry investigations were conducted between 1678 and 1708, with the busiest period occurring in the decade 1690–1701, when there were eighteen trials.[87] The specific concerns of some of these proceedings—and of many others that followed them, during the tenures of the auxiliary archbishop who followed Liñán, Francisco de Cisneros y Mendoza, and the archbishops Antonio de Soloaga (1714–1722), Diego Morcillo (1724–1730), and Antonio Escandón (1732–1739)—are treated in other chapters. What needs emphasizing is that the aims, findings, and means of idolatry

---

Segretaria di Stato, Lettere de Vescovi e Prelati, vol. 54, fol. 58, Melchior Archiepiscopus Limanus a Sanctissime Pater, Lima, 2 September 1681.

[85] AGI Lima 520, Liñán to the king, Lima, 18 October 1704.

[86] On Novoa, AGI Lima 304, Liñán to the king, Lima, 21 November 1690. On Castelvi, AGI Lima 520, the city of Lima to the king, Lima, 20 September 1682. One of Castelvi's visitas began on 20 April 1671, in the town of Cajatambo, in the district of the same name; AAL Legajo and expediente unnumbered (but Leg. 7, exp. 9 according to the new archival classification), Cajatambo. Another was conducted in nearby Mangas in the same year; AAL Leg. 4, exp. 41, and Leg. 5, exps. 10 and 17.

[87] L. Gutiérrez Arbulú, "Indice," pp. 126–28. The figure, however, should not be taken to signify anything more than a vague indication. As stated above, some trials were quick and others lengthy. Also, archival classification changes since 1989–1990 mean that documents which were often differentiated as separate "expedientes" are now sometimes lumped into the single investigation to which they most relate. For example, the idolatry investigation in La Concepción de Canta, Canta, in 1696 which by the previous classification was treated as three trials (AAL Leg. 5, exps. 25, and 26, and Leg. 4, exp. 46) is now AAL Leg. 9, exps. 6 and 8. With the same proviso about concluding too much from mere numbers of trials, in the holdings of the Archiepiscopal Archive of Lima one notes eleven idolatry investigations between 1708 and 1741, with at least another seven extant from after the latter date. L. Gutiérrez Arbulú, "Indice," pp. 128–30.

investigations of the 1690s or 1720s are recognizable in comparison with those of, say, the 1650s or 1660s. Pedro de Celis y Vega's visita to the parishes of Santiago de Maray, Checras (Chancay), and San Juan de Churín, Cajatambo, in 1724–1725, for instance, uncovered an intricate and functioning regional system of huaca worship.[88] And perhaps the most detailed surviving evidence of chanca worship comes from Toribio de Mendizábal's proceedings against Juan de Rojas, Francisco Libiac Condor, and others in and around Santiago de Carampoma, Huarochirí, in 1723.[89] Moreover, many of the punishments of idolaters in the late seventeenth or early eighteenth centuries resemble those of the 1650s or, for that matter, the era of Lobo Guerrero. Although some of the later trials did especially target individual offenders, this concentration was no more intense than before 1671. Finally, there are inquiries which are as voluminous and as complex in their many investigative strands and numbers of witnesses in the eighteenth as well as the middle of the seventeenth century.

Still, the resemblances between extirpating initiatives across the mid-colonial period do not mask the fact that a number of differences also emerge in the post-Villagómez investigations, not least those differences which cluster around noticeable changes in Andeans' capacities to defend themselves before their accusers and interrogators. Many late seventeenth- and early eighteenth-century communities had grown accustomed to the idea of an investigation of their religiosity and were aware of what surviving it would require. Individuals had grown conspicuously canny and conspicuously more able to demonstrate their Christianity. More than in earlier times, some people who appeared before extirpators demonstrated a nearly impeccable knowledge of the Christian doctrine, notable appetites for charity, and acts of personal and communal piety as evidence to counter idolatry accusations. An increasing number of principal accused among the Andean élite added to their model Christian citizenship a literacy in Spanish; many made impassioned written arguments for their innocence and against the injustices they claimed were perpetrated by their accusers and investigators. But the changes were not only on the Andean side.

Extirpation itself was changing in the post-Villagómez era. In some ways, though trials were less frequent than in the 1660s, the visita general de idolatría was becoming more systematic—even more like its methodological forebear, the Holy Office—in that there were more restrictions and checks in place than before. For example, Andeans increasingly took advantage of the special advocates and defenders, both in a given region and in Lima, who were in place for the Indians' benefit as protection from corrupt Spaniards and unwarranted accusations. These protectors could make complex legal arguments and assist in the presentation of a defendant's point of view. The Indians' *defensor* (advocate) countered and responded to the presentation of evidence assembled by the chief prosecutor of a given case, the *promotor fiscal*, in a fashion reminis-

---

[88] AAL Leg. 3, exp. 10, and Leg. 3, exp. 11; see Chapter Two above.
[89] AAL Leg. 3, exp. 9; see Chapter Three above.

cent of an inquisitorial trial. Defense officials were certainly not unknown during the Villagómez era, but Indian advocacy had been inconsistent. The role of defender, if it was taken up at all, was often left to a distant official in Lima known as the *protector general de los naturales*.

Finally, churchmen appear to have reached a consensus about the advisability of shifting more idolatry investigations to the central ecclesiastical court in Lima rather than leave them to be settled in the less easily monitored provincial villages and towns. Again, although some idolatry investigations were ultimately resolved in Lima during Villagómez's time, these had been exceptions. In Archbishop Liñán's time and thereafter, it became common for there to be no commissioned visitadores generales de idolatría. An idolatry trial might be begun in a local setting by a priest-extirpator who would gather initial charges and even hear testimonies, but only before transferring people and papers for conclusion and final sentencing in Lima. Thus, Bartolomé de Figueroa (the deputy [*teniente*] of the local priest) initiated the proceedings against one Domingo García in Santiago de Arahuay, Canta, in 1741–1742, in a case that was decided before Don Andrés de Munibe, the provisor and vicar general of the archdiocese. Also typically, the accused, García, was aided by Francisco Dávila y Torres, the *procurador de naturales*, one of the advocates noted above.[90]

The Extirpation that was revived by Pedro de Villagómez and that evolved in the years after his death attempted to answer its critics. This was because many churchmen believed it offered the best solution to persistent Andean religious error. What can too easily be obscured by the undeniable repressive side of the Christianity purveyed by extirpators is the element that was perhaps most central to its self-definition and sense of legitimacy in the face of diverse concerns, its perceived capacity to educate and encourage reform.

[90] AAL Leg. 3, exp. 17.

Reformation

THE IMAGE of the Extirpation of idolatry is justifiably a repressive one. The systematic visitations, interrogations, torture, punishments, and exiles carried out by the idolatry inspectors in the Archdiocese of Lima represent perhaps the most sustained religious persecution of indigenous peoples in the history of colonial Spanish America. Certain viceroys were ardent supporters, influential prelates were its benefactors and theoreticians, and many ranks of clergy and laymen were involved with, and even led, the visitas of idolatry in the Indian parishes. Although some of the investigations were clearly generated by conflict, competition, and self-interest within the parishes, there was also an overarching religious atmosphere in the Lima region that was self-perpetuating and that gave the Extirpation momentum.

In some ways, the Extirpation of idolatry was an example of theory being put into practice by Spanish representatives of the Roman Catholic Church in the New World. The Church's intermittent quest for purity and conformity in Peru and elsewhere connected attitudes framed in early Christian times, and developed in a variety of contexts thereafter, with approaches to heterodoxy and dissent in Counter-Reformation Spain and the Spanish world.[1] For the evangelist and extirpator of idolatry in Spanish America, Christian history was to be a powerful and malleable resource, a fount of authority and a practical guide. Just how the resource and guide was used, however, varied greatly. Generally speaking, the extirpating efforts of missionaries and priests across colonial Spanish America were inconstant. Much depended on individual churchmen's attitudes to the religious expressions of their parishioners, and on the climates of opinion encouraged by prelates and other officials.

Parish extirpating initiatives, as well as specific and more intensive examples such as the investigations of Cristóbal de Albornoz against the Taki Onqoy in south-central Peru in the 1560s, belong to different categories of religious repression than does the Extirpation. They were independently raised, and a response to a defined problem—something that Spanish officials saw as a movement and linked even to the political threat of the rebel neo-Inkas.[2] Beginning in the seventeenth century, for the first time in Peru, the religious crimes of baptized Andeans—their idolatry, heresy, and apostasy—were being

---

[1] Pioneering work that explores some of these lines is that of Sabine MacCormack. See especially *Religion in the Andes*, "Limits of Understanding," and "Ubi Ecclesia?"

[2] C. de Albornoz, "Instrucción," pp. 35–37. Among the many contemplations of the Taki Onqoy that followed after Luis Millones's work, and which particularly consider the fears it raised in Visitador Albornoz and the colonial state, see N. Wachtel, "Rebeliones y milenarismo," esp. p. 119. More generally, S. J. Stern, *Peru's Indian Peoples*, pp. 51–71, and R. Varón Gabai, "El Taki Onqoy."

systematically assaulted by a machinery of repression that was essentially a tamed version of the one that tried the crimes of heretics and deviants in contemporary Europe and Spanish America. The Extirpation's flaws and differences from what might be called classic inquisitorial form are less surprising when one considers the varied nature of the Inquisition's own methods in the many places and circumstances in which it made its presence felt. Pierre Duviols has accurately depicted the Extirpation an "Inquisition for Indians."[3]

The move toward judicial repression as a means of combating surviving Andean beliefs and perversions of Catholicism represented a victory for the impatient in the Peruvian context. In spite of the unevenness of evangelization efforts in early colonial times caused by such things as civil war, lust for treasure, and the inherent difficulties of the Andean terrain, in the minds of many seventeenth-century churchmen the mendicant orders had enjoyed over a century to finish their task: they had spread the Word of the True God and had introduced thousands of Indians to the Mother Church through baptism and elementary catechization; and they had done what they could to transform what the Europeans regarded as dispersed communities into a network of Christian parishes. Although disagreement and vacillation characterized Spanish Christian policy more than any clear shift in emphasis, for many churchmen it seemed time, even beyond time, for the mendicants to get out of the way.

For the apologists of extirpation, the next step would involve not only a more aggressive attitude toward the transfer of the *doctrinas de indios* administered by religious to secular clergy, but also a change of tack toward the systematic application of due force to encourage orthodoxy. The business of enforcing orthodoxy and punishing obstinate offenders belonged to the ecclesiastical justice system of the Church proper. Thus it was that the Extirpation of idolatry, a largely judicial and penal process with a jurisdiction over religious belief in the Indian regions, saw its inception. As I argued in Chapters One and Five, the so-called "discovery" of idolatry by the priest from Huarochirí, Francisco de Avila, and his careful direction of the theatrics that followed would have prompted no systematic extirpating initiative if there were not a broader climate of impatience with Andean religious error, and if like-minded prelates (especially Bartolomé Lobo Guerrero and Gonzalo de Campo, in the first instance, and Pedro de Villagómez, in the second) had not existed.

For over a decade after 1609–1610, again in 1625–1626, between 1646 and 1671, and occasionally thereafter until roughly 1750, archbishops of Lima either dispatched their specialized ecclesiastical judges and teachers, the visitadores de idolatría, or approved idolatry investigations by parish priests and the central ecclesiastical court. They tried and punished substantial numbers of Indians for a wide range of religious crimes. The intermittent declaration and acceptance of the need for so much extirpation was, in itself, something of an acknowledgement of failure for the Church. Quite apart from their demonstra-

---

[3] P. Duviols, *La Lutte*, pp. 217–26, and P. Duviols, ed., *Cultura andina*, pp. lxxiii–lxxvi. Pondering Duviols's line, see N. Griffiths, "Inquisition of the Indians?"

tion of the undeniable survival of many aspects of the prehispanic religious system, many of the Indians' spiritual offences suggested serious imperfections in the Christianization process. As many inquisitors of diverse parishioners in early modern Spain had also realized, punishment was often deserved more by the people's pastors than by the ignorant flock.[4] No matter how much the Devil or the incapacity of the Indians were invoked as part of the Spaniards' explanation for the suspect nature of Andean religion, recourse to the extirpating agenda implied a dissatisfaction with what had been accomplished, a rejection of the missionary approach as an adequate means of bringing the bulk of the indigenous population securely into the Christian fold.[5]

At some points in the seventeenth century, so striking is the swing of the Limeño Church's official attitude away from missionary persuasion toward openly sanctioning the use of methodical force against Indian idolatry that what is often forgotten, or passed over too quickly, is that the visita de idolatría was conceived of as a genuine effort at reformation, a reintegration of recalcitrant and misguided Indian Christians back into Christendom. The Extirpation's proponents presented their methods as those of persuasion, and they stressed their pastoral and reformative mission. The idolatry visitadores, the vicars and priests in Andean parishes were, Villagómez wrote in 1649, the "legitimate successors" of the apostles, teachers, and bearers of the same "sacred dignity." With such a mantle came an obligation, both to themselves and to "the inferior subjects." The Indians' salvations had become interconnected with those of the Spaniards through the process of evangelization. Anything that amounted to abandoning the former, he reminded his pastors, ensured the eternal damnation of both, the Spanish "for our negligence," and native Andeans "for their ignorance." Villagómez stressed the crying need for instruction in the archdiocese, just as in the time of Jesus Christ and Saint John the Baptist who had preached to the "gentiles," another people who, like the Andeans, did not understand religious matters in the same terms as their teachers, and who thus languished on the borders of the Holy Church. He emphasized the "helpful works of divine grace, by which we free our own souls and those of the people in our charge," and he exhorted his clergy not to be content as "forgetful listeners of the doctrine, who do not pass to the execution of it."[6]

The Church was accustomed to such predicaments, as Villagómez well knew. The message that turned inward to self-criticism in order to inspire Christian action and that also stressed pastoral aims in Peru differed little, for instance, from the message of the sixteenth-century Spanish Inquisitor General Fernando de Valdés, who sought not only to punish heretics but also to ensure that erring Christians would "cleave closer to the service of Our Lord," or that of

[4] See S. T. Nalle, *God in La Mancha*, especially the discussion of Juan de Collaga of Arbeteta who, accused of blasphemy and impiety, came before the inquisitors of Cuenca in 1556, on p. 104.

[5] S. MacCormack argues similarly in *Religion in the Andes*, esp. pp. 388–92. See also her "'The Heart Has Its Reasons.'"

[6] P. de Villagómez, *Carta pastoral*, ch. 1, pp. 3–4; 6–7; he returns to his theme in the final chapter of the first part, the exhortation; ibid., ch. 36, pp. 123–24.

Valdés's successor, Gaspar de Quiroga, who accentuated similarly his duty to make "good Christians."[7] Persons found guilty of the crime of idolatry in the Archdiocese of Lima might undergo a lengthy penance, suffer public shame and lashings, and even endure a lengthy exile for the things they said they believed and for the rituals in which they were thought to participate, but all this was done with a purpose. If at all possible, they were to be reformed. Moreover, they were to be intensively instructed (often re-instructed, it was underscored) in the faith and reconciled to active membership and worship in their parishes. In theory, even the most recalcitrant Andean ministers and dogmatizers sentenced to exile in the Casa de Santa Cruz were to mix their manual labor with regular education in the Catholic tenets, in anticipation of their repentance and a return to their communities. The lessons that Andean peoples were to learn from the whole procedure were thought to be numerous.

The Extirpation's instructive side presented the Indians with a Catholic Christianity that was neither the salvation-oriented variety of the sixteenth-century mass baptisms and "conversions" nor the patient and experimental faith of some other missionaries. Pablo José de Arriaga and, later, Pedro de Villagómez provided their own careful script. The evangelization efforts of the visitadores de idolatría were to be abrupt and intense doses of instruction supported by due force and exemplary punishment. Their instruction and efforts at persuasion were meant both as a warning and a dialectical process. The task was no longer conceived of as a first offering of Christianity, or even as part of a steady consolidation of the dialogue with the Savior that was said to have begun with baptism; a new evangelization was going on in the mid-colonial Andes. It was carried out by Church officials whose more coercive presence was seen as a necessary response to the fact that Indians, who had already received their introduction to Christianity, had strayed from the True Path and were leading others astray. The instructive aspect of the average visita de idolatría took on the character of a persuasion of apostates.[8] With the exception of the so-called "barbarous infidels" who still had the misfortune to live in ravines and jungles that remained beyond the reach of the parishes and mission stations, mid-colonial churchmen generally treated Andeans of the Archdiocese of Lima as a people who either knew, or had known, Christianity before falling away.[9] The extirpators spoke of, and were empowered to instill and enforce, a Catholic faith that, however unfamiliar it might actually be to many people in this part of the Andes, was supposed to have been planted years before. Voices which

[7] S. T. Nalle, *God in La Mancha*, pp. 63–64. At this point, Nalle is referring mostly to these officials' emphasis on "instilling higher standards of morality," but elsewhere she connects this emphasis to wider reform of both clerical sloth and popular ignorance of doctrine; see esp. ch. 4.

[8] In the context of the notorious sixteenth-century episode at Mani in Yucatán, Inga Clendinnen has argued that a similar, stepped-up intensity of Franciscan persecution can be explained in part by the Europeans' sense of paternal betrayal and disappointment with their persistently "idolatrous" Indian charges. See *Ambivalent Conquests*, pp. 112–26 and "Disciplining the Indians."

[9] On conceptions of and dealings with peoples beyond, and almost beyond, the reach of the gospel, see D. Block, *Mission Culture*, chs. 1 and 2.

argued that many Andean peoples were actually in need of more basic Catholic instruction than the Church was either admitting or preparing to offer were, during the Villagómez period in particular, mostly drowned out.

Archbishop Villagómez understood that the success of his attempt to rekindle systematic extirpation in the 1640s and 1650s would rest on his ability to disarm the critics of his plans. Thus, for reasons that certainly mixed zeal and expediency, he set out to meld a rebirth of the Extirpation of idolatry with an initiative of better instruction in the Christian faith. The first part of Villagómez's *Carta pastoral* of 1649 was an exhortation, composed to stir complacent priests and prospective visitadores into action and to guide them in their struggle against the idolatrous evil. The prelate devoted a full five chapters to refuting the arguments of those who, he claimed, did not believe that Andean religious error merited a coercive and systematic response, and who thus opposed his rekindled Extirpation. A further four chapters criticized lax and corrupt priests and recognized the failure of necessary instruction as one of the central reasons for persistent Indian idolatry.[10] Even in the second part of the work, the *instrucción*, largely borrowed from Arriaga's 1621 treatise and meant to guide his visitadores and priests in their eradication of suspect Andean beliefs and practices, he included substantial sections that argued for the indivisibility of the persuasion and reconciliation of religious offenders from their trial and punishment. Most of all, Villagómez could point his critics to a number of new books of bilingual sermons—one of which was appended to the *Carta pastoral*—designed to reach extirpators and parish priests and revitalize the evangelization of Indians throughout the realm. The anti-idolatry sermons were conspicuously commissioned and approved by his hand. The new archbishop was intent on proving his conviction that his Extirpation was the proper solution to Andean idolatry over one century after the Spanish had arrived in Peru. Due force was unavoidable. Some "idols" still had to be destroyed and the most troublesome "sorcerers" still had to be rooted out and banished from the parishes they were thought to corrupt. But Villagómez acknowledged that there remained much teaching to be done. And he made sure that others witnessed both his acknowledgement of and his efforts to remedy the perceived problem.

What follows is not a denial of repression but an examination of the lesser-known instructive side of the Extirpation. Pondering the extirpators' Christianity and their concomitant critique of Andean beliefs and practices amounts to an examination of a prominent kind of evangelization in the mid-colonial Archdiocese of Lima, and it also provides a foundation for my consideration of Andean response.

In their effort to win the hearts and minds of the indigenous population, the purveyors of the Extirpation were to employ their own versions of what were

---

[10] P. de Villagómez, *Carta pastoral*, chs. 8–12 and 25, and 20–24, respectively.

established missionary and pastoral tactics.[11] Much confidence was placed in the power of the Word, the gospel's inherent ability to win its own. That confidence, of course, had its origin in the apostolic days of the Christian faith in the Mediterranean world. Even in late medieval times, centuries after the preaching of the apostles, muttered recitations and garbled prayers and creeds were widely believed to have strange powers of seduction. Countless missions in the history of Christianity in Europe had initially operated on similar principles, as had the first missionaries to preach the faith in New Spain, Yucatán, and later, Peru.[12]

In the Andes, such was the apparent trust in the gospel's inherent powers that at times gatherings of Quechua- and Aymara-speaking peoples were preached to only in Spanish, and were asked to memorize Christian prayers in Latin. Of course, trust in the power of the Word was not the only reason for such practices. If the Hispanicization of the Indians was an ultimate goal then, as many argued, the Spanish language had a huge role to play. Moreover, the prospect of learning Andean languages, let alone translating the Catholic faith into them, seems to have dispirited many evangelists. In spite of the advice of Domingo de Santo Tomás, the experienced missionary and early lexicographer of the principal Andean tongue, Quechua, three sixteenth-century provincial councils at Lima had been anything but decisive regarding the use of indigenous vernaculars. The First Council of 1533 acknowledged that it was advisable for some priests to learn the indigenous tongues, but held that doctrinal instruction should continue in Spanish. In 1567, the Second Council decreed that Indians could pray in their own tongue if it was necessary for their understanding, and that priests who were not competent enough in the Indians' language to hear confession should appoint assistants who were. It was not until 1583 and the Third Provincial Council, however, that a constitution ordered that Indians not be required to pray in Latin. Another constitution noted the worrying prevalence of Indians whose confessions were not heard properly, if they were heard at all, because of their priests' linguistic incompetence (Figure 6).[13] By the middle of the seventeenth century most of the linguistic foot-dragging had ended, and priests were required to demonstrate functional knowledge of Quechua or Aymara (for southern regions) before receiving a benefice. Even so, the mid-century reports of Jesuit missionaries and others in

---

[11] I am indebted for inspiration for this examination of the extirpators' Christianity to Pierre Duviols's characteristically suggestive discussion of "means of persuasion" in *La Lutte*, pp. 270–95.

[12] E. Duffy, "Prayer, Magic and Orthodoxy," and *The Stripping of the Altars*. See W. H. C. Frend, "The Winning of the Countryside"; R. A. Markus, "Gregory the Great"; and C. H. Talbot, "St. Boniface." For similar effects of preaching in a later period, see W. A. Christian, *Local Religion*, pp. 53–54. On previous missions, see especially R. Ricard, *The Spiritual Conquest*, esp. pp. 83–132.

[13] See R. Vargas Ugarte, *Concilios limenses*, 1: 19, 26–27, 44, 230, 235, 247, 325, and 328. Particularly useful on these and other details of the language question is N. Meiklejohn, *La Iglesia y los Lupaqas*, pp. 149–52.

Figure 6. A priest and a bad confession. From Felipe Guaman Poma de Ayala, *El primer nueva corónica*, edited by John V. Murra and Rolena Adorno. Original manuscript in the Royal Library, Copenhagen.

the mountain areas affirmed repeatedly that many priests' linguistic abilities left much to be desired and that nominally Christian Indians sometimes went years without proper confession.

Christianity at this time was still very much meant to be heard. It was a religion that was predominantly heard by the majority of people in Western Europe into the seventeenth century, and its aural nature became especially pronounced in colonial Andean Peru, where only a tiny élite of indigenous nobles, scholars and ecclesiastical assistants were reading and writing. This fact along with earlier experiences in the evangelization of non-Christians, must have been persuasive in the Church's softening line toward instruction in Quechua. By the mid-colonial period in most of the Lima region the Christian doctrine classes were taught orally in Quechua. Thus potentially, at least, the new faith enjoyed the same medium, the people's language, as the Indians' tradiciones and sacred histories.[14]

There is no way of accurately determining how much Christianity was taught in Indian homes in this period. Evidence suggests, however, that the general level of domestic instruction in Christian tenets—spouses teaching each other, parents teaching and supervising their children, and so on—would have been extremely low. Even in the European experience, among people more familiar with the requirements of the faith, parishes took up the responsibility of educating children because most parents simply did not do it.[15]

The question of how involved Indian elders and community power structures (led by kurakas and camachicos) became in the Christianization of the different ayllus and families is easier to answer. In most villages and towns, evidence from the idolatry investigation reveals that there were often a few individuals who helped the priest and who even might encourage other parishioners to attend mass or to amend their behavior in some way. Yet many of these same people appear also to have participated in Andean observances, though they would often deny any involvement or forbidden allegiances to the visitadores. Their Christianity does not often appear to have been the faith of catechists, of indigenous people committed to the advance of an orthodox Christianity among their own people. In the mid-colonial Lima region most Andeans seem to have done little to assist the systematic spread of an orthodox Catholic faith. In fact, as I will discuss in Chapter Eight, many Andeans used their traditional authority to work against certain kinds and representatives of Christianity. Beyond obligatory attendance at Mass, the Easter duty of confession and communion, and the embrace that a mixture of nominal and genuine Christians gave to religious associations, the Indians' active participation in the

---

[14] These educated and Hispanicized Indians are discussed by Rolena Adorno in "Images of Indios Ladinos." On the development of written Quechua, see B. Mannhiem, *The Language of the Inka*. Work on these and other related themes is further advanced in colonial New Spain; see esp. L. Burkhart, *The Slippery Earth*; J. Lockhart, *The Nahuas after the Conquest*; and C.E. Dibble, "The Nahuatlization of Christianity."

[15] J. Bossy, *Christianity and the West*, pp. 117–19. R. L. Kagan concludes the same, after a closer examination of most Spanish homes of the time; see *Students and Society*, ch. 1.

Christian cult was ambivalent and, what is more, self-defined. For this predicament, the cautious Church had mostly itself—and the prevalence of deep-
seated theories of racial hierarchy and capacities—to blame. A wide literature
exists concerning one of the most serious aspects of this situation, the Catholic
Church's failure to ordain Christian Indians as priests before the late eighteenth century.[16]

The influx of Christianity into the Andean communities came largely from
limited and conspicuously European sources. In all but the most remote and
neglected of the parishes and annexes, either a Spanish or creole priest or one of
his assistants was responsible for ensuring that the baptized Indian parishioner
received regular instruction, principally through three established methods:
the repetition of the catechism; elementary classes in Christian doctrine (the
doctrina); and instruction from preaching.[17] These means formed the base of
Christian instruction that the seventeenth-century Quechua were supposed to
be receiving when the Extirpation sought to apply its own versions of the same.

The Jesuit Arriaga published the first comprehensive manual for extirpators
and their assistants in 1621, and Archbishop Villagómez's *Carta pastoral* of
1649 followed as an intensified revision. Among their many themes and preoccupations, both authors carefully outlined how a visita of idolatry should be
conducted. They recommended that the visitador's pursuance of his examinations and investigations should be accompanied by a rigorous regime of daily
instruction and preaching.[18] Special catechisms were in place that had been
drawn up with the supposed needs of Amerindian new converts in mind. Yet
the presentation of the catechism and doctrine to the indigenous peoples
would differ according to the competence and diligence of a given extirpator
and his entourage, even if their forms were meant to be more immutable than,
say, the sermons. Preaching was unmistakably the device that could best be
molded to the purpose of extirpation. Catechism, doctrine, and sermons—each
presented Catholic Christianity in a slightly different way to Andean peoples
during an idolatry inspection.

[16] See esp. C. R. Boxer, *The Church Militant*; R. Ricard, *The Spiritual Conquest*, pp. 217–35;
M. Mörner, *Race Mixture*, pp. 35–52; and J. L. Phelan, *The Kingdom of Quito*, pp. 55–58.

[17] To these, one could easily add penance, certainly thought to be an instructive and purposeful
sacrament. A useful survey of the Mesoamerican and Andean confessionals is Martine Azoulai's
"Para la historia de la evangelización en América." On the Andes, and with a provocative thesis, see
M. Barnes, "Catechisms and *Confesionarios*." A number of recent studies of this theme in the
Spanish world have taken inspiration from Michel Foucault's formulations in *The History of Sexu-
ality*, and have investigated how confession became a principal means of teaching aboriginal
peoples that they should abide by European sexual norms. In a growing literature, see especially a
perceptive and informative essay by Regina Harrison, "The Theology of Concupiscence"; on New
Spain, S. Gruzinski's "Individualization and Acculturation"; L. Burkhart, *The Slippery Earth*; J. J.
Klor de Alva, "Colonizing Souls," "Sin and Confession," and "Raconter des Vies"; and on the
Philippines archipelago, V. L. Rafael, "Confession, Conversion, and Reciprocity,"and *Contracting
Colonialism*, esp. ch. 3.

[18] J. de Arriaga, *La extirpación*, see esp. chs. 13 and 14, pp. 124–136; and P. de Villagómez,
Carta pastoral, chs. 50–54, pp. 182–203.

In Europe, the instruction of children in the faith by catechism was relatively new in the sixteenth and seventeenth centuries. Sara Nalle has noted recommendations of such instruction in late fifteenth-century synodal constitutions from Toledo, Spain, and the existence of printed catechisms meant for children before 1500. The development of "schools for doctrine" in which the children of the Morisco élite in Andalusia could be instructed in the faith also appears to have influenced Old Christians to improve the religious education of their own children.[19] And instruction in doctrine by catechism seems to have received yet another boost in Catholic Spain when similar methods were popularized by Protestants after the Reformation.[20] In keeping with the unsettled but generally paternal view that the Church took of its Indian faithful, the catechisms for Indians as well as the structure of the more explanatory doctrina were New World applications of European trends in introductory religious pedagogy. Yet especially in early colonial times it had proven just as difficult in Spanish America as it had been in Spain to control what priests taught to their charges. The pastors themselves were sometimes revealed to be founts of heresy and error. In his compilation of laws, Juan de Solórzano Pereira recalled to mind a royal cédula of 1551, as well as the 1550 Lima synod and subsequent provincial councils in Mexico and Peru. The law warned careless Dominican, Franciscan, and Augustinian friars that they must conform to the norms of the Christian doctrine and keep to the clear and approved catechisms. The presence of the law, as well as synodal and conciliar constitutions expressing concern, confirms that Spanish Christian authorities were as worried about the faith's purveyors in the New World as they were about its receivers.[21]

One learns of most of the earliest bilingual catechisms produced in the Andes—along with confessionals, sermons, and other pastoral complements—indirectly from citations in contemporary works.[22] In later versions that have survived, certain characteristics are common. The Christian mysteries were simplified, often condescendingly so, in an attempt to accommodate the teach-

---

[19] S. T. Nalle, *God in La Mancha*, p. 111. Nalle discusses the first schools for the children of Old Christians in the first half of the sixteenth century in Andalusia, other parts of Castile, and (established by Ignacio de Loyola himself) in the Basque country at pp. 111–12. See also A. Domínguez Ortiz and B. Vincent, *Historia de los moriscos*, pp. 97–99.

[20] J. Bossy, *Christianity and the West*, pp. 118–21. For more on the tradition see G. Strauss, *Luther's House of Learning*, and J. C. Dhôtel, *Les Origines du catéchisme moderne*.

[21] *Libro primero*, vol. 1, tit. 4, law 15, pp. 148–49. Sara Nalle includes a number of examples of aberrant teaching by ill-prepared or simply careless clergy in sixteenth-century Cuenca, Spain. Her impression is that the reformative measures decreed at Trent and then at the Provincial Council of Toledo led to a noticeable improvement in priestly standards. *God in La Mancha*, pp. 106–33 and 80–103.

[22] The religious primers, doctrinals, confessionals, and catechisms that remain unknown apart from what other authors either write about or borrow from them include Juan de Betanzos, *Doctrina christiana y dos vocabularios*; Francisco Churrón y Aguilar, *Cartilla, catecismo y sermones en la lengua general del Peru*; Diego Ortiz, *Doctrina cristiana y sermones en lengua quichua*; and Joducus de Ricke, *Doctrina cristiana y sermones en lengua peruana*. R. Harrison, "The Theology of Concupiscence," p. 138, working from P. Rivet and G. de Crequit-Montfort, eds., *Bibliographie*, 1: 23–25.

ings to what were conceived to be the lesser capacities of Indian congregations. The catechisms were clearly meant to be brief compendia of comprehensible truths, simple expositions of the essential articles of the faith. This learning device neither expanded upon difficult themes nor did it attempt to make its content particularly relevant to the world of the Indian neophyte. Its only significant adjustment to the peoples of the Andes was its simplification, especially in the case of shorter catechisms developed for peoples newest in the faith. Although constructed as an interrogation or dialogue between priest and parishioner, no deep speculation or exegesis was expected from the catecumen in his or her answers. In areas where priests organized regular catechetical instruction one can assume that the reponses became part of a rather familiar script. The *Catecismo breve para los rudos y ocupados*, the text approved by the Third Provincial Council of Lima in 1584–1585 and most widely used for the purposes of evangelization by priest-extirpators and others in mid-colonial times, began:

P. Tell me, is there a God?
R. Yes father, there is a God.
P. How many gods are there?
R. Only one, no more.
P. Where is this God?
R. In the sky, on the earth, and everywhere.

The short catechism was a reminder of one's essential beliefs when the achievement of a deeper understanding was judged to be either impossible or unlikely. It was not the medium for the kinds of explication designed to lessen the likelihood of serious problems for Andean interpreters. What, for example, did it mean to say that God was "in the sky, on the earth, and everywhere"? After establishing the elemental mystery of monotheism and its Trinity, and denying any other pretender to divine status with a single statement, the relationship of man to God was touched upon. Next, came a series of prescribed questions and answers on the subject of Jesus and the meaning of his death and resurrection, followed by a treatment of the necessity of keeping to God's commandments and Holy Sacraments.[23]

The *Catecismo mayor para los que son mas capaces* represented a considerable step forward from the *Catecismo breve*. Its exercises were spread over five sections and delved more profoundly into such additional subjects as the creeds, the Virgin Mary, the role of the Devil, the forms and significance of sin, and the act of prayer. Through repetition, these formulae were committed to memory; they were meant to become a personal meditation and examination with which a Christian could continually test his or her conscience.[24] Monica

---

[23] J. G. Durán, ed., *El catecismo*, pp. 382–85, fols. 13–18 of original; in the facsimile edition, *Doctrina Christiana*, see pp. 45–55.

[24] Ibid., pp. 388–410; fols. 25–73v, in *Doctrina Christiana*, pp. 69–166. Small notebooks con-

Barnes's suggestion that through incessant teaching and feats of memorization parish priests (and visitadores) were able to "insinuate . . . concepts into native belief systems" that would, in turn, inspire the religious imaginations of Andeans is an intriguing one to which I shall return.[25]

Perhaps even more than catechism, the very occurrence of the second element, the doctrina classes, and certainly their rigor and popular attendance, would have varied from investigation to investigation, just as from parish to parish. Yet in theory the elementary instruction or indoctrination was to provide the necessary and logical stride beyond simple recitation, and was thus considerably more important. This was where an Andean parishioner might clarify a problem such as the meaning of a God who was everywhere. During normal times, that is, not during a visita de idolatría, classes were to be convened at regular intervals by the parish priest or his assistants. Teaching was to be daily for children and any particularly recalcitrant elders, while adults who were considered lacking in knowledge were to attend three times a week (usually Wednesdays and Fridays in addition to Sunday after mass). Once a working man or woman was deemed to have achieved an acceptable level of understanding, according to the dictates of the Third Provincial Council of Lima their instruction could be lessened to once a week (except during the Lenten season, when the three weekly classes would resume in preparation for the obligatory confession of sins in time for Easter).

When the visita of idolatry arrived in a town or village, teaching was to occur daily and became more intensive. Ideally, the general populace received instruction every morning, and in the afternoons different ayllus would be separately taught and catechized until sunset. Parable readings and sessions of personal penance—to which the Indians were invited to bring their own sticks—might be added in the evenings. On Sundays, mass was to be held later to allow people to attend from the neighboring annexes of the parish, and the afternoon was taken up with more catechism, sermons, and perhaps a procession and some singing. Arriaga, who is the original and often the clearest source on procedure, allowed for some latitude in observing that, with respect to the sermons as well as other things, "when one is in town for a longer period . . . these things can be stretched out a bit."[26] One assumes that the pace of the

---

taining written versions of the catechism, doctrine, mysteries, commandments, prayers, sins, and virtues, as well as particularly edifying letters, were kept as devotional aids by European religious at the time. They demonstrate the breadth of knowledge required by the most exemplary and pious person. A Spanish Jesuit's book of this type, dated 1586 but with numerous dates between 1640 and 1648 scrawled inside its coverings (by a succession of owners?), survives in the British Library. See BL, Sloane Ms 796, "Modo de examinar la consciencia, que sirve para examen general y para confesarse. Va por pensamientos, palabras y obras." Some of the best work on such practical moral theology in Europe in this era appears in E. Leites, ed., *Conscience and Casuistry*.

[25] "Catechisms and *Confesionarios*," pp. 80 and 68.
[26] See P. J. de Arriaga, *La extirpación*, p. 128.

instruction régimes would have to lessen in certain circumstances; occasionally during the Villagómez period an idolatry investigation might last for months and even years.

The church bell, if one was to be had, tolled three times to call the people to doctrina. The most common setting for the instructive gatherings would have been the village church or, if this proved too small or otherwise insufficient, the adjacent plaza or patio.[27] Preaching and instruction in public places and in the wild, and the utilization of hastily constructed "chapels" and "oratories" near the spots where the Indians farmed or worked, might seem a way of reaching parishioners who would not otherwise attend mass or receive instruction, but such flexibility was thought by many churchmen to be irregular and dangerous.[28] Many people (African slaves, Mulattos, peninsular Spaniards, Creoles, Mestizos, and so on) in a region might require religious instruction but these occasions, irrespective of the presence of a visita, were meant exclusively for "Indians." In the increasingly mixed communities, especially in the valleys and nearer the Pacific coast, this separation would have been a constant reminder to Andean peoples of their differing status as new and inferior faithful.[29] In 1716, the archbishop of Lima, Antonio de Soloaga, cited a bull of Pope Pius V, a Tridentine constitution, and a decree from the First Provincial Council of Lima to reinforce his edict that in his realm Indian instruction was to occur on Wednesdays and Fridays, whereas "Spaniards and Mestizos and their families" could wait until Sundays.[30]

In the doctrine class the priest or visitador as pedagogue was to explore the meanings of the different aspects and mysteries of the faith that had only been brushed over during catechism. The doctrina cristiana used in mid-colonial Peru was itself supposed to be a set text, again one approved and issued by the Third Lima Council, and which ranged from the Lord's Prayer to a summary of all that was needed by a believer in the Catholic faith.[31] Beyond this skeleton of necessities, however, priests and extirpators would choose certain themes or texts into which to delve more deeply on each occasion. Lessons might explore, at least by allusion, matters of more immediate and emotional importance: perhaps moral and civil behavior (if, say, a recent feast day had been particularly raucous), respect for secular and religious authority (if an official had been shown disrespect), or guidance toward what was presented as a Christian

---

[27] A suitable setting was stipulated by Bishop Loaysa as early as 1545. See F. Mateos, "Constituciones para indios," pp. 9–10. Interesting on the use of open space in this part of early Spanish America is V. Fraser, *The Architecture of Conquest*, pp. 111–15.

[28] Archbishop Villagómez expressed his own fears on this subject, which had also bothered a number of his predecessors, at AGI Lima 303, Villagómez to the king, Lima, 16 September 1651.

[29] They were joined in this imposed status, of course, by African slaves. A beginning on the under-studied subject of the evangelization of African slaves both when they were destined for Peru and after their arrival is offered in F. P. Bowser's classic study, *The African Slave*.

[30] AGI Lima 520, "Edicto que las curas expliquen la doctrina christiana," Antonio de Soloaga, Lima, 12 November 1716.

[31] J. G. Durán, *El catecismo*, pp. 376–382; fols. 1–12v; in *Doctrina Christiana*, pp. 21–44.

way of life (if a notorious adulterer or thief had just been punished). Providing the teacher's Quechua was sufficient, indoctrination had at least the potential to take on a more informal, imaginative, and personable character than the more structured question-and-answer format of the catechism. This was the point, too, when such things as edifying plays and Bible stories performed by Indian actors in their own languages might be introduced as means of instruction, although these do not appear to have been as enthusiastically or experimentally employed in mid-colonial Peru as, for example, they had been by friars in mid-sixteenth-century New Spain.[32]

It is difficult to determine both the diligence of parish priests and visita officials in complying with their teaching obligations and the regularity of most Indians' attendance at their obligatory classes, but there are some hints if one looks hard enough. In 1622, for instance, the viceroy of Peru, the marquis of Guadalcázar, ordered that priests should keep parish registers of their parishio-ners, ostensibly to assist the regional corregidores' tribute collections and as-sessment of mita work forces.[33] If this decree had been followed, such registers would have provided useful references for priests concerned with the atten-dance of individuals at mass and doctrina. As it is, there are oblique indications that the doctrine classes were not likely to have been heavily attended in many Indian areas in mid-colonial times.

The fact that the sentences decreed by visitadores de idolatría at the close of their investigations often included supervised terms of doctrina classes for reli-gious transgressors provides a strong clue as to why. As Taylor has observed, mid-colonial priests who were also extirpators of idolatry (in New Spain and Peru) were inclined to see "instruction by love and by punishment . . . as a complementary pair." Teachers were necessarily also judges. Yet this equation of indoctrination and punishment cannot have contributed to the positive repu-tation of such instruction among Indian parishioners in Peru or anywhere else.[34] Although a sentence of required indoctrination was admittedly a lighter alternative to banishment to a convent or the sorcerers' prison in Lima, it was meant to carry the stigma of popular shame and ridicule in one's own commu-nity, which may have made it seem even worse. The image of the doctrina as carried by the Extirpation was that of something imposed from above, more akin to an eternal penalty and humiliation than an offering of understanding in

[32] On the employment of Nahuatl religious dramas in evangelization see F. Horcasitas, El teatro náhuatl; M. Ekdahl Ravicz, Early Colonial Religious Drama; R. Ricard, The Spiritual Conquest, pp. 194–206; J. M. Williams, El teatro del México colonial; and L. Burkhart, "A Nahuatl Religious Drama."

[33] Cited in G. Lohmann Villena, El corregidor de indios, p. 210. There is indication that this injunction was not universally observed. N. Meiklejohn writes that in 1635 the bishop of La Paz complained that none of the priests in his diocese had them; see La Iglesia, p. 166.

[34] See W. B. Taylor on the development of the tension between the competing conceptions (and self-conceptions) of priests, Magistrates of the Sacred, ch. 9. As an reaffirmation of the Extirpation's methodological inheritance, one should also recall that the Inquisition employed remedial instruc-tion as punishment for ignorant Spanish laymen and Morisco religious offenders in Spain; see S. T. Nalle, God in La Mancha, p. 104, and H. C. Lea, The Moriscos, p. 115.

a new faith. In his *Carta pastoral* Villagómez recommended that religious offenders who were not exiled be made to attend the children's doctrina every
day, in the mornings and afternoons, and that they should forever wear a
wooden cross around their necks.[35] In a typical example from 1725, an elder
and huaca minister living in San Antonio de la Lancha (in the parish of Andajes,
Cajatambo) named Antonio Tapaojo was sentenced to give up his independence and spend the rest of his days in the home of the Mercedarian friar and
priest in order that his punishment should be known by others and that he
might be carefully instructed in the faith.[36]

One does not learn of Antonio Tapaojo's feelings on the matter, but ultimately the best measure of the popular regard for, and the efficacy of, these
first two fundamental methods of Christian instruction comes from others like
him. Although visitadores were chiefly interested in hearing about "idolatrous"
beliefs and the locations of hidden gods and places of worship, they could not
help but wonder about the state of the Christian knowledge of the Indians they
interrogated. Indeed, as part of the established procedure borrowed from the
Inquisition, many investigators questioned people on the elemental Christian
mysteries and had them recite prayers and commandments. Some inevitable
exposures of ignorance resulted. While these exposures may seem unsurprising
to the modern reader, they underscored a crucial and embarrassing fact in their
day—a fact worth reiterating because it was so often avoided or denied: many
of the accused idolaters, people found incontrovertibly guilty of affirming Andean beliefs, practices, and traditions, had been baptized, instructed, and even
confirmed in the Christian faith. Indeed, during their ordeals before the visitador's tribunal, many Andeans demonstrated that they knew the requirements
of the European faith and the expectations of their judges well enough to
repent of their actions and claim to be poor *cristianos* who had erred.

From the perspective of the Church which, in the course of its idolatry
investigations, was inevitably also reviewing the state of its Christianization
efforts to date, the interrogatory showdowns in the seventeenth and eighteenth
centuries must have forced some uncomfortable thoughts. Of course, there
were always some apparent successes that one could recount and stress to
superiors, but even many of these did not leave one free from lingering doubts
and the knowledge of what they were deemphasizing. The consistent ambivalence of the mid-colonial Andeans' religious lives from the point of view of the
Spanish Christian is worth stressing here. Indians regularly reconciled observance of their traditional affiliations with their constant education in, and even
identification with, the Christian cult.[37]

[35] Ch. 63, p. 250. The offenders whose sentences included terms of imprisonment or confinement either in the villages or in some other place were also to be taught rigorously; ch. 64, p. 252.
[36] AAL Leg 3, exp 13, fols. 18–18v.
[37] See, for example, the case involving Francisco Gulca Rilpo, Petrona Apu Libia, and Martín
Champi from Carampoma, Huarochirí, AAL Leg. 3, exp. 15, 1730–1732, fols. 18–19, 23–23v, and
41; those from AAL Leg. 1, exp. 13, Santa María de Jesús de Huarochirí, 1700; AAL Leg. 3, exp. 9,
Santiago de Carampoma, Huarochirí, 1723; AAL Leg. 3, exp. 11, Santo Domingo de Nava, Ca-

Occasionally, life might require a choice between two religious systems. In 1662, Catalina Yauca Choque of Ambar, Cajatambo, for instance, explained to the visitador why she had lapsed into her old rituals of divination by noting the inefficacy she perceived in Christian measures. "All the masses that you ask to be said," she claimed, "do you no benefit, nor do they make [lost] blankets appear."[38] But more often, Catholicism and Andean religion appear to have been mixed together from the point of view of the Indian people, even if this mixing was denied or explained away, as in Huamantanga, Canta, in 1696. Here, the region's Indian official, Don Miguel Menacho, insisted that the people in his care were perfect Christians. "All the Indians of my reparti-miento," he said, "attend the doctrina and observe their Christian obligation. The time of my government of many years has been without notice of anything occurring that is opposed to the faith that, by the mercy of God, we profess." Yet the evidence from the visita held in this locality reveals widespread adher-ence to Andean religion, and general trust in Andean religious solutions for village conflicts.[39]

Much of what the visitadores found was thus inadvertent. Evidence of the "persistent paganism" of obstinate sorcerers and dogmatizers was sought, but far more complicated problems emerge. The Extirpation's gradual unveiling of the complex realities of colonial Andean religion in the Archdiocese of Lima proves a number of things, and not least that the evangelization process was suffering from something more serious than the cases mentioned above would indicate.

The case of an Andean governor (kuraka) named Don Juan Soclac (or, alter-natively, Soclam) of the town of San Juan de Huaral in the province of Chancay in 1676 is illustrative in this respect.[40] On the surface, the proceedings in this case provide yet another example of how idolatry accusations and the trials themselves could become conduits for preexisting village hatred and fear, as well as the rivalries for local political power (the kurakazgos). In Huaral, it was only after the ill will of an enemy had stirred up a cluster of rumors concerning such things as Don Juan's evil sorcery and purported ability to transform him-self into various kinds of animals that the kuraka finally found himself before the priest and appointed ecclesiastical judge of Chancay, Joseph Moran Col-lantes. An enmity with Juan Correa seems to have developed after Don Juan, as

---

jatambo, 1725: the declarations of Antonio Ripas fol. 4, Juana María of Nava fols. 5 and 7, Esteban Bentocilla fol. 5v, Francisco Quipo of Nava fol. 6; María Juana of San Sebastian de Tinta fol. 6v; Juan Bautista of Mallai fol. 7; Juana Beatrix of La Concepción de Oyon fol. 8; Martín Phelipe, Juan Ramos, Juana Juliana, and María Beatris of Pachangara fols. 9v, 10, 10v, and 10v–11, respectively; and Juana Agustina of San Francisco de Rapas fols. 11–11v.

[38] AAL Leg. 6, exp. 18, fol. 53 in succession.

[39] AAL Leg. 2, exp. 33, fol. 18; see also Chapter Eight below.

[40] AAL Leg. 5, exp. 14. This lengthy trial, pursued during the time of Archbishop Juan de Almoguera, was initiated by a priest from the villa of Chancay in his role as regional ecclesiastical judge. His methods did not differ greatly from those of an idolatry inspector, but he was not technically commissioned as a visitador general de idolatría, as would usually have been the case in the Villagómez period.

local governor, had punished the man's two sons. In addition to his expressed doubts about the legitimacy of Don Juan's governorship and allegations that this false kuraka had impeded the settlement of Huaral, much evidence was presented by Correa and a variety of other witnesses confirming and elaborating on fantasic tales of the man's evil powers. His garden, from which a slave had once stolen fruit on a dare, had taken on a mystique in the area and was said to be a place where strange voices were heard. Some said that Don Juan could turn himself into a snake and a horse. And there was a particularly engaging story told about the time he had appeared as a deer to a Jesuit padre out for a walk. Yet quite apart from the extraordinary stories and charges, what emerges as particularly interesting is the vision one gains of Don Juan's education in, and contacts with, Christianity.

The notary described Juan Soclac as sixty-five years old and *"muy ladino,"* which is to say well schooled and probably Hispanicized in dress and custom.[41] Petitions within the trial documentation written and signed in his own hand suggest considerable literacy. Given his proximity to Lima and Don Juan's status as a kuraka, like his father before him (and his son to follow), it is probable that he acquired this learning as a boy at the college for the sons of caciques (kurakas) that was administered by the Jesuits in the capital. He would have spoken Spanish as well as his mother tongue, Quechua, with ease and nothing in his general comportment would have made him seem anything but an assimilated, mid-colonial Andean noble to the Spanish investigators. Yet the display of his understanding of Christianity and, moreover, what was learned of his past, were less encouraging from a Catholic point of view.

A judge could examine impartially, and even sympathetically, the governor's plea that the charges against him—calling him an "idolater, witch, and sorcerer"—were "false and sinister," but what would he do with the evidence suggesting that Don Juan Soclac's knowledge of even elemental Christianity was seriously lacking? The third question put to the kuraka in his first appearance before Moran Collantes asked if he knew the Christian doctrine and mysteries of the faith. Don Juan's ready reply of "no" prompted a demand for his best attempt at their recitation. Despite the apparently high level of his Spanish in general, all he could manage was a stumbling repetition of the Ave Maria in Quechua. Moreover, an exploration of his understanding of the mysteries stalled soon after it had begun: in response to the elementary catechetical question "who is Jesus Christ?" Don Juan answered that he was "God the son and God the Holy Spirit."[42] During a second appearance, the judge found that the accused blundered even more seriously, this time over the Holy Trinity and the Incarnation.

The kuraka's twelve-year-old son and heir apparent in the governorship, Juan de la Cruz, was eventually brought forward, perhaps as a check on the Christian upbringing he was receiving from his father. The boy, too, was asked to

---

[41] Ibid., fols. 9v and 11.
[42] Ibid., fol. 9v.

demonstrate his doctrinal knowledge. After repeating "half the Pater Noster, the whole of the Ave Maria, half the Creed, and no other thing," he was asked "who is God?" He replied that he did not know how to respond, and noted, after being led in this direction by a question, that his father had not taught him. Young Juan then grew expansive. He revealed that the little he did know about the doctrina had been taught to him within the last few days by an African slave who was being held in the same jail as his father in the villa of Chancay.[43] During his visits to the jail to provide company and sustenance for his father, the boy—and perhaps Don Juan himself—had received basic instruction from the knowledgeable other prisoner. The father and son seem to have attempted to memorize enough of the basic Christian doctrine to satisfy their investigators. Had the boy not explained the desperate crash course convened by the incarcerated slave, and had the kuraka himself proved a better pupil (or the slave a more orthodox teacher), the scheme might just have worked. But it did not. And one is left uncertain about the ability of extended exposure to Hispanic cultural influences, and what must have been in Soclac's case considerable catechization for at least one portion of his life, to effect the required profound transformations in Andean thinking. The faith's presence in these people's lives and their knowledge of it were found seriously wanting.

How representative were Don Juan Soclac and his son of a wider condition of the Catholic faith among the Indians in their area? Why and how was it that in the late seventeenth century two such likely candidates for sound Christianization—Andean nobles in a well-traversed valley just north of Lima—were found so lacking? The answers contribute to one's improving vision of Christianity's varied place in this, and presumably other, areas of the archdiocese.

As part of his denunciation of the kuraka, Juan Correa recalled a certain Sunday (5 January, presumably 1676) when the interim parish priest, Gregorio de Zepeda, had flogged Soclac and his wife, "in punishment with other Indians . . . because they did not know how to pray." Bernabel de Arce, a tailor who lived in the same valley, testified that he had heard mass on the same day and had witnessed that "the other Indians," including the alcaldes (magistrates on the cabildo or municipal council), were all ignorant of the doctrina.

Arce attributed the people's general unfamiliarity with Christian tenets to the scattered nature of the majority of the population, "living in ravines and *haciendas* (landed estates)" and not in the town proper, where they might be more easily and regularly instructed. Martín Francisco, who served as *regidor* (alderman on the cabildo), said he had witnessed the public whipping of Don Juan Soclac, and that on this occasion the priest had asked him [Martín] "how it [the Christian doctrine] could be so forgotten." Martín Francisco was even more precise than the tailor had been: he claimed he had replied to the priest that, having lived outside the towns for some eighteen years working on various haciendas, these people simply did not hear mass and spent their entire time

[43] Ibid., fol. 15.

without doctrina. "It produces the same effect," he continued, "on the other Indians who are spread out working (*repartidos*) in the valley."[44]

The kuraka's enemies—for Juan Correa was not alone—blamed the depopulation of Huaral on Don Juan's alleged sorcery and impeding actions whereas this kuraka seems in truth to have unsuccessfully attempted to repopulate this lowland *reducción* (resettled town), whose original inhabitants had died out, and in which highlanders had never felt at home or prospered. Sebastián Félix, 102 years old, confirmed the story of the earlier depopulation, as did Francisco Exquibel Navarro.[45] The latter revealed further that he had seen Don Juan bring "four or five married couples, highland Indians (*serranos*)" to settle, but that the *temple* (the climate, broadly defined) in the area was so contrary to their nature that they had died off some twenty years before. Pedro de Villagómez, in his own information to the king twenty-two years earlier, stated that although the whole valley contained some two thousand parishioners, the annex of Huaral was home to "very few Indians."[46] If Don Juan had eventually come to the point of discouraging settlement, as the testimonies seem to indicate, he would have had ample reason.[47] Besides the inhospitable location from the Andeans' point of view, it was largely the ceaseless demand for labor in the haciendas of the valley that kept Indians from what, to Spanish minds, were the civilizing and Christianizing benefits that would accrue from a settled existence. A vital attachment to a huaca cult or the teachings of the elders does not play a central part in this case. In late seventeenth-century Huaral and environs the Indian people, through little fault of their own, had not heard Christian preaching or received instruction for some time.

Moreover, it seems that the Christian representatives who were immediately responsible for this portion of the Peruvian flock of new converts were contributing to the endurance of the faith's sorry condition. Don Juan Soclac revealed that when he confessed his sins each year, in accordance with the one obligatory precept, he was helped and guided by lenient confessors. Francisco Exquibel Navarro, who had known Don Juan for some forty years, confirmed that the kuraka had certainly complied with the sacrament of penance at the church in Huaral "in the time of Don Diego de Avila and some other priests." This provided a perfect opportunity for Don Juan's defensor, Manuel Carrasco, one of the officials increasingly used to assist the accused in idolatry trials in this period. Carrasco cannily wondered whether Don Juan's doctrinal errors might not have arisen from the "natural confusion . . . as occurs with many [Indians] . . . [for whom], having confessed and taken communion is not [necessarily] to have understood."[48] The lack of understanding of Christianity exhibited by a sixty-five-year-old ladino kuraka, the twelve-year-old boy who would be his suc-

[44] Ibid., fol. 6.

[45] See ibid., fols. 31 and 33v, respectively.

[46] AGI Lima 304, Villagómez to the king, Lima, 20 November 1664.

[47] See Martín Francisco's clear testimony that this was the case in response to the judge's second question to him; AAL Leg. 5, exp. 14, fol. 6.

[48] Ibid., fols. 11, 32v–33, and 20, respectively.

cessor, and presumably many others in a fertile valley just north of Lima was clearly not being monitored or remedied by normal parish evangelization. Just as importantly for the purposes of the present discussion, the situation was not improved by the idolatry visitas that had passed through Chancay in the years preceding the information collected by Moran Collantes in 1676.[49] The ignorance of Christianity only came to light as something of a subtext in 1676, when an ecclesiastical visitation arrived to investigate what seem to have been malicious allegations of diabolic sorcery.

For the apologists of the Extirpation at least one advantage could be derived from such exposures of the limits of evangelization in this part of the Andes. The repeated failures of parish priests and previous visitadores to solve the problem of suspect religiosity could be overlooked, whereas the persistence of idolatry and superstition, and the widespread occurrence of religious error and ignorance of Christianity, could be emphasized and fashioned into a justification of the renewed and improved visita de idolatría as an appropriate course of action. Idolatry could become a capacious concept, meaning whatever was deemed to be in error. This was especially the case when the proponents of the Extirpation's methods—with Archbishop Villagómez foremost among them—accentuated the instructive potential of the investigations. Arguably, the affair of Don Juan Soclac and many others like it justified drastic measures, the more dynamic and forceful forms of persuasion that the Extirpation represented. Yet however much basic teaching in the faith through catechism and doctrina could be intensified during the presence of a visita, these means were less adaptable than a third, infinitely more malleable, method of persuasion at the Extirpation's disposal. The face that the Catholic faith promoted at the times when the extirpating mentality held sway in the mid-colonial Archdiocese of Lima is best represented by the anti-idolatry sermons printed and preached in those years.

This is perhaps fitting, given the amount of inspiration and methodological influence the Extirpation owed to the Holy Office of the Inquisition. The *sermo* of the papal Inquisition of the Middle Ages became, in the Spanish context from the late fifteenth century onward, the *auto de fe*, the solemn spectacle of the religious criminals' sentencing and punishment. These public events were meant to evoke premonitions of the Day of Judgment to all who viewed them. The proceedings of an *auto* were customarily opened by a sermon (hence their designation as *sermo*) delivered by the Inquisitor or a friar famed for his oratory.[50]

The media of the sermon and *plática* (a shorter address) were widely used by missionaries and priests in Peru to teach Andean peoples, not to mention their other parishioners, about God and the necessity of adherence to Christianity,

---

[49] This part of Chancay was often visited by extirpators en route to Sayan. For investigations during 1662 see, for example, AAL Leg. 5, exps. 5, 7, and 8.

[50] H. C. Lea, *A History of the Inquisition*, vol. 3, bk. 7, ch. 5

long before the appearance of the Extirpation in the seventeenth century. But the standard book of thirty bilingual sermons for Indians collected and published by the Third Provincial Council of Lima in 1585 had been compiled in another climate of opinion in Lima, that presided over by Archbishop Toribio Alfonso de Mogrovejo. Only two of the thirty sermons printed by the Third Council dealt explicitly and at length with the problem of suspect Andean religiosity. P. José de Acosta, an influential figure and adviser to the council, had clearly not envisaged the need for sermons devoted to expounding upon, or extirpating, idolatry; he and his contemporaries at the Third Council had emphasized instruction in the Christian faith and the need to reform morality, among other things. The councillors seem to have assumed that most preachers would compose their own sermons, following approved and accessible models, yet in accordance with the needs of their particular parishioners and regions.[51] This must have continued to be the case well after more decidedly anti-idolatry sermons were being written and delivered by the Jesuits and priest-visitadores who took part in the early efforts of the Extirpation in the second and third decades of the seventeenth century. Even Padre Arriaga in his treatise on extirpation in 1621 only went so far as to suggest twelve hypothetical sermon titles for texts that would ideally be delivered in conjunction with an idolatry investigation.[52]

Early colonial priests and friars about whose sermons one knows little or nothing undoubtedly portended many of the themes and techniques that would become established during the mid-colonial extirpating years. Yet preaching in the Indian parishes of the Andes began to be self-consciously directed toward refuting and erasing error and bringing stray faithful back into the fold only in the era of Pedro de Villagómez, contemporaneous with the revival of the Extirpation. The printed sermonarios from this time were ostensibly meant as general medicine to assist and awaken all priests and ecclesiastical functionaries in the Indian parishes, and to make their preaching more effective. But their central role in the revived Extirpation was never much concealed. On their rounds of investigation, Villagómez's idolatry inspectors carried with them their archbishop's instructions, the *Carta pastoral*, and one collection of these special sermons.

Pedro de Villagómez would often assert that the enforcement of God's will

---

[51] For more on Acosta's attitudes see his *De Procuranda Indorum Salute*. See also P. Duviols's discussion in *La Lutte*, pp. 169–70. On the moral and sexual emphasis in the sermons, the accompanying "Tercero catecismo" and a number of later works, perhaps most notably Juan de Pérez Bocanegra's *Ritual formulario* of 1631, see R. Harrison, "The Theology of Concupiscence," esp. pp. 139–49 and n. 7. See also "Tercero catecismo."

For an idea of influences on a preacher slightly later, see the list of books in the library of Fernando de Avendaño in 1656, in P. Guibovich Pérez, "La carrera de un visitador," pp. 205–34. The popularity of works by Fray Luis de Granada, especially "Los seis libros de la retórica eclesiástica," and the "Memorial de la vida cristiana," are discussed by Irving Leonard generally, and Rolena Adorno with respect to influences on and citations in Guaman Poma. I. A. Leonard, "Best Sellers," and *Books of the Brave*, pp. 162–63 and 220; R. Adorno, *Guaman Poma*, ch. 3.

[52] *La extirpación*, pp. 126–28.

required no justification. But his actions and letters betray his bold rhetoric; especially in the 1650s and 1660s, he was a man in need of support and legitimacy for what he was doing. The production of the sermons and their inclusion as a complement to the *Carta pastoral* softened the repressive action that was questioned, both explicitly and implicitly, by opponents of systematic extirpation. Yet, as helpful as a dose of skepticism can be in reading the extirpating apologists' own representations of their enterprise, it should not prevent an appreciation for the convictions that attended even the most expedient remarks by mid-colonial churchmen. The extirpators' preaching was a serious part of the reformative mission. The anti-idolatry sermons are, above all, a reflection of the carefully conceived marriage of the judicial and penal with the edifying and instructive.

The sermon collections of Fernando de Avendaño and Francisco de Avila, which appeared almost simultaneously at the end of the 1640s, are enduring monuments to the mental atmosphere of the extirpating era in the Lima region.[53] As was the custom among notable preachers in contemporary Spain, these sermonarios were published late in the lives of both men, and thus represent a "personal selection" from a repertoire of texts that each had preached from, and added to, for many years.[54] Avendaño and Avila had served as curas in Indian areas and as visitadores, and each possessed an encyclopedic knowledge of indigenous rites and beliefs.

To reiterate briefly part of a story I have already told, in the late sixteenth and early seventeenth century Francisco de Avila had encouraged the collection of religious and mythical information in the area surrounding his parish of San Damián in Huarochirí. The resulting text, the so-called Huarochirí Manuscript, may not have been as voluminous or ambitious as, say, the earlier Franciscan-inspired compilations in New Spain, but its more free-flowing and eccentric style suggests that considerable rein was given to the spontaneous creativity of indigenous contributors.[55] Moreover, from marginalia by both Avila and the Andean redactors, as well as from the text itself, one notes a preoccupation with geographic information regarding the huacas and festivals

[53] F. de Avendaño, *Sermones*, and F. de Avila, *Tratado de los evangelios*. P. Duviols discusses anti-idolatry sermons and concentrates helpfully on a small sample of Avendaño's texts in *La Lutte*, pp. 270–95, but an adequate study of preaching in colonial Peru does not, to my knowledge, exist. The number of single sermons (*sueltos*) published for certain occasions or festivals in the era of Villagómez alone is astounding. See J. T. Medina, *La imprenta en Lima*. Another sermonario was written in 1649 by a Franciscan priest of Huánuco, in the Archdiocese of Lima, but it remained unpublished. The remains of Diego de Molina's badly deteriorated Lenten sermons, the "Sermones de la quaresma en lengua Quechua," reside in the Biblioteca Nacional del Perú in Lima. A useful summary of the work is C. A. Romero's "Un libro interesante."

[54] See H. D. Smith, *Preaching in the Spanish Golden Age*, and pp. 29–41.

[55] See B. Sahagún, *Florentine Codex* and, on this work and its compiler's techniques, J. J. Klor de Alva, H. B. Nicholson, and E. Quiñones Keber, eds. *The Work of Bernardino de Sahagún*. For the Huarochirí Manuscript see the edition by G. Taylor, tr. and ed., *Ritos y tradiciones*, and the edition that I have been citing, F. Salomon and G. L. Urioste, *The Huarochirí Manuscript* (hereafter *Huarochirí*).

being discussed, a preoccupation that points to the function for which Avila (but not necessarily all his assistants) intended the manuscript. Avila's ultimate objective was the extirpation of idolatry. His experiences and the compendium itself would have provided him with much first-hand information that would assist him not only in the practical act of attempting to destroy Andean religion but also in the composition of anti-idolatry sermons.

As for the other preacher, Avendaño's letters to the king and the reports of the trials in which he acted as visitador suggest a similar familiarity with the Andean religious world, combined with a less controversial past. In the preface to his *Tratado de los evangelios*, Avila would claim for himself the distinction of being the "discoverer" of idolatry. But Avendaño was the more seasoned veteran of the Extirpation, had been the confidant and close functionary of successive archbishops and, despite his age, it was Avendaño who was distinguished as Pedro de Villagómez's honorific superintendent of the Extirpation in the late 1640s.

It was also to Avendaño that the archbishop turned with his commission for a specially crafted sermonario to append to the *Carta pastoral* he had begun in 1647.[56] The preacher's work, particularly Book One, is extraordinary because of the concentration of its arguments and the breadth of its attack on Andean beliefs and practices (Figure 7). Avendaño's thematic focus, with each sermon playing its part in what was designed to be a gradual, persuasive dismantling of Andean religion and error, places this work firmly in the category described by Hilary Dansey Smith as *sermones de un tema*.[57]

Each of Avendaño's texts follows what is essentially an Aristotelian schema of rhetorical oration (*proposito, narratio, confirmatio,* and *peroratio*). Once the theme or *proposición* is stated, a text or analogy (*exemplum*) might follow. The *confirmación* makes up the body of the sermon, and offers a number of points as proof of the original proposition. A subsidiary part of the confirmación called the *confutación*, or "proof by contraries," was one of Fernando de Avendaño's favorite devices. The employment of what Stuart Clark calls an assymetrical or hierarchical "logic of binary opposition" in confronting and classifying an opposing religious system or rival appealed to Avendaño in Peru no less than it appealed to a host of other sixteenth- and seventeenth-century thinkers who faced witchcraft and religious dissent in Europe.[58] In the anti-idolatry sermon, the Spanish Christian could affirm Christianity both for his Indian audience

---

[56] F. de Avendaño, *Sermones.* Book One consists of ten sermons over 129 folios; Book Two is twenty-one sermons and ninety-four folios. On the probability of some rivalry between the two extirpating pioneers at the point of Villagómez's revival of the Extirpation, see A. Acosta, "Francisco de Avila," pp. 613–14.

[57] *Preaching in the Spanish Golden Age,* pp. 46–52. Smith admits that distinctions are controversial. Great contemporary preachers such as Fr. Luis de Granada and Cristóbal Suárez de Figueroa noted five and twelve types of sermons, respectively.

[58] I am indebted to Clark's generous sharing of thoughts that will appear in his *Thinking with Demons,* Part I, "Language." See his own explanation of the inspiration he has drawn from J. Derrida and work on dual classification in anthropology.

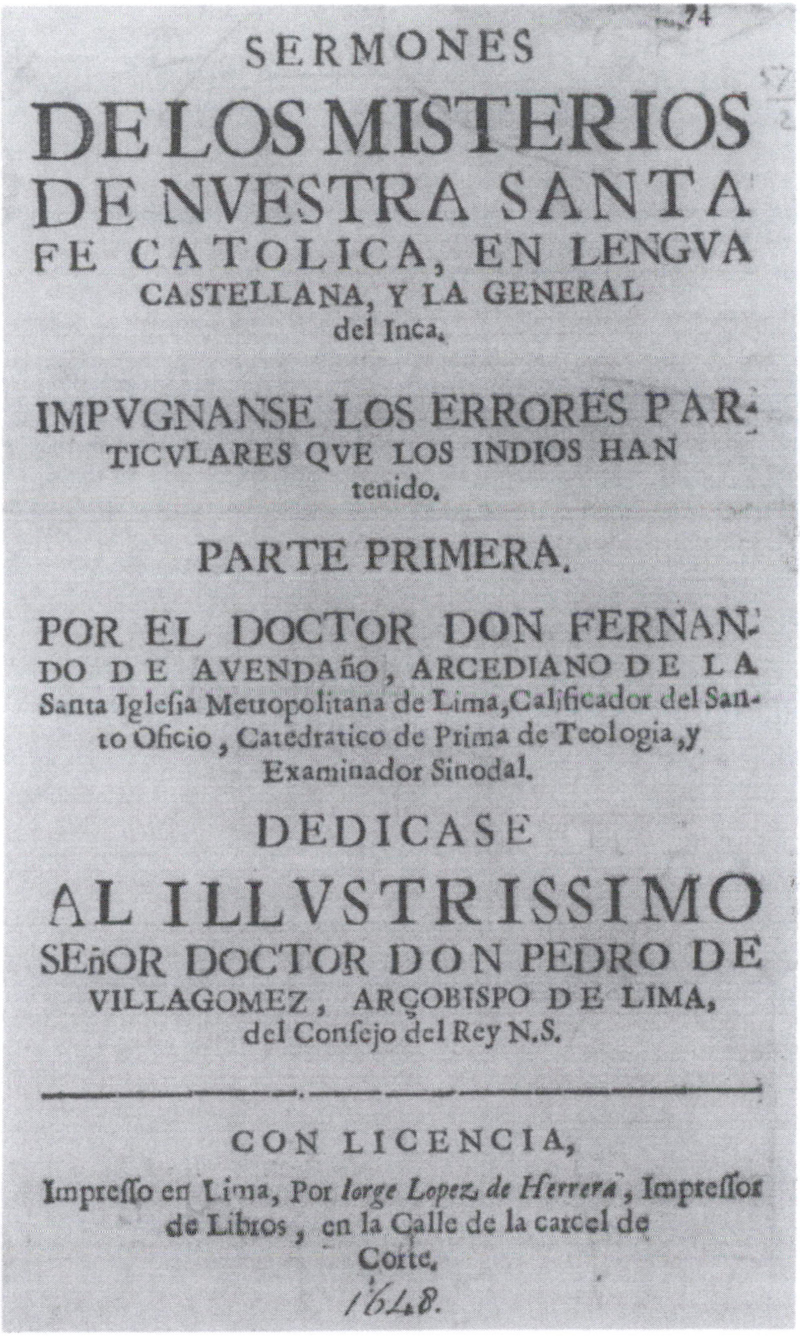

SERMONES

DE LOS MISTERIOS

DE NVESTRA SANTA

FE CATOLICA, EN LENGVA
CASTELLANA, Y LA GENERAL
del Inca.

IMPVGNANSE LOS ERRORES PAR-
TICVLARES QVE LOS INDIOS HAN
tenido.

PARTE PRIMERA.

POR EL DOCTOR DON FERNAN-
DO DE AVENDAño, ARCEDIANO DE LA
Santa Iglesia Metropolitana de Lima, Calificador del San-
to Oficio, Catedratico de Prima de Teologia, y
Examinador Sinodal.

DEDICASE

AL ILLVSTRISSIMO
SEñOR DOCTOR DON PEDRO DE
VILLAGOMEZ, ARÇOBISPO DE LIMA,
del Consejo del Rey N.S.

CON LICENCIA,

Impresso en Lima, Por *Iorge Lopez de Herrera*, Impressor
de Libros, en la Calle de la carcel de
Corte.

1648.

Figure 7. Title page of Fernando de Avendaño, *Sermones de los misterios* (1648). Courtesy of the John Carter Brown Library at Brown University.

and for himself through the negative caricaturization of Andean religion. The contraries advanced by Avendaño were the tenets he chose to surmise from colonial Indian religion, contraries selected and described in the interest of establishing the clear superiority of Christianity. The *peroración*, an epilogue in which the main points were repeated and concluded, was often dispensed with by Avendaño, though he was fond of making a single, summarizing point at the end of his sermons. Thus, his fourth sermon on how "the sun, moon and huacas are not God" concludes: "Reform yourselves, my children. No one should go back to look at the huacas, which are the inventions of the Devil. We will return to the True God with all our heart, asking for His mercy, and that He might grant us grace in this life and that we might come to enjoy glory in the next. Amen."[59]

Francisco de Avila's *Tratado de los evangelios* signaled some of its differences from Avendaño's *Sermones* with its very name. The contents of a *tratado* are bound in a freer, more "leisurely" form than the sermon proper. Avila could wander between points, unfettered by an initial proposition and the formulaic need to present his proof through contraries, though he, too, would often revert to this basic strategy. The tratado as a form had a reputation for popular and accessible references rather than argument by logic.[60] This is not to say that Avila, in choosing this form, abandoned structure; in fact, he chose to base his sermons, in an entirely customary way, on the Catholic festival cycle. The sermons expounded on the appropriate biblical texts through the calendar year. But these seasons and scriptures became launching points for a freer discourse. Because of the adherence to the conventional cycle, the emphasis upon the refutation of suspect Indian religiosity is less pronounced in the *Tratado* of Avila than in the *Sermones* of Avendaño. Yet if Avendaño's works are notable for the directness of their argumentation, then Avila's are more artful in the way they weave a subtle dissuasion from Indian beliefs into a cycle of scriptural instruction and elaboration. Avila's texts are full of surprises, whereas Avendaño's are often predictable. Duviols memorably took his comparison of the two preachers' styles to an emotional level. He refers first to Avendaño: "That which is probably most lacking in these sermons is Christian charity, or simply a feeling of humanity. The man is without a doubt dominated by his iconoclastic and apologetic zeal; he is skilled and brilliant, but his heart remains cold and hard. Of this we are fully convinced when we compare his sermons with those of Francisco de Avila."[61]

The seventeenth-century sermons for Indians from Arriaga's proposals to the mid-colonial finished products are, at their base, persuasive explications of the elemental mysteries of the catechism and doctrina. Although neither Avila nor

---

[59] F. de Avendaño, *Sermones*, fol. 50.
[60] H. D. Smith, *Preaching in the Spanish Golden Age*, pp. 43–44.
[61] *La Lutte*, pp. 279–80. See also the interpretation of G. de Dumezil, "Francisco d'Avila." Antonio Acosta comments upon the failings he sees in Avendaño's "logical elaboration" for both Andean audiences and, he claims, even "for a Western mind" in "Las extirpaciones," p. 191.

Avendaño was far removed from these other methods of evangelization, both preachers' texts were also compendia of formed opinion on Andean religion (and *lo andino* generally). In the anti-idolatry sermon, to a degree not seen in the other means, the articles of faith and the lessons of the Gospel merged with a mass of refutative arguments against Indian gods, beliefs, and practices. Christian presumption and representation of the rival take center stage. Intensive catechization and doctrine classes while a visita de idolatría was in town might replant the names and concepts of Christianity in the minds of the hearers and begin the task of explanation. But the sermons were the true opportunity to persuade an indigenous audience of their errors and move them emotionally and intellectually toward an orthodox faith. They emerge as the most telling portrait of the face of the extirpator's Christianity.

A common tactic in commencing a cycle of sermons was to argue that most Andean parishioners were good people who had only strayed from the True Path. All these new Christians needed was to be gently guided home. Andeans themselves were presented as natural Christians who had simply been misled, mostly by the Devil and his Andean agents in their midst. In this vein, Avendaño, echoing the contentions of some sixteenth-century friars and later scholars such as the Mestizo writer El Inca Garcilaso de la Vega, referred to Inka philosophers who, like the classical pagans of Europe, had glimpsed the one true God in their conception of Pacha Camac.[62] Yet many preachers before Indian assemblies, even as late as mid-colonial times, would feel the need to begin even more basically, as if presiding over an initial unveiling of a great truth, an exposure of blessed things too long obscured from the deprived Indian peoples. Avendaño's texts prepared also for this approach. Implicit in the beginning was the association of the Indian with a lesser capacity to understand. Avendaño addressed himself to those whom he called the "innumerable men who live as beasts without knowing there is a God who created them." "Men must know God," he continued in his second sermon, "to love him."[63] All the Indians had to do, he said, was to open their ears and their hearts.

The texts' larger purpose, to instill a genuine acceptance and worship of the Christian God, could be said to have been two-pronged: God's greatness and uniqueness had to be established and proven, and any rivals to his supremacy had to be refuted. The idea of a God or gods created some basic problems from the beginning. A notable contemporary of these sermons, the Jesuit Bernabé Cobo, in 1653 had pondered the apparent nonexistence of an appropriate

---

[62] See F. de Avendaño, *Sermones*, book 1, sermon 2, fol. 13, and the discussion by D. A. Brading in his "The Incas and the Renaissance." Similar claims about the monotheistic possibilities of another Andean deity, Vira Cocha, have enjoyed some modern popularity; see the discussion of P. Duviols, "Los nombres Quechua." Notwithstanding the similarities between many peoples' conceptions of divinity and the sacred, explored in the comparative work of Mircea Eliade and Jonathan Z. Smith among many others, I agree with F. Salomon, who has noted the "inherently inappropriate" nature of much of the effort to see the Andean divinity as some pre-Christian inkling of the Judeo-Christian God; see *Huarochirí*, ch. 15, sec. 199, note 389.

[63] F. de Avendaño, *Sermones*, book 1, sermon 2, fols. 12–12v.

Quechua concept to capture the idea of one god. Cobo noted almost reluctantly the early missionaries' failed search for a synonym and their eventual reliance on the Spanish word *Dios*; he himself could offer no other solution.[64] It does not hurt to reiterate here that like so many of the terms used to gloss Amerindian concepts, "god" was loaded with imposed connotations, and became a problematic and simplifying explanation for the numina and forces of Andean religion. The problem grew most acute when "god" was used in theological polemic, contributing to the illusion that Europeans were actually placing Andean supernatural beings, or gods, alongside the one Christian deity, even for the moment of negative comparison.[65]

The negative preconception, as well as the ubiquitous use of another loaded rubric, "idol" and thus "idolatry," to describe the Indians' alleged object of worship and their religion effectively precluded any possibility for genuine theological comparison.[66] Like the supposed idolaters in biblical times and Christian history, the Indians could gain little legitimacy in the eyes of their European judges because, among their many other faults, their religion was a priori false. Thus, from the extirpators' points of view, Andean religion was vainly polytheistic and denuded of any truth. This rhetorical approach tactically deprived Indian ways of legitimacy in the face of the practical evidence that might challenge such interpretations.

For instance, although Andean peoples clearly did not indulge in what Spanish commentators frequently called the "indiscriminate" worship of both natural and invented objects, indiscrimination became a common charge against Andean religion.[67] Thus a religious organization that had remained remarkably well defined, and that still sought to explain the world to its people in mid-colonial times, was degraded into something chaotic and impoverished. Any further explorations of Andean religious ideas by extirpators were not pursued so much out of curiosity or cultural interest as out of the practical need to know Indian ways in order to eradicate them more effectively, and the more all-encompassing need to establish Christian supremacy.

The result of intensified Christian self-centeredness was telling in the mid-colonial Andes. Spanish Catholic treatment of Andean religious ideas had long stemmed from a habitual inclination toward closing the mind. But, as they

[64] B. Cobo, *Historia del Nuevo Mundo*, book 13, ch. 4.

[65] A. R. Pagden charts the persistence and changing nature of this problem into the eighteenth century and Creole thought. See *Spanish Imperialism*, pp. 107–14. Of course, similar problems of language confront investigators of the effects of European religious expansion in many areas. In the Plains of North America, for instance, Wakantanka of the Lakota (or Western Sioux) was appropriated as a "God" figure, and was somewhat desperately called "Great Spirit" or "Great Mystery." See W. K. Powers, *Oglala Religion*. See my "Seeing God in Mid-Colonial Peru."

[66] A contemplation of these concepts and their contemporary application to Indian cultures in New Spain and Peru is C. Bernand and S. Gruzinski, *De l'idolâtrie*.

[67] See, for example, B. Cobo, *Historia del Nuevo Mundo*, book 13, ch. 11. S. MacCormack places Cobo's views in the context of the preceding ones of Acosta and Garcilaso in ch. 9.1 of *Religion in the Andes*.

went about their tasks and explained their own actions to themselves and supe-riors, most extirpators' capacities for intentional exploration became even more severely limited. A god that a visitador saw, or a spirit of which he heard tell, was not really considered at all. It was often not even confronted or legitimately pondered before being rejected; it was, after all, exactly what a visitador was looking for, with the purpose of eradication. As a result, the god's significance, the idea's own possibilities and wealth, were eclipsed.

Superficial understanding of another culture's divine forces and religious ideas, and the way they fit into that people's world view, led to the widespread inability of Spanish Christian observers to grant complexity and profundity to the originally non-Christian people, let alone their belief system. Instead of being represented as an alien people's vision of the world and their particular explanation of the human condition in relation to the forces believed present, Andean religion became "idolatry"—the worship of false gods. As I have stated above, idolatry was full of possibilities. But, above all, idolatry was something wild, dark, and uncivilized, a generic thing to be denigrated if one had to deal with it at all.

Simplifications of a complex enemy were, of course, not perpetrated only by the visitadores de idolatría. Especially in the middle of the seventeenth cen-tury, support for this kind of estimation of Andean religion came from the top levels of the Peruvian Church. Archbishop Villagómez, seeking royal support for his course of action when he and his methods were assailed by criticism, wrote to Philip IV in 1654 and informed him of the Indians' insidious sin "al-ways committed in secret, and most ordinarily in remote places (desiertos)." An armada that departed from Callao for Spain in 1651 carried a small box from the preacher and superintendent of the Extirpation himself, Fernando de Avendaño, also meant for the king. A separate letter reported that the box contained a number of "idols," along with comments on their "meanings and significance (significaciones)." Although one can only imagine the comments which accompanied these idols from Peru, Avendaño's sermons give no grounds to suppose that the gods were well represented. One must assume that his words were as promptly condemnatory, and perhaps as allusive to darkness and secrecy, as his prelate's. The gods, like the examples noted in the corre-spondence which treated the subject of Andean religion, were sent to Spain as curiosities and propaganda to assist their continued extirpation.[68]

Because of their low opinion of Andean religion and its functions in society, and the contrasting gratification they felt in the presence of their own religion's abstractions, the Extirpation's preachers saw a particular challenge in teaching the Indians to believe in a God they could not see. Andeans were not supposed to have had much capacity for abstract thinking. Thus, Avendaño combed the

[68] AGI Lima 303, Villagómez to king, Lima, 28 August 1654; AGI Lima 332, Letter from Avendaño to king, Lima, date unknown. During the first campaign, the viceroy of Peru, the prince of Esquilache, had made a similar but even larger remittance.

natural orders and limits of the visible world for signs and traces that might illustrate for his hearers the existence of the invisible "First Principle, Supreme Prince, [and] First Goodness upon which all depends."[69] His mid-colonial approach was not much different from that which can be discerned in the surviving *pláticas* (short addresses on a religious theme) of the Franciscan Bernardino de Sahagún from almost a century earlier in central Mexico, an indication of just how much Andeans were perceived to have lacked in their basic instruction in early colonial times.[70] An elementary course in the contemporary Church's vision of natural science and the order of things had begun.

God alone, the Indians were told, granted "life and being" and established the hierarchy of all things, including human society; for proof, it was only necessary to look around. The pebble could not be a diamond, the deer could not be a lion, and what Black slave or tributary Indian could ever aspire to the wealthy nobility?[71] God's "brand," the symbol of the cross, could be seen in many of his Andean creations (the condor with wings outstretched in flight, for instance), and who but a peerless God could perfect something as grand and elaborate as the bustling world at the same time as something so minute and intricate as the mosquito?[72] Duviols noted that this theme was part of a "sanctification of the colonial order," an underlying and paternalist message in the organization of public spectacles as well, encouraging the Indians to submit not only to the Christian religion but to the wider wishes of the Spanish Christian purveyors who clearly possessed the truth and knew what was best for them.[73]

There was also God's almighty power to be contemplated as proof of His existence. Avendaño invited Andean peoples to consider their own history for evidence of divine wrath and punishment in addition to the biblical instances of God's vengeance upon those who did not properly worship and respect him. On this score, the Indians' sacred histories suffer a fate worse than dismissal as preposterous delusions; the traditions were selectively appropriated and invoked as proof of the Christian God's wrath. Who, Avendaño asked rhetorically, had stricken from the face of the earth the superhuman giants recounted in the Indian *tradiciones*? The preacher did not linger over this momentary admission that huacas may have once existed. Who had sent the floods and fires that were said to have destroyed whole worlds and ages? And what had been the fate of the Inka nobles and the many other Indians who had perished and been de-

[69] F. de Avendaño, *Sermones*, book 1, sermon 2, fols. 13v and 15.

[70] R. Ricard, *The Spiritual Conquest*, includes discussion and selects a few passages from Sahagún at pp. 85–88.

[71] F. de Avendaño, *Sermones*, book 1, sermon 2, fol. 16. K. V. Thomas in *Man and the Natural World*, chs. 1 and 2, examines the use and rhetoric of these ideas of natural order in the roughly contemporary English context.

[72] F. de Avendaño, *Sermones*, book 1, sermon 2, fols. 14v–16 and 20v–21v; sermon 4, fol. 49; and sermon 6, fol. 63v.

[73] *La Lutte*, pp. 277–78. On the representation of order and consensus on public occasions, see C. S. Dean, "Painted Images of Cuzco's Corpus Christi."

feated after the Europeans' arrival?[74] In the face of so many signs of his power, who possessed the courage to maintain that the almighty God did not exist? Who had the courage even to ask?

God's invisibility, in contrast to the visibility of all his creations, was just another aspect of his greatness. The point was returned to over and over as Avendaño fashioned the faith that was to be presented to the recalcitrant idolaters who looked to their physical huacas, malquis, chancas, and conopas: God did not need to be seen. The image of the omnipresent God as a wise creator who was simultaneously a vengeful master was also built upon. Another of his predominant attributes, it seems, was jealousy.

The Andean gods were being rejected both explicitly and by inference as the glory of the God of the Christians was being established, but the teaching of monotheism—that there could be only one god—and of omnipotence—that only he had the power to do all manner of things—inevitably led the preacher toward more direct confrontations with indigenous divinities. The fundamental statement "There is one God who is omnipotent" (Avendaño's third sermon), and the rhetorical question "Who is God?" (from the fifth sermon) initiated a two-part demonstration. On the one hand, Avendaño elaborated on the supposed absurdity of more than one god and, on the other, he delivered a pointed analysis of who and what exactly could not be God, and why.

Once Avendaño had established the premise that a true God must necessarily be omnipotent, it followed that there could not be two rivals to total power; from this point, the prospect of thousands of gods, as he perceived in the Andean context, was absurd.[75] Sabine MacCormack's careful dissection of Bernabé Cobo's invaluable writings on the matter reveals the mid-colonial Jesuit's similar judgment. The Andeans are victims of confusion and deception who need to be saved from their nonsense and suffering. They worship, Cobo stated, "visible secondary causes" and not the "first and invisible cause."[76] To many Spanish Christian minds, the tendency toward such credulity was precisely what was delaying the spiritual conquest of Peru, complicating the Andean embrace of the strict monotheism of Christianity.

Extirpators could argue that the Church's preoccupation with neophyte comprehension of Christian mysteries was justified, confirmed by numerous Indian confessions from the period. To give but one example of a common phenomenon, a Jesuit provincial's annual letter to his Padre General in Rome in the early 1660s told of two missionaries' experience with an Indian in the Chinchay valley. When the man was asked the second question of the *Catecismo breve*, "How many gods are there?" he answered that there were four. Pressed to

[74] F. de Avendaño, *Sermones*, book 1, sermon 2, fols. 22–25.

[75] Ibid., sermon 3, fols. 28–29v.

[76] See *Religion in the Andes*, ch. 9.1, and especially p. 397 in discussion of Cobo's *Historia del Nuevo Mundo*, book 13, ch. 1, p. 147, and ch. 5, p. 157. Concentration on the Indians' supposed confusion with these causes was common among contemporary churchmen. See also A. de la Peña Montenegro, *Itinerario*, book 2, trat. 4, sess. 3, fol. 183.

think carefully about what he said, the man corrected himself, saying that indeed there were eight.[77]

Despite such basic problems, preachers in the Andes were urged to move from the subject of the one true God into a vigorous assault upon the actual objects which, in their enduring ignorance, the Indians worshiped. The sermons of Avendaño attempted to show the utter subordination of the things that Andeans took to be gods to the Christian God, and to devalue them before their people by portraying them as useless and absurd, inanimate and impotent. Lightning, the earth, the springs, the rivers, and the sea, Avendaño wrote, all moved, increased, and diminished in accordance with the will of God.[78] How could such things be gods?

The huacas, the cultural heroes whose great deeds and contributions to society were so central a part of local religion, became an especially favorite target for Christian derision. Even though the missionary wanderings and successive campaigns of extirpation meant that churchmen collectively had access to scores of Indian tradiciones that conveyed to them the importance and consequences of the huaca religion, their refutation in sermons rarely rose to an attentive level. Within the confines of extirpating rhetoric the huacas could be no more than "ugly stones."[79]

> Tell me brother, how can you put your hope in a rock as if it were the true God; do you not see that this stone does not have the wisdom to know what you ask? Do you not see that it has not the will to love you . . . no eyes to see you, no ears to hear, nor mouth to console you? And if it could talk it would say: "Indian, you are mad, you are blind to place your hope in me. I do not have any power; I cannot give you anything you ask of me. Do you not see that I am a stone, and that the birds and skunks soil me? If I am a stone, as you see that I am, how can I be God?" . . . There are many stones . . . wherever you go you will find stones, [but] there is only one True God.[80]

Fernando de Avendaño did not always go so far as to imagine a talking huaca (a dangerous tactic indeed when these gods were known for their responses to ministers). He more commonly urged priests and extirpators to point out the huacas' apparent inanimacy and powerlessness to achieve the desired effects. He poured scorn on the Indian ministers—whom he derided as hechiceros— and their claims that the huacas were creators who were capable of great deeds, and perpetual forces who could affect people's lives. In clear reference

---

[77] ARSI, Cartas anuas de 1660, 1661 y 1662, *Peru* 16, vol. 5, fol. 90. It is worth noting that this standard question, "how many gods are there?" appears to have led to similar problems for Jesuits elsewhere, raising the question of whether mistakes were not expected. In contemporary southern Italy, two shepherds near Eboli answered "a hundred" and "a thousand," respectively. P. Burke, *Popular Culture*, p. 32.

[78] F. de Avendaño, *Sermones*, book 1, sermon 5, fols. 51–52v.

[79] F. de Avendaño, *Sermones*, book 1, sermon 2, fol. 20v.

[80] Ibid., sermon 3, fols. 27–27v.

to the power of God the Father and the miracles of God the Son, which were regarded as scripturally revealed and thus proven, Avendaño asked what huaca could create all manner of living things, raise the dead, or give sight to the blind.[81] The Andean oral tradiciones had no legitimacy as equals to the Bible and the huacas were no serious rivals to the true God.

Other Andean divinities, the conopas for example, received similar but perhaps even more mocking treatment. In yet another return to the metaphor of the human life cycle in which Spanish Christians were adults and Indian Christians and potential Christians were children, a personal dimension of Andean religion was reduced to the most basic of levels. Conopas were likened to children's playthings. Knowingly or not, Avendaño resurrected a Las Casian argument that had employed classical models to show how Amerindian idolatry might be explained by a natural human inclination toward the worship of things, revealed perfectly in children's games and in their fondness for dolls.[82] Although Avendaño's invective often denied the huacas the physical attributes of eyes, mouths, and ears, in his attack on these smaller and generally more precisely formed gods of fecundity he was forced to admit the existence of these features, however muted. Only another quotation can begin to portray the preacher's subtle, methodical technique.

> This God [the Christians'] is the living God (*Dios vivo*), the others are dead gods (*dioses muertos*). Although they have mouths they do not speak, although they have ears they do not hear, although they have eyes they do not see, and although they have feet they do not move. Do you know what your conopas are? I will tell you. Have you not seen those dolls made of rags in the shape of a child, with eyes, mouth and hands? You buy them for a *real*, and when your little one is crying you give it to him and say: "here is your little child." And the little one takes it in his hands and kisses it, plays with it and feeds it, but the rag doll does not eat; he puts it to bed, but the doll does not sleep; he says that it walks, but the doll cannot move; and he speaks with it, but the doll does not hear or respond. Of the same ilk are your conopas. . . . Oh poor blind Indian, fool without reason! Do you not see that this conopa is like the doll with which you soothe your child that he will not cry?[83]

Another tack that was commonly pursued is related to the Christian rejection of Andean religious ideas, but represents a slightly more critical devaluation than the essentially emotional and dramatic one noted above. This prevalent charge against the huacas and other indigenous gods focused on their supposed temporality. It was an established criticism to proclaim, as these mid-colonial extirpators and preachers repeatedly did, that these were gods from

---

[81] Ibid., sermon 6, fol. 65v.

[82] B. de Las Casas, *Apologética historia*, 74, p. 386, as cited in S. MacCormack, *Religion in the Andes*, p. 237.

[83] F. de Avendaño, *Sermones*, book 1, sermon 5, fols. 62–62v.

whom the faithful could and did seek to derive only worldly benefit.[84] The proper Christian, the extirpators argued, looks to the good of the soul and to the reward of everlasting life after death. Thus he or she seeks a god who is spiritual and from whom a worshiper can reap spiritual sustenance, food for the soul. The Andean gods, in contrast, were propitiated by their faithful in the hope that they might provide temporary sustenance and things of the body. "The ancient Indians and the sorcerers," Avendaño asserted, "asked the huacas for material goods, . . . they asked them for good chacras, that the stock would not die, and that they would be given health—all this for the body. But for the good of their souls they asked not a thing, nor did they know what goods are those of the soul."[85]

Thus in addition to being portrayed as filthy rocks, soiled by animals and little boys, and as the equivalents of children's toys, the principal elements of Andean religion were denied any spiritual component by their extirpating critics. Andean conceptions of ancestral spirits and reciprocal forces in the world were not recognized, just as the subject of the local and regional religious systems' abilities to satisfy metaphysical concerns was not deemed worthy of consideration. As MacCormack has recently put it so eloquently in reference to a slightly earlier era, and with an expression that echoes aims in William Christian's work on the religiosity of late medieval and early modern inhabitants of rural Castile, "the issue of how a deity may touch a human being" was to be seen from a completely orthodox Spanish Christian point of view.[86]

It only remained for the Christians' belief in the utter inefficacy of huaca worship—rightly taken by the extirpators to be at the center of regional Andean religion—to be expounded, and this was duly done in connection with the fundamental assessment of shallowness and temporality. Through their sermons, the preachers of the extirpating era sought to convince the Indians that the rites and ceremonies that many continued to practice were in vain, and were in fact the deceptions of the Devil and his earthly agents, the Indian ministers and teachers. Sabine MacCormack, again working largely to capture Bernabé Cobo's analysis of Andean religion, dubbed the supposed deception of the sorcerer-charlatans "priestly fraud and pious make-believe" which, according to the Jesuit (but not, I think, MacCormack), went on "throughout the Andes."[87]

The measurement by which Andean religion consistently failed was, of course, ideal and Christian or, as it was just as often called, genuine or true religion. Francisco de Avila, in his sermon for Christ's nativity, contrasted the vigil that Christians observed on the day before Christmas with the abstinence from salt, ají, and sexual relations that the Indians kept in the days before the

---

[84] William Taylor has noted similar judgments about the religiosity of Indian parishioners in the Diocese of Guadalajara and the Archdiocese of Mexico. *Magistrates of the Sacred*, ch. 3.

[85] F. de Avendaño, *Sermones*, book 1, sermon 3, fol. 35v.

[86] *Religion in the Andes*, "Prologue," p. 7, and p. 14. See also W. A. Christian, *Apparitions*, p. 9.

[87] *Religion in the Andes*, p. 399.

collective worship of their gods.[88] Avila noted that the Indians attributed the failure of crops and work projects, sickness, and death to failed observance of the vigil. This, he said, was nothing but the treachery of the Devil "who, like a monkey, imitates God." And he built on this familiar, diabolic premise, for there was, in Avila's view, no end to the demonic parody of Christianity. For instance, just as the padres urged the congregations to sing in the church, the Devil instructed the Indians to sing in adoration of the hills, the peaks, and the rocks.[89]

Avendaño, too, preached on the futility of the fiestas of the huacas during which the Indians danced and sang, "invoking their [gods'] names" as they offered their valuable livestock and precious stones in sacrifice.[90] And in his own characteristic style he both replayed the child motif and echoed Avila's final attribution of blame for the cruel sham of a religion to the Devil.

> Some of you possess a very smooth little stone of lively color as your huaca, others a little beast made of silver, others a cob of maize, . . . others a small idol dressed in clothing of cumbe, and others a thousand silly things (*niñerias*) with which you offend and anger God. All because the honor that should go to the Almighty God is given to things so vile and obscene, the Devil is laughing and making a joke of you, whom, like senseless children, he has fooled with such tricks. . . . Who persuades you to worship the huacas? The Devil. He wants to take you prisoner. Who is it who sometimes speaks from within the huacas to your elders? The Devil, your enemy.[91]

There seem to have been occasions when such preaching could transcend the bounds of pure rhetorical persuasion and abet demonstrative extirpation. The *autos de fe* which, along with the pronouncement of sentences and processions of shame, characteristically brought visitas of idolatry to a dramatic close in the villages of the mid-colonial Archdiocese of Lima, must have been terrifying scenes. Here, the visitadores' agents burned the huacas, malquis, and religious implements that had been revealed and collected during the investigation in a public finale before the assembled Indian populations. The sermons, in close relationship to the *autos*, depended on the inspiration of a similar fear to convey their messages. In the realm of preaching and instruction, a controversial device noted for its exceptional emotional effect on audiences found its place amidst the Extirpation's evangelical arsenal. This was the so-called *sermón de aparato*, a sermon accompanied by display.[92]

There is no way to prove conclusively that Fernando de Avendaño comple-

---

[88] On Andean restrictions in the times of regular festivals in mid-seventeenth-century Cajatambo, see my *An Evil Lost to View?*, esp. ch. 5.

[89] F. de Avila, *Tratado de los evangelios*, "Sermon en la natividad del Señor," fols. 46–48.

[90] F. de Avendaño, *Sermones*, book 1, sermon 6, fol. 65v.

[91] Ibid., book 2, sermon 19, fols. 31–31v.

[92] Many preachers in contemporary Spain seem to have found the "spectacular surprises" of the so-called *sermones de aparato* crude and sensational, though they appear to have been widely used. See H. D. Smith, *Preaching in the Spanish Golden Age*, pp. 18 and 65–66.

mented the delivery of his sermon on the First Commandment with the destruction of an actual huaca before his congregations, but the text strongly suggests it. Moreover, the sermons were distributed to numerous other priests, all of whom were free to enlighten their parishioners with "educational theater" as they saw fit.[93] Avendaño's tone was sarcastic, even taunting. The following passage captures in concise form the drama and technique of one sermon text in particular. He began by asking: "Perhaps the huacas defended your ancestors from the viracochas (the Spaniards)?" and in the same tone he continued: "Give me a huaca here and I will crush it before you and turn it into dust. Why does it not respond? Why does it not speak? Why does it not defend itself? How . . . can something which does not defend or help itself manage to help you?"[94]

Robert Ricard, in his study of early evangelization methods in central Mexico, observed that the "very short catechumenate and the readiness with which they [the indigenous peoples of the region] were admitted to baptism," was a reflection not of missionary neglect, ill-preparedness, or even naïveté but of the friars' optimism and "respect for the soul of the natives." Even a cursory examination of the rich chronicles left by the friars upon whom Ricard principally focused reveals a more complicated situation than this one quotation suggests, a missionary optimism shadowed by preoccupation with the uncertain results of mass conversion and with the specter of religious mixture. And to his credit, Ricard himself recognized that minimal prebaptismal instruction would cause more problems later than it had solved at the time of the alleged conversions.[95] Yet Ricard was largely unyielding in his discernment of a fundamental respect and hopefulness in the attitudes of his historical subjects, the first missionaries of New Spain, toward the Indian new converts.

Few scholars would accept Ricard's portrayal of sixteenth-century evangelization in New Spain without revision. But it remains the case that the generally more experimental kinds of Christianity carried by early mendicants in Mexico were sustained by markedly fewer friars in the more troubled and geographically challenging setting of early colonial Peru. The bulk of early evangelization in the Andes was delayed and problematic. Moreover, Christianity bolstered its presence in Peru only after the decades of civil war, and in a markedly less optimistic climate than that in which the early evangelists of Mexico had operated. The consolidation of colonial Catholicism in the Andes came largely after the Council of Trent closed its last session in 1563, just as it was becoming increasingly apparent to Spanish Catholics that differences with the Protestants of northern Europe would not soon be reconciled, and when religious orthodoxy within Spain was steadily becoming more rigidly defined. Systematic extirpation, the recourse to coercive methods as a necessary means of enforcing

[93] R. Ricard, *The Spiritual Conquest*, p. 200.
[94] F. de Avendaño, *Sermones*, book 2, sermon 19, fol. 31v.
[95] R. Ricard, *The Spiritual Conquest*, p. 289.

orthodoxy, came quickly for most of the peoples new to the faith in the Arch-diocese of Lima; as Karen Spalding put it in her classic study of Huarochirí, there was "a cast to the temper and the actions of the Church in the Andes" that had not been so pronounced in earlier evangelization settings in Mesoamerica.[96]

What Ramsay MacMullen has claimed for the specific context of the late antique European setting also speaks to the Peruvian case I am describing. "What pagans saw *in* Christianity (in the sense of being drawn to it)," Mac-Mullen writes, "depended [at least in part] on what they saw *of* it."[97] What did colonial Andeans see of and in Christianity?

Monica Barnes and Regina Harrison, among others, draw attention to what catechization and the flow of Christian interpretations of the world, sin, and religious practice might have done to Andean minds. Barnes posits the ger-mination of change, writing that "with the mechanisms of repetition, suggestive questions, and memorization, they [priests and extirpators] were able to insinu-ate Renaissance concepts into native belief systems."[98] Harrison speculates in a more concentrated fashion on the problematic impact of determined clerical prying into matters of sexuality. "We may wonder," she writes, "if in fact the Church was not serving to disseminate knowledge of sexual pleasure that per-haps never had crossed the minds of their newly converted Quechua-speaking parishioners."[99] These inquiries are partly inspired by Foucault's formulations on the institutionalization of sexuality. They also seem influenced by what, for some time, scholars have been saying about the influence of the ideas of theo-logians and demonologists on accused witches in contemporary western Europe.[100]

In their investigations and refutations of Andean religion, extirpators in mid-colonial Peru, out of necessity, had to seek information, elaborate on, and dis-cuss dimensions of the forbidden religion. Perhaps, as has been suggested for a sixteenth-century Mexican context, Christian dissemination and refutation sug-gested opportunities for Amerindian resistance to Christianity.[101] Arguably, the investigations into Indian religious concepts, culture, and rituals in the two colonial heartlands (those of Sahagún, Landa, Alva, Ruiz de Alarcón, De la Serna, Avila, Arriaga, and the host of extirpators in Peru, and so on) for the purposes of more detailed teaching and more effective eradication may iron-ically have played a part in their survival.

But although it is certainly conceivable that Indians were "reminded" of

---

[96] K. Spalding, *Huarochirí*, p. 244; see also S. MacCormack, "'The Heart Has Its Reasons.'"

[97] "Two Types of Conversion," p. 174, emphasis added.

[98] M. Barnes, "Catechisms and *Confessionarios*," p. 80.

[99] R. Harrison, "The Theology of Concupiscence," p. 148. On how teaching about the Devil, in particular, might similarly backfire on the enforcers of Christian orthodoxy and on the interpreta-tions of Fernando Cervantes in this context, see Chapter Seven below.

[100] See S. Clark, *Thinking with Demons*, esp. Part I.

[101] I have in mind especially J. Jorge Klor de Alva; among his other articles, see especially "Nahua Colonial Discourse," pp. 30–31.

certain non-Christian rites and beliefs by their investigators, preachers, and judges, and that this spurred "traditional survival," in the mid-colonial Andes at least, people had more compelling and complicated reasons to survive. Responses were many, and were influenced by at least three factors. First, for many people in the Archdiocese of Lima, key dimensions of Andean religion, far from being in danger of being forgotten or becoming irrelevant, were adapting to new pressures. Second and simultaneously, elements of Christianity were proving useful and attractive, and these tended not to displace other elements in the emerging system. Third, and again at the same time, the Extirpation of idolatry carried into these realms an impatient kind of Christianity; its agents employed coercive means of persuasion and demanded complete orthodoxy.

Teaching—predominantly through catechism, indoctrination, and sermons but also through the regular administering of sacraments (penance in particular)—did much to determine the face of Christianity in the Andean parishes of the Archdiocese of Lima, both before and after visitas de idolatría, and while they were in progress. The image that Christian instruction had among the Indians in the mid-colonial period was generally bad and getting worse, but everything about Christianity was not universally repulsive.

Francisco de Avila, in his role as sermonizer, seems to have sensed the importance of this discrepancy between the various faces of Christianity. And this was in spite of both his crucial role in the earlier extirpation of idolatry in the Lima region and the legal complications of his own past. Avila's mid-colonial point of view in this respect provides another demonstration of the fact that contemporary Spanish Christian opinion was rarely simple, predictable, or necessarily unified on the matters of idolatry, its principal causes, and its most effective remedy. In his sermon for the first Sunday of Advent, Avila preached in a populist and sanctimonious fashion, over the heads of parish clergy like himself and directly to the Indians, whom he called "people possessing reason." Bad priests were like everyone else, he wrote; they would not escape the Last Judgment.

> I do not place much guilt on the Indians when it is said that they worship idols, consult maestros of idolatry for their needs, get drunk, cohabit out of wedlock, and commit other sins. Much of the guilt falls on the padres curas who do not teach you what you have to believe, and who do not make you understand the reasons for not committing these sins. If the priests worked at this it is without a doubt that you, as people possessing reason, would be convinced, and that you yourselves would be amused at the disparate things you believe and do. You would say: "Why do I do these crazy things?"[102]

Avila's appeal to the Indians' reasonableness and his attention to the negligence of parish instruction demonstrates that this extirpator, like Archbishop Villagómez and so many other churchmen, recognized there was more to blame

---

[102] F. de Avila, *Tratado de los evangelios*, fols. 11–12.

for the endurance of "idolatry" than Andean recalcitrance. Indeed, his words differed little from those of the people who opposed Villagómez's revival of the Extirpation. In identifying priestly ineptitude as an enduring and particular problem in mid-colonial times, Avila added his voice to an inward, self-critical refrain that had been especially prevalent among Catholic churchmen since the Council of Trent. The Third Provincial Council of Lima—through which Archbishop Mogrovejo had introduced Tridentine emphases to Peru—had included in the introduction to its confessional a statement not so different from the one Avila would later expound in his sermon:

> One of the reasons that the [Christian] belief has not taken is because of the scattered and unorganized way of teaching doctrine among many priests. As if these people were schoolboys or parrots, they happily have them recite Christian doctrine: and many times they tell them things about our beliefs without persuading them that they should believe it, nor making clear to them lies and tricks that the Devil has taught them.[103]

Avendaño's sermons are markedly more conservative and less critical of the Church's agents than Avila's. In his first and fifth texts from Book One and his fifteenth and twenty-third from Book Two, Avendaño compares parish priests with the apostles, representing them to the Indians as the "messengers of God" who must be respected and obeyed at all times.[104]

Avila's points were the more astute in that he tried to read Andean feelings and religious needs in mid-colonial times. His rhetoric sought to appeal to an Andean sense of injustice, and then to turn those feelings into a motivation that would spur personal and community reformation in spite of evil priests, bad Christian examples, and poorly sustained instruction. The early seventeenth-century Indian chronicler Felipe Guaman Poma de Ayala was a contemporary Andean Christian who had urged something similar. Guaman Poma's vivid criticisms of the priests and friars in the Indian parishes are well known. He gave specific and graphic examples of clergy in various states of incompetence, sin, and corruption. He portrayed priests who hindered the Indians' education the better to exploit them, and who then turned to expose the Indians' lack of knowledge. "When an Indian makes a complaint or demands justice," wrote Guaman Poma, "it is usual for the priest to retaliate by accusing him of ignorance of the Christian doctrina. He says: 'Tell me the doctrina, you troublesome Indian. Start talking at once!'"[105] The sheer amount of litigation and the number of sharp confrontations between priests and Indians in the seven-

---

[103] *Confessionario* [1585] in "Tercero catecismo y exposición," p. 200, as cited in R. Harrison, "The Theology of Concupiscence," p. 137.

[104] See F. de Avendaño, *Sermones*, book 1, fols. 1, 6, and 60; book 2, fols. 14v–15v and 46v.

[105] *El primer nueva corónica*, 2: 560–61, see also p. 558. The "padres" is one of the longest and most bitter in the entire chronicle. Guaman Poma seems to have framed most but not all of his work as a description of conditions before the Extirpation, because his depiction of visitadores generales includes significant praise for Cristóbal de Albornoz, the official who in the 1560s quelled the Taki Onqoy movement, and whom Guaman Poma personally assisted.

teenth and eighteenth centuries, in the Lima region as well as in other parts of Spanish America, confirms Guaman Poma's portrayal.[106] Moreover, such examples, frequently including acts of violence, only add to the impression that indoctrination had become inextricably linked to punishment in the Indians' minds. Guaman Poma's rendering of the actual efficacy of Christian preaching was not much kinder, even if it was slightly more ambiguous. In one of his most thought-provoking drawings, a cluster of Indian parishioners sit and kneel before their priest in his pulpit and demonstrate audience responses which range from deep sleep through casual boredom through rapt attention to obvious panic and tears (Figure 8). The effects of the visitas of idolatry and their contribution to the evangelization of Indians must be examined within this complex and troubled set of possibilities.

The Christian pastoral of the seventeenth and eighteenth centuries in the Archdiocese of Lima could not help but mirror the changes and uncertainties affecting the Church's larger policy toward suspect Andean religiosity. Missions and parish administration were one thing, and accompanying or at least supporting the agents of the Extirpation another. Yet many churchmen moved, both practically and intellectually, between the two. Perhaps predictably, the mid-colonial projection of Christianity moved just as tentatively between the poles of patient, paternal concern and aggressive eradication. That baptized Indians were worshiping forbidden gods and persistently turning to village adepts for religious solutions to pressing needs was cause for great concern, as were the obvious failings of parish clergy to offer remedies for the situation. The mid-colonial Church's intermittent vehicle to answer these problems, involving an assent to the systematic use of force, brought with it a forceful and focused language of dissuasion.

The Extirpation's preachers might expound on Christian mysteries and make simple explanations of why, for example, Catholic image worship was not idolatry, saying that the saints and Virgin were given reverence "for what they represent and not for what they are."[107] But the same distinctions and possibilities were not conceded the Andean huacas or ancestors. The point about the inherent divinity of Mexican painted images revived most recently by Serge Gruzinski is a seductive one in this context. Arguably, the Andean religious forms (huacas, conopas, chancas, among others), like the bright images produced by the Mexican *tlacuilos* (artist scribes) made divinity "physically present and palpable" for those who made offerings and sacrifices in their midst.[108]

---

[106] See the discussion in A. Acosta Rodríguez, "Los doctrineros," and the published guide to the *capítulos* section of Archiepiscopal Archive of Lima compiled by M. Tineo Morón, *La fe y las costumbres*. On litigiousness and confrontation between priests and parishioners in eighteenth-century New Spain, see William Taylor's discussion of a particular dispute in Ozoloapan, Temascaltepec, "Santiago's Horse," pp. 162–73.

[107] F. de Avendaño, *Sermones*, book 2, sermon 20, fols. 35v–36v, and my *An Evil Lost to View?*, ch. 6.

[108] *Painting the Conquest*, esp. pp. 15–16. The human *ixiptlas* of Mexico, too, are relevant to this line of inquiry into the sacred and representation. See I. Clendinnen, "Ways to the Sacred," pp. 122–26 and further discussion in the same author's *Aztecs*.

Figure 8. Indoctrination: a priest's sermon and his congregation. From Felipe Guaman Poma de Ayala, *El primer nueva corónica*, edited by John V. Murra and Rolena Adorno. Original manuscript in the Royal Library, Copenhagen.

But, in refusing to accept that huacas represented ancestors and ancestral deeds and in contending that they were stone forms venerated almost indiscriminately and for only material ends, most extirpators effectively avoided such taxing questions. In so doing they closed their minds and deprived themselves of a level of understanding that would seem to have been crucial to successful evangelization.

Indian religious expressions were denied both metaphor and subtlety. And this gave the instructive side of the Extirpation its fundamental negativity. Andean gods were required literally to eat and drink as their ministers claimed, and if they did not do so on command, they became the subjects of ridicule. The huacas were finally portrayed by Fernando de Avendaño, the quintessential Extirpation preacher, as laughable; the practical knowledge he possessed about the traditions and beliefs that surrounded them was used only to further their humiliation. The huacas' mythical transformations from Indians, ancient men and women, into stone figures that would last forever were viewed as an ungodly retrogression, when such moments of lithomorphosis were in fact steeped in sacred and historical meaning and often deemed a great honor.[109]

The critique of Andean beliefs that was so much a part of the face of mid-colonial Christianity, and which was so bound up in Spanish Christian identity in the eras of the Extirpation, involved more than intensified instruction and discursive degradation. As the intellectual dismantling of Andean concepts of the sacred and divine continued, there came many points when the extirpators felt they had proved the hopeless credulity and inferior capacities of the Indians. It followed that such *miserables* would also fall victim to even more serious deceptions than those caused by their ignorance and gullibility in the presence of charlatans.

[109] F. de Avendaño, *Sermones*, book 1, sermon 4, fols. 40, 43–43v. See also P. Duviols, *La Lutte*, pp. 280–95.

Deception and Delusion

THE ANCIENT INDIANS of Peru had not known the Christian revelation; most of the theories stating otherwise had, by the middle of the seventeenth century, fallen into disrepute. In terms of the dualistic Christian metaphor most frequently employed by early modern Spanish churchmen, pre-conquest Indians had lived in a state of darkness. Their post-conquest descendants were being offered the light, the word of God, and the prospect of eternal life. Even so, by the mid-colonial years, their enlightenment was proving a complicated process and their salvation was slow.

Most extirpators' explanations of Andean religion rested on the widely held belief in the intellectual inferiority of Indians; what but an ineffectual religion could be expected from peoples believed to possess a limited capacity for abstract thought and reason? Yet this interpretation of Andean religious ideas necessarily involved more than simply their degradation as futile and worthless conceptions. There was a point beyond which the phenomena of flawed religious development—all the false gods and vain rituals—required more definitive explanation. The Spanish could not but mine their own cultural and religious tradition for a readily accessible reason.

To the eyes of most Hispanic Peruvians, "idolatry" was more than another society's mistaken religion; it was the result of the interventions of a famous old enemy, the Devil. Satan and his cohorts provided an explanatory common denominator that explained the haunting familiarity of the Indians' religious perversions and misconceptions. The diabolically inspired inversions of the True Faith perceived in Peru were, after all, hardly Christianity's first brush with the Devil's mimetic ways; it would have been comforting, intellectually, to find that what occupied the attention of churchmen in the Peruvian present resembled evils against which the Church had struggled in the past. Pedro de Villagómez expressed the opinions of many in his time when he wrote that of the seven reasons he posited for the endurance of idolatry in Peru, the principal was the "great cunning and diligence of the Devil." According to the archbishop of Lima, as "the author of idolatry and all evil," Satan was a formidable adversary who faced few limitations; his powers of metamorphosis and capacity for spirit-like flight made it easy for him to deceive "such people as the Indians."[1]

The purveyors of the Christian faith to native Andeans had found many occasions that seemed to justify the systematic demonization of Andean gods and the rituals and practices associated with them. The first part of what one

---

[1] *Carta pastoral*, see ch. 12, pp. 41–42 and ch. 13, pp. 43–44. It was common for the cunning of the Devil to be linked to the credulity of the Indians in such explanations.

might call the standard demonizing equation involved the application of European intellectual assumptions about the Devil's powers over human minds and about Amerindian credulity. It is this aspect which has captured considerable attention in recent research on colonial Spanish America, and which has led to a concentration on the influences that shaped the ways in which Europeans interpreted unfamiliar religious concepts for themselves and their contemporaries.[2] But the second part of the equation—understanding what happened to the conceptualized Devil and demons on the ground in the Indian parishes—has proved more elusive for researchers.

Here, the rich variety of testimonial evidence from the visitas of idolatry in the Archdiocese of Lima offers new opportunities. The documentation allows for a closer examination of the complexity of the phenomena attributed to the Devil and demons in the Amerindian context, shedding light into some of the dimmer corners both of Hispanic demonization and its effects in the early modern period.

The role of the diabolic within the Spanish Christian interpretation of the Andean religious system was as inevitable as it was important. Satan and his demonic cohorts played an integral part in the explanatory cast for theologians, a pervasive evil force believed to play upon and amplify human weaknesses and credulity. As Sabine MacCormack has demonstrated, the assumption that demons could control matter and exploit the human "imagination" ran deep into the fibers of European learned tradition.[3] Investigators have consistently agreed with Sir John Elliott's general assertion that when sixteenth- and seventeenth-century Europeans in America confronted "the more puzzling features of alien societies"—many of which tended to be religious—they were inclined to believe in the answers provided them by the idea of a tireless Devil, the enemy of God and man, working among them.[4]

Satan had long since proven his capacity to tempt and deceive in the Old World. The temptation of Jesus on the mountain set a pattern, and there was every indication that the ambitions of the Devil involved constructing a similar theater of operations in America.[5] As a tempter and deceiver he afflicted even

---

[2] I am thinking particularly of one of the more prominent and rich strands in Sabine MacCormack's *Religion in the Andes*, and of the work of Fernando Cervantes on New Spain, especially *The Devil in the New World*, chs. 1 and 2, and "The Idea of the Devil." But see also his "The Devil in Colonial Mexico," and "The Devils of Querétaro."

[3] Using the sixteenth-century *Apológetica historia* of Las Casas as a central point of entry, MacCormack reflects upon how Aquinas, and particularly the Thomist commentary on Aristotle's distinction in *De Anima* between "sense perception" and "imagination," provided the basic framework within which demonic visions were understood by contemporary Spaniards in both Europe and America; see *Religion in the Andes*, esp. pp. 225–40.

[4] J. H. Elliott, "The Discovery of America," p. 59.

[5] Matthew 4:9. See also P. Brown, *Religion and Society*, pp. 119–46. For a view of Satan's central role in the early modern Iberian context see Fr. J. de los Angeles, *Diálogos de la conquista*, and BL, Egerton Ms. 2058, "Tratado y practica de las yllusiones del Demonio en que se traen casos particulares y notables sucedidos á diversas personas illusas" (1588), fols. 34–83v.

steadfastly Christian persons in both Europe and the Indies in ways that severely challenged their faith. Thus it was that in 1646 a Jesuit correspondent in
Lima recalled with horror the nocturnal ordeals suffered by a brother, P.
Agustín Lalumbrino, who on one occasion was visited in his "humble room" by
"a band of demons in the forms of women who sang and danced lasciviously"
and tormented his "most honest eyes."[6] MacCormack discusses the motif of
the seductive woman, that "stereotype of Christian ascetic theology," and its
employment by Las Casas, stemming especially from the famous experiences
of the hermit St. Anthony, who was tempted in a similar fashion.[7]

Yet not all apparitions were so obviously the work of the Devil and demons;
since late antique times Christian commentators noted that the fiends regularly
assumed the guise of the holy, coming as men of peace. As one late sixteenth-
century treatise affirmed, it was the demons' evil flexibility that made the illusory visions the most frightening aspect in their repertoire. Through manipulated visions, demons might "propose things so similar to that which God
communicates . . . that [people] can scarcely tell which are from God and
which are from the Devil, which of what they offer is true and which a lie."[8]

In a discussion of dreams within his treatise for parish priests the bishop of
Quito, Peña Montenegro, applied similar thoughts generally—and in their familiar Thomist terms—to the Indians of the Viceroyalty of Peru. Parts of his
work were clearly composed with the mid-seventeenth-century extirpators of
idolatry in mind. Dreams were of three types: those which were natural and
wholly permissible; those which were inspired by God (such as those of Gid-
eon, Daniel, Jacob, and Joseph in the Bible); and those which came from the
Devil, "exciting the fantasy in man . . . [causing people to] give them credit [for
things that happened] . . . and to order human actions according to them."[9]

Distinguishing between dreams which, on the one hand, filled the heart with
"good propositions" and "a certain flavor of the Divinity," and on the other,
engendered vice, boredom, and "a distaste for good things," made the task
sound remarkably easy. In reality, however, such distinctions depended on one's
cultural perspective and moral tradition. Anyone could conceivably be affected
by the third category of dream, the demonic illusion. But the Spanish Chris-

---

[6] ARSI, Carta anua de 1646, *Peru* 15, vol. 4, fols. 196v and 198.

[7] *Religion in the Andes*, p. 239 and pp. 30–35, and the depictions by Patinir and Bosch repro-
duced as Figures 5 and 6, pp. 32–33.

[8] BL, Egerton Ms. 2058, fol. 34. The author of this document argues that "great light can be
gained in the understanding of the Father of darkness and the cunning of his illusions" by attending to these cases, and proceeds to tell of how the Devil appeared to one man before the Holy
Sacrament in Seville, and to nuns in Córdoba, Granada, Seville, and Lisbon. S. MacCormack
discusses the heritage of the beliefs that surrounded demonic visions in *Religion in the Andes*, ch.
5. 2. On the mixed categories of beings that appeared to some Nahuas in central Mexico, see J. J.
Klor de Alva, "Nahua Colonial Discourse," pp. 20–21 and, in a wider swath of New Spain, F.
Cervantes, *The Devil in the New World*, esp. ch. 2.

[9] *Itinerario*, book 2, trat. 6, fols. 200–1. For discussion of how Aristotelian-Thomist doctrines on
dreams were applied by Hispanic commentators a century before Peña's writing, see S. MacCormack, *Religion in the Andes*, ch. 5, 2.

tian's unquestioning belief in a hierarchy of humankind meant that some people were thought to be more vulnerable to deception than others. Not everyone enjoyed the spiritual armaments of the Jesuit P. Lalumbrino, Christ on the mountain, or the hermit Saint Anthony, least of all the Indians.

Peña's views on Andeans' vulnerability to deception through dreams and visions conformed closely to José de Acosta's influential conception of Amerindians as members of the secondary and tertiary classes of heathens (beneath the Chinese and Japanese, in a categorization that depended largely on European criteria of political organization, forms of literacy, religious sophistication, and mode of living).[10] The Indians' "rusticity and simplicity," and their susceptibility to the "natural inclinations" that led to idolatry and sin prompted the bishop of Quito to proclaim that "if there are in the world a people who, in all truth, can be called *miserable*, it is the Indians of America."[11] In their unreasoning states, such *miserables* were the very credulous simpletons for which the Fiend was known to search. Peña made the connections between the Indians' perceived lesser capacities, their weakness for vices that deprived them of reason, and their general gullibility in concluding that "the Indians are consistently fooled into believing that what they have dreamed is infallibly true . . . and other times, [when] they chew coca and drink chicha to intoxicate themselves, they are persuaded that they must have dreamed the things . . . they desire to know for certain. All of this is to want to know by the instruction of the Devil."[12] The preponderance of questions about beliefs in dreams in the confessional for Indians designed by Juan Pérez Bocanegra as part of his *Ritual formulario* of 1631 further demonstrates that the European preoccupation with Andean delusion was far from simply an intellectual exercise.[13]

Because of the Indians' supposed ignorance and seemingly irremediable credulity, not to mention the fragility of their neophyte condition, in their midst the Devil became an especially potent and dangerous foe. According to Francisco de Avila, whose sermons pondered the Devil in great detail, the Enemy was a watchful and ever-present one who became most infuriated by the prospect of a Christian conversion. When the Devil saw an Indian beginning to keep the Commandments of God, he was said to strike immediately to thwart the process. The Andean parishioners were entreated to learn from the example set by Job in the Old Testament, for here was a common man just like

[10] J. de Acosta, *De Procuranda* and the *Historia*, esp. book 6, chs. 1–18, pp. 280–304. The best discussion of this element of Acosta's thought is A. R. Pagden, *The Fall of Natural Man*, pp. 162–97. See also J. H. Elliott, *The Old World and the New*, and J. D. Spence, *The Memory Palace of Matteo Ricci*.

[11] *Itinerario*, book 2, "Prologue," fols. 143 and 141. The common charge of immorality deserves a wider discussion of its own. For a beginning see my "Bad Christians."

[12] Ibid., fol. 200. On Spanish attitudes to Indian drinking in New Spain and the frequent connection with religious rituals that were being interpreted as the demonic see I. Clendinnen, "Ways to the Sacred," pp. 124–25, and W. B. Taylor, *Drinking, Homicide, and Rebellion*, pp. 33–34 and 39–40.

[13] *Ritual formulario*, see fols. 89–130, especially questions 7–20. And see further discussion below.

them, a man whom God allowed to endure all manner of suffering and temptation in order that he might prove his righteousness and Christian faith to a
beguiling Satan. Job, Avila asserted, had struggled against three great enemies:
the Devil, the flesh, and the world itself. The preacher implied that the Indians
were expected to do the same.[14]

The charged rhetoric of the sermons was also employed to warn the new
converts of the insidious ways of the Great Deceiver and his agents. Just what
the stirring language may have achieved is a matter for further discussion, but
at very least the preachers must have planted some vivid images in their
hearers' minds. Many of the preachers' demons conformed to standard artistic
and biblical representations of the Europeans' hellions, as in another of Avila's
sermons, a contemplation of the Last Judgment meant to be delivered on the
first Sunday of Advent.[15] These enemies were "frightful and shaking" creatures
with faces and hands "as black as coal." They breathed fire, cried blood, and
had scabbed and leprous bodies, the claws of a lion, and tails that set off sparks
as they lashed them to and fro.[16] Fernando de Avendaño was no less graphic in
his many animalistic comparisons. He alerted his congregations to a hateful
Devil who traveled the earth "as a hungry lion, looking for men to deceive
[and] to carry off to Hell,"[17] and he warned of the Devil as a hideous "black dog
tied up with iron chains" who harmed only those foolish enough to stray too
near.[18]

Yet Hispanic churchmen were all too aware that the Devil and his cohorts
were not confined by standard forms. They might stalk the world in any number of guises; correspondingly, experience had shown that there was no end to
the false cults they might inspire. Arguably, the Devil and his demons had
motivated the ancient religions of Judea and pagan Europe, they had held sway
among heretics in North Africa, the Catholic Alps and Pyrenees, they responded to calls from witches and assisted their evil purposes and, more recently in the European theater, they had induced a seemingly irreparable break
with the Protestant North. The confrontation with the Devil and demons in
America might thus be interpreted as only another chapter in the perpetual
struggle against evil in its various manifestations.

From the early years of the conquest, careful Spanish observers such as
Pedro Cieza de León did not balk at finding a "great multitude of demons"
responsible for religious practices in the Andes; that the demons would have
assumed the forms of Andean gods to enhance their legitimacy among the

---

[14] See Job 1:1 to 2:10 and Avila's *Tratado de los evangelios*, "Sermon del Glorioso Protomartyr
San Estevan," fols. 68–69.

[15] See for example the illustrations within a late fifteenth-century French treatise in BOD, Ms.
Douce 134, *Le Livre de la Vigne Nostre Seigneur*, fol. 99.

[16] *Tratado de los evangelios*, fols. 28, 2 and 39.

[17] Villagómez also employed this common depiction from 1 Peter 5:8, in which the true Christian is warned to raise his guard: "Be sober, be vigilant; because your adversary the Devil, as a
roaring lion, walketh about, seeking whom he may devour." See the *Carta pastoral*, ch. 2, pp. 9–10.

[18] *Sermones*, book 1, sermon 7, fols. 80–80v.

Indians was only to be expected.[19] Sabine MacCormack has concentrated on a comparison with the prime oracle of Apollo in classical Greece to illustrate a similar argument. She argues that, from the point of view of orthodox Catholic tradition, the ecstatic experience of the Pythia at Delphi and the mediation of a huaca's responses by a Indian minister in the Andes were both instances of the same kind of grand deception.[20] The Devil's flexibility and greedy omnipresence through the ages provided a frame for the interpretation of the unfamiliar—one of the means, in Anthony Pagden's terms, of making commensurable the incommensurable.[21] Whether or not the South American demons did their deeds in familiar European forms becomes an issue of little importance. It was well within the Devil's powers and character to innovate. The demonological system that had been inherited from early Christian commentators and the friars and inquisitors of medieval Europe, and refined by their Renaissance and early modern successors, could be used to incorporate the "idolatry" of America.

There was no doubting the Devil's heterogeneous existence and role in the Andes. This fact was made manifest as much in the actions that will be my main focus as in the thoughts expressed in contemporary treatises. The established traditions and experiences of their Church provided Peruvian missionaries and extirpators with justifying precedent and proper procedure when confronting what was perceived to be the diabolic. One fundamental example of the interest in and attention to precedence is the ways in which the sacred spaces of non-Christians shrines were initially appropriated for God and thus from the clutches of the Devil. The necessity of expelling demons had made exorcists a necessary component of late fourth-century churches in Europe; Ambrose of Milan is said to have noted their positions "just below the subdeacon."[22] Similarly, in preparing the abbot Mellitus for his journey to Britain in 601, Pope Gregory the Great had instructed him to "convert" pagan temples "from the worship of Devils to the service of the true God" by sprinkling holy water and erecting altars.[23] More than a millennium later, when padres from the Jesuit college at Cusco entered the provinces of Maraypití, Cotabambas, and Yanaguras, they conducted "exorcisms" at some twenty-eight shrines (*adoratorios*), "expelling the Devils from them."[24] Similarly, when visitadores of idolatry confronted huacas and the cave tombs of malquis, and responded by commanding rites of purification, the erection of wooden crosses, and the

---

[19] *La crónica*, ch. 84, pp. 229–30. See also ch. 64, p. 190.

[20] MacCormack discusses how Plato's, Lucan's, and especially John Chrysostom's interpretations of the Delphic oracle influenced Las Casas's thinking with regard to demonic possession. See *Religion in the Andes*, pp. 229–31. For another example of this application to Peruvian "oracles," see the anonymous Jesuit's sixteenth-century discussion of the "*furor diabólico* which they call Utirayay" in the *Relación de las costumbres antiguas de los naturales del Perú*.

[21] *European Encounters*, pp. 17–49.

[22] Cited in P. Johnson, *A History of Christianity*, p. 108.

[23] Bede, *Ecclesiastical History of the English Nation*, book 1, ch. 30, pp. 52–53.

[24] ARSI, Carta anua de 1649, *Peru* 15, vol. 4, fols. 235v–36.

conferment of saintly place names, they followed a long-established practice of claiming for God space that had previously belonged to the Devil.

The demonization of persistent Indian religious concepts and practices became a common and operative aspect in the contemporary European critique of Andean religion both because it conformed to a pious standard and because it was convenient. The idea of the Devil offered a potentially universal explanation for what was otherwise only partly explicable, and it justified almost any Christian recourse and remedy. Although some mid-colonial extirpators clearly became less satisfied with the diabolic explanation for Andean error in the face of the evidence they collected, it provided many others with the answers and official responses they needed.

For the Andean peoples afflicted by the visitas of idolatry, the apparent heterogeneity of the Christian Devil and his demons, and their burgeoning explanatory role, brought an even more ambiguous mix of explanations and problems. Initially, the Devil might offer Indians an escape from blame. If the Indians' religious errors were perceived to be the Devil's responsibility, the fruits of his deceptions among yet another set of credulous *miserables*, it was conceivable that they might be punished relatively lightly as ignorant followers. As Elliott has suggested, the paradox of "the diabolical explanation" might become a saving grace in which Indians could be portrayed by those who judged them as "deluded rather than deficient."[25] Indeed, the defensores of those "idolaters" accused of pacts with demons frequently employed this defense for their parties. Much depended on the inclinations of the judges and how they utilized these elastic demonic explanations.

In the mid-colonial Archdiocese of Lima, the principal investigators in question were, of course, the particular visitadores de idolatría and, later, the priests and appointed ecclesiastical judges. The fate of many individuals depended on how influenced these people were by theological contentions that colonial Andean religion was part of the insidious demonic milieu. The Devil remains a steady part of the background in most mid-colonial Spanish Christian minds, even if it becomes a much less frequent explanation for Andean religious error, particularly in the eighteenth-century trials that have survived. Yet for some extirpators, persistent huaca worship and belief in magical agency—especially in the seventeenth century—was little separated from voluntary demonolatry and the willful practice of diabolic arts. From these investigators' perspective, many Indians admitted to active worship of what were, for all intents and purposes, manifestations of the Devil. To the judge who was indifferent to or impatient with the complexities involved in assessing the penetration of Christian concepts into the Andean context, Indians who spoke of demons and devils (or the appropriated Quechua concept Supay) could be taken at their word, and might be treated as the worst of a bad lot of religious offenders.

Scarcely less serious were the offences of Indians who by mid-colonial times were thought to know better: those who were believed to be withholding the

[25] J. H. Elliott, "The Discovery of America," p. 60.

fact that demonic powers, and perhaps even a diabolic pact, were behind the ostensibly Andean practices they described in their testimonies. Such Indian parishioners were perceived to have committed even graver sins than apostasy; arguably, they had made a conscious choice of a path not only away from God but toward the Devil. Their offense was no longer merely an adherence to paganism stemming from a regrettable ignorance of Christianity. By the seventeenth century, when the Devil and his demons had fully entered the field of possibilities in the struggle against idolatry, many visitadores focused their attacks. And, in spite of complicating evidence, most were not in the habit of finding the Church's own efforts at fault.

Demonization had a rigidifying effect on explanation. It often proved even more stifling to the process of understanding than the discursive degradation of Andean religious tenets. If diabolical inversion was enlisted to explain any religious function or aspect that vaguely resembled a rite of Christianity, the entire religious system soon became, a priori, the province of the contrary, a place in which the Devil reigned freely.[26] Descriptions of Andean religion could become rife with diabolic connections; everything from an act of offering to the most basic ceremony or observance might be given a dark demonic tinge or be viewed as a shameful parody of Christianity. A few typical illustrations of this prevalent line of thinking make this point more vividly.

In the vicinity of Santiago de Maray, Checras, in 1724–1725 the apparent consumption of diverse offerings by the great Apu Libiac and Libiac Cancharco were interpreted, not dismissively as "priestly frauds," but as real deceptions of the Devil.[27] In the words of the prosecutor in this investigation, Matheo Salazar y de la Serna, the maize cakes and jerky that the 115-year-old maestro, Pedro Quiñones, placed before the gods would slowly disappear "by diabolic device." Moreover, Quiñones' "special and frequent" communications with another god, Apu Quichunqui, were defined as "speaking with the Devil." Similarly, when the collective worship of three gods with the names Apo Bilca,

[26] John Elliott called demonization "an obstacle to deeper understanding" in "The Discovery of America," p. 60. Stuart Clark, examining such explanations from the points of view of contemporary scholars in both Protestant and Catholic Europe, discusses just how much the demonic was a legitimate "intellectual resource"; see *Thinking with Demons*. Diabolical inversions had long been perceived in Europe. See particularly S. MacCormack's attention to the early sixteenth-century Spanish treatises of M. de Castañega and P. Ciruelo, the *Tratado de las supersticiones* (1529) and *Reprobación de las supersticiones y hechicerías* (c. 1530), respectively, in *Religion of the Andes*, pp. 36–49. Similar charges became universal among the early observers in New Spain as well as Peru, and were duly taken up by later extirpators. See, for example, the discussion of the influence of Juan de Torquemada's *Monarquía indiana* in D. A. Brading, *The Origins of Mexican Nationalism*, p. 8 ff., and F. Cervantes on José de Acosta in "The Devil in Colonial Mexico," pp. 36–40. On the influence of Castañega's theories about demonic inversion upon those expressed in the 1550s by Fr. Andrés de Olmos in Mexico in his *Tratado de hechicerías y sortilegios*, see Cervantes, "The Idea of the Devil," pp. 18–19.

[27] "Priestly frauds," the reader will recall, was MacCormack's phrase to describe P. Bernabé Cobo's treatment of the supposed trickery of spiritual charlatans; *Religion in the Andes*, pp. 398–99.

Canin Bilca, and Ango Bilca conducted in a home of the ancients in the old town of Canin Tacray was described, the proceedings were said to have been directed by a priestess dressed in a "black cassock" with her hair done, Salazar added, "in the way of the Devil."[28]

Fernando Cervantes's examination of Hispanic demonization in New Spain has suggested that post-Tridentine demonology drew a crucial dividing line between the natural and the supernatural ("nature and grace"). He argues that the influence of Nominalist thinkers in the late Middle Ages came to supplant a Thomist or more "naturalistic explanation" of Amerindian religious expression. Among other things, what this shift in Hispanic analyses of Amerindian religion meant was a more active and central role for the Devil. The explanatory inclinations of the mid-colonial visitadores de idolatría in Peru confirm this general trend, but less comfortably. The Devil is prevalent as an explanation, but the dividing line between what one might identify as Thomist and Nominalist attitudes in reaction to Indian religion is less definite among the body of visitadores than Cervantes' comparison of the great thinkers Las Casas and Acosta has suggested.[29] Demonization was, not surprisingly, less tidy in practice.

Individual extirpators might have espoused some recognizably Nominalist views when preaching in their parishes and when winning their spot in the extirpating campaigns in Lima, but none could predict what challenges practical involvement in the visitas de idolatría would hold in store. The idolatry interrogations were a considerably less calculable medium for advancing a philosophical line than an apologetic or treatise. In the visitadores' statements, petitions, interrogations, and sentences, one can identify a number of intellectual influences that these Hispanic Peruvian priests and extirpators would have absorbed in the Jesuit schools and seminaries, at San Marcos University, and during their years spent in the administration of Indian parishes. But for my purposes, more useful than scrutinizing the Peruvian trial evidence for the mixed, and often contradictory, strands of these larger European streams of thought is the evaluation of the extirpators' demonization on its own terms, as it was employed to explain incidences of idolatry and to meet specific interpretative challenges.

Once in the parishes of the Archdiocese of Lima, the visitadores de idolatría seem to have conceived of at least two broad and sometimes simultaneous roles for the Devil and demons in the context of the colonial Andean religion they

---

[28] AAL Leg. 3, exp. 10, fol. 31 and Matheo Salazar y de la Serna at fol. 32.

[29] *The Devil in the New World*, two sections within ch. 1, pp. 17–25 and 25–33. This Nominalist reaction to scholastic metaphysics found its most influential representative in William of Ockham (died 1349). Cervantes chooses to focus especially on the differences between Las Casas's essentially Thomist reading of Amerindian religion, and what he terms the Nominalist aspects in the thought of Acosta. He discusses the generalizing limits involved in contrasting the views of these two prototypes, and notes the shift toward more widespread demonizing tendencies at pp. 34–35. He himself challenges prevailing assumptions about the ubiquity of the rise of Reason in the later seventeenth century with the memorable case study at the center of his ch. 4. An earlier version appeared as "The Devils of Querétaro."

were charged to extirpate. The first was as an evil force that worked like an unseen hand, a behind-the-scenes source of corruption and error. This Devil was the one who prevailed in the background of some extirpators' minds.[30] The second role involved the Devil and demons as real presences—audible advisers, participatory familiars, and even physical objects of worship. Even these two broad forms of demonization might not always be separate; Archbishop Villagómez, in a perfect example of the possible ambiguity, was able to conceive of an overarching "author of idolatry" as the very same force that might assume various shapes and fly through the air. At different interpretive moments in their investigations, idolatry inspectors often inclined toward seeing the Devil in one way or the other; this inclination was often crucial to the development of the trial and the interpretation of the evidence.

The first demonological explanation was present in many contemporary interpretations of Andean religion. Belief in the Devil as a behind-the-scenes source of negative causal energy was amply exemplified in the language of description employed by visitadores, and by their tendency automatically to attribute the incomprehensible in Andean belief and practice to diabolic artifice. Thus Visitador Sarmiento de Vivero, in a characteristically protracted preface to his interrogation of Ana María of Ambar, Cajatambo, in 1662 confidently informed her that she and her companion "sorceresses (*hechiceras*)" were "deceived by the Devil." In San Blas in Tarama, the annual offering of a llama at the banks of a spring "to which they [the community] gave worship as to God" became, for Visitador Pedro de Cardenas y Arbieto, a "superstitious anniversary of the Devil."[31] The very language is a powerful expression of the fact that in such cases the diabolic became a given, a force that was assumed, almost without thinking. The Devil exerted a generally corrupting influence that inspired and maintained all error and superstition. For some extirpators the role of the diabolic in explaining Andean religion might well stop here.

Juan Sarmiento de Vivero, famed for his rigor, provides one mid-seventeenth-century example of an idolatry inspector who believed in the reality of a behind-the-scenes adversary, but who would usually resist taking the demonic explanations any further. His most common stance can be seen most clearly in his attitudes toward testimonies concerning dreams and mystical imaginings, the very experiences that often inspired Hispanic distrust of the Indians' visionary prudence and commonly prompted the most obsessive forms of demonization.

One learns from numerous colonial sources that divination from dreams had

---

[30] This type of demonization seems much like the "symbolic view of the Devil" discussed by Sir Keith Thomas in the context of the positions advanced by mid- to late seventeenth-century English thinkers. In this context, the Devil and demons were not denied the capacity for spiritual assaults and sinister influence, but the idea that they could assume corporeal forms was greeted with increasing skepticism. See *Religion and the Decline of Magic*, especially pp. 566–67 and 682–83.

[31] AAL Leg. 6, exp. 18, folio without number but fol. 36 in succession; and AAL Leg. 4, exp. 37, 1668–1669, fols. 5v–6. See discussion of this spring in Chapter Two above.

long been the province of Andean specialists who fulfilled vital religious functions.[32] The mid-colonial idolatry evidence confirms the main assertions of the chronicles, treatises, and catechisms that treat the subject: native Andean peoples of many regions had eloquent dreams; they encouraged and developed this faculty; and from these dreams many people continued to seek meanings and important messages in the colonial years.[33]

In Sayan, Chancay, in 1662 Felipe Capcha, it seems, had fallen asleep on a riverbank while fishing. There, he had dreamt that his soul had been taken from his body to a busy sacrificial meal; the dreamer confessed the guiding presence of two horsemen as well as the obscure participation of some blacksmiths and silversmiths. Another of Sarmiento's declarants, however, said it was commonly believed that Felipe's soul had been taken inside a nearby huaca, and that within he had been protected by a Franciscan friar during some sort of interview with the king (presumably of Spain). Knowledge of various versions of Felipe's dream seems to have spread throughout the community, and it seems probable that people talked and widely believed the experience to have special significance. The visitador, however, was remarkably restrained and level-headed. His notary recorded that, "knowing by the subject and sincerity of his [Felipe's] words that this was not a thing of malice, . . . the said Señor Visitador told him not to believe in dreams because it was only the sun which had given him a fever and made him delirious."[34] Visitador Juan Sarmiento dismissed the different versions of Felipe's dream experience with a strong rebuke and an expression of disbelief in the dream's significance. The last factor, the import the Indians seemed to have given the experience, appears to have been what most preoccupied Sarmiento.

In the same province and year, again before Juan Sarmiento, an accused named Pedro Guamboy admitted to worshiping a huaca called, in the coastal Yunga language, Viñiqui at a place named Puchucau on the road between Quintay and Cochamarca.[35] His father had taught him the proper forms of observance, and as a boy he recalled dropping to his knees and kissing the stone, which then elicited the distinctive response, "*vi vi vi*," which had startled him at first. Pedro was asked why he and his father had gone to Viñiqui, and

---

[32] B. Mannheim makes a thorough survey of a number of these sources in "A Semiotic of Andean Dreams," see particularly pp. 137–40. Mannheim ingeniously uses Pérez Bocanegra's information on dreams alongside his own field data from late twentieth-century Andahuaylillas to examine the changes that befell Andean dream signs and their analysis in the space of over four hundred years.

[33] See, for instance, the Jesuit padres' description of the specialists whom people consulted after dreams in ARSI, Carta anua de 1617, *Peru* 14, vol. 3, fols. 52v–53. Similar functions were filled among many native cultures in the Americas. See, for example, A. F. C. Wallace, "Dreams and the Wishes of the Soul."

[34] AAL Leg. 5, exp. 7, Capcha and Sarmiento at fols. 18v–19; see also Rafaela de los Ríos at fols. 1v–2.

[35] AAL Leg. 5, exp. 8, fol. 12v. At fol. 13 he also told of another stone in a corral near Quintay to which he made similar offerings and requests. This is the same Guamboy who is discussed in Chapter Four above.

why he continued to visit the rock with offerings of maize and chicha. He said that it was "to ask to travel (*andar*)." It emerged that Pedro flew "like a turkey buzzard (*gallinaso*) . . . [with] wings on his arms," while his body slept at home. The trips were taken, Pedro continued, "because the rocks commanded it"; Viñiqui himself had expressly instructed him: "travel where you wish, from pueblo to pueblo." The man's journeys seem to have continued for some time; only when the blame for another Indian's mysterious death had fallen upon him had Pedro thought it wise to curtail his flying. In response to the leading questions that such experiences elicited from almost any contemporary visitador de idolatría, Pedro declared he had seen the Devil some ten times, in the form of "a very large shadow that seemed to come from the sky" and which would appear to him on the road at night. The Devil spoke to him on these occasions, providing directions that resembled those which the huaca Viñiqui was said to have given—although possibly more precise—which the notary glossed as: "You go there, I will go here."[36]

Here was an even more imposing intellectual challenge for Sarmiento than Felipe Capcha's dream. In the case of Pedro Guamboy there would be no naturalistic attribution of blame to the heat of the sun and hopeless Indian credulity. Yet notably, although Visitador Sarmiento could hardly avoid asking about the Devil and acknowledging diabolic machinations, in a case in which he might have let his imagination run wild he confined the Devil to a background role, as a Father of Lies. Pedro Guamboy was charged first, and commonly, with idolatry, the crime of depriving the Christian God of the worship owed to him by giving reverence to things falsely taken to be gods, in this case outcroppings of rock. Second, he was accused of "asking permission [from Viñiqui] to fly through the air." Sarmiento explained the role of the diabolic in this latter offense about as precisely as one might hope. "In this, the Devil, Our Enemy, used his industry to deceive him [Pedro] into thinking that stones were powerful and that they could make him fly if he pretended with his arms."[37]

Sarmiento conceived of the Devil as an illusory force that made the false god Viñiqui seem to speak, and that caused Pedro to believe that the huaca gave him the ability and charter to fly where he pleased. But even though this visitador saw the deception of the Devil as the cause behind the Indian's erroneous suppositions about his experiences, and even though the confession of flight might have summoned witches and sabbats to mind, he resisted the crucial next step in his interpretation and sentence. Sarmiento might have allowed the diabolic a more active role in his explanation of the huaca and its perceived powers, and thus disassociated Pedro's experiences further from their mid-colonial Andean religious context; but, he did not. Viñiqui remained, for him, a false Andean god, a stone that was worshiped in vain because of the Devil's general powers of artifice. Even the shadows in the sky which Pedro had seen

---

[36] Ibid., fols. 12v–13v.
[37] Ibid., Sarmiento's *Auto de Prueba* at fol. 36.

from the road at night and to which Pedro himself had referred as the Devil failed to set Sarmiento off on a diabolical tangent.[38]

Many of the visitador's contemporaries, when presented with similarly and less provocative confessions, succumbed readily to the temptation of the second broad form of demonization: interpreting the Devil and demons as participatory beings and forces. This second intellectual position was far from radical in its day either in Europe or America, as Cervantes's work has made clear. Belief in an active Devil was supported, after all, by the established sanctions of Catholic history and tradition. Andean beliefs in the phenomena of human flight and metamorphosis could comfortably be interpreted not only as signs of the Devil's illusory work among simple minds but in the familiar terms associated with European witch beliefs. Although extirpators did not normally extend the rumor-filled testimonies concerning such experiences far enough to hypothesize that Indian parishioners were flying to the Andean equivalents of diabolically convened witches' sabbats, the activities of a recognizable Devil might still be found.[39] Regardless of whether he was thought to be the one who granted the powers of flight and metamorphosis or the one who deceived people into believing that such things occurred while they slept, the Devil could become a paramount, and ultimately obscuring, force. Mid-colonial Andean beliefs and practices, of course, became eclipsed in the process of this more active form of demonization.

The steady flow of testimonies from persons interrogated by the Extirpation's agents produced enough information on certain kinds of experiences to confirm the demons' more participatory role in the minds of many extirpators. Sometimes it took little more than a witness's turn of phrase or a person's

---

[38] There are other examples of Andeans who were said to make mysterious flights and even communicate with the Devil, but whose investigations were not completely subverted by suggestions of the diabolic. See the trials of Juan de Vetanços, questioned by Br. Sebastián de Vitoria in the Dominican parish of La Xapallanga, Jauja (modern Sapallanga), AAL Leg. 5, exp. 11, 1665, esp. fols. 3v–4; another trial conducted by Sarmiento de Vivero at Ambar, Cajatambo, in 1662, involving Francisca Leonor of the Valley of Jayba, AAL Leg. 6, exp. 19, esp. fols. 2v–3 and 3v–4; and the case of Isabel in the same parish, also in 1662, AAL Leg. 4, exp. 32, esp. Agustín Capcha's accusation at fol. 1.

[39] The sabbat analogy, however, was well known and was made on occasion. In the mid-colonial period, see most importantly ch. 43, pp. 155–56 of Archbishop Villagómez's *Carta pastoral*. The archbishop's interpretation of Andean "killing witches" echoed both Arriaga's statements in his 1621 treatise and Arriaga's and P. Luís de Teruel's earlier treatments. The two Jesuits freely borrowed from the tradition of the witches' sabbat presided over by the Devil and involving followers who attended and worshiped him. P. Duviols discusses similar matters and also the possible influence of ideas of the sabbat spreading from France, influencing the Zugarramurdi witch trial at Logroño in 1610, which in turn influenced the interpretations within the Peruvian chronicle of the Augustinian Antonio de la Calancha, the *Corónica moralizada del orden de San Augustín en el Perú*, (1639): see vol. 1 of A. de la Calancha and B. de Torres, *Crónicas agustinianas del Perú*. Calancha discusses the sabbatlike findings of the Jesuit Teruel at La Barranca in the Huaura valley to the north of Lima. See the Spanish edition of Duviols, *La destrucción*, pp. 32–34. On the more skeptical results in the aftermath of the Basque trial, see G. Henningsen, *The Witches' Advocate*.

mention of what was to certain Spanish Christian minds a diabolically suggestive theme to prompt a torrent of interrogation along these lines. For these
investigators, many Indians' declarations simply documented on the ground
what they had long believed about demons and devils in theory. Here, confirmed, was the diabolic capacity actively to corrupt the indigenous peoples of
the Andes. By conjuring such things as flight and dreams, their deception had
only begun. The demonic adversaries, after all, were unfettered masters of
disguise who could embody the huacas and impersonate all manner of things.

It seems useful to ask if the extirpator's inclination not only to devalue but to
demonize Andean beliefs and practices was augmented by what the Indians
said they believed, for it seems that it was. Some mid-colonial Indians maintained what might be called largely Andean explanations, even amid the deluge
of diabolic suggestion from some Hispanic extirpators and missionaries. In
1661, Don Francisco Laxa Luana of Lunahuana, Cañete, for example, rejected
a Spaniard's claim that what Francisco had described as his huaca-ancestors'
mythic arrangement of the stones which determined the path of the community's irrigation channel could only have been accomplished by "the art of the
Devil."[40] But other Andeans responded quite differently. When they found
themselves before the Extirpation's tribunals many Indians' testimonies, together with corroborating evidence, suggests that some people had assimilated
the concepts of the Devil and demons into their own explanations of their
religious beliefs. The issue of what this kind of assimilation meant to them is
quite another matter, and there is the ever-present possibility that the visitador
or notary was reading things into an Andean's testimony, so an approach to
these apparent appropriations of the idea of the Devil in the mid-colonial
Andes must be made carefully.

First, a mid-colonial Indian's employment of the words "Devil" or "demon,"
or his or her borrowing from a collection of stereotypical demonic traits to
describe sacred things or religious experience, could be very different from an
actual incorporation of these concepts into an evolving or eclectic religious
framework. Appropriations could be superficial, and with widely divergent
meanings for different Spaniards and Andeans.[41] Second, the motivations that
might have inspired Indians' admission of the demons into their explanatory
frameworks must be considered; the assimilation of Spanish Christian interpretations could be feigned out of pragmatism or fear, in the hope of escaping
blame or at least gaining leniency. At times, the plea of diabolic deception was
very clearly a ploy for mercy by Indians who astutely recognized one of the few
benefits that might accrue from *miserable* status. Numerous Indians provided
details of strongly held Andean beliefs before transparently agreeing in the end
that the Devil had deceived them all along.[42] The defenders and advocates of

---

[40] AAL Leg. 7, exp. 1, 1661, Alonso de Belásques at fol. 6v.

[41] S. MacCormack argues similarly; *Religion in the Andes*, pp. 406–7.

[42] A typical example is that of Juan Chapa of Pilas, Yauyos in AAL Leg. 1, exp. 2, 1660, fols. 7v–
8.

"idolaters" so active in the post-Villagómez investigations also frequently utilized the diabolic line of defense in a fashion that had changed little since
benevolent chroniclers such as Garcilaso de la Vega had employed it to explain
away what seemed to them inconvenient facets of prehispanic Andean culture.
In 1723, for instance, Melchor de Caraval's defense of the chanca ministers
Juan de Rojas and Francisco Libiac Condor described them as "rustic people
(*personas miserables*) . . . disturbed by the Devil's suggestion."[43]

In still other cases, a devil or demon seems to have become a genuine part of
the peoples' conceptual framework. Some Indians appear to have internalized
the connection that the doctrine classes and extirpating sermons had repeatedly stressed, the connection between their gentility and the earthly activity of
the demonic hordes. The Devil spoke through the huacas; demons could take
many forms; Indian religious ministers and specialists were the agents of the
Enemy whom they worshiped; all traditional observances were envious par-
odies of Christian worship: these messages would have been well known to the
people of the mid-colonial parishes of the Archdiocese of Lima.

The ambivalence and sheer playfulness of many Andean divinities and religious conceptions would have eased any gradual internalization of the Devil by
some Andeans. A point that William Taylor has stressed about the divergence
between Christian and native conceptions of duality is as appropriate in the
colonial Andes as in the colonial Mexican setting. Indian peoples conceived of
such apparent (to the more dualistic Christians) oppositions as good and evil,
creation and destruction, and natural and supernatural monistically rather than
dualistically. Thus an Indian god might embody, in Taylor's words, "opposite
tendencies . . . even as beliefs and practices were modified and confused by
Christian teachings." The gradual acceptance of some Christian concepts (the
Devil is simply one recognizable example) into local religious practices and
understandings might not disturb monistic ways of seeing such things.[44]

Thus it was that by 1725 Antonio Ripas of Navan in the parish of Churín,
Cajatambo, could describe a well-known Andean agricultural ceremony as a
time when "they [the people] would dress as devils and dance the Airigua."[45]
Even earlier, there are moving depictions of Indians who, in genuine psychological torment, seem to have faced down their Andean religious allegiances—
now represented by the forms of demons and the fires of Hell—in the shadow
of death. The most famous example is that of Don Gerónimo Cancho Huaman,
whose story is told in chapter twenty of the collection of myths and religious
information from Huarochirí. The tale is told from a Christianized Andean
point of view, but one that still does not hide a deep ambivalence: Don Gerónimo scorned the demonic huacas, only to be assailed and perhaps even "deceived" by them one last time on his deathbed. Once again, the idolatry information offers vivid corroboration. There was Juan de Salazar of Quinti,

[43] AAL Leg. 3, exp. 9, Carampoma, Huarochirí, 1723, fols. 49–50.
[44] *Magistrates of the Sacred*, ch. 3.
[45] AAL Leg. 3, exp. 11, fol. 6v.

Huarochirí, in 1660, who only confessed the true sins of others to the visitador in his final hours because, as he put it, "I am dying and . . . I do not want the Devil to take me." In 1690, in the Franciscan parish of Mito, Jauja, the ritual specialist Diego Yacan was driven to such despair during his imprisonment by the Extirpation that he was visited by the Devil and seems to have attempted suicide. Diego was said to have confessed to his captors that he had thrust a dagger into his stomach because the Devil had deceived him, only to appear again to him as "a face," which had made the specialist want even more to die.[46]

The possibility that some native Andeans had enlisted their own version of the Christians' Satan as an intermediate deity, a kind of anti-Christian special agent, is worth considering. In the mid-1660s, Jesuit missionaries from Cusco encountered Aymara-speaking Indians in southern Peru to whom a demon had allegedly appeared, claiming that he was the younger brother of Christ. The demon had taught that while God the son was the Lord of the Christians, he, as Christ's younger brother, was the rightful god of the Indians. Other padres from Juli met with news of a devil named Iuaha (or Juaha) in Pucara who, among other things, also claimed to be "almighty" and the sibling of Jesus.[47] The Jesuit provincial wrote to Rome explaining that although he himself was a missionary of some thirty years' experience, he had never heard anything that could compare with this. His evident alarm and the way the account is worded suggests that this report provoked in him an old and genuine fear from deep in Christian demonological and heretical traditions, a fear that the Devil was capable of anything in his quest to be the unfettered Lord of the Earth.

It is tempting to make much of such examples. For here, arguably, are the results of the inroads—albeit within a confused and heretical interpretation—made by a Christian concept, the Devil, into the Indian religious sphere. Here, perhaps, is evidence of a Satan who had been manipulated by Indian interpretation, and who was now an aggressive part of the assailed native religious system. Working largely from Oaxacan evidence and information about Indians gleaned from Inquisition trials in New Spain, Fernando Cervantes has presented an engaging argument that pivots on a recognition of the Indians' contribution to their own demonization. The friars' and priests' constant teaching that the Devil, in the guise of an indigenous god or spiritual force, was the beneficiary of misguided Indian veneration, becomes a backdrop to the process through which fundamental aspects of Christianity are reconceptualized by Indian parishioners. Cervantes notes other possibilities and exceptions, and he is careful not to overstate his case, noting that there were times when the people's "increasing identification of Indian practices with demonic activity"

---

[46] On Gerónimo Cancho Huaman, see *The Huarochirí Manuscript*, edited by and translated by F. Salomon and G. L. Urioste (hereafter *Huarochirí*), ch. 20, sec. 247, and Salomon's insightful note 493; on Juan de Salazar see AAL Leg. 2, exp. 23, fol. 11; and on Diego Yacan, AAL Leg. 1, exp. 9, fols. 10v–11 and 14v–15.

[47] ARSI, Carta anua de 1664, 1665 y 1666, *Peru* 16, vol. 5, fols. 140v, 179–179v.

were "in no way part of an effort to oppose Christianity." Yet in his overall description of the complicated process of reinterpretation in colonial Mexico, Cervantes conceives of the Devil mostly as an idea that might be used by Indians to counter the success of the invader's faith and as a vehicle for the survival of prehispanic religious practices. He emphasizes the opportunities that the Devil and worship of him offered certain Indians consciously "to oppose Christianity," and to keep their own religion. "It is likely," Cervantes writes, "that the Indians would have come to see the Devil as crucially important in the effort to protect and continue their sacrificial rituals."[48]

A different evangelization experience in Peru makes such a position of dubious assistance here. Systematic Christian teaching had come later in Peru than in Mexico and, even after it had begun, it continued to be remarkably ragged in its extension. Compared with New Spain, less effort and less time were spent in making a deep missionary impression. Along with many other Christian concepts, the Devil had received fewer opportunities to find a comfortable or even heretical home in most Andean hearts and minds.

By the mid-seventeenth century there were forces or spirits in the world that some Andean people in the Archdiocese of Lima had come to call demons and devils, but they were rarely very "Satanic," and only very rarely is there evidence to suggest that Andeans thought of them as strict opponents to Christianity. Some extirpators, on the other hand, were often most content to apply their polarizing categories, and to see the Devil and his agents in the only manner they knew, as the enemies of Christianity and the Indians' souls.

Notably, some Indian witnesses before the Extirpation used the Quechua word, *Supay*, which had—rather unwisely—been appropriated by missionaries to express the diabolic. Some of the demons took the forms and exhibited the behavior of the familiar enemies of the Christians about which the Indians had undoubtedly learned in doctrina and from sermons. Even superficial demonic resemblances revealed in some Indian testimonies were often enough to prompt the visitadores' imaginations. Certain extirpators heard what they expected to hear, and manipulated the idolatry trials they presided over in accordance with their opinions.

A close scrutiny of these same trials and Indian testimonies reveals that these devils and demons were in fact deeply ambivalent, surprising and frequently contradictory beings. Their likeness to Satan and his charges was not imagined so much by the Indians as by the Hispanic observers and judges who possessed few other ways of understanding them. The second form of the demonization

---

[48] *The Devil in the New World*, pp. 46, 47, and 53. The cases of Diego Luis (an Indian denounced as a "master of idolatries" to the bishop of Oaxaca in 1656) and Mateo Pérez (a late seventeenth-century governor of Santiago de Atitlán in the parish of Juquila, Oaxaca) are highlighted as examples of this tendency. An earlier pass at the subject is "Christianity and the Indians." Cervantes's argument about the Devil's place in the Indians' colonial religious system is partly influenced by Hugo Nutini's thesis, which hypothesizes the Indians' gradual merging of prehispanic gods into Christian saints in a series of stages. See *The Devil in the New World*, pp. 54–57, and H. G. Nutini, "Syncretism and Acculturation," pp. 306–7.

of dimensions of Andean religion, involving the belief in a participatory Devil and demons, was almost inevitable because of the things that colonial Indians appear to have said.

The most memorable deceivers in the Archdiocese of Lima seemed to appear to Indians in the very ways that Hispanic churchmen most feared they would. Demons came as illusions, visions, and as beings in dreams. And they came in any number of forms. Their behavior and intentions among the Indians, though often unconventional from a strictly European point of view, were easily countenanced because the Devil's repertoire was fabulously elastic. Indeed, given the high measure of belief in the diabolic presence and of the Devil's ultimate culpability in Indian religious error, one might reasonably ask what the Andean gods could possibly have done that would not have recalled familiar demonic wiles and seen them fitted into the Christian category. For example, when Peruvian Indians spoke of demons who appeared to them as old Indian men, in typically Indian garb, the description meshed comfortably enough with the common demonic form of the dark and sinister man.[49]

Hernando Caruachin, the *ministro mayor* in Huamantanga, Canta, confessed to Pedro de Quijano Zevallos in 1656 that some eighteen years before he had seen the Devil numerous times in succession. On at least two of these occasions the Devil had appeared as an old Indian man who wielded a stick and beat him over the back and shoulders. The first time Hernando was attending to the irrigation of his chacra named Lloquepampa, and the second occurred a week later when he was collecting firewood on a hill called Caniar. Although Hernando assured his judge that he had not been drinking on either occasion, he confessed that just before and during the demon's visits he had felt "affected" and stunned, "as one who is drunk." The old man was dark (*azambado*), with an evil face and "eyes that looked very ugly, shining brightly like candles." He had long black hair that hung over his shoulders and a sparse, long, brown beard. His fingers, Hernando remembered, were very long. He wore no trousers, but only a brown shirt that reached to his knees. His general aspect was unmistakably that of an Indian, though he was conspicuously without the customary manta and sling (*guaraca*).[50]

Similarly, Juana Ycha of Pomacocha in the Mercedarian parish of Caujo, Canta, described one of the forms assumed by a "demon" named Apo Parato, to whom I shall return in more detail below. His name was that of an Andean god—*apo* or *apu* meaning lord or father, and frequently referring to the huacas of mountain peaks. Juana described him to Antonio de Cáceres, a *teniente de cura* who was investigating her beliefs in 1650. Apo Parato had also appeared like an Indian, dark in complexion, and he always kept himself so thoroughly

---

[49] See, for example, J. Caro Baroja, *The World of the Witches*, p. 85, and K. V. Thomas, *Religion and the Decline of Magic*, pp. 561, 565–67.

[50] AAL Leg. 2, exp. 11, fols. 4v–5v. I am translating *azambado* as derived from *zambo*, which refers to a person of partly African descent.

wrapped in his black manta that Juana said she could not tell if he wore a *cusma* or shirt. He was thin, and his legs and feet were like those of "a rooster."[51] Ynes Carua Chumbi, another woman from Pomacocha, knew a demon with another lordly Andean name, Capac Quircay (or Apo Quircay) of Chinchay Cocha. One learns that he, too, appeared in Indian garb—though again it is remarked that the demon was without a sling—and with a white manta wrapped up even to his face.[52]

It was also a familiar demonic trick to assume less mysterious but equally familiar human shapes, as in the mocking impersonation of men of the religious orders. Both Leonor Rimay of San Martín de Ama in Canta and an anonymous Indian described in a Jesuit letter to Rome claimed that demons had appeared to them disguised as friars.[53]

It was not just the demons' appearances that struck idolatry investigators so forcefully. For some extirpators the negative aspects in the demonic visitors' general demeanor must have sealed the issue of their accordance with European diabolic conceptions. The Christian Devil and demons were often supposed to be miserable and envious outcasts, and handy parallels were quick to present themselves in the Andes. And yet if one recalls the huacas of the Huarochirí manuscript, these were also beings who were said to have appeared in settlements as ragged beggars, to have expected sustenance, and to have wreaked vengeance on those who failed them. Apo Parato, for instance, appears a sad and lonely wanderer. When Juana asked him why he did not bring her foods, Apo Parato explained "that he traveled about the countryside and had nowhere from which he could give her anything." He was every bit as laconic and short-tempered as Hernando Caruachin's stick-wielding demon; Apo Parato's only companionship came from the meals he regularly took with Juana Ycha. Juana said that when he was not content with the food she provided, he would shout: "Where is the *mazamorra* (maize porridge); give me mazamorra and chicha." If she was not quick enough in satisfying his request, it was his custom to beat her.[54]

Irene Silverblatt has contended that, unlike the "powerful European Devil, whose virtue lay in his ability to provide food and clothing to the desperate," in the Andean case, "unable to fulfill the expectations of their native worshippers, huacas had become diabolic."[55] Her interpretation presents Apo Parato and his minister Juan Ycha, as well as others like them, as quintessentially European demonic outcasts. It implies at least two related things about the mid-colonial Andeans' religion: first, that people had assimilated European demonological

[51] AAL Leg. 4, exp. 14, fol. 12v. Olivia Harris discusses the connection between mountain spirits and the Devil's "evil sphere" in "The Dead and Devils," p. 66.

[52] AAL Leg. 2, exp. 10, 1650, fols. 2, 5; Chinchay Cocha was a lake nearby.

[53] AAL Leg. 2, exp. 11, 1656, fol. 16; "a very old bearded padre" had appeared to Leonor Rimay on a number of occasions. ARSI, Carta anua de 1646, *Peru* 15, vol. 4, fol. 202v.

[54] AAL Leg. 4, exp. 14, fols. 11v–12. For similar examples of other demons' propensity for violence see AAL Leg. 2, exp. 11, fols. 2–11, 11–13, and 15v–16v.

[55] *Moon, Sun, and Witches*, pp. 185 and 194.

theories in a straightforward manner and to a relatively high degree (that is, their gods had been effectively and consistently demonized not only by Spanish extirpators but also in the Andean peoples' own minds) and second, that people's recollection of the customary behavior and reciprocal relationships demanded by Andean gods had largely passed away. These implications misrepresent the Andean "demons," who, like the indigenous gods and forces that they were, continued to bring divine assistance and powerful knowledge to their ministers and various specialists. Many of the supposed demons were clearly forthcoming as providers of just the sort of material things which Apo Parato was unable to provide. Ynes Carua Chumbi, for example, testified that she had not been to the market in four years, because her "demon" delivered ample supplies of both maize and *maca* (a root crop) to her home.[56]

It may be that one of the most noteworthy aspects of the trial of Juana Ycha is the gulf between what the Indian confessant was saying and what the investigator came to ask and subsequently demanded to hear. The scale of this misunderstanding came into the sharpest relief in this case and many others when the idolatry inspectors attempted to substantiate diabolic compacts. Women were often religious ministers and specialists in Andean societies. But women, and particularly poverty-stricken old widows—the most enfeebled of the sex assumed to be weak-willed and vulnerable—were also believed by many extirpators to be the demons' favorite points of entry into the world. Once again, the Indians' accounts of certain experiences vividly recalled the exploits of the European Devil to the extirpators' minds.

The trial of Juana Ycha of Pomacocha provides an illuminating example. Early in her first confession, Juana had confessed to the teniente Cáceres that in her dreams her deceased husband would return to her, asking "where are you?" Twice, she dreamt that she had received him (the implication is as a lover).[57]

A reverence for, and a belief in the possibility of interaction with, the dead was common in the Andes. Elaborate fasting and ceremonies followed deaths, and the bodies of the deceased received annual offerings. The spirits of the dead were believed to linger close to the dwellings of living relatives, especially at night. If there were signs in the morning of some movement across a grain-strewn floor, if supplies had been tampered with, or if chicha had been drunk, it was surely the dead who were responsible.[58] By the mid-seventeenth century, extirpators were acquainted with many variations of the Indian beliefs surrounding death. Archbishop Villagómez, borrowing from Arriaga's text as closely as ever on Andean rites, devoted the better part of a chapter of his *Carta Pastoral* to the description of the death vigils, and of how the souls of the deceased were later temporarily welcomed back to their homes with food and

---

[56] See AAL Leg. 2, exp. 10, 1650, fol. 5.

[57] AAL Leg. 4, exp. 14, fol. 7.

[58] See esp. R. Hernández Príncipe, "Idolatrías en Recuay," p. 499, and C. D. Valcárcel, "Supay (sentido)," p. 37.

drink. Thus Juana's dreams of her returning husband, similar to another of her expressed beliefs on the subject—that the souls of her dead children and relatives regularly visited her in the form of whirlwinds seeking to allay their hunger and thirst—should not have been too surprising to her investigator.[59]

Yet soon after Juana's revelation of the existence of the demon Apo Parato, who frequently visited as a man, first Cáceres' enquiry and subsequently Juana Ycha's story underwent a marked transformation. The presence of the familiar demon, a dreaded incubus, focused the extirpator's mind. Interest in what would have been regarded as fanciful Andean superstitions about the exploits of the spirits of the dead vanished. Cáceres began a rigorous interrogation to establish the nature and details of Juana Ycha's relationship with Apo Parato.[60] Sexual intercourse was thought to be the most common way for a demon to seal his compact with his earthly agents. Thus contemporary investigations of European witches tirelessly endeavored to gain evidence and the details of actual sexual unions with the Devil.[61] In Canta, Peru, the husband's returning soul gradually became the familiar demonic visitor in the extirpator's mind, and the experience that initially had been described as a dream was effectively erased because of the Devil's assumed ability to simulate this sort of encounter.[62]

The pressure, the fear, and perhaps the growing realization that her confession of experiences with returning souls and vivid dreams of her dead husband were not being accepted by Cáceres, produced confusion, desperation, and ultimately contradiction in Juana Ycha's testimony. She came to describe the dream as a real experience and the dream vision as a demon. The being was now described indecisively as "her husband or he who said he was her husband." Finally, in response to repeated questioning, she proceeded to tell the extirpator what he most expected to hear. It had been the demon Apo Parato all along; his nocturnal advances had only seemed like those of her husband. Even earlier contradictions could suddenly be explained away: "when she confessed the first time, the Devil must have tricked her." Similar patterns held true in other investigations that involved Indian women to whom demons appeared in human form.[63]

Andean religious elements were being overshadowed by demonizing explanations that seemingly knew few bounds. The extent to which the extirpators' demonization might reach may be seen vividly if one follows up the Apo Parato example. This demon's deeply Andean character and true potential are done considerable injustice by the narrowing of Antonio de Cáceres's investigation after he had stumbled upon familiar terms and situations: Apo Parato, the

[59] P. de Villagómez, *Carta pastoral*, ch. 46, pp. 170–71; AAL Leg. 4, exp. 14, fol. 10.

[60] See ibid., fols. 9–9v, 10, and 17v.

[61] Examples abound, but see particularly the examination of María de Zozaya in G. Henningsen, *The Witches' Advocate*, pp. 164–65.

[62] See A. de la Peña Montenegro, *Itinerario*, fol. 201.

[63] AAL Leg. 4, exp. 14, fol. 10. See particularly the notaries' records of the interrogations and testimonies of Ynes Carua Chumbi's experiences with Capac Quircay at AAL Leg. 2, exp. 10, 1650, fol. 5v and María Ticlla Guacho's at AAL Leg. 2, exp. 11, 1656, fol. 12.

supernatural being, was invoked in fire; he was regularly offered a food prepared for Andean gods, *milcapa* and the ritual chicha; he was venerated as a spider in Andean rituals of healing and divination; and Apo Parato habitually traveled, like the souls of the dead, in whirlwinds.[64] Most strikingly of all, Apo Parato, the demonized huaca of the mountains, seems to have exhibited the complicated characteristics of a little-understood Andean being, a spirit known in Quechua as Supay.[65]

Juana Ycha actually referred to Apo Parato thus on one occasion in her testimony, imploring her gruff visitor: "Supay, why are you maltreating me when I give you so much to eat?"[66] The instance probably stands out as a reflection of Juana's actual choice of word because of its departure from the notary's otherwise unflagging usage of "the demon (*el demonio*) Apoparato." Although Spanish lexicographers and churchmen tended to follow the example of Diego González Holguín in appropriating the alien concept of Supay (Çupay) as an approximation of "the Devil," even a brief examination of the complexities of its meaning reveals the danger of this assumption.[67] Supay offers a good example of the kind of monistic conception that would consistently defy Christian attempts to fit it into dualistic doctrine. Although Supay implies the capacity for evil and destruction, and seems the consummate trickster, its similarities with the orthodox Catholic figure of Lucifer should be carried no further—especially in the seventeenth century.

Supay was an omnipresent force representing a world of coexisting good and evil, simultaneous doing and undoing, growth and decay, birth and death—a spiritual expression of the contradictions involved in life itself. Apo Parato, for instance, was present when Juan Ycha helped women with the births of their children. And Apo Parato, like Supay, could be invoked through fire, rauran or

[64] For fire, see Juana's description of the teachings of her two maestros, Catalina and Alonso Caja Guaranga, and of the ritual feedings and mediations that they supervised; AAL Leg. 4, exp. 14, fols. 15–15v and 30, and fols. 7 and 14, respectively. Milcapa consisted of llama fat, *sanco* (a soft maize cake), crushed black and white maize, ground stones, and the colored feathers of mountain birds. The collection of offerings, though often mentioned, are only referred to as milcapa once, at AAL Leg. 4, exp. 14, fol. 30. For the spider, see AAL Leg. 4, exp. 14, Phelipe Curichagua at fol. 2, and Juana's descriptions of the rites at fols. 7v–8 and 17v–18. For more general information on the predictions and prognoses of ritual specialists known as *pacharicuccs* see P. J. de Arriaga, *La extirpación*, or P. Villagómez, *Carta pastoral*, ch. 43, p. 153. For travel in whirlwinds, see AAL Leg. 4, exp. 14, the description of his "arrivals" at fols. 8v–9 and 29v.

[65] Supay has not been neglected by modern scholars, even if absolute certainty about it is next to impossible. The elusive significance of Supay and its connection with the flying soul is analyzed most perceptively by P. Duviols in "Camaquen, Upani." See also G. Taylor, "Supay," C. D. Valcárcel, "Supay (sentido)," and F. Salomon's speculations in *Huarochirí*, ch. 7, sec. 91 at note 164. S. MacCormack surveys the commentaries on the concept in *Religion in the Andes*, pp. 254–57, and with interesting additions to what Duviols had already discussed in *La Lutte*, pp. 37–39.

[66] AAL Leg. 4, exp. 14, fols. 9–9v.

[67] D. González Holguín, *Vocabulario*, pp. 88 and 477. P. Duviols notes that the earlier lexicon of Fr. Domingo de Santo Tomás included a more rounded attempt at defining Supay, capturing it as a "good or bad angel," a demon or spirit that was not exclusively evil; *La Lutte*, p. 38 and n. 58.

rauranchini.[68] The connection between Apo Parato and fire became most vivid in Juana's healing practices. On one occasion, when called upon to cure a small child, the specialist and minister passed llama fat into a fire, saying "Fire Apo Parato, take and eat this illness of the one whom I have healed."[69] Carlos Valcárcel writes that "fire is the perfect manifestation of Supay. Supay is real, he lives because he eats . . . at the same time as he destroys he gives light and heat, the generators of life."[70] Even in the clandestine circumstances of much colonial Andean observance, fire was what devoured the offerings to Andean gods. It was the creative act by which the food of sacrifice was taken, the medium through which a sacred beings' nourishment might be achieved, that the gods, in turn, might prove benevolent to crops, herds, and men and women as they went about their lives. Like other divine forces in the Andes, Supay was only to be dreaded if one had grown slack in one's social and religious obligations.[71] Like any huaca or malqui, Apo Parato was treated improperly at one's peril. When wishes and promises solicited of him did not come to pass, Juana Ycha put the blame squarely on her clients or herself for not nourishing him correctly. To the religiously attentive, however, it was clear that there might come powerful assistance.

Most mid-colonial demonios, in spite of their characteristics that so provoked some visitadores, served particular and notably Andean functions after their appearances. The pattern of Juana Ycha's relationship with Apo Parato offers one detailed case in point. Juana would invoke the being with offerings; he would appear in one of his forms; she would feed him his usual ritual mixture and then claim the right to make requests of him. The majority of Juana's objectives pertained to the healing of persons who came to her (and to whom she was called), and were similar to the objectives of the love and curse specialists.[72] The demon became an instrument of personal vengeance only when some outstanding wrong was deemed to have been committed. More generally, Juana and Apo Parato provided an integral divine service to the community in Pomacocha.

The list of their local functions seems as varied as it is endless. A shepherd named Lorenzo Yana wished to make smooth a troublesome departure from Pomacocha; Pedro Mosco wanted to be free from suspicion in the solving of a series of local crimes; a tribute collector sought Apo Parato's counsel through Juana to locate a certain Indian; a coca seller wondered how his business would fare; three persons sought the return of lost mules—the recovery of animals and property being one of the classic ends of colonial Andean divination; and a chief claimant to regional authority (the kurakazgo) sought to enlist Juana and

---

[68] D. González Holguín, *Vocabulario*, p. 314.
[69] AAL Leg. 4, exp. 14; see fols. 16v and 20.
[70] "Supay (sentido)," p. 35.
[71] See the case of Pedro Guaman's mistress at AAL Leg. 4, exp. 14, fols. 18v–19.
[72] See AAL Leg. 4, exp. 14, 1650.

her demon on his side in a political dispute.[73] What is perhaps the most striking example of the supposed demon's range of functions came whenever Juana served as a midwife. On such occasions, Apo Parato accepted both an active and advisory role. At the delivery of Leonor Yarro's baby, Juana explained how the "demon" had calmly judged that although the woman had a narrow birth canal, she would be able to give birth and not die. When ritually invoked with offerings during the difficult labor of Juana Chumpi, Apo Parato had recommended that the mother and the child, who was being born feet first, would have to be assisted by pulling.[74]

Many native Andean women and men confessed to their judges of experiences in which similar beings imparted some special power or knowledge. The majority of the divine visitors do not seem any more clearly diabolic, in the western European sense, than Apo Parato. Their frequent involvements in the transfer of secrets and wisdom were means and ends that can be viewed as largely Andean, though such a view does not negate the possibility of the additional influences of imported diabolism on native minds. What is certain is the clear discomfort that many extirpators felt in the presence of such phenomena. Mid-colonial priests and ecclesiastical judges distrusted the Indians' abilities to differentiate imaginative (and thus dangerous) deception from the permissible or revelatory, and this discomfort and distrust often clouded their interpretations.

For example, when he appeared before a tribunal in Lima in 1710, the healer Juan Básquez related how, as a small child in Cajamarca (in the north central Andes), an old man had appeared to him in a dream and taught him the virtues of a host of different flowers and herbs.[75] Visions and divine demonstrations of herbs and powders would differ slightly from one teller to the next, but many colonial Andeans revealed that healing arts among other things had frequently been learnt from huacas in similar ways. Although Básquez had gone on to heal many people (in what to many contemporary Christian observers seemed a strikingly pious and unselfish manner) during his life—and although he had received encouragement from his Franciscan confessors—diabolical rumors about his practices and the inclinations of most of his investigators and their learned advisors, produced overwhelming suspicions that Juan Básquez had made a pact with a demon.

Although it is sometimes tempting to guess that the Devil or demons to which these documents refer were not so named by Indian accused and witnesses, there is often as much evidence pointing in the other direction. Although they were encouraged by leading questions and by the obsessive focus the interrogation might take once the diabolic was sensed, native Andeans might facilitate the ready demonization of their testimonies by providing the

---

[73] Ibid., fols. 19–19v, 20–21, 23v, 24, 23–23v, and 21v–22, respectively.
[74] Both ibid., fol. 22v.
[75] AAL Leg. 3, exp. 6, fols. 24v–25v.

demonic terms of reference themselves. This does not mean, however, that the spiritual forces concerned had radically shifted; their ways and functions are recognizably, and sometimes, blatantly Andean. There was, for example, the demon who had come as a scolding old Indian in Quipan, Canta. He was thus named and had apparently provided Hernando Caruachin with a number of tiny beads, some black and others blue, strung on a plait of black hairs. This demon had told Hernando always to be faithful to the sun and to his huacas, and that he should carry these beads with him that he might offer them in sacrifices to restore the health of the sick and use them in making medicines, for divining the future, and for a host of other things. Some two months later, Hernando had his first opportunity to try out the beads that the demon had given him when he healed a shepherd named Francisco Capa Erachi, who had been afflicted by a huaca who was a vengeful spring.[76] Hernando's demon was a strikingly Andean force, directly comparable with what one can learn of the huacas and active Andean spirit world, that recommended the maintenance of Andean worship and ritual practices. Yet Hernando's own naming of him as a demon, together with the being's form and manner, recalled the diabolic to the extirpator.

Any misgivings in some extirpators' minds about the validity of their application of demonic suspicions would usually vanish when one especially prevalent feature of the Andean demons' existence came to light: their apparently negative attitudes toward Christianity. Whether the demons inspired rude mockeries of Catholicism or whether they worked as the active agents of its downfall, their obstacles to proselytization provided the indisputable proof that the enemies which afflicted the Indians were familiar ones. For some churchmen, here at last was an explanation powerful (and convenient) enough to account for the unmistakable failure of the gospel to win its own in Peru after well over a century of Catholic evangelization and, in some areas, repeated visits by the Extirpation. Missionaries and extirpators knew that the Devil, in his envy and hatred of men and women, had always sought to inflict on them the greatest injury: the frustration of their salvation. The testimonial information received by extirpating churchmen in mid-colonial Peru was often judged accordingly, with the theories of the Devil's machinations and ultimate aims firmly in mind.

The missives from Jesuit provincials in Lima to the Father General in Rome are another body of sources that feature the standard inversion rhetoric which so characterized the hard line of contemporary demonization. The Jesuits often wrote of Andean communities where the Christian cult, right down to its clerical vestments and altar, was degraded by the vile renditions of diabolically inspired rites and ceremonies.[77] Satan and his agents were thought to make a

---

[76] AAL Leg. 2, exp. 11, fol. 5v.

[77] See, for example, ARSI, Carta anua de 1638, *Peru* 15, vol. 4, fols. 141–41v and Carta anua de 1641, 1642 y 1643, *Peru* 15, vol. 4, fol. 183.

particular assault upon the Holy Sacraments and Christian doctrine in blatant bids to snatch for themselves the worship owed to God.[78] The sacrament of penance, if not always imitated, was said to be especially flouted. For example, just south of Lima, Jesuit padres had encountered a man who said that a devil had instructed his grandparents and parents, as well as him and his own immediate family—three successive generations—not to tell of their idolatry in their obligatory confessions to the priest.[79] The even more personal stories unearthed by mid-colonial extirpators would have only verified such information in many churchmen's minds.

In 1656, the huaca minister María Ticlla Guacho of Huamantanga explained how the demon who came to her conspicuously whenever she worshiped the huaca Mallmay, and communicated with her in a style that must have seemed to her judge, Pedro Quijano de Zevallos, the crudest parody imaginable of the simple catechism. The demon stressed, she said, "that there was only the huaca to worship without suggesting that there is another God," to which she would reply "like this it shall be." The same demon sought veneration for himself, although it is unclear whether this was seen as separate from Mallmay's cult by María or by Quijano and his notary. On three occasions the demon was said to have administered what undoubtedly would have been construed as an obnoxious mockery of the Holy Communion before offering a temptation to illicit (but, again, conspicuously Andean) powers. According to the notary's rendering, he gave María a piece of black excrement, saying "take this and eat it. With this neither will you be able to forget me nor will you reconcile yourself to God. You will be wise and know the future; you will overcome all and do what you wish." He also reprimanded and flogged her for believing in the God of the Spaniards and for praying as Spanish Christians did. Yet, once María returned to his fold, he rewarded her with colored earths, saying that these would bring her health, land, and food, and that they would allow her to do as she wished.[80]

If Andean demons could not destroy Christianity through mockery, it seems that they would avoid the Spaniards' faith while attempting gradually to instill their antipathy in the hearts of the Indians. The chief minister Hernando Caruachin of Quipan twice had been savagely beaten by a demon for straying from the practice of his "sorceries." Leonor Rimay of Huamantanga found that she lost her allegedly demon-given talent to divine as soon as she received the Holy Sacrament.[81]

The demon Apo Parato's aversion to Christianity in 1650 Canta is even more clearly documented. The Spaniards' religion and its representatives seem polluted from the Andean demon's point of view. Juana Ycha said that when the friars were near he would fly off in a whirlwind as he had come. On one other

[78] Existing summaries of belief in derisive demonic parody are written by J. Caro Baroja, *The World of the Witches*, pp. 70–71, and H. R. Trevor-Roper, *The European Witch-Craze*, pp. 112–15, among many others. But see especially Stuart Clark's forthcoming *Thinking with Demons*.

[79] ARSI, Carta anua de 1664, 1665 y 1666, *Peru* 16, vol. 5, fols. 103–103v.

[80] AAL Leg. 2, exp. 11, 1656, fols. 11v–12.

[81] Ibid., fols. 5–5v and 16v.

occasion, Apo Parato had refused to help Juana advise a woman because her concerns involved the priest's mule, a beast that had been sullied by its attendance at Christian funerals and masses. When once Juana's ten-year-old son, Pedro Quispe, had cowered in the grass and cried "*a la lay Jesús a la lay*" in his fear of the great noise and stir made by "the demon Apo Parato, who came in that wind," the being pointedly rejected the offering they had laid out for him. Even more graphically, Juana said that Apo Parato impeded her from saying the few Christian prayers she had learned from a Spanish lady for whom she had once worked. Moreover, Juana Ycha secretly kept a crucifix given to her by a visiting archbishop, as well as her rosary, wrapped in an old rag and hidden among her clothing and balls of wool in a corner of her home. She was careful "that Apo Parato did not know," because if he did, she said, he would "give her a thump."[82]

When the townspeople went to church, Juana said she was in the habit of feigning illness and making excuses. She refused to pray, as mentioned above, and she had not taken communion for many years. When she was forced to confess her sins to the friars she noted that she concealed, as the notary put it, "all that was essential in her evils." Juana repeated that Apo Parato had advised that she neither pray nor attend the doctrina classes. But the teniente Cáceres was curious about Apo Parato's reaction after the occasions when Juana was pressured to take part in Catholic rites and worship. When the officials had made sure of her presence in the church, she told Cáceres that she could hear the demon come and show his displeasure by creating a clamor outside. As she and the rest of the congregation left their prayers, Apo Parato would disappear, only to return to Juana in the privacy of her home, to be nourished and to reaffirm their reciprocal relationship. He would take his meal in his usual sullen way, off the floor, covered in his black manta.[83]

The numerous fragments of information about mid-colonial Andean demons express similar realities. In general terms, they highlight difficult moments in the lives of Indians who were, like the more famous examples in the collection of religious information from the region of Huarochirí, assailed by pressures to change.[84] They show, moreover, that the huacas and Supay were not losing significance to many people—ministers, specialists, clients, and ordinary faithful included—despite Christian influences, attributes, and sometimes names. Yet at the same time, for Andeans skeptical of the old ways, persistent Andean beliefs and practices might be explained by demonic instigation and participation in the hope that they might be more easily and justifiably eradicated. Perhaps most importantly, some of the serious failings of Christian evangeliza-

---

[82] AAL Leg. 4, exp. 14, fols. 22–22v, 13, and 16v, respectively. The archbishop probably would have been Hernando Arias de Ugarte, who made lengthy tours of his see in the 1630s.

[83] Ibid., fols. 10v and 11–11v.

[84] See Frank Salomon's suggestive analysis of *Huarochirí*, chs. 20 and 21, in "Nightmare Victory."

tion and its reputation among mid-colonial Indian parishioners could be conve-
niently reburied by churchmen beneath diabolic explanations and an ever-
developing condemnation of colonial Andean religion. One can connect the
themes of patchy evangelization and the demonization of Andean religion even
more effectively by returning one last time to Pomacocha.

In the course of the proceedings, the investigator Antonio de Cáceres
learned that Juana Ycha had been baptized and that she knew who her god-
father was. Yet she had grown up in a home where "neither her father nor her
mother knew how to pray."[85] Despite learning some prayers at one point in her
life from a Spanish woman, other stronger loyalties militated against their
maintenance. Her increasingly anxious attitude toward the annual confession
of her sins and obligatory attendance at mass have already been discussed.
Juana's relationship with and understanding of Christianity were, like her crucifix and rosary, hidden away and pushed into a corner of her everyday life. But
this is vastly different from saying that certain Christian ideas and practices had
not been contemplated by her or other Indians, or that Catholic conceptions
had never merged with Andean ways of seeing and making sense of things by
mid-colonial times.

Popular rumor had informed teniente Cáceres that Juana Ycha believed that
the images of Christ and the saints in the church were only wood and that the
true God was up above and all-seeing. In a bold statement that might recall the
attitude of a certain Italian miller to some readers, Juana confirmed these contentions, stating "that no one had taught it to her, only that she understood it to
be so."[86] Hers was a common rebuttal of some of Catholicism's claims in the
mid-colonial Andes; it employed a similar logic to that which was argued by
Andean dogmatizers and huaca ministers in other parts of the archdiocese.
What were the saints, Hernando Chaupis Condor asked during his testimony
before Visitador Bernardo de Novoa in Acas, Cajatambo, in 1656, "but the
Spaniards' huacas and creators?"[87] But Antonio de Cáceres was not capable of
interpreting Juana's words and actions in a way that would admit misunder-
standings and religious expressions that were outside his control—not after
what he had heard about Apo Parato. Instead, like the visitador investigating
the chanca priest and his wife discussed in Chapter Three, he chose the ordeal.

With cords tightened onto her arms, Juana Ycha was persuaded to contradict
herself yet again. As with the dream of her deceased husband's returning spirit,
she was made to affirm that it was "the demon Apo Parato himself" who had
taught her the heresy about the mute images. With the instruments of torture
in operation, Cáceres followed up another related charge in the same fashion,
the charge that Juana performed a rite which invoked "Ucupacha Mamay," an

[85] AAL Leg. 4, exp. 14, fols. 16–16v.

[86] Ibid., fols. 28–29. For a telling of the miller Menocchio's story, see C. Ginzburg, *The Cheese
and the Worms*.

[87] On the Cajatambo dogmatizers' messages see my *An Evil Lost to View?*, ch. 6. "Dogmatizer"
is my tentative gloss of *dogmatizador*, the term employed by the notaries. These persons were
teachers, guardians, and tellers of sacred histories, as well as ministers and ritual adepts.

expression that the notary rendered and then translated as "mother hell." Juana was, however, soon virtually unable to answer further queries with anything but agreement. The notary recorded the result in a way that is strongly suggestive of the coercion which this Mercedarian friar's assistant and his agents applied to gain her assent. He wrote that "she was exhausted from all the questions they made to her. Now she knows that it was the temptation of the demon, and that everything is deception except for God, Our Father, and His Holy Mother, the Virgin of the Rosary."[88] The investigation was satisfied only by the achievement of an explanation that the demon Apo Parato and his hostility to God's truth had led Juana into ignorance and error.

Juana Ycha spent days in confession before the extirpator's tribunal and came to understand that her inquisitor only accepted what made sense to him. If Apo Parato was a demonized Andean god who, like so many other indigenous divinities and forces, had come to embody a natural Andean response to the imposition of Christianity, it is doubtful that Juana—or anyone else— would have been aware of, or been able to articulate, the subtle and gradual transformations that had brought about this complex religious reality. In any event, sitting before the Extirpation's tribunal was no place to sort out religious discrepancies. As Juana grew more tormented and desperate, she chose the common path of people in her unenviable position: she started to confess in a deferential way to gain relief and some form of escape. The truth, along with Apo Parato, began to fade away.

For his part, Antonio de Cáceres was perplexed by the fact that Apo Parato, who could evidently do so much, had not come to rescue Juana when she was put in the stocks or when she was imprisoned in the church by his idolatry investigation.[89] Juana replied that she had not invoked Apo Parato then because she feared that the "great noise" he always made would wake the Extirpation officials who slept nearby. But, she implied later, he had come anyway. While she was held in the church, Juana confessed, she had heard Apo Parato pass outside in his customary way, "as a whirlwind with much noise." At midnight, he was up against the door of the church, and through the hinges she heard him say *"pay pay"* in what she recognized to be "his voice like other times." Juana said that she had told him to be gone, that she was now "in the hands of God" and had decided "to follow him (God) and the Mother of God [the Virgin] of the Rosary." As he left the door of the church, she said that Apo Parato had spoken to her one last time, saying: "I want to return to where I am, above Cajapalca [a village nearby] to a great hill, the one with the lake called Cochayoc on top." Juana also told of how he had come in his *manta* many times before, wanting to take her with him to this place.[90]

---

[88] AAL Leg. 4, exp. 14, fol. 29.

[89] As appears to have often been the case in the towns of rural Mexico, in Peru rooms in churches were often used by visitadores de idolatría as the most secure places for temporary incarceration; on Mexico, see W. B. Taylor, *Magistrates of the Sacred*, ch. 9.

[90] AAL Leg. 4, exp. 14, fols. 11v, 17, and 29v–30.

It is, of course, impossible to judge how genuine Juana Ycha's professed choice of Christianity was. Was her whole account of shunning her relationship with the Andean god nothing but a desperate fabrication? The twin pleas of credulity and deception by the Devil were, as I have noted, common ones from Indians and experienced advocates before certain extirpators, and Juana may well have availed herself of this escape. But, it is interesting that, through Juana's own words (for the specifics, at least, could not have come from the notary or Cáceres), one learns of Apo Parato's parting and his chosen place of refuge—or at least Juana's representation of this. He had been verbally spurned by his minister, who was imprisoned in the church and who was choosing Christianity, though perhaps only out of fear or in hope of lessening her imminent sentence. Yet Juana did not have the abandoned Apo Parato descend, shaking a leprous fist, into some fiery chasm as the teniente might have thought appropriate; the demon climbed to a place near a mountain lake, the acknowledged domain of the Andean gods.

In one sense, the demonization of Andean religious ideas demonstrates some of the complicated ways in which Indians in colonial times assimilated aspects and interpretations of Christian ideas and forms into their own emerging conceptions. But the fruits of the search for such demonstrations are limited and generalizations are dissatisfying. Any search for a demonic prototype, in the Archdiocese of Lima at least, is ultimately futile. The mid-colonial Andean "demons" are the enemies of easy summary. Indeed, in their refusal to be essentially diabolic, in the persistently ambiguous exhibitions of their powers, these beings of which the Indians spoke must have puzzled even the extirpators who, in the official record, seem content to view them in the narrowest of terms.

In a dream, a demon had once come to Hernando Caruachin of Quipan, Canta, as a donkey that proceeded to carry him on an exhausting tour of all the churches of Lima. The colonial capital was over seventy-five kilometres to the southwest of Quipan. The same fiend was a frequent visitor, who returned "in diverse forms, sometimes with horns, other times in the figure of lion, or else as a condor or a fox." Although the first two creatures might suggest common European demonic forms, the condor and fox were popular heroes in Andean myths. Hernando asserted that his various personal communications with demons were not so extraordinary; they were, in his view, no more than what other Indians in Huamantanga also experienced.[91]

His words rang true even beyond his Cantan parish. But although Andean demons might serve general functions and assist some Indians in the manner of the gods they were, for the many Indians who had entered a new religious space that one might tentatively characterize as beyond the two religious systems, and for those who had chosen Christianity, there was greater spiritual

---

[91] AAL Leg. 2, exp. 11, fols. 4v–6. See *Huarochirí* and G. Urton, ed., *Animal Myths and Metaphors*.

confusion and torment to come. Many huacas, the gods who remained the most powerful regional symbols of the Andean religious imagination, found it impossible to live with their people's betrayal. Widespread messianic uprisings inspired by the huacas' ministers might have been out of the question in the middle of the seventeenth century, but Andean beliefs and practices had found a far more complex medium for their religious survival than full-scale rebellion: transformation. The examples come not only from the years of Villagómez's Extirpation and those which followed until the mid-eighteenth century. Even nominally Christian Indians like Cristóbal Choque Casa from Huarochirí suffered fierce doctrinal contests with the demonic manifestations of huacas who were far from forgotten, and whose importance in their communities had been assaulted but not erased.[92]

The examination of demonizing tendencies enlightens the whole approach to the eradication of Andean religion in these times. The acceptance of the Devil's role, alongside Indian credulity, as a fundamental basis for religious interpretation provided much-tested and convenient reasons for the things that were conceived to be at error, and thus evil, in the Andes. The conception of Andean demons where the Indians' gods once had been was, of course, a natural reaction for early modern Spanish Christians. Yet there was no denying that demonization simultaneously served less pious ends in Peru. It furnished a shrewd sanction for the boldest actions of the Church and the state, as demons and Devils and witches had long done in Europe.[93] The Devil and his apparently steady assumption of Andean religious forms helped both Archbishop Villagómez and his visitadores meet their constant need to justify the forceful response of extirpation and an increasing set of demands for cultural change on Andean peoples.

Demonization, however, would not always be made to fit. One may note a tinge of discouragement and skepticism in the records of idolatry investigators such as Juan Ignacio de Torres y Solis in León de Huánuco in 1662 or Juan de Saavedra y Osorio in Huamantanga, Canta, in 1697, both of whom were deprived of diabolic explanations in the examination of different Indian religious crimes. In Huánuco, despite grave suspicions, a septuagenerian healer named Agustín Carvajal was finally judged guilty of "fraudulent practices (*embuste*), without acting in concert with the Devil."[94] Over three decades later in Huamantanga, where a number of Indians were tortured and repeatedly questioned about the forms assumed by the Devil and about the pacts he made with them and other local people, a string of resolute denials was broken only by the admission of María Pilco Suyo. She told of a "spirit" which regularly rested on

[92] See *Huarochirí*, chs. 20 and 21, esp. secs. 234–36 and 240–42, and F. Salomon, "Nightmare Victory."

[93] On the Devil as a "sanction for Christian orthodoxy," see K. V. Thomas, *Religion and the Decline of Magic*, p. 568. On the enticing connection to political theory, S. Clark's forthcoming *Thinking with Demons*.

[94] AAL Leg. 3, exp. 3, 1662, fol. 15.

her left shoulder and whispered instructions and assistance in her regional performances of divination.[95] The spirit was not referred to as a demon; indeed, if one needed a Catholic equivalent it seemed more like a guardian angel. But in a situation in which another people's religious subtleties were as consistently distorted as in the extirpators' approach to colonial Andean religion, demon was perhaps close enough.

[95] AAL Leg. 5, exp. 25, 1696–1697, fols. 19–19v.

Colonial Andean Religion

COLONIAL Andean religion, as I am calling it, has inspired a good deal of scholarly speculation. In 1928, in one of his famous essays on Peruvian identity, José Carlos Mariátegui argued that the "Catholic conquest" of the sixteenth and seventeenth centuries had failed to impose Christianity on the peoples who had formerly lived under the Inka. What endured of the Spanish efforts, he claimed, was only "the liturgy," "the cult," and the "spiritual and abstract religiosity," while indigenous religion survived beneath the Catholic veneer. The historian Luis E. Valcárcel could be said to have expanded upon this thesis but to have worked within its bounds in matters of Andean religiosity. Even George Kubler's 1946 treatment of the colonial Quechua agreed with this conception of the Indians' Catholicism as superficial even after the "divine essence" had left "the components of Quechua religion." A second interpretation came from authors who were more apologetic toward the Catholic efforts at evangelization. They felt, as Fernando Armas Medina did, that the rugged geography of the Andes had been the principal factor preventing total success and that, in any event, "the soul of the Indian" had become "essentially Christian."[1] In spite of an increasing complication in argument and no small rise in jargon, important later work has tendered solutions which more or less conform to these two lines of argument.

The most intriguing challenges to these sweeping views have explored the explanatory possibilities of syncretism. Many Andeanists have been influenced by Nathan Wachtel's 1971 portrayal of a "juxtaposition" of belief systems. For Wachtel, the religious encounter between Spanish Christians and native Andeans proceeded roughly as follows: two world views clashed, adapted as necessary, and then continued on in a parallel coexistence with "acculturation elements [only masking] a division between the European and Indian worlds." However much such Christian elements as church-centered dance and festivals offered attractive spiritual space for Indians, there was enough fundamental opposition between the two systems to preclude widespread mixture. "Acculturation elements" are the engines of religious change in the native societies, but they do not much change the "destructuration" without "restructuration" underlying Wachtel's scheme.[2]

---

[1] J. C. Mariátegui, *Siete ensayos de interpretatación*, p. 172. See particularly Valcárcel's *Ruta cultural del Perú*, pp. 165 and 184; and G. Kubler, "The Quechua," p. 403. F. Armas Medina, *Cristianización del Perú*, especially p. 596.

[2] *The Vision of the Vanquished*, p. 157, and more generally pp. 85–168. Wachtel's title, *La vision des vaincus* (Paris, 1971), repeats the Mesoamericanist Miguel León-Portilla's *Visión de los vencidos*, translated into English as *The Broken Spears*.

Manuel Marzal's *La transformación religiosa peruana*, published in 1980, is a remarkable contribution, valuable not only for its treatment of Andean religious change (the visions "of the vanquished") but also for its original scrutiny of colonial ecclesiastical policy and difference of opinion. Marzal conceives of a religious "crystallization" in the Andean parishes in the late seventeenth century, an arrival at a moment when certain elements of Christianity were accepted as legitimate Andean sacra, a moment when a syncretic "conversion" was, for the most part, reached.[3] Marzal's work is perhaps the best example in Andeanist circles of a wider inclination among investigators of religious syncretism in the core areas of colonial Spanish America, an emphasis William Taylor has characterized as a tendency among students of religion and change toward finding "a stable, homogenous mixture or fusion . . . an end state of completion and wholeness." Taylor continues, noting that in many studies although "process is invoked, . . . there has been little examination of what it entails beyond the addition or fusion of Catholic elements into a native world view, producing a stable, 'syncretic' religion."[4] Marzal, it should be noted, ultimately complicates his own formulation of a crystallization, in leaving room for elements of both Christianity and the Andean religious system that would resist integration into a syncretic result.[5] Wachtel's juxtaposed religious worlds and Marzal's moment of nearly complete crystallization offer enticing propositions that go some way toward explaining religious survival and change.

Wachtel himself noted the deep influence of studies which, often from the isolated perspectives of Church history or histories of the "target" societies, treat processes like Christianization, acculturation, and resistance as having not only beginnings and perhaps problematic middles, but also what Taylor calls "end states of completion and wholeness." Wachtel's ponderings, linked to Marzal's inclusion of the resistant half moons, resemble Taylor's words in their central message:

> It is sometimes suggested that in order to avoid . . . [a] fragmentation of history and of cultures, attention should be focused on the end-result of the process (syncretism, assimilation, rejection) or, in a more refined analysis, on the degrees of acculturation, the various steps or stages, definition of which consequently reintroduces a static framework. This may well be a useful analytic approach *in the first instance*, but what about the process itself? What happens between the steps? How is one to identify choices, conflicts or creations? In short we are faced with an

---

[3] M. M. Marzal, *La transformación religiosa peruana*. Along related lines, Manuel Burga conceives of Andean "mental change" and a late seventeenth-century "triumph of Christianity" in Part 2 of his thought-provoking *Nacimiento*. See also A. Meyers and D. E. Hopkins, *Manipulating the Saints*, esp. pp. vii–viii.

[4] *Magistrates of the Sacred*, ch. 3.

[5] "the two circles of the two religious systems in contact, the Catholic and the Andean, [were] almost superimposed, but there remained two small half moons representing aspects of the Catholic system which never managed to insert themselves into the Indian world (for example, the priesthood) or aspects of Andean religion which were never Christianized (for example, the worship of Pacha Mama)." *La transformación religiosa peruana*, p. 440.

antimony, a contradiction: to isolate the elements is to fail to grasp the culture as a whole; to define the stages of a process is to neglect the dynamics of acculturation. . . . it illustrates a dual pressure: the tension between the abstraction of theoretical analysis and the apprehension of living reality.[6]

Enrique Dussel, for one, envisaged some contradictions and mysterious shades of meaning in the "living reality." Dussel dubbed the resulting religious situation in the Andes a "chiaroscuro" where, on the one hand, simple ignorance of Christian concepts was thought to be evidence of relapsed paganism and, on the other, Indians were accepted as suitably Christian on the basis of little more than their baptism and a rudimentary understanding of a few central tenets.[7] Dussel's formulation comes in the midst of a wide-ranging study, and it is all too brief and without much assembled evidence to drive it home. But it is intriguing in its lack of closure—its acknowledgement of uncertainty, distortions and limits to understanding.

Other treatments of the religion of Indians in colonial Peru and elsewhere—albeit usually as parts of wider studies—have been less inclined toward constructing all-encompassing explanations, ambitious typologies of change, or syncretic models to describe a complicated religious reality.[8] Studies such as those by Luis Miguel Glave, Luis Millones, and Fernando Iwasaki Cauti have taken the encouraging step of viewing colonial Andean religion, as well as attitudes to it, as connected to the wider religious atmospheres of which they were a part.[9]

Understanding has also been greatly enriched by the gradual intellectual digestion of the Huarochirí collection of myths and religious information, and also by recent work on the idolatry trials, particularly those from the province of Cajatambo.[10] Investigators have been attracted by the phenomenal dura-

---

[6] *The Vision of the Vanquished*, p. 5, emphasis added.

[7] *A History of the Church*, p. 68.

[8] A few of the major monographs are: K. Spalding, *Huarochirí*, pp. 239–69; S. J. Stern, *Peru's Indian Peoples*, pp. 51–79; L. Millones, *Historia y poder*, esp. chs. 2 and 3; M. Burga, *Nacimiento*, Part 2; A. Flores Galindo, *Buscando un Inca*, ch. 2; I. Silverblatt, *Moon, Sun, and Witches*, chs. 9 and 10; N. M. Farriss, *Maya Society*, esp. ch. 10; S. Gruzinski, *The Conquest of Mexico*, chs. 4–6; and F. Cervantes, *The Devil in the New World*, ch. 2.

[9] See especially the essays by Millones and Iwasaki Cauti within L. Millones, *Una partecita del cielo*. Iwasaki's contribution is also published elsewhere: "Mujeres al borde de la perfección"; see also, his "Fray Martín de Porras," and L. M. Glave, "Santa Rosa de Lima".

[10] For a recent reading of the Huarochirí collection, see F. Salomon's introductory essay to *The Huarochirí Manuscript*, edited and translated by F. Salomon and G. L. Urioste. In the text itself see, for instance, the suggestive contrast of Doctor Avila's act of destruction and Capac Huanca's staying power in ch. 25, sec. 347. The idolatry material from Cajatambo has attracted both independent archival work and useful compilations of documents. Duviols's edited collection, *Cultura andina* (1986) first made accessible in print a number of fascinating seventeenth-century idolatry investigations from the province. To add to the corpus of primary sources from the region, this time with a sampling of documents stretching from 1622 to 1807, is *Ofensas a Dios*, edited by J. C. García Cabrera (1994). A. Sánchez's edited collection of trials, *Amancebados, hechiceros y rebeldes* (1991) shifts attention to seventeenth-century Chancay. Each of the three collections has a substan-

bility of regional Andean gods in the hearts and minds of their faithful in spite of actions that destroyed their physical representations. There is no doubting the importance of this point to any understanding of colonial Andean religion and the confrontations with its enemies, as churchmen grew anxious over evidence that suggested that huacas and other Andean gods might not need to be physically present to command the attention of their peoples.

Ultimately, however, focus upon these examples of religious survival leaves the investigation of the mid-colonial Andean religion incomplete, and even misrepresented. The magnetism both of apparent resistance and of the prospect of survivals of prehispanic religion should inspire as much caution as interest. The peoples of mid-colonial Cajatambo are not generic Andeans. Whether through certain visitadores' diligence in comparison with other investigators' abilities and methods of detection or, more likely, a host of internal factors that promoted Andean religious survival in places like Acas, Otuco, and Mangas, or a combination of both, the information from these trials is extraordinary in a number of respects. The vitality of the cults of the dead, the sheer numbers of revered malquis that were discovered, the intact ayllu ministries and ceremonial cycles, and the overall extent of the Andean dogmatizers' rhetorical and practical resistance to Catholic inroads stand out in the Archdiocese of Lima. Trial information from, say, Canta or Huarochirí might detail similar organizations, and are often as rich or richer in certain other aspects. There is also the issue of what people are concealing or misrepresenting for their own reasons. Even in these seventeenth-century Cajatambo pueblos, where Indian religious survival is well documented, the dynamic survival of Andean cults did not negate the presence of other religious options. The place of Christianity was different in various settings in this emerging colonial religious world.

A simple and strict adhesion to traditional Andean practices and worship—however transformed—was impossible for most Indian people, even if it had been the desired option. As a consequence, over the entire Archdiocese of Lima, it was perhaps the least viable and most uncommon religious alternative. Some small groups and isolated individuals seem to have fled to the punas and remote ravines in an effort to live virtually undisturbed by Spanish demands, but for the vast majority of Indians in the mid-colonial Lima region membership and participation in a Catholic parish was both presumed and accepted. No matter what hesitation they felt, no matter what reconciliations they had made between the Andean and Christian belief systems, most people heard mass, attended doctrine classes, and observed at least the basic sacraments.

In many cases, Christian symbols and rituals had become more than simply meaningless forms or resented obligations in the Indian pueblos. The Church was becoming a source of sacred power in the Andes, and personal identifica-

---

tial intoduction by the editor. For interpretations that focus on parts of the Cajatambo material see S. MacCormack, *Religion in the Andes*, ch. 9.2; M. Burga, *Nacimiento*, esp. pp. 138–96; my *An Evil Lost to View?*; and two theses, M. E. Doyle, "The Ancestor Cult," and G. Cock Carrasco, "El sacerdote andino."

tion with at least some rendering of Catholic Christianity represented more than just prudence or an instinct for self-preservation. The challenge, of course, is to understand how this religious situation came about and how it worked in people's lives. The evidence is such that it is not satisfying to produce a simple model to explain a subtle and varying process, or to conclude in a broad manner that Christianization occurred gradually, in accordance with an Indian agenda, or that Indians reinterpreted Christianity. As true as such conclusions might be, they are in danger of saying not very much at all. Rather than invoke dim images of religious change, I want to try to reconstruct what colonial Andean religion was like.

The extirpators confronted Andean religious ideas with condemnatory shows of force. The justification for these measures was found in the supposed vanity, diabolic inspiration, and corrupt nature of all that they destroyed. Yet it is possible to turn away briefly from the face the Church presented to the Indians during the anti-idolatry campaigns to recall another age of the faith. However fleetingly, Christianity had enjoyed, and was enjoying, other more persuasive standard bearers in the Andes. This is not to claim that the mendicant orders, the Jesuits, and the secular clergy did not engage in acts of religious coercion or that they had not extirpated idolatry on their own initiatives but only to stress the fact that neither the aggressive stance of the Villagómez years—a time of intensely centralized control—nor the contagious hysteria over the evil of idolatry in his and later times was typical. The systematic campaigns of the Extirpation were stern, temporary measures, shows of force among supposedly recalcitrant idolaters in order to restore the possibility of normal parish life.

One can assume that during times which can tentatively be designated as normal, when crusading Christian authorities and visitas de idolatría were nowhere to be seen, the process of religious change was more harmonious. Although the theoretical prospect of attempting to mold Christianity, and even the holy scriptures, to fit the Indians' needs and expectations was officially rejected, in practice missionaries and churchmen frequently adapted the Christian metaphors and parables to suit their congregations and validate the new religion in the new converts' eyes. It was during these moments of persuasion that Christian ideas might begin to be "insinuated" into the Andean religious imagination or, alternatively, to be guided into an expanding religious framework by individuals and groups.[11] Available documentary evidence on these earliest improvisations or the incorporative process in any given area is limited. Much of the change was gradual and virtually unconscious. Moreover, most mid-colonial Andeans' allusions to the early colonial period are fleeting and frequently placed within the playful and confusing context of the people's vivid tradiciones. The mid-colonial testimonies before the visitadores principally tell of beliefs and practices in a present and recent past that might only evoke ancient times. However, from these relatively fixed points of testimonial

---

[11] Monica Barnes uses "insinuated" in "Catechisms and *Confessionarios*," p. 80.

reference some extrapolations about how certain conceptions and customs came into being seems warranted, particularly in cases of apparently voluntary religious intermixture.

In most of the parishes there were groups of people who described themselves as Christians, but who also recognized the importance of observing native ceremonial practices (Figure 9). What might initially appear as religious duality, however, shows itself rarely to have been so. Religious concepts and principles had a way of intermingling in everyday life. The idolatry sources are particularly enlightening with respect to the activities of the Indians in an expanding religious common ground, a terrain composed of people whose religious behavior drew from pools of religious options that had officially been declared incompatible.[12]

This meant that effectively, if not purposefully, many Andeans lived religious lives that contravened the precise and guiding commands both of their Indian dogmatizers and their parish priests. Inga Clendinnen has questioned the temptation for scholars to examine later sixteenth-century Indian religion in Mexico in accordance with what she calls "that familiar mix and match model of 'syncretism.'" This approach, she observes, "subjects a 'lived religion' to vivisection, carving it into transportable, stateable, teachable propositions: a disturbing, dispiriting, and finally effectively disabling business."[13] Instead of shuffling around parts of that "lived religion" (reminiscent of what Wachtel named "living reality"), looking for Spanish and Andean ingredients, let us open up the uncommonly abundant and descriptive archive of religious information, without confining it to tight models or discussing change as a progression through stages in one particular direction. The testimonial sources from mid-colonial Peru provide information about religion as practiced and lived by Andeans in the mid-colonial period. These sources are the very post-conquest "experiential scripts" which are needed to proceed in the observance-based manner Clendinnen suggests.[14]

The multifariousness of colonial Andean religion can be confirmed in the range of attitudes that Andeans seem to have adopted to Christianity. In pursuing this avenue perhaps the obvious challenge is interpreting the possibility of religious contention in the parish context. What basis is there to think of a polarity of religious feeling in mid-colonial Indian society, a growth of local rivalry, competition, and factionalism along religious lines?

---

[12] The Dominican Diego Durán's use of the Nahuatl term *nepantla* to describe the religious situation of many native people in early colonial central Mexico has greatly influenced views of religious change in colonial Spanish American historiography. "Nepantlism" refers to a transitory condition "in between" traditional beliefs and practices and adherence to Christianity. It is usually portrayed as a time of confusion and unease. Exploring this interpretative model and a host of others, is J. J. Klor de Alva, "Spiritual Conflict," pp. 353–55. But see the reflections of W. B. Taylor in *Magistrates of the Sacred*, ch. 3.

[13] "Ways to the Sacred," p. 109. Clendinnen notes the influence of anthropology, especially Victor Turner's work, and the formulations in William Christian's writing about local religion in Spain in particular at n. 14. For Christian's own thoughts on "religion as lived," see particularly "Folk Religion," p. 371.

[14] "Ways to the Sacred," p. 110 and notes 14 and 15.

Figure 9. A Christian Andean. From Felipe Guaman Poma de Ayala, *El primer nueva corónica*, edited by John V. Murra and Rolena Adorno. Original manuscript in the Royal Library, Copenhagen.

In seeking answers to this question, the assumptions of contemporary Spanish churchmen push attention in only one direction. There is little doubt that it was in terms of a clear-cut rivalry that many mid-colonial missionaries and extirpators would have preferred to interpret the religious reality in areas where recalcitrance seemed a problem despite the Indians' long-standing relationship with Christianity. Conceiving of a dualistic struggle between those who had been won over by the gospel, and who defended it, and those who wickedly resisted the advance of truth was a standard and convenient Augustinian line. Jesuit missives to Rome, in particular, were inclined to stress dramatic instances in which the two camps of light and darkness could be delineated among the Indians. In the Archdiocese of Lima, the clerical attitude that preferred a state of clear opposition was reflected most clearly in the Church's long term fixation upon the removal of hechiceros, the leaders of a perceived evil fifth column, from the communities in which they were said to corrupt others.[15]

Much of what the Andean teachers and ministers (dogmatizers) asserted could fall into what their Spanish Christian interpreters would rather comfortably classify as a religiously suspicious statement—what in inquisitorial language was called a *proposición*. Such statements either explicitly or implicitly challenged a tenet or practice of the Catholic Church.[16] Thus the teachings that could be attributed to some of these persons would have contributed significantly to their condemnation. Some Indian dogmatizers were confrontational toward the claims of Catholicism, often acknowledging the need for their faithful to adapt to some sort of deceptive coexistence. The well-known contentions of some of the dogmatizers within the Cajatambino religious élite, which interpreted the holy images as the "Spaniards' huacas," which blamed Indian poverty and depopulation on the neglect of the needs of the Indians' huacas and malquis, and which recommended strategies to trick Catholic confessors, are dramatic cases in point.[17] Their tones were typical of committed traditionalists in neighboring areas. Among other things, Andean dogmatizers might point out the inefficacy of Christianity in comparison with the relevance and strength of Andean religion, or the rigidity of Christian moral strictures in comparison with the more relaxed demands of what was presented as the na-

[15] See accounts of evildoers and organized "Christian killing" near Cusco in ARSI, Carta anua de 1649, *Peru* 15, vol. 4, fols. 236 and 236v. Apart from being a common aim of the extirpators, the attitude toward hechiceros can be traced back to the sixteenth-century provincial councils. For perhaps the most influential post-conquest depiction of the Andean hechiceros, and the one included among the pastoral complements of the "Tercero catecismo" of the Third Provincial Council of Lima, see J. Polo de Ondegardo, "Los errores y supersticiones," pp. 469–71, and in *Doctrina Christiana*, pp. 274–76.

[16] Note the similar approaches to perceived religious offenders in Spain discussed by S. Nalle, *God in La Mancha*, pp. 60–61.

[17] See the pioneering study by L. Huertas Vallejos, *La religión en una sociedad*; also, my *An Evil Lost to View?*, ch. 6. For the striking similarities between these leaders' messages and those preached by the messianic *taquiongos* (itinerant religious mendicants) of the central Andes in the 1560s, see L. Millones, ed., *El retorno de las huacas*, pp. 11–18.

tive moral code; they often advised Indians of useful strategies to conceal their forbidden beliefs and practices in the face of regular confession and interrogation on idolatry charges.[18]

The huaca ministers and dogmatizers were intelligent innovators who frequently changed just as much as they needed to counter their perceived rival, and to keep intact a recognizably Andean religion. For these stands and because of their enduring power, they commanded respect in many mid-colonial communities. Yet there could be a sizeable gap between their views and those of the many others who were not maestros of the old ways and who did not conceive of themselves as guardians of ancient knowledge in the face of the new pressures of colonial times. Many people were neither in a state of resistance or opposition, nor were they consciously accommodating. These people were more eclectic, even experimental, tending to mix religious elements gradually rather than to substitute or replace. Their religious decisions may have been less conscious than has often been supposed, and by their very nature part of processes of change and mixture that were in motion and thus incomplete. People's lived religion in mid-colonial times does not comfortably stick to either of the poles that seem originally to have been suggested by the churchmen themselves. The idolatry evidence moves discussion of Andean religion away from generalizations and polarizing tendencies toward what may seem to outsiders like the more ambiguous "colonial combinations" of individuals.[19]

When points of contention between Christianity and Andean religion arose in people's minds they seem to have been phrased in personal terms, reduced, as it were, to an individual's choice between the possible solutions to life's problems. For example, Don Diego Pacha, a kuraka from Cañas in the parish of Sayan, Chancay, revealed to a visitador in 1662 that anxiety over the illness of his son had caused him to accede to the entreaties of a specialist and minister named Hernando Niño. The Andean governor had provided a pitcher of chicha to placate a local huaca which the local minister claimed was "consuming" the governor's children in punishment for Don Diego's religious negligence. Once he had made the offering before the huaca and presumably received some sort of message or sign (about which one does not learn), Niño informed the kuraka that they had started too late: "there was [now] no cure for the young boy." When the minister began to tell him of the other ancient shrines that they might consult, Don Diego claimed that he had rejected the hechicero and his prognosis. Moreover, he had denounced Niño's "wickedness" to the parish priest, Gregorio de Utrilla, to whom he then turned in the hope of restoring the health of his son. In addition to the service he provided in revealing the activities of Niño and the locations of a number of local huacas, Don Diego gave the

---

[18] Other examples from outside Cajatambo are discussed above. See also the teaching of Lorenzo Llacxa Guaroc of Carhuamayo in Junin; AAL Leg. 4, exp. 8, 1631, Felipe Nuna Vilca at fols. 2–2v. For a transcription and introduction to the Junin trial see my "Persistencia religiosa."

[19] The phrase is William Taylor's from *Magistrates of the Sacred*, ch. 3.

priest twenty *reales* in alms, asking him to sing a mass for the recovery of his son.[20]

The issue of whether Hernando Niño was an exploitative or somewhat illegitimate example of his kind is, in this instance, less interesting than the consideration of the actions of Don Diego Pacha. The kuraka's self-portrayal before the visitador as one who had suffered a momentary weakness before realizing that the only healing power in the world came from God and the only intercession through the accepted channels of the Holy Mother Church, seems to have been a ploy for mercy. In reality, it is probable that in times of need at least two religious paths would have seemed open to the Indian governor and others like him. No matter what he asserted to a Spanish investigator after the fact, Don Diego seems at the time both to have sought and to have been content to accept divine assistance from wherever it would come—although it is perhaps significant that the huaca was approached with a cantarillo of chicha before twenty *reales* were donated to the priestly coffers.

There are, however, indications that other Indians had accepted Christianity's exclusive claims and were trying to encourage similar views in their pueblos. It emerged in 1660 in Omas, Yauyos, for example, that Doña Catalina, the kuraka's wife, had berated the healer Francisca Maivai for her apparent religious duality. How was it, Catalina was said to have ventured, that this *embustera* (liar or impostor) could "deceive the Virgin in [confessing and] taking communion each year" while making sacrifices to the local mountain huaca, Maguaca Coto?[21]

In most parishes the option of Christianity was as close as the village church; the Catholic faith's praises were repeated in sermons and in doctrine classes. Yet Christianity's dominant position and monopoly on at least the official propaganda could not ensure that it would strike Indians as the unique answer to their spiritual and physical needs. One can recall the people who detailed their considerable loyalties to huacas, chancas, and conopas in terms of their faith in the power of these deities to produce good effects in life's pursuits, or the sheer number of clients served by the specialists in these regions. Or one can remember the case of Catalina Yauca Choque in Ambar, Cajatambo, in 1662, who declared her skepticism that saying masses would do anything to make lost and stolen blankets appear. She, for one, would trust in the indigenous rites of divination.

In any event, the evidence suggests that for the overwhelming majority of native Andeans in the Archdiocese of Lima there was rarely a compelling need to make such a clear choice between religious rivals. It was the presence and pressure of the visitador and his assumptions, not to mention the hope of leniency, that often seems to have forced people to compartmentalize and try to present themselves as on one side or the other. In terms of the example from

---

[20] AAL Leg. 5, exp. 5, Diego Paha at fols. 1v–2. Diego also led Utrilla to the huacas so that they could be destroyed.

[21] AAL Leg. 2, exp. 18, fol. 32v.

Omas cited above, people were closer to Francisca Maivai's religious situation (regularly taking communion and confessing her sins, while continuing to make offerings to a local huaca) than to the one attributed to the scolding kuraka's wife, Doña Catalina (requiring exclusive adherence). Although the entrance of Christianity into Andean religious thinking and practice is undeniable and readily apparent in a number of spheres, and although the Christianization of people can often be said to have increased with the passage of time, this was no simple process for one to plot as a steady rising line on a graph. Moreover, as I will show further below, things were happening to parts of Christianity as they became portions of colonial Andean religious life. To repeat Frank Salomon's phrase in reference to the peoples of Huarochirí, colonial people were "making the found world their own."[22] The most experienced and reflective missionaries and extirpators of idolatry could not remain blind to the unpredictable realities of Andean responses to the many faces of Christian evangelization. What can be detected from the pen of the Jesuit Arriaga onward to the descriptions of idolatry investigations in mid-colonial times is not so different from what a perceptive earlier commentator in New Spain, Diego Durán, had observed in his setting; such Spanish Christians had an uneasy awareness of the fact that the enemy of straight Christian conversion in the Indian parishes and missions was increasingly complicated.

At times, religious change is only superficially evident, and it is difficult to know how deeply it pervaded. A certain amount of conceptual borrowing might take place even when rituals and central beliefs do not seem to have been altered. Andean peoples have consistently shown the ability to accept various "symbols of a dominant political authority" into their own expanding religious and conceptual framework.[23] This process was not simply a matter of the extirpators' notaries employing Christian vocabulary to express otherwise alien religious practices. The word choices differ and are not sufficiently standardized into Catholic terms to suggest that this was always the case; moreover, the witnesses' descriptions were sometimes so Andean as to make necessary Spanish glosses or even Quechua words and phrases in the attempt to capture meaning. Of course, these ongoing attempts to capture meaning and represent difficult concepts were also made by Andeans themselves. I believe that for many Indian declarants, what might appear to a modern reader to be suspiciously Catholic descriptions of native religion were, in fact, natural expressions for the people themselves. Just as huacas might be referred to as demons by some witnesses, different Andean rites could be explained through use of the increasingly familiar concepts and terminology of the Christian religion. Juan Paria Vilca of Chorrillo, Huarochirí, could hardly have been more explicit. He told Sarmiento de Vivero in 1659 "that his father and mother were sorcerers (*hechiceros*), that his father made sacrifices in the same way as a priest

---

[22] Salomon himself is borrowing from Waud Kracke; "Nightmare Victory," p. 5. See W. Kracke, "Myths in Dreams," and p. 18 n.12 above.

[23] L. Millones observes this in "Los ganados," p. 142.

(*cura*), and that his father ordered him about, as a priest does his sacristan, asking him for things." What is more, when Juan watched over the chacras of maize he recalled that in order to keep the fog, mist, and harming frost (cold) away from his crops his father would blow some powders which they called "Hallelujah (*Aleluía*)" into the air.[24]

To many Spanish Christians, a more potent form of religious mixture was the apparent tendency of the Indians to celebrate traditional rites and festivals in conjunction with Catholic worship and feast days. Approaches to the sacred that were supposed to be in opposition were often performed if not at the same time then at least on the same days. For instance, Ysabel Chumbi of Ihuari, Chancay, revealed in 1665 that directly after hearing mass in the church the people of her village would enter a nearby corral to make complicated divinations for the well-being of the community with the spiders that they had brought with them (presumably to mass as well) in their *llicllas* (shawls).[25] One learns no more in many such cases, and can only wonder at the possible relationship between these two Sunday ritual participations. Perhaps the answer is simple: the sabbath had become a special day for the Indians' observances according to transforming religious traditions that were becoming less and less separated in people's minds.

The evidence is clearer concerning the coexistence of festivals. Throughout the Archdiocese of Lima, key points in the crowded Catholic calendar came at or near the traditional celebrations of the Andean religious and agricultural cycle. Eventually, as had happened during the first centuries of the Church's expansion in Europe, many of these festivities came to coincide.[26] In 1657 in Acas, Cajatambo, for example, it emerged that through their ministers the huacas seem to have granted formal permission to the villagers to attend the Catholic feast of Saint Peter, whose own standard appears to have been integrated into traditional religious activities. Practices that Visitador Novoa judged as the height of irreverence and profanity in the presence of a Holy Image seem to have been a manifestation of the fact that San Pedro's religious patronage of the village had been truly accepted by the Indians, who were integrating their interpretation of the saint into local religious life. Yet Novoa, like many of his extirpating colleagues, saw such inroads of religious change only as blasphemous religious error.[27] Visitador Pedro de Cárdenas y Arbieto, after an idolatry investigation in San Blas, Tarama, in 1668–1669, might have written for many extirpators when he expressed his conviction that priestly vigilance would have to be greatly increased on Catholic feast days. In this case, Cárdenas had discovered that a huaca-spring was annually worshiped with the

---

[24] AAL Leg. 6, exp. 14, fols. 3v and 4.

[25] AAL Leg. 5, exp. 12, fol. 2.

[26] Following Peña, a useful list is compiled in G. Kubler, "The Quechua," p. 406.

[27] See further discussion in my *An Evil Lost to View?*, ch. 4. Irene Silverblatt's interpretation of this same event is similar to that of Novoa (in this case) and other extirpators, finding that "the saints were profaned by Andean ritual"; "El surgimiento de la Indianidad," esp. p. 475. See also the similar but slightly revised formulations in her "Becoming Indian," esp. p. 288.

sacrifice of a llama and great jubilation, all in conjunction with the day of the patron, San Blas. The surveillance of a careful priest, Cárdenas wrote, was the only way to restrain the Indians from their "natural inclination" on saints' days, a tendency which he summarized as their desire "to refresh their memories of ancient times." Similar discoveries occurred throughout the period. In 1660 in Pilas, Yauyos, the peak Cataacaca was propitiated on the feast of San Juan and at Christmas. In both 1723 and 1730 in the parish of Carampoma, Huarochirí, Andean rites seem to have been held in conjunction with the festivals of Santiago and San Bartolomé.[28]

Yet as evocative as the numerous examples of festival coexistence are, there are other less well-known and equally interesting indications of Andean religious change. The practices of the specialists are particularly indicative and important in this respect. Once one surmounts the extirpators' almost constant disparagement of these individuals, they emerge as vital functionaries in mid-colonial Andean religious life. Their contact with the many people whom they served over wide regions was frequent and intimate, making them potentially the most influential facilitators of religious transformation in the Indian parishes. A half century ago, George Kubler hinted that this might be the case. The rites of colonial Andean practitioners, he pointed out, frequently employed "Christian formulas." But without the evidence to move further, he qualified his prescient speculations on the religious nature—Quechua / Christian—of these practitioners, and placed them finally on a nonreligious periphery. "The sorcerers played a role in the formation of Quechua Catholicism, while bringing support to Quechua idolatry. In essence, however, their crafts were contrary to religion whether Quechua or Christian, in that their magic was illicit, infrasocial, and proliferant without relation to doctrine."[29] More recently others, in particular Luis Millones, have also pointed out the vitality and persistence of these specialists, their rituals, and invocations in Andean religious life.

The Andean specialists' reputations rested largely upon their perceived abilities to represent people's needs and concerns before the supernatural forces that influenced the world. Their realm of ritual and mystery was not removed from that of religion. Healers provide a particularly illustrative example in this respect. Like ministers to the gods (which they often were as well), healers frequently integrated the propitiation and consultation of Andean numina in vital human affairs and in matters of life and death. Thus the gradual inclusion of Christian symbols and rites into what healers did among their people was no trivial accretion.

The entrance of Catholic concepts and prayers into Andean rituals and techniques begs a brief comparison with some well-known cases of popular healing

[28] AAL Leg. 4, exp. 37, fols. 17–17v; see also fols. 4v and 5; AAL Leg. 1, exp. 2, fol. 6v; AAL Leg. 3, exp. 9, 1723, fols. 6, 7, and 9, and AAL Leg. 3, exp. 15, 1730, fols. 12 and 12v.
[29] See "The Quechua," p. 398.

traditions in contemporary Europe, many of which made unorthodox or "syncretic" use of Christian ideas and rites. A common scholarly tendency when faced with such matters, has been to follow the opinions of early modern theologians. Most churchmen considered the supposedly garbled rites of local "magicians" and "healers" as the decentralized and insidious rivals of the orthodox solutions to such things as illness and calamity which were offered by the clergy and European men of medicine.[30] In Andean Peru, as in parts of Europe, a creativity in healing rituals was deemed superstitious and thus frowned upon as a corrupting influence in a given community or region. Since then, the healers' rites have risked being tossed, along with the practices of so-called sorcerers, into a degenerated jumble. In the mid-colonial Andean context, healers and their various repertoires bear closer examination. The superstitious or vaguely syncretic explanations attached to their use of Christian elements in native practices can distort too easily our view of the persistence and centrality of what were changing, but still Andean, traditions.

Examined from another angle, Christian inclusions into healers' beliefs and practices signified that from the perspectives of these practitioners—immensely influential points of view in the local and regional contexts—the sources from which sacred power could be drawn were expanding. The practices of six healers from four different regions of the archdiocese illustrate this expansion. Although the idolatry trial evidence does not always allow one to map the transformation of each healer's techniques and self-perception over time, the different pieces of information often inform each other. Moreover, because the six span well over sixty years (1661–1723), they are suggestive of a general nature of change.

Native Andeans were not, of course, the only ones experiencing change in these years. It becomes evident that over time it grew increasingly difficult for extirpators to punish healers whose practices fell more and more within the ambit of fervent—albeit popular—Christian piety. This hesitancy would usually be said to have reflected both a softening of the Church's attitude after the Villagómez years and the increasing penetration of Christian ideas and rites into the Andean religious picture, but the evidence does not support so clear a shift. There was no tidy transition between a mentality that would condemn Indian healers as superstitious idolaters out of hand, and one that would look beyond their traditional Andean connotations and ridiculed theories of causation at their virtues and increasingly Christian character. The religious mixture personified by the healers continued to provoke heated controversy in the course of the eighteenth-century trials I discuss, further evidence against viewing the 1660s as a mental or historical watershed.

Fernando de Avendaño, in a sermon for Indians on the subject of charity,

---

[30] M. R. O'Neil, "Magical Healing," pp. 89–91. Such denigration was widespread in European relations with Amerindian peoples. In northeastern North America, for instance, the Jesuits freqently referred to Iroquios shamans as "jugglers." See discussions in J. Axtell, *The Invasion Within*, esp. pp. 99–104, and M. Dennis, *Cultivating a Landscape of Peace*, p. 92.

alms, and love, could be said to have captured the Catholic position on the matter of Andean healers in the mid-colonial era: "He who knows how to heal without superstition [should] heal the poor and sick by the love of God and thus shall he be well compensated in Heaven."[31] Yet Avendaño's point might as well have been made in a vacuum. In practice, few Andean healers, some of whom were remarkably "Christian" in both word and deed, could ever manage to appear untainted by the wide assortment of things that many mid-colonial churchmen were calling superstition or idolatry. Thus in the persons of these Christianized Indian healers the Church Militant in Peru frequently faced the increasingly commmon but nevertheless distressing task of confronting the repercussions of its own presence. The extirpators' time-worn escapes from such dilemmas often lay in conventional interpretations of the offending aspects of the specialists' arts. For example, the healer's practices could be viewed as filled with error or diabolically inspired. Popular Christian elements in his or her technique could be passed off as heretical and thus offensive to God. Although some extirpators would come to question such ready explanations as the zealous flotsam of another age, such views were not completely abandoned in this era.

In the first case from 1661, an investigation found that Magdalena Callao (alias Condoriana) of Lunahuana in Cañete cured people using *sanco* (the nourishment of the gods) and a mixture of compresses and massage. On one particular occasion Callao claimed that she had healed a cripple named María Magdalena by employing crushed white maize, coca, llama fat, and warm wine in a curative rub. The wine was the only material addition to what seemed otherwise an account of a number of native Andean healing procedures. Yet when Magdalena was asked if she incanted any words to assist her results, the addition is more substantial. She replied that "she rubbed in the name of Our Father and Our Lady."[32]

Almost thirty years later in Mito, Jauja, Pedro Guaman was described as a "doctor" who traveled over a large region, like other regional specialists. He carried a bundle called *quipe*, within which were coca leaves and a seed called *vilca tauri* which he used for his cures. Yet, in spite of these and other traditional implements, he was said to have sought to bring about a cure for the regional kuraka by "asking it of God."[33] The case of Pedro Vilca Guaman, a specialist accused of being a "witch" from Huarochirí in 1700, is even more striking. Here was a specialist who removed harmful curse objects (*hechizos*) from the thatched ceilings of sick people's homes who, at the same time, adamantly defended himself as a Christian wonder-worker before his prime accuser. He was neither a witch nor a murderer, he pleaded; it was simply that "God had shown him favor (*gracia*) and given him the power to resuscitate

---

[31] *Sermones*, book 2, sermon 28, fol. 70.
[32] AAL Leg. 7, exp. 1, fols. 24v–25 and 26–26v.
[33] AAL Leg. 1, exp. 9, 1690, fols. 20v–21 and 9–9v.

those who were dying." One can speculate about the origin of his self-image. Pedro's language—speaking of receiving God's grace and reviving those who seemed lost to this world—is strikingly reminiscent of the way in which contemporary preachers portrayed the miracles of Christ, the apostles, and the saints as examples whom the Indians should strive to emulate.[34]

In spite of the pious strivings and the obvious Christian elements in the practices and identities of these three healers, some of their other pursuits, and certainly their accoutrements, were certainly Andean—which is to say idolatrous in the view of the extirpators. Moreover, the religious atmosphere in seventeenth-century Lima was not yet so lenient as officially to consider indigenous curing practices legitimate among Christians. Folk healing practices were thought suspicious in contemporary Spain as well. Fray Pedro Ciruelo, an inquisitor from Saragosa in the early sixteenth century, for example, demonstrated how worried clerical authorities were that Spanish specialists used curses and garbled versions of Christian prayers in healing the sick. Ciruelo observed in his well-known treatise, the *Reprovación de las supersticiones y hechicerías* (c. 1530), that although it was a mortal sin for a curer to pray while healing, a patient might pray to relieve pain while being healed. But, as Fernando Iwasaki Cauti has shown brilliantly in his study of attitudes to healing in seventeenth-century Lima, Spanish views on such matters were complicated and ambivalent; they might easily be applied inconsistently, particularly, one might add, in the context of the Extirpation's operations against disparaged specialists in the Indian parishes of Peru. In this respect, the Church's concern with Andean idolatry was causing it to lag behind a generally more curious scientific regard for indigenous medical knowledge in the colonial era.[35] Extirpators gave little ground at first, despite some classificatory difficulties. If Indian healers, as devalued specialists, were not conceived as interconnected with the keepers of the Andean gods—the formal idolaters—then they were to be included within the ranks of those specialists, the hechiceros and brujos, who thronged beneath the lesser banner of superstition. The healers' frequent use of Christian words and rituals, and even their protestations and corroborated acts of Christian charity, could often be added to their list of offenses against God.

Yet a degree of change in these interpretative patterns can be gradually discerned in the examples from the early eighteenth century. Rather in the way that the Devil began to lose some of his explanatory potency in the Andes at

---

[34] AAL Leg. 1, exp. 13, fol. 14. See, for example, F. de Avendaño, *Sermones*, book 1, sermon 1, fols. 7v–8; sermon 2, fol. 18v; and sermon 5, fol. 62.

[35] P. Ciruelo is cited and discussed in F. Iwasaki Cauti, "Fray Martín de Porras," esp. pp. 166–67. As Iwasaki shows, Martín de Porras, who would later be canonized, said prayers, "invoking God and the Virgin Mary," while he healed, thus breaking the rules upheld in other cases by Lima's inquisitors. For evidence of early interest in indigenous knowledge and practice, see I. A. Leonard's survey of a range of sixteenth-century studies of the subject in *Books of the Brave*, pp. 188–89 and 201.

about the same time, Andean healing began slowly to shed its evil image. Indian healers showed signs of being too Christian (which might also mean detached from what was conceived to be Andean religion) for this to be denied any more; officials in the ecclesiastical court involved in extirpation, in particular, clearly began increasingly to feel scruples about taking the standard repressive action against such people.

In 1701, the procurador general Melchor de Carvajal defended a healer from Huarochirí named Jerónimo Poma Yauri against various charges of idolatry by portraying him as a "good Christian" of over twenty years' standing. Jerónimo reportedly obeyed the dictates of the church, heard mass, attended doctrina regularly, and what was more went about "his work" in peace. Carvajal did not attempt to deny that, for a Christian, his party made unorthodox medical prognoses; he did not dispute the fact that Jerónimo cured one woman by rubbing her entire body with a cuy. The defender passed over the controversial details quickly, both to diminish their importance and because he, for one, appears to have rejected any interpretation that might portray them as evil. Forty years earlier, in the time of Villagómez, a defender of an Indian accused of idolatry or superstition would not have dared such a legitimating line; it was common for defenders to admit how deceived and ignorant their parties were before moving on to defensive strategies. In 1700 too, the case of the healer from Huarochirí had proceeded rather too quickly in the opinion of another man, the promotor fiscal, whose conservative arguments won the day on this occasion. Yet even though Jerónimo Poma Yauri still languished in the jail of the ecclesiastical tribunal in Lima as the documentation of this case terminated on 14 April 1701, his complete lack of malice and the obvious extent of his Christianity had exposed a telling difference of opinion and demonstrated new concerns.[36]

A long trial in 1710 involved a healer named Juan Básquez, a native of Cajamarca who had come to work as a button maker on the Calle de Malambo in Lima. Once again it is this person's combination of Christian piety and native Andean healing practices—in his case, including divinatory prognoses taken from saliva in the palm of his hand, rubbings with cuyes, blood offerings, and the preparation of medicinal beverages—that allow him to be presented as something of a prototype.

Juan Básquez refused to accept any payment for his curing services, saying that his knowledge was a gift from God. In a statement he would later be forced to retract, Juan confessed even more about the perceived source of his powers. He told of a vision in a dream which he had experienced as a child in Cajamarca: an old man with a cross whom he identified as Saint John had appeared to him and indicated the virtues of a host of flowers and plants. The next day, while playing with his friends, the youth had noticed four black marks in the sign of a cross on his arm, which had caused him to remember his dream

---

[36] AAL Leg. 4, exp. 49, Huarochirí, 1700–1701, fols. 38–38v, 40, and 40v.

and, eventually, to try out his vocation. Later in his life, when he was already in Lima, he had a second vision, this time of a child angel who directed him to a particular *yerba* (medicinal plant).[37]

Many of the people Juan healed after he had settled in Lima—a few of whom were Spanish priests—were interrogated, and duly emphasized his use of Christian prayers, creeds, and acts of contrition in his curing sessions. Juan's successes were many; in fact, he had become famous. Those actions which seemed most remarkable, such as his healing of cripples, greatly enhanced his reputation in the streets of Lima. In keeping with his piety, Básquez even confessed of his powers out of fear that he had sinned. But after some initial reservations, his Franciscan confessor had come to encourage the healing practices as pious and beneficial.[38] Evidently, in the opinion of his confessor and a number of other Spanish Christians who benefited from his knowledge and powers, Juan was healing "by the love of God," as Avendaño had advised.

One priest, however, a certain Don Bartolomé de Alberca, whose eyesight the healer had failed to assist, led a faction of witnesses who were skeptical of Juan Básquez's legitimacy and were bent on his ruin. As if undecided as to the best manner of defaming him before the ecclesiastical tribunal, the group portrayed him alternatively as a superstitious charlatan and as one who employed an army of demons (eighteen to be exact) and secret knowledge of the huacas in his healing sessions.[39] The proceedings that ensued from these lively beginnings are suggestive in a number of respects, not least in the challenge which Juan Básquez, a veritable embodiment of mixed religiosity, represented to different Spanish investigators at the end of the first decade of the eighteenth century.

The case against Básquez became labored even if it finished with a flourish. The promotor fiscal, Juan Martín de Castro, began his statement by adopting an argumentative line familiar in extirpating circles. The prosecutor held, among other things, that Juan Básquez exhibited "credulity" and "damnable superstition" in believing in the dream he had experienced in Cajamarca to be some sort of guidance; the *imágenes* or *fantasmas* which he thought had instructed him in visions, Martín de Castro posited, were caused by "the illusions of demons." In other words, he wrote out a stock representation linking familiar theories about diabolically inspired dreams and Indian credulity. Martín de Castro concluded by adding that he found the healer's use of prayers in his healing sessions (*curaciones*) unacceptable, "idolatrous by the abuse of such divine invocations." Again, ones notes what was by this point a standard line on how simple folk might pervert Catholicism.

Still, the fiscal relented slightly on the most serious charge of all. He admitted he was unable to state categorically that Juan had called upon the Devil to

---

[37] AAL Leg. 3, exp. 6; see especially Don Juan Chacon at fols. 10v–11. AAL Leg. 3, exp. 10, fols. 24v–25v, 26v.

[38] AAL Leg. 3, exp. 6, fols. 27–27v.

[39] Ibid., see esp. Alberca at fols. 14–16 and Joseph Fernández at fols. 16–17v.

aid his healing or divinatory practices. The official cautiously mined the conventional wisdom on what constituted heresy and a compact with the Devil. As he understood it, such an act of "heresy depends upon the inner consent (*consentimiento interior*) of the agent (*operante*)." The prosecutor's repeated examinations of the Andean healer had revealed nothing of the kind. On the contrary, Castro had found that, apart from a few small errors in doctrine, Juan Básquez was "steadfast in the faith."[40]

The fiscal called for the assistance of men more expert than himself in such difficult matters. He passed the witnesses' testimonies and confessions on to two Dominican friars in the city, Fray Pedro de la Peña and Fray Martín Calderón, for their learned perusal. After reviewing the proceedings, their verdict, unlike Martín de Castro's own, was unequivocal. The Dominicans found Juan Básquez's actions "suspicious of *vehementi infide*, which is to say, of heresy and of an explicit pact with the Devil." Beyond that, the aspect which was most offensive, in their opinion, was "the mixture of sacred prayers and vain observance," in other words, the confounding of true religion and superstition.[41]

Seemingly undeterred by the friars' intervention, Melchor de Carvajal gamely set about the healer's defense. Among many other things, he emphasized that Juan Básquez had been persuaded to recant his stories about the guiding visions and the stigmata on his arm. Thus amended to orthodoxy, Carvajal continued, Juan now stated that his powers came by "a special grace from God Our Father." The defender then reminded the judge that this Indian healer's examination of saliva and pulses "to know illnesses" was not such a suspicious "novelty" when one considered that European physicians who "acquired their knowledge by letters" also recognized sickness through bodily fluids. Moreover, the defense vindicated herbal knowledge in an equally rational way, providing examples of many other peoples in the world who had discovered the medicinal values of certain plants that were strange to Europeans. Most importantly, the procurador defended Juan Básquez against the two friars' strong presumptions by emphasizing the inherent charity in Juan's actions, his sense of guilt, and his exemplary dedication to confession before and after his acts of healing.[42]

Martín de Castro greeted the advocate's onslaught shrewdly—with caution and, despite his misgivings, without total dismissal. In demonstration of his new interpretative dilemma, he was done with friars and now turned to science. He ordered the consultation of another set of professionals, this time calling in three professors of medicine from the University of San Marcos. After a period of study and presumably some fieldwork, Doctor Francisco Bermejo y Rodan and his assistants pronounced that the herbs which were named in this investigation did possess natural virtues that the Indians' ancestors might well have mastered. Yet, apart from that one statement, the professors remained pru-

---

[40] Ibid., see his entire *auto* at fols. 40–42.
[41] Ibid., fol. 43.
[42] Ibid., fols. 44–46.

dently academic. They refrained from offering any opinions on what the prisoner did with the herbs. That, in Bermejo y Rodan's words, was "a point of religion."[43]

The interrogation of an expanded field of witnesses that followed, now employing sets of questions prepared by both Castro and Carvajal, did little to clarify the multiple shades of doubt and worry in the upper reaches of the early eighteenth-century Limeño Church. The see was then vacant, in anticipation of the arrival in 1714 of the archbishop-elect, Antonio de Soloaga. Otherwise, this lengthy trial might well have drawn an archbishop's judgment to bring it to a conclusion. Even the glowing testimony of Don Pedro Capcha, the kuraka of Guacho in the parish of Churín, Cajatambo, where Juan had worked as a shepherd for a short time on his way from Cajamarca to Lima, failed to swing the decision completely in the healer's favor. Básquez had reportedly been a solid Christian in the village, joining the confraternity and even buying a bell for the local church at his own expense. Juan Básquez was judged guilty of healing with a combination of "sacred words, prayers, observations of God . . . [and] superstition." He was ordered to spend two years under the care and instruction of the friars of the Bethlehemite order, to cease his healing practices forever, and to avoid all discussion of herbs and the curing arts.[44]

By 1723, a similar investigation of a healer from the province of Huarochirí would see a markedly different ending. Juan Mango of San Juan de Yris in the parish of Casta was apprehended by the priest of Carampoma and sent to Lima to be interrogated along with a number of others. Before Don Pedro de la Peña, the presiding provisor, Mango proclaimed himself "a Christian by the grace of God," a statement that the concerned priest of Casta, Nicolás Flores de Molina, affirmed in a letter penned on his parishioner's behalf. Juan Mango admitted to healing in the ways of "the ancient Indians," with among other things herbs and ointments from medicinal plants, but he assured the provisor that it was also his custom to employ the Lord's Prayer and the Ave Maria, and to call for the help of the souls of the dead. In the end, this healer was released into the care of his priest not only on the recommendation of the defence, the same battle-weary advocate Melchor de Carvajal, but on the opinion of another prosecutor, Matheo Salazar y de la Serna.[45]

The measure of Christian elements within the healers' mixed repertoires was, if anything, increasing over time, as was the intensity of their self-description as Christians. However, such a measurement is largely an historian's problem; the issue of how Christian they were would have come as a surprise to some specialists, been treated indifferently by a few, even as it might have delighted still others. If one believes what the Indians said at their trials and, if one takes their ritual actions as a reflection of their religious feelings, a halting process of what might be called self-Christianization was on the rise and

---

[43] Ibid., fol. 48.
[44] Ibid., fols. 71–71v and Don Gregorio de Loaysa at fols. 80–80v.
[45] AAL Leg. 3, exp. 9, fols. 32v, 42–43v., and 65–65v.

largely, it seems, despite the Extirpation. By the eighteenth century, the kinds of "advances" of the faith that appear in the healers' cases were mirrored in many other spheres of Andean religious life.

The healers' Christianities forced at least a few extripating churchmen to take more than a glance at some of the realities of evangelization, realities that were all too easily denied at other times. Yet, the mid-colonial Spanish capacity to appreciate and build upon the Andean religiosity emerging from within ranged from minimal to nonexistent. Neither in the post-Villagómez period nor in the eighteenth century do matters appear to have changed significantly; an Andean specialist or huaca minister might get off more lightly, but not necessarily, and not without still being treated as a religious offender.

One can recall the niche or "chapel" in the home of Juan de Rojas in Carampoma, Huarochirí, in 1723 for a nearly-perfect illustration. In this case, although the investigator zealously concentrated upon the chanca and conopa allegiances that clearly survived, and on the gatherings of worshipers that he had uncovered, much else was overlooked or interpreted in the narrowest of fashions. It was determined, almost parenthetically, that Juan de Rojas knew his prayers and doctrina well, and that he confessed and took communion at regular intervals. Yet these protestations of faith, recollections of the mysteries, and even his protection of the confraternity's cattle, were seen as flawed because of his apparently mixed loyalties, because of his concomitant attachment to what seemed to be distressingly ambiguous religious solutions. Scrutiny of Juan's home turned up no fewer than six Christian images, three of which were of the Christ and one of Saint Mark. Yet the prosecutor emphasized the startling (to him) coexistence of stone Andean gods with Christian holy images. He pointed out the subterfuge and irreverence which he perceived in the Indian's personal chapel and in the people's regular gatherings in the home; moreover, he was not one to resist the opportunity to include a weighty allusion or two. The idolatrous niche was concealed, he wrote, "behind a stone." Even worse, the niche was blasphemously "at the foot of a Holy Crucifix."[46]

Native Andeans were determined to incorporate a little of themselves—which inevitably meant a little of their religious culture and traditions—into any acceptance of Christianity into their spiritual lives. When Domingo García of Arahuay in Canta was imprisoned by an extirpator in the early 1740s, one of the charges against him was that he planned to smear llama's blood on the foundations and adobe walls of a new local church "to make it strong." The provisor in Lima asked him how a "Christian" could do such a thing; Domingo answered that it was standard procedure in constructing a church. He even noted that his forefathers had done the same when building the church at Pampacocha. Under pressure from his interrogator, Domingo eventually attempted to back down a little, claiming that this practice was only "a tradition he had acquired from his ancestors." Anyway, he assured his judge, when he had purchased a

[46] Ibid., fols. 10v–11, 23, and 34.

second llama for the purpose, he had been careful to offer its sacrificial blood only to the church floor. This kind of example contributes more than a post-script to an improving comprehension of the effects of widespread church-building and the process of the Indians' reduction into villages and towns.[47]

The entry of Andean peoples into a deepening relationship with Christianity began with the baptisms and teachings of the first missionaries in the sixteenth century. It continued in the day-to-day relations between priests and their Andean parishioners, relations that were outside the purview of most idolatry inspectors of the seventeenth and early eighteenth centuries.[48] The nature of this relationship was different in the Andes from, for example, parts of central Mexico. The numbers of friars in New Spain were greater from the beginning and many of their attitudes toward the evangelization of Indians had been formed in earlier, more optimistic times.[49] Moreover, in central Mexico such difficulties as decades of civil war and immense geographical constraints, which were immediately present in the Andes, raised fewer obstacles to missionary endeavor. Finally, the Christianization of Andeans was clearly not limited solely by self-imposed restraints, by an invincibility of Indian religious tradition, or a presumed recalcitrance. Andeans were active agents in the challenges that beset their lives, but the particular face of the Christianity that was epitomized by the idolatry visitas also contributed to ongoing religious outcomes. The official Church in Lima failed to recognize the religious needs of the Andean new converts in the mid-colonial era. Indians, even more than peasants in Europe, were expected to resign themselves to being second-class Catholics, barred from all but the simplest mysteries and sacraments. Moreover, at the very time when unorthodox but nonetheless nascent forms of Andean Christianity were, in effect, staring them in the face, the most powerful churchmen in the Lima region espied idolatry and superstition and responded with more visitas de idolatría. To some native Andeans—especially influential figures such as the healers and other specialists—it may have seemed nothing less than betrayal: Guaman Poma's critique and ringing charge of hypocrisy against so many Spanish Christians did not have to be heard by native Andeans to be widely endorsed.[50]

There were countless public religious occasions when Indian actions so devi-

---

[47] AAL Leg. 3, exp. 17, 1741–1742, fols. 2–2v, 6v, and 7. For an interpretation of sixteenth-century efforts, see V. Fraser, *The Architecture of Conquest*. With very different emphases, see also A. M. Wightman, *Indigenous Migration*.

[48] For preliminary studies of priests and parishoners, though with a much later focus, see C. Hunefeldt, "Comunidad, curas y comuneros," and D. Cahill, "Curas and Social Conflict." For a particularly rich treatment of these relations in late colonial Mexico, see W. B. Taylor, *Magistrates of the Sacred*.

[49] See esp. R. Ricard, *The Spiritual Conquest of Mexico*; J. L. Phelan, *The Millennial Kingdom*; E. Sylvest, *Motifs of Franciscan Mission Theory*; and L. Gómez Canedo, *Evangelización y conquista*.

[50] See R. Adorno, *Guaman Poma*, esp. pp. 140–143.

ated from Catholic norms as to demand official reprisals by visitadores.[51] Indians would not be trusted, especially with control over the observances of the Catholic faith. Like native peoples in other parts of colonial Spanish America, Andeans were assumed to need constant guidance and, in mid-colonial times, forceful instruction. Such an attitude blended pessimism and disillusionment with impatience. And it would spawn a number of ramifications for the colonial future, not least of which was the decision not to ordain Indians as priests, which was reversed only in the late eighteenth century. Close scrutiny of the indigenous parishioners consistently disappointed the investigators. The Indians' understanding of what was deemed morally and religiously acceptable appeared to be fundamentally flawed. Their natural behavior seemed too inclined toward irreverence and vice for them to merit the Church's most blessed confidences. What was the point of reform? Fernando de Avendaño seems to have reasoned as much in a sermon in which he explained to his rural congregations why only those properly "prepared" could receive Holy Communion. Avendaño concluded that he found it impossible to gain enough confidence in the judgment of most Indians to include them in such sacred mysteries. To trust them and attempt their inclusion, he preached to the very people he demeaned, "would be to cast gold and precious stones into a hill of dung."[52] The impact of such messages, which were wedded to the central actions of extirpation, become the subject of the next chapter.

This chapter's focus on healers and the arguments of the fiscales, defensores, and procuradores involved in their trials through the mid-colonial period capture something of the Church's evolving perspectives in its struggle with colonial Andean religion and grudging confrontation with the limits of evangelization. The methodical campaigns against idolatry may have slowed and altered in certain ways after Villagómez's death but extirpation did not end, either in theory or in practice. The relatively tolerant outlook toward enduring Andean beliefs and practices taken by a procurador such as Melchor de Carvajal was neither perfectly nor widely shared by the middle of the eighteenth century. The day when an Indian who fulfilled his Christian obligations, who was a church benefactor, and who belonged to the local religious association could be openly defended as the very same person who condoned, and even observed, mixed religious practices was some time off.

When faced with this very challenge in the person of an Indian principal named Don Pablo Guaman Charic in 1657, the advocate Domingo Mautino maintained the following. He argued that if one of the Indians whom he was defending had acquiesced in an act of idolatry it could only have been in drunkenness, or when some other impediment had deprived the said person of his or

---

[51] See the case evidence in my "Bad Christians," and also the voluminous trial at BNP, B612: "Testimonio del expediente sobre la denuncia de incesto, idolatría y otros excesos cometidos por el cacique de Santiago de Aija, Don Diego Yaruparia," 1672; the case of Don Francisco Gamarra from Ihuari, Checras, at AAL Leg. 1, exp. 5, 1668; and that of Don Francisco Llaxa Luana from Lunahuana, Cañete, from 1661, AAL Leg. 7, exp. 1.

[52] *Sermones*, book 2, sermon 14, fol. 13.

her judgement and *"entera capacidad."*[53] That was about the best defence that could be raised in 1657, but it might well have been proferred by a defender even fifty years later. For the changes in clerical attitudes, like the changes in colonial Andean religion, were anything but abrupt. If suspect Andean religiosity was no longer deemed to be formal idolatry, it was superstition. Both had flexible definitions that were deep reflections of the religious confrontation in the extirpating era, and deep reflections of mid-colonial Spanish Christian attitudes toward Amerindians and their transforming religious constructs. Both terms were like blankets, implying an indisposition or a weakness suffered by a lesser people, and they encouraged little exploration of what might be emerging underneath.

[53] AAL Leg. 2, exp. 12b, San Juan de Machaca (parish of Acas), Cajatambo, fols. 26–26v and Novoa's sentence at fol. 34. See also P. Duviols, ed. *Cultura andina*, pp. 265–290.

Extirpation

THE ELABORATE edifice of justification that Archbishop Villagómez and others had built upon the reforming elements in the idolatry investigations was clearly meant to disarm concern and criticism. Yet the programs of instruction were consistently overshadowed by coercive actions. The visitadores' punitive and destructive operations during the course of their idolatry investigations, usually known as *diligencias*, were central to the intended reform of the parishes of the mid-colonial Archdiocese of Lima. By means of such actions, religious offenders could be isolated by the Spanish Christian authorities in order to be disciplined and ridiculed before their own people, and the so-called instruments of idolatry—the false gods, the ancestors' remains, and the sacrificial materials—could be physically destroyed. In fact, nothing was thought to be more instructive for the Indians, or more symbolic of their spiritual fate, than the religious spectacles that featured the destruction of their forbidden cults. Accordingly, almost all idolatry trials featured diligencias of some description.

Often, these operations were the culmination of a visita's stay in a parish, occurring after the judicial proceedings. A whole range of public acts of punishment (usually floggings of persons who had been shorn, tied, and stripped), penance, and "processions of shame" (in which the guilty were often dressed in the conspicuous pointed headgear known as *corozas*, made to carry crosses in their hands, and attended by criers to broadcast the religious crimes) were administered to those with the heaviest sentences.[1] Some of those deemed most dangerous and least likely to reform their ways—the so-called sorcerers (*hechiceros*) and witches (*brujos*), the ministers of Andean gods, and the religious specialists—would be publicly banished to the Casa de Santa Cruz in Lima or to the care of some convent, in an effort to ostracise both their persons and their reputations from the places where they held spiritual sway. And there were *autos de fe* at which any object both idolatrous and transportable would be burned before the people who had been assembled in the local plazas.

The fact that memories of these destructive acts lingered so long is the greatest testament to their brutal effect. Scholars have noted the power of similar recollections among indigenous peoples in New Spain.[2] Andean declarants be-

---

[1] The public nature of the punishment of Andean rebels and religious offenders had roots not only in Europe but in symbolic castigations in sixteenth-century Peru. For a discussion of the execution of the last Inka rebel Tupac Amaru in 1572, and on the processions of shame used by Cristóbal de Albornoz in his suppression of the Taki Onqoy, see S. MacCormack, *Religion in the Andes*, pp. 249–254.

[2] S. Gruzinski, "Le filet déchiré: sociétés indigènes, occidentalisation et domination dans le Mexique central, XVIe-XVIIIe siècles" (thèse de doctorat, Paris, 1986), pp. 254 and 289, cited and

fore visitadores in the 1660s frequently recalled in vivid detail the deeds of extirpators almost half a century before; the visits seem to have become negative reference points in the people's recollection of the past, remembered in much the same way as particularly bad droughts or the outbreaks of a killing disease.[3]

Through public punishment, demolition of religious objects and places, and the attempted appropriation of immovable Andean huacas to Catholic purposes, the process of instruction through destruction and humiliation continued. Indeed, theatrical coercion became something of a constant even when an extirpating prelate such as Villagómez was no longer supporting a centralized initiative. There was, for instance, little difference between the methods of the idolatry inspector Felipe de Medina in Cajatambo in 1652 and those of Toribio de Mendizábal in Huarochirí in 1723, or of Pedro de Celis in Chancay in 1724. Medina dealt harshly with "an obstinate backslider and formal idolater," Don Jerónimo Julca, who was found to have concealed entire families of sacred malquis from earlier visitas. Julca was exiled to Lima and his home was burned to the ground, "so that the others might see who had been a hechicero."[4] In eighteenth-century Carampoma (Huarochirí), Mendizábal confronted the backsliding indigenous minister Juan de Rojas in a similar manner. After all the "idols" had been burned before the villagers' eyes in an *auto de fe*, Rojas's house was then flattened and "a cross was erected in memory."[5] Similarly, in 1724 Pedro de Celis assembled four hundred Indians of all ages in the plaza of San Pedro de Pacho in Chancay to watch an *auto* of cult objects, and in the course of the same investigation Pedro Quiñones, the experienced minister of many Andean gods in neighboring Pachangara, reported that on numerous occasions throughout his life he had been publicly whipped for his relapses into idolatry.[6] An approach toward the eradication of Andean religion, which historians have long associated mostly with the seventeenth-century campaigns of the Extirpation, proves to have been alive and well in the more sporadic initiatives of the eighteenth century.

In spite of all their intended edification and solemnity, the mid-colonial diligencias revealed the most vulnerable point of the Extirpation: the point where

---

supported in F. Cervantes, "Christianity and the Indians," p. 181. A considerably shorter, recent adaptation of Gruzinski's thesis is *The Conquest of Mexico*.

[3] Such examples abound. See, for example, recollections of Francisco de Avila as "he who destroyed and burnt everything," and who directed destructive missions from San Damián, in Quinti, Huarochirí in 1660 (AAL Leg. 2, exp. 21, fol. 8, and Leg. 4 exp. 32, fol. 7); or the memory in Xapallanga, Jauja, in 1665 of punishments meted out by Diego Barreto de Castro; AAL Leg. 5, exp. 11, fol. 1. There is a sad similarity here to the way that contemporary Andean peoples in the Ayacucho region (and in many other areas) identify negative "epochs" in their recent past, so marred by both guerrilla and army violence. I was prompted to this comparison by B. J. Isbell, "The Texts and Contexts of Terror."

[4] AAL Leg. 6, exp. 9, Cajatambo, Cajatambo, 1652, fols. 2–2v.

[5] AAL Leg. 3, exp. 9, fol. 14 ff.

[6] AAL Leg. 3, exp. 10, Santiago de Maray, Checras, 1724–1725; see fol. 12 and fols. 7v–8 and 8v, respectively.

idealism came face to face with reality. The results of the exercises were very different from the hopes that attended them. Common assumptions about the influence of the Devil on Indian beliefs and practices, and preconceptions about Indian immorality and mental inferiority, proved serviceable to visitadores in the course of most idolatry trials. Enemies of the faith and of the advancement of Christianity in the Andean communities could be defined, interpreted on a familiar grid, and castigated accordingly. Theory and theological opinion supplied comfort to faith and fired the ambitions of extirpators whose rewards were often slight payment for the rigors of their labors in remote regions. But the enemies sometimes slipped through the interpretative grid, events did not always proceed as planned, and the effectiveness of punishments and coercive actions was often uncertain. In the performance of their duties, extirpators of idolatry and their notaries, perhaps more than any other first-hand observers and recorders of the mid-colonial realities of the Andean world, were pushed outside the regulated, prejudicially constructed environments of the treatise or of a letter to a superior. In their operations the visitadores confronted ambiguous physical manifestations of a changing Andean religiosity that they imperfectly understood, yet were bound to obliterate. Granted, when their actions were complete, extirpators and their officials might retreat to the familiar domain of the written word. Many, as they defined the Indians' sins and pronounced sentence, were clearly reviewing the sheaves of Indian testimony from within the refuge offered by the established conceptual canon. But the notaries' accounts of the destructive excursions of the visitadores, provide less scripted sources for the examination both of these events and of the information on colonial Andean religion that they contain.

For there were occasions when the discoveries made in the course of extirpating operations or in their aftermath must have made the act of orthodox interpretation distinctly uncomfortable. It is worth recalling at this point how much the Andean world had been affected by over a century of Spanish domination. Disease, warfare, dislocation, the disruption of the people's reciprocal patterns of economic exchange and social order, greater demands for labor and tribute being made from fewer people, occasional abandonment by Hispanicized Indian élites, had all taken their toll on Indian society.[7] The imposition of a parish structure, the lure of a powerful new religion, and the uneven spread of evangelizing efforts had drawn some Indians closer to, and often into, the Christian fold. Their introduction to Christianity had usually come through the teaching and example of mendicant friars and, after about 1570, also of the Jesuits. Even in the Andes, where missionary numbers and enthusiasm were not those of early New Spain, many Indian communities had at least a fleeting

---

[7] On the population decline see N. D. Cook, *Demographic Collapse*, esp. chs. 9, 11, and 12; Andean reciprocity and land use is described by J. V. Murra in *Formaciones económicas y políticas*, esp. ch. 3; and on the Toledan resettlement program see A. Málaga Medina, "Las reducciones en el Perú"; on the complicated roles of Andean kurakas as intermediaries see especially Karen Spalding, "El kuraka en el sistema"; and ch. 2 of S. J. Stern, *Peru's Indian Peoples*.

contact during the sixteenth century with a more heterodox and experimental Christianity than that of later times. Moreover, as the Crown's policy of racial segregation proved impossible to enforce, there was plenty of unofficial Christianization accompanying general cultural exchange. Increased opportunities for contact with Spaniards, Mestizos, and Africans, and with the diverse brands of Christianity they practiced, offered Indians much inadvertent religious direction.[8]

Because of its capacity to absorb and make something of new influences, the Andean religious system was emerging a good deal less impoverished than might have been expected. The transformations of Andean religious ideas and practices, and the indisputable penetrations of Christianity into an evolving Andean religious framework, seem to have owed little to coercive tactics such as those of the Extirpation. Indeed, the institution pitted itself as much against alleged perversions of orthodoxy—what one might call popular Catholicism or emergent Andean Christianity—as against huaca worship and ritual "superstition." What exactly the Indians believed was unknown and dangerous, an inadvertent hybrid with recognizably Christian traits, for which the earlier mendicant orders and Jesuits, and ultimately the Church itself, would find it difficult to deny some responsibility.

The uneasy encounter between the extirpators' orthodox idealism and the realities of the Indians' increasingly complex religious lives is often revealed in the course of a diligencia, particularly the kind of diligencia that sent solemn excursions into the Andean hinterland to destroy and appropriate Andean huacas and other sacred places. For at few points were the agents of the Extirpation more exposed to the limits and realities of both Catholic efficacy and colonial Andean religion than when its agents ventured away from the churches, plazas, and grid-pattern streets of the resettled Indian pueblos in pursuit of their investigations.

The image of the extirpators leaving the familiar order of the resettled villages is an important one. Their excursions possessed a symbolic equivalence to the spate of churchbuilding, resettlement, and town foundation that had gripped Andean Peru about a century before.[9] The towns and cities were designed to do more than make Europeans feel at home. The ambitious urbanization, as well as assisting tribute collection and the organization of Indian

---

[8] On the breakdown of the *república de indios* in different settings see M. Mörner, *Region and State in Latin America's Past*, pp. 19–32. On the transfer of more diverse forms of Spanish Catholicism in the Viceroyalty of New Spain: S. Gruzinski, *The Conquest of Mexico*, esp. pp. 197–200; F. Cervantes, "Christianity and the Indians," and, more expansively, the same author's *The Devil in the New World*, chs. 1 and 2. Even further afield, Richard White's *The Middle Ground*, though concerned principally with the very different context of Indian-French relations in the *pays d'en haut*, is an interesting exploration of exchange and re-creation.

[9] For an interesting contemplation of what the architecture and town foundation meant for Spanish builders, friars, and residents see V. Fraser's *The Architecture of Conquest*. Important connections between urbanization and evangelization were suggested almost fifty years ago by George Kubler in *Mexican Architecture*, 1: 68–104.

laborers, sought to extend a Hispanic brand of civility among the newly converted. The Indians were meant to be drawn in wonder to these designs, to fall
upon their knees in pious awe beneath the arches of the churches they themselves had built for a new god. But the patterned Christian environments in the
Andes, the ordered centers that reach rectilinearly outward from the village
plazas and church façades, began to dissipate at the edges. Likewise, the organization into towns had wrought changes in Andean society which, however
striking in their economic effects, are ultimately poor indicators of religious
transformation. In the Archdiocese of Lima at least, many Indians had been
resettled not far from their ancestors' plots of land, their mythical places of
origin (*pacarinas*), their physical and spiritual homes. The ancient settlements
that the notaries called *pueblos viejos* (old towns), often near to the huacas and
the machayes or cave tombs of the malquis, remained well within reach. As
José María Arguedas has observed, the principal cities and towns established
by the Spaniards in the sixteenth century were located on or very near the
places where Andean populations had been focused in Inkaic and even pre-
Inkaic times.[10] Apart from the migrants and workers who had to leave for long
stints in mines and in other duties, and who thus grew more detached from
land and kin, people inhabited a familiar landscape, the meanings of which
changed with them. Moreover, villages and towns of resettled Indians, established especially by the viceroy Francisco de Toledo after about 1570, had not
always held together perfectly. For example, the idolatry inspector Juan Sarmiento de Vivero wrote from Guañec in the province of Yauyos in 1660, complaining of Indians who had been absent from their resettled communities for
some twenty years, living instead in the ravines and high plateaux of Paria
Caca.[11]

The seventeenth-century extirpators learned much about the persistence of
the religious, social, and economic connections between the people and the
surrounding landscape in the Lima region. Irrespective of how much of this
information would be appreciated by active extirpators, it was clear—even to
the crusading Christian—that in the post-conquest years the Indians' contact
with their rich ancestral mythology and fundamental dimensions of their religious system had been strained but not broken.[12] The aim of the Extirpation's
diligencias was thus to finish a drawn-out task, to sever these roots—in some
cases quite literally. But persuasion continued to coexist with force, both before
and after some churchmen grew disillusioned with the prospect of genuine

[10] *Formación de una cultura*, esp. pp. 148–50.

[11] AAL Leg. 4, exp. 26, fols. 1–1v. Irene Silverblatt emphasizes Indian desertions of the
seventeenth-century reducciones in *Moon, Sun, and Witches*, esp. chs. 9 and 10. And similar
situations are described in colonial Guatemala by W. G. Lovell in *Conquest and Survival*,
pp. 82–89.

[12] In addition to the religious information from idolatry trials see G. Taylor, ed., *Ritos y tradiciones*, and F. Salomon and G. L. Urioste, trs. and eds., *The Huarochirí Manuscript* (hereafter
Huarochirí). I am indebted to William Taylor for encouraging me to reflect on the comparison
elaborated in this paragraph and the next.

Indian conversions. Destructive actions against indigenous shrines and the raising of crosses had gone on since the first *entradas*—the rapid, surprise entries
of the Spanish conquerors into unknown lands. And efforts at peaceful conversion and sustained religious instruction were pursued in the seventeenth and
eighteenth centuries. When visitadores penetrated the more remote reaches
and climbed to the pueblos viejos, a purpose and idealism, that one century
earlier would have prompted a pair of visiting friars to press for a local labor
force to build an adobe church in a newly founded village, had come to require
solemn forays to fell idols, peer in caves, dig up bones, and erect tall crosses.
My point is to emphasize the comparable spirit of early colonial efforts at
Christianization and the both destructive and consecratory diligencias of the
middle colonial period. Like the person who organized the building of a first
church or who rode in a conquering expedition, the seventeenth-century extirpator on diligencia participated in a new beginning, a potential Christian triumph and appropriation in foreign territory. In his mind at least, a visitador's
acts of destruction and re-consecration in the mountains might be cause for a
kind of optimism. Something was being started where nothing but evil and
perhaps dormant potential were thought to exist.

Yet in the diligencia there was often, at the same time, cause for pessimism.
To varying degrees, indigenous gods and Andean religious organization had
survived the attempted spiritual conquest; the need for idolatry investigations
in general—and their destructive actions in particular—was evidence enough.
The seventeenth-century diligencia was a rearguard action, an imperfect, late
advance by churchmen into an unconquered countryside, with the expectation
of a retreat to the safety and order of their urban bases. Although many of
them, as experienced priests, knew the realities of the mid-colonial Andean
parishes as well as any Spaniard in the viceroyalty, the visitadores frequently
showed signs of feeling ill at ease during their destructive operations outside
the towns. They could recognize in the diligencia a desperation, perhaps even
an admission of defeat.

Of all the officials conducting idolatry investigations in the Villagómez period, Visitador Juan Sarmiento de Vivero may have been the most careful to
ensure that an attending notary recorded his devotion to duty and the hard-
ships he was forced to endure. As a fortunate consequence, descriptive accounts of a number of his diligencias have survived, written on the spot while
memories and excitement were fresh.[13] A first example occurred in the high-

---

[13] Sarmiento was fifty-six years old in 1664, the year in which the events to be described below
occurred; his age was about average for an idolatry inspector active in the time of Archbishop
Villagómez. Of noble Spanish stock in Lima (according to papers presented to the Council of the
Indies by his brother Jerónimo, an ancestor had participated in the military conquest of Peru), he
was educated by the Jesuits and ordained in 1637 at the age of twenty-nine. He went on to obtain a
bachelor's degree in canon law from the Royal University of San Marcos in 1653. In addition to
spending a number of years as chaplain to the Convent of the Incarnation in Lima, Sarmiento
accepted from his prelate at least two commissions as *visitador general* (in 1649 to visit the diocese
of Huamanga and in 1655 as inspector of the archdiocese of Lima). He was named *visitador de*

lands northeast of Lima, in the parish of Huamantanga, Canta, in
Sarmiento and a sizeable entourage resolved to visit the old town of
ayllu and a number of other places in the surrounding area. A dec
the regional Indian governor, Don Rodrigo Rupay Chapa, and a der....ciation
by a woman named Ana María had given the visitador reason to believe that his
efforts would be rewarded.[14] On 1 June, Whitsunday (the *Pascua del Espíritu
Santo*), the notary recorded that Sarmiento, mounted on a mule, set out for the
ancient settlement of the Sigual accompanied by an interpreter, the ecclesiastical prosecutor, two local magistrates, and "many other Indians."

The ancient settlement was perched high above Huamantanga, and by three
in the afternoon the mules had passed as far as they might. Guided by the
Indians, the party gained the summit on foot. They came upon some dilap-
idated homes and a small open area formed inside man-made walls of stone,
from the edge of which Huamantanga could be seen far below. Inside this
plazuela was an old and abundant tree that produced colored flowers. The
"roots" of this tree, Sarmiento discovered from the Indians, "were those of the
people." While the visitador ordered the same people to pull up the tree and
destroy its roots, he and the others spent the remaining daylight hours exploring a number of covered enclosures just below the open space, which were
found to contain numerous ancestors' remains.[15] In due course, all were incin-
erated in a public *auto de fe*. Three days later, the visitador returned with a
work party to erect a large wooden cross, nearly three meters in height. In
standard fashion, the place was renamed as that of the Holy Spirit, because
"on that day the idolatry of the pueblo had been revealed." It was not, perhaps,
the appropriate moment to recall that similar idolatrous revelations by previous investigators had checkered this parish's recent past; the notary recorded
only the pious hope that the cross would become a place "where all might
worship."[16]

Another example from the same visita, though featuring different challenges, confirms the general pattern of the operations. In the afternoon, Sar-

---

idolatría in 1660. Sarmiento was atypical in not having served as a priest (*doctrinero*) in an Indian
parish before his participation in the Extirpation. See Archivo General de Indias, Seville, Audiencia
de Lima 303, Villagómez to king, Lima, 28 Aug. 1658, Villagómez to king, Lima, 8 June 1663; *ibid.*,
304, Villagómez to king, Lima, 5 Dec. 1664. Sarmiento de Vivero was Villagómez's busiest idolatry
inspector by far. Of some fifty-four visitas that he conducted in the Lima region, seven (all from the
district of Chancay) are transcribed in *Amancebados, hechiceros, y rebeldes*, edited by A. Sánchez.
Many accounts of other inspectors' *diligencias* come only from the more detached and self-
congratulatory medium of letters and informaciones de servicios written after the fact. As with so
many colonial officials, visitadores often filled these accounts with boasts of their zeal and of the
beneficial results of their services; see, for example, the case of Bernardo de Novoa reported in the
document in AGI Lima 333, printed in *Cultura andina*, edited by P. Duviols, pp. 423–35.

[14] AAL Leg. 1, exp. 3, see the kuraka at fol. 11v, and Ana María at fols. 1–1v and 6–7.

[15] What the people called the flowers on the tree was rendered only in Castilian as "*canto con
las hojas*." AAL Leg. 1, exp. 3, fols. 3v–4.

[16] The *auto* took place on 8 October 1664. The elaborate process is recorded in some detail at
ibid., fols. 17v–19; see also fol. 8.

miento set out with the pueblo's officials, a Mercedarian friar, and some "sixteen Indians armed with spades, sticks, and three large wooden crosses." Before long they came upon a number of bountiful plots of land. Overlooking these was a great pinnacle of rock "in the form of a human head," the features of which the notary felt especially obliged to remark upon. When they were questioned, the Indians explained that this was Vicho Rinri (the notary's rendering), a huaca ancestor who was much celebrated in dances and songs.[17] Three attempts to dislodge the huaca with sticks and levers—the last of which involved a new, thicker lever, an invocation of God, and the addition of the exertions of the visitador—finally sent Vicho Rinri plummeting into the ravine below. Sarmiento ordered that a cross be fashioned out of the largest implement, and that it be erected and shrouded in flowers. The place of Vicho Rinri was then renamed in honor of the Holy Sacrament. The diligencia ended only after the party had worshiped before the cross and the notary had made a record of the day's events.[18]

These are official outlines of what happened, meant to be repetitive—triumphantly repetitive—and carefully prepared in order to record zealous endeavor and to demonstrate a visitador's diligence in acting upon information that the Indians had supplied about Andean religion. The patterned coercive maneuvers against Andean sacred places of course followed long-established Catholic practice in the struggles against pagan shrines. They resembled, for instance, the procedures recommended over one thousand years earlier by a man whom Archbishop Villagómez greatly admired and often quoted in his writings, Pope Gregory the Great.[19] Yet, in spite of the desires of Villagómez and some of his visitadores to assure themselves of a place in the grand sweep of Christian history, the documentation from the Archdiocese of Lima offers considerably more than a formulaic addition to the Church's long struggle against paganism and the corrupting influence of the Devil. There were also moments of unease, times when the things which the extirpator encountered in

---

[17] Ibid., fols. 10–10v. They reportedly sang "*Vicho Rinri papa* [potato], *Vicho Rinri oca* [another edible South American tuber, either *Oxalis O. crenata* or *O. tuberosa*]". "Rinri" means ear and "vicho" or "vichu" could be what the Quechua lexicographer Diego González Holguín calls "Vicçu," meaning "tuerto" in colonial Spanish, or "twisted (either inside out or back to front)" in English. It is possible that the notary who, along with the visitador, had the features of this anthropomorphic god's "head" explained to him, may have taken a description of a distorted feature to be the name of the divinity; or the huaca may simply have had an ear that was twisted. Yet the mention of the song that included the name, along with what one can learn about other huaca names in the region, suggests otherwise. A possible if crude translation of the huaca's name might thus be "Twisted Ear." See D. González Holguín, *Vocabulario*, pp. 318 and 351. I am grateful to Frank Salomon for help in arriving at these suggestions. A number of regional huaca histories (often called *tradiciones* in the documentation from the idolatry trials) about similar beings and places interlace *Huarochirí*.

[18] AAL Leg. 1, exp. 3, fols. 10v–11. On 24 June 1664, a similarly equipped party was led along the royal road toward Canta to yet another great stone embedded in a hill. Since this huaca proved impossible to topple, a cross was erected and the spot was appropriately named after St. John the Baptist: fols. 11–12.

[19] See especially R. A. Markus, "Gregory the Great."

the Andean landscape were intellectually and practically more cumbersome than the survival of purely Andean religious forms.

One can consider, for instance, what occurred just after the sacred tree above Huamantanga was uprooted and replaced with a cross. On this occasion, the denunciator, Ana María, interrupted the pious tenor of the moment to observe that the wall beside which they stood was very near to the recess where she and another witness had seen an accused "sorcerer," Cristóbal Chumbi Guaman (alias Llaguas), performing a suspicious act of worship. Cristóbal, who was also in the extirpator's company, protested that she lied, but Ana María proceeded to describe how she had seen him in that protected place, naked from the waist up, upon his knees, with his arms raised skyward, muttering to himself.[20] Viewing the recess for himself, the visitador discovered an upright piece of wood nearly three meters in height, with a horizontal groove in which a second piece of wood would have rested. The Indian magistrates informed Sarmiento that these were the remains of a cross that had been erected eight years earlier by another visitador de idolatría, Don Pedro de Quijano.[21] In this way, the triumphal and edifying story—the comprehensible, almost surgical act of desecration and reconsecration—are interrupted not so much by persistent Andean religion as by the traces of a more confusing kind of religious error. An extirpator's regional victory for Christianity over "idolatry" is complicated by the undecipherability of mid-colonial Indian practice.

Yet if the discovery of the somewhat sorry traces of a predecessor's efforts at that site troubled the mind of Juan Sarmiento, one does not learn of it in the notary's record. The subsequent find of a quantity of human bones and skulls in the same recess, behind the remnants of the cross, concentrated his attention upon the alleged idolatry (that is, Andean religious practices) of Cristóbal Chumbi Guaman and upon the numerous other zealous tasks at hand.[22] There was no return to the intriguing matter of what went on in the recess in the old town that was now flanked by two of the Extirpation's crosses. As is so often the case with the idolatry documentation, one must look to neighboring regions for more information.

Two years earlier, in somewhat similar circumstances, the disquiet of Visitador Juan Sarmiento is less elusive. In late August 1662, Sarmiento was guided on a seven-point tour of the environs of *el paraje de Cañas* in the parish of Sayan, Chancay, by the region's kuraka, Don Diego Pacha. The diligencia followed the standard pattern of demolition, cross erection, and Christian con-

---

[20] The details of the confrontation are at AAL Leg. 1, exp. 3, fol. 8. See also Ana María at fols. 6–7.

[21] Pedro de Quijano Zevallos conducted an eventful visita in Huamantanga in 1656. See AAL Leg. 2, exp. 11.

[22] AAL Leg. 1, exp. 3, fols. 8–8v. This case is made even more interesting by the fact that both Ana María and Cristóbal escaped from Huamantanga and sought to influence the proceedings by appealing to Archbishop Villagómez in Lima. One learns that preexisting enmity had motivated Ana María's denunciation to the visitador, thus increasing the possibility that Cristóbal had been wrongfully accused; see AAL Leg. 1, exp. 1, 1664.

secration, but at two of the huacas the visitador's party discovered the familiar traces of the previous extirpating and sanctifying efforts of a parish priest. In both cases old crosses stood a few paces away from huacas that were massive outcroppings of rock which could not be brought down or otherwise destroyed. The state of the first of these places evidently satisfied Sarmiento, for, as the notary recorded, "they did not find any signs that superstitions or sacrifices had been performed there in those [recent] times."[23]

But the second site was more disturbing to the visitador's conscience. His concern over the fate of the religious ground that had been distinguished by a predecessor's cross was natural; after all, previous extirpating actions were among the few yardsticks he had to evaluate the efficacy of the actions he solemnly continued. A previous testimony taken in the village had revealed the belief that the huaca at this place had been "consuming" (or stealing the health of) the children of the kuraka, Don Diego Pacha, because he had not been honoring the god in the proper way.[24] Moreover, the great white rock with its accompanying cross stood in the midst of an ancient settlement in which they also found, in the notary's words, a "large cave," the ceiling of which featured "a great number of different figures of demons in the form of animals with horns, painted in black." Although Sarmiento seemed to accept that this same kuraka who now guided him had reformed his thinking with respect to the devouring huaca, the investigator clearly wondered about what had been the effect on the minds of other Indians of the cross that stood at that place. Standing in the pueblo viejo staring at the central Christian symbol in the shadow of the immovable rock whose Andean significance and supposed divine outrage (at the kuraka's ritual negligence) were only dimly perceived, surrounded by other huacas and painted figures that had been called demons, might possibly have led Sarmiento to a sobering contemplation of the efficacy both of the policy of repeated visitas de idolatría and, more immediately, of his own diligencias among the Indians.[25] The notary registered that the visitador became preoccupied with "a quantity of small stones which appeared to have been placed by hand" at a point on the rock face which proved impossible to reach by climbing. Because a cross had already been erected, Sarmiento could only ease his apparent dissatisfaction with what was being achieved by naming the place after "the glorious St John the Baptist."[26]

[23] AAL Leg. 5, exp. 5, fol. 4v. The main diligencias were conducted on 25 and 30 August. Each of the stops on this tour of the community's huacas can be examined in the transcription in *Amancebados, hechiceros y rebeldes*, edited by A. Sánchez, pp. 67–71.

[24] AAL Leg. 5, exp. 5, fol. 1v.

[25] Following Arriaga's recommendations, Villagómez argues in his *Carta pastoral* that the visitas in the Indian parishes, including whatever punishments and destruction of Andean *sacra* (sacred places and things) proved necessary, should be repeated; see esp. pp. 25–33, 80–85, 105–26.

[26] AAL Leg. 5, exp. 5, fols. 4v–5. The cross had been erected by the parish priest, Gregorio de Utrilla. It was common for small smooth stones to be included in offerings to mountain huacas. See for example AAL Leg. 4, exp. 8, Carhuamayo, Junin, Felipe Nuna Vilca (at fol. 2), transcribed in my "Persistencia religiosa," pp. 227–28.

The actions of the extirpators in these instances from Canta and Chancay in the early 1660s suggest a number of questions. Although most of the questions defy certain answers, taken together they begin to penetrate to the heart of what was occurring in the mid-colonial Archdiocese of Lima. One can consider the ayllu's ancient settlement perched above but not out of reach of the resettlement of Huamantanga. What did this place, and others like it, mean to Indians in the mid-colonial era? Before this visita occurred, what had been the attitude of the Mercedarian friars—who were the people's priests, doctrineros, and confessors—toward continued devotion and commitment to the place? What were the effects of the visita's diligencias that physically uprooted the ancient flowering tree, the roots of which were said to be "those of the people," and the incineration of the ancestors' bones, and innumerable acts like these throughout the archdiocese? And what of the successive efforts by the visitadores to erase and supplant the significance of Andean sacred places through the erection of crosses and propitious christenings?

The huge stone presence, the ancestor Vicho Rinri, whose sanctuary does not appear to have been assaulted until Sarmiento's visit, offers another challenge for analysis. Even the admittedly slim evidence that one has in his particular case indicates that Vicho Rinri, like so many other huacas in the Andes, was a religious survivor, a manifestation of the fact that Catholic domination in the community and region did not negate Andean religious affiliations. In 1664 the reference to dancing and singing in his name suggests that his benevolence, and probably even his mythical past, were regularly commemorated. Like others of his ilk from neighboring regions where different and more abundant details survive in the documentary evidence, one can imagine that Vicho Rinri was given offerings and consulted by a faithful minister, and that he was attended by others who depended on his protection and favor.

But one must further explore the intricacies of the changing religious situation of which this Andean ancestor-being had increasingly become a part. Vicho Rinri, like so many other surviving huacas, would have transformed himself in colonial times, mirroring the needs of his people. He acquired an expanded range of functions, a meaning and a relationship with people who increasingly participated in Christian and Andean religious frameworks. One can recall that Apullana Guara and Mama Guanca, two similar beings from Churín (Cajatambo) discussed in Chapter Two, were approached by their people not only to bring agricultural and pastoral abundance but also to prevent the abuses of a parish priest and corregidor.[27] Guaman Cama, a principal huaca of Acas in mid-seventeenth-century Cajatambo, among the many other entreaties to him, was asked by his people for permission to attend the Catholic festival of the village patron, St Peter.[28] Although some Andean religious forms would prove less adaptable to the exigencies of the seventeenth century, Vicho Rinri from Canta was a familiar force in these times, both a traditional guardian of

---

[27] AAL Leg. 3, exp. 11, 1725, fol. 6.
[28] See Chapter Eight above, and my *An Evil Lost to View?*, pp. 61–83.

agricultural prosperity and a pragmatic, evolving protector. The image of a huaca retaining importance through transformation, demonstrating the capacity to absorb innovation and expand a spiritual repertoire, can be viewed as a regional expression of what was occurring in the mid-colonial Andean religious system as a whole.

How did the methods of the Extirpation fare against so variable and elastic a rival? Vicho Rinri's fall into the ravine, like the destruction of other gods, was meant by the extirpators to be a finalizing event, a resolution. But how would the act of destruction have been interpreted by the Indians who had assisted the deed, or those who heard of it later? And would recollection of the event have affected their conception of the destroying lever-cum-cross that was meant to be the huaca's symbolic substitute? The central questions persist, and are not merely rhetorical.

While one can readily appreciate what was meant to be achieved by the diligencia operations, there are considerable indications that these acts of destruction and re-consecration did not inspire as much real confidence in extirpating circles as was often claimed for official and justificatory purposes. At times, once the crust of triumphalism is broken through, there is a sense of futility before an insurmountable problem. There is a feeling of resignation, even desperation. When little else could be done to advance the faith, the ceremony of fashioning and raising the supreme Christian symbol was made to suffice. Perhaps the ceremonial reconsecrations by the extirpators of Andean sacred places were even some extirpators' expressions of ultimate failure—acts of giving in, but with some dignity.[29]

For their tasks were, more often than not, physically if not religiously impossible. Extirpators frequently lamented the fact that many huacas were "born of the hills themselves"; others, although detached from the mountainsides, were so large or impossibly placed that they also proved indestructible.[30] Moreover, although in theory most diligencias set out against specific gods and places, in practice the actions could take on a weary and wanton character (like an early entrada) crushing whatever was found. Ecclesiastical judges felt a need to justify the considerable effort involved in mounting the visitas by achieving some—and sometimes any—material result. For example, in the parish of Omas, Yauyos, in 1660, no person seemed willing to lead the visitador to the "stone . . . in the form of a person" in the Yanapati ravine—not even knowledgeable Pedro Chumbi, who had confessed its existence; so the investigators contented themselves by ravaging an ancient burial site that had been found along the way. As has been suggested from evidence even beyond the limits of the Lima region, Indians became practiced at sating the extirpators' almost

---

[29] I am indebted to Peter Brown and his knowledge of similar extirpation methods in late antique and early Christian Europe for stimulating me to explore further this possibility.

[30] AAL Leg. 7, exp. 1, Lunahuana, Cañete, fol. 4 on a corregidor's efforts to destroy it. See also Sarmiento's recorded confrontation with a massive stone outside Andacoto in Canta; AAL Leg. 4, exp. 22, Atavillos, Canta, 1659, fols. 1v–2.

indiscriminate appetite for "idols" while at the same time guarding what was most important.[31]

The apparent physical results of the efforts that found their particular targets are equally contentious. The meaning and presence of a huaca that was taken away, smashed into pieces, burned in a plaza, or heaved into a ravine were not necessarily forgotten. In fact, the actions of contemporary churchmen betrayed their growing anxiety over Andean religious allegiances that seemed impossible to extinguish. It became established procedure to dispose secretly of all pieces, dust, and ashes of the huacas and malquis that had been demolished, for fear of the Indians' continued worship of "relics." As Andrés Guaman Pilpi of San Pedro de Acas, Cajatambo, explained to Bernardo de Novoa in 1657, the survival of the local huaca Marcayan could be accounted for because "although it had been burnt, the 'spirit' [the gloss of the Quechua concept *camaquen*] of the said idol lived."[32]

If the success of the destructive exercises against huacas was frequently in doubt, then equally so were efforts at reconsecration. One cannot say with certainty what roles were assumed by the seemingly innumerable crosses that were meant to extinguish old Andean loyalties and point the spiritual way forward, but one can readily state what a few of those roles were supposed to be. For the most Hispanicized and Christian members of Andean communities the crosses were to be a gift of encouragement; here was God's most powerful sign, His holy brand upon another part of his world.[33] Even more than that, the crosses commemorated the great acts of destruction and resanctification. The symbols were to provide the extirpators with an assurance of permanent effect that they desperately needed, just as they were to provide the Indians with strong memories of their huacas' humiliation and defeat. The words of Sarmiento's notary confirm that renaming the places where crosses were erected was undertaken to turn the localities into perpetual reminders of the day when idolatry had been banished and Christianity had triumphed. The actions in the mountains and ancient settlements made it seem possible for the extirpators, in Anthony Pagden's phrase, "to transform the un-possessable."[34]

But, of course, for most indigenous people it was hardly so simple. The triumphal outline, the show of assured mastery, is a screen obscuring a more fluid reality. Many early missionaries seem to have recognized the fluidity of Indian religious constructs; this reality inspired caution in some, whereas

---

[31] AAL Leg. 2, exp. 18, San Pedro de Pilas, Yauyos, fols. 24–26. See A. M. Wightman, "Diego Vasicuio," and F. Salomon, "Ancestor Cults."

[32] For accounts of careful Jesuit actions in Cajatambo and Huamanga see ARSI, Carta anua de 1664, 1665 y 1666, *Peru* 16, vol. 5, fols. 108 and 138, respectively. For Guaman Pilpi's testimony see P. Duviols, ed., *Cultura andina*, p. 185, and discussion in S. MacCormack, *Religion in the Andes*, pp. 409–11. On the divine energy *camaquen* that extirpators frequently glossed as "soul" or "spirit," see esp. P. Duviols, "Camaquen, Upani."

[33] See F. de Avendaño, *Sermones*, book 1, sermon 2, fols. 20–21v. For more on the intended symbol, the cross as Christ's victory, see G. Aulen, *Christus Victor.*

[34] *European Encounters*, p. 27 and 17–49.

others clearly tried to manipulate it in the interest of Christian conversion. According to Bernal Díaz del Castillo, Fray Bartolomé de Olmedo, who accompanied Hernán Cortés in the early days of the Spanish presence in Mexico, was inclined to be more cautious than the conqueror about the erection of crosses as reminders of the Spaniards' early teaching and their efforts to extirpate native cults. "In my opinion," Olmedo is said to have told Cortés, "it is too early to leave a cross in these people's possession . . . . What you have told them is enough until they are better acquainted with our holy religion." Ramón Gutiérrez's interpretation of the "confabulation" of Christian crosses with indigenous prayer sticks in the early contacts between Spaniards and Pueblos in New Mexico would seem to underscore Olmedo's point. According to Gutiérrez, some Franciscans in New Mexico proceeded as many of their earlier brethren had done in New Spain, salvaging aspects of the Indian religiosity that were already present, and employing these supposed parallels for Christian ends. Indigenous peoples in the region would come to recognize "the power of the men who brandished crosses" and from that point it would take little effort "to convince them to worship the cross."[35] Perhaps. But it is dangerous to look for and think with the very parallels between European and Indian religions that colonial Spanish churchmen sought. Moreover, exactly what the "worship" of the symbol meant to a seventeenth-century Puebloan or, to return to present concerns, an Andean religious imagination in the mid-colonial years, remains open to question.

The idolatry trial evidence from mid-colonial Peru reminds one that the roles of crosses in the Indian religious world—the roles of elements of Christianity in general—should inspire caution in historians. Among the many possible variables, these roles were affected by the nature of previous evangelization, exposure to persuasive anti-idolatry preaching, and the rival messages of any Andean dogmatizers who might exist. As a result, the functions of Christian symbols and concepts depended on the decisions, and sometimes even the opportunistic whims, of a varied indigenous society. Often, the "holy places" in the countryside do not appear to have been confined to their roles as the nonurban markers or outposts of Christianity in the Andean parishes. They seem, instead, to have been places were other Christianities—different from the ones represented by the extirpators and even from those centered in the parish churches—were beginning to assert themselves.[36]

---

[35] *The Conquest of New Spain*, translated by J. M. Cohen, p. 137. R. Gutiérrez, *When Jesus Came*, pp. 82–83. For a more nuanced discussion of the possible meanings of crosses and crucifixes to sixteenth-century native peoples in Mexico, see I. Clendinnen in "Ways to the Sacred," pp. 128–29. On methods in New Spain in general see R. Ricard, *The Spiritual Conquest of Mexico*. Gutiérrez's *When Jesus Came* offers a typical example of the search for compatibility between Indian and European beliefs and practices to help in the explanation of gradual Christianization. An interesting, much earlier example of the approach is U. Lamb's "Religious Conflicts." For an emphasis on the "predisposition" of the Indians to convert see also S. Cline, "The Spiritual Conquest Reexamined," esp. p. 477, and J. Lockhart, *The Nahuas after the Conquest*, pp. 203–4.

[36] William Christian's conception of a "paganization (from *pagus*, country) of Christianity—a

As we have now seen, it can be misrepresentative to follow contemporary extirpators too closely in tending to see a strict polarity of religious feeling among mid-colonial Andean parishioners. The time of a visita's presence in an Indian community was an abnormal time of fear and tension, a time of unreality when an artificial dualism might be imposed. Extirpators were usually priests from outside, who arrived in a community to speak and act without the spirit of patience or compromise; there was a careful procedure that many of them took pains to observe, but within these bounds they committed acts of sporadic violence in an attempt to encourage submission. Idolatry denunciations in the Andean communities multiplied when they were encouraged, and when the climate of opinion was such that something might easily be gained through them. The preoccupation, defensiveness, and animosities they encouraged descends like a thick fog, often making the time of an idolatry inspection a time when the ordinary rules and habits of daily life changed, when things that had once been admissible were suddenly offenses that might be concealed or used as weapons against others.[37]

Religious boundary lines and the eccentricities of local belief structures that were transforming during the colonial years were not usually policed so tirelessly. When the visita moved on—depending, of course, on such crucial variables as the views of a parish priest and the nature of Andean religious survival—there could be a return to what I have tentatively called normal times. As other students of the colonial period have observed, many local priests saw the encouragement of religious "convergence" between native and Christian religious forms as the best recipe not only for the Indian parishioners' gradual Christianization but also for peaceful parish life.[38] Religious ideas, like peoples, mixed, often through unconscious facilitators of change such as the religious specialists and healers. Spaniards like Doña Ursula in Cajatambo and Creoles like the Dancer in Chancay, sought love with the help of the powers of Andean wisepersons and practitioners. Native Andeans showed many signs of having been touched by aspects of Christianity. Catalina Yauca Choque of Ambar, Cajatambo, noted the difficulty presented by the special flowers used in the procurement of love when flowers were meant only to adorn the Virgin Mary. In another case María Puyron asked what was wrong with an Andean Christian helping to bring about marriages among the people. Individual

---

kind of encoded recapitulation of the process by which rural pre-Christian notions of a sacred landscape reasserted themselves over an initially cathedral- and parish-centered religion," is helpful here. Indeed, what Christian suggests may be even better suited to conditions in mid-colonial Peru (in which pre-Christian times and influences were less remote, or, at least, less transformed by generations of Christian presence) than late medieval and early modern rural Spain. See W. A. Christian, *Apparitions*, p. 20, but also pp. 21 and 149.

[37] William Christian has observed similar phenomena in contemporary Spain: see *Apparitions*, p. 158.

[38] See W. B. Taylor, *Magistrates of the Sacred*, ch. 3. On the debate over how far certain elements of Franciscan encouragement in New Spain might have gone, and how intentional it might have been, see H. G. Nutini, "Syncretism and Acculturation," and F. Cervantes, *The Devil in the New World*, esp. pp. 54–57.

priests or friars, perhaps in the interests of village tranquillity or because of a tolerance bred by experience, might overlook certain forms of Indian error. Indians, free from the pressure to conform absolutely, might actively seek the benefits and solace offered by their growing pools of religious opportunities. Colonial Andean religious life, the interaction between indigenous and Spanish religious conceptions and practices, could be less constrained and more harmonious than is often implied.

This is not to suggest that competition and conflict between Spanish Catholic and Indian leaders over religious (and secular) power in the parishes was eliminated or lacked significance. In many communities there were clearly Indians who, through their testimonies, demonstrated that they were allies of the priests, and that as committed Christians they were opponents of colonial Andean religion. And there were ardent traditionalists who articulately opposed the religious assimilations they could discern and who actively disputed the growing place for forms of Christianity in the Indian communities. In Acas, Cajatambo, Andean ministers warned that if the huacas and malquis were not nourished by offerings the people would "lose their plots of land . . . and their irrigation canals and springs would dry up" and they would be condemned "to walk poor and desolate and . . . all waste away."[39] Such stark warnings were not made without reason, for few people faced Christianity with an attitude of either complete acceptance or steadfast opposition.

Although the entrance or incorporation of elements of Christianity into Andean religious thinking and practice are undeniable and are increasingly apparent in a number of spheres, these aspects of the Europeans' faith became part of colonial Andean religious framework by an uneven agenda, varying from place to place, individual to individual, and usually without clearly eclipsing the existing religious connections. The crosses erected by the visitadores, near or on top of the regional huacas, take their place amidst these complicated realities in the mid-colonial Andean parishes.

Once they had been stuck in the soil at the base of a cliff or propped up in a pile of stones in a pueblo viejo, and once the visita had moved on, the holy crosses became ambiguous monuments, supremely Catholic symbols in deeply Andean contexts.[40] Their new meanings must have formed gradually, as part of a developing process.[41] The partially disfigured cross that Sarmiento found standing in the old town above Huamantanga may have meant nothing. More probably, however, it had a function and significance that remain unknown to us. In that case, ill will and procedural complications obscure any serious clues as to what the place with the cross had come to mean and what rites might have been observed there, if not by the accused, Cristóbal Chumbi Guaman, then

[39] Francisco Poma y Altas and Juan Raura in P. Duviols, ed., *Cultura andina*, pp. 189 and 192, respectively. For further discussion see my *An Evil Lost to View?*, pp. 105–26.

[40] For a synthetic interpretation of the symbol's accumulated meanings in current Andean society see J. L. González, *El huanca y la cruz*, esp. pp. 43–85.

[41] Serge Gruzinski's idea of post-conquest Indian painting in New Spain demonstrating an "identity in gestation" conceptualizes a similar state of flux; *The Conquest of Mexico*, p. 26.

perhaps by others. Comparable information from neighboring regions provides some suggestive complements, even if the interpretative task remains a difficult one.

Many people who came before the visitadores de idolatría were conspicuously reticent about the fate of the huacas and important places that had come to the extirpators' attention and been Christianized by a cross and perhaps a name. Examples abound of mid-colonial Indian witnesses who, having experienced previous idolatry investigations, had learned how to face an extirpator or zealous priest. Veterans of the extirpation process grew adept at strategic silence, at concealing what would surely draw rebuke and punishment, and protecting what mattered. The meaning of the places would remain a mystery, were it not for the fact that the people's muteness and obfuscation in the face of persistent interrogation are not always as unhelpful as they might seem.

Juan Paria Vilca of Lanca in the parish of el Chorrillo, Huarochirí, for instance, was insistently questioned by Juan Sarmiento in 1659 about a place in the Lanca ravine called Acora (or Acoia) where an earlier visitador, "Dr Ramírez," had erected a cross. When Sarmiento asked, "had the ancients worshiped (*mochado*) at it?" Juan answered obliquely that the Indians of Chorrillo were angered with those of his village because the latter "spoke so freely and would confess to the Jesuits who then destroyed all the errors."[42] The man, not wishing to substantiate his neighbors' charges, remained evasive or completely silent. A year later María Chumbi Ticlla of Guancari in the parish of Quinti, Huarochirí, was denounced for her practices on a great hill named Guaya Manco where Francisco de Avila had raised a cross. Although she denied it, the prosecutor, Don Diego Bartolomé, claimed that she "cried in voices in the custom of the elders and ancients," and that others too, "cried out the ancient names on that hill." María said that she did not know if the hill had ever been a *mochadero* (a place for Andean offerings and worship). But she was conspicuously quick to deny another alarming allegation that came up against her, namely, that she and others prayed with rosaries and engaged in self-flagellation (*disciplinas*) on the hill. In her own defense, she claimed that she performed her acts of Christian penance only in her home or in the church.[43] María Casa Suyo of Quinti was similarly cryptic concerning her many visits to the place called Guaychipan where there was a huaca named Raypa Nusca. Although two Jesuits, P. Salazar and P. Clavero, had erected crosses and consecrated the place with holy water, María disingenuously claimed not to know why the missionaries would have gone to that effort.[44] And when in 1696 Juan Saavedra y Osorio questioned the well-known specialist Juan Baptista about a huaca

[42] AAL Leg. 6, exp. 14, fol. 4. Diego Ramírez was commissioned at the same time as Fernando de Avendaño and was at his busiest in the second decade of the seventeenth century; see P. Duviols, *La Lutte*, pp. 156–59, 234, and 308, and commentary of his diligence in P. J. de Arriaga, *La extirpación*, pp. 8–10.

[43] See AAL Leg. 2, exp. 22, one small loose folio and fol. 2.

[44] AAL, Legajo and expediente unnumbered, San Lorenzo de Quinti, Huarochirí, 1660, fol. 9v. The trial proceedings took place between 12 March and 23 May 1660.

marked by a cross on the road near the village of Marco in Canta, the notary recorded only "that he answered in the negative as he had done for the preceding question."[45]

The most intriguing characteristics that El Inca Garcilaso de la Vega had attributed to huacas as he struggled to define them for his readers and posterity were their astonishing variety and versatility. The most illuminating single source for colonial Andean religion, the Huarochirí manuscript, concurs, even telling of how the "visible forms" of some huacas might be rediscovered in colonial times.[46] Some of the crosses erected on or in place of huacas by the Extirpation's diligencias may have gradually become if not huacas themselves at least elements integrated into a religious system which was, according to place and specific conditions, deep in the process of creative change.

The reluctance of Andeans to tell of the histories and redefined significance of the Christianized shrines, springs, and caves is eminently understandable. These religious transformations, even if they could be articulated, were rewarded only with lashings, banishments, and shame. The changes in Indian religious life that I am documenting represent the beginnings of what one might call an Andean Christianity; but this complex entity was, by any definition, at variance with the demands of the purveyors of the official faith during the years of extirpation. The Extirpation sought to enforce a rupture with the past in the Indian communities, not only the prehispanic past but also the past since the Spanish conquest, because years of religious mixture, conflict, and reformulation were generating a host of new meanings in the Andean world. Domingo García of Arahuay in Canta, the man who made offerings of llama's blood to strengthen his village church in the early 1740s, appears to have only been persuaded of his error after considerable effort by his judges.[47]

Holy crosses, patron saints, invocations, coexistent terminology and concepts, Christian penance, and rites associated with feast days in what were now Andean Christian calendars—all of these things were becoming part of the religious activities and observances that continued at Andean religious places. This much Indian witnesses could only partially conceal, but this much most mid-colonial extirpators proved unable to face. The physical excursions into the Andean hinterlands, and the destruction and strategic placement of crosses that were the material results, were meant to inspire in the Indians a final acceptance of prescribed Catholic devotions and a dread at the thought of the diabolically motivated errors of the past. The huacas, malquis, the chancas and conopas, and the specializations and rituals, were being required to disappear in deference to the almighty Christian rival. The fact that generally speaking they did not—even for Indian people who professed to be Christian—is a

[45] AAL Leg. 5, exp. 25, fols. 14–14v.

[46] Garcilaso de la Vega, *Royal Commentaries*, book 2, chs. 4 and 5; *Huarochirí*, ch. 20. On the possibility of colonial huacas with localized, recent histories see the arguments of Gary Urton in *The History of a Myth*.

[47] AAL Leg. 3, exp. 17, 1741–1742, fols. 2–2v, 6v, and 7.

reflection of the failure of the process of the Extirpation to be what its greatest proponent Pedro de Villagómez claimed it was: the ultimate antidote to suspect Andean religiosity.

The impact of intermittent, systematic extirpation and its concomitant pastoral message on the Indians' attitudes and outlook can only be the subject of speculation. But the idolatry evidence suggests that, along with other factors, the Extirpation encouraged an aversion to what was being trumpeted as official Christianity and an atmosphere in Andean parishes which allowed for myriad forms of religious mixture. The Extirpation's forms of coercion may have also fostered a lack of self-confidence, a need to withdraw, and a deep distrust and hatred that would brew until an outlet was found in later rebellions.[48] And it is not so difficult to know how to interpret an indigenous response which is more common in the evidence from the eighteenth century, that of guarded silence.[49] We know that in at least one region elders had learned a valuable lesson by 1725: they instructed people to keep their true beliefs to themselves.

[48] See S. J. Stern, "New Approaches" and J. Szeminski, "Why Kill a Spaniard?" On a number of Indian risings in the eighteenth century that did occasionally exhibit religious undertones see chs. 2 and 3 in S. O'Phelan Godoy's *Rebellions and Revolts*.

[49] See evidence from San Juan de Churín, Cajatambo, in AAL Leg. 3, exp. 11, 1725, fols. 4, 9v, and 10.

The following non-English terms appear in the text, where they are defined briefly at first mention. Definitions in the text and in the glossary pertain to the contexts in which the words are used in this book, and are not intended to cover all wider usages in other times and places. They are predominantly words of Spanish and Quechua origins, although some were formulated in colonial times and might be more accurately designated Hispanicized Quechua. A few others are of Latin and other origin. The spelling of written Quechua terms varies perhaps even more among modern authors than it did among colonial scribes; when it seems helpful I include principal variants after the spelling I have employed in the book. All entries are in the singular.

aclla — chosen woman, the chosen one.
ají — hot pepper.
alcalde — local magistrate.
alcalde del crimen — chief criminal judge on the audiencia.
apu — lord, also god or "spirit," often a reverential term of address for a high mountain peak.
anexo — hamlet or small settlement affiliated with the principal town (*cabecera*) of a parish.
araguai — black maize, here grown especially for a huaca's chicha.
aucache — Andean religious office of "confessor" of wrongs, usually held within an ayllu.
audiencia — regional governing body and court, consisting of judges and a president; also refers to this court's territorial jurisdiction.
ayllu — a localized social group of extended kin.
brujo and *bruja* — male and female witch; a term of opprobrium for Andean ministers and specialists, especially those thought to cause the misfortune and deaths of others.
cabecera — a principal town in a parish or region.
cabildo — municipal council.
cacique — term used generically by the Spanish to refer to the ruler of a native polity. See *kuraka*. (Hispanicized Arawakan).
camachico — head of a lineage group, ayllu or, occasionally, a small community.
camote — sweet potato.
capilla — small "chapel" or home shrine.
cédula — *real cédula*, a decree issued by the Crown to one or a number of secular and religious officials.
Cercado — here refers to a walled district in Lima inhabited mostly by native Andeans who worked in and around the capital city.
chacra or *chakra* — a plot of cultivable land.

chacrayoc — lord of a *chacra*; usually addressed to a huaca or huanca who watches over the land and its farmers.

chanca — a lineage god, of particular significance to the well-being of a specific social group or extended family; in colonial times, often a named stone in the care of a chanca minister.

chicha, asua, or *aka* — thick maize beer.

choclo — maize cob

coadjutor — priest's assistant, frequently synonymous with teniente de cura

coca — *Erythroxylon coca*, low tropical bush, the leaves of which are among the common sacred offerings to gods; chewed as a stimulant during work and travel.

cofradía — Catholic religious association of lay men and women centering on the devotion to a particular holy image; the image is cared for and carried in procession by its members.

colca — a storehouse for grains.

colegio mayor — a house of education or college within Spain's principal universities.

conopa (illa in south-central Andean parlance) — personal god of fecundity, the sculpted or natural form of which depicted its creative function.

consultor — one of an assembly of expert officials who assisted a judge of the Inquisition in passing judgment.

converso — a "new convert" to Christianity from Judaism.

coroza — conspicuous pointed headgear worn by Indian religious offenders in local processions of shame; borrowed from the Inquisition, which required penitents to wear *corozas* at autos de fe.

corregidor — a district administrator appointed by the Spanish Crown. A *corregidor de indios* was in charge of a rural, Indian region, whereas a *corregidor de españoles* oversaw an urban, Spanish population.

corregimiento — a district (within a larger audiencia) under the purview of a corregidor.

criollo — Creole; a person of, or claiming, Spanish descent born in the new world.

cumbe, cumbi, or *qumpi* — a fine and intricately woven fabric, often worn for ritual occasions.

cura — a secular priest of the Roman Catholic Church.

curandero — healer.

cusma — sleeveless shirt or tunic.

cuy or *kuwi* — an Andean guinea pig raised in homes, important for blood offerings to gods and for healing purposes.

defensor — advocate or defense attorney.

demonio — a demon, or the Devil. Term applied to Andean gods themselves, and/or to the evil force said to be behind them.

diligencia — here, a destructive or punitive operation associated with an idolatry investigation in a local setting.

doctrina — i) elementary Christian doctrine that parishioners were taught repeatedly and expected to commit to memory. ii) a parish of Indians; technically, a parish in which newly converted parishioners are receiving indoctrination.

doctrinero — the Catholic priest administering to a doctrina, an Indian parish. Might be a member of a religious order or a secular priest.

dogmatizador — dogmatizer. Andean teacher, guardian, and teller of sacred histories, as well as minister and ritual adept.

encomendero — Spaniard to whom a group or groups of Indians have been "entrusted." He might demand manual labor and tribute from the Indians, theoretically in exchange for payment, protection, and religious instruction.

encomienda — a grant of labor and tribute rights from the crown to an encomendero over specified groups of Indians.

entrada — an act of entry into a region hitherto unknown; most often associated with friars' and soldiers' movements beyond frontiers of Spanish settlement and principal economic interests.

espinas — thorns or bristles.

fiscal — i) prosecutor in a trial; crown attorney; ii) church or cofradía assistant; see *mayordomo*.

hacienda — a large landed estate, in which ranching and farming normally occurs.

hechicero — sorcerer; general Spanish term of opprobrium for an Indian minister or specialist.

hechizo — spell, curse.

huaca, w'aka, or *guaca* — a local or regional sacred place and divinity; often, but not exclusively, an ancestor being and "founder" in the surrounding landscape, regularly nourished with offerings and given reverence, whose deeds and histories make sense of a region and are recounted by the people who are his or her progeny.

huacanqui — a striking object assembled by a love specialist and believed to influence human passions.

huacapvillac — a huaca minister, literally one who speaks with a huaca and interprets its messages.

huacsa — Andean minister who dances and reenacts a huaca's life and adventures.

huanca — a large stone in the landscape, often acting as specialized protector of a chacra.

íchu — a tough, strawlike bunch grass of the puna, eaten by the camelids (alpacas, llamas, and vicuñas).

idolatría — "idolatry"; refers especially to surviving prehispanic beliefs and practices, but often to all suspect Andean religion and culture, including alleged perversions of Christianity.

illa — southern Andean term for conopa.

ingenio — sugar plantation and mill.

instrucción — manual or instructions on procedure.

kuraka — native lord of non-Inka Andean people; in colonial times a regional Andean governor, playing an intermediary role between Spanish authorities and native Andeans. *Kuraka* was often used interchangeably with *cacique*, a term of Caribbean origin that the Spanish used generally to refer to an Amerindian lord or chief.

kurakazgo — office of kuraka.

ladino — an Indian Hispanicized in dress, culture, and behavior; Usually literate in Spanish, and speaking Spanish as well as Quechua.

letrado — a bureaucrat in the Spanish world, most often trained in a university in civil or canon law, and, occasionally, in the humanist tradition.

llacta — a hamlet or small Andean settlement before Spanish resettlement schemes, the inhabitants often claiming descent from a common founder.

lliclla — a native Andean woman's woven shawl.

maca or *maka* — probably *Lapidium mayenii*; a tuber cultivated at very high altitude, said to have aphrodisiacal properties.

marcayoc — a local religious leader.

machay — a resting place of a malqui, a mummified ancestor; often a cave tomb.

maestra — a female teacher.

malqui or *mallqui* — an ancestor whose body has been mummified; a god of regional significance, and like the huaca, regularly nourished with offerings and commemorative, festive attention.

manta — blanket or cloak.

mate — gourd.

mayordomo — a rotating position as chief attendant or "foreman" in a church or religious association.

mazamorra — maize porridge.

mestizo — descendant of a Spanish and an Indian parent.

micuy — food, nourishment.

milcapa — a mixture of food prepared for Andean divinities, including llama fat, sanco, crushed black and white maize, ground rock, and colored feathers.

mingador — here, a person seeking the services of an Andean specialist.

ministro mayor — the principal Andean minister in a community or region.

miserable — poor and rustic person; often with pitying connotations, but also frequently containing the assumption of lesser intelligence.

mita — Spanish adaptation of a labor rotation system employed by the Inkas.

mochadero — a place of Andean "worship"; one of the Spaniards' adapted blanket terms for Andean sacred places.

mochar — a kisslike gesture, with hands moving out and upward from lips, to express reverence to an Andean god.

mullu — *Spondylus*; warm water mollusk; shell used in offerings to Andean gods.

natural — here, a person native to the Andes, although, generally speaking, a *natural* is a native of any place.

obraje — small-scale factory run by Indian labor, most often producing textiles.

oca — *Oxalis O. tuberosa*, an edible tuber.

oposición — competition for a parish or another clerical or university post.

pacarina — place of origin and to which one returns, venerated by native Andeans.

pachakuti — "the world turned upside down," term denoting chaos or radical change.

pacha — earth.

pampa — open grassy area.

papa — potato.

pariona or *parihuana* — *Phoenicpterus chilensis*, the Chilean flamingo; pink wading bird of the high plateaux.

parpa — cake or ball of cooked white maize.

patacón — coin.

patronato real — royal patronage; crown control of the church.

peninsular — a person born in the Iberian peninsula who has come to America.

plática — a short religious discourse.

poco — powders from a sea shell; a sacrificial food.

principal — a local notable.

procuración — an allowance for maintenance while a *visitador* is on duty.

procurador general — legal defender of Indian accused before the ecclesiastical court in Lima.

promotor fiscal — chief prosecutor in a trial.

proposición — i) the stated theme of a sermon, stated first; also ii) a statement thought by Spanish Christian authorities to be suspicious of heresy or at least error.

protector general de los naturales — Protector of the Indians; Spanish official charged with monitoring the treatment of Indians and looking out for their welfare.

pueblo — general term for community or town; here, refers to a resettlement of a number of ayllus into a reducción, except in the case of *pueblo viejo*.

pueblo viejo — old town; The settlement of Andean ancestors before the colonial reduction of peoples into pueblos and cities. In the Archdiocese of Lima, it was frequently near to the Andean divinities and within walking distance of the reducción.

puna — high Andean plateau and habitat of llamas and alpacas; a cold altitudinous subregion dominated by tundra, alpine, and subalpine conditions; treeless pasture dotted with springs, rocks, and marshy places.

puquio or *pukyu* — a spring; sometimes a huaca.

quipu, *quipo*, or *k'ipu* — a mnemonic device consisting of a connected series of colored, knotted strings.

reducción — a forced resettlement of native Andean groups in colonial times.

regidor — alderman and administrative office holder on a cabildo.

relapso — a baptized person who has lapsed into former errors.

repartimiento — here, a regional administrative district; also a system for the exaction of Indian labor.

sacristán — sexton or church assistant, but used often in idolatry documentation to describe native Andean assistants and "apprentice-ministers" in non-Christian practices.

sanco, or *sango* — a small, soft cake or ball of maize; often prepared with blood offerings for the Andean divinities.

sapo — toad.

sermo, as in *sermo generalis* — an inquisitor's discourse on the accusations against religious defendants, preceding the pronouncement of sentence at an auto de fe.

sermonario — book or cycle of sermons.

serrano — mountain person, highlander. Can be derrogatory, similar to "hillbilly."

supay or *çupay* — Andean force or "spirit" with good and evil properties, sometimes described as a flying soul of a relative. Appropriated by some Spanish missionaries and lexicographers as a gloss for the Christian idea of the Devil.

Taki Onqoy — a native religious movement in the south-central Andes in the 1560s, the dancing messengers of which traveled in search of adherents with a message foretelling the end of Spanish Christian domination.

taqui or *taki* — a ritual dance, often accompanied by music and song.

taquiongo — the itinerant spokespersons or "preachers" of the Taki Onqoy, described as becoming possessed by huacas angered by the rise of the cult of the Christian god, and who prophesied the end of his and the Spaniards' power in the Andes.

Tawantinsuyu or *Tahuantinsuyu* — land of the four quarters; the Inkaic term for the Inka empire.

tembladera — a wide, round dish or vessel, often of thin silver and sometimes decorated, with two handles on the sides.

teniente de cura — an assistant to a parish priest.

ticti — chicha residue; a food for Andean divinities.

tinaja — a large earthen jar, often with iconographic information, and here used for sacred chicha.

tradición — tradition; here, the common gloss for an Andean sacred history regularly told by minister-dogmatizers and performed in dance and song at festivals of the gods whose deeds the tradiciones often recounted.

tratado — treatise; here, also a collection of sermons.

tupu — large silver brooch which fastens lliclla.

villa — a small town.

villca — demigod or high-ranking huacalike human watched over by the huacas in sacred histories.

viracocha — an indigenous term for Spaniards, derived from name for an Andean creator god.

visita general — administrative tour of inspection (secular or religious).

visita general de idolatría or *visita de idolatría* — a trial or investigation of colonial Andean religion conducted by a Catholic priest with the commission of visitador general de idolatría.

visitador general de idolatría or *visitador* — An inspector and judge of idolatry; an extirpator; a Catholic priest specially commissioned as an ecclesiastical investigator of "suspect" Andean religion.

yanacona — in colonial times, a displaced native Andean without local ayllu affiliations, usually the servant of a Spaniard.

yanca — a hereditary huaca minister and specialist of regional importance.

yaya — father.

yerba, hierba — herb, medicinal plant.

My list divides unpublished manuscripts and printed works. When a work has been reprinted, the date given is that of the edition consulted, with the date of original publication in parentheses after the title.

Manuscript Sources

Specific manuscripts cited in the text are listed here when this practice seems helpful to the reader, as in the case of the documents from the Archiepiscopal Archive of Lima (AAL). In the case of well-known bodies of documentation, such as the Audiencia de Lima papers from the General Archive of the Indies, I list the relevant sections; reference to individual documents is made in the notes.

AAL: Archivo Arzobispal de Lima, Lima, Peru; Sección de idolatrías y hechicerías, Legajos 1–7
"Idolatry trials" cited in the text are listed in chronological order according to the classification system in place in 1989–1990 when the archive was under the direction of Mario Ormeño. A new director, Laura Gutiérrez Arbulú, has since changed this system of classification. See her "Indice de la sección hechicerías e idolatrías del Archivo Arzobispal de Lima," in Ramos and Urbano, eds., *Catolicismo*, 105–36.

Legajo 2 Expediente 8: Santa María de Jesús de Huarochirí, Huarochirí (26 September 1642)
Legajo 4 Expediente 11: San Jerónimo de Pampas (Yautan), Huaylas (29 December 1646–27 January 1647)
Legajo 6 Expediente 8: San Jerónimo de Pampas, Huaylas (27 December 1646–26 November 1648)
Legajo 4 Expediente 14: Caujo (Nuestra Señora de la Limpia Concepción de Pomacocha), Canta (9 March 1650–16 April 1650)
Legajo 2 Expediente 10: Caujo (Nuestra Señora de la Limpia Concepción de Pomacocha), Canta (4 April 1650–22 April 1650)
Legajo 5 Expediente 1: Huarmey, Santa (5 December 1650–25 March 1651)
Legajo 6 Expediente 9: Santa María Magdalena de Cajatambo, Cajatambo (5 April 1652)
Legajo 6 Expediente 4: San Juan de Caujul, Cajatambo (22 May 1652)
Legajo 2 Expediente 11: La Advocación de Nuestra Señora de la Natividad de Huamantanga, Canta (8 April 1656–17 September 1656)
Legajo 2 Expediente 12(b): San Pedro de Hacas (San Juan de Machaca), Cajatambo (starting date unknown–12 April 1657)
Legajo 4 Expediente 20: Various towns, Tarama (Jauja) (22 April 1657)
Legajo 4 Expediente 21: San Juan de Lampian, Canta (5 June 1659–14 July 1659)
Legajo 4 Expediente 22: San Juan de Atavillos (San Jerónimo de Andacoto), Canta (28 June 1659)
Legajo 4 Expediente 23: San Juan de Lampian, Canta (22 July 1659–16 August 1659)

Legajo 6 Expediente 12: San Juan de Lampian (San Pedro de Caras), Canta (28 July 1659)

Legajo 6 Expediente 13: San Juan de Lampian (San Pedro de Caras), Canta (28 July 1659)

Legajo 6 Expediente 14: San José de Chorillo, Huarochirí (14 December 1659–18 December 1659)

Legajo 2 Expediente 15: San Lorenzo de Quinti, Huarochirí (11 January 1660–23 April 1660)

Legajo 2 Expediente 19: San Lorenzo de Quinti, Huarochirí (16 January 1660–12 May 1660)

Legajo 2 Expediente 21: San Lorenzo de Quinti, Huarochirí (25 January 1660–26 May 1660)

Legajo 4 Expediente 32: San Lorenzo de Quinti, Huarochirí (29 January 1660–23 April 1660)

Legajo 4 Expediente 33: San Lorenzo de Quinti, Huarochirí (30 January 1660–28 April 1660)

Legajo 2 Expediente 22: San Lorenzo de Quinti, Huarochirí (1 February 1660–27 May 1660)

Legajo 2 Expediente 23: San Lorenzo de Quinti, Huarochirí (1 February 1660–25 April 1660)

Legajo 2 Expediente 25: San Lorenzo de Quinti, Huarochirí (5 February 1660–11 May 1660)

Legajo 2 Expediente 26: San Lorenzo de Quinti, Huarochirí (20 February 1660)

Without number: San Lorenzo de Quinti, Huarochirí (12 March 1660–23 May 1660)

Legajo 4 Expediente 24: San Lorenzo de Quinti, Huarochirí (1 April 1660–12 May 1660)

Legajo 4 Expediente 25: San Lorenzo de Quinti, Huarochirí (22 April 1660–4 May 1660)

Legajo 2 Expediente 13: San Lorenzo de Quinti, Huarochirí (17 May 1660)

Legajo 2 Expediente 16: San Lorenzo de Quinti, Huarochirí (28 May 1660–13 August 1660)

Legajo 4 Expediente 26: San Cristóbal de Huañec, Yauyos (1 June 1660)

Legajo 2 Expediente 18: San Jerónimo de Omas, Yauyos (8 October 1660–date unknown)

Legajo 1 Expediente 2: San Jerónimo de Omas (San Pedro de Pilas), Yauyos (9 November 1660–17 December 1660)

Legajo 4 Expediente 29: San Jerónimo de Omas (San Pedro de Pilas), Yauyos (6 December 1660–7 December 1660)

Legajo 7 Expediente 1: Santiago de Lunahuana, Cañete (27 April 1661–28 May 1661)

Legajo 3 Expediente 3: León de Huánuco, Huánuco (7 August 1662–16 September 1662)

Legajo 6 Expediente 18: La Asunción de Nuestra Señora de Ambar, Cajatambo (3 June 1662–24 November 1662)

Legajo 5 Expediente 5: San Jerónimo de Sayan (Canas), Chancay (8 June 1662–30 August 1662)

Legajo 5 Expediente 8: San Jerónimo de Sayan, Chancay (11 June 1662–7 October 1662)

Legajo 5 Expediente 7: San Jerónimo de Sayan, Chancay (4 September 1662–11 October 1662)

Legajo 6 Expediente 20: La Asunción de Nuestra Señora de Ambar, Cajatambo (17 October 1662–2 November 1662)

Legajo 6 Expediente 17: La Asunción de Nuestra Señora de Ambar, Cajatambo (24 October 1662)

Legajo 4 Expediente 34: La Asunción de Nuestra Señora de Ambar, Cajatambo (30 October 1662–18 November 1662)

Legajo 6 Expediente 19: La Asunción de Nuestra Señora de Ambar, Cajatambo (12 November 1662–18 December 1662)

Legajo 6 Expediente 21: La Asunción de Nuestra Señora de Ambar, Cajatambo (19 November 1662)

Legajo 1 Expediente 3: La Advocación de Nuestra Señora de la Natividad de Huamantanga, Canta (21 October 1664–date unknown)

Legajo 1 Expediente 4: La Advocación de Nuestra Señora de la Natividad de Huamantanga, Canta (21 October 1664–24 December 1664)

Legajo 5 Expediente 10: San Juan de Lampian, Canta (17 January 1665)

Legajo 6 Expediente 23: San Pedro de Acas, Cajatambo (9 April 1665–24 April 1665)

Legajo 5 Expediente 12: San Francisco de Ihuari, Checras (Chancay) (May 1665–12 August 1665)

Legajo 5 Expediente 11: Xapallanga, Jauja (26 May 1665–28 May 1665)

Legajo 4 Expediente 35: Pachas, Huamalies (24 November 1665–6 September 1667)

Legajo 6 Expediente 24: Santo Domingo de Ocros, Cajatambo (15 December 1665–6 June 1669)

Legajo 7 Expediente 6: Lima, Lima (date unknown, 1668)

Legajo 4 Expediente 37: San Juan de los Sondores, Tarama (Tarma) (6 June 1668–5 February 1669)

Legajo 1 Expediente 5: San Francisco de Ihuari, Checras (Chancay) (10 July 1668–16 August 1668)

Legajo 2 Expediente 30: Lima, Lima (18 August 1668–8 November 1668)

Legajo 4 Expediente 38: Lima, Lima (date unknown, 1669)

Without number: Santa María Magdalena de Cajatambo, Cajatambo (20 April 1671)

Legajo 1 Expediente 6: San Francisco de Ihuari, Checras (Chancay) (6 January 1675)

Legajo 5 Expediente 14: Villa de Chancay (San Juan de Guaral), Chancay (26 April 1676–12 November 1676)

Legajo 7 Expediente 6: La Asención de Mito, Jauja (Concepción) (26 October 1689–28 May 1691)

Legajo 1 Expediente 9: La Asención de Mito, Jauja (Concepción) (16 November 1690–11 December 1690)

Legajo 7 Expediente 21: La Rinconada de Late, Lima (26 October 1695–29 October 1695)

Legajo 6 Expediente 2: La Advocación de Nuestra Señora de la Natividad de Huamantanga, Canta (1 October 1696)

Legajo 5 Expediente 26: La Concepción de Canta, Canta (3 October 1696–8 October 1696)

Legajo 2 Expediente 33: La Advocación de Nuestra Señora de la Natividad de Huamantanga, Canta (9 October 1696–23 April 1697)

Legajo 5 Expediente 25: La Advocación de Nuestra Señora de la Natividad de Huamantanga, Canta (12 October 1696–27 February 1697)

Legajo 1 Expediente 13: Santa María de Jesús de Huarochirí, Huarochirí (24 July 1700–29 July 1700)

Legajo 4 Expediente 49: Santa María de Jesús de Huarochirí, Huarochirí (date unknown–14 April 1701)

Legajo 3 Expediente 5: Santiago de Lunahuana, Cañete (4 October 1704–11 March 1705)

Legajo 3 Expediente 6: Lima, Lima (20 January 1710–9 August 1710)

Legajo 3 Expediente 9: Santiago de Carampoma, Huarochirí (29 April 1723–24 September 1723)

Legajo 3 Expediente 10: Santiago de Maray, Checras (Chancay) (18 September 1724–22 January 1725)

Legajo 3 Expediente 11: San Juan de Churín, Cajatambo (12 April 1725–7 May 1725)

Legajo 3 Expediente 13: Santiago de Andajes, Cajatambo (11 November 1725–26 November 1725)

Legajo 3 Expediente 15: Santiago de Carampoma, Huarochirí (28 December 1730–4 November 1732)

Legajo 3 Expediente 17: San Juan de Quivi (Santiago de Arahuay), Canta (10 October 1741–1 May 1742)

ACS: Archivo de la Santa Metropolitana y Patriarchal Iglesia Catedral de Sevilla, Seville, Spain; Sección I
Secretaría: Pruebas de sangre
Secretaría: Autos capitulares

AGI: Archivo General de Indias, Seville, Spain
Audiencia de Lima

AHN: Archivo Histórico Nacional, Madrid, Spain
Sección de Inquisición

ARSI: Archivum Romanum Societatis Iesu, Rome, Italy
Annuae Litterae Provinciae Peruanae Societatis Iesu

ASV: Archivio Segreto Vaticano, Rome, Italy
S. Congr. Concil. Relationes 450, Ad Limina, Limana, Civitatis Regum
Segretario di Statto, Lettere di Vescovi e Prelati

BL: British Library, London, Great Britain
Egerton, Additional, and Sloane MSS

BNM: Biblioteca Nacional de España, Madrid, Spain
MS. 3124, Fernando Montesinos, "Memorias antiguas i nuebas del Pirú," 1642
MS. 5938, "Sobre la escritura de los indios del Perú, por el doctor Murillo de la Cerda," 1589, fols. 433–35.

BNP: Biblioteca Nacional del Perú, Lima, Peru
B 612, "Testimonio del expediente sobre la denuncia de incesto, idolatría y otros excesos cometidos por el cacique de Santiago de Aija, Don Diego Yaruparia. Santiago de Aija, 26 de enero de 1672"
B 1742, Villagómez, Pedro de "Constituciones sinodales de Pedro de Villagómez. Cuaderno no. 22, Arequipa, 5 de mayo de 1639." From synod of 1638 in Arequipa

Molina, Diego de. "Sermones de la Quaresma en Lengua Quechua, Huánuco, 1649" (badly deteriorated)

BOD: Bodleian Library, Oxford, Great Britain
MS. Douce 134, *Le Livre de la Vigne Nostre Seigneur.*

PRINTED SOURCES

Acosta Rodríguez, Antonio. "Los clérigos doctrineros y la economía colonial (Lima, 1600–1630)." *Allpanchis* 16: 19 (1982): 117–49.

———. "Los doctrineros y la extirpación de la religión indígena en el arzobispado de Lima, 1600–1620." *Jahrbuch für Geschichte von Staat, Wirtschaft und Gesellschaft Lateinamerikas* 19 (1982): 69–109.

———. "La extirpación de las idolatrías en el Perú. Origen y desarrollo de las campañas. A propósito de *Cultura andina y represión* de Pierre Duviols." *Revista andina* 9: 1, (July 1987): 171–95.

———. "Francisco de Avila, Cusco 1573(?)-Lima 1647." In *Ritos y tradiciones*, edited by Gerald Taylor, pp. 551–616. Lima: Instituto de Estudios Peruanos and Institut Français d'Etudes Andines, 1987.

———. "El pleito de los indios de San Damián contra Francisco de Avila, 1607." *Historiografía y bibliografía americanistas* 23 (1979): 3–33.

Acosta, José de. *De Procuranda Indorum Salute* [1588]. Madrid: Consejo Superior de Investigaciones Científicas, 1984.

———. *Historia natural y moral de las indias en que se tratan de las cosas notables del cielo, elementos, metales, plantas y animales dellas, y los ritos y ceremonias, leyes y gobierno de los indios* [1590], edited by Edmundo O'Gorman. Mexico: Fondo de Cultura Económica, 1940.

Adorno, Rolena. *Cronista y Príncipe. La obra de don Felipe Guaman Poma de Ayala.* Lima: Pontificia Universidad Católica del Perú, 1989.

———. *Guaman Poma: Writing and Resistance in Colonial Peru.* Austin: University of Texas Press, 1986.

———. "Images of *Indios Ladinos* in Early Colonial Peru." In *Transatlantic Encounters: Europeans and Andeans in the Sixteenth Century*, edited by Kenneth J. Andrien and Rolena Adorno, pp. 232–70. Berkeley and Los Angeles: University of California Press, 1991.

———. Introduction to *Books of the Brave. Being an Account of Books and of Men in the Spanish Conquest and Settlement of the Sixteenth-Century New World*, by Irving A. Leonard [1949]. Reprint, Berkeley and Los Angeles: University of California Press, 1992.

———. ed. *From Oral to Written Expression: Native Andean Chronicles of the Early Colonial Period.* Syracuse: Maxwell School of Citizenship and Public Affairs, Syracuse University, 1982.

Albornoz, Cristóbal de. "Instrucción para descubrir todas las guacas del Pirú y sus camayos y haciendas" [c. 1582], edited by Pierre Duviols. *Journal de la Société des Américanistes* 56: 1 (1967): 17–39.

Aldea Vaquero, Quintín, and Tomás Marín Martínez, eds. *Diccionario de historia eclesiástica de España.* Madrid: Instituto Enrique Flórez, Consejo Superior de Investigaciones Científicas, 1972.

Angeles, Juan de los. *Diálogos de la conquista del reino de Dios.* Prologue and notes by Ángel González Palencia. Madrid: Biblioteca selecta de clásicos españoles, ser. 2, vol. 1, 1946.

Andrien, Kenneth J., and Rolena Adorno, eds. *Transatlantic Encounters: Europeans and Andeans in the Sixteenth Century*. Berkeley and Los Angeles: University of California Press, 1991.

Ankarloo, Bengt, and Gustav Henningsen, eds. *Early Modern Witchcraft Centres and Peripheries*. Oxford: Clarendon Press, 1990.

Anonymous Jesuit (Blas Valera). *Relación de las costumbres antiguas de los naturales del Perú*. In *Tres relaciones de antigüedades peruanas* [1879]. Reprint, Asunción, Paraguay: Editorial Guaranía, 1950.

Arguedas, José María. "Folklore del pueblo de Araguay." *Antropológica* (Lima) 5 (1987): 357–78.

———. *Formación de una cultura nacional indoamericana*. Mexico: Siglo Veintiuno Editores, 1975.

Arias de Ugarte, Hernando. "Constituciones sinodales del Arçobispado de Los Reyes en el Perú, 1636." In *Sínodos de Lima*, edited by Horacio Santiago-Otero and Antonio García y García, pp. 247–457. Madrid: Consejo Superior de Investigaciones Científicas, and Salamanca: Universidad Pontificia de Salamanca, 1987.

Armas Medina, Fernando de. "El clero en las guerras civiles del Perú," *Anuario de estudios americanos* 7 (1950): 1–46.

———. *Cristianización del Perú (1532–1600)*. Seville: Escuela de Estudios Hispano-Americanos, 1953.

———. "La pervivencia de la idolatría y las visitas para extirparla." *Boletín del Instituto Riva-Agüero* 7: 7 (1966–1968): 7–28.

Arriaga, Pablo José de. *La extirpación de la idolatría en el Perú* [1621]. Colección de libros y documentos referentes a la historia del Perú, ser. 2, vol. 1, edited by Horacio H. Urteaga. Lima: Imprenta y Librería San Martín, 1920.

———. *The Extirpation of Idolatry in Peru* [1621], translated by L. Clark Keating. Lexington: University of Kentucky Press, 1968.

———. *Rhetoris Christiani Partes Septem Exemplis cum Sacristum Philosophicis Illustratae*. Lyons: Sumptibus Horatii Cardon, 1619.

Augustine. *City of God* [426], translated by Henry Bettenson. Harmondsworth: Penguin Books, 1972.

Aulen, Gustaf. *Christus Victor: An Historical Study of the Three Main Types of the Idea of Atonement* [c. 1969]. New York: MacMillan Publishing Company, 1972.

Avendaño, Diego de. *Thesaurus Indicus seu generalis Instructor pro Regimine Conscientiae, in Iis Quae ad Indias Spectant*. Antwerp (Antverpiae): Apud Iacobum Meursium, 1668–1675.

Avendaño, Fernando de. *Sermones de los misterios de nuestra santa fe católica, en lengua castellana y en la general del Inca impugnanse los errores particulares que los indios han tenido*. Lima: Jorge López de Herrera, 1649.

Avila, Francisco de. *Dioses y hombres de Huarochirí: Narración quechua recogida por Francisco de Avila [¿1598?]*, translated and edited by José María Arguedas. Lima: Instituto Francés de Estudios Andinos e Instituto de Estudios Peruanos, 1966.

———. *Tratado de los evangelios que nuestra Madre la Yglesia nos propone en todo el año. Desde la primera dominica de Adviento hasta la última Missa de Difuntos. Explicase el Evangelio, y en cada uno se pone un sermon en lengua castellana y la General de los Indios deste Reyno del Perú, y donde conviene da lugar la materia se refutan los errores de idolatría*. Lima: 1648.

Axtell, James. *The Invasion Within: The Contest of Cultures in Colonial North America*. New York and Oxford: Oxford University Press, 1985.

Azoulai, Martine. "Para la historia de la evangelización en América: Los confesionarios." *Allpanchis* 13: 22 (1983): 127–41.

Bandin Hermo, Manuel. *El Obispo de Quito Don Alonso de la Peña Montenegro (1596–1687)*. Madrid: Consejo Superior de Investigaciones Científicas, 1951.

Barmby, James, tr. and ed. "The Book of Pastoral Rule and Selected Epistles of Gregory the Great, Bishop of Rome." In *Nicene and Post-Nicene Fathers of the Christian Church*, 2nd ser., vol. 12. Oxford: James Parker and Company, 1885.

Barnadas, Josep M. "The Catholic Church in Colonial Spanish America." In *The Cambridge History of Latin America*, vol. 1, edited by L. Bethell, pp. 511–40. Cambridge: Cambridge University Press, 1984.

Barnes, Monica. "Catechisms and *Confessionarios*. Distorting Mirrors of Andean Societies." In *Andean Cosmologies through Time*, edited by Robert V. H. Dover, et al., pp. 67–94. Bloomington: Indiana University Press, 1992.

Barriga, Victor M., ed. *Los Mercedarios en el Perú en el siglo XVI: documentos del Archivo General de Indias de Sevilla, 1518–1600*. 5 vols. Arequipa: Establecimientos Gráficos La Colmena, 1942.

Bartlett, Robert. *The Making of Europe: Conquest, Colonization, and Cultural Change 950–1350*. Princeton: Princeton University Press, 1993.

Bartra, Enrique T., ed. *Tercer Concilio Limense 1582–1583, versión castellana original de los decretos con el sumario del Segundo Concilio Limense*. Lima: Facultad Pontificia y Civil de Teología de Lima, 1982.

Bastien, Joseph W. *Mountain of the Condor: Metaphor and Ritual in an Andean Ayllu* [1978]. Reprint, Prospect Heights, Illinois: Waveland Press, 1985.

Bede. *Ecclesiastical History of the English Nation* [731], translated by J. Stevens and revised by J. A. Giles. London: J.M. Dent and Sons, 1910.

Behar, Ruth. "Sexual Witchcraft, Colonialism, and Women's Powers: Views from the Mexican Inquisition." In *Sexuality and Marriage in Colonial Latin America*, edited by Asunción Lavrin, pp. 178–206. Lincoln: University of Nebraska Press, 1989.

———. "The Visions of a Guachichil Witch in 1599: A Window on the Subjugation of Mexico's Hunter-Gatherers," *Ethnohistory* 34: 2 (Spring 1987): 115–38.

Bernand, Carmen, and Serge Gruzinski. *De l'idolâtrie: un archéologie des sciences religieuses*. Paris: Editions du Seuil, 1988.

Bertonio, Ludovico. *Vocabulario de la lengua aymara* [1612]. Cochabamba, Bolivia: Centro de Estudios de la Realidad Económica y Social, 1984.

Bethell, Leslie, ed. *The Cambridge History of Latin America*. 11 vols. Cambridge: Cambridge University Press, 1984–1995.

Blair, Emma H., and James A. Robertson, eds. *The Philippines Islands*. 55 vols. Cleveland: Arthur H. Clark, 1903–1909.

Block, David. *Mission Culture on the Upper Amazon: Native Tradition, Jesuit Enterprise, and Secular Policy in Moxos, 1660–1880*. Lincoln: University of Nebraska Press, 1994.

Borah, Woodrow. *Justice by Insurance: The General Indian Court of Colonial Mexico and the Legal Aides of the Half-Real*. Berkeley and Los Angeles: University of California Press, 1983.

Borges, Pedro. *El envío de misioneros a América durante la época española*. Salamanca: Universidad Pontificia de Salamanca, 1977.

———. *Métodos misionales de la cristianización de América, Siglo XVI*. Madrid: Consejo Superior de Investigaciones Científicas, 1940.

Bossy, John. *Christianity and the West, 1400–1700*. Oxford: Oxford University Press, 1985.

Bouysse-Cassagne, Thérèse, and Phillippe Bouysse. "Volcan indien, volcan chrétien. A propos de l'éruption de Huaynaputina en l'an 1600." *Journal de la Société des Americanistes* 70 (1984): 43–68.

Bouysse, Thérèse, and Olivia Harris. "Pacha. Entorno al pensamiento aymara." In *El pensamiento andino*, edited by T. Bouysse-Cassagne et al., pp. 11–59. La Paz: HISBOL, 1987.

Bouysse-Cassagne, Thérèse, V. Cereceda, Olivia Harris, and Tristan Platt, eds. *El pensamiento andino en el Qullasuyu: tres reflexiones*. La Paz: HISBOL, 1987.

Bowser, Frederick P. *The African Slave in Colonial Peru, 1524–1650*. Stanford: Stanford University Press, 1974.

Boxer, Charles R. *The Church Militant and Iberian Expansion, 1440–1770*. Baltimore: Johns Hopkins University Press, 1978.

Brading, David A. *The First America. The Spanish Monarchy, Creole Patriots, and the Liberal State 1492–1867*. Cambridge: Cambridge University Press, 1991.

———. "The Incas and the Renaissance: The *Royal Commentaries* of the Inca Garcilaso de la Vega," *Journal of Latin American Studies* 18: 1 (1986): 1–23.

———. *The Origins of Mexican Nationalism*. Cambridge Latin American Miniatures. Cambridge: Cambridge University Press, 1985.

Bradley, Peter T. *Society, Economy and Defence in Seventeenth-Century Peru: The Administration of the Count of Alba de Liste (1655–61)*. Institute of Latin American Studies, University of Liverpool, Monograph Series no. 15. Liverpool: Institute of Latin American Studies, 1992.

Brantley, C. "An Historical Perspective of the Giriama and Witchcraft Control." *Africa* 49: 2 (1979): 112–33.

Brown, Peter. "Aspects of the Christianization of the Roman Aristocracy." *Journal of Roman Studies* 51 (1961): 1–11.

———. *The Cult of the Saints: Its Rise and Function in Latin Christianity*. Chicago: University of Chicago Press, 1981.

———. "The Problem of Christianization." The Raleigh Lecture on History read at Nottingham, England, 22 October 1992. *Proceedings of the British Academy* 82 (1993): 89–106.

———. *The Rise of Western Christendom: Triumph and Diversity, A.D. 200–1000*. Oxford: Blackwell, 1996.

Brown, Peter, ed. *Religion and Society in the Age of St. Augustine*. London: Faber and Faber, 1972.

Burga, Manuel. *Nacimiento de una utopía: Muerte y resurrección de los incas*. Lima: Instituto de Apoyo Agrario, 1988.

Burke, Peter. *History and Social Theory*. Cambridge and Oxford: Polity Press, 1992.

———. "Overture: The New History, Its Past and Its Future [1991]." In *New Perspectives on Historical Writing*, edited by Peter Burke, pp. 1–23. Cambridge: Polity Press, 1992.

———. *Popular Culture in Early Modern Europe* [1978]. Reprint, Aldershot: Wildwood House, 1988.

Burke, Peter, ed. *New Perspectives on Historical Writing*. Cambridge and Oxford: Polity Press, 1992.

Burke, Peter, and Roy Porter, eds. *The Social History of Language*. Cambridge: Cambridge University Press, 1987.

Burkhart, Louise. "A Nahuatl Religious Drama from Sixteenth-Century Mexico," *Princeton University Library Chronicle* 53: 3 (1991–1992): 264–86.

————. *The Slippery Earth: Nahua-Christian Moral Dialogue in Sixteenth-Century Mexico*. Tucson: University of Arizona Press, 1989.

Cahill, David. "Curas and Social Conflict in the Doctrinas of Cuzco, 1780–1814," *Journal of Latin American Studies* 16 (1984): 241–76.

Cahill, David, and Scarlett O'Phelan Godoy. "Forging Their Own History: Indian Insurgency in the Southern Peruvian Sierra, 1815." *Bulletin of Latin American Research* 11 (1992): 125–67.

Caro Baroja, Julio. *The World of the Witches* [1961], translated by Nigel Glendinning. London: Weidenfeld and Nicolson, 1964.

Calancha, Antonio de la, and Bernardo de Torres. *Crónicas agustinianas del Perú*. [c.1639–1651], edited by Manuel Merino. 2 vols. Biblioteca Missionalia Hispánica no. 17. Madrid: Consejo Superior de Investigaciones Científicas, 1972.

Castañeda Delgado, P. "Don Bartolomé Lobo Guerrero, tercer arzobispo de Lima." *Anuario de estudios americanos* 33 (1976): 57–103.

Castañega, Martín de. *Tratado de las supersticiones y hechicerías* [1529]. Madrid: Sociedad de Bibliófilos Españoles, 2nd ser., vol. 17, 1946.

Cavillac, Michel. *Gueux et marchands dans le Guzmán de Alfarache (1599–1604): roman picaresque et mentalité bourgeoise dans l'Espagne su siècle d'or*. Bordeaux: Institut d'Études Ibériques et Ibéro-Américaines de l'Université de Bordeaux, 1983.

Cervantes, Fernando. "Christianity and the Indians in Early Modern Mexico: The Native Response to the Devil." *Historical Research* 66 (1993): 177–96.

————. "The Devil in Colonial Mexico: Cultural Interaction and Intellectual Change (1521–1767)." Ph.D. dissertation, Cambridge University, 1989.

————. *The Devil in the New World: The Impact of Diabolism in New Spain*. New Haven and London: Yale University Press, 1994.

————. "The Devils of Querétaro: Scepticism and Credulity in Late Seventeenth-Century Mexico." *Past and Present* 130 (February 1991): 51–69.

————. "The Idea of the Devil and the Problem of the Indian: The Case of Mexico in the Sixteenth Century." University of London, Institute of Latin American Studies Research Papers no. 24, 1991.

Cevallos-Candau, Francisco Javier; Jeffrey A. Cole; Nina M. Scott; and Nicomedes Suárez-Aráuz, eds. *Coded Encounters: Writing, Gender, and Ethnicity in Colonial Latin America*. Amherst: University of Massachusets Press, 1994.

Christian, William A., Jr. *Apparitions in Late Medieval and Renaissance Spain*. Princeton: Princeton University Press, 1981.

————. "Folk Religion: An Overview." In *The Encyclopedia of Religion*, edited by Mircea Eliade. 5: 370–74. New York: Macmillan, 1987.

————. *Local Religion in Sixteenth-Century Spain*. Princeton: Princeton University Press, 1981.

Cieza de León, Pedro. *La crónica del Perú* [1553], edited by Manuel Ballesteros. Madrid: Historia 16, 1984.

Cirac Estopañán, Sebastian. *Los procesos de hechicerías en la Inquisición de Castilla la Nueva: tribunales de Toledo y Cuenca*. Madrid: Consejo Superior de Investigaciones Científicas, Instituto Jerónimo Zurita, 1942.

Ciruelo, Pedro. *Reprobación de las supersticiones y hechicerías, del maestro Pedro Ciruelo*. [c. 1530]. Madrid: Joyas Bibliográficos, 1952.

Clark, Stuart. "The Rational Witchfinder: Conscience, Demonological Naturalism and Popular Superstitions." In *Science, Culture and Popular Belief in Renaissance Eu-

rope, edited by Stephen Pumfrey et al., pp. 222–48. Manchester: Manchester University Press, 1991.

———. *Thinking with Demons: The Idea of Witchcraft in Early Modern Europe*. Oxford: Oxford University Press, forthcoming.

Clendinnen, Inga. *Ambivalent Conquests. Maya and Spaniard in Yucatan, 1517–1570*. Cambridge: Cambridge University Press, 1987.

———. *Aztecs: An Interpretation*. Cambridge: Cambridge University Press, 1991.

———. "Disciplining the Indians: Franciscan Ideology and Missionary Violence in Sixteenth-Century Yucatan." *Past and Present* 94 (February 1984): 27–49.

———. "Landscape and World View: The Survival of Yucatec Maya Culture under Spanish Conquest." *Comparative Studies in Society and History* 22 (1980): 374–93.

———. "Ways to the Sacred: Reconstructing 'Religion' in Sixteenth-Century Mexico." *History and Anthropology* 5 (1990): 105–41.

Clifford, James, and George E. Marcus, eds. *Writing Culture: The Poetics and Politics of Ethnography*. Berkeley and Los Angeles: University of California Press, 1986.

Cline, Sarah L. "The Spiritual Conquest Reexamined: Baptism and Christian Marriage in Early Sixteenth-Century Mexico." *Hispanic American Historical Review* 73: 3 (1993): 453–80.

Cobo, Bernabé. *Historia del Nuevo Mundo* [1653]. In *Obras de P. Bernabé Cobo*. edited by Francisco Mateos. 2 vols. Biblioteca de autores españolas 91 and 92. Madrid: Real Academia Española, 1956.

Cock Carrasco, Guillermo. "El sacerdote andino y los bienes de la divinidades en los siglos XVII y XVIII." Bachelor's thesis. Pontificia Universidad Católica del Perú, Lima, 1980.

Cock Carrasco, Guillermo, and Mary Doyle. "Del culto solar a la clandestinidad de Inti y Punchao." *Historia y Cultura* 12 (1979): 51–73.

Collier, George A., Renato I. Rosaldo, and John D. Wirth, eds. *The Inca and Aztec States, 1400–1800: Anthropology and History*. New York: Academic Press, 1982.

Cólogan, Tomás. *De la Inquisición de Granada al arzobispado de Lima. Santo Toribio Alfonso Mogrovejo*. Granada: Imprenta de F. Román Camacho, 1953.

Columbus, Claudette Kemper. "Immortal Eggs: A Peruvian Geocracy; Pariaqaqa of Huarochirí." *Journal of Latin American Lore* 16: 2 (1990): 175–98.

"Confessionario" [1585]. In *Tercero catecismo y exposicion de la doctrina christiana por sermones. Corpus Hispanorum de Pace*. 2: 189–250. Madrid: Consejo Superior de Investigaciones Científicas, 1985.

Consejo de la Suprema Inquisición: Catálogo de las informaciones genealógicas de los pretendientes a cargos del Santo Oficio. Valladolid: Imprenta "Casa Social Católica," 1928.

Contreras, Jaime. "The Impact of Protestantism in Spain, 1520–1600." In *Inquisition and Society in Early Modern Europe*, edited by Stephen Haliczer, pp. 47–63. London and Sydney: Croom Helm, 1987.

Cook, Noble David. *Demographic Collapse. Indian Peru, 1520–1620*. Cambridge: Cambridge University Press, 1981.

Córdova y Salinas, Diego de. *Corónica de la religiosíssima provincia de los doze apóstoles del Perú, de la Orden de N. P. San Francisco*. Lima: Jorge López de Herrera, 1651.

Cummins, Victoria H. "Blessed Connections: Sociological Aspects of Sainthood in Colonial Mexico and Peru." *Colonial Latin American Historical Review* 3:1 (Winter 1994): 1–18.

Curatola, Marco. "El culto de crisis del Moro Oncoy." In *Etnohistoria y antropología andina*, edited by M. Koth de Paredes and A. Castelli, pp. 179–92. Lima: Museo Nacional de Historia, 1978.

D'Acosta, Blas. *Sermon en la solemníssima colocación de la sagrada reliquia del santo lignum crucis que la Santidad de Urbano VIII de felice recordación embio a la Santa Iglesia de Lima*. Lima: Luis de Lyra, 1649.

Dammert Bellido, José. "Procesos por supersticiones en las provincias de Cajamarca en la segunda mitad del siglo XVII." *Allpanchis* 6 (1974): 179–200.

———. "Procesos por supersticiones en la provincia de Cajamarca en la segunda mitad del siglo XVIII." *Allpanchis* 20 (1984): 177–84.

Dash, Robert C., ed. *Mesoamerican and Chicano Art, Culture and Identity*. Salem, Oregon: Willamette Journal of the Liberal Arts Supplemental Series 6 (bilingual ed.), 1994.

Davenport, F. G., ed. *European Treaties Bearing on the History of the United States and Its Dependencies to 1648* [Washington, D.C: Carnegie Institution of Washington, 1917]. Reprint, Gloucester, MA.: Peter Smith, 1967.

Dean, Carolyn Sue. "Painted Images of Cuzco's Corpus Christi: Social Conflict and Cultural Strategy in Viceregal Peru." Ph. D. dissertation. University of California, Los Angeles, 1990.

Dedieu, Jean-Pierre. "L'Inquisition et le droit. Analyse formelle de la procedure inquisitoriale en cause de foi." *Mélanges de la Casa de Velázquez* 23 (1987): 227–51.

Delgado de Thays, Carmén. *Religión y magía en Tupe (Yauyos)*. Cuernavaca: Centro Intercultural de Documentación, 1968.

Delumeau, Jean. *Catholicism between Luther and Voltaire: A New View of the Counter-Reformation* [1971], tr. by Jeremy Moiser. London: Burns and Oates, and Philadelphia: Westminster Press, 1977.

Dening, Greg. *Islands and Beaches: Discourse on a Silent Land: Marquesas 1774–1880*. Chicago: Dorsey Press, 1980.

Dennis, Matthew. *Cultivating a Landscape of Peace: Iroquois-European Relations in Seventeenth-Century America*. Ithaca: Cornell University Press, and Cooperstown: New York State Historical Association, 1993.

Descripción del virreinato del Perú: crónica inédita de comienzos del siglo XVII, edited by Boleslao Lewin. Rosario, Argentina: Universidad Nacional del Litoral, Facultad de Filosofía, Letras y Ciencias de la Educación, 1958.

Dhôtel, Jean-Claude. *Les origines du cátechisme moderne d'après les premiers manuels imprimés en France*. Paris: Aubier, 1967.

Díaz del Castillo, Bernal. *The Conquest of New Spain*, translated by J. M. Cohen. Harmondsworth: Penguin Books, 1963.

Dibble, Charles E. "The Nahuatlization of Christianity." In *Sixteenth-Century Mexico*, edited by Munro S. Edmonson, pp. 225–33. Albuquerque: University of New Mexico Press, 1974.

Dirks, Nicholas B., ed. *Colonialism and Culture*. Ann Arbor: University of Michigan Press, 1992.

Doctrina Christiana y catecismo para instrucción de indios. Corpus Hispanorum de Pace. Vol. 26–2, edited by Luciano Pereña et al. Madrid: Consejo Superior de Investigaciones Científicas, 1985.

Domínguez Ortiz, Antonio, and Bernard Vincent. *Historia de los moriscos: Vida y tragedia de una minoría*. Madrid: Alianza Editorial, 1978.

Douglas, Mary. *Purity and Danger: An Analysis of Concepts of Pollution and Taboo*. London: Routledge and Kegan Paul, 1966.

Dover, Robert V. H.; Katherine E. Seibold; and John H. McDowell, eds. *Andean Cosmologies through Time: Persistence and Emergence*. Bloomington: Indiana University Press, 1992.

Doyle, Mary E. "The Ancestor Cult and Burial Ritual in Seventeenth- and Eighteenth-Century Peru." Ph.D. dissertation, University of California, Los Angeles, 1988.

Dransart, Penny. "Fibre to Fabric: The Role of Fibre in Camelid Economies in Prehispanic and Contemporary Chile." D.Phil. dissertation, Oxford University, 1991.

Dransart, Penny, ed. *Andean Art: Visual Expression and Its Relation to Andean Beliefs and Values*. Aldershot: Avebury, 1995.

Dudden, Frederick Homes. *Gregory the Great: His Place in History and Thought*. London: Longmans, Green, 1905.

Duffy, Eamon. "Prayer, Magic and Orthodoxy in Late Medieval Catholicism." Paper presented at the Conference on Popular Religion in Europe and the Americas, 15th–18th Centuries, Institute of Latin American Studies, University of London. 2 June 1990.

———. *The Stripping of the Altars: Traditional Religion in England c.1400–c.1580*. New Haven: Yale University Press, 1992.

Dumézil, Georges. "Francisco d'Avila: le bon pasteur (Sermon de Pâques 1646) traduit du quechua," *Diogène* 20 (1957).

Durán, Diego. *Historia de las Indias de Nueva España e islas de la Tierra Firme*, edited by Angel María Garibay. 2 vols. Mexico: Biblioteca Porrúa, 1967.

Durán, Juan Guillermo, ed. *El catecismo del III concilio provincial de Lima y sus complementos pastorales (1584–1585)*. Buenos Aires: Facultad de Teología de la Pontificia Universidad Católica Argentina "Santa María de los Buenos Aires," 1982.

Durkheim, Emile. *The Elementary Forms of Religious Life* [1912]. London: Allen and Unwin, 1954.

Dussel, Enrique. *A History of the Church in Latin America: Colonialism to Liberation (1492–1979)*. Grand Rapids, Mich.: William B. Eerdmans, 1981.

Duviols, Pierre. "'Camaquen, Upani': Un concept animiste des anciens peruviens." In *Estudios americanistas, I. Homenaje a H. Trimborn*, edited by Roswith Hartmann and Udo Oberem, 1: 132–44. Collectanea Instituti Anthropos, no. 20. St. Augustin: Haus Völker und Kulturen, Antropos-Institut, 1978.

———. "Estudio bio-bibliográfico." In *Dioses y hombres de Huarochirí*, translated and edited by J. M. Arguedas, pp. 219–40. Lima: Instituto Francés de Estudios Andinos e Instituto de Estudios Peruanos, 1966.

———. "Huari y Llacuaz. Agricultores y pastores: un dualismo prehispánico de oposición y complementaridad." *Revista del museo nacional del Perú* 39 (1973): 153–91.

———. *La Lutte contre les réligions autochtones dans le Pérou colonial*. Lima: Institut Français d'Etudes Andines, 1971. In Spanish with some revision as *La destrucción de las religiones andinas (conquista y la colonia)*, translated by Albor Maruenda. Mexico: Universidad Nacional Autónoma de México, 1977.

———. "Los nombres Quechua de Viracocha, supuesto 'Dios Creador' de los evangelizadores," *Allpanchis* 10 (1977): 53–64.

———. "Un Procès d'idolâtrie au Pérou: Arequipa, 1671." *Colloque d'Études Péruviennes* 61 (1967): 101–19.

———. "Un Symbolisme de l'occupation, de l'aménagement et de l'exploitation de l'espace. Le monolithe 'huanca' et sa fonction dans les Andes préhispaniques." *L'Homme* 19: 2 (April-June 1979): 7–31.

Duviols, Pierre, ed. *Cultura andina y represión. Procesos y visitas de idolatrías y hechicerías Cajatambo, siglo XVII.* Cusco: Centro de Estudios Rurales Andinos "Bartolomé de Las Casas," 1986.

Edmonson, Munro S., ed. *Sixteenth-Century Mexico: The Work of Sahagún.* Albuquerque: University of New Mexico Press, 1974.

Egaña, Antonio de, S. J. *Historia de la Iglesia en la América española desde el descubrimiento hasta comienzos del siglo XIX. Hemisferio Sur.* Madrid: Biblioteca de Autores Cristianos, 1966.

Ekdahl Ravicz, Marilyn. *Early Colonial Religious Drama in Mexico: From Tzompantli to Golgotha.* Washington D.C.: Catholic University Press of America, 1970.

Eliade, Mircea. *Shamanism. Archaic Techniques of Ecstasy* [1951]. Translated by Willard R. Trask. Princeton: Princeton University Press, 1964.

Eliade, Mircea, ed. *The Encyclopedia of Religion.* New York: Macmillan, 1986.

Elliott, Sir John H. "The Court of the Spanish Habsburgs: A Peculiar Institution?" In John H. Elliott, *Spain and Its World,* pp. 142–61. New Haven: Yale University Press, 1989.

———. "The Discovery of America and the Discovery of Man." In John H. Elliott, *Spain and Its World,* pp. 42–64. New Haven: Yale University Press, 1989.

———. *Europe Divided, 1559–1598.* London: Fontana Press, 1968.

———. "Final Reflections: The Old World and the New Revisited." In *America in European Consciousness, 1493–1750,* edited by Karen Ordahl Kupperman, pp. 391–408. Chapel Hill: University of North Carolina Press, 1995.

———. *The Old World and the New, 1492–1650.* Cambridge: Cambridge University Press, 1970.

———. "Spain and America in the Sixteenth and Seventeenth Centuries." In *The Cambridge History of Latin America,* vol. 1, edited by Leslie Bethell, pp. 287–340. Cambridge: Cambridge University Press, 1984.

———. *Spain and Its World, 1500–1700: Selected Essays.* New Haven: Yale University Press, 1989.

Espinosa Galarza, Max. *Topónimos quechuas del Perú.* Lima: Comercial Santa Elena, 1973.

Farriss, Nancy M. *Maya Society under Colonial Rule: The Collective Enterprise of Survival.* Princeton: Princeton University Press, 1984.

Febvre, Lucien, and H. J. Martin. *The Coming of the Book. The Impact of Printing, 1450–1800.* London: NLB Foundations of History Library, 1976.

Fernández-Santa María, J. A. *Reason of State and Statecraft in Spanish Political Thought, 1595–1640.* Lanham, Md.: University Press of America, 1983.

Flint, Valerie I. J. *The Rise of Magic in Early Modern Europe.* Princeton: Princeton University Press, 1991.

Flores Galindo, Alberto. *Buscando un Inca: Identidad y utopía en los Andes* [1986]. Reprint, Lima: Editorial Horizante, 1988.

Flores Ochoa, Jorge A. "Enqa, enqaychu, illa y khuya rumi." In *Pastores de puna uywamichuq punarunakuna,* edited by J. A. Flores Ochoa, pp. 211–37. Lima: Instituto de Estudios Peruanos, 1977.

———. *Los pastores de Paratía. Una introducción a su estudio.* Mexico: Instituto Indigenista Interamericano, 1968.

Flores Ochoa, Jorge A., ed. *Pastores de puna uywamichuq punarunakuna.* Lima: Instituto de Estudios Peruanos, 1977.

Foucault, Michel. *The Archaeology of Knowledge,* translated by A. M. Sheridan Smith. London: Tavistock Publications, 1972.

————. *The History of Sexuality*, translated by Robert Hurley. 3 vols. Harmondsworth: Penguin Books, 1978–1986.

Fraser, Valerie. *The Architecture of Conquest: Building in the Viceroyalty of Peru, 1535–1635*. Cambridge: Cambridge University Press, 1990.

Frend, W. H. C. "The Winning of the Countryside." *Journal of Ecclesiastical History* 18: 1 (April 1967): 1–14.

Ganster, Paul Bentley. "A Social History of the Secular Clergy of Lima during the Middle Decades of the Eighteenth Century." Ph.D. dissertation, University of California, Los Angeles, 1974.

García Ayluardo, Clara, and Manuel Ramos Medina, eds. *Manifestaciones religiosas en el mundo colonial americano*. Vol. 1: *Espiritualidad barroca colonial: santos y demonios en América*. Mexico: Universidad Iberoamericano, 1993.

García Cabrera, Juan Carlos, ed. *Ofensas a Dios, pleitos e injurias: Causas de idolatrías y hechicerías, Cajatambo siglos XVII–XIX*. Cusco: Centro de Estudios Regionales Andinos "Bartolomé de Las Casas," 1994.

García y García, Antonio, and Francisco Maseda, eds. *Doctrina cristiana y catecismo para instrucción de los indios: Introducción*. Madrid: Consejo Superior de Investigaciones Científicas, 1986.

Garcilaso de la Vega, El Inca. *Royal Commentaries of the Incas and General History of Peru* [1609], translated by Harold V. Livermore. Austin: University of Texas Press, 1987.

Gareis, Iris. "Brujos y brujas en el antiguo Perú: aparencia y realidad en las fuentes históricas." *Revista de Indias* 53 (1993): 583–613.

————. "Extirpación de idolatrías e Inquisición en el virreinato del Perú," *Boletin del Instituto Riva-Agüero* 16 (1989), pp. 55–74.

————. "La 'idolatría' andina y sus fuentes históricas: reflexiones en torno a *Cultura andina y represión* de Pierre Duviols." *Revista de Indias* 50 (1990): 607–26.

————. "Religión popular y etnicidad: La población indígena de Lima colonial." *Allpanchis* 40: 2 (1992): 117–43.

————. "Religiöse Spezialisten des zentralen Andengebietes zur Zeit der Inka und während der spanishen Kolonialherrschaft." Ph.D. dissertation, Ludwig-Maximilans Universität zu München, Munich, 1987.

Gayangos, Don Pascual de, ed. *Catalogue of the Manuscripts in the Spanish Language in the British Library*, [1875]. 4 vols. Reprint, London: British Museum Publications, 1976.

Gibson, Charles, ed. *The Spanish Tradition in America*. Columbia: University of South Carolina Press, 1968.

Ginzburg, Carlo. *The Cheese and the Worms: The Cosmos of a Sixteenth-Century Miller*, translated by John and Anne Tedeschi. Baltimore: Johns Hopkins University Press, 1980.

————. "The European (Re)discovery of Shamans." *London Review of Books*, 28 January 1993, pp. 9–11.

————. *The Night Battles. Witchcraft and Agrarian Cults in the Sixteenth and Seventeenth Centuries*, translated by John and Anne Tedeschi. Baltimore: Johns Hopkins University Press, 1983.

Glave, Luis Miguel. "Santa Rosa de Lima y sus espinas: la emergencia de mentalidades urbanas de crisis y la sociedad andina (1600–1630)." In *Manifestaciones religiosas en el mundo colonial americano*, vol 1: *Espiritualidad barroca colonial: santos y de-*

monios en América, edited by C. García Ayluardo and M. Ramos Medina, pp. 53–70. Mexico: Universidad Iberoamericano, 1993.

Goffman, Erving. *The Presentation of Self in Everyday Life*. New York: Doubleday, 1959.

Gómez Canedo, Lino. *Evangelización y conquista: experiencia franciscana en Hispanoamérica*. Mexico: Editorial Porrúa, 1977.

González, José Luis. *El huanca y la cruz: creatividad y autonomía en la religión popular*. Lima: Tarea, 1989.

González de Avila, Gil. *Teatro eclesiástico de la primitiva Iglesia de las Indias Occidentales*. Madrid: Diego Díaz de la Carrera, 1649–1655.

González Holguin, Diego. *Vocabulario de la lengua general de todo el Perú llamada lengua Qquichua o del Inca* [1608]. Lima: Universidad Nacional Mayor de San Marcos, 1989.

Gossen, Gary H.; J. Jorge Klor de Alva; Manuel Gutiérrez Estévez; and Miguel León-Portilla, eds. *De palabra y obra en el nuevo mundo*, vol. 3: *La formación del otro*. Mexico and Madrid: Siglo XXI editores, 1993.

Granada, Luis de. "Memorial de la vida cristiana" [1566]. In *Obras de fray Luis de Granada* edited by Buenaventura Carlos Aribau, 2: 203–411. Biblioteca de Autores Españoles, vol. 8. Madrid: Atlas, 1945.

———. "Los seis libros de la retórica eclesiástica, o de la manera de predicar" [1576]. In *Obras de fray Luis de Granada*, edited by Buenaventura Carlos Aribau, 3: 488–642. Biblioteca de Autores Españoles, vol. 11. Madrid: Atlas, 1945.

Greenleaf, Richard E. "The Inquisition and the Indians of New Spain: A Study in Jurisdictional Confusion." *The Americas* 22 (1965–1966): 138–66.

———. *Zumárraga and the Mexican Inquisition 1536–1543*. Washington D.C.: Academy of American Franciscan History, 1962.

Griffiths, Nicholas. "Los *hechiceros idólatras* del Perú colonial." In *Actas del Primer Congreso Anglo-Hispano*, vol. 3: *Historia*, edited by Richard Hitchcock and Ralph Penny, pp. 261–73. Madrid: Association of Hispanists of Great Britain and Ireland y Editorial Castalia, 1994.

———. "'Inquisition of the Indians?': The Inquisitorial Model and the Repression of Andean Religion in Seventeenth-Century Peru." *Colonial Latin American Historical Review* 3: 1 (Winter 1994): 19–38.

Gruzinski, Serge. *La colonisation de l'imaginaire: Sociétés indigènes et occidentalisation dans le Mexique*. Paris: Editions Gallimard, 1988. Translated by Eileen Corrigan as *The Conquest of Mexico: The Incorporation of Indian Societies into the Western World, 16th-18th Centuries*. Cambridge and Oxford: Polity Press, 1993.

———. "Individualization and Acculturation: Confession among the Nahuas of Mexico from the Sixteenth to the Eighteenth Century." In *Sexuality and Marriage in Colonial Latin America*, edited by Asunción Lavrin, pp. 97–117. Lincoln: University of Nebraska Press, 1989.

———. *Man-Gods in the Mexican Highlands: Indian Power and Colonial Society, 1520–1800*, translated by Eileen Corrigan. Stanford: Stanford University Press, 1989.

———. *Painting the Conquest: The Mexican Indians and the European Renaissance*, translated by Deke Dusinberre. Paris: Flammarion and Unesco, 1992.

Guaman Poma de Ayala, Felipe. *El primer nuevo corónica y buen gobierno* [c. 1613], edited by John V. Murra and Rolena Adorno. 3 vols. Mexico: Siglo XXI editores, 1980.

Guibovich Pérez, Pedro. "La carrera de un visitador de idolatrías en el siglo XVII: Fernando de Avendaño (1580?–1655)." In *Catolicismo y Extirpación de idolatrías, siglos XVI–XVIII: Charcas, Chile, México, Perú*, edited by Gabriela Ramos and Henrique Urbano, pp. 169–240. Cusco: Centro de Estudios Regionales Andinos "Bartolomé de Las Casas," 1993.

———. Evangelización y sociedad en el Perú de XVII: La instrucción de sacerdotes del obispo Almoguera." *Revista Teológica Limense* 26: 1 (1992): 82–94.

Gutiérrez Arbulú, Laura. "Indice de la sección hechicerías e idolatrías del Archivo Arzobispal de Lima." In *Catolicismo y extirpación de idolatrías*, edited by Gabriela Ramos and Henrique Urbano, pp. 105–36. Cusco: Centro de Estudios Regionales Andinos "Bartolomé de Las Casas," 1993.

Gutiérrez, Ramón. *When Jesus Came, the Corn Mothers Went Away: Marriage, Sexuality, and Power in New Mexico, 1500–1846*. Stanford: Stanford University Press, 1991.

Gwassa, G. "Kinjikitele and the Ideology of the Maji Maji." In *The Historical Study of African Religion*, edited by Terence O. Ranger and I. M. Kimambo, pp. 202–17. London: Heinemann, 1972.

Haliczer, Stephen, ed. and tr. *Inquisition and Society in Early Modern Europe*. London and Sydney: Croom Helm, 1987.

Hamilton, Bernard. *The Medieval Inquisition*. New York: Holmes and Meier, 1981.

Hanke, Lewis. *The Spanish Struggle for Justice in the Conquest of America*. Philadelphia: University of Pennsylvania Press, 1949.

Hanke, Lewis, ed. *History of Latin American Civilization*, vol. 1: *The Colonial Experience*. Boston: Little, Brown, 1967.

Hansen, Leonardo. *Vida admirable de Santa Rosa de Lima. Patrona del Nuevo Mundo*, translated by Jacinto Parra. Lima: Tipografía de "El Santísimo Rosario," 1895.

———. *Vita mirabilis et mors pretiosa venerabilis sororis Rosa de Sa. Marie Limensis*. Rome: Typis Nicolo Angeli, 1664.

Harris, Olivia. "'The Coming of the White People.' Reflections on the Mythologisation of History in Latin America." *Bulletin of Latin American Research* 14:1 (1995): 9–24.

———. "The Dead and the Devils among the Bolivian Laymi." In *Death and the Regeneration of Life*, edited by Maurice Bloch and Jonathan Parry, pp. 45–73. Cambridge: Cambridge University Press, 1982.

———. "The Earth and the State: The Sources and Meanings of Money in Northern Potosí, Bolivia." In *Money and the Morality of Exchange*, edited by Jonathan Parry and Maurice Bloch, pp. 232–68. Cambridge: Cambridge University Press, 1989.

———. "De la fin du monde: Notes depuis le Nord-Potosí." *Cahiers des Amériques Latines* 6 (1987): 93–118.

Harrison, Regina. "The Theology of Concupiscence: Spanish-Quechua Confessional Manuals in the Andes." In *Coded Encounters: Writing, Gender, and Ethnicity in Colonial Latin America*, edited by F. J. Cevallos-Candau et al., pp. 135–50. Amherst University of Massachusets Press, 1994.

Harrod, Howard L. "Blackfeet." In *Native American Religions*, edited by Lawrence E. Sullivan, pp. 35–38. New York: Macmillan, 1989.

Harvey, L. P. *Islamic Spain, 1250–1550*. Chicago: University of Chicago Press, 1990.

Henningsen, Gustav. *The Witches' Advocate: Basque Witchcraft and the Spanish Inquisition (1609–1614)*. Reno: University Press of Nevada, 1980.

Henningsen, Gustav, and John Tedeschi, eds. *The Inquisition in Early Modern Europe: Studies on Sources and Methods*. DeKalb: Northern Illinois University Press, 1986.

Hernández Príncipe, Rodrigo. "Idolatrías in Recuay, provincia de Huailas (1622)." In

Cultura andina y represión, edited by Pierre Duviols. Cusco: Centro de Estudios Rurales Andinos "Bartolomé de Las Casas," 1986.

Hillgarth, J. N., ed. *Christianity and Paganism, 350–750: The Conversion of Western Europe*. Rev. ed. Philadelphia: University of Pennsylvania Press, 1986.

Hitchcock, Richard, and Ralph Penny, eds. *Actas del Primer Congreso Anglo-Hispano*, vol. 3: *Historia*. Madrid: Association of Hispanists of Great Britain and Ireland and Editorial Castalia, 1994.

Hoberman, Louisa, and Susan Socolow, eds. *Cities and Society in Colonial Latin America*. Albuquerque: University of New Mexico Press, 1986.

Horcasitas, Fernando. *El teatro náhuatl: Épocas novohispana y moderna*. Mexico: Universidad Nacional Autónoma de México, 1974.

Howard-Malverde, Rosaleen. "The Speaking of History: 'Willapaakushayki' or Quechua Ways of Telling the Past." University of London, Institute of Latin American Studies Research Paper no. 21, 1990.

Howard-Malverde, Rosaleen, and William Rowe, eds. *Textuality in Amerindian Cultures: Production, Reception, Strategies*. Oxford: Oxford University Press, forthcoming.

Huertas Vallejos, Lorenzo. *Dioses mayores de Cajatambo*. Ayacucho: Universidad Nacional de San Cristóbal de Huamanga, 1978.

———. *La religión en una sociedad rural andina (siglo XVII)*. Ayacucho: Universidad Nacional de San Cristóbal de Huamanga, 1981.

Hulme, Peter. *Colonial Encounters: Europe and the Native Caribbean, 1492–1797* [1986]. London: Routledge, 1992.

Hultkrantz, Åke. "The Religious Life of Native North Americans." In *Native American Religions*, edited by Lawrence E. Sullivan, pp. 3–18. New York: Macmillan, 1989.

Hunefeldt, Christine. "Comunidad, curas y comuneros hacia fines del periódo colonial: Ovejas y pastores indomados en el Perú." *HISLA: Revista Latinoamericana de Historia Económica y Social* 2 (1983): 3–31.

Isbell, Billie Jean. *To Defend Ourselves: Ecology and Ritual in an Andean Village*. Austin: University of Texas Press, 1978.

———. "The Texts and Contexts of Terror in Peru." In *Textuality in Amerindian Cultures: Production, Reception, Strategies*, edited by R. Howard-Malverde and W. Rowe. Oxford: Oxford University Press, forthcoming.

Iwasaki Cauti, Fernando. "Fray Martín de Porras: Santo, ensalmador y sacamuelas." *Colonial Latin American Review* 3: 1–2 (1994): 159–84.

———. "Mujeres al borde de la perfección: Rosa de Santa María y las alumbradas de Lima." *Hispanic American Historical Review* 73: 4 (November 1993): 581–613.

Johnson, Paul. *A History of Christianity*. Harmondsworth: Penguin Books, 1976.

Kagan, Richard L. *Students and Society in Early Modern Spain*. Baltimore: Johns Hopkins University Press, 1974.

Kamen, Henry. *Inquisition and Society in Spain in the Sixteenth and Seventeenth Centuries*. Bloomington: Indiana University Press, 1985.

Kedar, Benjamin Z. *Crusade and Mission: European Approaches toward the Muslims*. Princeton: Princeton University Press, 1984.

Klor de Alva, J. Jorge. "Colonizing Souls: The Failure of the Indian Inquisition and the Rise of Penitential Discipline." In *Cultural Encounters*, edited by M. E. Perry and A. J. Cruz, pp. 3–23. Berkeley and Los Angeles: University of California Press, 1991.

———. "Martín Ocelotl: Clandestine Cult Leader." In *Struggle and Survival in Colo-*

nial America, edited by David G. Sweet and Gary B. Nash, pp. 128–41. Berkeley and Los Angeles: University of California Press, 1981.

————. "Nahua Colonial Discourse and the Appropriation of the (European) Other." In *Archives des Sciences Sociales des Religions* 77 (January-March 1992): 15–35.

————. "Raconter des Vies: L'autobiographie confessionnelle et la reconstruction de l'être nahua." In *Archives des Sciences Sociales des Religions* 77 (January-March 1992): 111–24.

————. "Sahagún and the Birth of Modern Ethnography: Representing, Confessing and Inscribing the Native Other." In *The Work of Bernardino de Sahagún*, edited by J. Jorge Klor de Alva et al., pp. 31–52. Austin: University of Texas Press, 1988.

————. "Sin and Confession among the Colonial Nahuas: The Confessional as a Tool for Domination." In *La ciudad y el campo en la historia de México*, edited by Ricardo A. Sánchez Flores et al., 1: 91–101. Mexico: Instituto de Investigaciones Históricas, Universidad Nacional Autónoma de México, 1992.

————. "Spiritual Conflict and Accomodation in New Spain: Toward a Typology of Aztec Responses to Christianity." In *The Inca and Aztec States, 1400–1800: Anthropology and History*, edited by George A. Collier et al., pp. 345–66. New York: Academic Press, 1982.

Klor de Alva, J. Jorge; H. B. Nicholson; and Eloise Quiñones Keber, eds. *The Work of Bernardino de Sahagún: Pioneer Ethnographer of Sixteenth-Century Aztec Mexico*. Austin: University of Texas Press, distributors for the Institute for Mesoamerican Studies, the State University of New York, Studies on Culture and Society, 1988.

Koepcke, María. *The Birds of the Department of Lima, Peru*, translated by Erma J. Fisk. Wynnewood, Pennsylvania: Harrowood Press, 1970.

Koth de Paredes, M., and A. Castelli, eds. *Etnohistoria y antropología andina: Primera jornada del museo nacional de historia*. Lima: Museo Nacional de Historia, 1978.

Kracke, Waud. "Myths in Dreams, Thoughts in Images. An Amazonian Contribution to the Psychoanalytic Theory of Primary Process." In *Dreaming*, edited by Barbara Tedlock, pp. 31–54. Cambridge: Cambridge University Press, 1987.

Kubler, George. *Mexican Architecture of the Sixteenth Century*. 2 vols. New Haven: Yale University Press, 1948.

————. "The Quechua in the Colonial World." In *The Handbook of South American Indians*, edited by Julian H. Steward, 2: 331–410. Washington D.C.: United States Government Printing Office, 1946.

Kupperman, Karen Ordahl, ed. *America in European Consciousness, 1493–1750*. Chapel Hill: University of North Carolina Press, 1995.

Lamb, Ursula. "Religious Conflicts in the Conquest of Mexico," *Journal of the History of Ideas* 17 (1956), pp. 526–539.

Landa, Diego de. *Relación de las cosas de Yucatán*. Introduction by Ángel María Garibay K. 10th edn. Mexico: Editorial Porrúa, 1973.

Larner, Christina. *Enemies of God: The Witch-hunt in Scotland*. London: Chatto and Windus, 1981.

Las Casas, Bartolomé de. *Apologética Historia* [c. 1559], edited by Edmundo O'Gorman. 2 vols. Mexico: Universidad Nacional Autónoma de México, 1967.

Lavallé, Bernard. *Las promesas ambiguas: Ensayos sobre el criollismo colonial en los Andes*. Lima: Instituto Riva-Agüero de la Pontificia Universidad Católica del Perú, 1993.

Lavrin, Asunción. "Female Religious." In *Cities and Society in Colonial Latin America*, edited by Louisa Hoberman and Susan Socolow, pp. 165–95. Albuquerque: University of New Mexico Press, 1986.

———. "Women and Religion in Spanish America." In *Women and Religion in America*, edited by Rosemary R. Ruether and Rosemary S. Kueller, 2: 42–78. San Francisco: Harper and Row, 1983.

Lavrin, Asunción, ed. *Sexuality and Marriage in Colonial Latin America*. Lincoln: University of Nebraska Press, 1989.

Lea, Henry Charles. *A History of the Inquisition in Spain*. 4 vols. New York: Macmillan, 1906–1907.

———. *The Moriscos of Spain: Their Conversion and Their Expulsion* [1901]. Reprint, New York: Macmillan, 1968.

Leites, Edmund, ed. *Conscience and Casuistry in Early Modern Europe*. Cambridge: Cambridge University Press, 1988.

Lemlij, Moisés, and Luis Millones, eds. *El umbral de los dioses*. Lima: Biblioteca Peruana de Psicoanálisis, 1991.

Le Roy Ladurie, Emmanuel. *Jasmin's Witch*, translated by Brian Pearce. Harmondsworth: Penguin Books, 1990.

———. *Montaillou: The Promised Land of Error*; translated by Barbara Bray. New York: Vintage Books, 1979.

León-Portilla, Miguel, ed. *The Broken Spears: The Aztec Account of the Conquest of Mexico*. Expanded and updated edition of the 1962 translation by Lysander Kemp. Boston: Beacon Press, 1992.

———. *Visión de los vencidos*. Translated by Ángel María Garibay K.. Mexico: Universidad Nacional Autónoma de México, 1959.

Leonard, Irving A. "Best Sellers of the Lima Book Trade." *Hispanic American Historical Review* 22 (1942): 5–33.

———. *Books of the Brave: Being an Account of Books and Men in the Spanish Conquest and Settlement of the Sixteenth-Century New World* [1949]. Reprint, with a new introduction by Rolena Adorno. Reprint, Berkeley and Los Angeles: University of California Press, 1992.

Levillier, Roberto. *Don Francisco de Toledo: Supremo organizador del Perú. Su vida, su obra (1515–1582). Años de andanzas y de guerras (1515–1572)*. 2 vols. Madrid: Espasa-Calpe, 1935.

———. *Santo Toribio Alfonso Mogrovejo, Arzobispo de Los Reyes (1581–1606). Organizador de la iglesia en el virreinato del Perú*. Madrid: Riva de Neyra, 1920.

Levillier, Roberto, ed. *La organización de la iglesia y órdenes religiosas en el virreinato del Perú en el siglo XVI. Documentos del Archivo de Indias*. Madrid: Sucesores de Riva de Neyra, 1919.

Lima, Mesquitela. "Fetishism." In *The Encyclopedia of Religion*, edited by Mircea Eliade, 5: pp. 314–17. New York: Macmillan, 1987.

Lisi, Francesco Leonardo, tr. and ed. *El Tercer Concilio Limense y la aculturación de los indígenas sudamericanos: Estudio crítico con edición, traducción y comentario de las actas del concilio provincial celebrado en Lima entre 1582 y 1583*. Salamanca: Ediciones Universidad de Salamanca, 1990.

Lobo Guerrero, Bartolomé, and Fernando Arias de Ugarte. *Sínodos de Lima de 1613 y 1636*, edited by Horacio Santiago-Otero and Antonio García y García. Madrid: Centro de Estudios Históricos del Consejo Superior de Investigaciones Científicas, and Salamanca: Instituto de Historia de la Teología Española de la Universidad Pontificia de Salamanca, 1987.

Lockhart, James. "Charles Gibson and the Ethnohistory of Postconquest Central Mexico." Institute of Latin American Studies, La Trobe University, occasional paper no. 9, 1989.

———. *The Men of Cajamarca*. Austin: University of Texas Press, 1972.

———. *The Nahuas after the Conquest: A Social and Cultural History of the Indians of Central Mexico, Sixteenth through Eighteenth Centuries*. Stanford: Stanford University Press, 1992.

———. "Sightings: Initial Nahua Reactions to Spanish Culture." In *Implicit Understandings*, edited by Stuart B. Schwartz, pp. 218–48. Cambridge: Cambridge University Press, 1994.

Lockhart, James, ed. and trans. *We People Here: Nahuatl Accounts of the Conquest of Mexico*. Berkeley and Los Angeles: University of California Press, 1993.

Lohmann Villena, Guillermo. *El corregidor de indios en el Perú bajo los Austrias*. Madrid: Ediciones Cultura Hispánica, 1957.

Long, Charles H. *Significations: Signs, Symbols, and Images in the Interpretation of Religion*. Philadelphia: Fortress Press, 1986.

Lovell, W. George. *Conquest and Survival in Colonial Guatemala: A Historical Geography of the Cuchumatán Highlands, 1500–1821*. Rev. ed. Montréal and Kingston: McGill-Queen's University Press, 1992.

———. "Re-membering America: The Historical Vision of Eduardo Galeano." *Queen's Quarterly* 99: 3 (Fall 1992): 609–17.

———. "Surviving Conquest: The Maya of Guatemala in Historical Perspective." *Latin American Research Review* 23: 2 (1988): 25–58.

MacAloon, John J., ed. *Rite, Drama, Festival, Spectacle: Rehearsals Toward a Theory of Cultural Performance*. Philadelphia: Institute for the Study of Human Issues, 1984.

MacCormack, Sabine. "Atahuallpa and the Book," *Dispositio* 14: 36–38 (1989): 141–68.

———. "Atahualpa y el libro," *Revista de Indias* 48 (1988): 693–714.

———. "From the Sun of the Incas to the Virgin of Copacabana." *Representations* 8 (Fall 1984): 30–60.

———. "'The Heart Has Its Reasons': Predicaments of Missionary Christianity in Early Colonial Peru." *Hispanic American Historical Review* 65 (1985): 443–66.

———. "Limits of Understanding: Perceptions of Greco-Roman and Amerindian Paganism in Early Modern Europe." In *America in European Consciousness, 1493–1750*, edited by Karen Ordahl Kupperman, pp. 79–129. Chapel Hill: University of North Carolina Press, 1995.

———. "*Pachacuti*, Miracles, Punishments, and Last Judgment: Visionary Past and Prophetic Future in Early Peru." *American Historical Review* 93:4 (1988): 960–1,006.

———. *Religion in the Andes: Vision and Imagination in Early Colonial Peru*. Princeton: Princeton University Press, 1991.

———. "Ubi Ecclesia? Perceptions of Medieval Europe in Spanish America." *Speculum* 69: 1 (January 1994): 74–100.

Málaga Medina, Alejandro. "Las reducciones en el Perú." *Historia y cultura* 8 (1974): 141–72.

Mannheim, Bruce. *The Language of the Inka Since the European Invasion*. Austin: University of Texas Press, 1991.

———. "A Semiotic of Andean Dreams." In *Dreaming*, edited by Barbara Tedlock, pp. 132–53. Cambridge: Cambridge University Press, 1987.

Mariátegui, José Carlos. *Siete ensayos de interpretación de la realidad peruana* [1928]. Reprint, Lima: Biblioteca Amauta, 1985.

Markus, R. A. *The End of Ancient Christianity*. Cambridge: Cambridge University Press, 1990.

———. "Gregory the Great and a Papal Missionary Strategy." In *Studies in Church History*, edited by G. J. Cuming, 6: 29–38. Cambridge: Cambridge University Press, 1970.

Martín, Luis. *The Intellectual Conquest of Peru: The Jesuit College of San Pablo, 1568– 1767*. New York: Fordham University Press, 1968.

Martín, Luis, and Jo Ann Pettus, eds. *Scholars and Schools in Colonial Peru*. Dallas: Southern Methodist University Press, 1973.

Marzal, Manuel M., S. J. "Una hipótesis sobre la aculturación religiosa andina." *Revista de la Universidad Católica* 2 (1977): 95–131.

———. *La transformación religiosa peruana* [1983]. Reprint, Lima: Pontificia Universidad Católica del Perú, 1988.

———. *La utopía posible: Indios y jesuitas en la América colonial (1549–1767)*. 2 vols. Lima: Pontificia Universidad Católica del Perú, 1992.

Mateos, Francisco. "Constituciones para indios del primer Concilio Limense." *Missionalia Hispánica* 7 (Madrid, 1950): 5–44.

McKenzie, Don F. "The Sociology of a Text: Oral Culture, Literacy and Print in Early New Zealand." In *The Social History of Language*, edited by Peter Burke and Roy Porter, pp. 161–97. Cambridge: Cambridge University Press, 1987.

McMullen, Ramsay. "Two Types of Conversion to Early Christianity." *Vigiliae Christianae* 37 (1983): 174–88.

Mecham, J. Lloyd. "The Church in Colonial Spanish America." In *Colonial Hispanic America*, edited by A. Curtis Wilgus, pp. 200–39. New York: Russell and Russell, 1963.

Medina, José Toribio. *La imprenta en Lima (1584–1824)* [1904–1907]. 4 vols. Reprint, Amsterdam: N. Israel, 1965.

———. *La imprenta en Méjico (1539–1821)*. 8 vols. Santiago de Chile: Impreso en la casa del autor, 1907–1912.

Meiklejohn, Norman. *La iglesia y los Lupaqas de Chucuito durante la colonia*. Cusco: Centro de Estudios Rurales Andinos "Bartolomé de Las Casas," 1988.

Melendez, Juan. *Tesoros verdaderos de las Indias en la historia de la gran provincia de San Juan Bautista del Perú de la Orden de Predicadores*. 3 vols. Rome: Imprenta de Nicolás Angel Tinassio, 1681.

Mendiburu, Manuel de. *Diccionario histórico biográfico del Perú*. 11 vols. Lima: Librería e Imprenta Gil, 1931–1934.

Meyers, Albert, and Diane Elizabeth Hopkins, eds. *Manipulating the Saints. Religious Brotherhoods and Social Integration in Postconquest Latin America*. Hamburg: Wayasbah, 1988.

Middendorf, Ernst W. *Die einheimischen Sprachen Perus*. Leipzig: F. A. Brockhaus, 1890.

Miller, Joseph C. "Listening for the African Past." In *African Past Speaks*, edited by Joseph C. Miller, pp. 1–59. Folkestone, Eng.: W. Dawson, and Hamden, Conn.: Archon Books, 1980.

Miller, Joseph, ed. *African Past Speaks: Essays on Oral Tradition and History*. Folkestone, Eng.: Dawson, 1980.

Millones, Luis. "Los ganados del señor: mecanismos de poder en las comunidades andinas, siglos XVIII y XIX," *América Indígena* 39: 1 (January-March 1979): 107–45.

———. *Historia y poder en los Andes centrales: desde los orígenes al siglo XVII*. Madrid: Alianza Editorial, 1987.

———. *El Inca por la Coya*. Lima: Fundación Friedrich Ebert, 1988.

———. "Introducción al estudio de las idolatrías." *Letras* 78–79 (1969), Universidad Nacional Mayor de San Marcos, Lima, Instituto de Literatura Papel no. 27, pp. 5–40.

———. "Un movimiento nativista del siglo XVI: el Taki Onqoy." *Revista peruana de cultura* 3 (1964): 134–40.

———. *Una partecita del cielo: La vida de Santa Rosa de Lima narrada por Don Gonzalo de la Maza a quien ella llamaba padre*. Lima: Editorial Horizante, 1993.

———. "La religión indígena en la colonia." In *Historia del Perú*, vol. 5: *Perú colonial*. Lima: Editorial Juan Mejía Baca, 1980.

———. "Religion and Power in the Andes: Idolatrous Curacas of the Central Sierra." *Ethnohistory* 26: 3 (1979): 143–263.

———. "Shamanismo y política en el Perú colonial: los curacas de Ayacucho." *Histórica* 8: 2 (1984): 131–49.

Millones, Luis, ed. *Las informaciones de Cristóbal de Albornoz: documentos para el estudio del Taki Onqoy*. Mexico: Centro Intercultural de Documentación, 1971.

———. *El retorno de las huacas. Estudios y documentos sobre el Taki Onqoy, siglo XVI*. Lima: Instituto de Estudios Peruanos y Sociedad Peruana de Psicoanálisis, 1990.

Millones, Luis, and Moisés Lemlij, eds. *En el nombre del Señor: Shamanes, demonios y curanderos del norte del Perú*. Lima: Biblioteca Peruana de Psicoanálisis y Seminario Interdisciplinario de Estudios Andinos, 1994.

Millones, Luis, and Mary Pratt. *Amor brujo: Imagen y cultura del amor en los Andes*. Lima: Instituto de Estudios Peruanos, 1989.

Millones, Luis, and G. Solari. "Males del cuerpo y males del alma." *Cielo Abierto* (Lima) 3: 7 (1980): 3–12.

Mills, Kenneth. "Bad Christians in Colonial Peru.," *Colonial Latin American Review* 5: 2 (1996): forthcoming.

———. "Especialistas en rituales y resistencia cultural en la región norcentral del Perú, 1646–1672." In *En el nombre del Señor*, edited by L. Millones and M. Lemlij, pp. 148–83. Lima: Biblioteca Peruana de Psicoanálisis y Seminario Interdisciplinario de Estudios Andinos, 1994.

———. *An Evil Lost to View? An Investigation of Post-Evangelisation Andean Religion in Mid-Colonial Peru*. Institute of Latin American Studies, the University of Liverpool, Monograph Series no. 18. Liverpool: Institute of Latin American Studies, 1994.

———. "The Limits of Religious Coercion in Mid-Colonial Peru." *Past and Present* 145 (November 1994): 84–121.

———. "Persistencia religiosa en Santiago de Carhuamayo (Junin), 1631." In *Testimonios, cartas y manifiestos indígenas (época colonial y primer periódo republicano)*, edited by Martín Leinhard, pp. 222–31. Caracas: Biblioteca Ayacucho, 1992.

———. "Seeing God in Mid-Colonial Peru." In *Andean Art*, edited by Penny Dransart, pp. 302–17. Aldershot, Eng.: Avebury Publishers, 1995.

"Misión a las provincias de Ocros y Lampas del corregimiento de Cajatambo (Letras Annuas de la Compañía de Jesús, Provincia del Perú. Real Academía de la Historia, Madrid [1619])." In *Cultura andina y represión*, edited by Pierre Duviols, pp. 449–57. Cusco: Centro de Estudios Rurales Andinos "Bartolomé de Las Casas," 1986.

Molina, Cristóbal de (el Cusqueño). *Relación de las fábulas y ritos de los Ingas*. Colección de libros y documentos referentes a la historia del Perú [1575], edited by Horiacio H. Urteaga, 1: 1–103. Lima: Imprenta y Librería Sanmarti, 1916.

———. *Relación de las fábulas y ritos de los Incas*. In *Fábulas y mitos de los incas*, edited by Henrique Urbano and Pierre Duviols. Madrid: Historia 16, 1989.

Moore, R. I. *The Formation of a Persecuting Society: Power and Deviance in Western Europe, 950–1250*. Oxford: B. H. Blackwell, 1987.

Moreno Yañez, Segundo, and Frank Salomon, eds. *Reproducción y transformación de las sociedades andinas, siglos* XVI–XX. 2 vols. Quito: Ediciones ABYA–YALA y Movimiento Laicos para América Latina, 1991.

Mörner, Magnus. *Race Mixture in the History of Latin America*. Boston: Little, Brown, 1967.

———. *Region and State in Latin America's Past*. Baltimore: Johns Hopkins University Press, 1993.

Muchembled, Robert. *Culture populaire et culture des élites (XVe–XVIIIe siècles)*. Paris: Flammarion, 1978.

Muldoon, James. *The Americas in the Spanish World Order: The Justification for Conquest in the Seventeenth Century*. Philadelphia: University of Pennsylvania Press, 1994.

———. *Popes, Lawyers, and Infidels: The Church and the Non-Christian World, 1250–1550*. Philadelphia: University of Pennsylvania Press, 1979.

Murra, John V. "Una apreciación etnológica de la visita." In *Visita hecha a la provincia de Chucuito por Garci Diez de San Miguel en el año 1567*, paleographic version by Waldemar Espinosa Soriana, pp. 419–44. Lima: Ediciones de la Casa de la Cultura del Perú, 1964.

———. "El 'control vertical' de un máximo de pisos ecológicos en la economía de las sociedades andinas." In Iñigo Ortiz de Zúñiga, *Visita de la provincia de León de Huánuco en 1562*. 2: 429–76. Huánuco: Universidad Nacional Hermilio Valdizan, 1972.

———. *Formaciones económicas y políticas del mundo andino*. Lima: Instituto de Estudios Peruanos, 1975.

Nader, Helen. *The Mendoza Family in the Spanish Renaissance 1350 to 1550*. New Brunswick, N.J.: Rutgers University Press, 1979.

Nalle, Sara T. *God in La Mancha: Religious Reform and the People of Cuenca, 1500–1650*. Baltimore and London: The Johns Hopkins University Press, 1992.

Nandy, Ashis. *The Intimate Enemy: Loss and Recovery of Self Under Colonialism*. Delhi: Oxford University Press, 1983.

Ni-Chatháin, P. and M. Richter, eds. *Ireland and Christendom*. Stuttgart: Klett-Cotta, 1987.

The New Catholic Encyclopedia. 17 vols. New York: McGraw-Hill, 1967.

Nolasco Pérez, Pedro. *Historia de las misiones Mercedarias en América*. Madrid: n.p., 1966.

Nutini, Hugo G. "Syncretism and Acculturation: The Historical Development of the Patron Saint in Tlaxcala, Mexico (1519–1670)." *Ethnology* 15: 3 (July 1976): 301–21.

Olmos, Andrés de. *Tratado de hechicerías y sortilegios*, translated and edited by Georges Baudot. Mexico: Mission Archeologique et Ethnologique Française au Mexique, 1979.

O'Neil, Mary R. "Magical Healing, Love Magic and the Inquisition in Late Sixteenth-Century Modena." In *Inquisition and Society*, edited by Stephen Haliczer, pp. 88–114. London: Croom Helm, 1987.

———. "Superstition." In *The Encyclopedia of Religion*, edited by Mircea Eliade, 14: 163–66. New York: Macmillan, 1986.

Ong, Walter. *The Presence of the Word*. New Haven: Yale University Press, 1967.

Oñate, Pedro de (Onnate, Petrus de). *De Contractibus in genere. (De contractibus lu-*

crativis.) Nova methodo ex iuris utriusque legibus et theologorum et iurisperitorum placitis concinnati. Rome: F. Caballi, 1646–1647.

O'Phelan Godoy, Scarlett. *Rebellions and Revolts in Eighteenth-Century Peru and Upper Peru.* Cologne: Bohlau, 1985.

Ossio, Juan M., ed. *Ideología mesiánica del mundo andino.* Lima: Ignacio Prado Pastor, 1973.

Pacheco, J. M. "Don Bartolomé Lobo Guerrero, arzobispo de Santafé de Bogotá." *Ecclesiastica Xavieriana* 5 (1955): 123–201.

Padilla, Juan de. "Trabajos, agravios e injusticias que padecen los indios en lo espiritual y temporal." [1657]. In R. Vargas Ugarte, *Historia general del Perú.* Vol. 3, appendix. 2nd rev. ed. Lima: Editor Carlos Milla Batres, 1971.

Pagden, Anthony. *European Encounters with the New World.* New Haven: Yale University Press, 1993.

———. *The Fall of Natural Man: The American Indian and the Origins of Comparative Ethnology.* Rev. ed., Cambridge: Cambridge University Press, 1986.

———. "*Ius et Factum*: Text and Experience in the Writings of Bartolomé de Las Casas." *Representations* 33 (Winter 1991): 147–62.

———. *Spanish Imperialism and the Political Imagination. Studies in European and Spanish American Social and Political Theory, 1513–1830.* New Haven: Yale University Press, 1990.

Parry, Jonathan, and Maurice Bloch, eds. *Money and the Morality of Exchange.* Cambridge: Cambridge University Press, 1989.

Paso y Troncoso, Francisco del, ed. *Tratado de las idolatrías, supersticiones, dioses, ritos, hechicerías y otras costumbres gentílicas de las razas aborígenes de México.* 2 vols. 2nd ed. Mexico: Librería Navarro, 1953.

Pease G. Y., Franklin. *Curacas, reciprocidad y riqueza.* Lima: Edubanco, 1992.

———. *El dios creador andino.* Lima: Mosca Azul Editores, 1973.

Peñaherrera del Aguila, Carlos et al., eds. *Atlas histórico geográfico y de paisajes peruanos.* Lima: Instituto Nacional de Planificación, 1963–1970.

Peña Montenegro, Alonso de la. *Itinerario para parochos de indios en que se tratan las materias más particulares tocantes a ellos para su buena administración.* Madrid: Joseph Fernández de Buendía, 1668.

Pérez Bocanegra, Juan. *Ritual formulario e institución de curas para administrar a los naturales de este reyno, los santos sacramentos del baptismo, confirmación, eucaristía y viatico, penitencia, extrema unción y matrimonio, con advertencias muy necesarias.* Lima: Jerónimo de Contreras, junto al convento de Santo Domingo, 1631.

Perry, Mary Elizabeth, and Anne J. Cruz, eds. *Cultural Encounters: The Impact of the Inquisition in Spain and the New World.* Berkeley and Los Angeles: University of California Press, 1991.

Peters, Edward. *Inquisition.* Berkeley and Los Angeles: University of California Press, 1988.

Phelan, John Leddy. *The Kingdom of Quito in the Seventeenth Century: Bureaucratic Politics in the Spanish Empire.* Madison: University of Wisconsin Press, 1967.

———. *The Millennial Kingdom of the Franciscans in the New World. A Study of the Writings of Gerónimo de Mendieta (1525–1604).* Berkeley and Los Angeles: University of California Press, 1956.

Platt, Tristan. "The Andean Soldiers of Christ: Confraternity Organization, The Mass of the Sun and Regenerative Warfare in Rural Potosí (18th–20th Centuries)." *Journal de la Société des Américanistes* 73 (1987): 139–92.

Polo de Ondegardo, Juan. "Los errores y supersticiones de los indios sacadas del tratado y averiguación que hizo el Licenciado Polo" [1585]. In *El catecismo*, edited by J. G. Durán, pp. 459–78. Buenos Aires: Facultad de Teología de la Pontificia Universidad Católica Argentina "Santa María de los Buenos Aires," 1982.

———. "Instrucción contra las ceremonias y ritos que usan los indios conforme al tiempo de su infidelidad" [1585]. In *El catecismo*, edited by J. G. Durán, pp. 447–55. Buenos Aires: Facultad de Teología de la Pontificia Universidad Católica Argentina "Santa María de los Buenos Aires," 1982.

Ponce, Pedro. *Breve relación de los dioses y ritos de la gentilidad* [c.1629–1634]. In *Tratado de las idolatrías*, edited by F. del Paso y Troncoso, 1: 369–80. Mexico: Librería Navarro, 1953.

Poole, Stafford. *Pedro Moya de Contreras: Catholic Reform and Royal Power in New Spain, 1571–1591*. Berkeley and Los Angeles: University of California Press, 1987.

Powers, William K. *Ogala Religion*. Lincoln: University of Nebraska Press, 1977.

Prakash, Gyan. *Bonded Histories: Genealogies of Labor Servitude in Colonial India*. Cambridge: Cambridge University Press, 1990.

Prakash, Gyan, ed. *After Colonialism: Imperial Histories and Postcolonial Displacements*. Princeton: Princeton University Press, 1995.

Pumfrey, Stephen; Paolo L. Rossi; and Maurice Slawinski, eds. *Science, Culture and Popular Belief in Renaissance Europe*. Manchester: Manchester University Press, 1991.

Quiroga, Pedro de. *Libro intitulado Coloquios de la verdad. Trata de las causas e inconvenientes que impiden la doctrina o conversión de los indios de los reinos del Perú, y de los daños e males e agravios que padecen* [c. 1563], edited by Julián Zarco Cuevas. Biblioteca Colonial Americana, vol. 7. Seville: Tipografía Zarzuela, 1922.

Rafael, Vicente L. "Confession, Conversion, and Reciprocity in Early Tagalog Colonial Society." In *Colonialism and Culture*, edited by Nicholas B. Dirks, pp. 65–88. Ann Arbor: University of Michigan Press, 1992.

———. *Contracting Colonialism: Translation and Christian Conversion in Tagalog Society under Early Spanish Rule*. Ithaca: Cornell University Press, 1988.

Ramírez, Susan R. "The '*dueño de indios*': Thoughts on the Consequences of the Shifting Bases of Power of the '*curaca de los viejos*' under the Spanish in Sixteenth-Century Peru." *Hispanic American Historical Review* 67: 4 (November 1987): 575–610.

Ramos, Gabriela, and Henrique Urbano, eds. *Catolicismo y Extirpación de idolatrías, siglos XVI–XVIII: Charcas, Chile, México, Perú*. Cusco: Centro de Estudios Regionales Andinos "Bartolomé de Las Casas," 1993.

Ranger, Terence O. "The Problem of Evil in Eastern Africa." Lectures given at St. Antony's College, Oxford, 2 and 7 November 1988.

Ranger, Terence O., and I. M. Kimambo, eds. *The Historical Study of African Religion*. London: Heinemann, 1972.

Recopilación de leyes de los reynos de las Indias [1681]. 4 vols. 4th edn. Madrid: Gráficas Ultra, 1943.

Relación de la religión y ritos del Perú hecha por los primeros religiosos Agustinos que allí pasaron [c. 1560]. Colección de documentos inéditos relativos al descubrimiento, conquista y colonización de las posesiones españolas en América y Oceania, 3: 5–58.

Rezabel y Ugarte, José. *Biblioteca de los escritores que han sido individuos de los seis colegios mayores: de San Ildefonso de la Universidad de Alcala; de Santa Cruz de la Valladolid; de San Bartolomé; de Cuenca; san Salvador de Oviedo; y del Arzobispo de Salamanca*. Madrid: La Imprenta de Sancha, 1805.

Ricard, Robert. *The Spiritual Conquest of Mexico. An Essay on the Apostolate and the Evangelizing Methods of the Mendicant Orders in New Spain: 1523–1572* [1933], translated by Lesley Byrd Simpson. Berkeley and Los Angeles: University of California Press, 1966.

Rivera Cusicanqui, Silvia. "El Mallku y la sociedad colonial en el siglo XVII: el caso de Jesús de Machaca." *Avances: Revista Boliviana de Estudios Históricos y Sociales* 1 (1978): 7–27.

Rivet, Paul, and Georges de Crequit-Montfort, eds. *Bibliographie des langues aymara et kicua*, vol. 1: *1540–1875*. Paris: Institut d'Ethnologie, 1951.

Rodríguez Valencia, Vicente. *Santo Toribio de Mogrovejo, organizador y apóstol de Sur-América*. 2 vols. Madrid: Consejo Superior de Investigaciones Científicas, Instituto de Santo Toribio de Mogrovejo, 1956–1957.

Romero, Carlos A. "Don Pedro de Villagómez. Nota biobibliográfica." Colección de libros y documentos, vol. 12, edited by Horacio H. Urteaga, pp. v–xi. Lima: Imprenta y Librería San Martín, 1919.

———. "Un libro interesante." *Revista histórica* (Lima) 9 (1928): 51–87.

Romero, Emilio. *Tres ciudades del Perú*. Lima: Imprenta Torres Aguire, 1929.

Rosaldo, Renato. "From the Door of His Tent: The Fieldworker and the Inquisitor." In *Writing Culture*, edited by J. Clifford and G. E. Marcus, pp. 77–97. Berkeley and Los Angeles: University of California Press, 1986.

Rostworowski de Diez Canseco, María. *Estructuras andinas del poder: ideología religiosa y política*. Lima: Instituto de Estudios Peruanos, 1983.

———. *La historia de Tawantinsuyu*. Lima: Instituto de Estudios Peruanos, 1989.

———. "Mitos andinos relacionados con el origen de las subsistencias." *Boletín de Lima* 37 (año 7, January 1985): 33–37.

Rubio Merino, Pedro, ed. *Archivo de la Santa Metropolitana y patriarcal Iglesia Catedral de Sevilla*. Madrid: Fundación Ramon Areces, 1987.

Ruether, Rosemary R., and Rosemary S. Kueller, eds. *Women and Religion in America*. 3 vols. San Francisco: Harper and Row, 1981–1986.

Ruiz de Alarcón, Hernando. "Tratado de las supersticiones y costumbres gentilicas que hoy viven entre los naturales de esta Nueva España" [1629] In *Tratado de las idolatrías, supersticiones, dioses, ritos, hechicerías y otras costumbres gentílicas de las razas aborígenes de México*, edited by Francisco del Paso y Troncoso. 2 vols. 2nd edn. 2: 17–180. Mexico: Librería Navarro, 1953.

———. *The Treatise of Ruíz de Alarcón*, [1629], translated and edited by J. R. Andrews and Ross Hassig. Norman: University of Oklahoma Press, 1984.

Sahagún, Bernardino de. *The Florentine Codex: General History of the Things of New Spain*, translated from Nahuatl and edited by Arthur J. O. Anderson and Charles E. Dibble. 13 vols. Santa Fe, N.M.: School of American Research and University of Utah, 1950–1982.

———. *Historia general de las cosas de Nueva España*, edited by Ángel María Garibay K. 3rd ed. Mexico: Editorial Porrúa, 1975.

Sallnow, Michael J. *Pilgrims of the Andes: Regional Cults in Cusco*. Washington, D.C.: Smithsonian Institution Press, 1987.

Salomon, Frank. "Ancestor Cults and Resistance to the State in Arequipa, ca. 1748–

1754." In *Resistance, Rebellion and Consciousness*, edited by Steve J. Stern, pp. 148–65. Madison: University of Wisconsin Press, 1987.

———. "Chronicles of the Impossible: Notes on Three Peruvian Indigenous Historians." In *From Oral to Written Expression: Native Andean Chronicles of the Early Colonial Period*, edited by Rolena Adorno, pp. 9–39. Syracuse: Maxwell School of Citizenship and Public Affairs, Syracuse University, 1982.

———. *Native Lords of Quito in the Age of the Incas: The Political Economy of North Andean Chiefdoms*. Cambridge: Cambridge University Press, 1986.

———. "Nightmare Victory: The Meanings of Conversion among Peruvian Indians (Huarochirí, 1608?)." Department of Spanish and Portuguese, University of Maryland, Working Papers no. 7. College Park, Md., 1990.

———. "Oral and Redactorial Make-up of a 'Native Chronicle.'" Unpublished manuscript, 1990.

———. "The Picture Outside the Frame: Some Protagonists of *Runa Yndio Niscap* as Seen in Unpublished Sources." Paper presented at the 47th International Congress of Americanists, New Orleans, July 1991.

———. "Shamanism and Politics in Late Colonial Ecuador." *American Ethnologist* 10: 3 (1983): 413–28.

Salomon, Frank, and George L. Urioste, tr. and eds. *The Huarochirí Manuscript. A Testament of Ancient and Colonial Andean Religion*. Austin: University of Texas Press, 1991.

Sánchez, Ana. "Mentalidad popular frente a ideología oficial: el Tribunal de la Inquisición de Lima y los casos de hechicería (siglo XVII)." Paper presented at the II Coloquio Internacional del Grupo de Trabajo CLASCO, Historia y antropología andina "Poder y Violencia en los Andes." Quito, 1990.

Sánchez, Ana. ed. *Amancebados, hechiceros y rebeldes (Chancay, siglo XVII)*. Cusco: Centro de Estudios Regionales Andinos "Bartolomé de Las Casas," 1991.

Sánchez Flores, Ricardo A.; Eric Van Young; and Gisela von Wobeser, eds. *La ciudad y el campo en la historia de México: Memoria de la VII Reunión de Historiadores Mexicanos y Norteamericanos*. 2 vols. Mexico: Instituto de Investigaciones Históricas, Universidad Nacional Autónoma de México, 1992.

San Pedro, Juan de. *La persecución del demonio. Crónica de los primeros agustinos del norte del Perú* [c. 1560], edited by Eric E. Deeds; preliminary studies by Luis Millones, John Topic, and José Luis González. Málaga: Algazara y CAMEI editores, 1992.

Santa Cruz Pachacuti Yamqui, Juan. "Relación de antigüedades deste reyno del Perú" [1613]. In *Crónicas peruanas de interés indígena*. Biblioteca de Autores Españoles, no. 209. Madrid: Ediciones Atlas, 1968.

Santo Tomás, Domingo de. *Léxico o vocabulario de la lengua general del Perú llamada quechua* [1563]. Lima: Universidad Nacional Mayor de San Marcos, 1951.

Schäfer, Ernesto. *El Consejo Real y Supremo de las Indias. Su historia, organización y labor administrativa hasta la terminación de la Casa de Austria*. 2 vols. Seville: Escuela de Estudios Hispano-Americanos, 1935–1947.

Schama, Simon. *The Embarrassment of Riches: An Interpretation of Dutch Culture in the Golden Age* [1987]. Reprint, London: Fontana Press, 1991.

Schwaller, John F. *The Church and Clergy in Sixteenth-Century Mexico*. Albuquerque: University of New Mexico Press, 1987.

———. "The Extirpation of Idolatry in New Spain, 1524–1650: A New Look at an Old Topic." Paper presented at the Joint Meeting of the Rocky Mountain Council on

Latin American Studies and the Pacific Coast Council on Latin American Studies, Las Vegas, Nevada, 7 March 1995.

Schwartz, Stuart B., ed. *Implicit Understandings: Observing, Reporting, and Reflecting on the Encounters between Europeans and Other Peoples in the Early Modern Era*. Cambridge: Cambridge University Press, 1994.

Seed, Patricia. "'Failing to Marvel': Atahualpa's Encounter with the Word." *Latin American Research Review* 26: 1 (1991): 7–32.

Serna, Jacinto de la. "Manual de ministros de indios para el conocimiento de sus idolatrías y extirpación de ellas." [1656]. In Colección de documentos inéditos para la historia de España, 104: 1–267. Madrid: Imprenta de José Perales y Martínez, 1892.

Silverblatt, Irene. "Becoming Indian in the Central Andes of Seventeenth-Century Peru." In *After Colonialism: Imperial Histories and Postcolonial Displacements*, edited by Gyan Prakash, pp. 279–98. Princeton: Princeton University Press, 1995.

———. *Moon, Sun, and Witches: Gender Ideologies and Class in Inca and Colonial Peru*. Princeton: Princeton University Press, 1987.

———. "El surgimiento de la Indianidad en los Andes del Perú Central: El nativismo del siglo XVII y los muchos significados de 'indio'." In *De palabra y obra en el nuevo mundo*, vol. 3: *La formación del otro*, edited by G. H. Gossen, J. J. Klor de Alva, M. Gutiérrez Estévez, and M. León-Portilla, pp. 459–81. Madrid: Siglo XXI editores, 1993.

Smith, Hilary Dansey. *Preaching in the Spanish Golden Age. A Study of Some Preachers of the Reign of Philip III*. Oxford: Oxford University Press, 1978.

Solórzano Pereira, Juan de. *Libro primero de la recopilación de las cédulas, cartas, provisiones y ordenanzas reales* [1622]. 2 vols. Buenos Aires: Instituto de Historia del Derecho Argentino, 1945.

———. *De Indiarum Jure sive de justa Indiarum Occidentalium Inquisitione, Acquisitione, et Retentione*. 2 vols. Madrid: Ex typographia Francisci Martinez, 1629–1639.

———. *Política indiana* [1647], edited by Miguel Ángel Ochoa Brun. Biblioteca de autores españoles desde la formación del lenguaje hasta nuestros días. 5 vols. Madrid: Ediciones Atlas, 1972.

Soto Rábanos, José María. "Sínodos de Lima de 1613 y 1636: Contexto histórico." In *Sínodos de Lima de 1613 y 1636*, by B. Lobo Guerrero and F. Arias de Ugarte, edited by H. Santiago-Otero and A. García y García, pp. ix–ciii. Madrid: Centro de Estudios Históricos del Consejo Superior de Investigaciones Científicas, and Salamanca: Instituto de Historia de la Teología Española de la Universidad Pontificia de Salamanca, 1987.

Southern, Sir Richard W. *Western Society and the Church*. Pelican History of the Church, 2. Grand Rapids: Eerdmans, 1970.

Spalding, Karen. "Defendiendo el suyo. El *kuraka* en el sistema de producción andina." In *Reproducción y transformación de las sociedades andinas, siglos XVI–XX*, edited by Segundo Moreno Yañez and Frank Salomon, 2: 401–14. Quito: Ediciones ABYA-YALA y Movimiento Laicos para América Latina, 1991.

———. "*Kurakas* and Commerce: A Chapter in the Evolution of Andean Society." *Hispanic American Historical Review* 54: 4 (November 1973): 581–99.

———. *Huarochirí: An Andean Society under Inca and Spanish Rule*. Stanford: Stanford University Press, 1984.

———. "Social Climbers: Changing Patterns of Mobility among the Indians of Colonial Peru." *Hispanic American Historical Review* 50: 4 (November 1970): 645–64.

Spence, Jonathan D. *The Memory Palace of Matteo Ricci*. Harmondsworth: Penguin Books, 1984.

Stern, Steve J. "New Approaches to the Study of Peasant Rebellion and Consciousness: Implications of the Andean Experience." In *Resistance, Rebellion and Consciousness*, edited by S. J. Stern, pp. 3–25. Madison: University of Wisconsin Press, 1987.

———. *Peru's Indian Peoples and the Challenge of Spanish Conquest: Huamanga to 1640*. Madison: University of Wisconsin Press, 1982.

Stern, Steve J., ed. *Resistance, Rebellion and Consciousness in the Andean Peasant World, 18th to 20th Centuries*. Madison: University of Wisconsin Press, 1987.

Steward, Julian H., ed. *The Handbook of South American Indians*, vol. 2. Washington, D.C.: United States Government Printing Office, 1946.

Strauss, Gerald. *Luther's House of Learning: Indoctrination of the Young in the German Reformation*. Baltimore: Johns Hopkins University Press, 1975.

Straw, Carole. *Gregory the Great: Perfection in Imperfection*. Berkeley and Los Angeles: University of California Press, 1988.

Sullivan, Lawrence E., ed. *Native American Religions. North America*. Selections from *The Encyclopedia of Religion*, edited by Mircea Eliade [1987]. New York: Macmillan, 1989.

Sweet, David G. and Gary B. Nash, eds. *Struggle and Survival in Colonial America*. Berkeley and Los Angeles: University of California Press, 1981.

Sylvest, Edwin E. *Motifs of Franciscan Mission Theory in Sixteenth-Century New Spain*. Washington, D.C.: Academy of American Franciscan History, 1975.

Szeminski, Jan. "Why Kill a Spaniard? New Perspectives on the Andean Insurrectionary Ideology in the 18th Century." In *Resistance, Rebellion and Consciousness*, edited by S. J. Stern, pp. 166–91. Madison: University of Wisconsin Press, 1987.

Talbot, C. H. "Saint Boniface and the German Mission." In *Studies in Church History*, vol. 6, edited by G. J. Cuming, pp. 45–57. Cambridge: Cambridge University Press, 1970.

Taussig, Michael. *The Devil and Commodity Fetishism in South America*. Chapel Hill: The University of North Carolina Press, 1980.

Taylor, Gerald. "Supay." *Amerindia* 5 (1980): 47–63.

Taylor, Gerald, tr. and ed. *Ritos and tradiciones de Huarochirí: Manuscrito quechua de comienzos del siglo XVII*. Lima: Instituto de Estudios Peruanos e Institut Français d'Études Andines, 1987.

Taylor, William B. "Colonial Religion and Quincentennial Metaphors: Mexican Santiagos and *Cristos de Caña*." In *Mesoamerican and Chicano Art, Culture, and Identity*, edited by Robert C. Dash, pp. 26–49. Salem, Oregon: Willamette Journal of the Liberal Arts Supplemental Series 6 (bilingual edition), 1994.

———. *Drinking, Homicide, and Rebellion in Colonial Mexican Villages*. Stanford: Stanford University Press, 1979.

———. *Magistrates of the Sacred: Priests and Parishioners in Eighteenth-Century Mexico*. Stanford: Stanford University Press, forthcoming.

———. "Santiago's Horse: Christianity and Colonial Indian Resistance in the Heartland of New Spain." In *Violence, Resistance, and Survival in the Americas*, edited by W. B. Taylor and F. Pease G.Y., pp. 153–89. Washington, D.C.: Smithsonian Institution Press, 1994.

Taylor, William B., and Franklin Pease G. Y., eds. *Violence, Resistance, and Survival in the Americas: Native Americans and the Legacy of Conquest*. Washington, D.C.: Smithsonian Institution Press, 1994.

Tedlock, Barbara, ed. *Dreaming: Anthropological and Psychological Interpretations*. Cambridge: Cambridge University Press, 1987.

"Tercero catecismo y exposicion de la doctrina christiana por sermones" [1585]. In *Doctrina Christiana y catecismo para instrucción de indios*. Corpus Hispanorum de Pace, vol. 26–2, edited by Luciano Pereña et al., pp. 333–777. Madrid: Consejo Superior de Investigaciones Científicas, 1985.

Thomas, Keith V. *Man and the Natural World: Changing Attitudes in England, 1500–1800*. London: Penguin Books, 1983.

———. *Religion and the Decline of Magic: Studies in Popular Beliefs in Sixteenth- and Seventeenth-Century England* [1971]. Reprint, Harmondsworth: Penguin Books, 1978.

Tibesar O. F. M., Antonine. *Franciscan Beginnings in Colonial Peru*. Washington, D.C.: Academy of American Franciscan History, 1953.

Tineo, Primitivo. *Los concilios Limenses en la evangelización latinoamericana: Labor organizativa y pastoral del Tercer Concilio Limense*. Pamplona: Ediciones Universidad de Navarra, 1990.

Tineo Morón, Melecio, ed. *La fe y las costumbres: Catálogo de la sección documental de Capítulos (1600–1898), Archivo Arzobispal de Lima*. Cuadernos para la historia de la evangelización en América Latina, no. 9. Cusco: Centro de Estudios Regionales Andinos "Bartolomé de Las Casas," 1992.

Titu Cusi Yupanqui. *Relación de la conquista del Perú* [1570], edited by Francisco Carrillo. Lima: Biblioteca Universitaria, 1973.

Torres Rubio, Diego de. *Arte y vocabulario de la lengua quichua general de los indios de el Perú. Que compuso el padre Diego de Torres Rubio de la Compañía de Jesús. Y añadio el P. Juan de Figueredo de la misma Compañía* [1619]. Lima: La Imprenta de la Plazuela de San Christoval, 1754.

Trevor-Roper, Hugh R. *The European Witch-Craze of the Sixteenth and Seventeenth Centuries* [1967]. Reprint, Harmondsworth: Penguin Books, 1978.

Turner, Victor W. "Liminality and the Performative Genres." In *Rite, Drama, Festival, Spectacle*, edited by John J. MacAloon, pp. 19–41. Philadelphia: Institute for the Study of Human Issues, 1984.

Turner, Victor W., and Edward M. Bruner, eds. *The Anthropology of Experience*. Urbana and Chicago: University of Illinois Press, 1986.

Uhle, Max. "Las llamitas de piedra del Cuzco." *Revista Histórica* 1 (1906): 388–92.

Urbano, Henrique. "Estudio preliminar." In *La fe y costumbres*, compiled by Melecio Tineo Morón, pp. 7–12. Cusco: Centro de Estudios Regionales Andinos "Bartolomé de las Casas," 1992.

———. "Introducción: Idolos, figuras, imágenes. La representación como discurso ideológico." In *Catolicismo y extirpación de idolatrías, siglos XVI-XVIII*, edited by G. Ramos and H. Urbano, pp. 7–30. Cusco: Centro de Estudios Regionales Andinos "Bartolomé de Las Casas," 1993.

Urbano, Henrique, and Pierre Duviols, eds. *Fábulas y mitos de los Incas*. Crónicas de América 48. Madrid: Historia 16, 1989.

Urteaga, Horacio H. "Ynformación de vita et moribus del Dotor Francisco de Avila, fecha el año de 1607." *Revista del Archivo Nacional del Perú* 9: 2 (1936): 177–209.

Urton, Gary, ed. *Animal Myths and Metaphors in South America*. Salt Lake City: University of Utah Press, 1985.

————. *The History of a Myth: Pacariqtambo and the Origin of the Inkas.* Austin: University of Texas Press, 1990.

Valcárcel, Carlos D. "Supay (sentido de la manera autóchtona)," *Revista del Museo Nacional del Perú* 11: 1 (1942), pp. 31–39.

Valcárcel, Luis E. *Ruta cultural del Perú.* Mexico: Fondo de Cultura Económica, 1945.

Van Young, Eric. "The Cuautla Lazarus: Double Subjectives in Reading Texts on Popular Collective Action." *Colonial Latin American Review* 2: 1–2 (1993): 3–26.

Vargas Ugarte, Rubén. *Biblioteca Peruana.* 12 vols. Lima and Buenos Aires: Tipografía de la Empresa Periodística La Prensa, 1935–1957.

————. *Historia de la Iglesia en el Perú.* 5 vols. Vol. 1, Lima: Imprenta Santa María, 1953; Vols. 2–5, Burgos: Imprenta de Aldecoa, 1959–1962.

————. *Historia del Perú Virreinato.* 4 vols. Buenos Aires: Imprenta López, 1949–1958.

————. *Historia general del Perú.* Vol. 3. 2nd edn. Lima: Editor Carlos Milla Batres, 1971.

Vargas Ugarte, Rubén, ed. *Concilios Limenses (1551–1772).* 3 vols. Lima: Juan Cardenal Guevara, Arzobispo de Lima, 1951.

————. *Pareceres jurídicos en asuntos de Indias: 1601–1718.* Lima: Compañía de Impresiones y Publicidad, 1951.

Varón Gabai, Rafael. "Cofradías de indios y poder en el Perú colonial: Huaraz, siglo XVII." *Allpanchis* 17 (1982): 127–46.

————. *Curacas y encomenderos: acomodamiento nativo en Huaraz, siglos XVI y XVII.* Lima: P. L. Villanueva, 1980.

————. "El Taki Onqoy: las raíces andinas de un fenómeno colonial." In *El retorno de las huacas,* edited by L. Millones, pp. 331–405. Lima: Instituto de Estudios Peruanos and Sociedad Peruana de Psicoanálisis, 1990.

Vásquez de Espinosa, Antonio. *Compendio y descripción de las indias occidentales* [1623], edited by B. Velasco Bayón. Biblioteca de Autores Españoles no. 231. Madrid: Ediciones Atlas, 1969.

Vega, Feliciano de. *Constituciones sinodales del Obispado de Nuestra Señora de La Paz del Perú, 1638.* Sínodos diocesanos, second series, no. 9, Cuernavaca: CIDOC, 1970.

Vega Bazán, Estanislao. *Testimonio auténtico de una idolatría muy sutil que el demonio avia introducido entre los indios.* Lima: Julian Santos, 1656 Rockefeller Library, Brown University. Medina Collection of microfilm FHA.210.5.

Villagómez, Pedro de. *Carta pastoral de exortación e instrucción acerca de* [sic: *contra*] *las idolatrías de los indios del arzobispado de Lima* [1649]. Colección de libros y documentos referentes a la historia del Perú, vol. 12, edited by Horacio H. Urteaga. Lima: Imprenta y Librería San Martín, 1919.

Vitoria, Francisco de. *Political Writings,* edited and translated by Anthony Pagden and Jeremy Lawrance. Cambridge: Cambridge University Press, 1991.

Vivero, Domingo de, and José Antonio Lavalle. *Galería de retratos de los arzobispos de Lima (1541–1891).* Lima: Imprenta y Litografía de la Librería Clásica y Científica, 1892.

Von Tschudi, Juan Jacobo. *Die Kechua-Sprache. Dritte Abtheilung,* vol. 2. Vienna: Aus der Kaiserlich-Königlichen Hof- und Staatsdruckerei, 1853.

Wachtel, Nathan. "Rebeliones y milenarismo." In *Ideología mesiánica del mundo andino,* edited by J. M. Ossio, pp. 103–42. Lima: Ignacio Prado Pastor, 1973.

————. *The Vision of the Vanquished: The Spanish Conquest of Peru through Indian Eyes, 1530–1570* [1971], translated by Ben and Siân Reynolds. Hassocks: Harvester Press, 1977.

Wallace, A. F. C. "Dreams and the Wishes of the Soul: A Type of Psychoanalytic Theory Among the Seventeenth-Century Iroquois." *American Anthropologist* 60: 2 (1958): 234–48.

Weber, David J. *The Spanish Frontier in North America*. New Haven: Yale University Press, 1992.

White, Richard. *The Middle Ground: Indians, Empires and Republics in the Great Lakes Region, 1650–1815*. Cambridge: Cambridge University Press, 1991.

Wightman, Ann M. "Diego Vasicuio: Native Priest." In *Struggle and Survival in Colonial America*, edited by David G. Sweet and Gary B. Nash, pp. 38–48. Berkeley and Los Angeles: University of California Press, 1981.

———. *Indigenous Migration and Social Change: The Forasteros of Cuzco, 1520–1720*. Durham and London: Duke University Press, 1990.

Wilgus, A. Curtis, ed. *Colonial Hispanic America*. New York: Russell and Russell, 1963.

Wilkerson, S. Jeffrey K. "The Ethnographic Works of Andrés de Olmos, Precursor and Contemporary of Sahagún." In *Sixteenth-Century Mexico*, edited by M. S. Edmonson, pp. 27–77. Albuquerque: University of New Mexico Press, 1974.

Williams, Jerry M. *El teatro del México colonial: época misionera*. New York: Peter Lang, 1992.

Wood, Ian. "Pagans and Holy Men, 600–800." In *Ireland and Christendom*, edited by P. Ni-Chatháin and M. Richter, pp. 347–61. Stuttgart: Klett-Cotta, 1987.

Wright, A. D. *Catholicism and Spanish Society under the Reign of Philip II and Philip III*. Lewiston, N.Y. and Lampeter, Wales: Edwin Mellen, 1991.

Yule, Paul. *The New Incas*, with an Introduction by John Hemming. London: Robert Hadrill at New Pyramid Press, 1983.

Zarzar, Alonso. *"Apo Capac Huayna, Jesús Sacramentado": mito, utopia y milenarismo en el pensamiento de Juan Santos Atahualpa*. Lima: Centro Amazónica de Antropología y Aplicación Práctica, 1989.

About the Author

KENNETH MILLS is Assistant Professor of History
at Princeton University.

Made in the USA
Middletown, DE
28 June 2015